T0139809

Human–Computer Interaction Series

The Human – Computer Interaction Series, launched in 2004, publishes books that advance the science and technology of developing systems which are effective and satisfying for people in a wide variety of contexts. Titles focus on theoretical perspectives (such as formal approaches drawn from a variety of behavioural sciences), practical approaches (such as techniques for effectively integrating user needs in system development), and social issues (such as the determinants of utility, usability and acceptability).

HCI is a multidisciplinary field and focuses on the human aspects in the development of computer technology. As technology becomes increasingly more pervasive the need to take a human-centred approach in the design and development of computer-based systems becomes ever more important.

Titles published within the Human–Computer Interaction Series are included in Thomson Reuters' Book Citation Index, The DBLP Computer Science Bibliography and The HCI Bibliography.

Orestis Georgiou · William Frier · Euan Freeman ·
Claudio Pacchierotti · Takayuki Hoshi
Editors

Ultrasound Mid-Air Haptics for Touchless Interfaces

Editors
Orestis Georgiou 🆔
Ultraleap
Bristol, UK

William Frier 🆔
Ultraleap
Bristol, UK

Euan Freeman 🆔
School of Computing Science
University of Glasgow
Glasgow, UK

Claudio Pacchierotti 🆔
Institut de Recherche en Informatique et
Systèmes Aléatoires (IRISA)
Centre national de la recherche scientifique
(CNRS)
Rennes, France

Takayuki Hoshi
Pixie Dust Technologies, Inc.
Tokyo, Japan

ISSN 1571-5035   ISSN 2524-4477   (electronic)
Human–Computer Interaction Series
ISBN 978-3-031-04045-0   ISBN 978-3-031-04043-6   (eBook)
https://doi.org/10.1007/978-3-031-04043-6

This Springer imprint is published by the registered company Springer Nature Switzerland AG
The registered company address is: Gewerbestrasse 11, 6330 Cham, Switzerland

Foreword

The haptic sense, the sense of touch, always occurs when a person touches an object. This common sense is about to change with ultrasound mid-air haptic displays. The emerging research field of creating human–computer connections through non-contact haptic displays is referred to as *mid-air haptics*. Airborne ultrasound is a promising medium for non-contact haptic stimulation. In principle, it can freely reproduce various sensations under certain limitations on the displayed maximum force. Such non-contact haptic reproduction can drastically change the use of human haptic senses in daily life.

An ultrasound mid-air haptic display removes the constraint that a device is required to transmit intentions to a computer. Imagine operating switches and levers or entering characters via a keyboard or touch panel. Tactile feel is always necessary for efficient operation. Mid-air haptics enables such interactions without the need to touch any physical devices. Gesture control has long been explored as a device-free method. With mid-air haptic feedback, gesture control becomes more efficient and intuitive. This is the main topic of this book, and the basic concepts and results are summarised.

Applications in human–computer interaction (HCI) are spreading to various fields through short- and long-term developments. Device control in automobiles is a promising application in the near future. Visual information combined with mid-air haptic interaction will also bring a new effect to digital signage. Practical tactile technologies will evolve with advances in aerial imaging technology.

Another aspect is the reproduction of realistic haptic sensations in virtual reality (VR). Visual reproduction of VR using a head-mounted display (HMD) has been popular since the mid-2010s, but touch still lags behind. Non-contact stimulation offers the practical advantage of not having to hold anything in your hand and is also an effective strategy for creating a realistic haptic sensation. The calculated data for the ultrasonic transducers can create the desired force patterns anywhere on the skin. Although the technology is still in development, everything is programmable. Eventually, it will produce realistic sensations from various VR objects that can be freely grasped and manipulated.

The haptic sensation generated offers a new way of communicating with the sense of touch. Moreover, such non-contact haptic stimulation has the potential to lead to new applications of haptic perception. Haptic stimulation of faces is useful for alerting people who need to concentrate at work. Stimulation of the hand can control hand movement. When a person begins to fall asleep, a pleasant tactile sensation leads to deep sleep. Such pleasant stimulation can also be useful at work.

In addition, mid-air haptics advances scientific studies of human haptic perception. In conventional haptics research, the reproducibility of haptic stimulation is a constant problem. Conditioning the contact between the skin and the tactile display device during experiments remains a challenge. Non-contact ultrasound stimuli can stably produce the desired stimuli. This reproducibility is a necessary condition for healthy scientific studies of haptics.

Finally, I would like to mention the uncultivated area of haptic senses: haptic art. It is not unrealistic for people to enjoy the comfortable haptic stimulation produced by non-contact haptic displays because a variety of spatiotemporal patterns are stably programmed in a large area of the skin. Recall that the recent music is created as an auditory art by high-tech instruments and did not exist in ancient times. I look forward to enjoying and being moved by haptic art in the future, and the activities of haptic art have already begun. Haptic stimulation integrated into interaction systems will have a profound impact on the human mind.

Although mid-air haptics is a new technology, it has been more than a decade since our laboratory at the University of Tokyo demonstrated the first ultrasonic mid-air haptics in 2008. Thereafter, the University of Bristol team pioneered the sound field rendering and founded the leading mid-air haptics company *Ultrahaptics* (renamed *Ultraleap* in 2019) in 2013. Practical use of mid-air haptics is limited to only a subset of potential applications. However, research and development have made great strides in the last decade. The possibilities of mid-air haptics have expanded dramatically.

This book was conceived by Dr. Orestis Georgiou, Ultraleap Limited, and his co-editors to identify the progress made to date and the prospects for future mid-air haptics. Many authors have contributed to this book, including experienced and young researchers who have only recently entered the field. It is difficult to find words to express my pleasure at the completion of this book.

The technologies and their nature are discussed in the first half of the book. It also explains the importance of haptic feedback in HCI systems, focusing on gesture interfaces and automotive applications. In addition, VR/multimodal interactions and new aspects of non-contact haptic displays are summarised.

The second half of the book presents fundamental studies for future applications. Technical issues related to ultrasonic devices and the synchronisation of multiple phased arrays, the inverse problem of sound field reproduction, and basic properties of haptic perception are summarised. In addition, device prototyping, the basic theory of ultrasound, and safety standards are explained.

This textbook is ideal for anyone looking to get started with mid-air haptics or understand the potential of mid-air haptics. I am confident that mid-air haptics will make significant leaps forward in the near future, with endless potential for growth. I hope many young people will enter this field and reap the rewards.

When we started researching mid-air haptics, I was sure that it would be one of the critical components of information technologies. However, the haptic sensations in the early prototypes were weak and limited to specific vibration sensations. The experiences created by the prototypes often disappointed people and made them feel far from their goals. The focus of our laboratory during these 10 years has been to improve haptic qualities in VR scenarios. The achievements were very successful and much more than I expected in 2008. During the studies, it was fortunate that the academic societies for haptics, VR, and HCI all endorsed this technology. In particular, the activities of Ultraleap (Ultrahaptics), the University of Bristol, the University of Sussex, and the University of Glasgow have led the mid-air haptics studies in HCI and related sciences. Thanks to Ultraleap, these devices are widely available and open to young researchers for future development. The plenary session at the IEEE World Haptics Conference 2021 was successful and marked the beginning of a new phase in mid-air haptics that is now evolving with many players in interdisciplinary fields. I look forward to this technology exceeding my imagination in the future.

Again, I would like to express my sincere appreciation to Dr. Orestis Georgiou, the Ultraleap team, the editors, all authors of this book, and finally, all collaborators and students in my laboratory.

Prof. Hiroyuki Shinoda
The University of Tokyo
Tokyo, Japan

Preface

When we touch a physical object, a sequence of mechanical events occurs whereby vibration is transmitted via the hard and soft tissues of the hand. The signals generated during object manipulation are then transduced into neural signals via ascending sensory pathways that our brain interprets as touch. When combined with signals from our other senses, memories, and opinions, this information influences our realisation of the physical world.

Touch is essential for our normal functioning, affecting how we feel, perceive, and interact with our environment. Touch is not just a functional utility, however. It is also a remarkably powerful driver of human experience and emotion. For example, touching a business card made of high-quality paper can instill a sense of trust and influence our decision to collaborate or purchase. Similarly, a gentle caress on the forearm can evoke a sense of compassion and influence our decision to form friendship bonds or share our thoughts and emotions with the other person. These, often subtle tactile sensations can have a visceral effect on us.

With modern technology, it is possible to generate digital environments and experiences with breath-taking graphics and immersive 3D sounds. However, without stimulating our sense of touch, these experiences can ultimately feel hollow and fictitious, like something is missing. Meanwhile, the COVID-19 pandemic and the rapid digitisation of work and many services have further accentuated the 'touch-gap' between the physical and digital.

Haptic technologies are a direct response to this touch-gap and have recently been experiencing an explosion of interest. This is mostly driven by the ever-increasing integration of haptics into consumer devices such as smartphones and a keen adoption by the medical and automotive industries. Because of their diverse applicability in different markets, haptic technologies come in many different shapes and sizes: they can be wearable, grounded, surface mounted, chemical, embedded, or mid-air.

This is a book about mid-air haptics, generated by ultrasound phased arrays, and the novel human-computer interaction (HCI) paradigms it enables. Since the first prototypes in the early 2010s, mid-air haptic technology has been explored and advanced by many research labs producing 100s of academic papers and commercialised by companies like Ultraleap and Pixie Dust in a variety of settings, including automotive, VR, and digital signage. Yet, there are many unexplored and unanswered questions, many of which are spread across geographic silos of academic pockets and a plethora of publications. Mid-air haptics is also hugely multidisciplinary, spanning the fields of engineering, computer science, design, neuroscience, and psychology. This multi-compartmentalisation prevents the interchange of knowledge and makes it difficult for new people and ideas to enter this research space, ultimately slowing down the integration of mid-air haptics into commercial solutions and holding back our knowledge of this technology.

Predecessors to this book have included three workshops hosted at the ACM Conference on Human Factors in Computing Systems (CHI) in 2016 (Subramanian et al. 2016), 2018 (Giordano et al. 2018), and 2019 (Georgiou et al. 2019). Each of these full-day workshops had approximately 20 participants from the haptics and HCI community, and included interactive demos, brainstorming, discussions, presentations, and scenario building exercises. These workshops were captured by a visual note-taker, Dr. Makayla Lewis. A selection of the resulting sketches is shown in Figs. 1, 2, 3, 4, and 5, illustrating some of the key challenges and questions at the time. In addition to these three HCI workshops, there have also been several hackathons and symposia that took place at the IEEE WorldHaptics, EuroHaptics, and AsiaHaptics conferences, directly engaging with the scientific haptics community, and leaving behind a digital trail of papers, demos, and online videos. Finally, a recent survey of mid-air haptics and its applications has been presented in (Rakkolainen et al. 2020), highlighting the wealth and breadth of this emerging technology and the vibrant scientific community surrounding it.

Motivated by all the above, and being passionate about learning, good science, and the exchange of ideas, we assembled an editorial team of five active researchers and innovators and proposed this book to Springer Nature, and specifically the Human-Computer Interaction Series. Our international co-editorial team is composed of a mix of industry and academic experts who have been pioneering and driving mid-air haptic technology forward since day one. Combined, our backgrounds span the areas of HCI, haptics, physics, and robotics.

Fig. 1 Illustrations by Makayla Lewis at CHI 2016. https://makaylalewis.co.uk/

Fig. 2 Illustrations by Makayla Lewis at CHI 2018. https://makaylalewis.co.uk/

Fig. 3 Illustrations by Makayla Lewis at CHI 2018. https://makaylalewis.co.uk/

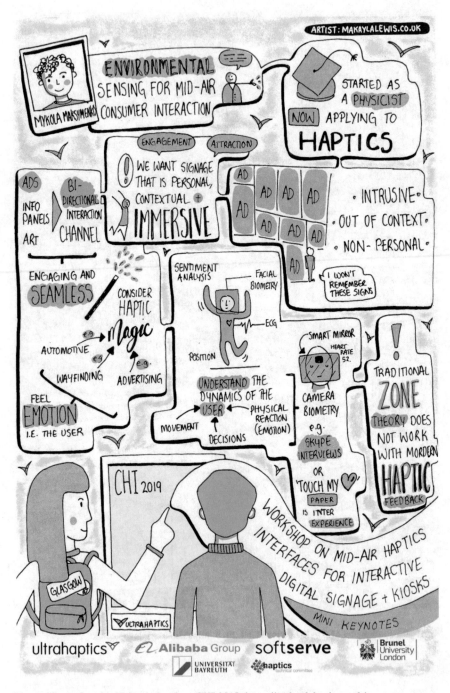

Fig. 4 Illustrations by Makayla Lewis at CHI 2019. https://makaylalewis.co.uk/

Fig. 5 Illustrations by Makayla Lewis at CHI 2019. https://makaylalewis.co.uk/

Our ambition, when we first started talking about this book towards the end of 2020, was to bring the different research communities, their ideas, insights, methods, and challenges together, and literally bind them together into this editorial volume. Almost two years later, our vision has finally been realised. The book includes both retrospectives (reflecting on seminal work in this emerging technology) and perspectives (looking ahead to how this technology will change our interactions with technology). Each contributed chapter is written by expert researchers covering both introductory and advanced topics on the theory of ultrasound-phased arrays (Chaps. "Introduction to Ultrasonic Mid-Air Haptic Effects" and "The Physical Principles of Arrays for Mid-Air Haptic Applications"), hardware prototypes (Chaps. "Multiunit Phased Array System for Flexible Workspace" and "Prototyping Airborne Ultrasonic Arrays"), temporal and spatial haptic rendering (Chaps. "Modulation Methods for Ultrasound Midair Haptics" and "Sound-Field Creation for Haptic Reproduction"), user experience (Chaps. "User Experience and Mid-Air Haptics: Applications, Methods, and Challenges"–"Opportunities for Multisensory Mid-Air Interactions Featuring Ultrasound Haptic Feedback"), safety in ultrasound exposure (Chaps. "Safety of High-Intensity Ultrasound" and "Ultrasound Exposure in Mid-Air Haptics"), and many different HCI applications (Chaps. "Augmenting Automotive Gesture Infotainment Interfaces Through Mid-Air Haptic Icon Design"–"Touchless Tactile Interaction with Unconventional Permeable Displays", "Superimposing Visual Images on Mid-Air Ultrasonic Haptic Stimulation" and "Ultrasound Mid-Air Haptic Feedback at the Fingertip"). These 17 chapters include new results and findings, new insights and fresh perspectives on prior work, as well as short opinion pieces on the past and future challenges of this exciting topic. Finally, in Chap. "Mid-Air Haptics: Future Challenges and Opportunities" we give our own perspective of the road ahead.

The contributed chapters have been compiled by expert authors, 30 in total, who have responded to invitations and open calls sent out in February 2021. Each of these chapters underwent two review cycles, from at least three editors, to ensure quality and consistency. Our aim was to include chapters by people with diverse backgrounds and expertise in developing, evaluating, and applying the technology. We welcomed contributions from both academic and industrial backgrounds as well as practitioners of varying juniority and seniority, interests, and expertise. As a result, we have managed to cover a wide spectrum of topics and disciplines, weaving together these different contexts and perspectives while maintaining a clear focus on HCI.

Crucial to the formation of this book have been the EU projects Levitate, H-Reality, and Touchless, funded by the Future and Emerging Technologies (FET) programme within the Horizon 2020 research and innovation programme, grant agreement numbers 737087, 801413, and 101017746, respectively. These projects enabled mid-air haptic technological innovation to advance rapidly, and iterate alongside user-centred design, while also branching out and being influenced by the broader scientific communities in a truly interdisciplinary and international manner.

We hope that you will enjoy reading this edited volume on mid-air haptics and also hope that the contributed chapters will inspire new research ideas and directions for the successful deployment of this new and enabling touchless technology.

Orestis Georgiou
Head of R&D Partnerships at Ultraleap
Bristol, UK
orestis.georgiou@ultraleap.com

William Frier
Lead Haptics Researcher at Ultraleap
Bristol, UK
william.frier@ultraleap.com

Euan Freeman
Lecturer at University of Glasgow
Glasgow, UK
Euan.Freeman@glasgow.ac.uk

Claudio Pacchierotti
Institut de Recherche en Informatique
et Systèmes Aléatoires (IRISA)
Centre national de la recherche
scientifique (CNRS)
Rennes, France
claudio.pacchierotti@irisa.fr

Takayuki Hoshi
CRO at Pixie Dust Technologies, Inc.
Tokyo, Japan
star@pixiedusttech.com

Acknowledgments We stand on the shoulders of giants, some of which have contributed to this volume.

References

Georgiou O, Limerick H, Corenthy L, Perry M, Maksymenko M, Frish S et al (2019, May) Mid-air haptic interfaces for interactive digital signage and kiosks. In: Extended abstracts of the 2019 CHI conference on human factors in computing systems (pp 1–9)
Giordano M, Georgiou O, Dzidek B, Corenthy L, Kim JR, Subramanian S et al (2018, April) Mid-air haptics for control interfaces. In: Extended abstracts of the 2018 CHI conference on human factors in computing systems (pp 1–8)
Rakkolainen I, Freeman E, Sand A, Raisamo R, Brewster S (2020) A survey of mid-air ultrasound haptics and its applications. IEEE Trans Haptics 14(1):2–19

Subramanian S, Seah SA, Shinoda H, Hoggan E, Corenthy L (2016, May) Mid-air haptics and displays: systems for un-instrumented mid-air interactions. In: Proceedings of the 2016 CHI conference extended abstracts on human factors in computing systems (pp 3446–3452)

Contents

Editors and Contributors

About the Editors

Orestis Georgiou received a Ph.D. in Mathematics from the University of Bristol in 2012. In 2013, he was a postdoc at the Max Planck Institute of Complex Physics in Dresden. He then moved from academia to industry, first working for Toshiba Telecommunications Research Lab as a Senior Researcher (2013–2017), and later for Ultraleap as Head of R&D Partnerships (2017–present) where he is the PI on several publicly funded R&D projects. He is the author of five patents and over 90 academic papers published in leading journals and conferences of Mathematics, Physics, Computer Science, Engineering, and Medicine. Orestis has been awarded a Marie Curie Individual Fellowship hosted at the University of Cyprus (2019–2021), is an author of two best paper awards (ISWCS'2013 and AutoUI'2018), is a Senior IEEE member, and the recipient of the prestigious IEEE Heinrich Hertz Award in 2019.

William Frier received a Ph.D. in Informatics from the University of Sussex, UK, in 2020. He is currently the Lead Haptics Researcher at Ultraleap. He has been working with Ultraleap technology for over 6 years and has published and patented extensively on the foundational aspects of mid-air haptics. William has been a key investigator in studying the perception of mid-air haptics which led to various publications in HCI and Haptic conferences. He has studied Electrical and Electronic Engineering at ESIGELEC (France) and Intelligent System and Robotics at University Pierre and Marie Curie (France), making him a key person in the development and integration of modular ultrasound mid-air haptic devices for human–machine interfaces.

Euan Freeman received a Ph.D. in Computing Science from the University of Glasgow, UK, in 2016 for a thesis focused on mid-air interaction techniques and usability. He was a postdoctoral Research Associate at the University of Glasgow until 2019, doing research into non-visual interaction techniques (EU-funded ABBI project), mid-air interaction techniques for VR (funded by Nokia), and mid-air multi-modal interfaces (EU-funded Levitate project). He then became a Lecturer (Assistant Professor) at the University of Glasgow, where he continues to do leading research on mid-air interaction and ultrasound haptics.

Claudio Pacchierotti received a Ph.D. in Information Engineering from the University of Siena, Italy, in 2014. He is currently a Researcher of the CNRS at IRISA and Inria RBA, Rennes, France. He held a postdoctoral position with the Italian Institute of Technology, Genoa. He visited the Penn Haptics Group, University of Pennsylvania, Philadelphia, PA, USA, in 2014; DIMEG, University of Padua, Padua, Italy, in 2013; and MIRA, University of Twente, Enschede, The Netherlands, in 2014. Dr. Pacchierotti received the 2014 Eurohaptics Best Ph.D. Thesis Award. He is the Senior Chair of the IEEE Technical Committee on Haptics and Secretary of the Eurohaptics Society.

Takayuki Hoshi received a Ph.D. (Information Science and Technology) from the University of Tokyo in 2008. After working as JSPS Research Fellowship for Young Scientists DC2/PD (2007–2009), Assistant Professor at Kumamoto University (2009–2011), Nagoya Institute of Technology (2011–2016), and the University of Tokyo (2016–2017), he founded Pixie Dust Technologies, Inc. in 2017. He is an expert on wave control technology based on full use of physics and mathematics. He developed the world-first scannable prototype of airborne ultrasound tactile display in 2008, and he demonstrated the world-first 3D acoustic manipulation in 2013. He was awarded Significant Contribution to Science and Technology in 2014 by NISTEP, MEXT, Japan. He is currently working on social implementation of wave control technology through industry–academia collaboration and open innovation.

Contributors

Battista Andrew Di Ultraleap Ltd, Bristol, England

Brewster Stephen University of Glasgow, Glasgow, UK

Brown Eddie Ultraleap Ltd, Bristol, UK

Burnett Gary University of Nottingham, Nottingham, England

Cornelio Patricia University College London, London, UK

Drinkwater Bruce W. Department of Mechanical Engineering, University of Bristol, Bristol, UK

Freeman Euan School of Computing Science, University of Glasgow, Glasgow, Scotland

Frier William Ultraleap Ltd., Bristol, UK

Georgiou Orestis Ultraleap Ltd, Bristol, UK

Hasegawa Keisuke Graduate School of Information Science and Technology, The University of Tokyo, Tokyo, Japan

Hoshi Takayuki Pixie Dust Technologies, Inc., Tokyo, Japan

Howard Thomas University of Rennes, Inria, IRISA, CNRS, Rennes, France

Inoue Seki The University of Tokyo, Kashiwa, Chiba, Japan; University of Tokyo, Tokyo, Japan

Kim Jin Ryong Department of Computer Science, The University of Texas at Dallas, Richardson, TX, USA

Large David R. University of Nottingham, Nottingham, England

Limerick Hannah Ultraleap Ltd, Bristol, UK

Makino Yasutoshi The University of Tokyo, Kashiwa, Japan

Marchal Maud University of Rennes, INSA, IRISA, Inria, CNRS, Rennes, France; IUF, Paris, France

Marzo Asier UpnaLab, Institute of Smart Cities, Public University of Navarre, Navarre, Spain

Matsubayashi Atsushi University of Tokyo, Tokyo, Japan

Pacchierotti Claudio Institut de Recherche en Informatique et Systèmes Aléatoires (IRISA), Centre national de la recherche scientifique (CNRS), Rennes, France

Pan Kevin Computer Science, Swansea University, Swansea, UK

Raisamo Roope Tampere University, Tampere, Finland

Rakkolainen Ismo Tampere University, Tampere, Finland

Sahoo Deepak Computer Science, Swansea University, Swansea, UK

Sand Antti Tampere University, Tampere, Finland

Schneider Oliver Faculty of Engineering, University of Waterloo, Waterloo, Canada

Shinoda Hiroyuki The University of Tokyo, Kashiwa, Chiba, Japan; Graduate School of Frontier Sciences, The University of Tokyo, Chiba-ken, Japan

Surakka Veikko Tampere University, Tampere, Finland

Suzuki Shun The University of Tokyo, Kashiwa, Chiba, Japan

Introduction to Ultrasonic Mid-Air Haptic Effects

Takayuki Hoshi

Abstract In this chapter, we discuss the basic physical principles of ultrasonic mid-air haptics. Our aim is to provide a holistic introduction to the technology, facilitate a better understanding of these principles, and help newcomers to join this exciting field of research in following the rest of this book. To that end, we have assumed a simplified and idealized situation and divide our discussion into four sub-topics: acoustic radiation pressure, phased array focusing, vibrotactile stimulation, and by-product audible sounds.

1 Introduction

Ultrasonic mid-air haptics is realized by exploiting several physical phenomena and control methods. It is necessary for researchers and engineers of this technology to understand those underlying principles, and such knowledge is also advisable for haptic designers, even if they are not from an engineering background. This chapter briefly introduces the principles of ultrasound mid-air haptics and acts as a gateway to the more advanced topics covered elsewhere in this book.

We will focus on four principles, leaving deeper discussions on specific aspects and application of this technology to other chapters or research papers. To grasp the essence, we assume the simplest conditions and describe the phenomena from a theoretical standpoint. The differences between theory and practice, e.g., due to approximations and simplification of the acoustic theory or due to the complexities of the hardware electronics, are not discussed in this chapter. The four topics we believe form a good starting point are as follows:

1. Acoustic radiation pressure: The force acting on the skin originates from the acoustic radiation pressure, a nonlinear effect caused by high-intensity sound waves. It is known that the acoustic radiation pressure is proportional to the acoustic energy density in front of the skin surface. We derive the acoustic

T. Hoshi (✉)
Pixie Dust Technologies, Inc., Tokyo, Japan
e-mail: star@pixiedusttech.com

© The Author(s), under exclusive license to Springer Nature Switzerland AG 2022
O. Georgiou et al. (eds.), *Ultrasound Mid-Air Haptics for Touchless Interfaces*,
Human–Computer Interaction Series, https://doi.org/10.1007/978-3-031-04043-6_1

1

radiation pressure by starting from the kinetic theory of gases to determine the origin.

2. Phased array focusing: Mid-air haptics is usually delivered by an array of hundreds of ultrasonic transducers. Although each transducer cannot radiate an intense ultrasonic wave, the phases of the transducers can be appropriately controlled to generate focal points as a result of the principle of superposition. We discuss the case of a single ultrasonic focal point and then briefly consider that of multiple focal points.

3. Vibrotactile stimulation: Human tactile perception is more sensitive to vibrations than to static pressure due to the underlying mechanoreceptors in the skin. In ultrasonic mid-air haptics, the focal point is usually amplitude-modulated (AM) to provide a vibrotactile sensation. Different modulation techniques exist and can be used to design different tactile feelings and experiences.

4. Audible sound radiation: The amplitude modulation of ultrasound waves can also cause unwanted audible sounds to be created. This is another nonlinear effect of high-intensity sound waves. The rapid movement of a focal point is another origin of audible sound, as the discontinuity of phase changes leads to fluctuations in the amplitude of the ultrasound. We consider methods for suppressing these noises.

2 Acoustic Radiation Pressure

2.1 Mathematical Expression

When an intense sound wave is blocked by an object, a force acts in the wave direction pushing the surface of the object. This effect is due to the acoustic radiation pressure, and it is one of the nonlinear effects of sound waves (Awatani 1955; Hasegawa et al. 2000). Iwamoto et al. first introduced this effect into mid-air haptics (Iwamoto et al. 2008) with the following explanation:

"The acoustic radiation pressure P [Pa] is described as

$$P = \alpha E = \alpha \frac{I}{c} = \alpha \frac{p^2}{\rho c^2}$$

where E [J/m^3] is the energy density of the ultrasound, I [W/m^2] is the sound power, c [m/s] is the sound speed, p [Pa] is the sound pressure of the ultrasound, and ρ [kg/m^3] is the density of the medium. α is a constant ranging from 1 to 2 depending on the reflection properties of the surface of the object. In case the surface of the object perfectly reflects the incident ultrasound, the value of α is 2, while if it absorbs the entire incident ultrasound, the value of α is 1. ... When the airborne ultrasound is applied on the surface of the skin, almost all the incident ultrasound is reflected."

(Note: p is the root mean square (RMS) value, that is, $1/\sqrt{2}$ of the peak amplitude [Pa] of a sinusoidal wave.)

The above explanation indicates that the acoustic radiation pressure is proportional to the square of the sound pressure. This means that the acoustic radiation pressure is too small to be felt on our skin when the sound pressure is small and becomes prominent when the sound pressure reaches a certain sound pressure level (SPL), such as approximately 140 dB or more. The perceptual thresholds for ultrasound are presented in Chap. "Ultrasound Exposure in Mid-Air Haptics". The sound pressure level (SPL) is a relative value of the RMS sound pressure p [Pa] to the RMS reference sound pressure $p_0 = 20\,\mu$Pa, and it is calculated through $20\log_{10}(p/p_0)$ [dB].

2.2 Derivation Based on Kinetic Theory of Gases

Our understanding of the phenomenon is as described above; however, it is difficult to grasp the physical intuition of it just by looking at the equation. We therefore take a step back and look at the kinetic theory of gases, and from there derive the acoustic radiation pressure.

We assume an ideal gas, which is a large number of identical submicroscopic particles, all of which are in constant, rapid, random motion. We consider the situation shown in Fig. 1 to derive the pressure on a wall whose area is S [m^2]. Although each particle has a different speed, we assume the average speed normal to the wall of the particle, v [m/s]. The total mass of the particles hitting and rebounding from the wall during time Δt [s] is calculated as a product of the density ρ and volume $Sv\Delta t$. Then, the impulse $F\Delta t$ [kg m/s] that the wall receives is calculated as a product of the total mass and the average speed, as follows:

$$F\Delta t = 2\rho S v^2 \Delta t$$

Here, "2" denotes a perfectly elastic collision, where v turns into $-v$ (i.e., the change in the average speed is $2v$) owing to the collision. From this equation, the atmospheric pressure P_0 [Pa] acting on the wall is obtained as follows:

$$P_0 = \frac{F}{S} = 2\rho v^2$$

Fig. 1 Illustration of a single molecule

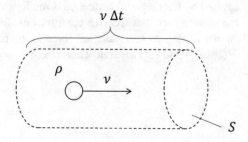

Next, we add a sound wave whose particle velocity is u [m/s], propagating normal to the wall. By replacing v in the above equation with $v + u$, the total pressure $P_{tot} = P_0 + P$ is given as follows:

$$P_{tot} = 2\rho(v + u)^2 = 2\rho v^2 + 4\rho vu + 2\rho u^2$$

Then, by taking the time average of P_{tot}, we can obtain an equation as follows:

$$\langle P_{tot} \rangle = \langle 2\rho v^2 \rangle + \langle 2\rho u^2 \rangle = P_0 + 2\rho u_{rms}^2$$

In the above, $\langle \cdot \rangle$ denotes the time average. The time average of $4\rho vu$ is zero, because $4\rho v$ is constant, and u is sinusoidal. The squared RMS value u_{rms}^2 gives the time-averaged squared value $\langle u^2 \rangle$ by definition. Finally, assuming a plane wave whose acoustic impedance is ρc, that is, $u = p/\rho c$, we have reached the same equation as explained in Iwamoto et al. (2008):

$$P = 2\frac{p_{rms}^2}{\rho c^2}$$

This final form is equal to $2E$, i.e., twice the acoustic energy density. This derivation process indicates that the origin of the acoustic radiation pressure is not the acoustic energy density itself, but rather the product of the momentum (containing u) and the number of particles hitting and rebounding from the wall (containing another u).

2.3 Diagonal Incidence

In the above derivation, we considered the case in which ultrasonic waves are incident normally on a flat surface. Here, we consider the case where they are incident diagonally, as discussed in Awatani (1955). In that study, it was shown that the radiation pressure normal to the wall was $(\cos\theta)^2$ times when the incident angle was θ. This was obtained by substituting $u\cos\theta$ with u in the above derivation.

Notably, if the width of the incident ultrasonic beam is limited to S, the total force applied by the diagonal incidence is multiplied by a factor of $\cos\theta$. This is because the surface area that receives the ultrasonic beam becomes larger (i.e., $S/\cos\theta$), as shown in Fig. 2. The radiation force is the product of the radiation pressure (i.e., $P(\cos\theta)^2$) and surface area. Therefore, we have a force of $P S\cos\theta$.

Fig. 2 Incident and reflected beams of ultrasound at the angles of incidence and reflection, θ. The surface area within the beam is $1/\cos\theta$ times of the cross-sectional area of the beam, S

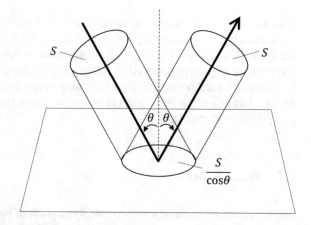

2.4 Acoustic Streaming

In ultrasonic mid-air haptics, not only the radiation pressure is felt but also a feeling of air flow. This effect is referred to as acoustic streaming, a nonlinear phenomenon of high-intensity sound waves. It is often assumed that the sound wave does not move the medium, and only the sound energy propagates through it when the amplitude is small. However, when the wave amplitude increases, a part of the acoustic energy acts as a driving force, and a flow in the medium is generated. This is initially a laminar flow, and then, it becomes a turbulent flow as it develops. Users of ultrasonic mid-air haptics may feel not only the sense of pressure owing to the radiation pressure, but also a sense of wind owing to acoustic streaming. Further details of this phenomenon are provided in Chap. "The Physical Principles of Arrays for Mid-Air Haptic Applications".

3 Phased Array Focusing

In the previous section, we demonstrated that high-intensity ultrasound can push against objects. The next issue we discuss concerns how to generate high-intensity ultrasound. Conventionally, a bolt-clamped Langevin-type transducer (BLT) has been used to generate high-intensity ultrasonic waves. For example, Ito achieved an SPL of 178 dB at the center of a focal point by combining a BLT with a properly designed concave reflector for converging the ultrasonic wave (Ito 2015). Another method of achieving a high-intensity ultrasonic wave in the air is to use a large number of transducers that cannot individually output such high-intensity ultrasonic waves. Together, these transducers can generate a high-intensity focal point by appropriately controlling their phases (Hoshi et al. 2010). For example, Hoshi et al. achieved an SPL of 162 dB at the center of a focal point with 285 ultrasonic transducers.

This was sufficiently intense to make people feel tactile sensations (Hoshi 2014). Furthermore, we can move the position of the focal point electronically by controlling the transducer phases. Therefore, the device that generates these focal points and control their respective positions is called a phased array.

Below, we describe the sound pressure distribution generated by a phased array in the case where a single focal point is generated. The first step toward multiple focal points is also introduced.

3.1 Focal Point

The spatial distribution of an ultrasonic focal point of pressure p [Pa] on the focal plane coordinates (x_f, y_f) at the focal length r [m] generated by $N \times N$ transducers arranged in a square lattice at interval d [m] is given by the following equation.

$$p(x_f, y_f) \approx \sqrt{2} p_r N^2 \frac{\mathrm{sinc}\left(\frac{Ndv_x}{2}, \frac{Ndv_y}{2}\right)}{\mathrm{sinc}\left(\frac{dv_x}{2}, \frac{dv_y}{2}\right)} e^{j\{\varphi(x_f, y_f) - \omega t\}}$$

Here, we have ignored the directivity of the transducer and assumed that a spherical wave is radiated from each transducer. Transducer directivity is considered in Chaps. "The Physical Principles of Arrays for Mid-Air Haptic Applications" and "Prototyping Airborne Ultrasonic Arrays". The parameter definitions and some derivations are provided in Appendix A. The following are notable points from the above equation of $p(x_f, y_f)$.

- The sound pressure at the center of the focal point is the product of the sound pressure traveled from a single transducer p_r and the number of transducers N^2.
- The spatial distribution of the ultrasound on the focal plane follows the sinc function, i.e., $\mathrm{sinc}(x, y) \equiv \sin(x)\sin(y)/xy$.

The focal point as represented by the sinc function described above has a spatial distribution of the ultrasound, as shown in Fig. 3. The diameter w [m] of the region with the largest amplitude (main lobe) is expressed by the following equation using three parameters: the wavelength λ [m] of the ultrasonic wave, size of the phased array Nd, and focal length r:

$$w = 2\lambda \frac{r}{Nd}$$

The above equation is derived from the condition that the sinc function of the numerator of the equation of the sound pressure distribution $p(x_f, y_f)$ first becomes zero. From this equation, it can be seen that if the phased array is too small or the focal length is too large, the focal point will be blurred, i.e., the ultrasonic waves will be dispersed, and a high-intensity ultrasound will not be obtained. This is determined

Fig. 3 Spatial distribution of ultrasound (absolute value) on the focal plane generated by a square-shaped phased array (close-up shot: $40 \times 40 \, \text{mm}^2$). The array size is 170 mm, and the focal length is 200 mm

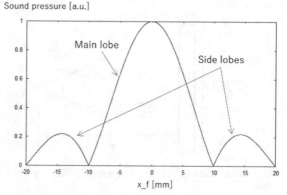

Sound pressure [a.u.]

(a) 1D cross-sectional plot of focal point ($y_f = 0$).

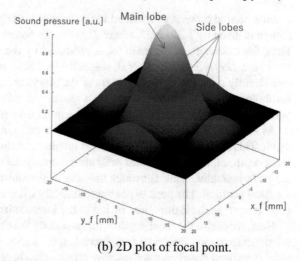

(b) 2D plot of focal point.

by the interference of the waves and is related to numerical values in the field of optics such as the diffraction limit, F value, and the numerical aperture.

Although the main lobe is surrounded by multiple side lobes (see Fig. 3), it is called a focal point because the side lobes are often too weak to be felt and are therefore ignored. For example, the diameter of the focal point (the full width at the zero intensity of the main lobe) is calculated as 20 mm when the wavelength is 8.5 mm (40 kHz ultrasonic wave in air), the length of one side of the square-shaped phased array is 170 mm, and the focal length is 200 mm. Notably, the area in which the radiation pressure is sufficiently strong to evoke a tactile sensation may be narrower than the calculated diameter.

The shape of the focal point here is the sinc function, because the shape of the phased array is square. These shapes are in the relationship of a Fourier transform, and the shape of the focal point changes if the shape of the phased array changes. For example, we have a focal point represented by the Airy pattern when we use a

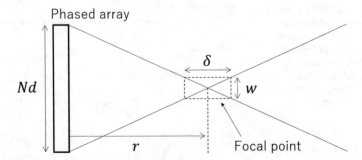

Fig. 4 Width and depth of the focal point © IEEE. Reprinted, with permission, from Hoshi et al. (2010)

circular phased array. As explained in the field of lens optics, the radius of the Airy pattern is given by $1.22\lambda r/D$, where D is the diameter of the circular wave source. Thus, the diameters of the main lobes produced by the square and circular phased arrays are $2\lambda r/Nd$ and $2.44\lambda r/D$, respectively. These are not the same, but are not significantly different if the diameters of the arrays are similar, that is, if $Nd = D$. As another example, in the case of a hexagonal phased array, the shape of the focal point is radial in six directions, i.e., it will exhibit 6 smaller side lobes.

As shown above, a focal point is not truly a point, and it has both a width and depth. This means that the users can feel tactile sensations on their hand within the focal depth, although the sound pressure gradually decreases as the distance from the peak increases. This alleviates the accuracy required for the depth control of the focal position. The peak exists approximately a few centimeters before the focal point (target) in the Z direction, owing to the limited size of the phased array.

Here, we derive the focal depth δ [m], assuming the situation shown in Fig. 4. The relationship among the array size, focal length, width, and half depth of the focal point is derived based on the similarity relationship between triangles, as follows:

$$\frac{Nd}{r} = \frac{w}{\delta/2}$$

By substituting $w = 2\lambda r/Nd$ as obtained in Sect. 3.1, the focal depth δ is given as follows:

$$\delta = \frac{4\lambda r^2}{N^2 d^2}$$

For example, $\delta = 47$ mm when the wavelength of the ultrasonic wave is 8.5 mm, the length of one side of the square-shaped phased array is 170 mm, and the focal length is 200 mm.

3.2 Grating Lobes

Attention should be paid to when the interval between the centers of neighboring transducers is larger than the wavelength of the ultrasonic waves. This is because regions called grating lobes are generated having a large amplitude comparable to the focal point (main lobe) (see Fig. 5). The distance l [m] between the main lobe and the first grating lobe is given by the following equation,

$$l = \lambda \frac{r}{d}$$

Fig. 5 Spatial distribution of ultrasound (absolute value) on the focal plane generated by a square-shaped phased array (long shot: $400 \times 400\,\text{mm}^2$). The transducer interval is 10 mm, and the focal length is 200 mm.

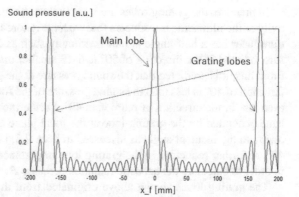

(a) 1D cross-sectional plot of main and grating lobes $(y_\text{f} = 0)$.

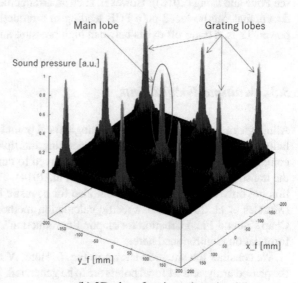

(b) 2D plot of main and grating lobes.

This is derived from the condition that the sinc function of the denominator of the equation of the sound pressure distribution $p(x_f, y_f)$ first becomes zero. For example, the grating lobes are generated at $l = 170$ mm in the X and Y directions, that is, in the direction of $40°$ with respect to the main lobe when the transducers are arranged at an interval $d = 10$ mm, the wavelength of the ultrasonic wave is 8.5 mm, and the focal length is 200 mm. This angle ($40°$) is determined by the ratio of the transducer interval to the ultrasonic wavelength and becomes larger as the spacing decreases. They finally disappear when the interval becomes shorter than the wavelength, because the condition for the generation of the grating lobes is no longer fulfilled. This disappearance of the grating lobes cannot be explained by l as shown above, because l was derived under the paraxial and Fresnel approximations.

In practice, the grating robes are weaker than the main lobe, owing to the directivity of the ultrasonic transducers that we have ignored in our discussion. An actual transducer has a half-angle at half maximum, such as $50°$. That is, the sound pressure radiated in the direction of $50°$ is 6 dB smaller than that in the direction of $0°$. From this, it is predicted that the sound pressure at the grating lobe appearing in the direction of $40°$ is less than the sound pressure of the focal point by nearly 6 dB, and even less in the direction of more than $40°$. Furthermore, the radiation force on the hand generated by the grating lobe at the focal plane also suffers from a reduction owing to the incident angle as discussed in Sect. 2.3, i.e., approximately -2 dB for $40°$. A further reduction in the grating lobe importance is due to the squaring of p in order to calculate the acoustic radiation pressure P.

The grating lobes shown above originated from the periodic placement of the transducers and the inter-transducer distances. It is known that arrays whose transducers are not arranged in a periodic manner mitigate the grating lobes (for example, see Price and Long (2018)). However, such an arrangement reduces density of transducers that can be laced on a PCB leading to a reduction in the output ultrasonic power. Thus, a trade-off exists between high pressure and grating lobes.

3.3 Multiple Focal Points

Although an example of generating a single focal point is shown in the above calculation, there are also algorithms for generating multiple focal points. In the most commonly used case, a matrix equation is solved to determine adequate phases of the transducers (Carter et al. 2013; Long et al. 2014). This is an important calculation not only for mid-air haptics, but also for acoustic levitation (for example, see (Morales et al. 2019)). The specific calculation methods are discussed further in Chap. "Sound-Field Creation for Haptic Reproduction", and only the essence of the formulation is introduced here.

We consider the situation shown in Fig. 6. Here, N transducers are arranged on the phased array, and M focal points are to be generated. The controllable parameters of the n-th transducer are the amplitude x_n and phase α_n of the driving signal. Then, all of the initial sound waves radiated from the transducers can be represented as

Fig. 6 Formulation of
multiple focal points. Here,
as an example, N transducers
generate two focal points

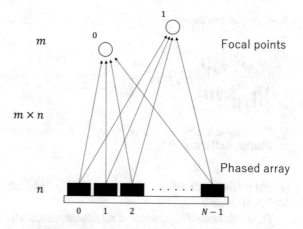

a vector $x = \{x_n e^{j\alpha_n}\}$. Similarly, the parameters of the m-th focal point are the amplitude b_m and phase β_m of the sound pressure giving the vector $b = \{b_m e^{j\beta_m}\}$. The propagation of a sound wave is represented as $e^{jkr_{m,n}}/r_{m,n}$, where $r_{m,n}$ [m] is the distance from the n-th transducer to the m-th focal point. Assuming a propagation matrix $A = \{e^{jkr_{m,n}}/r_{m,n}\}$, we have a linear equation that maps x onto b via:

$$b = Ax$$

Now the problem comes down to solving this matrix equation and how to obtain the inverse matrix of A efficiently and under some constraints and conditions. One simple solution is using the pseudo-inverse matrix $A^+ = (A^T A)^{-1} A^T$, where superscripts T and -1 denote the transpose and the inverse, respectively. Then, x is obtained as $x = A^+ b$. However, this solution has not been optimized in terms of the overall spatial distribution of ultrasound, i.e., only the amplitudes at the focal points are designed, and the other areas are not considered. Therefore, additional processing, such as regularization and iterative calculations, may be required to brush up the solution.

4   Vibrotactile Stimulation

In the case of most ultrasonic mid-air haptic devices, the force applied on a reflective surface by the high-intensity ultrasound is slightly greater than 10 mN within an area of several centimeters in diameter. If this is continuously applied to the skin surface, the nerves of the mechanoreceptors under the skin will adapt, and the tactile sensation will no longer be felt. AM of the ultrasound is usually used to provide a vibrotactile stimulation (Fig. 7) which can be more efficiently sensed by the receptors embedded in our skin. Recently, different modulation methods other than AM have also been

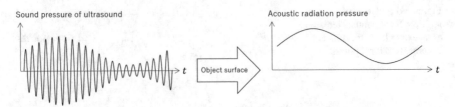

Fig. 7 Acoustic radiation pressure acting on the object surface produced by the amplitude modulation (AM) ultrasound

proposed; these are discussed further in Chap. "Modulation Methods for Ultrasound Midair Haptics".

The modulation frequency and waveform used at a focal point can affect the texture of the tactile sensations related to human tactile perception characteristics. Thus, the frequency content of any vibrotactile stimulus needs to match the characteristics of the human tactile sensory channels, which are approximately in the range of 10–500 Hz (Bolanowski et al. 1988). Therefore, a modulation of 100–200 Hz is usually used for mid-air haptics. Notably, the spatial resolution and the perceived tactile sensation differs depending on the stimulus frequency (Vallbo and Johansson 1984). For example, the focal point at 200 Hz feels larger and more blurred than one at 50 Hz (Hoshi 2015). There is many degrees-of-freedom and many trade-offs that one needs to consider when designing modulation techniques as they will each induce a different tactile sensation. This is an active research space where different authors have begun to build up a library of mid-air haptic sensations.

5 Audible Sound Radiation

Audible sounds originating from AM ultrasound have been reported. Even though the ultrasound itself is inaudible, such audible sounds can sometimes worsen the experience. This side effect is caused because the tactile frequency range (approximately 10–500 Hz) of the mid-air haptic stimulus overlaps with the audible frequency range (approximately 20 Hz to 20 kHz). Here, the mechanism of the audible sound generation is explained, and methods for suppressing noise are introduced.

5.1 Self-demodulation

The audible frequency range varies from person to person, but it is generally from 20 Hz to 20 kHz. Sounds higher than 20 kHz are usually called ultrasound. For example, 40 kHz is twice as high as the audible range; hence, the human ear usually

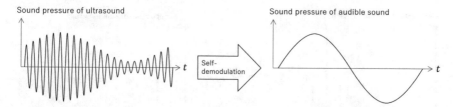

Fig. 8 Audible sound radiated from the AM ultrasound

hears nothing from a constant 40 kHz signal. However, it is known that when ultra-sound is more intense than a certain sound pressure level and the ultrasound fluctuates at frequencies in the audible range, the fluctuation is radiated as an audible sound. In other words, as the modulated ultrasonic waves propagate through the air, they are demodulated by the nonlinearity of the air as seen in Fig. 8. The result is that the space in which the ultrasonic waves exist behaves as a source of audible sound; a kind of self-demodulating effect.

The audible sound p_s [Pa] produced by self-demodulation can be expressed by a differential equation, as follows (Yoneyama et al. 1983):

$$\left(\nabla^2 - \frac{1}{c^2}\frac{\partial^2}{\partial t^2}\right)p_s = -\frac{\beta}{\rho c^2}\frac{\partial^2}{\partial t^2}p^2$$

Here, ρ is the density of air, c is the speed of sound, and β is the nonlinear parameter used in nonlinear acoustics ($\beta = 1.2$ for air). The left-hand side of this differential equation is the wave equation for audible sound. The right side indicates that the time change of the ultrasound acts as a driving force. It is a nonlinear phenomenon that is driven by the time-second derivative of the square of the sound pressure of the ultrasound p signal.

Here, we will briefly examine this phenomenon based on mathematical formulas. In the case of AM by a sinusoidal wave envelope, the modulated ultrasound is expressed as follows:

$$p = (P_c + P_m \cos \omega_m t) \cos \omega_c t$$
$$= P_c \cos \omega_c t + \frac{P_m}{2} \cos(\omega_c + \omega_m)t + \frac{P_m}{2} \cos(\omega_c - \omega_m)t$$

In the above, P and ω are the amplitude and angular frequency, respectively, and the subscripts c and m denote the "carrier" (i.e., usually 40 kHz) and "modulation" (i.e., the frequency lower than the carrier wave). As the second line shows, the resulting AM signal p has three frequency components, ω_c, $\omega_c + \omega_m$, and $\omega_c - \omega_m$, shown in Fig. 9, left. We can then investigate how this signal acts as a sound source by substituting the modulated ultrasound p into the right side of the self-demodulation differential equation from above:

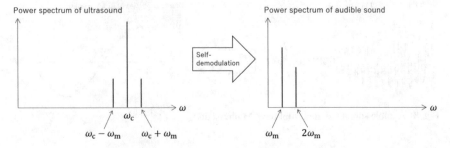

Fig. 9 Power spectrums of the AM ultrasound and radiated audible sound

$$-\frac{\beta}{\rho c^2}\frac{\partial^2}{\partial t^2}p^2 = -\frac{\beta}{\rho c^2}\frac{\partial^2}{\partial t^2}(P_c + P_m\cos\omega_m t)\cos\omega_c t$$

$$= \frac{\beta}{\rho c^2}\Big\{P_c P_m\omega_m^2\cos\omega_m t + P_m^2\omega_m^2\cos 2\omega_m t$$

$$+ \big(2P_c^2\omega_c^2 + P_m^2\omega_m^2\big)\cos 2\omega_c t$$

$$+ \frac{4P_c P_m\omega_c^2 + P_c P_m\omega_m^2}{2}[\cos(2\omega_c + \omega_m)t + \cos(2\omega_c - \omega_m)t]$$

$$+ 2P_c P_m\omega_c\omega_m[\cos(2\omega_c + \omega_m)t - \cos(2\omega_c - \omega_m)t]$$

$$+ \frac{P_m^2\omega_c^2 + P_m^2\omega_m^2}{2}[\cos(2\omega_c + 2\omega_m)t + \cos(2\omega_c - 2\omega_m)t]$$

$$+ \frac{P_m^2\omega_c\omega_m}{2}[\cos(2\omega_c + 2\omega_m)t - \cos(2\omega_c - 2\omega_m)t]\Big\}$$

As shown above, various frequency components are included in the driving force. When we omit the frequency components in the ultrasonic range, we have the frequency components of ω_m and $2\omega_m$ in the audible range (Fig. 9, right). It is also shown that the radiated sound has a frequency dependency of ω_m^2, that is, the lower frequency is less radiated (-12 dB when the modulation frequency is half). Notably, a higher frequency is also less radiated, owing to the narrow resonant frequency band of the ultrasonic transducer (e.g., -6 dB at approximately 1.5 kHz away from the resonant frequency).

Possible ways to reduce this noise include making the modulation waveform as close to a sinusoidal wave as possible to reduce the extra frequency components, and setting the modulation frequency lower than the audible range, so that users cannot hear the by-product sound. Recently, it has been reported that the lateral modulation (spatial movement of the focal point on the skin surface) is less noisy than AM (Suzuki et al. 2020). This is an idea based on using spatial control instead of temporal control and on employing a gradual phase change to reduce the noise, as discussed in the next subsection.

5.2 Movement of Focal Point

The movement of the focal point is achieved by appropriately changing the phase command value of each transducer. However, the transducer being a resonant system, it exhibits a transient response when its input signal is stepwise switched. Specifically, it can be seen from simulating an equivalent circuit of an ultrasonic transducer that the pressure amplitude experiences a significant dip because of this phase switching during a movement of the focal point. This change in amplitude produces an audible sound. While the audible sound generated by one transducer is small, it becomes significant and perceivable when hundreds of transducers are synchronized in the phased array. To reduce this effect, it is sufficient that the phase change rate is small. Thus, a method of updating the position change of the focal position with a high spatial resolution and high update rate should be considered. Although this is effective when the intended focal movement trajectory is nearly continuous, the effect of this method is limited when the focal point hops between discrete positions. To suppress any noise artifact in that case, a method of gradually changing the phase has been proposed (Hoshi 2016; Hoshi, 2020), and a noise suppression of approximately 10 dB was achieved in that case.

Here, we observe the effect of gradually changing the phase of the driving signal by simulation. A resonant electric circuit is modeled, and three types of driving signals of the resonance frequency (here, 40 kHz) are input into the circuit. Although the phase change is the same ($\pi/4$) for all three situations, the transitions are different: the phase changes instantly, gradually over seven cycles, and gradually over 14 cycles. The results are shown in Fig. 10, where the amplitude change occurs shortly after

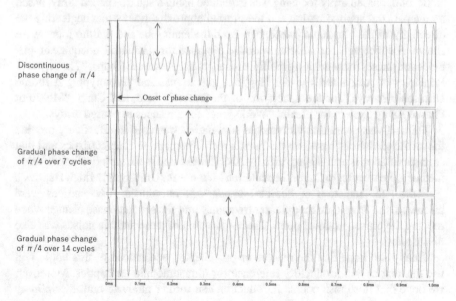

Fig. 10 Simulation of amplitude changes induced by discontinuous or gradual phase changes

the phase change, and the amplitude change decreases as the phase changes slowly. This control method takes a longer time than an instant phase change; however, the transient period is approximately 1.0 ms at the maximum, and it is therefore negligible for the purposes of mid-air haptics.

6 Conclusion

Multiple physical phenomena are involved in the generation process of ultrasonic mid-air haptic sensations, such as the acoustic radiation pressure that impinges the skin surface, phased array focusing algorithms based on interference, modulation techniques to induce a vibrotactile effect, and self-demodulation that radiates audible sound. These phenomena are usually discussed in the form of mathematical equations. While such equations are useful for diving into deeper discussions and engineering, they are not easy to understand and pose an entry barrier to newcomers of the field of mid-air haptics. To that end, we have attempted to explain the principles of ultrasonic mid-air haptics using simplifying assumptions, visual representations, and basic physical argumentation.

First, the origin of the acoustic radiation pressure was shown, based on the kinetic theory of gases, assuming an ideal gas and plane ultrasonic wave. The effect of the incidence angle was discussed. Another effect known as acoustic streaming was also introduced. Please refer to Chap. "The Physical Principles of Arrays for Mid-Air Haptic Applications" for further discussion.

Second, phased array focusing was explained using a square-shaped array, based on the paraxial approximation and the Fresnel approximation, while neglecting the directivity of the ultrasonic transducer. Both the main lobe and grating lobes were shown. A conceptual formulation was also provided for calculating adequate amplitudes and phases for generating multiple focal points. Please see Chaps. "The Physical Principles of Arrays for Mid-Air Haptic Applications" and "Prototyping Airborne Ultrasonic Arrays" for the generation of the acoustic field, and Chap. "Multiunit Phased Array System for Flexible Workspace" for advances in phased arrays.

Third, it was noted that vibrotactile stimulation was used to effectively provide the tactile sensations based on the human tactile perception characteristics and that such stimulation is usually provided by AM. If interested in the variety of modulation methods, please refer to Chap. "Modulation Methods for Ultrasound Midair Haptics".

Fourth, the radiation of audible sounds was introduced. Two sources were discussed, the amplitude modulation frequency and the sudden phase change when moving the ultrasonic focal point. The suppression of these audible noises was also discussed.

Finally, we hope that the readers of this chapter, and indeed of this book, will use this text as an introductory reference for ultrasonic mid-air haptics. Moreover, we hope that this crash course introduction can further motivate multidisciplinary research in hardware, software, waveform, and haptic experience design, thus accelerating the advancement of mid-air haptic technology and its uptake in novel human computer interaction applications and use cases.

Acknowledgements We would like to thank Editage (www.editage.com) for English language editing.

Appendix

A. Derivation of Spatial Distribution of Ultrasound on Focal Plane

The process by which a phased array forms a single ultrasonic focal point can be expressed using the following mathematical formulas. We assume the coordinate system shown in Fig. 11. The XY coordinate is on the surface of the phased array (x, y). The focal plane, (x_f, y_f), is separated by the distance r [m] from the surface. Let the center coordinate of the m-th and n-th transducers in the X and Y directions, respectively, be $(x_m, y_n, 0)$, and the center coordinate of the focal point be (x_c, y_c, r).

Here, we ignore the directivity of the transducer, and assume that a spherical wave is radiated from each transducer with an appropriate phase to generate a single focal point. The RMS ultrasonic sound pressure p_r [Pa] (inversely proportional to r) is produced on the focal plane by each transducer and is a paraxial approximation. A square-shaped phased array is assumed; this is the shape of the majority of current ultrasonic mid-air haptic devices. The N transducers are lined up in both the X and Y directions. At this time, the distribution of ultrasonic sound pressure generated on the focal plane is given as follows:

Fig. 11 Coordinate system for the formulation of phased array focusing © IEEE. Reprinted, with permission, from Hoshi et al. (2010)

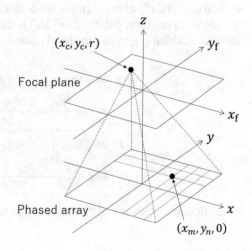

$$p(x_f, y_f) = \sum_{m=0}^{N-1}\sum_{n=0}^{N-1} \sqrt{2}\, p_r e^{-jkr'} e^{j(kr''-\omega t)}$$

$$\approx \sqrt{2}\, p_r e^{-j\omega t} e^{j\{\frac{k}{2r}(x_f^2+y_f^2-x_c^2-y_c^2)-\xi(v_x+v_y)\}} \sum_{m=0}^{N-1} e^{-jdmv_x} \sum_{n=0}^{N-1} e^{-jdnv_y}$$

$$= \sqrt{2}\, p_r e^{-j\omega t} e^{j\{\frac{k}{2r}(x_f^2+y_f^2-x_c^2-y_c^2)-\xi(v_x+v_y)\}} \left(\frac{1-e^{-jNdv_x}}{1-e^{-jdv_x}}\right)\left(\frac{1-e^{-jNdv_y}}{1-e^{-jdv_y}}\right)$$

$$= \sqrt{2}\, p_r e^{-j\omega t} e^{j\{\frac{k}{2r}(x_f^2+y_f^2-x_c^2-y_c^2)-\xi(v_x+v_y)\}} e^{-j\frac{(N-1)d}{2}(v_x+v_y)}$$

$$\times \left(\frac{e^{j\frac{Ndv_x}{2}}-e^{-j\frac{Ndv_x}{2}}}{e^{j\frac{dv_x}{2}}-e^{-j\frac{dv_x}{2}}}\right)\left(\frac{e^{j\frac{Ndv_y}{2}}-e^{-j\frac{Ndv_y}{2}}}{e^{j\frac{dv_y}{2}}-e^{-j\frac{dv_y}{2}}}\right)$$

$$= \sqrt{2}\, p_r\, e^{j\{\varphi(x_f,\, y_f)-\omega t\}} \frac{\sin\frac{Ndv_x}{2}}{\sin\frac{dv_x}{2}}\frac{\sin\frac{Ndv_y}{2}}{\sin\frac{dv_y}{2}}$$

$$= \sqrt{2}\, p_r\, e^{j\{\varphi(x_f,\, y_f)-\omega t\}} \left(\frac{\frac{Ndv_x}{2}\frac{Ndv_y}{2}}{\frac{dv_x}{2}\frac{dv_y}{2}}\right)\frac{\sin\left(\frac{Ndv_x}{2}\right)\sin\left(\frac{Ndv_y}{2}\right)/\left(\frac{Ndv_x}{2}\frac{Ndv_y}{2}\right)}{\sin\left(\frac{dv_x}{2}\right)\sin\left(\frac{dv_y}{2}\right)/\left(\frac{dv_x}{2}\frac{dv_y}{2}\right)}$$

$$= \sqrt{2}\, p_r\, N^2 \frac{\mathrm{sinc}\left(\frac{Ndv_x}{2},\frac{Ndv_y}{2}\right)}{\mathrm{sinc}\left(\frac{dv_x}{2},\frac{dv_y}{2}\right)} e^{j\{\varphi(x_f,\, y_f)-\omega t\}}$$

In the above, j is an imaginary unit. k [rad/m] and ω [rad/s] are the wavenumber and angular frequency, respectively. t [s] is the time. The definition of the sinc function is $\mathrm{sinc}(x, y) \equiv \sin(x)\sin(y)/xy$.

The first line represents the operation of multiplying the spherical wave coming from a transducer $\sqrt{2}p_r e^{j(kr''-\omega t)}$ by the phase control factor to focus the waves $e^{-jkr'}$ and then adding them together. In the second line, the Fresnel approximation is applied to r' and r'', where r' [m] is the distance from the m-th row and n-th column transducer to the focal point, and r'' [m] is the distance from the transducer to the arbitrary position (x_f, y_f) on the focal plane.

$$r' \equiv \sqrt{(x_m - x_c)^2 + (y_n - y_c)^2 + r^2}$$

$$\approx r + \frac{(x_m - x_c)^2 + (y_n - y_c)^2}{2r}$$

$$r'' \equiv \sqrt{(x_m - x_f)^2 + (y_n - y_f)^2 + r^2}$$

$$\approx r + \frac{(x_m - x_f)^2 + (y_n - y_f)^2}{2r}$$

Furthermore, changes of the variables are applied as follows:

$$v_x \equiv \frac{k}{r}(x_f - x_c)$$

$$v_y \equiv \frac{k}{r}(y_f - y_c)$$

Then, the positions of the m-th and n-th transducers are written in another form, that is, $(x_m, y_n) = (md + \xi, nd + \xi)$, using the interval between the centers of neighboring transducers d [m] and an offset $\xi = -(N-1)d/2$. The third line is obtained by the summation formula of the geometric series, i.e., $\sum_{n=0}^{N-1} \alpha^n = (1 - \alpha^N)/(1 - \alpha)$. The fourth line is the middle of the formula transformation to the fifth line. By extracting $e^{-j\alpha/2}$ from $(1 - e^{-j\alpha})$, a form of $(e^{j\alpha/2} - e^{-j\alpha/2})$ is obtained. The fifth line is derived because $(e^{j\alpha/2} - e^{-j\alpha/2}) = 2j\sin(\alpha/2)$. $\varphi(x_f, y_f)$ is the phase delay and depends on the position on the focal plane:

$$\varphi(x_f, y_f) \equiv \frac{k}{2r}\left(x_f^2 + y_f^2 - x_c^2 - y_c^2\right) - \left\{\xi + \frac{(N-1)d}{2}\right\}(v_x + v_y)$$

The sixth line is again the middle of the formula transformation to the seventh line. By extracting $\alpha/2$ from $\sin(\alpha/2)$, a form of $\sin(\alpha/2)/(\alpha/2)$ is obtained; thus, the sinc function finally appears in the seventh line.

References

Awatani J (1955) Studies on acoustic radiation pressure. I. (General considerations). J Acoust Soc Am 27(2):278–281

Bolanowski SJ Jr, Gescheider GA, Verrillo RT, Checkosky CM (1988) Four channels mediate the mechanical aspects of touch. J Acoust Soc Am 84(5):1680–1694

Carter T, Seah SA, Long B, Drinkwater B, Subramanian S (2013) UltraHaptics: multi-point haptic feedback for touch surfaces. In: Proceedings of 26th annual ACM symposium on user interface software and technology (UIST'13), pp 505–514

Hasegawa T, Kido T, Iizuka T, Matsuoka C (2000) A general theory of Rayleigh and Langevin radiation pressures. Acoust Sci Technol 21:145–152

Hoshi T Low-noise ultrasonic wave focusing apparatus. U.S. Patent, US20170144190A1, 2020-02-25

Hoshi T, Takahashi M, Iwamoto T, Shinoda H (2010) Noncontact tactile display based on radiation pressure of airborne ultrasound. IEEE Trans Haptics 3(3):155–165

Hoshi T (2014) Noncontact tactile display using airborne ultrasound. In: Proceedings of 21st international display workshops, pp 1529–1533

Hoshi T (2015) Variation of tactile feelings of focused ultrasound: modulation frequency and hand movement. In: Proceedings of ACM SIGGRAPH Asia 2015, workshop on haptic media and contents design. Article 18

Hoshi T (2016) Gradual phase shift to suppress noise from airborne ultrasound tactile display. In: ACM CHI 2016 workshop on mid-air haptics and displays: systems for un-instrumented mid-air interactions, session 2: provide visual and haptic feedback

Ito Y (2015) High-intensity aerial ultrasonic source with a stripe-mode vibrating plate for improving convergence capability. Acoust Sci Technol 36:216–224

Iwamoto T, Tatezono M, Shinoda H (2008) Non-contact method for producing tactile sensation using airborne ultrasound. In: Haptics: perception, devices and scenarios: 6th international conference, Eurohaptics 2008 proceedings (lecture notes in computer science), pp 504–513

Long B, Seah SA, Carter T, Subramanian S (2014) Rendering volumetric haptic shapes in mid-air using ultrasound. ACM Trans Graph 33:181:1–181:10

Morales R, Marzo A, Subramanian S, Martínez D (2019) LeviProps: animating levitated optimized fabric structures using holographic acoustic tweezers. In: Proceedings of 32nd annual ACM symposium on user interface software and technology (UIST'19), pp 651–661

Price A, Long B (2018) Fibonacci spiral arranged ultrasound phased array for mid-air haptics. In: Proceedings of IEEE international ultrasonics symposium (IUS), pp 1–4

Suzuki S, Fujiwara M, Makino Y, Shinoda H (2020) Reducing amplitude fluctuation by gradual phase shift in mid-air ultrasound haptics. IEEE Trans Haptics 13(1):87–93

Vallbo ÅB, Johansson RS (1984) Properties of cutaneous mechanoreceptors in the human hand related to touch sensation. Hum Neurobiol 3:3–14

Yoneyama M, Fujimoto J, Kawamo Y, Sasabe S (1983) The audio spotlight: an application of nonlinear interaction of sound waves to a new type of loudspeaker design. J Acoust Soc Am 73(5):1532–1536

User Experience and Mid-Air Haptics: Applications, Methods, and Challenges

Orestis Georgiou⬤, William Frier⬤, and Oliver Schneider

Abstract Mid-air haptic feedback presents exciting new opportunities for useful and delightful interactive systems. However, with these opportunities come several design challenges that vary greatly depending on the application at hand. In this chapter, we reveal these challenges from a user experience perspective. To that end, we first provide a comprehensive literature review covering many of the different applications of the technology. Then, we present 12 design guidelines and make recommendations for effective mid-air haptic interaction designs and implementations. Finally, we suggest an iterative haptic design framework that can be followed to create a quality mid-air haptic experience.

1 Introduction

Interaction design for novel human-computer interfaces has been met with increasingly complex challenges due to the advancements made by novel input technologies. Keyboard and mouse input has in many cases been replaced or complemented by touchscreen input, while since 2010 with the release of Microsoft Kinect and Leap Motion in 2014, advances in hand-tracking algorithms and devices (mostly camera based) have been challenging developers and interaction designers to explore the use of 3D mid-air hand gestures and their capabilities in a range of products and services. For example, hand- and finger-tracking sensors have been embedded in car infotainment systems for a more intuitive and comfortable input that is also less visually distracting; in virtual and augmented reality (VR/AR) head mounted displays

O. Georgiou (✉) · W. Frier
Ultraleap Ltd., Bristol, UK
e-mail: orestis.georgiou@ultraleap.com

W. Frier
e-mail: william.frier@ultraleap.com

O. Schneider
Faculty of Engineering, University of Waterloo, Waterloo, Canada
e-mail: oliver.schneider@uwaterloo.ca

(HMDs) for controller-free games and more immersive experiences; and in digital signage or self-service kiosks for a more hygienic and pleasant touchless operation.

All these touchless technologies enable novel and more natural interactions with the digital world; however, they lack physicality as they do not stimulate our sense of touch. Ultrasonic mid-air haptic technology is a direct response to this *touch gap*, aiming not only to re-instill physicality to touchless user interfaces, thereby improving their functionality, but also to enhance user experience (UX), thereby improving various non-functional aspects of the interface.

Since the early prototypes emerging out of academic research labs in Japan (Hoshi et al. 2010) and later in the UK (Carter et al. 2013), ultrasound mid-air haptics have received a lot of academic and commercial interest and is an active area of research in the HCI and haptics communities (see recent survey here Rakkolainen et al. 2020). The main advantage of this technology compared to other mid-air haptic alternatives, such as air jets, plasmas, and lasers, is that ultrasound mid-air haptic hardware platforms can be electronically programmed to display multiple points of vibrotactile stimulation with a high degree of spatial and temporal resolution and can do so in a controllable and safe manner (Di Battista 2019). Moreover, the tactile sensation is presented almost instantaneously and can be accurately targeted to the users' palms, fingers, face, lips, forearms, and chest in the form of a short burst, or continuously over a large 3D workspace. Finally, various modulations and rendering techniques of the ultrasound waveforms can be used to further imbue the tactile sensation with rich touch information such as shape, stiffness, curvature, and roughness.

Many of these aspects and associated challenges are discussed in more detail in the following chapters of this book. In this chapter, we will instead approach the topic from a UX perspective, by first giving an overview of the different applications of the technology (Sect. 2) and then presenting some guidelines (Sect. 3) and methods (Sect. 4) for the design of useful mid-air haptic-enabled interactive systems. Finally, we will discuss future challenges and give our vision for mid-air haptic user experience enhancement (Sect. 5).

2 Applications

2.1 Automotive

The global automotive human machine interface (HMI) market size was valued at USD 14.8 billion in 2017 and was projected to reach USD 33.6 billion by 2025, registering a compound annual growth rate (CAGR) of 11.1% from 2018 to 2025. According to market research reports, the key drivers behind this projected growth are observed to be enhanced UX and entertainment in vehicles and an increased focus on driver assistance systems. To that end, haptics have traditionally been applied in the automotive domain in many forms, notably the steering wheel, the seat, and the foot pedals, primarily for providing safety-related benefits to the driver. Increasingly however, and in line with the market research reports, haptics are also applied in other interactive areas of the car, such as surfaces and touchscreens to improve UX, to enable new features, and to improve the perceived quality of the car itself (Burnett and Irune 2009). Despite their ability to emulate, e.g., a 'click' touch sensation when in contact with a screen, haptic-enabled touchscreens are absent of contours and hence lack genuine tactile guidance, resulting in them being visually demanding during operation. This is also the main reason why touchscreen use in vehicles has been shown to increase driver distraction and crash risk (Green 2000; Horrey and Wickens 2007; Klauer et al. 2006; Olson et al. 2009; Pitts et al. 2010).

Therefore, a lot of research has in recent years focused on In-Vehicle Infotainment Systems (IVISs) and how to make large touchscreens more usable while driving, without taking the driver's visual attention away from the road (Rümelin and Butz 2013). One promising alternative has been the use of touchless gesture input technologies (Alpern and Minardo 2003; Pickering 2005), with several car manufacturers like BMW, VW, Jaguar, Mercedes-Benz, Cadillac, PSA, and Hyundai, all investing in mid-air gesture interfaces (Hermann 2018). The key advantage of gesturing in mid-air is that it engages our proprioception (kinesthetic haptics Freeman et al. 2017), thereby potentially enabling eyes-free operation interaction with the IVIS, especially when feedback is provided through a multimodal combination of visual, audible, and/or tactile information (Shakeri et al. 2017). Gesture interfaces are also more hygienic, leaving no fingerprints or dirt transfer onto the center console of the car.

Despite the core advantage of relieving visual distraction, gesture input technology in cars comes with its own challenges, such as potential cultural nuances (Loehmann et al. 2013), the learning associated with more complex gestures (Garber 2013), the lack of a standard gesture set (Villarreal-Narvaez et al. 2020), a restricted 3D interaction space above the gearshift (Riener et al. 2013), the need for user acceptance (Detjen et al. 2021), the reliability of the gesture recognition system itself, and of course the loss of haptic feedback (Cornelio Martinez et al. 2017), a key ingredient toward the sense of agency (SoA)—the subjective experience of voluntary control over your actions. Meanwhile, speech and non-speech audio feedbacks have been proposed to offset this lack of tactile feedback (May et al. 2014); however, these methods are not as effective and also interfere with other audio signals and external noise (e.g., due to an open window) while also disrupting passenger conversations.

Currently, most interactive hand-gesture input implemented in prototypes, concepts, and production IVISs includes the index pointing gesture, pinch and drag, palm-swipe to reject, rotating index finger to adjust volume, downward push, grab and pull, and the 'v' for victory gesture being user-defined. It has been argued that adding mid-air haptic feedback to these and/or other gestural interactions in cars can add value by: increasing interface usability, improving gesture learning and recall, reducing cognitive load, enhancing a sense of agency, reducing visual distraction, reducing eyes-off-road time especially during target locating, supporting error recovery, providing an experiential alternative to audio feedback, enabling new IVIS features and applications, and being more inclusive to deaf or hard-of-hearing

Fig. 1 Experimental setups from Shakeri et al. (2018) (left), Harrington et al. (2018) (middle), and Young et al. (2020) (right)

drivers. In addition to all these potential functional and usability benefits, there are experiential aspects such as expressivity, immersion, realism, autotelic, and harmony as presented by Kim and Schneider (2020) that can enhance how the IVIS feels to the user, and not just how well it works.

Research efforts in better understanding and establishing some of the above claims are underway, with automotive being an active yet currently under-explored use case of mid-air haptics. Here, we briefly review some of the reported literature on the topic and highlight some gaps and unanswered questions.

Georgiou et al. (2017) presented a first prototype demo created by Ultrahaptics (now Ultraleap) for a mid-air haptified hand-gesture IVIS using just two input functions and hand gestures (volume and fan speed up/down and a switch between the two). Harrington et al. (2018); Large et al. (2019) explored the human factors and benefits associated with adding mid-air haptics to gesture interfaces through user studies in a high-fidelity driving simulator. Importantly, they showed the potential of haptified hand gestures toward reducing visual demand and perceived workload, improving secondary task performance and vehicle control when gesturing at the IVIS while driving, as compared to the non-haptic gesture and touchscreen input cases. It should be stressed that their results were not unanimous in all test cases; however, they were generally encouraging and positive, indicating that if designed and implemented properly, mid-air haptic gesture input could indeed mitigate many of the key concerns about touchscreens and gesture input for human-car interactions. The study by Shakeri et al. (2018) echoed many of these encouraging findings, while also further arguing in favor of multimodal feedback (auditory and peripheral vision) in combination to mid-air haptics. The experimental setups of these studies are shown in Fig. 1.

A study by Korres et al. (2020) used a holographic (floating) interactive display (rather than a standard LCD) together with mid-air haptic gesture input and showed that the addition of mid-air haptic feedback to the interactions with the IVIS improved driving performance (the average speed error, spatial deviation, and the number of off-road glances), improved the secondary task of IVIS interaction (reach time), and improved overall quality of user experience, as compared to no tactile feedback. Also using floating displays, Rümelin et al. (2017) studied pointing gestures with haptic feedback directed onto the index finger. This interaction and a mid-air haptic display were prototyped and built into BMW's concept car shown at CES 2017 in Las Vegas that was branded as 'HoloActive Touch' (Etherington et al. 2017). Rümelin's work varied the amplitude modulation (AM) frequency and stimulus duration of the feedback presented during a holographic button press. Subjective ratings 200 Hz as the best stimulus frequency combined with a duration between 50 and 130 ms.

Motivated by former evaluations of button sounds and their perceived associations with the quality of a product, Rümelin's paper also looked at evaluating a vocabulary of adjectives used to describe the presented mid-air feedback pointing gesture and grouped them under: valence precision, attractiveness, resolution, and intensity. The most descriptive words that emerged were as follows: effortless, sharp, desirable, deep, pleasant, artificial, coarse, and strong.

Combining prior results and knowledge from prototypes, psychophysical, and human factors studies, Young et al. (2020) developed a more advanced mid-air haptic gesture-enabled user interface for human-vehicle interactions. The prototype comprised of a graphical user interface and information architecture (i.e., a menu) with four functions (1. music control, 2. temperature and fan control, 3. navigation map control, and 4. phone-call answer/reject), while using just 5 hand gestures (pinch and move, tap, grab-release, swiping, and hand twist) to ease learnability (Cowan 2001), and applied multimodal feedback (visual and audio) in combination to a variety of haptic feedback and feedforward sensations. The paper did not only present the prototype but also proposed a set of UX requirements for the mid-air haptic IVIS called REQUEST (Reliable, Quick, Useful, Easy, Safe, and realisTic) and documented the design process considerations during the development process. These included an online survey, business development insights, background research, and three agile prototype iterations and user testing on a simplified driving simulator.

Finally, motivated by human-centered design, the expressivity afforded by mid-air haptics and the need to improve the learnability of IVISs, Brown et al. (2020) proposed a method to design an exemplar set of robust, function-associated haptic gestures, aka Ultrahapticons, that leverages drivers' mental models of interactions. This work is further described in Chap. "Augmenting Automotive Gesture Infotainment Interfaces Through Mid-air Haptic Icon Design."

Automotive brands, OEMs, suppliers, and HMI design agencies want to create in-car experiences which are differentiating, easy to use and update, and are cost-appropriate and safe. Mid-air haptic technology presents a compelling solution to the automotive use case wants; however, most published research studies to date have largely focused on validating the technology and its associated benefits. They are essentially singular findings that do not naturally generalize to a broader automotive user context; perhaps such activities are better suited to industrial R&D settings. Going forward, studies should shift their focus on optimizing both individual parts of mid-air haptic integration into IVIS but also how they all fit and work together. For example, there are no studies on the optimal set of ergonomic product design and placements of ultrasonic arrays within a car dashboard. With the exception of Young et al. (2020), there are no studies on how best to design and implement mid-air haptic sensations (along with any accompanying sounds and visuals) to support the user in searching and operating IVIS control elements. To that end, the methods we will present in Sect. 4 could be followed to map out the interaction design and how mid-air haptics can be better leveraged to add value to IVISs and their users. Moreover, while much of the haptic use cases in automotive have been limited to the finding and confirmation of input control actions, other use cases could also be explored such as warning mechanisms during high visually and cognitively loaded conditions such as high traffic density (Mizutani et al. 2019).

2.2 Touchless Displays in Public Spaces

2.2.1 Digital Signage, Pervasive, and Accessible Displays

Digital signage and pervasive displays use technologies such as LCD, LED, projection, and e-paper to display things like images, video, Web pages, weather data, restaurant menus, or text, usually in public spaces like train stations, airports, malls, and theaters. Making these large screens interactive has promised to transition such platforms from simple broadcast systems to rich digital media for targeted and bi-directional communication, e.g., through interactive experiences that enhance brand engagement. However, touchscreen technologies do not naturally lend themselves to this use case due to the need to ensure: hygiene and cleaning requirements, robustness against extended use and potential damage, needs for securing access to the display control panel, responsiveness, and finally reachability requirements that compromise viewability and location (Davies et al. 2014).

It is worth noting here that the global digital signage market was estimated at USD 16.3 billion in 2021 and projected to reach USD 27.8 billion by 2026, rising at a CAGR of 11.2% during the forecast period. According to market research reports, much of this growth is driven by an increasing adoption of digital signage in commercial applications and settings, while a key opportunity observed is the growing demand for contactless engagement in the post-COVID-19 era. Advances in computer vision (face, gaze, facial expression, body, and hand-gesture recognition) and mid-air haptics have thus stepped in to enable new ways of distal interactivity with digital content. These however also come with their own challenges. Namely, it is not clear how the interactivity of these displays is communicated to the passerby audience and future user, how to initialize an interaction, and once the audience have engaged, how the interactive affordances are communicated across, both of which are fundamental UX questions. Sub-challenges that permeate and affect the above aspects include display blindness, interaction blindness, interaction design, awkward or embarrassing gestures in public, ergonomic design, and the spatial positioning of the signage. Many of these were explored by Limerick (2020) during an 8-week in-the-wild experiment in LA that led to a set of solutions and design guidelines, e.g., the use of animated idle screens showing hand gestures that people would mirror to initiate interaction, simplified instructional panels, footprints on the floor to signify where users should stand, but also the use of mid-air haptics to enhance user engagement and help offer more compelling experiences (see Fig. 2). In a different

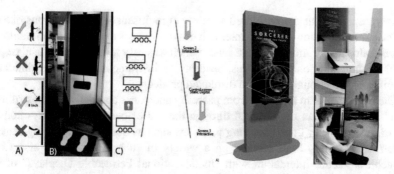

Fig. 2 Left: Instructional panel images shown on side of screen. **b** Footprints on the floor beneath the interactive poster. **c** Layout of the deployment interactive posters (green) and the control poster (black) in movie theater corridor. Right: **a** Example with interactive poster setup, haptic interaction zone in green, and hand-tracking zone within white sphere. **b** Example of hand location for interaction. **c** Example of two-handed interaction. Reproduced from Limerick (2020)

but similar study, also by Limerick et al. (2019), participants reported significantly more focused attention and experienced greater levels of reward when mid-air haptic feedback was present than without it.

Rutten et al. (2020) challenged the sustained positive UX effect of mid-air haptic to such experiences. They found that the added value of valence was due to a novelty effect as it was only significantly elevated during initial use and fell after repeated use. However, the added value of mid-air haptic feedback in terms of enjoyment, engagement, and arousal remained elevated over the course of their study (five weeks).

Corenthy et al. (2018) presented a demonstrator further including gamification aspects to the touchless experience, while using different mid-air haptic stimuli to indicate discrete events that were congruent with audio-visual stimuli (e.g., as laser blasts) but also haptic-only stimuli that conveyed hidden signals to the user (e.g., the direction of an incoming asteroid). Notably, continuous haptic stimuli were also displayed to indicate system responsiveness and the invisible tethered control of a user's hand and the game on the screen. Finally, an initialization haptic was used to guide the user toward positioning their hand in the right place and height, approximately at the center of the interaction zone in front of the display.

Kim et al. (2019) presented a demonstrator for a new retail shopping experience which they called Refinity (see also Chap. "Multimodal Interaction with Mid-Air Haptics"). In their vision, customers could directly select and explore realistic virtual products using auto-stereoscopic 3D displays combined with mid-air haptics and hand and finger tracking. Haptic gestures were introduced to enable natural interaction with products: point to identify, grab to select, rotate to preview, swipe to browse other options, and push back to place the items back in the virtual shelf. Notably, sensory substitutions via haptics and audio were used to tackle the visual-physical conflict when interacting with the 3D screen. Further, in addition to the visual and mid-air vibrotactile haptic feedback presented by the ultrasonic arrays in the Refinity prototypes, Kim et al. also explored a variety of multisensory combinations like different smells, heat flow, and rich interactive auditory cues to create a memorable and joyful multisensory shopping experience which was easy to walk up and use, i.e., not requiring any additional wearables, headsets, or instrumentation, while simulating the different functionalities of the displayed products.

Gaining maximum attention from passerby audiences and delivering a strikingly novel experience can be achieved through the use of permeable displays consisting of tiny, flowing, light scattering particles, such as dust, smoke, or fog. Rakkolainen et al. (2015) have worked on a variety of such systems (see also Chap. "Touchless Tactile Interaction with Unconventional Permeable Displays" of this book) where a thick laminar air flow is created along a plane within which particles are injected and are protected by the surrounding air flow, thus keeping the screen flat and enabling high-quality images and videos to be projected onto them thus creating a hovering holographic effect. While images floating in thin air are a common theme in science fiction, they are still relatively rare in everyday life and are thus easily noticed by the audience whose attention and imaginations are intrigued. Enhancing such floating displays with ultrasound haptic feedback can be utilized for the efficient information transfer on tactile displays, e.g., the presentation of interactive buttons or tactile images through tapping, swiping, grasping, and dwell time gesture input. To that end, (Inoue et al. 2014; Makino et al. 2016; Monnai et al. 2014) have been using floating images produced by projecting through transmissive mirrors, also referred to as aerial imaging plates which double up as a reflector of ultrasound waves that focus and provide tactile feedback to the optical holographic images. These techniques and challenges are further discussed in Chap. "Superimposing Visual Images on Mid-air Ultrasonic Haptic Stimulation" of this book.

Finally, motivated by the increased unwillingness to touch self-service touchscreens in public places due to the COVID-19 pandemic, Huang et al. (2020) presented a touchless Customer Feedback Kiosk (happy, OK, bad, terrible), like those deployed after security checks at airports. Their study results pointed out that even for simple touchless interfaces like these, there are many new and unexplored design questions that present implementation challenges such as the optimal distance between buttons, the size of the virtual hands to reduce error rates, and the need for training instructions, akin to those presented by Limerick (2020) but further appropriated for the quick and direct input interactions necessitated by self-service touchless kiosk interfaces.

Also motivated by COVID-19, Singhal and Phutane (2021) designed an interactive simulation of a contactless elevator panel with mid-air touch feedback and comprehensive accessibility considerations. Users could not only feel mid-air haptic feedback on contact with the panel buttons corresponding to the different floors, but could also feel their Braille representations using a similar implementation to that described by Paneva et al. (2020). Additional interactions such as responsive button magnification to assist people with low vision, intuitive gestures for opening or closing doors, and audio feedback were also presented in their prototype.

2.2.2 New Media, Art, Science Communication, and Museums

Museums and art galleries have traditionally been at the forefront of integrating and stimulating multiple human senses, not only to explore new ways of representing arts, but also to increase the wider public interest in the artifacts being displayed. Within this context, Vi et al. (2017) worked with a team of curators artists and designers to create and deploy a six-week multisensory display called Tate Sensorium that was exhibited to over 2500 people at the Tate Britain art gallery in London. This was the first time that mid-air haptic technology was used in a museum context over a prolonged period of time and integrated with sound to enhance the experience of visual art. Participants expressed that experiencing art with the combination of mid-air haptics and sound was immersive and memorable and provided an up-lifting experience of touching without touch.

Trotta et al. (2020) created a multisensory science exhibit that was presented at the London Science Museum aimed at communicating abstract concepts in cosmology and astrophysics in a more accessible and inclusive manner. Different experiences evoking all five of our senses were designed, with touch and particularly the mal-leability offered by mid-air haptics were used for producing tactile sensations that represented the change in dark matter wind during an earth-year, and its density profile in our galaxy. Participants voted on which of the five sensory channels had the most significant influence on one of five personal responses: Awareness, Enjoyment, Interest, Opinion forming, and Understanding (also known as the AEIOU framework) with the touch experience performing comparatively well in the Awareness, Enjoyment, and Understanding dimensions.

Going beyond this single exhibit, Daniel et al. (2020) explored how mid-air haptics technology could play a role in communicating a variety of scientific concepts. In their work, they prototyped six mid-air haptic probes for three thematic areas: particle physics, quantum mechanics, and cell biology and also describe guidelines on how to do so most effectively through the use of cognitive and tactile metaphors. Then, through three qualitative focus group sessions with domain experts and science communicators, the team identified how dynamic features afforded by mid-air haptics could convey scientific concepts through metaphors and stories. For example, dynamic tactile feedback on the palms of both hands was presented to simulate the process of particle collisions in the large hadron collider (LHC). Similarly, a growing haptic sensation that then splits into two smaller haptic sensations was used to simulate the process of meiosis (a type of cell division). It was further discovered that dialog around the haptic probes (post-experience) naturally resulted in a co-discovery process and that shared exploration of scientific phenomena contributed to the enjoyment of mid-air haptics technology for public engagement therefore complementing formal learning.

In contrast to previous studies where the haptic experience was created to match a specific graphic or semantic interaction space, Ablart et al. (2017) designed generalized mid-air haptic patterns to enhance movie experiences. The authors then assessed their effects through physiological measurements (respiration, heart rate, skin conductance level) and questionnaires (SAM and Immersion Questionnaires) which hinted toward increased immersion, improved overall UX, and potentially the ability to influence the viewer's emotions. The latter opportunity (emotions) with the exception of the work by Obrist et al. (2015) has yet remained largely unexplored due to the complexity and difficulty of customizing the haptic stimulus and presenting it at the right time and place. The former opportunity (immersion) was further developed and successfully deployed by O'Conail et al. who created an immersive yet accessible (blind, deaf, or wheelchair) movie experience that is currently (2021) in use at the Aquarium of the Pacific in LA (O'Conaill et al. 2020). Their development process followed agile and design thinking principles, cycling through design, implementation and user testing at each phase or cycle, resulting in both a finished installation and valuable insights about how to design and match haptic sensations to different environmental themes (here aquatic) and using audio-visually synchronized dynamic haptic patterns that achieve semantic congruence (similar to Hajas et al. (2020)). An unexpected finding of their study was a role reversal, where deaf or blind viewers who observed the mid-air haptic-enhanced experience of the movie would enthusiastically explain or describe their experience to family members.

2.3 Augmented, Virtual, and Mixed Reality

With AR and VR finally breaking through the novelty barrier and reaching increasingly more markets and applications (gaming, employee training, health care, education, and entertainment), almost all major HMD vendors are beginning to integrate outward facing camera systems into their headsets in what appears to be an effort to unlock a controller-free interaction paradigm. One reason for this is that the capabilities offered by hand-tracking technologies in AR and VR environments have demonstrated remarkable advancements in the last few years with tracking accuracies down to just a few centimeters (Schneider et al. 2020) and latencies of less than 20 ms. Another reason is that hand controllers are an added cost to the HMD.

Fig. 3 Left: Tactile bio-hologram by Romanus et al. (2019). Middle: AR car design simulation and customization demo by Dzidek et al. (2018). Right: VR with a head mounted mid-air haptic array by Sand et al. (2015)

With virtual and physical worlds merging into the metaverse, and with hand and gesture interactions in AR/VR becoming increasingly feasible, the opportunity to physicalize and enrich virtual and augmented content through mid-air haptics has been identified and explored by several authors. Perhaps one of the earliest efforts was that by Sand et al. (2015) who built an ultrasound mid-air haptic device and mounted it onto a VR HMD (see Fig. 3). Through their testing of that new hybrid platform, it was not observed that the inclusion of tactile feedback resulted in interaction speed or accuracy improvements, but rather that the key benefits of this technology in this use case were a qualitative improvement in UX. Participants reported that they preferred to experience mid-air tactile feedback, rather than not, and felt slightly less mentally and physically tired.

Similar observations were made by Pinto et al. (2020) who explored pick-and-place tasks within a mixed reality robotic teleportation environment. In their implementation, the authors were looking to teach a robotic arm how to perform such tasks without using any kinematic or programming languages, but instead through human hand guidance, i.e., mimicking of user movements. In order to replicate the experience of physical hand guidance more closely, ultrasonic mid-air haptics were introduced since hand grasping movements are reported to be more realistic and ergonomic in the presence of tactile feedback. Pick-and-place grasping tasks in VR were also studied by Frutos-Pascual et al. (2019), who concluded that while task completion time was mostly unaffected through the addition of mid-air haptics to the interaction, grasping accuracy, UX, and overall preference were improved, particularly for small objects.

2.3.1 VR Instruments and Games

Motivated by the prospect of enhancing UX, Hwang et al. (2017) developed a musical piano in VR whose keys were emulated through ultrasonic mid-air haptic feedback. Follow-up user studies of their AirPiano VR prototype confirmed that adding mid-air haptic feedback significantly improved the UX. Their adaptive tactile intensity feedback during key pressing further increased clarity, reality, enjoyment, and user satisfaction.

In a similar musical VR environment, Georgiou et al. (2018) presented a rhythm game akin to playing the bongo drums that leveraged hand-tracking and mid-air haptic technologies. It is worth noting here that VR rhythm games are very popular, with the likes of the Beat Saber rhythm game achieving sales of up to USD 180 million as of February 2021 since its launch in May 2018. In their implementation of the VR bongo rhythm game, the mid-air haptic stimuli were not designed to accurately mimic the physical shape of what was seen on the screen during the game, but rather to convey its dynamics and motion. For instance, tapping tactile sensations presented at the middle of the palm were synchronized with tapping gestures and congruent audio-visual effects, while moving stimuli were presented during swiping gestures (similar to those used in automotive IVISs Young et al. 2020).

Following a similar approach, where dynamic haptic stimuli are used to accompany and enhance VR experiences, Martinez et al. (2018) sought to haptify abstract and supernatural notions like the shooting of lightning bolts from the user's hands (so-called Special Effects as discussed in Chap. "Ultrasound Haptic Feedback for Touchless User Interfaces: Design Patterns"). The challenge there was to design haptic sensations that were temporally congruent with audio-visual cues, and that felt somehow similar to what one might expect or imagine such supernatural experiences should feel like on their hands. To that end, four tactile stimuli were designed and projected to the center of the user's palm during a variety of interactions to represent the touching of a magic orb (a tactile focal point skipping through multiple random haptic points), casting a lightning spell (rapidly moving the haptic point from the wrist to the index fingertip), and finally casting a fire spell (spiral following the infinity path).

2.3.2   AR/VR/MR Training and Simulation

Looking beyond gaming and entertainment use cases, perhaps the most pivotal VR application is that of training and simulation. According to market research, the virtual training and simulation market size were valued at USD 262.36 million in 2020 and projected to reach USD 628.62 million by 2028, growing at a CAGR of 13.30% from 2021 to 2028. A key driver to this projected growth has been the ability of VR simulators to include human action recognition methods, which provide students with an engaging and immersive training environment. To that end, Balint and Althoefer (2018) have presented a VR training procedure to palpate the body with one hand and place the stethoscope with the other hand on different body parts. During this interaction, mid-air haptics were used to convey touch sensation to a healthcare trainee while they would touch and feel the body of a virtual patient (e.g., to examine the size, consistency, texture, location, and tenderness of different organs and body parts). To further heighten user immersion, their VR system was programmed in a way that the user's hands cannot penetrate the patient's body or other objects in the simulated world. This pseudo haptic effect (i.e., the visual illusion of a solid object) combined with the vibrotactile haptic feedback generated by the ultrasound device was argued to adequately create the illusion of a physical interaction as required during a VR medical simulation and training environment.

While no prototype was created nor tested, the concept and premise for a mid-air haptically enhanced VR flight simulator were proposed and discussed for the first time by Girdler and Georgiou (2020). Indeed, while an entire industry exists that installs real-life flight decks, displays, and visual systems that replicate flight conditions for pilot training, novel mixed reality alternatives have been stepping in to provide low-cost, flexible, and more accessible simulation environments. Already, mixed reality display products such as Collins Aerospace's Coalescence or CAE's Sprint VR Trainer, for example, allow not only a synthetic environment to be viewed, but also the user's hands, props, and real-world view. The authors argue that the number of props can be significantly reduced, virtualized, and mid-air haptified, therefore reducing cost and increasing flexibility and accessibility of the training and simulation platform. Note that the Airbus A330 has over 200 buttons on the overhead panel alone, while the Boeing 737 cockpit has undergone dozens of iterations over the past 50 years. Haptic feedback in training and simulation environments can aid in the learnability of a specific cockpit layout and facilitate for faster and more accurate hand interactions within the peripheral visual field of the pilot. While such hypothesis need to be vigorously tested, mid-air haptic-enhanced VR simulators also need to be FAA certified before trainees and pilots can officially log flight training time and maintain instrument flight rules (IFR) currency.

On a slightly less stringent road map, AR headsets and their ability to overlay digital content and virtual user interfaces on top of real environments have presented interesting new opportunities for product design and brand engagement, among many others. Here, users can see and interact with AR holograms, receive additional information, select actions by tapping on virtual screens, and use hand gestures or verbal commands to interact with the digital content while also being able to interact with the real world around them. To that end, Dzidek et al. (2018) presented a prototype AR car design simulation and customization demo and describe five mid-air haptic sensations that were applied to different hand-gesture interactions (see also Fig. 3). Each haptic sensation was further customized to better match the intended interaction. For example, during the demo the user could reach out, touch, feel, and hear the car engine rev. During that interaction, the audio waveform was used to dynamically modulate the base envelope of the mid-air haptic intensity profile, aiming to achieve good audio-haptic congruence.

External sensory data can also be used to alter the haptic sensation; for example, Romanus et al. (2019) (see also Fig. 3) used an expanding haptic circle sensation that was displayed at the same frequency as the heart rate recorded by a wearable sensor (60–100 beats per minute). An AR hologram of a beating heart was also shown to the user in synchrony with the haptics and measured heart rate, thus creating a so-called tactile bio-hologram.

Finally, while all previously described AR, VR, and MR mid-air haptic experiences are table-top and therefore suffer from reduced interaction volumes, Brice et al. (2019) and Howard et al. (2019) have proposed and demonstrated methods of mounting ultrasound mid-air haptic devices on robotic arms or rotating platforms, thus enlarging the effective workspace for room-scale mixed reality experiences.

2.4 Touchless Computer Interfaces in Hospitals

Providing surgeons with control over medical images while maintaining sterility has motivated a number of research initiatives that explore novel ways of interacting with imaging technologies without touching them. Initially, this was enabled through the use of gesture and voice control (Pauchot et al. 2015). Many of these novel interface

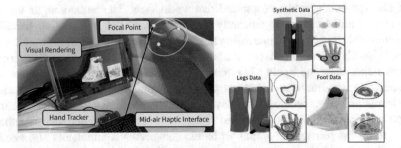

Fig. 4 Left: Experimental setup showing the user interacting with a 3D hologram of a CT scan. First, the user defines a region of interest; then, a haptic rendering algorithm produces a set of tactile patterns which represent the internal structures of the region selected that can be explored and felt in real time by the user. Right: The volumetric data are converted into a tactile periphery render and is displayed to the user's hand. Reproduced from Jang et al. (2021)

ideas and challenges were discussed by O'Hara (2014) under the theme of touchless interaction surgery, later expanded and reviewed by Cronin and Doherty (2019) under the more general theme of touchless computer interfaces in hospitals. The four key motivators for introducing touchless control in medical environments according to the scientific literature have included (i.) sterility (up to 95% of hospital keyboards have been shown to be contaminated), (ii.) enhanced 3D applications (e.g., navigating 2D and 3D data and images), (iii.) new and more efficient input methods (e.g., to speed up of specific tasks), and (iv.) tele-medicine and rehabilitation (e.g., using hand-gesture recognition for post-stroke rehabilitation Li et al. 2017). Recently, some of these use cases have taken on a whole new dimension enabled by HMDs such as the Hololens and Magic Leap that come with inbuilt hand-tracking technologies enabling additional functions such as remote training of medical staff.

When designing touchless interfaces in medical environments for use by medical professionals, one needs to be very careful and aware of the key target outcomes and expectations of the user that if adequately met will accelerate the introduction and integration of the proposed new technology into the realms of standard practice. From Cronin and Doherty (2019), some of the key metrics and target outcomes stated include ease of use, task completion time, accuracy, reliability, scalability, learnability, responsiveness, and UX. While many of these key targets relate to the overall touchless system's performance, and therefore depend on a complex set of sub-components and their interactions, several UX studies of ultrasound mid-air haptics have reported relevant benefits, thus motivating their use in touchless medical prototype systems with haptic-enhanced gesture input. For example, studies have demonstrated how mid-air haptics can help localize and interact with floating widgets (Freeman et al. 2019; Vi et al. 2017), enhance grasping of virtual objects in VR (Frutos-Pascual et al. 2019) and AR (Vaquero-Melchor and Bernardos 2019), improve the sense of agency (Cornelio Martinez et al. 2017), enhance perceived physicality of holograms (Pinto et al. 2020), and improve usability and aesthetic appeal (Limerick et al. 2019).

Exploring the use of mid-air haptics in touchless computer interfaces in hospitals therefore makes sense and however is significantly under studied.

Hung et al. (2013) developed a mid-air haptic system in 2013 to train cardiologists to search for a pulse. The prototypes called UltraSendo and UltraPulse were piloted at Glan Clwyd Hospital in Wales where multiple clinicians evaluated its efficacy with mixed responses (Hung et al. 2014). Balint and Althoefer (2018) implemented a training and simulation setup in 2018 in VR using ultrasound mid-air haptics to emulate the palpation of a virtual patient and train staff. Romanus et al. (2019) presented a mid-air haptic bio-hologram, where the user can see, touch, and feel a holographic projection of a user's heart beating (see also Fig. 3). Data about the heart rate were wirelessly streamed live from a wearable sensor. Finally, Jang et al. (2021) presented a demonstrator that combined a 3D holographic display and mid-air haptics to enable users to explore anatomical data (CT scans of a human body), where elements like bones and vessels are rendered by different tactile effects in mid-air (see Fig. 4).

In summary, the use of mid-air haptics for medical applications and training is very much in an exploratory phase, with a variety of one-off demonstrators and indirectly studied benefits. One reason for this is that this use case is highly interdisciplinary requiring a lot of medical or industry specific expertise and insights as well as the integration with a variety of immersive display technologies.

2.5 Neuroscience Research Studies

Neuroscience is the scientific study of the nervous system and is a hugely multi-disciplinary science. The emergence of powerful new measurement techniques such as neuroimaging, EEG, MEG, and electrophysiology has allowed scientist to probe and then measure so as to understand how cognition and emotions are mapped to specific neural substrates. Specifically for touch, neuroscientists are interested in understanding how the somatosensory system processes tactile information.

The ability of mid-air haptics to produce complex spatial and temporal tactile stimuli has thus presented neuroscientists with uncharted new territories for research and knowledge generation. For example, Perquin et al. (2021) asked whether the tactile system can be used to perceive complex whole hand motion stimuli, and whether it exhibits the same kind of established perceptual biases as reported in the visual domain. To that end, they designed user studies that confirmed human hand ability to discriminate tactile motion direction and affirmed the presence of a tactile 'Oblique Effect' (analogous to that observed in vision) where users are both better and more confident at discriminating motion in the vertical and horizontal axes of the hand, compared to those stimuli moving obliquely. In another example, Karafotias et al. studied whether VR and mid-air ultrasound tactile stimulation could reduce perceived pain simulated via the cold pressor test (Karafotias et al. 2017) and showed that mid-air haptic stimulation plays a significant role in increasing pain tolerance time. In contrast, Nakajima et al. (2019) leveraged the thermal grill illusion together with mid-air ultrasonic haptics and some mist vapor to display tactile pain or cooling sensations to the forearm.

Lehser et al. (2018) used EEG recordings to demonstrate the feasibility of eliciting somatosensory evoked potentials (SEPs) with ultrasonic haptic stimuli in mid-air, and that more complex tactile stimuli (e.g., shapes) tend to elicit a larger EEG wavelet phase synchronization stability indicating that a greater attentional effort is needed to solve more complex tactile recognition tasks (Lehser and Strauss 2019). It is worth noting that Carcagno et al. (2019) who performed a similar study to see if people could hear the ultrasound emitted by a mid-air haptic device did not detect any EEG phase locked activity. Therefore, EEG and SEPs could potentially be used to provide objective evaluation metrics for mid-air haptic feedback in different HMI settings. To that end, Brice et al. (2021) created a mid-air haptically enhanced VR environment where users were exposed to virtual spiders (in jars, near them, or on their hands) and used EEG recordings and skin conductance levels to measure changes in anxiety and distress. Their results were then contrasted to self reported data obtained through the Fear of Spiders Questionnaire.

Going beyond EEG and in order to use advanced neural monitors such as microneurography, Hayward et al. (2020) developed an electromagnetic shielding (Faraday cage) that can encapsulate the ultrasonic mid-air haptic device therefore reducing any electromagnetic interference (EMI). This is important since microneurography uses metal microelectrodes to detect neural traffic in nerves leading to or coming from muscle and skin receptors, a process which is very sensitive to EMI. Moreover, microneurography can discriminate between the type of mechanoreceptors being stimulated by mid-air haptics (i.e., Merkel disks (SA1), Meissner corpuscles (RA1), Pacinian corpuscles (RA2), and Ruffini endings (SA2)) (Moore et al. 2021) but also help study afferent neural pathways relevant to affective touch (McGlone et al. 2014).

Finally, to aid in the design of mid-air haptic stimuli, especially for research purposes, Mulot et al. (2021) developed an open-source framework called DOLPHIN that enables easy control of the different haptic rendering parameters.

3 Design Guidelines for Effective Mid-Air Haptic Interfaces

Clearly, mid-air haptic technology has been used in a variety of applications ranging from automotive, to VR, to public displays in retail, to touchless interfaces in hospitals and museums, and even in the home (Van den Bogaert et al. 2019). Moreover, it holds great research potential in deepening our understanding of how our brain works and interprets touch. Closing the loop and bringing that understanding back into the applications presented in the previous subsections and beyond is an even greater but highly desirable challenge. From a UX perspective however, it is paramount to extract design guidelines and best practices from the plethora of applications and prototypes built to date—which is the focus of the present section.

As shown in the previous section of this chapter, ultrasound mid-air haptic technology can be used in a variety of applications to enhance touchless control interfaces, by providing the end user with a sense of touch in mid-air. In such settings, the sense of touch is vital for control in at least two key ways: *(1) confirmation*—conveying that an action has been recognized by the system and *(2) presence and affordance*—conveying information about the physical requirements of control, i.e., where the control is located (presence) and what actions are required from the user to assert control (affordance).

We can see both concepts embodied by physical controls in the real world, e.g., the tactile cues one experiences when pressing a light switch. Mechanical feedback from the switch confirms the action has taken place and the physical properties of the switch (e.g., its shape, current state) are the affordances that help the user discover how to use it. A good user interface should therefore aim to give confirmation feedback and convey affordances, while also supporting a user's internal locus of control (i.e., the degree to which people believe that they, as opposed to external forces, have control over the outcome of events in their lives) which is one of Shneiderman's 8 golden rules of interface design (Shneiderman et al. 2016).

Mid-air tactile cues can address the requirements for control (confirmation, presence, and affordance) and therefore support the user's internal locus of control by (1) enabling control and (2) enhancing the feeling of control (an idea explored further in Chap. "Opportunities for Multisensory Mid-air Interactions Featuring Ultrasound Haptic Feedback"). Moreover, repeated use of a new mid-air interface that combines multimodal feedback (e.g., visual, haptic, audio, and olfactory) can result in the build up of a user's experience with the interface and can translate into a feedforward loop that primes their expectations for their next interactions and accelerates familiarization via muscle memory, interface learning, mental models, etc. (Breitschaft et al. 2019). Below, we present some of the ways that an interaction designer can leverage mid-air haptics to their advantage while also highlighting some of the key challenges and considerations. These design recommendations are derived from findings in the literature and best practices adopted by the ultrasound haptics community.

3.1 Presence of Controls

Guideline 1: use haptic feedback to convey the presence and location of mid-air controls (e.g., buttons, slider elements, dials).

Tactile cues can signal the presence and location of a mid-air control interface, subtly indicating to the user that their hand is in the correct location for making a particular action. Vo and Brewster (2015), for example, showed that when providing haptic feedback to indicate the location of a mid-air control, users were able to find and interact with it about 50% more accurately compared to providing visual feedback

Fig. 5 Presence of controls. This image illustrates that a mid-air button, slider, and general haptic feedback presence can be represented in mid-air making it easy for a user to find and interact with

alone. Such improvements afforded to touchless interfaces by mid-air haptics can decrease the minimum recommended widget size from $2\,\text{cm}^2$ to $1\,\text{cm}^2$; since users can more accurately localize controls with haptic feedback, touchless interfaces can provide more functionality within a given size of workspace. This is especially important if the use case requires the user to be visually attending to another element of the interaction, such as during driving, or if the interaction volume is small or the input interface is dense, e.g., for a virtual keyboard such as in Hwang's AirPiano (Hwang et al. 2017). Figure 5 illustrates some examples of mid-air controls that can be displayed using ultrasound mid-air haptic feedback.

3.2 System Status and Changes

> Guideline 2: use haptic feedback to inform the user of system status and changes to system state.

The first principle in Nielsen's 10 usability heuristics (Nielsen 2005) is to convey system status, so that the user understands the current state of the system. Adhering to this heuristic ensures that the user feels informed and in control. This is typically achieved in interface design by using Shniederman's third golden rule—offering informative feedback. Informing the user of ongoing operations and system state is important, especially when actions do not have an immediately noticeable outcome. For example, graphical user interfaces often employ progress indicators to show when the system is loading or carrying out lengthy operations, letting the user know they can expect a slight delay while the system processes information.

In a similar way, tactile feedback can be used to convey system status to users, e.g., through changes in haptic parameters and sensations. For example, a progress indicator can be represented haptically to a user by drawing a line or a circle on the palm of their hand, analogous to a graphical progress indicator (like in Fig. 6). The chosen haptic sensation should aim to convey or trigger some kind of semantic meaning or relevance that is congruent to the action or system state itself. This is the principle behind the Ultrahapticons concept (Brown et al. 2020), further detailed in

Fig. 6 The system status of a loading time being conveyed through tactile information

Chap. "Augmenting Automotive Gesture Infotainment Interfaces Through Mid-air Haptic Icon Design" of this book.

3.3 Confirmation

> Guideline 3: use haptic feedback to give confirmatory feedback about input actions.

Tactile cues can be used to provide haptic feedback to confirm that the system has recognized the user's input actions. Confirmation is perhaps the most commonly considered and applied use of tactile cues in interface design, especially during user input as it can enhance the user's sense of agency (Cornelio Martinez et al. 2017). For example, haptic feedback during smartphone keypad input is now commonplace, a subtle 'buzz' or 'pop' vibration for every screen tap, or a burst of vibrations when adjusting a slider.

Intuitive confirmation haptics can improve the user experience and progressively establish trust between the interface and the user who feels in control. The same concept carries over to mid-air haptic feedback and gesture input and can be particularly useful in reducing the amount of time users need to perform the input accurately, or glance at the screen for additional visual feedback; reducing glance time is particularly important for car infotainment systems.

Cornelio Martinez et al. (2017) and Evangelou et al. (2021) have studied the enhancements in the sense of agency imbued due to mid-air haptics during discrete input events such as pressing a mid-air button followed by a haptic feedback confirmation sensation. Young et al. (2020) have applied several such mid-air haptic feedback sensations, often enhanced with additional functional information such as directional and dynamic haptics to match the corresponding hand gesture. In a similar automotive setting, Georgiou et al. (2017) considered agency and control during their haptic design of automotive touchless user interfaces by applying haptics throughout the interaction, not just during the input action. This was achieved by incorporating a solution for pre-emptive gestures: On entrance of a hand into the active interaction region of the interface, the user's palm is met with a continuous haptic sensation that fixes itself onto the palm and moves with the hand. Akin to lightly touching a keyboard key before pressing it, this sensation lets the user know that the system is engaged and ready for their input. Once the user initiates an action gesture (e.g., a tap or a swipe), the mid-air haptics delivers a powerful pulse to indicate confirmation of a click. Congruence between mid-air haptic design and hand gestures has been hypothesized to improve UX, but no evidence has yet been presented to support that.

3.4 Latency and Timing

> Guideline 4: aim to provide the *right haptic feedback* at the *right time* in the interaction.

Tactile cues must be well timed to facilitate effective control. We see from psychological studies that the perception of time and control are linked during our interaction with technology (Limerick et al. 2014). Therefore, one needs to consider two key timing questions: How much latency can the interaction afford, and should haptic cues be presented before, during, or after the interaction takes place?

The latency between when the user makes an action and when the feedback is actually provided is an important parameter to consider when designing for mid-air haptic control interfaces. As a general rule, this latency should not exceed 100 ms and should be as small as possible (Kaaresoja et al. 2011). Excessive latency may lead the user to attempt an operation again because they were unsure if their action was recognized (i.e., missing confirmation feedback), for example, when a person continues pressing a button in a lift if the doors have not started to close.

In most gesture interaction scenarios, the computer must first recognize the user's action before it can generate a response, thus making it difficult to achieve instantaneous feedback, especially if the input gesture is long or complex. Therefore, it is important to consider the type of gesture to be used in an interface, together with the type of mid-air haptic feedback that should be given, since these may sometimes be incompatible or result in excess latency due to the necessary gesture recognition time. This continues to be an issue, despite advancements and capabilities brought forward by machine learning approaches that enable the prediction of the intended gesture before the gesture completes (Ahmad et al. 2015). Pickering et al. (2007) for example classified gesture input into pre-emptive, function associated, context sensitive, global shortcut, and natural dialog. From these, one might expect that functional, context sensitive, and natural dialog type of gestures will generally be more complex and take longer to complete or action, therefore delaying gesture recognition and making the application of instantaneous haptic feedback difficult and prone to delays.

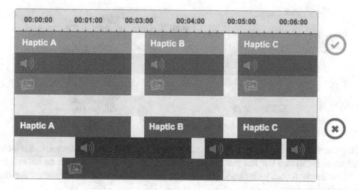

Fig. 7 Timing illustration of haptic, auditory, and visual playback cues. Generally, these should be congruent in time and space; however, sometimes applying a short delay can be beneficial

Choosing a suitable time to present tactile cues is also important and can be difficult to design for. If tactile cues are presented at the wrong time during the interaction, it can be confusing and frustrating to the user. Therefore, the best time to provide the tactile cue depends on the role it plays in the interaction. If its purpose is to guide or pre-empt the user prior to some input action, then providing tactile cues *before* their action begins can help indicate that their hand is in the correct location or that the system is engaged. If its purpose is to represent the physicality of the control interface (e.g., the size, shape, or location of control elements), then feedback should be given instantaneously with as little delay as possible. If haptic cues are intended as confirmation feedback for an input action, e.g., pressing a button or adjusting a slider, then preliminary evidence suggests that a greater sense of agency is achieved when haptics are presented at the time of the *outcome* resulting from activation, as opposed to being presented at the time of the activating gesture itself. If the haptic interaction purpose is to represent the state or the function of a particular control element, then just like with hover-over gesture interactions, a small delay could be applied before haptics are displayed. Finally, how haptic feedback or feedforward stimuli are triggered and timed relative to other visual or audio stimuli is an important UX consideration (see Fig. 7).

3.5   Interaction Zone and Hand Positioning

Guideline 5: use haptic feedback to reveal the interaction zone so users know where to provide input.

A key principle when designing a good interactive experience is that hand position and gesture are ergonomic for comfortable use (Nielsen et al. 2003). Hand position also has important implications for the quality of input sensing and mid-air haptic

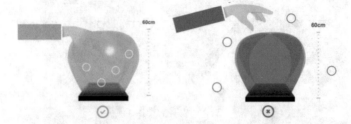

Fig. 8 The green diagram shows that the user's hand and the haptic interactive elements of the experience must be within the interaction zone to feel the optimum strength of haptic sensations. The red image shows a badly designed experience, where the interactive elements are outside the optimum interaction zone

feedback quality (Freeman et al. 2019). A well-positioned hand can help to optimize the extent to which the user feels a haptic sensation. Ultrasonic mid-air haptic feedback requires a line of sight between the emitting phased array and the target region on the hand. Moreover, it is important that the hand is within range of both the tracking and haptic devices; otherwise, input sensing is degraded. Therefore, one needs to choose hand gestures that expose the right parts of the hand in a suitable mid-air position, thereby enabling good tracking and good haptics. For example, a fist/punch hand gesture is difficult to track by most gesture recognition algorithms and will also occlude the palmar region of the hand which is the most sensitive to ultrasonic vibrotactile stimulation. One also needs to consider where the haptic and tracking devices are positioned relative to the interaction region while also considering any use case specific limitations and UX constraints.

The interaction zone is the volume of space above the ultrasound array in which the haptic sensation can be felt and where the hand-tracking device will track the hand. The haptic designed thus must ensure that the interactions and the haptic objects in the experience are within the interaction zone, and anything outside of this zone will be weak or not felt at all. Figure 8 shows the typical interaction zone for a 16×16 transducer phased array. The interaction volume increases with transducer count and can take different shapes when multiple non-planar arrays are used.

The angle at which the focused pressure interacts with the hand is also an important consideration. Roughly, the acoustic radiation pressure applied to the hand will vary with $\cos^2 \theta$, where θ is the angle between the source and the target surface on the hand and is equal to $\theta = 0$ when they are parallel. Therefore, to ensure maximum haptic sensation, the experience design should encourage the user to have an open hand with their palm facing the array when inside the interaction zone. For example, if the array is placed pointing upwards on a table, the palm faces down. Conversely, if the array is facing downwards, acoustic pressure is directed downwards and the user should place their hand with their palm facing up. More complex gestures can of course be used, and the angle θ need not be exactly zero. For example, a swipe gesture that exposes the palm to the haptic source is preferred to one that does not. Therefore, the UI/UX and haptic designer need to consider this limitation during both

Fig. 9 Green images show the correct hand positioning within the interaction zone with the palm open and facing the array. Red images showing sub-optimal hand positioning

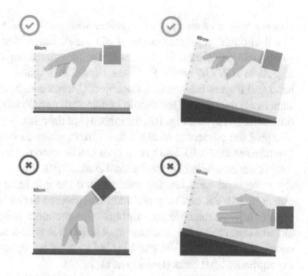

the interaction design and the physical design (where to place ultrasound emitters) of the experience (see Fig. 9).

3.6 Haptic Congruence

Guideline 6: maximize congruence between haptic sensations and other sensory modalities.

Ensuring that there is good congruence between haptic sensation and audio-visual cues, as well as being congruent with the system status, is an important and challenging consideration. In the simplest case, one should aim to match primary interface properties such as the interactive object's location, size, and function. Virtual buttons or widgets for example should look, sound, feel, and react similarly, e.g., they can be 'snappy' and 'clicky.' The mid-air haptics applied should therefore also imbue a similar 'click' or 'pop' sensation and should be fairly localized, either as a single focal point on the fingertip or somewhere on the palm. Detailed consideration and suggestions about the different haptic design patterns and when or how they relate to different types of interaction are discussed in more detail in Chap. "Ultrasound Haptic Feedback for Touchless User Interfaces: Design Patterns" of this book.

Mid-air haptic sensations stimulate our cutaneous haptic sense (i.e., are vibrotactile) and lack a strong kinesthetic force, a crucial element in our interactions with the physical world captured by Newton's third law. Thus, mid-air haptics will by definition fail to recreate accurate physical touch sensations of a holographic object.

Despite this, mid-air haptics, together with audio and visual feedback, can create 'good enough' representations of 3D touch interactions, especially if we follow some basic guidelines. For instance, when manipulating or grasping 3D holographic objects in AR/VR, haptic feedback should be applied to the contact regions of the hand and fingers intersecting the object (Matsubayashi et al. 2019), salient features such as corners and edges should be haptically emphasized (Hajas et al. 2020; Martinez et al. 2019) (see Fig. 10), the intensity of the ultrasound haptics can be modulated to adjust the perceived changes in stiffness when an object is pressed or squeezed (Marchal et al. 2020), and visual cues can be used to further indicate when a grip is formed successfully (Frutos-Pascual et al. 2019). It has also been argued that applying some semi-transparency shaders onto the graphical representation of a virtual object in AR/VR can help maintain congruence between a penetrable holographic object and a vibrotactile mid-air haptic interaction that lacks force feedback. This is already observed when contrasting AR and VR with a force-feedback apparatus of equal intensity where VR graphics led to them being perceived as 60% stiffer than the equivalent AR ones (Gaffary et al. 2017).

Following this line of thought, Beattie et al. (2020) proposed that the visually inferred tactile expectations of a virtual object, i.e., how we imagine that an object will feel before actually touching it, should be congruent to with the mid-air haptic effect applied. Beattie et al. (2020) demonstrated this idea by using machine learning to match the visual perception of roughness to haptic rendering algorithm to produce visuo-haptic congruent textures. It is expected that visuo-haptic and audio congruence would further enhance the tactile reproduction of textures (Mc Gee et al. 2000) and of other hand-object interactions, with audio in particular influencing how some mid-air haptic sensations are perceived (Freeman 2021). In fact, through multimodal synthesis and haptic design, it is possible to supplement or augment a number of tactile and haptic experiences to either create supernatural experiences of abstract notions, e.g., magic spells (Martinez et al. 2018) or can lead to the creation of so-called tactile illusions (Lederman and Jones 2011).

3.7 Improving Perceived Haptic Intensity

> Guideline 7: use knowledge of haptic perception to maximize perceived intensity of haptic stimuli.

As with other perceptual modalities (e.g., visual, auditory), the perceived intensity (strength) of the haptic stimulus is primarily due to the maximal stimulation of the corresponding sensory receptors, which in this case depend on frequency selectivity, and spatial and temporal summation effects (Gescheider et al. 2002). It is therefore important to know how one should modulate and leverage the available control parameters of mid-air haptics to maximize the perceived strength of the tactile stim-

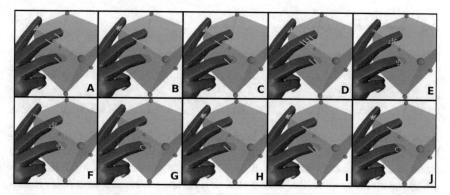

Fig. 10 Image showing where mid-air haptic feedback should be applied during hand-object interactions while also emphasizing salient features of the object. Reproduced from Martinez et al. (2019)

ulus. When using amplitude modulation, a stationary amplitude modulated (AM) focal point is felt stronger at frequencies of about 150–200 Hz (Hasegawa and Shinoda 2018; Rümelin et al. 2017), which corresponds to the peak sensitivity of the PC mechanoreceptors. Also, similar to visual and auditory stimuli, the duration and intensity of mid-air haptics can be interchanged for a similar perceptual outcome. In fact, according to Driller et al. (2019) who tested short impulses of a mid-air haptic point presented for 100–700 ms, it was observed that longer duration stimuli were generally perceived as more intense than shorter duration stimuli, i.e., a *temporal summation* effect was observed. Similarly, when utilizing more advanced haptic rendering techniques like lateral modulation (LM) and spatiotemporal modulation (STM), described in more detail in Chap. "Modulation Methods for Ultrasound Midair Haptics," one can take advantage of the so-called *spatial summation* effect, where the size of the mid-air haptic stimulus being presented will impact its perceived strength, i.e., the larger the stimulus against the hand, the stronger it will feel. Care needs to be taken here, however, as a larger stimulus will reduce the total pressure output capacity of a mid-air haptic device, resulting in a trade-off between the applied radiation pressure (Newtons per square meter) and the stimulus area.

To address this trade-off, LM and STM techniques propose to rapidly move a single focal point along a trajectory (e.g., a line or circle) thereby increasing the effective stimulus area while maintaining the instantaneous total applied radiation pressure. Further optimizing the sampling interval of STM paths can maximize the perceived strength of the vibrotactile stimuli (Frier et al. 2019). Additionally, optimizing the focal point motion speed to match the surface wave velocity of vibrations on human skin (in the range of 5 to 8 m/s) can cause wave-front constructive interference, thereby increasing skin indentation and amplifying the perceived intensity of the stimulus (Frier et al. 2018). Known characteristics of haptic perception like these can be used to increase perceived intensity, without any changes to the haptic device or its driving software.

3.8 Shape Recognition

Guideline 8: select an appropriate rendering approach for the desired haptic shapes.

Accurate shape representation has been one of the earliest and most studied challenges associated with this technology, motivated through the presentation of haptic icons in car interfaces (Brown et al. 2020), science communication (Daniel et al. 2020), menu navigation (Rocchesso et al. 2019), and interaction with AR/VR digital and immersive worlds (Kervegant et al. 2017). As such, there are multiple approaches toward the rendering of haptic shapes, which can be generally grouped under three distinctly different approaches: (1) placing multiple AM focal points along the perimeter of the shape (Long et al. 2014); (2) using a single STM focal point to rapidly trace out the shape (Martinez et al. 2019); and (3) using a single AM focal point that moves to dynamically draw the intended shape while briefly pausing at salient features such as the shape corners (Hajas et al. 2020). In the following sections, we review each of these in more detail.

Multiple refinements and modifications to these methods exist and are also ongoing in state-of-the-art research, while their implementations differ in complexity, effectiveness, and suitability to each specific use case. Note that the difference in the three implementations can be illustrated when the acoustically rendered shape is projected onto an oil bath using the apparatus described by Abdouni et al. (2019). Figure 11 shows a similar apparatus to that of Abdouni et al. (2019). In the bottom right sub-figure, one can clearly observe an STM circle pressure field being applied to the thin layer of oil bath. The caption of Fig. 11 describes how one can reproduce this apparatus and view mid-air tactile holography.

3.8.1 Multiple AM Points Forming a Perimeter

Long et al. (2014) presented the first implementation and successful user study of volumetric rendering of 3D shapes (e.g., cube, cone, pyramid, etc.) with an 80% recognition rate using a novel multi-point solver of ultrasound mid-air haptics. While the user was unable to enclose a 3D shape in a traditional sense due to the lack of force feedback, the 3D object, such as a sphere or pyramid, could be explored from all sides using the palm and fingertips. In their implementation, the user's hand was represented as sixteen planes (a palm polygon and three separate polygons for each finger). When some of these planes intersect an object in the 3D scene, the hand-object intersections are found as line segments and processed into continuous arcs. Multiple ultrasonic focal points are then sampled along the arcs at appropriate spacings and presented onto the user's hand by a 320x phased transducer array. Repeating this procedure which takes a few milliseconds to compute would re-position the focal points dynamically during active exploration or manipulation of 3D digital objects

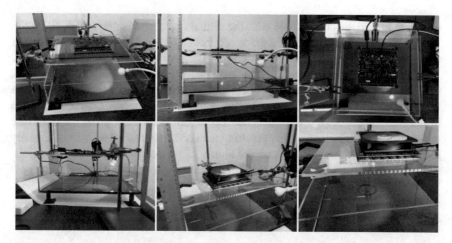

Fig. 11 Oil bath apparatus for visualizing mid-air haptic shapes and sensation. An array is suspended approximately 15 cm above the oil bath. The oil is between 2 and 5 mm deep and of the correct consistency: viscous enough to show dispersion, fluid enough to be responsive. We have found that a 50:50 mix of olive oil and pumpkin seed oil give good results. The oil bath must be level and raised approximately 3 cm above a white surface or table. A bright single light source is used from above or at an angle to project the shadow of the distorted oil onto the white surface. If the light is bright enough, it can reflect onto a wall to create a screen. The room must be as dark as possible to achieve the best effect. If operating the array for long, it is advisable to use a cooling fan to suck out hot air and avoid over heating

by the user's hands therefore enabling real-time haptic sensations and dynamically changing shapes. Each focal point was amplitude modulated (AM) 200 Hz; however, multiple focal points were grouped together into two groups, with one of the groups modulation pattern shifted by $\pi/2$ as to improve the array efficiency.

In a different setting where participants were prohibited to move their hand freely during the mid-air tactile interaction (passive touch) and using just a 100x transducer phased array, Korres and Eid (2016) used a similar implementation to Long et al. and studied 2D shape recognition (circle, triangle, line, and plus sign) and reported an average accuracy of about 60% with a mean recognition time being 14 s. In yet a slightly different setting, Rutten et al. (2019) also used a similar implementation to Long and studied how identifiable mid-air haptic shapes (4 static and 4 dynamic) were. These were presented to an older group of people than in previous studies for just 1 s using a 196x transducer phased array. They observed a 44% recognition rate which is quite low, thus suggesting that participant age, the short stimulus time, a smaller array, and the large variety of shapes presented could all have a negative impact on shape recognition. However, they also concluded that line-based patterns were generally better recognized than circular ones and that dynamic sensations made of a moving focal point were more accurately recognized than static shapes made by multiple focal points. Further improvements have been reported when the acoustic pressure distribution applied to different parts of the hand surface is controlled to mimic the contact area with the virtual object (Matsubayashi et al. 2020). This however requires larger transducer counts capable of more precise control of the acoustic fields and more complex computations of the hand-object interactions.

A slightly different approach is that achieved by Morales et al. (2021) where a modified Gerchberg–Saxton algorithm is used to produce a target acoustic amplitude field by iteratively back- and forward-propagating with a discretization masking step in between. Even though the mathematical algorithm is very different from that of a multi-focal point solver, the resulting acoustic field resembles that of densely packed AM points. User studies on the ability of such algorithms to produce well-recognizable tactile shapes in mid-air have not yet been conducted.

3.8.2   Single STM Point Rapidly Tracing Out a Shape

Mid-air haptic devices utilizing phased arrays are limited in the amount of acoustic energy they can output, thus limiting the number of focal points they can display simultaneously. To mitigate this shortcoming, STM rendering techniques were proposed by Kappus and Long (2018) whereby a single focal point at maximum pressure output is rapidly ($\sim$7 m/s) moved along a path or a set of so-called polylines which trace a geometric shape resembling the hand-object intersection profile (Martinez et al. 2019). Howard et al. studied the ability of people to discriminate the orientation of a haptic STM straight line presented at different angles ($\alpha = \{0°, 45°, 90°, 135°\}$) to the palm of a user and observed quite high recognition rates of 92–99.3% (Howard et al. 2019). When displaying more complex shapes however such as a circle, a triangle, or a square, Hajas et al. (2020) observed a shape recognition of just 51.7% and 57.3% for passive and active touch explorations, respectively. These studies seem to suggest that the STM shape rendering approach is not robust enough and therefore not well suited for the tactile presentation of 2D and 3D shapes in mid-air. However, the above studies have only considered holographic shapes which are of diameters of a few centimeters being projected onto the user's palm during active or passive explorations. In contrast, Matsubayashi et al. (2019) applied STM rendering along micro-paths tracing the perimeter of finger-object contact cross-sections and observed an average shape recognition of 65%, an improvement of about 25% compared to a stationary AM focus point located at the center of the finger-object contact point. It should be stated however that Matsubayashi et al. were using a very large array with 3984 transducers and only compared between four local shapes (curved, flat, edge, corner).

3.8.3   Single AM Point Dynamically Drawing a Shape

Currently, the most effective method for presenting complex tactile shapes using ultrasound mid-air haptic devices (84.7 and 88%) has been reported by a dynamic rendering method described by Hajas et al. (2020) and Rocchesso et al. (2019), both of which leverage AM points to dynamically draw a given shape or icon on the user's palm, akin to a pencil writing on paper. This method is known as *dynamic tactile pointer* (DTP). Slowing down the speed of the DTP according to the curvature of the trajectory, or even pausing completely for 300–450 ms at corners, helps the user identify salient features of the shape or count its corners. Note that corner identification was a key failure point mentioned by users in a study by Marti et al. (2021) who used a 196-transducer array to project static tactile shapes (circle, square, point) and match them to visual or verbal representation probes. While DTP successfully manages to convey corners thus helping with the discrimination between circles and polygons, one issue with this method is that it can take a few seconds for the icon/shape to be fully dynamically rendered, thus introducing a minimum delay in recognition time. Adding a second AM focal point that draws on the palm simultaneously can address that in some cases, depending on the path being drawn, e.g., for the equals and times symbols (= and ×). Indeed, it was recently shown that it was significantly easier to identify stimuli that are rendered at a slower pace (i.e., longer duration) regardless of the number of draw repetitions (Sand et al. 2020). It is noted that recognition accuracy and time can be improved when the set of icons chosen are somehow meaningful to the actions they are supposed to trigger or relate to specific mental models of their application (Brown et al. 2020). Therefore, the choosing and the design process of the specific icons that constitute a mid-air haptic interface are as important as the rendering method used.

3.9 Haptic Switching Duration

> Guideline 9: use a brief gap between different haptic sensations to help users recognize change.

Pauses between mid-air haptic sensations can be as noticeable and perceptible as the sensation itself. Rather than presenting a series haptic effects in sequence, brief pauses or gaps can be used to increase impact and make changes more noticeable, e.g., when moving from one button on a mid-air control interface to another. This delay, known as the *haptic switching duration*, can support better recognition of the change in haptic sensation. When switching between haptic patterns, leaving a delay of at least 200 ms is advisable; however, a rigorous investigation of the optimal gap duration has not yet been conducted.

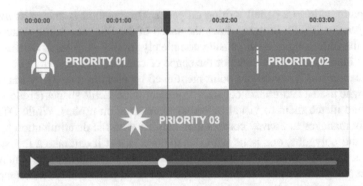

Fig. 12 Illustrating the haptic priority principle where the highest priority haptic will play

3.10 Haptic Sensation Priority

> Guideline 10: prioritize haptic sensations so that users receive the most important or salient feedback.

When multiple haptic sensations need to be presented simultaneously, it is logical to only present the one which is most dominant or important to the user experience. This is similar to visual hierarchy principles in visual design, when dominance conveys something critical about the experience. For example, the mid-air game experience described by Corenthy et al. (2018) used the hand's movements to represent the position of a spaceship and applied different mid-air haptic effects to present a number of different game actions and events, such as lasers fired from the user's space ship and entering or jumping between scenes. However, when the spaceship got hit by enemy fire, its haptic sensation was prioritized over others to represent the explosion, which was a more important and rare game event, as illustrated in Fig. 12. Therefore, depending on different events in and during an interaction, the priority will shift and should be considered by the UX and haptic designer.

3.11 Static or Moving?

> Guideline 11: consider if your mid-air haptic interface should remain in position, or follow the user's hand movements.

This question refers to the way that mid-air haptics are applied to the user's hand while also leveraging the capabilities of the hand-tracking system. A static control panel

Fig. 13 (1) *Static:* three buttons fixed in space within the interaction zone. The user will move their hand between these buttons, but the haptic for each button will be fixed in space. (2) *Dynamic:* the button follows the user's hand. The user will feel a button wherever their hand is located within the interaction zone. Then, a 'click' sensation is projected when the user taps one of the three static buttons or the dynamic button

composed of a matrix of buttons for example was implemented in the automotive study by Harrington et al. (2018) where the driver would feel the relative locations of buttons arranged in a 2 × 2 grid and then choose which one to activate via a pressing down gesture. Such an implementation is robust and does not require advance hand-tracking algorithms as a simple proximity sensor could suffice. In contrast, a moving control panel where the buttons 'come to you' was implemented in an automotive setting by Young et al. (2020) where a gesture was detected and a set of haptic sensations were accurately projected toward the user's palm or fingers as long as they were within a predefined interaction region. The two scenario are illustrated in Fig. 13. Static mid-air haptic interfaces are therefore generally easier and more straightforward to implement and comprehend as they represent a more direct one-to-one mapping between physical space and holographic touch interactions, while dynamic ones require a robust implementation of gesture input yet facilitate for a more natural 3D spatial interaction. Choosing which of the two types of haptics is more suitable will strongly depend on the use case and available hardware capabilities. Chap. "Ultrasound Haptic Feedback for Touchless User Interfaces: Design Patterns" further considers the use of static vs moving haptic interfaces.

3.12 Multimodal Feedback and Synthesis

Guideline 12: combine mid-air haptics with other sensory modalities to create a richer user experience.

Other sensory modalities (visual, audio, olfactory, and even gustatory) can be combined with that of haptics to enhance utilitarian or functional aspects of an interaction, as well as its experiential qualities. For example, peripheral visual feedback can be leveraged to aid users in finding where to place their hand for improved mid-air interaction (better accuracy and faster interaction time) (Freeman et al. 2019). Here, the authors used an LED strip that interpolated between green and white hues as a function of the proximity distance between a target and the user's hand position. A similar arrangement was used by Shakeri et al. in an automotive setting, where the LED strip would pulse briefly in white when the user's hand would enter the interaction region, and blue lights would animate from the ends of the strip toward its center during a 'v' gesture, while yellow and blue lights would animate to the left or right during a swipe or circular gesture (Shakeri et al. 2018). The inclusion of such peripheral visual feedback together with mid-air haptics was shown to significantly reduce the average eyes-off-the-road time and the subjective workload during a driving task. Even better results were however reported for the combination of haptics plus audio feedback which were ranked as the most preferred form of feedback in their study (Shakeri et al. 2018). These examples leveraged multiple sensory modalities to make user interface feedback more salient.

In a different, more immersive setting, mid-air haptic feedback was combined with different sound cues that were triggered by tapping and swiping hand gestures to create a VR rhythm game for playing the bongo drums (Georgiou et al. 2018). As rhythm games in general require tight synchronicity between visual, audio, and haptic cues, the author's demonstrator showed that mid-air haptics can be reliably and pleasantly displayed in real time and in sync with audio-visual cues in an immersive VR setting thereby increasing the user's sense of being in control and feeling of interacting with a more responsive system (Cornelio Martinez et al. 2017). This example used multimodal feedback for a higher quality user experience.

Mid-air haptics can also have a significant effect on several experiential and perceptual dimensions (e.g., intensity, roughness, regularity, roundness, and valence) when displayed in conjunction with different audio and visual stimuli. Early evidence by Ablart et al. (2019) suggested that when congruent stimuli, e.g., mid-air haptics and audio stimuli that were rated as both being quite 'round' are presented simultaneously a general enhancement effect was reported, while incongruent stimuli could alter or augment the perception of the bimodal (audio/visual plus haptic) stimuli. Indeed, in a recent study by Freeman it was shown that adding white noise audio (emanating from the haptic device itself) increased the perceived roughness of a mid-air tactile sensation, while pure audio tones had a small but opposite effect (Freeman 2021). These examples demonstrate the potential benefits of using congruent, or deliberately incongruent, sensations from different modalities to influence the haptic experience.

Additional guidelines on how to best combine auditory and mid-air haptic feedback in a simple light-switch interaction were recently presented by Ozkul et al. (2020). Not only did they demonstrate the added value of multimodality with mid-air haptic feedback in influencing pleasantness, the authors results also suggested that adding more sensory components resulted in more pleasantness (trimodal > bimodal > unimodal) while mid-air haptics and visual feedback were the preferred bimodal pair composition. Further, it was shown that longer haptic stimuli and the use of designed sounds (as opposed to digital click sounds) led to higher perceived pleasantness and clarity.

In a more creative yet real-world setting (i.e., outside of a controlled laboratory) comprising interactive art installation, Vi et al. (2017) reported on how to design art experiences while considering all the senses (i.e., vision, sound, touch, smell, and taste). The authors identify that touch, as displayed through a mid-air haptic device, was rated by the 2500 visitors as the most important sense during the whole experience, as opposed to scent and taste, and that the combination of mid-air haptics and sound was immersive and provided an up-lifting experience of an art painting. Thus, as more such findings are explored and documented for different use cases, we can anticipate that UX and haptic designers will be able to tailor the parameters of different mid-air haptic stimuli (size, shape, frequency etc.) to deliver richer tactile and multimodal experiences that better reflect the desired outcome effect and will be potentially able to modulate and control various experiential aspects of the different interactions and applications. While this is a fascinating future vision with great potential, guidelines of exactly how one should synthesize multimodal feedback are however still in an early exploration phase with very few clear cut examples. Namely, while mid-air haptics have been integrated in short movie experiences and have been shown to improve valence, arousal, and liking ratings, design guidelines on how to best present and time them are still under-explored.

3.13 Summary

In this section, we have reviewed numerous aspects of mid-air haptic design and presented 12 guidelines, which make recommendations for effective haptic design and prompt designers to consider how to make the best use of mid-air haptic technology for their intended user experience. In the following section, we suggest an iterative haptic design process that can be followed to create a quality mid-air haptic experience.

4 Methods

When designing a mid-air haptic experience, you can follow a general interaction design process and employ methods and techniques used in other areas of UX design. However, there are additional special challenges to be considered, which may not be encountered in other fields of interaction design. In this section, we review some of these challenges and make recommendations about how to overcome them.

Our general process follows the four key activities often found in a typical interaction design process, specifically based on the model by Sharp et al. (2002): (1) establish requirements, (2) design alternatives, (3) prototype solutions, and (4) evaluate them (see Fig. 14). Hapticians can use this section as a crash course in how

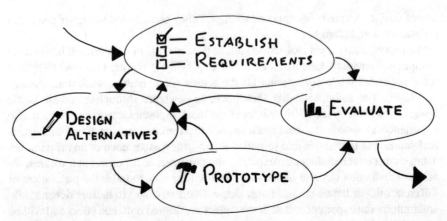

Fig. 14 The major interaction design activities, as adapted from Sharp, Preece, Rogers (Sharp et al. 2002). Interaction designers rapidly iterate between gathering requirements, designing alternatives, prototyping potential designs, and evaluating those prototypes

to think about interaction design, and interaction designers can use this section to adapt their craft when designing for a mid-air haptic interface. While this section is described in the order one might encounter these activities, the overall process is highly iterative and can be blended or rearranged as needed.

4.1 Why Care About User Experience Design?

Haptic technology often faces a crisis of justification. The costs are high, and in many application areas, the main added value comes from subtle experiential benefits that are difficult to link to the bottom line (Schneider et al. 2017). However, recent work has started to study the impact of haptic feedback on experience, especially in digital media. Work by Maggioni et al. (2017) showed that adding mid-air haptic or vibrotactile feedback can improve UX as measured by the AttrakDiff questionnaire (Hassenzahl et al. 2003); specifically, movies with mid-air haptic and vibrotactile feedback were rated as more pleasant, unpredictable, and creative than movies without haptic feedback. Other recent studies highlight the benefits of haptic feedback from other types of haptic device. For example, Pauna et al. (2018) worked with motion seat feedback in movies, finding physiological signals of positive emotions increased. Singhal and Schneider (2021) examined video games, showing that vibrotactile feedback can improve player experience as measured by the Player eXperience Inventory (PXI) questionnaire (Abeele et al. 2020)—specifically increasing measures of appeal, immersion, and meaning, with some moderation by visual effects.

Ultimately, haptic feedback, including mid-air haptics, can enable more tasks, make many interfaces more usable, and have value simply by being a better experience, if designed correctly.

4.2 Establish Requirements

The commonly stated first step in any interaction design process is to engage with stakeholders and understand their needs and then use this to establish requirements (Sharp et al. 2002). Doing this step early is essential; otherwise, you might design a solution to the wrong problem, and fixing core design problems after delivery is more costly than addressing them during the requirements and design phase (Boehm and Port 2001). From a design standpoint, immediately jumping to a solution risks 'tunnel vision' and can limit the number of solutions considered, potentially missing out on more suitable alternative designs. Most design processes advocate starting by considering as many options as possible.

However, when hapticians talk to people, there are major barriers to communication. Interviews with expert hapticians tells us that people 'do not really know what to do with [haptics],' even though there is an expectation that it will add value to the user experience (Schneider et al. 2017). Similarly, it can be challenging to communicate about haptics because there is such a varied (and ambiguous) vocabulary used to talk about tactile experiences (Obrist et al. 2013). When clients do come in with questions, they are often inscrutable, such as creating the design as being 'variable.' To that end, it is essential that hapticians have existing demos and examples to help communicate with the various stakeholders of their projects and establish their understanding of what tactile experiences are (and are not) possible.

After engaging the various people involved in your project, an important activity early in the interaction design process is to consolidate the project's goals. In interaction design, these goals are often split into pragmatic goals (utility and usability) like 'easy and quick to use' and hedonic (experiential) goals like 'immersive' or 'surprising.' As we have already covered in this chapter, mid-air haptic feedback can help improve utility (e.g., with reduced eye-off-the-road in automotive applications Harrington et al. 2018; Large et al. 2019), usability (e.g., with tasks like shape recognition Hajas et al. (2020) or widget localization Vo and Brewster (2015), Freeman et al. (2019)), experience (e.g., with movies Ablart et al. (2017)), and engagement (e.g., with digital signage displays Limerick (2020)). However, designers may often consider additional or alternative design goals. For example, Kim and Schneider recently tried to formalize a specific construct of 'haptic experience (HX)' (Kim et al. 2020). Their HX model is intended to guide UX goals across different haptic devices and capabilities. While it is not yet evaluated with mid-air ultrasound haptics, a study of over 260 participants experiencing vibrotactile feedback provides initial evidence that the HX model's 5 factors form different, but coherent, goals when rated (Sathiyamurthy et al. 2021). These goals may be suitable in your next haptics project.

In summary, two key tasks when establishing design requirements for a haptic experience are to:

1. Find ways to effectively communicate about haptics with stakeholders, e.g., using modifiable demonstrators and
2. Define goals and application requirements, both pragmatic and hedonic.

4.3   Design Alternatives

Once goals have been identified, many designers instinctively launch into building a prototype. However, pausing to deliberately think through what you might design will help create the most effective designs and mitigate hidden risks. There are two ways to deliberately think about your designs: (1) conceptually (top-down) and (2) through device exploration (bottom-up).

4.3.1   Top-Down: Employ a Conceptual Model

It can be valuable to step away from the device you are using and think about the concepts that might be used in your design. This is known as conceptual design or conceptual modeling (Johnson and Henderson 2002, 2011). Novices to haptic design, especially those with an engineering-focused background, are often unaware of conceptual design, leading to a common misstep in haptic design (Seifi et al. 2020).

A conceptual model is a 'high-level description of how a system is organized and operates' involving major metaphors and analogies (e.g., the desktop interaction metaphor with files and folders), task-domain concepts (e.g., a computer file has a date created, last modified, file size), and relationships between concepts (e.g., folders contain 0 or more folders and files) (Johnson and Henderson 2002). A conceptual model can take several forms, from diagrams to a defined lexicon, and can inform application vocabulary and documentation, while initiating and focusing the implementation, thus saving time and money by reducing development time (Johnson and Henderson, 2011). In haptic design, conceptual models include decisions like how haptics fit in with other sensory feedback (is it primary or secondary? synchronized or complementary to other senses? cf. with some of the guidelines presented in Sect. 3) and how the user is represented (are they an idealized invisible observer or linked to a object with an impact in the environment?). For more ideas, MacLean et al. (2017) offer a selection of frameworks for multisensory haptic interactions, while Seifi et al. (2020) document an in-depth set of design decisions and consequences for novices with force-feedback design.

Once you have established the conceptual design, you can then start to map concepts to how they are represented in the *concrete design*. Concrete design is what most people think about when they think about design, for example, the colors, fonts, materials, and layouts used in a visual interface. In haptics, this involves making careful choices about when to deploy haptics, and how to set the technical parameters that result in the intended experience. Many practical examples about mid-air haptics were given in the previous section of this chapter. While your specific conceptual model will inform the right concrete design, you may be able to leverage existing research to determine the right mapping. For example, Obrist et al. (2013) document a vocabulary used to describe different frequencies and amplitudes for mid-air feed-

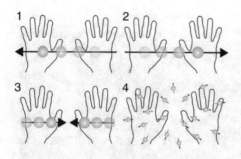
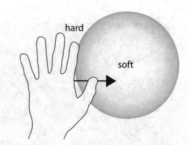

(a) A particle collision effect, where the user's two hands passively feel dynamic particles moving, then colliding and exploding.

(b) A cell nucleus effect, where the user's one hand actively moves to feel the structure of the nucleus.

Fig. 15 Two examples of mid-air haptic experiences for science outreach (Hajas et al. 2020). These two designs employ very different conceptual models and interaction modalities, both intentionally designed before implementation. Reproduced with permission from Hajas et al. (2020)

back; if you need to represent a 'strong' or 'weak' sensation, you might have natural concrete design decisions to represent those variations (Fig. 15).

An excellent example of conceptual design for mid-air haptics is that by Hajas et al. (2020), which includes six designs of scientific concepts that were brought to science educators. One design demonstrated a dynamic experience, specifically, a particle collision. The user puts two hands over the device, holding them steady, then feels three effects in sequence: (1) a particle moving left across both hands, (2) a second particle moving right across both hands, and then (3) two particles moving toward the middle, followed by a 'sparkly explosion.' In this example, the user passively feels the experience with both hands, the device needs to render a particle that moves, and an explosion effect. This was then rendered as a concrete design using two Ultraleap devices, one for each hand. Impulses were sent with 200 ms delay to evoke movement, with the particles rendered 200 Hz using amplitude modulation (AM). The 'explosion' was rendered by randomly moving points 30 Hz using spatiotemporal modulation (STM). A second design was intended to represent the structure of a cell nucleus—in this demonstration, the cell nucleus was statically rendered, and the user could use a single hand to explore its haptic representation, which had a 'hard' exterior and a 'soft' interior. The concrete design was a disk pattern rendered 80 Hz frequency for the cell exterior, and a pattern 10 Hz frequency in the middle to represent the 'soft' interior. These two exemplar designs use the same haptic device and are from the same domain (i.e., science communication), but the interaction modality and conceptual models are quite different and are bespoke for the intended application goals.

4.3.2 Bottom-Up: Use Examples

One of the best ways to explore what is possible with mid-air haptic design is to look at existing examples and demonstrators. In more mature fields like graphic design,

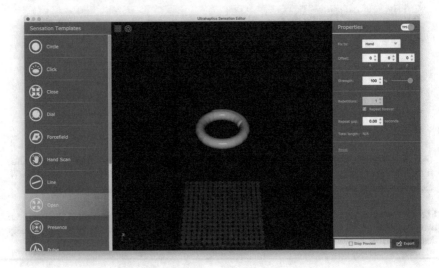

Fig. 16 The Ultraleap Sensation Editor demonstrating existing examples for mid-air haptic designs. These are incorporable into designs because they can be edited. Incorporable examples provide a direct starting point for anyone creating a new sensation and an indirect way to learn how to design new effects by observing patterns used by others Schneider and MacLean (2016)

example viewing at specific times (early and repeated) has been linked to more novel and common elements (Kulkarni et al. 2014), and dedicated support with example browsing tools has the potential to improve outcomes (Lee et al. 2010). In other fields of haptics, such as vibrotactile design, examples have been linked to several benefits in design. Schneider and MacLean (2016) presented several interfaces with different ways of incorporating examples into a wearable vibrotactile design, with several key insights of how to effectively use examples. First, when provided with examples, designers tend to inspect all provided examples, find the closest to their intended design, and then use it as a starting point. Second, providing incorporable, visible examples (examples that are 'open source' and can be changed and inspected) not only helps designers get started (e.g., by copying then modifying the closest design sample), but also helps them learn how to work with the tactile modality by observing existing patterns.

With mid-air haptics, you can draw inspiration from existing libraries of effects. At the time of writing, several examples include those found in the Ultraleap Sensation Editor (Fig. 16) or Unity examples[1] and tutorials.[2]

---

[1] https://github.com/ultraleap/UnityExamples.

[2] https://developer.ultrahaptics.com/kb/unity.

In summary, the main advice for exploring design possibilities is to:

1. Engage with conceptual design by deliberately thinking about the conceptual elements of the intended design and how they relate to each other (top-down design).
2. Gather examples of designs, devices, and materials to provide potential starting points, build your repertoire of ideas, and identify compelling candidate designs that are possible with the available haptics hardware (bottom-up design).

4.4 Prototype

Prototyping is the process of taking your designs from initial conception to (near-) final execution. To create effective and successful prototypes, you will need to generate many different prototypes of different scope, searching the design space to come up with a suitable final implementation that satisfies the initial design goals and experience requirements.

To arrive at a suitable design, you must juggle two competing goals: exploring as wide a range of possible solutions as possible and developing those solutions into final proposals. The way to achieve this is through iterative *elaboration* and *reduction*.

Laseau's funnel (Fig. 17) visualizes this process as a 'funnel' that widens/closes as ideas are explored and evaluated (Greenberg et al. 2011). An *elaboration* phase is used to explore different ideas and implementations from a starting point, through brainstorming and variation—i.e., widening the design funnel. Its aim is to go for *quantity*, not quality. Once you have several ideas, you then *reduce* the design space, prioritize, compare, and combine ideas into a smaller set of top candidates—i.e.,

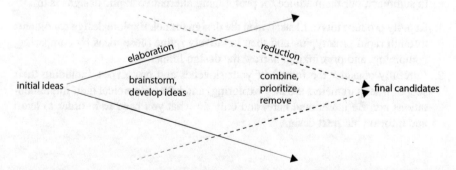

Fig. 17 Laseau's funnel, adapted from Greenberg et al. (2011). When moving from early designs to prototypes, you begin with your conceptual design, examples, or other starting point and then rapidly generate new ideas to explore as wide a space as possible. Once you have a variety of prototypes, you then reduce them by combining, prioritizing, or removing ineffective designs. This is then repeated with your reduced set until you have a final candidate prototype

reducing the design funnel. This process can iterate until you have reached promising final designs, guided by prototyping.

To accomplish this in a manageable time period, prototypes need to be generated quickly and only need to be sufficient for testing the design ideas (rather than being of final production quality). Lim et al. (2008) propose principles to help guide prototyping activities. The first is the fundamental prototyping principle: Prototypes filter the qualities in which designers are interested without distorting the whole. This means that your prototypes can view different aspects of your design—perhaps, different frequencies and sizes of a mid-air button to choose those parameters and then different dynamic properties on how it reacts when pressed. Both prototypes are simpler than a fully implemented design, but arrive at a final solution. The second principle is the economic principle of prototyping: The best prototype is the simplest and most efficient while also achieving its goals and requirements. There is great value in low-fidelity prototypes as they enable to get initial ideas extremely cheaply and rapidly, then exerting more time and effort only when there is more confidence in an outcome.

Haptics tend to be more difficult for prototyping than other technologies. It is heavily reliant on other modalities and the rest of the system, so it is more difficult to apply these principles. However, careful decisions about what you prototype will speed up your design process. You can find inspiration in Simple Haptics (Moussette 2012), which demonstrates the attitudes of sketching expressed in hardware to inform haptic interaction design. In this approach, you move from prototypes implemented in seconds to those implemented in minutes, hours, and eventually days, starting with household objects and puppetry then moving toward more sophisticated technology. This iterative and progressive prototyping process was used by Young et al. (2020) when designing mid-air haptic gesture controlled user interfaces for cars. Their first prototype consisted of visual non-interactive wireframes, slowly and iteratively built up toward a multimodal interactive user interface.

In summary, our main advice for prototyping alternative haptic designs is to:

1. Rapidly produce lots of ideas: widen the design funnel. Explore design candidates through rapid prototyping and then iteratively refine those ideas by comparing, combining, and prioritizing: narrow the design funnel.
2. Carefully consider the format of your sketches and prototypes, including their scope (what parameters are they exploring) and how economical their implementations are. Be intentional here, and only do what you need to in order to learn and inform your next design.

4.5   Evaluate

Evaluation may be the least formally developed activity in haptic experience design. Typically, expert hapticians use qualitative methods such as focus groups and interviews, or simply trusting the judgment of designers and developers who iterate until a haptic experience 'just feels right' (Schneider et al. 2017). However, short of trusting your own intuition, there are some ways to receive feedback in a principled way.

First, evaluations are best framed in terms of the design goals articulated when gathering requirements. These goals can inform suitable questions and metrics for both informal and formal evaluation. For informal evaluation, try bringing your prototypes to colleagues or potential users whenever you can, to evaluate and inform your next iteration. If your prototypes can be rapidly adapted in response to feedback, this will help you achieve a common understanding of what can be done (Schneider et al. 2017). For formal evaluation, quantitative metrics can complement qualitative feedback. Task completion time and error rate are common metrics for usability and for example have been used for evaluating and comparing the added benefits of mid-air haptics when interacting with an automotive infotainment system (Large et al. 2019). Usability and UX questionnaires are other common tools for general usability and experiential goals; for example, (Maggioni et al. 2017) used the AttrakDiff questionnaire to quantify improvements to aspects of the experience of watching movies with haptics. In industry, custom scales are often used (Kim et al. 2020). Other widely used methods include removing the haptic feedback after people experience it to see if they want it back (often users do not notice haptic feedback until it has been removed), and trusting people whose design sense has a track record of results.

In summary, our advice for evaluating haptics is to:

1. Relate evaluations back to the intended experience goals and requirements, established earlier in the design process.
2. Collect rapid feedback through informal evaluation methods.
3. Use formal feedback methods such as UX questionnaires and interaction metrics.

5 Conclusion

This book chapter aspires to equip the reader with an understanding of the many different applications of ultrasonic mid-air haptics studied to date (see Sect. 2), the guidelines and best practices which have been derived from said applications (see Sect. 3), and methods for the design of useful and delightful interactive systems (see Sect. 4). To that end, we have presented five key application themes (automotive, public displays, virtual and mixed reality, health care, and neuroscience R&D) that we hope provide useful context when reading the later chapters in this book. We also presented mid-air haptic design guidelines and a general UX design framework, to inspire and inform your own mid-air haptic designs.

Throughout this chapter, we have highlighted compelling challenges and open questions for future research. Importantly, we have identified the need for more advanced, integral, and system-level UX studies which look at the interplay of mid-air haptics independently but also in unison together with other technologies and sensors. Moreover, we have stressed the lack of application-specific prototypes and

UX studies in the areas of health care and VR training. We have also highlighted the need for more fundamental research on touch and the transfer of that knowledge back into applications and enhanced experiences. Finally, we have hinted toward the need for generative UX design tools that leverage our current know-how, and possibly artificial intelligence (AI) predictive capabilities to automatically create multiple creative mid-air haptic options that meet certain application-related constraints and requirements thereby making the design process shorter and less uncertain.

Acknowledgements This project has received funding from the European Union's Horizon 2020 research and innovation programme under grant agreements No 801413 (H-Reality), and 101017746 (Touchless).

References

Abdouni A, Clark R, Georgiou O (2019) Seeing is believing but feeling is the truth: Visualising mid-air haptics in oil baths and lightboxes. In: International conference on multimodal interaction, pp 504–505

Abeele VV, Spiel K, Nacke L, Johnson D, Gerling K (2020) Development and validation of the player experience inventory: a scale to measure player experiences at the level of functional and psychosocial consequences. Int J Human-Comput Stud 135:102370

Ablart D, Frier W, Limerick H, Georgiou O, Obrist M (2019) Using ultrasonic mid-air haptic patterns in multi-modal user experiences. In: IEEE international symposium on haptic, audio and visual environments and games (HAVE). IEEE, pp 1–6

Ablart D, Velasco C, Obrist M (2017) Integrating mid-air haptics into movie experiences. In: Proceedings of the 2017 ACM international conference on interactive experiences for TV and online video, pp 77–84

Ahmad BI, Murphy JK, Langdon PM, Godsill SJ, Hardy R, Skrypchuk L (2015) Intent inference for hand pointing gesture-based interactions in vehicles. IEEE Trans Cybernet 46(4):878–889

Alpern M, Minardo K (2003) Developing a car gesture interface for use as a secondary task. In: CHI'03 extended abstracts on Human factors in computing systems, pp 932–933

Balint P, Althoefer K (2018) Medical virtual reality palpation training using ultrasound based haptics and image processing. Proc Jt Work New Technol Comput Assist Surg

Beattie D, Frier W, Georgiou O, Long B, Ablart D (2020) Incorporating the perception of visual roughness into the design of mid-air haptic textures. ACM Sympos Appl Percept 2020:1–10

Boehm B, Port D (2001) Risk-based strategic software design: how much cots evaluation is enough? In: Proceedings of the third international workshop on economics-driven software engineering research. Toronto, Canada. Citeseer

Breitschaft SJ, Clarke S, Carbon C-C (2019) A theoretical framework of haptic processing in automotive user interfaces and its implications on design and engineering. Front Psychol 10:1470

Brice D, Gibson Z, Mcguinness F, Rafferty K (2021) Using ultrasonic haptics within an immersive spider exposure environment to provide a multi-sensorial experience. Front Virtual Real 2:707731

Brice D, McRoberts T, Rafferty K (2019) A proof of concept integrated multi-systems approach for large scale tactile feedback in vr. In: International conference on augmented reality, virtual reality and computer graphics. Springer, pp 120–137

Brown E, Large DR, Limerick H, Burnett G (2020) Ultrahapticons:"haptifying" drivers' mental models to transform automotive mid-air haptic gesture infotainment interfaces. In: 12th international conference on automotive user interfaces and interactive vehicular applications, pp 54–57

Burnett G, Irune A (2009) Drivers' quality ratings for switches in cars: assessing the role of the vision, hearing and touch senses. In: Proceedings of the 1st international conference on automotive user interfaces and interactive vehicular applications, pp 107–114

Carcagno S, Di Battista A, Plack CJ (2019) Effects of high-intensity airborne ultrasound exposure on behavioural and electrophysiological measures of auditory function. Acta Acust United Acust 105(6):1183–1197

Carter T, Seah SA, Long B, Drinkwater B, Subramanian S (2013) Ultrahaptics: multi-point mid-air haptic feedback for touch surfaces. In: Proceedings of the 26th annual ACM symposium on user interface software and technology, pp 505–514

Corenthy L, Giordano M, Hayden R, Griffiths D, Jeffrey C, Limerick H, Georgiou O, Carter T, Müller J, Subramanian S (2018) Touchless tactile displays for digital signage: mid-air haptics meets large screens. In: Extended abstracts of the. CHI conference on human factors in computing systems, pp 1–4

Cornelio Martinez PI, De Pirro S, Vi CT, Subramanian S (2017) Agency in mid-air interfaces. In: Proceedings of the 2017 CHI conference on human factors in computing systems, pp 2426–2439

Cowan N (2001) The magical number 4 in short-term memory: a reconsideration of mental storage capacity. Behav Brain Sci 24(1):87–114

Cronin S, Doherty G (2019) Touchless computer interfaces in hospitals: a review. Health Informat J 25(4):1325–1342

Daniel H, Damien A, Schneider O, Obrist M (2020) I can feel it moving: science communicators talking about the potential of mid-air haptics. Front Comput Sci

Davies N, Clinch S, Alt F (2014) Pervasive displays: understanding the future of digital signage. Synthesis Lect Mob Pervas Comput 8(1):1–128

Detjen H, Faltaous S, Pfleging B, Geisler S, Schneegass S (2021) How to increase automated vehicles' acceptance through in-vehicle interaction design: a review. Int J Human-Comput Int 37(4):308–330

Di Battista A (2019) The effect of 40 kHz ultrasonic noise exposure on human hearing. Universitätsbibliothek der RWTH Aachen

Driller KK, Frier W, Pont SC, Hartcher-O'Brien J (2019) Mid-air ultrasonic stimulations of the palm-the influence of frequency and stimulus duration on perceived intensity. In: WHC 2019: IEEE world haptics conference

Dzidek B, Frier W, Harwood A, Hayden R (2018) Design and evaluation of mid-air haptic interactions in an augmented reality environment. In: International conference on human haptic sensing and touch enabled computer applications. Springer, pp 489–499

Etherington D (2017) Bmw's holoactive touch in-car interface offers tactile feedback on a floating display

Evangelou G, Limerick H, Moore J (2021) I feel it in my fingers! sense of agency with mid-air haptics. In: IEEE world haptics conference (WHC). IEEE, pp 727–732

Freeman E (2021) Enhancing ultrasound haptics with parametric audio effects. In: Proceedings of the 23rd ACM international conference on multimodal interaction-ICMI, vol 21

Freeman E, Vo D-B, Brewster S (2019) Haptiglow: helping users position their hands for better mid-air gestures and ultrasound haptic feedback. In: IEEE world haptics conference (WHC). IEEE, pp 289–294

Freeman E, Wilson G, Vo D-B, Ng A, Politis I, Brewster S (2017) Multimodal feedback in HCI: haptics, non-speech audio, and their applications. In: The handbook of multimodal-multisensor interfaces: foundations, user modeling and common modality combinations. Morgan & Claypool

Frier W, Ablart D, Chilles J, Long B, Giordano M, Obrist M, Subramanian S (2018) Using spatiotemporal modulation to draw tactile patterns in mid-air. In: International conference on human haptic sensing and touch enabled computer applications. Springer, pp 270–281

Frier W, Pittera D, Ablart D, Obrist M, Subramanian S (2019) Sampling strategy for ultrasonic mid-air haptics. In: Proceedings of the 2019 CHI conference on human factors in computing systems, pp 1–11

Frutos-Pascual M, Harrison JM, Creed C, Williams I (2019) Evaluation of ultrasound haptics as a supplementary feedback cue for grasping in virtual environments. In: International conference on multimodal interaction, pp 310–318

Gaffary Y, Le Gouis B, Marchal M, Argelaguet F, Arnaldi B, Lécuyer A (2017) AR feels "softer" than VR: haptic perception of stiffness in augmented versus virtual reality. IEEE Trans Visual Comput Graph 23(11):2372–2377

Garber L (2013) Gestural technology: moving interfaces in a new direction [technology news]. Computer 46(10):22–25

Georgiou O, Biscione V, Harwood A, Griffiths D, Giordano M, Long B, Carter T (2017) Haptic in-vehicle gesture controls. In: Proceedings of the 9th international conference on automotive user interfaces and interactive vehicular applications adjunct, pp 233–238

Georgiou O, Jeffrey C, Chen Z, Tong BX, Chan SH, Yang B, Harwood A, Carter T (2018) Touchless haptic feedback for VR rhythm games. In: 2018 IEEE conference on virtual reality and 3D user interfaces (VR). IEEE, pp 553–554

Gescheider GA, Bolanowski SJ, Pope JV, Verrillo RT (2002) A four-channel analysis of the tactile sensitivity of the fingertip: frequency selectivity, spatial summation, and temporal summation. Somatosens Motor Res 19(2):114–124

Girdler A, Georgiou O (2020) Mid-air haptics in aviation–creating the sensation of touch where there is nothing but thin air, arXiv preprint arXiv:2001.01445

Green P (2000) Crashes induced by driver information systems and what can be done to reduce them. Tech, Rep, SAE Technical Paper

Greenberg S, Carpendale S, Marquardt N, Buxton B (2011) Sketching user experiences: the workbook. Elsevier

Hajas D, Pittera D, Nasce A, Georgiou O, Obrist M (2020) Mid-air haptic rendering of 2d geometric shapes with a dynamic tactile pointer. IEEE Trans Hapt 13(4):806–817

Hajas D, Ablart D, Schneider O, Obrist M (2020) I can feel it moving: science communicators talking about the potential of mid-air haptics. Front Comput Sci 2

Harrington K, Large DR, Burnett G, Georgiou O (2018) Exploring the use of mid-air ultrasonic feedback to enhance automotive user interfaces. In: Proceedings of the 10th international conference on automotive user interfaces and interactive vehicular applications, pp 11–20

Hasegawa K, Shinoda H (2018) Aerial vibrotactile display based on multiunit ultrasound phased array. IEEE Trans Hapt 11(3):367–377

Hassenzahl M, Burmester M, Koller F (2003) Attrakdiff: ein fragebogen zur messung wahrgenommener hedonischer und pragmatischer qualität. In: Mensch Computer, Springer, pp 187–196

Hayward N, Lewis E, Perra E, Jousmäki V, Saarinen V-M, McGlone F, Sams M, Nieminen H (2020) A novel ultrasonic haptic device induces touch sensations with potential applications in neuroscience research. In: IEEE international ultrasonics symposium (IUS). IEEE, pp 1–4

Hermann DS (2018) Automotive displays-trends, opportunities and challenges. In: 25th International workshop on active-matrix flatpanel displays and devices (AM-FPD). IEEE, pp 1–6

Horrey WJ, Wickens CD (2007) In-vehicle glance duration: distributions, tails, and model of crash risk. Transp Res Rec 1:22–28

Hoshi T, Takahashi M, Iwamoto T, Shinoda H (2010) Noncontact tactile display based on radiation pressure of airborne ultrasound. IEEE Trans Hapt 3(3):155–165

Howard T, Marchal M, Lécuyer A, Pacchierotti C (2019) Pumah: pan-tilt ultrasound mid-air haptics for larger interaction workspace in virtual reality. IEEE Trans Hapt 13(1):38–44

Howard T, Gallagher G, Lécuyer A, Pacchierotti C, Marchal M (2019) Investigating the recognition of local shapes using mid-air ultrasound haptics. In: IEEE world haptics conference (WHC). IEEE, pp 503–508

Huang S, Ranganathan SP, Parsons I (2020) To touch or not to touch? comparing touch, mid-air gesture, mid-air haptics for public display in post covid-19 society. SIGGRAPH Asia Posters 1–2

Hung GM, John NW, Hancock C, Gould DA, Hoshi T (2013) Ultrapulse-simulating a human arterial pulse with focussed airborne ultrasound. In: 35th annual international conference of the IEEE engineering in medicine and biology society (EMBC). IEEE, pp 2511–2514

Hung GM, John NW, Hancock C, Hoshi T (2014) Using and validating airborne ultrasound as a tactile interface within medical training simulators. In: International symposium on biomedical simulation. Springer, pp 30–39

Hwang I, Son H, Kim JR (2017) Airpiano: enhancing music playing experience in virtual reality with mid-air haptic feedback. In: IEEE world haptics conference (WHC). IEEE, pp 213–218

Inoue S, Kobayashi-Kirschvink KJ, Monnai Y, Hasegawa K, Makino Y, Shinoda H (2014) Horn: the hapt-optic reconstruction. In: ACM SIGGRAPH. Emerging Technologies, pp 1–1

Jang J, Frier W, Georgiou O, Park J (2021) Using mid-air tactile patterns in interactive volume exploration. In: 2021 IEEE world haptics conference—demo paper. IEEE

Johnson J, Henderson A (2002) Conceptual models: begin by designing what to design. Interactions 9(1):25–32

Johnson J, Henderson A (2011) Conceptual models: core to good design. Synthesis Lect Human-Centered Inf 4(2):1–110

Kaaresoja T, Anttila E, Hoggan E (2011) The effect of tactile feedback latency in touchscreen interaction. In: IEEE world haptics conference. IEEE, pp 65–70

Kappus B, Long B (2018) Spatiotemporal modulation for mid-air haptic feedback from an ultrasonic phased array. J Acoust Soc Am 143(3):1836–1836

Karafotias G, Korres G, Teranishi A, Park W, Eid M (2017) Mid-air tactile stimulation for pain distraction. IEEE Trans Hapt 11(2):185–191

Kervegant C, Raymond F, Graeff D, Castet J (2017) Touch hologram in mid-air. In ACM SIGGRAPH. Emerging technologies, pp 1–2

Kim JR, Chan S, Huang X, Ng K, Fu LP, Zhao C (2019) Demonstration of refinity: an interactive holographic signage for new retail shopping experience. In: Extended abstracts of the. CHI conference on human factors in computing systems, pp 1–4

Kim E, Schneider O (2020) Defining haptic experience: foundations for understanding, communicating, and evaluating HX

Kim E, Schneider O (2020) Defining haptic experience: foundations for understanding, communicating, and evaluating hx. In: Proceedings of the 2020 CHI conference on human factors in computing systems, pp 1–13

Klauer SG, Dingus TA, Neale VL, Sudweeks JD, Ramsey DJ et al (2006) The impact of driver inattention on near-crash/crash risk: an analysis using the 100-car naturalistic driving study data

Korres G, Eid M (2016) Haptogram: ultrasonic point-cloud tactile stimulation. IEEE Access 4:7758–7769

Korres G, Chehabeddine S, Eid M (2020) Mid-air tactile feedback co-located with virtual touchscreen improves dual-task performance. IEEE Trans Hapt 13(4):825–830

Kulkarni C, Dow SP, Klemmer SR (2014) Early and repeated exposure to examples improves creative work. Design Thinking Research. Springer International Publishing, Cham, pp 49–62

Large DR, Harrington K, Burnett G, Georgiou O (2019) Feel the noise: mid-air ultrasound haptics as a novel human-vehicle interaction paradigm. Appl Ergonom 81:102909

Lederman SJ, Jones LA (2011) Tactile and haptic illusions. IEEE Trans Hapt 4(4):273–294

Lee B, Srivastava S, Kumar R, Brafman R, Klemmer SR (2010) Designing with interactive example galleries. In: Proceedings of the 28th international conference on Human factors in computing systems - CHI '10. ACM Press, New York, New York, USA, p 2257

Lehser C, Wagner E, Strauss DJ (2018) Somatosensory evoked responses elicited by haptic sensations in midair. IEEE Trans Neural Syst Rehabil Eng 26(10):2070–2077

Lehser C, Strauss DJ (2019) Attentional correlates in somatosensory potentials evoked by ultrasound induced virtual objects in mid-air. In: 2019 9th international IEEE/EMBS conference on neural engineering (NER). IEEE, pp 933–936

Li W-J, Hsieh C-Y, Lin L-F, Chu W-C (2017) Hand gesture recognition for post-stroke rehabilitation using leap motion. In: International conference on applied system innovation (ICASI). IEEE, pp 386–388

Lim Y-K, Stolterman E, Tenenberg J (2008) The anatomy of prototypes. ACM Trans Comput-Human Interact 15(2):1–27

Limerick H (2020) Call to interact: communicating interactivity and affordances for contactless gesture controlled public displays. In: Proceedings of the 9TH ACM international symposium on pervasive displays, pp 63–70

Limerick H, Coyle D, Moore JW (2014) The experience of agency in human-computer interactions: a review. Front Human Neurosci 8:643

Limerick H, Hayden R, Beattie D, Georgiou O, Müller J (2019) User engagement for mid-air haptic interactions with digital signage. In: Proceedings of the 8th ACM international symposium on pervasive displays, pp 1–7

Loehmann S, Knobel M, Lamara M, Butz A (2013) Culturally independent gestures for in-car interactions. In: IFIP conference on human-computer interaction. Springer, pp 538–545

Long B, Seah SA, Carter T, Subramanian S (2014) Rendering volumetric haptic shapes in mid-air using ultrasound. ACM Trans Graph (TOG) 33(6):1–10

MacLean KE, Schneider OS, Seifi H (2017) Multisensory haptic interactions: understanding the sense and designing for it. In: The handbook of multimodal-multisensor interfaces: foundations. User modeling, and common modality combinations, vol 1, pp 97–142

Maggioni E, Agostinelli E, Obrist M (2017) Measuring the added value of haptic feedback. In: 2017 ninth international conference on quality of multimedia experience (QoMEX). IEEE, pp 1–6

Makino Y, Furuyama Y, Inoue S, Shinoda H (2016) Haptoclone (haptic-optical clone) for mutual tele-environment by real-time 3d image transfer with midair force feedback. CHI 1980–1990

Marchal M, Gallagher G, Lécuyer A, Pacchierotti C (2020) Can stiffness sensations be rendered in virtual reality using mid-air ultrasound haptic technologies? In: International conference on human haptic sensing and touch enabled computer applications. Springer, pp 297–306

Martinez J, Griffiths D, Biscione V, Georgiou O, Carter T (2018) Touchless haptic feedback for supernatural vr experiences. In: 2018 IEEE conference on virtual reality and 3D user interfaces (VR). IEEE, pp 629–630

Martinez J, Harwood A, Limerick H, Clark R, Georgiou O (2019) Mid-air haptic algorithms for rendering 3d shapes. In: IEEE international symposium on haptic, audio and visual environments and games (HAVE). IEEE, pp 1–6

Marti P, Parlangeli O, Recupero A, Sirizzotti M, Guidi S (2021) Touching virtual objects in mid-air: a study on shape recognition. In: European conference on cognitive ergonomics, pp 1–6

Matsubayashi A, Makino Y, Shinoda H (2019) Direct finger manipulation of 3d object image with ultrasound haptic feedback. In: Proceedings of the 2019 CHI conference on human factors in computing systems, pp 1–11

Matsubayashi A, Makino Y, Shinoda H (2020) Rendering ultrasound pressure distribution on hand surface in real-time. In: International conference on human haptic sensing and touch enabled computer applications. Springer, pp 407–415

Matsubayashi A, Oikawa H, Mizutani S, Makino Y, Shinoda H (2019) Display of haptic shape using ultrasound pressure distribution forming cross-sectional shape. In: IEEE world haptics conference (WHC). IEEE, pp 419–424

May KR, Gable TM, Walker BN (2014) A multimodal air gesture interface for in vehicle menu navigation. In: Adjunct proceedings of the 6th international conference on automotive user interfaces and interactive vehicular applications, pp 1–6

Mc Gee MR, Gray P, Brewster S (2000) The effective combination of haptic and auditory textural information. In: International workshop on haptic human-computer interaction. Springer, pp 118–126

McGlone F, Wessberg J, Olausson H (2014) Discriminative and affective touch: sensing and feeling. Neuron 82(4):737–755

Mizutani S, Fujiwara M, Makino Y, Shinoda H (2019) Thresholds of haptic and auditory perception in midair facial stimulation. In: IEEE international symposium on haptic, audio and visual environments and games (HAVE). IEEE, pp 1–6

Monnai Y, Hasegawa K, Fujiwara M, Yoshino K, Inoue S, Shinoda H (2014) Haptomime: midair haptic interaction with a floating virtual screen. In: Proceedings of the 27th annual ACM symposium on user interface software and technology, pp 663–667

Moore W, Makdani A, Frier W, McGlone F (2021) Virtual touch: sensing and feeling with ultrasound. bioRxiv

Morales R, Ezcurdia I, Irisarri J, Andrade MA, Marzo A (2021) Generating airborne ultrasonic amplitude patterns using an open hardware phased array. Appl Sci 11(7):2981

Moussette C (2012) Simple haptics: sketching perspectives for the design of haptic interactions. Ph.D. dissertation, UmeåUniversitet

Mulot L, Gicquel G, Zanini Q, Frier W, Marchal M, Pacchierotti C, Howard T (2021) Dolphin: a framework for the design and perceptual evaluation of ultrasound mid-air haptic stimuli. ACM Sympos Appl Percept 2021:1–10

Nakajima M, Makino Y, Shinoda H (2019) Displaying pain sensation in midair by thermal grill illusion. In: IEEE international symposium on haptic, audio and visual environments and games (HAVE). IEEE, pp 1–5

Nielsen J (2005) Ten usability heuristics

Nielsen M, Störring M, Moeslund TB, Granum E (2003) A procedure for developing intuitive and ergonomic gesture interfaces for HCI. In: International gesture workshop. Springer, pp 409–420

Obrist M, Seah SA, Subramanian S (2013) Talking about tactile experiences. In: Proceedings of the SIGCHI conference on human factors in computing systems, pp 1659–1668

Obrist M, Subramanian S, Gatti E, Long B, Carter T (2015) Emotions mediated through mid-air haptics. In: Proceedings of the 33rd annual ACM conference on human factors in computing systems, pp 2053–2062

O'Conaill B, Provan J, Schubel J, Hajas D, Obrist M, Corenthy L (2020) Improving immersive experiences for visitors with sensory impairments to the aquarium of the pacific. In: Extended abstracts of the. CHI conference on human factors in computing systems, pp 1–8

O'Hara K et al (2014) Touchless interaction in surgery. Commun ACM 57(1):70–77

Olson RL, Hanowski RJ, Hickman JS, Bocanegra J et al (2009) Driver distraction in commercial vehicle operations. United States. Department of Transportation. Federal Motor Carrier Safety. . ., Technical Report

Ozkul C, Geerts D, Rutten I (2020) Combining auditory and mid-air haptic feedback for a light switch button. In: Proceedings of the 2020 international conference on multimodal interaction, pp 60–69

Paneva V, Seinfeld S, Kraiczi M, Müller J (2020) Haptiread: reading braille as mid-air haptic information. In: Proceedings of the 2020 ACM designing interactive systems conference, pp 13–20

Pauchot J, Di Tommaso L, Lounis A, Benassarou M, Mathieu P, Bernot D, Aubry S (2015) Leap motion gesture control with carestream software in the operating room to control imaging: installation guide and discussion. Surg Innovat 22(6):615–620

Pauna H, Léger P-M, Sénécal S, Fredette M, Courtemanche F, Chen S-L, É. Labonté-Lemoyne, Ménard J-F (2018) The psychophysiological effect of a vibro-kinetic movie experience: the case of the d-box movie seat. In: Information systems and neuroscience. Springer, pp 1–7

Perquin MN, Taylor M, Lorusso J, Kolasinski J (2021) Directional biases in whole hand motion perception revealed by mid-air tactile stimulation. Cortex

Pickering CA, Burnham KJ, Richardson MJ (2007) A research study of hand gesture recognition technologies and applications for human vehicle interaction. In: 3rd Institution of engineering and technology conference on automotive electronics. IET, pp 1–15

Pickering C (2005) The search for a safer driver interface: a review of gesture recognition human machine interface. Comput Cont Eng J 16(1):34–40

Pinto AR, Kildal J, Lazkano E (2020) Multimodal mixed reality impact on a hand guiding task with a holographic cobot. Multimodal Tech Interact 4(4):78

Pitts MJ, Burnett GE, Williams MA, Wellings T (2010) Does haptic feedback change the way we view touchscreens in cars?. In: International conference on multimodal interfaces and the workshop on machine learning for multimodal interaction, pp 1–4

Rakkolainen I, Sand A, Palovuori K (2015) Midair user interfaces employing particle screens. IEEE Comput Graph Appl 35(2):96–102

Rakkolainen I, Freeman E, Sand A, Raisamo R, Brewster S (2020) A survey of mid-air ultrasound haptics and its applications. IEEE Trans Hapt 14(1):2–19

Riener A, Ferscha A, Bachmair F, Hagmüller P, Lemme A, Muttenthaler D, Pühringer D, Rogner H, Tappe A, Weger F (2013) Standardization of the in-car gesture interaction space. In: Proceedings of the 5th international conference on automotive user interfaces and interactive vehicular applications, pp 14–21

Rocchesso D, Cannizzaro FS, Capizzi G, Landolina F (2019) Accessing and selecting menu items by in-air touch. In: Proceedings of the 13th biannual conference of the Italian SIGCHI chapter: designing the next interaction, pp 1–9

Romanus T, Frish S, Maksymenko M, Frier W, Corenthy L, Georgiou O (2019) Mid-air haptic bio-holograms in mixed reality. In: 2019 IEEE international symposium on mixed and augmented reality adjunct (ISMAR-Adjunct). IEEE, pp 348–352

Rümelin S, Butz A (2013) How to make large touch screens usable while driving. In: Proceedings of the 5th international conference on automotive user interfaces and interactive vehicular applications, pp 48–55

Rümelin S, Gabler T, Bellenbaum J (2017) Clicks are in the air: how to support the interaction with floating objects through ultrasonic feedback. In: Proceedings of the 9th international conference on automotive user interfaces and interactive vehicular applications, pp 103–108

Rutten I, Frier W, Van den Bogaert L, Geerts D (2019) Invisible touch: how identifiable are mid-air haptic shapes? In: Extended abstracts of the. CHI conference on human factors in computing systems, pp 1–6

Rutten E, Van Den Bogaert L, Geerts D (2020) From initial encounter with mid-air haptic feedback to repeated use: the role of the novelty effect in user experience. IEEE Trans Hapt

Sand A, Rakkolainen I, Isokoski P, Kangas J, Raisamo R, Palovuori K (2015) Head-mounted display with mid-air tactile feedback. In: Proceedings of the 21st ACM symposium on virtual reality software and technology, pp 51–58

Sand A, Rakkolainen I, Surakka V, Raisamo R, Brewster S (2020) Evaluating ultrasonic tactile feedback stimuli. In: International conference on human haptic sensing and touch enabled computer applications. Springer, pp 253–261

Sathiyamurthy S, Liu M, Kim E, Schneider O (2021) Measuring haptic experience: elaborating the HX model with scale development. World Haptics '21, p 6

Schneider OS, MacLean KE (2016) Studying design process and example use with macaron, a web-based vibrotactile effect editor. In: 2016 IEEE haptics symposium (HAPTICS). IEEE, pp 52–58

Schneider O, MacLean K, Swindells C, Booth K (2017) Haptic experience design: what hapticians do and where they need help. Int J Human Comput Stud 107:5–21

Schneider D, Otte A, Kublin AS, Martschenko A, Kristensson PO, Ofek E, Pahud M, Grubert J (2020) Accuracy of commodity finger tracking systems for virtual reality head-mounted displays. In: 2020 IEEE conference on virtual reality and 3D user interfaces abstracts and workshops (VRW). IEEE, pp 804–805

Seifi H, Chun M, Gallacher C, Schneider O, MacLean KE (2020) How do novice hapticians design? a case study in creating haptic learning environments. IEEE transactions on haptics 13(4):791–805

Shakeri G, Williamson JH, Brewster S (2017) Novel multimodal feedback techniques for in-car mid-air gesture interaction. In: Proceedings of the 9th international conference on automotive user interfaces and interactive vehicular applications, pp 84–93

Shakeri G, Williamson JH, Brewster S (2018) May the force be with you: Ultrasound haptic feedback for mid-air gesture interaction in cars. In: Proceedings of the 10th international conference on automotive user interfaces and interactive vehicular applications, pp 1–10

Sharp H, Preece J, Rogers Y (2002) Interaction design: beyond human-computer interaction

Shneiderman B, Plaisant C, Cohen MS, Jacobs S, Elmqvist N, Diakopoulos N (2016) Designing the user interface: strategies for effective human-computer interaction. Pearson

Singhal T, Phutane M (2021) Elevating haptics: an accessible and contactless elevator concept with tactile mid-air controls. In: Extended abstracts of the. CHI conference on human factors in computing systems, pp 1–4

Singhal T, Schneider O (2021) Juicy haptic design: vibrotactile embellishments can improve player experience in games. In: CHI '21, p 10

Trotta R, Hajas D, Camargo-Molina JE, Cobden R, Maggioni E, Obrist M (2020) Communicating cosmology with multisensory metaphorical experiences. J Sci Commun 19(2)

Van den Bogaert L, Geerts D, Rutten I (2019) Grasping the future: Identifying potential applications for mid-air haptics in the home. In: Extended abstracts of the. CHI Conference on human factors in computing systems, pp 1–6

Vaquero-Melchor D, Bernardos AM (2019) Enhancing interaction with augmented reality through mid-air haptic feedback: architecture design and user feedback. Appl Sci 9(23):5123

Vi CT, Ablart D, Gatti E, Velasco C, Obrist M (2017) Not just seeing, but also feeling art: mid-air haptic experiences integrated in a multisensory art exhibition. Int J Human-Comput Stud 108:1–14

Villarreal-Narvaez S, Vanderdonckt J, Vatavu R-D, Wobbrock JO (2020) A systematic review of gesture elicitation studies: what can we learn from 216 studies? In: Proceedings of the 2020 ACM designing interactive systems conference, pp 855–872

Vo D-B, Brewster SA (2015) Touching the invisible: localizing ultrasonic haptic cues. In: IEEE world haptics conference (WHC). IEEE, pp 368–373

Young G, Milne H, Griffiths D, Padfield E, Blenkinsopp R, Georgiou O (2020) Designing mid-air haptic gesture controlled user interfaces for cars. In: Proceedings of the ACM on human-computer interaction, vol 4, no EICS, pp 1–23

Ultrasound Haptic Feedback for Touchless User Interfaces: Design Patterns

Euan Freeman ⓘ

Abstract Touchless user interfaces enable people to interact with digital services and information without physically touching an input device. There are numerous benefits to touchless interaction (including convenience, hygiene and the potential for more expressive input), and sensing technologies have advanced significantly in recent years. As a result, touchless user interfaces have been adopted on a wider scale across a variety of application areas, e.g. automotive, digital signage and gaming. However, usability remains a key concern; touchless gesture input poses several interaction challenges, many related to uncertainty and the inherent loss of tactile cues. Ultrasound haptic feedback has shown promise in helping users overcome such interaction challenges, restoring the missing sense of touch and closing the feedback loop for effective haptic interaction. This chapter explores how ultrasound haptic feedback has been used in touchless user interface design and presents design patterns used by industry and academia alike.

1 Introduction

Touchless user interfaces have the potential to radically change how people interact with technology. For example, users can interact in more 'natural' and expressive ways, leveraging more degrees of freedom for input sensing than are available using contact-based alternatives like touchscreens (Sridhar et al. 2015). Touchless user interfaces also offer convenience. For example, users can interact without reaching for a screen or input device, without washing messy hands and without taking attention away from other tasks. Finally, touchless user interfaces can address hygiene concerns with shared input devices (Corenthy et al. 2018). Whilst this can help in contexts

E. Freeman (✉)
School of Computing Science, University of Glasgow, Glasgow G12 8RZ, Scotland
e-mail: euan.freeman@glasgow.ac.uk

© The Author(s), under exclusive license to Springer Nature Switzerland AG 2022
O. Georgiou et al. (eds.), *Ultrasound Mid-Air Haptics for Touchless Interfaces*,
Human–Computer Interaction Series, https://doi.org/10.1007/978-3-031-04043-6_3

where sterility is a concern (e.g. in hospitals (Cronin and Doherty 2019; O'Hara et al. 2014)), the COVID-19 pandemic has led to increased awareness of using shared touch surfaces and increased interest in using touchless alternatives for accessing digital information and services.

These potential benefits have led to the adoption of touchless technologies across a variety of market sectors, as seen throughout this book. Many chapters examine particular use cases in detail: e.g. automotive user interfaces (Chap. "Augmenting Automotive Gesture Infotainment Interfaces Through Mid-air Haptic Icon Design"), mixed reality (Chap. "Ultrasound Mid-Air Tactile Feedback for Immersive Virtual Reality Interaction") and input for novel displays (Chap. "Touchless Tactile Interaction with Unconventional Permeable Displays", Chap. "Superimposing Visual Images on Mid-air Ultrasonic Haptic Stimulation"). However, touchless gesture input has usability challenges that affect its use more generally, e.g. the challenge of knowing where to provide input Freeman et al. (2016, 2019), uncertainty about whether the system is responding (Freeman et al. 2014) and a limited feeling of control over interaction (Cornelio-Martinez et al. 2017).

Suitable feedback about interaction can help users overcome these issues, and ultrasound haptic feedback is ideally suited to this, allowing tactile feedback to be given directly to users' hands as they gesture in air. There are many user experience benefits from using ultrasound haptic feedback in a touchless user interface. Such feedback has been found to address some of the usability challenges inherent with touchless input, e.g. guiding users so they can find where to provide input (Freeman et al. 2019) and creating a feeling of control over user interface widgets (Cornelio-

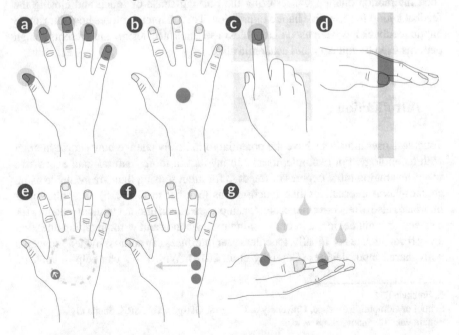

Fig. 1 This chapter presents seven ultrasound haptic design patterns: **a** Tracked Fingertips, **b** Tracked Palm, **c** Floating screen, **d** Forcefield, **e** Object outline, **f** Motion patterns, **g** Special effects

Martinez et al. 2017). Mid-air haptics can also help enhance touchless interaction by giving interaction designers access to another sensory modality, which can increase user engagement (Limerick et al. 2019). These usability benefits are being applied across a diverse range of application areas, including automotive HCI, mixed reality and interactive advertising (Rakkolainen et al. 2020).

A growing body of academic research has helped to improve our understanding of how ultrasound haptic feedback is perceived, has established its benefits to user experience and evaluated its use across a variety of application areas (Rakkolainen et al. 2020). All highlight the compelling benefits and exciting potential of this novel haptic technology. Less clear, however, is the question of where to begin. **How can designers, developers and researchers start to incorporate ultrasound haptic feedback into a touchless user interface design?** This chapter begins to address this question by creating a collection of design patterns for ultrasound haptic feedback, previewed in Fig. 1. These design patterns represent common solutions used by the ultrasound haptics community, which can be used to kick-start the mid-air haptic feedback design process.

2 Background

Ultrasound haptic devices can be used to present a variety of tactile sensations against the hand. The basic unit of output is a **focal point**, a region of intense focused sound pressure in mid-air that imparts a subtle force against the hand upon contact Iwamoto et al. (2008). These focal points are generally not strong enough to be perceived on their own, but can be purposefully modulated in a way that greatly improves perception, so that users can feel distinct tactile sensations. It is not necessary to understand modulation approaches (see Chap. "Modulation Methods for Ultrasound Midair Haptics") or haptic rendering to read this chapter, because the design patterns will be described in terms of what the user experiences against their hands. Indeed, there may be several modulation methods that can produce similar tactile sensations, and by the time you read this, novel rendering methods may have replaced the current state of the art. Haptic designers and practitioners will likely have software tools at their disposal that streamline the development process and take care of the nuances of rendering, and so their responsibility is to choose the 'best' design for a given problem, to meet the needs of those who will use their touchless user interface. This chapter aims to inform this selection.

Design patterns and their intended tactile experience will be described using **haptic points** and **haptic patterns** as design primitives.

Haptic points are focal points, the smallest unit of perceptible output from an ultrasound haptics device. Multiple independent focal points can be positioned in 3D space above an ultrasound haptics device, and their size corresponds to the sound frequency; most devices use 40 kHz sound, creating focal points that are approximately 8.6 mm in diameter (Carter et al. 2013).

Haptic patterns are composed from one or more focal points, which change position in a deterministic way over time. For many of the design patterns described in this chapter, haptic patterns will be simple shapes, e.g. lines and polygons. There are numerous methods for creating such shapes, e.g. distributing multiple focal points along the outline of the shape (Long et al. 2014) or rapidly moving a single focal point along that outline (Frier et al. 2018; Takahashi et al. 2018, 2019) to elicit different tactile sensations (Freeman and Wilson 2021; Frier et al. 2018, 2019). To understand this chapter, it is sufficient to know the concept of a haptic pattern without understanding how such a pattern is created, especially since cutting edge research improves our understanding about how to improve rendering (Hajas et al. 2020).

Recent work has proposed simple design spaces that formally categorise and describe ultrasound haptic experiences. Rakkolainen et al. (2020) identified four categories of mid-air haptic output: sensations of motion, shapes, textured surfaces and abstract dynamic patterns. Dzidek et al. (2018) identified five categories of perceptual sensation: field sensations, edge detection, focused sensations, spherical sensations and fingertip sensations. This chapter takes a retrospective view of ultrasound haptics research to explore common haptic designs, but it is *not* an exhaustive overview and does not attempt to cover all designs found in the literature in a formal design space.

3   Ultrasound Haptic Design Patterns

This section presents a collection of design patterns for ultrasound haptic feedback. These represent commonly used interaction metaphors and feedback designs, which satisfy many usability needs and allow the creation of a variety of engaging user experiences. These are designs that designers, developers and practitioners may find useful—'recipes' for a good touchless user interface experience.

Each design pattern will be described in its own section. There will be a summary box that explains **what** the design pattern is, **why** it may be used in a touchless user interface, **where** it is rendered, and **when** the haptic feedback may be presented. Finally, there will be questions that designers need to consider if using these design patterns, and examples of research where they have been described and used.

3.1   Tracked Fingertips

In this design pattern, haptic points are positioned at one, or more, fingertips, like in Fig. 2. When the user moves their hand or fingers, the haptic points are repositioned in 3D to remain in contact. This pattern implies the use of hand tracking which is capable of multi-finger location relative to the haptic device. One aim of this haptic

Fig. 2 Tracked Fingertips: haptic points are given against the fingers and are linked to the fingertip positions

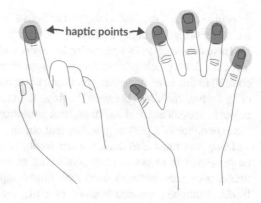

design is to create the experience of touching something in mid-air; for example, to let the user know they have touched a user interface element or a virtual object. In this case, the presence of feedback is enough to enhance the user experience, because users can feel where and when they have touched an interactive object in mid-air. Another aim of this haptic design is to inform users that their fingers are actively being tracked and that the system is responding to their movements. In this case, the presence of feedback shows 'system attention' (Bellotti et al. 2002), reassuring users that they are providing input in a suitable position (Freeman et al. 2014).

3.1.1 Design Considerations

Haptic feedback can be presented against one or more fingertips. Designers need to choose which number of fingers is most appropriate for their interaction design, as this may affect the strength of the haptic feedback. When a single haptic point is created, the ultrasound haptic device can maximise feedback intensity; as more points are added, the intensity of all points will typically be reduced. Presenting additional unnecessary points can therefore have a detrimental effect on the overall strength of the haptic feedback.

> Tracked Fingertips (**UHDP1**)
> *What?* Haptic points that are linked to one, or more, fingertip positions.
> *Why?* To create the experience of touching something. To confirm that the system is actively responding to the user's actions.
> *Where?* One or more fingertips.
> *When?* In response to input (event-driven), or continuously, or to show system attention.

In most cases, a single haptic point is sufficient. A common touchless gesture design is to use a single extended index finger for input, e.g. to control an on-screen cursor or to 'tap' virtual buttons. For this, a single haptic point at the extended fingertip can be sufficient to support effective input, and it confirms to the user that the correct finger is being tracked by the user interface.

There are situations where multiple fingers will require haptic feedback. For example, consider a pinch gesture between index finger and thumb, used to drag a slider control; in this case, presenting feedback to each fingertip may enhance the sensation of 'grasping' the slider between the fingers. Likewise, if the user is holding a virtual object in a touchless user interface, then presenting feedback at all fingertips supports the experience of a person grasping that object.

Designers must also decide when feedback should be given. Haptic points can be presented in response to actions using an event-driven feedback model (e.g. a user experiences feedback once their finger 'taps' a mid-air button). Alternatively, feedback can be presented at all times whilst the hand is within range of the device. The most appropriate choice here depends on the intended user experience. In an event-driven input model (e.g. pressing buttons, grasping objects), feedback can be presented in short bursts (e.g. after a button press) or continually (e.g. whilst grasping a virtual object). For other user experiences, users may feel more confidence if feedback is presented continuously whilst their hands are within the interaction volume, so that they know when their hands are being tracked.

In this design pattern, haptic feedback is presented as one or more discrete points. Amplitude modulation (Iwamoto et al. 2008) and lateral modulation (Takahashi et al. 2019) are suitable rendering methods for this design pattern, as they enable perceptible feedback at fixed-position points. The perceived size of the focal point corresponds to the wavelength of the sound wave; for 40 kHz ultrasound, this is approximately 8.6 mm (Rakkolainen et al. 2020). When the focal point is positioned appropriately, users will feel like the entire fingertip is being stimulated.

3.1.2 Questions for Designers

When using this design pattern, consider:

- How many fingertips should receive haptic feedback?
- When should haptic feedback be presented, and for how long?

3.1.3 Examples

One of the first examples of the Tracked Fingertips design pattern can be seen in work by Carter et al. (2013), who presented a touchless user interface that was capable of tracking multiple fingers and targeting them with independent points of haptic feedback. Haptic feedback was used in their system to mimic the sensation of touching a screen in mid-air, an experience we will look at in more detail in Sect. 3.3. Shakeri et al. (2018) used discrete event-driven haptic feedback, presenting a 500 ms pulse against two fingertips to confirm recognition of the 'victory' gesture

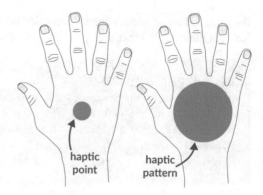

Fig. 3 Tracked Palm: haptic points (left) or patterns (right) are given against the palm and are linked to the palm position

(i.e. extended index and middle fingers). In this instance, event-driven feedback was given to inform the user that their input gesture was recognised. As can be seen by contrasting these examples, event-driven feedback may be better suited to confirming response to a user's actions, whilst continuous feedback may be more appropriate for creating the sensation of touching something.

3.2 Tracked Palm

In this design pattern, a haptic point or pattern is positioned on the palm of the hand, like in Fig. 3. When the user moves their hand, the haptic output is repositioned to remain in contact with the hand. This is very similar to the Tracked Fingertips design pattern, except haptic feedback is presented against the palm (or whole hand), rather than just the fingertips. This offers the same potential benefits as the Tracked Fingertips design pattern, i.e. letting the user know when they are touching a virtual object, or informing them when their hand is being actively tracked for input.

3.2.1　Design Considerations

One of the first things designers should consider is whether to use this or the Tracked Fingertips design pattern. Both aim to give the same benefits to the user, so the most appropriate choice will likely be informed by the choice of tracking technology and the intended interaction metaphor. Targeting haptic points at fingertips requires precise finger tracking, which may not always be available. In this situation, targeting haptic feedback at the palm will be more straightforward as this requires a lower resolution sensor that only needs to be able to roughly estimate hand position (e.g. like in work by Hoshi (2011)). Choice of design pattern will also be influenced by the intended interaction metaphor. If the palm position is used as input to the system (rather than a fingertip position), then it makes more sense to target haptic feedback at the palm. Likewise, if the intended sensation is for users to grasp a virtual object and feel it in their whole hand, then presenting feedback on the palm will be appropriate.

> **Tracked Palm (UHDP2)**
> *What?* Haptic points or patterns linked to the palm position.
> *Why?* To create the experience of touching something. To confirm that the system is actively responding to the user's actions.
> *Where?* On the palm, typically centred.
> *When?* In response to input (event-driven), or continuously.

A key decision with this design pattern is the choice of tactile sensation to render on the palm. An individual haptic point or a spatially modulated pattern could be presented (e.g. circles). Choice may be limited by the haptic device and its driving software: haptic points are more straightforward to render, whereas continually moving haptic points require higher sample rates, more complex calculations, etc. From a usability perspective, there is likely to be little difference between the choice of tactile sensation; the presence of haptic feedback will be more important than its shape or tactile qualities. There will be a perceptual difference, however: patterns can feel more intense than fixed-position points (Frier et al. 2018; Takahashi et al. 2019), and so these may be the best choice if available.

Similar to the Tracked Fingertips design pattern, designers need to consider when feedback should be presented. As discussed before, the most appropriate choice depends on the intended user experience and the reader should refer to Sect. 3.1.1 for more insight.

3.2.2   Questions for Designers

When using this design pattern, consider:

- Should this design be used, or is Tracked Fingertips more appropriate?
- What should be presented against the palm—haptic point, pattern?
- If using a haptic pattern, what should be rendered?
- When should haptic feedback be presented, and for how long?

3.2.3   Examples

The Tracked Palm design has been widely used to give users feedback that confirms the touchless user interface is actively tracking their hand movements in air, although there are subtle variations in how this experience is created. Hoshi (2011) and Georgiou et al. (2018), for example, both presented a continuous haptic point against the centre of an open palm to confirm the system was tracking the hand. In the latter system, additional haptic patterns targeted other regions of the hand in an event-driven model, e.g. to confirm when gestures were recognised. An advantage of presenting a single point like this is that it leaves other parts of the hand free for presenting additional feedback.

Alternatively, larger patterns can be presented against the palm. For example, Freeman et al. (2019) presented a continuous circular pattern against the palm, which dynamically resized to guide hand movements in mid-air. Shakeri et al. (2018) also presented a circular pattern, although this was only presented briefly after input gestures were recognised. As can be seen by contrasting these examples, event-driven feedback is typically more appropriate when feedback is given in response to a user action, whilst continuous feedback will be more appropriate when feedback aims to guide users or confirm that the system is tracking their hands correctly.

3.3 Floating Screen

Touchless user interfaces often mimic the behaviour of touchscreens, allowing users to 'tap' buttons and icons on a virtual screen in mid-air. A virtual screen is generally defined as a flat surface that is oriented and positioned in air in front of a real display. Users' hands are tracked and mapped to the position of an on-screen cursor, which can be used to make selections by reaching forward, breaking the surface and effectively 'tapping' the floating screen. This interaction metaphor leverages familiarity with touchscreens and, from a more pragmatic perspective, can be easier to retrofit to existing user interfaces (effectively using the hand or finger position to control a mouse pointer). Ultrasound haptic feedback is naturally suited to these floating virtual touchscreens because it can provide the missing sense of physical contact that supports effective touchscreen input (Freeman et al. 2014), overcoming a usability issue with floating screens (Waugh and Robertson 2021).

In this design pattern, haptic feedback is positioned in order to create the experience of the hand or fingers touching the virtual screen, like in Fig. 4. One aim of this haptic design is to inform users of where the floating screen is positioned, so they know how far they must reach to activate its user interface elements (Vo and Brewster 2015). Another is to give confirmation to users that their input actions were recognised by the system, because even the brief presentation of a focal point after a button activation gesture can be effective (Cornelio-Martinez et al. 2017). This can be considered a special case of the Tracked Fingertips and Tracked Palm design patterns, where haptic feedback is presented when targeting controls in a touchless user interface, with the intention of mimicking contact with a touchscreen.

Fig. 4 Floating screen:
haptic feedback is given
when users touch a virtual
screen surface, or buttons on
the surface. For example,
feedback on the fingertip
(left) or palm (right)

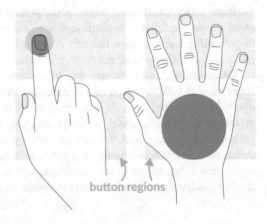

3.3.1 Design Considerations

Haptic feedback can be presented against a fingertip, the palm or the whole hand. The most appropriate choice is the part of the hand used to activate content on the floating screen, so users know how to target user interface elements effectively. For example, if an extended index finger is used to 'tap' buttons, then haptic feedback should be positioned at the index fingertip, or if the centre of the palm is used to detect a whole-hand button 'press', then haptic feedback should be positioned at the centre of the palm.

Floating Screen (UHDP3)
What? Haptic feedback given when the hand is targeting a virtual screen.
Why? To reveal the position of the virtual screen surface. To give feedback about activating screen controls.
Where? At the point of contact with the screen, typically at the part of the hand used for input tracking.
When? In response to screen activation (event-driven), or continuously.

Screen contact can be conveyed using both haptic points and haptic patterns, although the most appropriate choice will depend on the input gesture design: e.g. a haptic point is sufficient for a single fingertip, whereas a haptic pattern may be more suitable if the screen is activated by the palm. In some touchless user interface designs, it may be possible to represent the shape and size of the button as a haptic pattern, creating cross-modal congruence between visual and haptic feedback. Whilst this may create a richer interaction experience, the main usability benefits will come from simply feeling the feedback in the first place, as this conveys the screen position and informs the user that they have made contact.

Designers need to decide when feedback should be given, a choice that will be informed by the floating screen design. Touchless buttons on a floating screen can be activated in numerous ways; for example, when a hand contacts its surface, when a hand hovers in front of it for a short period of time or when a finger performs a 'tap' motion in front of it. When buttons are activated through contact or tapping gestures, event-driven feedback will likely be most appropriate, because the onset of haptic feedback informs the user that the activation gesture has been acted upon. When buttons are activated via hover, it may be more suitable to present feedback continuously whilst the hand is hovering, to inform users that they are controlling an active cursor and an unintended selection may take place.

Button activation method will also influence the hand positions where haptic feedback should be given. If buttons are activated through contact or tapping gestures, haptic points or patterns should be positioned at the surface of the screen and oriented towards the hand. This is a natural complement to the event-driven feedback model: haptic feedback will only be experienced by the user when their hand reaches towards the screen to activate a user interface element. Alternatively, for continuous feedback, haptic feedback should be given at all times when the hand is actively being tracked: e.g. whilst the activation timer is enabled for dwell activation.

3.3.2 Questions for Designers

When using this design pattern, consider:

- Which part of the hand should be used as input to the floating screen?
- What should be presented against that part of the hand—haptic point, pattern?
- If using a haptic pattern, what should be rendered—the button shape and size?
- How should floating buttons and other user interface elements be activated?
- When should haptic feedback be presented, and for how long?

3.3.3 Examples

This is a widely used design pattern, and numerous examples can be found in the literature; however, for brevity I focus on a few examples that highlight how this design can be varied. Hoshi (2011) and Carter et al. (2013) used the Floating Screen design pattern and targeted the palm and fingertips, respectively. In both examples, the floating screen surface was positioned directly in front of a visual display.

Floating screens can be placed in other positions, however. For example, Freeman et al. (2014) used a floating screen in an offset position, with users gesturing *beside* a small screen instead of directly in front of it (to avoid occluding the display content). Sand et al. (2015) used this design pattern in virtual reality, using a hand tracker and haptics device mounted on a virtual reality headset, such that users felt contact with a floating screen when their hands touched it in virtual reality. This design pattern has also been used with mid-air holographic displays, e.g. by Monnai et al. (2014).

Fig. 5 Forcefield: haptic feedback is used to create a 'forcefield' surface that users must reach through

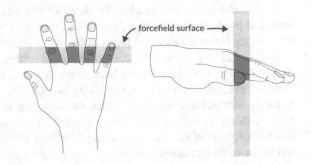

This design pattern can also be used in interactive experiences that do not mimic interaction with traditional graphical user interfaces; for example, Hwang et al. (2017) describe a novel example whereby users can play a piano in virtual reality, tapping piano keys instead of user interface buttons.

3.4 Forcefield

A key usability challenge with touchless interaction is knowing where to perform input gestures. Physical input devices that users touch or grasp have affordances that help users discover how to direct their input, but touchless user interfaces do not—the interaction volume is not visible, and users cannot be expected to know where their hands can, and cannot, be sensed (Freeman et al. 2016). Users may not even know that touchless interaction is available (Limerick 2020), especially if a touchless input device is used alongside an existing touchscreen display.

In this design pattern, ultrasound haptic feedback is used to convey the boundaries of a touchless user interface by creating a 'forcefield', a haptic surface that users feel as they reach through it (like in Fig. 5). One aim of this haptic design is to help users discover the boundaries of a touchless interaction volume; reaching into this volume—by breaking through the forcefield—creates a perceptible change in state, letting users know that *this* is where interaction begins. At the same time, the presence of the forcefield reveals the otherwise invisible touchless user interface, which users may have previously been unaware of; the touchless haptic feedback conveys interactivity in the space in front of the display and may prevent them reaching for the screen.

There are similarities between this and the Floating Screen design pattern, in that both utilise the concept of a surface in a fixed position in mid-air. The key distinction between them is that users are intended to interact *on the surface* of a Floating Screen and interact *on the other side* of the Forcefield. An alternative means of revealing a touchless user interface would be to use continuous haptic feedback linked to the hand (i.e. Tracked Fingertips or Tracked Palm). However, the advantage of using a fixed position Forcefield is that users only experience a tactile sensation when they reach through the surface; once their hand is inside the interaction volume, haptic feedback can then be used for other purposes, e.g. to give feedback about touchless gestures, or to render haptic representations of virtual objects.

3.4.1 Design Considerations

When creating an ultrasound haptic forcefield, two of the first design considerations are where to place it and how to orient it. A forcefield will typically be used alongside a visual display, and if the intention is to convey the boundaries of the touchless user interface, then it will make the most sense to align the forcefield with the screen. As a result, the forcefield surface will generally be the same distance in front of all regions of the screen, aligned like a Floating Screen. That distance between screen and forcefield depends on the intended interaction metaphor: does the forcefield define where the interaction area begins (i.e. after crossing this point, touchless input sensing is active), or ends (i.e. after crossing this point, touchless input sensing will stop)? Perhaps even both, using two forcefields to show both boundaries?

Forcefield (UHDP4)

What? Haptic feedback that represents a surface that users must reach through.
Why? To indicate the boundaries of the interaction volume, so users know where to provide input or can feel the transition between two interface states.
Where? On a line segment across the hand, where the hand intersects the forcefield surface.
When? When the hand intersects the forcefield surface.

An ultrasound haptic forcefield will be placed in a fixed position and orientation in space, but users' hands will approach it from different positions and at different angles. In some cases, it may be more appropriate to choose a curved forcefield surface rather than a flat one. For example, a flat haptic surface is ideally suited to a flat screen, but a curved surface might suit other configurations, e.g. for a touchless interface in a vehicle where the user does not receive any visual feedback on a screen (Georgiou and Griffiths 2017; Shakeri et al. 2018). The choice of surface shape will impact how the forcefield is presented against the user's hand: a touchless user interface needs to calculate the intersection between the hand and the surface, taking hand height and orientation into consideration. The intersection can then be used as the trajectory for one or more focal points to move along, creating the sensation of a surface that remains in place whilst the hand passes through.

3.4.2   Questions for Designers

When using this design pattern, consider:

- What does entering the forcefield mean—entering the interaction zone, leaving the interaction zone, both?
- What is the shape of the forcefield—spherical surface, flat surface?
- How is the forcefield oriented—aligned with input sensor or visual display?

3.4.3   Examples

This design pattern exists as a template within the Ultraleap Sensation Editor (Ultraleap 2019) but has seen little use in the academic literature so far. A similar design was described by Shakeri et al. (2018), who evaluated a touchless user interface for in-car interaction. In their system, ultrasound haptic feedback was briefly presented against the palm when it entered the interaction volume. Whilst this rendering did not create the sensation of a solid surface being broken by the hand, it had the same intention of conveying the boundary between interactive and non-interactive regions in space.

3.5   Object Outline

An alluring capability of ultrasound haptic feedback is its ability to take simple focal points and use them to render patterns of varying shape and size. A compelling use of this capability is to create haptic representations of virtual objects, so that users can 'feel' the visual content they see on a display. Rendering haptic shapes that can be accurately recognised is a challenge (Hajas et al. 2020; Korres and Eid 2016; Long et al. 2014; Rutten et al. 2019), although a corresponding visual representation of the shape can help users make sense of the haptic feedback.

In this design pattern, ultrasound haptics is used to create a haptic representation of a virtual object shown on a visual display. Whilst there are many ways to achieve this, the most common is to render the outside edge of the object, where it intersects the hand. For example, Fig. 6 shows examples of how a haptic circle may be presented using discrete focal points (left) or spatially modulated focal points (right). Users can only perceive a 2D shape on their palm at any one time, but by dynamically scaling the shape outline, users can experience the illusion of moving their hand *through* a 3D object. Consider a sphere: as a user moves their hand through a virtual sphere, its circular cross-section on the palm will increase, reach maximum size at the midpoint and then decrease as the hand approaches the opposite side (Long et al. 2014).

This design pattern aims to help users locate virtual objects in mid-air and support haptic exploration (e.g. by conveying shape and size). The addition of haptic feedback

Fig. 6 Object outline: haptic feedback represents the edge of a virtual object, e.g. using a series of points (left) or a moving focal point (right) to render a circle on the palm

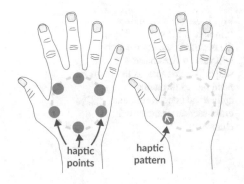

can also create a more engaging user experience, through the addition of another sensory modality that allows users to 'feel' what they see on screen.

3.5.1   Design Considerations

An object outline pattern needs to resemble the shape of the corresponding virtual object, so there are less design parameters for designers to consider. However, a key decision will be how to represent the outline shape. Haptic shapes can be presented using several haptic points distributed around the outline (e.g. Fig. 6–left) or using spatially modulated patterns, where haptic point(s) rapidly traces the outline (e.g. Fig. 6–right).

> **Object Outline (UHDP5)**
> **What?** Haptic feedback resembling the outline of a virtual object.
> **Why?** To help users locate virtual objects. For haptic exploration. To increase engagement and enhance content shown on screen.
> **Where?** On the region of the hand that intersects the object.
> **When?** When the hand is intersecting the virtual object.

We cannot recommend a 'best' method for presenting haptic shapes, as research into improved shape rendering is ongoing and recommendations will change over time—as will be discussed in Sect. 3.5.3. It is worth noting, however, that most research into haptic shape perception investigates shape recognition with haptic-only presentation. In practice, the Object Outline design pattern is most likely to be used with a visual representation on the screen, which is likely to make the haptic shapes more easily recognisable, such that subtle variation in shape rendering approach become less important.

When creating 3D virtual objects for a touchless user interface, the virtual object will likely have to be fixed in position. This allows the user's hand to move 'through'

Fig. 7 As the hand moves
'through' a 3D virtual object,
the outline of the intersection
will vary in size and/or
shape. For example, as the
hand moves through a
cylindrical cone, its circular
cross-section diameter will
change

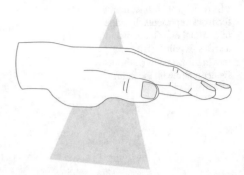

the object, experiencing the varying shape and size as a result of the changing intersection between hand and virtual object (e.g. Fig. 7).

Presenting 2D outlines is more straightforward as the shape and/or size of the
outline does not vary (although may change position or orientation as the hand
moves). Consequently, 2D shapes need not be fixed in position and could be linked
to the hand, so that users perceive them from any hand position (a special instance
of Tracked Palm).

3.5.2 Questions for Designers

When using this design pattern, consider:

- What visual cues, if appropriate, can be given to aid shape perception?
- How large should the haptic object be—will it fit on the palm?
- Will 2D shapes be fixed in position, or should they be linked to hand position?

3.5.3 Examples

In one of the earliest explorations of this design pattern, Long et al. (2014) described a
novel method for rendering volumetric 3D objects by creating several disconnected
haptic points around the edge of the 2D cross-section with the palm. Frier et al.
(2018) presented a more sophisticated rendering method for polygons, where one
focal point rapidly and repeatedly traverses the outline. Whilst this works fine for
circles, object outlines with corners are more difficult to accurately perceive (e.g.
squares, triangles). Hajas et al. (2020) discussed a novel extension of Frier's method,
where the moving focal point briefly pauses at corners before changing direction.
This helped to emphasise the corners and edges of the object, so that users could
more accurately recognise the shapes.

Fig. 8 Motion Patterns: haptic patterns that are perceived as movement across the hand, e.g. lines that scan across the palm (left) or points moving along circular paths (right)

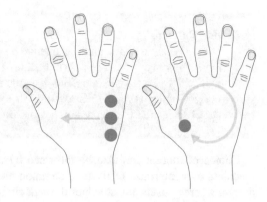

3.6 Motion Patterns

In the design patterns described so far, the haptic sensations have been fixed in position: some are fixed on the hand (e.g. Tracked Fingertips and Tracked Palm) whilst others are fixed in space (e.g. Floating Screen and Forcefield). Users may experience sensations of haptic movement when interacting with fixed-position haptic feedback, like when they reach through a Forcefield, but that motion is a result of the user's actions and not deliberate movement intended by the designer.

In this design pattern, ultrasound haptic feedback is used to create a deliberate and controlled sensation of motion on the hand (like in Fig. 8). This is distinct from other designs because the motion is consistent and intentional, controlled by the touchless user interface and not a result of inherent hand movement. One aim of this design is to convey a change in system state, informing the user that *something has happened* through animated haptic sensation. This form of feedback can be perceptibly distinct from other designs that may be used in the same touchless interface, e.g. a static Tracked Palm sensation given to confirm active hand tracking. Another aim of this design is to create more engaging user experiences, e.g. by synchronising haptic motion with effects shown on screen.

3.6.1 Design Considerations

Most ultrasound haptic feedback primitives can be used to create a sensation of motion on the palm, e.g. by moving haptic points, lines and shapes. Designers thus need to identify the most appropriate motion patterns for their touchless user interface design. If Motion Patterns are being used to give feedback in response to input gestures, it is often most appropriate to align the motion with the action that caused it. For example, if users swipe their hand to the left or right, feedback patterns could confirm input recognition with a corresponding haptic sensation, that moves to the left or right across the hand (Shakeri et al. 2018).

Motion Patterns (UHDP6)
What? Dynamic haptic patterns that are perceived as motion on the hand.
Why? To convey change in system state. To encode information. To give
feedback. To create engaging and dynamic user experiences.
Where? Typically on the palm, but may move across the fingers too.
When? In response to screen activation (event-driven), or continuously.

Choice of motion can also be informed by interaction metaphors used in the
touchless user interface. Dials are a common metaphor in touchless user interface
design, whereby users adjust values through circular motions (Freeman et al. 2016)
or 'grasping and turning' gestures Freeman et al. (2015). Circular motion of haptic
points can extend this metaphor to the haptic feedback. For example, a haptic point
moves clockwise when values increase or anticlockwise when values decrease (Georgiou and Griffiths 2017). Motion can also be paired with animated feedback shown
on screen, creating a sense of cohesion between mid-air haptics and the visual content
on a distant display.

After choosing appropriate motion patterns, designers need to think about where
and when to present them against the hand. Motion patterns are typically targeted
at the palm of the hand, since it is a contiguous space across which motion can be
perceived (unlike the fingers, which may be spread apart). Motion patterns can be
presented continuously (e.g. when synchronised with on-screen animations), but will
mostly likely be event-driven, presented in response to an action by the user, a change
in system state, etc.

There are many ways that sensation of motion can be created. One of the earliest
demonstrations of perceived motion used a perceptual illusion known as apparent tactile motion (Wilson et al. 2014). This sensation was created by presenting a sequence
of three haptic points in order, with a slight delay, such that people perceived continuous movement between those points. Contemporary rendering approaches can use
actual motion, updating the position of a haptic point thousands of times per second,
so that it actually moves across the skin (Frier et al. 2018). This, in turn, can elicit
the sensations of dynamic and 'static' haptic patterns (Freeman and Wilson 2021).

3.6.2   Questions for Designers

When using this design pattern, consider:

- Which types of motion should be presented to the user?
- Where should the motion pattern be presented?
- When should it be presented, and for how long?

Fig. 9 Special Effects: haptic patterns intended to create the sensation of touching unfamiliar yet recognisable experiences, like touching fire (left) or lightning (right)

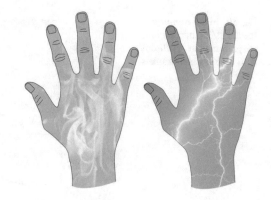

3.6.3   Examples

Motion Patterns can be used to convey a change in touchless user interface state; for example, (Georgiou and Griffiths 2017) used clockwise and anticlockwise circle patterns to indicate increasing and decreasing values, respectively. Motion can also be used to give feedback confirming the recognition of hand motion gestures; for example, Shakeri et al. (2018) and Georgiou et al. (2018) both used motion patterns after mid-air swipe gestures, e.g. haptic points that moved across the palm in the same direction the user had swiped for input. Many examples of Motion Patterns can be found in the Ultraleap Sensation Editor (Ultrahaptics 2017), e.g. scanning lines across the hand or presenting circles that 'expand' and then 'contract'.

3.7   Special Effects

In the haptic design patterns discussed so far, haptic sensations have been grounded in *familiar* interaction experiences: e.g. the sensation of touching user interface elements or virtual representations of physical objects. Due to the unique design capabilities of this technology and its lack of mechanical constraints, ultrasound haptic feedback can also be used to create radically new and unfamiliar tactile sensations: best described as special effects, or 'supernatural experiences' (Martinez et al. 2018).

In this design pattern, haptic feedback is used alongside visual and audio to create multisensory special effects (like in Fig. 9), e.g. the feeling of touching lightning, holding a ball of fire and casting magical spells (Limerick et al. 2019; Martinez et al. 2018). Unlike other design patterns, the haptic rendering itself may seem irregular, using random and disjointed movement to create sensations that 'feel right' for the intended effect. The success of these special effects comes from an effective coupling between multiple sensory modalities. Unsurprisingly, these effects have the ability to capture users' imagination and increase engagement with a touchless user interface Limerick et al. (2019) and could be compelling for entertainment applications, e.g. video games (Georgiou et al. 2018; Martinez et al. 2018) and movies (Ablart et al. 2017).

Fig. 10 In the *raindrop* special effect, haptic points are presented in synchrony with visible water droplets

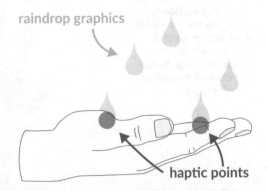

3.7.1 Design Considerations

Creating ultrasound haptic special effects is not straightforward, because there is no systematic way of defining the tactile experience of touching a flame, holding a hand under running water, etc. Most design patterns discussed in this chapter can be defined using geometric primitives (points, lines, shapes) and the spatial relationship between the user's hand and touchless user interface (e.g. fixed position vs linked to the hand), but this is not possible for special effects. Instead, a more exploratory approach is needed, to find suitable spatial and temporal characteristics for the intended effect.

Special Effects (UHDP7)
What? Dynamic patterns intended to create recognisable tactile experiences, not grounded in the physical world.
Why? To create an engaging experience that captures the imagination.
Where? Where the hand intersects the visual effects.
When? In synchrony with visual and/or audible effects.

Since little systematic guidance can be offered for creating new special effects, this section instead looks at case studies of existing special effects, to give insight into possible approaches. What is notable about these examples is the haptic effects are always presented in synchrony with visual and audio effects. These other sensory modalities help users attribute meaning to a tactile experience that may otherwise difficult to describe. In other words, the graphics and audio help to sell the illusion.

One of the first ultrasound haptic special effects was the sensation of raindrops falling on the palm, described by Hoshi et al. (2010). In their system, a holographic display showed falling raindrops landing on the user's hand, which were synchronised with the presentation of haptic points against the palm (like in Fig. 10). Although these simple haptic points did not feel like water, the temporal coincidence between visual and haptic effects contributed to the experience of rain falling on the hand.

Fig. 11 In the *lightning spell* special effect, a haptic point moves along the palm and a finger, to coincide with an electrical arc graphic that extends from the fingertip

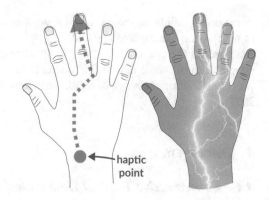

haptic point

In their paper on 'supernatural experiences', Martinez et al. (2018) describe numerous haptic special effects. One of these is the experience of casting a lightning bolt from the fingertips, in a virtual reality spellcasting game. Their lightning spell effect was created using haptic points that follow an erratic path from the base of the palm to the fingertip (like in Fig. 11), coinciding with visual and audible cues in the virtual reality game. The combined feeling of motion across the palm and other sensory information created a convincing and engaging user experience of casting magical spells.

3.7.2   Questions for Designers

When using this design pattern, consider:

- *'What elements of the audio-visual [design] should one look to haptically enhance and/or augment?'* (Corenthy et al. 2018)
- Are there spatial or temporal characteristics in the visual effects that can be replicated via haptics?

3.7.3   Examples

Ultrasound haptic special effects—'supernatural experiences' (Martinez et al. 2018)—have mostly been used to increase user engagement during gameplay. For example, Martinez et al. (2018) describe a virtual reality game where users cast magic spells, feeling the elemental sensations of wind, fire and lightning. Limerick et al. (2019) used haptic special effects for interactive digital advertising, e.g. to experience the sensation of firing lasers from a spaceship or feeling electrical static against the palm. Similar effects exist within the Ultraleap Sensation Editor (Ultrahaptics 2017), e.g. to mimic the sensations of rippling water or electrical sparks. Haptic special effects have also been paired with holographic content: e.g. Hoshi et al. (2010) created the effects of raindrops falling on the palm and a small animal walking across the hand, both of which were accompanied by mid-air graphics from a holographic display. Recent work shows the potential for combining ultrasound haptic sensations with audio effects from the same device (Hirayama et al. 2019), which could be a promising way of expanding the range of tactile sensations for haptic special effects (Freeman 2021).

4 Discussion

4.1 Retrospective Look at Haptic Design

This collection of design patterns shows seven widely used haptic interaction designs found in human-computer interaction research and in real-world deployments of this technology. Whilst the main aim of this chapter is to help designers identify suitable haptic designs for a touchless user interface, these design patterns also give insight into how this technology has been used and the user experience benefits it offers.

In the earliest years of this technology, the Tracked Fingertips and Tracked Palm designs were common. Amplitude modulation (Iwamoto et al. 2008) was the predominant rendering method at the time and was best suited for stationary haptic points, in a fixed position in mid-air or on the hand. Targeting the fingertips or centre of the palm was a straightforward way of creating a consistent user experience, and this often created a coupling between the input and output: i.e. presenting haptic feedback against the location on the hand that was being tracked for input. This was a simple yet effective design, creating a sense of presence in a touchless user interface; the haptic feedback both revealed the presence of a haptic user interface in mid-air and provided reassurance to users that their actions were being tracked.

Over the past decade, the predominant use of ultrasound haptic feedback has been to create a haptic embodiment of a touchless user interface and its interactive elements. Floating Screen provides the experience of pressing a 'touchless screen' in mid-air, with feedback about familiar user interface components like buttons and sliders. Forcefield represents the boundaries between interactive and non-interactive space, analogous to a window in a graphical user interface. Finally, Object Outline conveys the shape and size of user interface elements and other virtual objects. Collectively, these haptic designs convey the position of touchless user interface elements and give feedback about interactions with them.

More recently, Motion Patterns and Special Effects have emerged as compelling use of ultrasound haptic feedback. These 'animated' haptic patterns take advantage of improved rendering methods and increasingly more capable technology. These are predominantly used to give users feedback about interaction, or to enrich interaction and increase engagement through the use of an extra sensory modality. Special Effects, in particular, are an exciting departure from the geometric primitives that dominated the early use of ultrasound haptic technology (i.e. the points, lines and shapes used in numerous haptic design patterns). It is exciting to imagine what might come next—perhaps the design patterns of the future will bear no resemblance to those presented here, e.g. by using focal points in novel ways or by moving away from focal points entirely to exploit ultrasound pressure in different ways.

4.2 Selecting Design Patterns

A key question addressed by this chapter is **where to start?**—how should one identify design patterns for a new touchless user interfaces? Table 1 shows a suggested mapping between design patterns and six common user experience objectives in a touchless user interface, intended to guide readers towards a suitable design pattern. Whilst these objectives can be satisfied through numerous designs, this table gives suggestions about which patterns may be the most effective.

Reveal Interactivity means haptic feedback is intended to inform users about the presence of a touchless user interface. **Confirm Tracking** means haptic feedback is intended to give reassurance that the system is correctly sensing their actions. **Action Feedback** means haptic feedback is intended to confirm response to a user's input actions (e.g. feedback about mid-air gestures). **Object Representation** means haptic feedback is intended to represent virtual objects in a touchless user interface, and **UI Representation** is a special case where the virtual object is a user interface element (e.g. a screen, button or slider). **Engagement** means haptic feedback intends to engage and excite users through novel multisensory effects.

4.2.1 Case Study: Touchless Button Menu

When designing a touchless user interface, it may be necessary to employ multiple haptic designs to support different usability needs. As a case study, consider a touchless user interface with a gesture-activated button menu. Users' hands are tracked in 3D, and buttons can be activated at any distance from the screen, by hovering a hand in front of them and then 'pushing' the palm towards the screen.

This touchless interface would benefit from feedback that (i) reveals touchless interactivity, (ii) confirms that users' hands are actively being tracked when within range of the touchless interface, (iii) represents the touchless buttons in their mid-air position and (iv) gives feedback about button activation gestures. As can be seen from Table 1, many patterns could be chosen to satisfy these interaction needs. However, not all combinations will make sense to users and they may have difficulty differentiating between feedback designs. A suitably chosen combination of design patterns must therefore be cohesive, so that users can recognise different interface states through clearly perceptible differences in feedback design.

Table 1 Suggested mapping of ultrasound haptic design patterns to user experience objectives in a touchless user interface

	Reveal Interactivity	Confirm Tracking	Action Feedback	Object Representation	UI Representation	Engagement
Tracked Fingertips	✓	✓				
Tracked Palm	✓	✓				
Floating Screen			✓		✓	
Forcefield	✓				✓	
Object Outline				✓	✓	
Motion Patterns			✓			✓
Special Effects			✓			✓

One combination that satisfies our feedback needs in this case study example would be the Tracked Palm, Floating Screen and Motion Patterns designs:

- Tracked Palm: a haptic point presented against the centre of the palm when the user's hand is within range of the input device reveals interactivity and informs the user that their hand is being tracked (Fig. 12a). As corresponding visual feedback, a model of the user's hand would be shown in the user interface.
- Floating Screen: when the user places their hand over the position of a mid-air button, a circular pattern is presented against the palm, so they feel the button's position in mid-air (Fig. 12b). This feedback informs the user that their hand is targeting a button; visual feedback would show the hand model in front of the button, with an animation that invites them to 'push forward'.
- Motion Patterns: when the user pushes their hand forward to activate a button, the diameter of the circle pattern changes, so that the user feels it contracting to a point on the palm (Fig. 12c) and then expanding back to full size (Fig. 12d). This haptic animation shows a dynamic response to the button activation gesture.

These three designs are intended to represent three states of the touchless user interface: (i) being tracked by the interface but not targeting a button, (ii) actively targeting a button by hovering the hand over it and (iii) targeted button has been activated by the push gesture. The transitions between these states will be noticed by perceptible changes in the feedback. When the user moves over a button, the single haptic point on their palm is replaced by the circle pattern, which stimulates a larger area of the hand and feels more intense (Takahashi et al. 2019). Likewise, when the user activates a button, they will perceive the circle contracting and expanding. When the user moves away from a button (or if the interface transitions to a new window), the haptic feedback resets to a haptic point in the centre of the palm.

This simple feedback vocabulary combines three design patterns to give haptic feedback before, during and after button activation; the transitions between these designs reflect transitions in user interface state, a haptic accompaniment to visual feedback that would be shown on screen. Other design patterns could have been

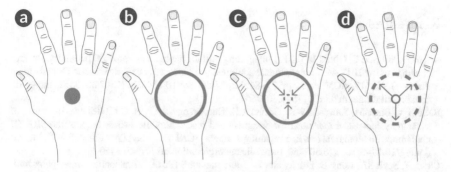

Fig. 12 Haptic feedback designs for the case study example: **a** a haptic point in the centre of the palm confirms tracking when within range; **b** a haptic circle is presented when the user hovers over mid-air buttons; **c–d** when the user pushes forward to 'press' a button, the circle contracts **c** then expands **d** again to confirm recognition

selected for the same purpose, e.g. a haptic Forcefield to inform the user when they have entered the interaction space, rather than continuous Tracked Palm feedback, suggesting the so-called 'best' combination is a challenge for future research.

5 Conclusion

This chapter presented seven ultrasound haptic design patterns, which illustrate the variety of ways that interaction designers and researchers are using this technology in touchless user interface design. This serves three aims: (i) to reflect on the evolution of this technology (and our understanding of it); (ii) to highlight the many ways that ultrasound haptic feedback can improve usability and user experience; and (iii) to inform the design of future touchless user interfaces. The set of design patterns presented in this chapter is by no means complete. Ultrasound haptic technology is continually advancing, and so is our understanding of touchless interaction and haptic perception. In turn, design patterns will evolve and new ones will emerge, to make better use of ultrasound haptic feedback and to pave the way to more engaging and usable touchless interaction experiences.

Acknowledgements I have been fortunate enough to be a part of this community for a relatively long time. I am grateful to those who have helped me along the way, including Tom Carter, Sriram Subramanian, Stephen Brewster, Graham Wilson and many friends at Ultraleap.

References

Ablart D, Velasco C, Obrist M (2017) Integrating mid-air haptics into movie experiences. In: Proceedings of the 2017 ACM international conference on interactive experiences for TV and online video—TVX '17, ACM Press, pp 77–84, https://doi.org/10.1145/3077548.3077551, https://dl.acm.org/citation.cfm?id=3077548.3077551

Bellotti V, Back M, Edwards WK, Grinter RE, Henderson A, Lopes C (2002) Making sense of sensing systems: five questions for designers and researchers. In: Proceedings of the SIGCHI conference on human factors in computing systems—CHI '02, ACM Press, pp 415–422. https://doi.org/10.1145/503376.503450, http://dl.acm.org/citation.cfm?id=503450

Carter T, Seah SA, Long B, Drinkwater B, Subramanian S (2013) UltraHaptics: multi-point mid-air haptic feedback for touch surfaces. In: Proceedings of the 26th symposium on user interface software and technology—UIST '13. ACM Press, pp 505–514, https://doi.org/10.1145/2501988.2502018, http://dl.acm.org/citation.cfm?id=2502018

Corenthy L, Giordano M, Hayden R, Griffiths D, Jeffrey C, Limerick H, Georgiou O, Carter T, Müller J, Subramanian S (2018) Touchless tactile displays for digital signage. In: Extended abstracts of the 2018 CHI conference on human factors in computing systems—CHI '18. ACM Press, p Demo 103. https://doi.org/10.1145/3170427.3186533, http://dl.acm.org/citation.cfm?doid=3170427.3186533

Cornelio-Martinez PI, Pirro SD, Vi CT, Subramanian S (2017) Agency in mid-air Interfaces. In: Proceedings of the 2017 CHI conference on human factors in computing systems—CHI '17, ACM Press, pp 2426–2439. https://doi.org/10.1145/3025453.3025457, http://dl.acm.org/citation.cfm?id=3025457

Cronin S, Doherty G (2019) Touchless computer interfaces in hospitals: a review. Health Informatics J 25(4):1325–1342. https://doi.org/10.1177/1460458217748342, https://journals.sagepub.com/doi/full/10.1177/1460458217748342

Dzidek B, Frier W, Harwood A, Hayden R (2018) Design and evaluation of mid-air haptic interactions in an augmented reality environment. In: Proceedings of EuroHaptics 2018 in LNCS 10894—EuroHaptics '18, Springer International Publishing, pp 489–499. https://doi.org/10.1007/978-3-319-93399-3_42, https://link.springer.com/chapter/10.1007/978-3-319-93399-3_42

Freeman E (2021) Enhancing ultrasound haptics with parametric audio effects. In: Proceedings of the 2021 international conference on multimodal interaction. Association for Computing Machinery, New York, NY, USA, ICMI '21, pp 692–696. https://doi.org/10.1145/3462244.3479951, https://doi.org/10.1145/3462244.3479951

Freeman E, Wilson G (2021) Perception of ultrasound haptic focal point motion. In: Proceedings of the 2021 international conference on multimodal interaction. Association for Computing Machinery, New York, NY, USA, ICMI '21, pp 697–701. https://doi.org/10.1145/3462244.3479950, https://doi.org/10.1145/3462244.3479950

Freeman E, Brewster S, Lantz V (2014) Tactile feedback for above-device gesture interfaces: adding touch to touchless interactions. In: Proceedings of the 16th international conference on multimodal interaction—ICMI '14. ACM Press, pp 419–426. https://doi.org/10.1145/2663204.2663280, http://dl.acm.org/citation.cfm?id=2663280 http://dl.acm.org/citation.cfm?doid=2663204.2663280

Freeman E, Brewster S, Lantz V (2015) Towards In-Air Gesture Control of Household Appliances with Limited Displays. In: Proceedings of INTERACT '15 in LNCS 9299, IFIP, pp 611–615, https://doi.org/10.1007/978-3-319-22723-8_73, http://link.springer.com/10.1007/978-3-319-22723-8_73

Freeman E, Brewster S, Lantz V (2016) Do that, there: an interaction technique for addressing in-air gesture systems. In: Proceedings of the 2016 CHI conference on human factors in computing systems—CHI '16. ACM Press, pp 2319–2331, https://doi.org/10.1145/2858036.2858308, http://dl.acm.org/citation.cfm?doid=2858036.2858308

Freeman E, Vo DB, Brewster S (2019) HaptiGlow: helping users position their hands for better mid-air gestures and ultrasound haptic feedback. In: Proceedings of the IEEE world haptics conference 2019, the 8th joint Eurohaptics conference and the IEEE haptics symposium, IEEE, pp 289–294, https://doi.org/10.1109/WHC.2019.8816092, https://ieeexplore.ieee.org/document/8816092

Frier W, Ablart D, Chilles J, Long B, Giordano M, Obrist M, Subramanian S (2018) Using spatiotemporal modulation to draw tactile patterns in mid-air. In: Proceedings of EuroHaptics 2018. Springer, Berlin

Frier W, Pittera D, Ablart D, Obrist M, Subramanian S (2019) Sampling strategy for ultrasonic mid-air haptics. In: Proceedings of the 2019 CHI conference on human factors in computing systems proceedings—CHI '19. ACM Press, p Paper 121, https://doi.org/10.1145/3290605.3300351, https://dl.acm.org/citation.cfm?id=3290605.3300351

Georgiou O, Griffiths D (2017) Haptic in-vehicle gesture controls. In: Adjunct proceedings of the 9th international ACM conference on automotive user interfaces and interactive vehicular applications—AutomotiveUI '17, ACM Press, pp 233–238. https://doi.org/10.1145/3131726.3132045

Georgiou O, Jeffrey C, Chen Z, Tong BX, Chan SH, Yang B, Harwood A, Carter T (2018) Touchless haptic feedback for VR rhythm games. In: Proceedings of 25th IEEE conference on virtual reality and 3D user interfaces—IEEE VR '18. IEEE, pp 2–3, https://doi.org/10.1109/VR.2018.8446619, https://ieeexplore.ieee.org/document/8446619

Hajas D, Pittera D, Nasce A, Georgiou O, Obrist M (2020) Mid-air haptic rendering of 2D geometric shapes with a dynamic tactile pointer. IEEE Trans Haptics 13(1):1–12. https://doi.org/10.1109/TOH.2020.2966445

Hirayama R, Martinez Plasencia D, Masuda N, Subramanian S (2019) A volumetric display for visual, tactile and audio presentation using acoustic trapping. Nature 575

Hoshi T (2011) Development of aerial-input and aerial-tactile-feedback system. In: Proceedings of the 2011 IEEE world haptics conference, IEEE, pp 569–573. https://doi.org/10.1109/WHC.2011.5945548, http://ieeexplore.ieee.org/lpdocs/epic03/wrapper.htm?arnumber=5945548

Hoshi T, Takahashi M, Iwamoto T, Shinoda H (2010) Noncontact tactile display based on radiation pressure of airborne ultrasound. IEEE Trans Haptics 3(3):155–165

Hwang I, Son H, Kim JR (2017) AirPiano: enhancing music playing experience in virtual reality with mid-air haptic feedback. In: 2017 IEEE world haptics conference—WHC '17. IEEE, pp 213–218. https://doi.org/10.1109/WHC.2017.7989903, http://ieeexplore.ieee.org/document/7989903/

Iwamoto T, Tatezono M, Shinoda H (2008) Non-contact method for producing tactile sensation using airborne ultrasound. In: Proceedings of EuroHaptics 2008. Springer, Berlin, pp 504–513. https://doi.org/10.1007/978-3-540-69057-3_64, http://www.springerlink.com/index/X41J595757401387.pdf

Korres G, Eid M (2016) Haptogram: ultrasonic point-cloud tactile stimulation. IEEE Access 4:7758–7769

Limerick H (2020) Call to interact: communicating interactivity and affordances for contactless gesture controlled public displays. In: Proceedings of the 9th ACM international symposium on pervasive displays—PerDis '20, pp 63–70. https://doi.org/10.1145/3393712.3395338

Limerick H, Hayden R, Beattie D, Georgiou O, Müller J (2019) User engagement for mid-air haptic interactions with digital signage. In: Proceedings of the 8th ACM international symposium on pervasive displays—PerDis '19. ACM Press, p to appear

Long B, Seah SA, Carter T, Subramanian S (2014) Rendering volumetric haptic shapes in mid-air using ultrasound. ACM Trans Graphics 33(6):Article 181. https://doi.org/10.1145/2661229.2661257, http://dl.acm.org/citation.cfm?id=2661257

Martinez J, Griffiths D, Biscione V, Georgiou O, Carter T (2018) Touchless haptic feedback for supernatural VR experiences. In: Proceedings of the 25th IEEE conference on virtual reality and 3D user interfaces, pp 629–630. https://doi.org/10.1109/VR.2018.8446522

Monnai Y, Hasegawa K, Fujiwara M, Yoshino K, Inoue S, Shinoda H (2014) HaptoMime: mid-air haptic interaction with a floating virtual screen. In: Proceedings of the 27th symposium on user interface software and technology—UIST '14. ACM Press, pp 663–667. https://doi.org/10.1145/2642918.2647407, http://dl.acm.org/citation.cfm?id=2642918.2647407

O'Hara K, Gonzalez G, Sellen A, Penney G, Varnavas A, Mentis H, Criminisi A, Corish R, Rouncefield M, Dastur N, Carrell T (2014) Touchless interaction in surgery. Commun ACM 57(1):70–77

Rakkolainen I, Freeman E, Sand A, Raisamo R, Brewster S (2020) A survey of mid-air ultrasound haptics and its applications. IEEE Trans Haptics 14(1):2–19

Rutten I, Frier W, Van de Bogaert L, Geerts D (2019) Invisible touch: how identifiable are mid-air haptic shapes? In: Proceedings of extended abstracts on human factors in computing systems on—CHI EA '19 p LBW0283

Sand A, Rakkolainen I, Isokoski P, Kangas J, Raisamo R, Palovuori K (2015) Head-mounted display with mid-air tactile feedback. In: Proceedings of the 21st ACM symposium on virtual reality software and technology—VRST '15. ACM Press, pp 51–58. https://doi.org/10.1145/2821592.2821593, http://dl.acm.org/citation.cfm?doid=2821592.2821593

Shakeri G, Williamson JH, Brewster S (2018) May the force be with you: ultrasound haptic feedback for mid-air gesture interaction in cars. In: Proceedings of automotive UI 2018—AutoUI '18. ACM Press

Sridhar S, Feit AM, Theobalt C, Oulasvirta A (2015) Investigating the dexterity of multi-finger input for mid-air text entry. In: Proceedings of the SIGCHI conference on human factors in computing systems—CHI '15. ACM Press, pp 3643–3652. https://doi.org/10.1145/2702123.2702136, https://dl.acm.org/citation.cfm?id=2702136

Takahashi R, Hasegawa K, Shinoda H (2018) Lateral modulation of midair ultrasound focus for intensified vibrotactile stimuli. In: Proceedings of EuroHaptics 2018 in LNCS 10894—EuroHaptics '18. Springer International Publishing, pp 276–288. https://doi.org/10.1007/978-3-319-93399-3_25, http://link.springer.com/10.1007/978-3-319-93445-7

Takahashi R, Hasegawa K, Shinoda H (2019) Tactile stimulation by repetitive lateral movement of midair ultrasound focus. IEEE Trans Haptics

Ultrahaptics (2017) Sensation Editor: The first 10 sensation templates. https://developer.ultrahaptics.com/knowledgebase/the-first-10-sensation-templates/

Ultraleap (2019) UCA tutorial 8: the forcefield sensation. https://developer.ultrahaptics.com/knowledgebase/unity-tutorial-eight/

Vo DB, Brewster S (2015) Touching the invisible: localizing ultrasonic haptic cues. In: Proceedings of world haptics conference 2015—WHC '15, IEEE, pp 368–373. https://doi.org/10.1109/WHC.2015.7177740, http://ieeexplore.ieee.org/xpl/login.jsp?tp=&arnumber=7177740

Waugh K, Robertson J (2021) Don't touch me! a comparison of usability on touch and non-touch inputs. In: Proceedings of the IFIP conference on human-computer interaction—Interact '21. Springer, Berlin, pp 400–404. https://doi.org/10.1007/978-3-030-85607-6_46

Wilson G, Carter T, Subramanian S, Brewster S (2014) Perception of ultrasonic haptic feedback on the hand: localisation and apparent motion. In: Proceedings of the SIGCHI conference on human factors in computing systems—CHI '14. ACM Press, pp 1133–1142. https://doi.org/10.1145/2556288.2557033, http://dl.acm.org/citation.cfm?id=2557033

Opportunities for Multisensory Mid-Air Interactions Featuring Ultrasound Haptic Feedback

Patricia Cornelio

Abstract Mid-air technology is not well studied in the context of multisensory experience. Despite increasing advances in mid-air interaction and mid-air haptics, we still lack a good understanding of how such technologies might influence human behaviour and experience. Compare this with the understanding, we currently have about physical touch, which highlights the need for more knowledge in this area. In this chapter, I describe three areas of development that consider human multi-sensory perception and relate these to the study and use of mid-air haptics. I focus on three main challenges of developing multisensory mid-air interactions. First, I describe how crossmodal correspondence could improve the experience of mid-air touch. Then, I outline some opportunities to introduce mid-air touch to the study of multisensory integration. Finally, I discuss how this multisensory approach can benefit applications that encourage and support a sense of agency in interaction with autonomous systems. Considering these three contributions, when developing mid-air technologies can provide a new multisensory perspective, resulting in the design of more meaningful and emotionally-loaded mid-air interactions.

Keywords Multisensory experiences · Multisensory integration · Sense of agency

1 Introduction

We live in a world that is increasingly characterised as a fusion of physical and digital/virtual events. Today, contactless technology involving mid-air interactions (e.g. virtual reality, holograms, and volumetric displays) is being designed for application scenarios commonly found in daily life, such as in shops, hospitals, museums, and cars. Importantly, emerging digital technology is enabling interaction with digital worlds where the human senses are as important and prominent as they are in people's daily life (Velasco and Obrist 2020). For example, multisensory technology

P. Cornelio (✉)
University College London, London, UK
e-mail: patricia.cornelio@ultraleap.com

© The Author(s), under exclusive license to Springer Nature Switzerland AG 2022   99
O. Georgiou et al. (eds.), *Ultrasound Mid-Air Haptics for Touchless Interfaces*,
Human–Computer Interaction Series, https://doi.org/10.1007/978-3-031-04043-6_4

is more connected to our body, emotions, actions, and biological responses in realistic scenarios that are no longer limited by audio-visual experiences but also include touch, smell, and taste experiences (Cornelio et al. 2021).

However, mid-air technology is not well studied in the context of multisensory experience. Despite the increasing development of mid-air interactions (Vogiatzidakis and Koutsabasis 2018; Koutsabasis and Vogiatzidakis 2019) and particularly of mid-air haptics (Rakkolainen et al. 2020), we still lack a good understanding of the influence of this technology on human behaviour and experiences, in comparison with the understanding we currently have about physical touch (Cornelio et al. 2021). For instance, the crossmodal processing of mid-air touch with other senses is not well understood yet. Additionally, the impact of mid-air interaction on human behaviour, such as emotions, agency, and responsibility, remains unclear. Considering the growing development of mid-air technology and the importance of multisensory cues in both our daily life and our interaction with technology (Velasco and Obrist 2020), we need to gain a rich and integrated understanding of multisensory experiences for mid-air technology in order to design interfaces that support more realistic and emotionally engaging digital experiences.

In this chapter, I discuss opportunities of mid-air interactions in the context of multisensory experience (see Fig. 1). I particularly emphasise three areas of development: (1) *mid-air tactile dimensions*—in which I highlight the ability of our brain to associate information perceived from different senses, and I discuss the opportunities to exploit this ability to engage mid-air touch with other sensory modalities; (2) *multisensory integration*—in which I highlight the lack of studies involving mid-air touch in the broad literature of multisensory integration and discuss opportunities to advance our understanding of mid-air touch to the extent to which we understand physical touch; and (3) *agency and responsibility*—in which I highlight how

Fig. 1 Mid-air interaction that involves the human senses, behaviour, and experiences

we live in a world that is increasingly automated and integrated to our body, and I discuss possibilities of using multisensory mid-air interactions to promote a feeling of control and responsibility in a world in which intelligent algorithms (e.g. autonomous systems and autocomplete predictors) assist us and influence our behaviour. Finally, I conclude with a reflection on how multisensory experiences can be included as a part of future ethics guidelines for mid-air interactions. Readers are encouraged to consider how ultrasound haptics can become part of meaningful multisensory mid-air experiences, which positively influence behaviour.

2   Mid-air Touch in an Emerging Contactless World

The COVID-19 pandemic has demonstrated that touchless systems have the potential to significantly impact our interactions with technology in two relevant ways. First, unlike contact-based devices such as touchscreens, contactless activation (e.g. doors, taps, toilet flush, payments, etc.) can provide a more hygienic solution for reducing the spreading of pathogens. Second, physical distancing and national lockdowns have produced an acceleration towards digital experiences that enable us to interact with others remotely. The digitalisation and transformation of business and education practice have taken place over a matter of weeks, resulting in an increased human–computer symbiosis. However, these online experiences and activities often lack realism compared with their physical counterparts, as they only use limited sensory cues (mainly vision and audio). Mid-air technologies can significantly enhance such digital experiences, that otherwise are limited to being seen or heard (e.g. virtual tours through a museum), through the addition of a haptic component (e.g. haptic interactions or contactless haptic feedback). Whilst it has been argued that mid-air technologies can become ubiquitous in the future, as depicted in sci-fi movies (e.g. Minority Report), the current situation is accelerating the need for more meaningful digital experiences and making evident the advantages of touchless interactions in physical and virtual spaces.

These recent events provide a unique opportunity for research and development innovation around mid-air technology. There is a need to apply the principles of human–computer interaction (HCI) and multisensory experience to enhance interaction with contactless technologies (e.g. gesture recognition, body tracking, ultrasound haptic output) in order to, first, study how multiple senses can be engaged with mid-air interactions and thus design novel and more meaningful touchless paradigms, and second, apply the knowledge gained to help in emerging applications that support not only technical innovation but also societal responsibility in the context of an accelerated digital human-technology integration.

Current advances in mid-air technologies, however, have been mostly focussed on the context of software and hardware development in order to advance engineering methods related to accuracy (Matsubayashi et al. 2019), recognition (Sridhar et al. 2015), and rendering (Long et al. 2014). However, whilst recent research has explored mid-air technologies in the context of human perception (e.g. emotions (Obrist et al.

2015)), little is known about how these technologies influence human behaviour and how human perception can be exploited to improve the interaction with such technologies. For example, ultrasound has enabled rich tactile sensations (e.g. 3D shapes in mid-air), however, different questions remain—how does the user perceive those shapes? Is it sufficient to display a 3D shape of a button for the user to perceive a button shape? How can that perception be exploited to engage with other senses? And finally, how can this technology help society?

3 Opportunities for Multisensory Mid-air Haptics

Humans are equipped with multiple sensory channels to experience the world (Stein and Meredith 1993). Whilst Aristotle taught us that the world is dominated by 5 basic senses (sight, hearing, touch, smell, and taste), research in philosophy suggests that we have a lot more (anywhere between 22 and 33 senses) (Smith 2016). Some examples are the sense of proprioception (the perception of spatial orientation), kinaesthesia (the sense of movement), the sense of agency (the sense of control), amongst many others. Whilst there are increasing efforts to design digital experiences that go beyond audio-visual interactions, involving for instance, smell (Maggioni et al. 2018), and taste (Narumi et al. 2011), mid-air technologies still lack a multisensory perspective. In the future of mid-air interaction, this view can change how mid-air technologies are studied, aiming to account for multisensory information.

In the next sections of this chapter, I describe three areas of development that consider human multisensory perception to advance the study of mid-air haptics. To do so, I focus on three main challenges of developing multisensory mid-air interactions. First, I describe how crossmodal correspondences could improve the experience of mid-air touch. Second, I outline opportunities to introduce mid-air touch to the study of multisensory integration. Finally, I discuss how this multisensory approach could benefit application scenarios that require a sense of agency in the interaction with autonomous systems. This chapter highlights the potential benefits of integrating ultrasound haptics into multisensory experience, from both a research and application perspective.

3.1 Challenge 1: Mid-air Tactile Dimensions

Mid-air haptic feedback produced by focussed ultrasound can be effectively rendered in the form of 3D shapes (Long et al. 2014) and textures (Frier et al. 2016) that can be felt by users without direct contact. For example, people could "touch and feel a hologram of a heart that is beating at the same rhythm as your own" (Romanus et al. 2019) through such technologies. However, despite the great levels of possible control over haptic patterns (Martinez Plasencia et al. 2020) and the ability to render complex shapes (Long et al. 2014), "mid-air haptic shapes do not appear to be easily identified" (Rutten et al. 2019). This difficulty of precisely identifying shapes and patterns produced by mid-air haptics can be caused by the lack of other sensory cues (e.g. visual feedback) that help to confirm the perceived shape of an object or the texture of a tactile pattern. Adding extra sensory cues perceived through different channels could help the identification of haptic information (Ozkul et al. 2020; Freeman 2021). For instance, combining a sphere rendered on the hand with a visual display showing the same shape, or combining a rough texture pattern with a rough sound. However, it could be possible to produce a multisensory experience with only the haptic feedback itself using crossmodal associations.

The human brain has the ability to associate crossmodal information from different senses. This is well supported by the broad body of literature in crossmodal correspondences (CCs) research. CCs are defined "*as a tendency for a sensory feature, or attribute, in one modality, can be matched (or associated) with a sensory feature in another sensory modality*" (Spence and Parise 2012). These associations have been widely employed in design, marketing, and multisensory branding (Spence and Gallace 2011). For instance, it has been shown that the shape of a mug can influence the coffee taste expectations (Van Doorn et al. 2017), that colours and sounds influence our perception of temperature (Velasco et al. 2013; Ho et al. 2014), and that our sensation of touch can be influenced by odours (Dematte et al. 2006). These CCs have not yet been explored for mid-air touch. For instance, it is unclear how people associate tactile patterns produced by focussed ultrasound on the skin with different sensory features such as sounds, smells, temperature, moisture, emotions, amongst others. This can be explored by building on prior studies in the literature. A rich variety of robust CCs have been demonstrated between various pairs of sensory modalities (Parise 2016). Particularly relevant in this chapter, a number of studies have found CCs involving tactile features such as heaviness, sharpness, thickness, angularity, and temperature that are associated with other sensory features.

For example, it has been shown that the perception of heaviness is associated with dark and low-pitched cues, whilst the perception of sharpness is associated with high-pitch sounds (Walker et al. 2017). Similarly, textures can be associated to adjectives referring to not only tactile features but also to visual and auditory domains. For example, smooth textures are associated to adjectives such as "bright", "quiet", and "lightweight" whilst rough textures with adjectives such as "dim", "loud", and heavy (Etzi et al. 2016). Additionally, there is evidence suggesting that certain shapes can be associated to different temperatures attributes (Van Doorn et al. 2017; Carvalho and Spence 2018).

These CCs are also common when referring to the chemical senses (smell and taste). Studies have shown that angular shapes are associated to sour tastes whilst rounded shapes with sweet tastes (Salgado Montejo et al. 2015). Similarly, angular shapes have been found to be associated to lemon and pepper odours whilst rounded shape with raspberry and vanilla odours (Hanson-Vaux et al. 2013).

Emotions also play an important role in CCs when referring to tactile features. Research has shown that soft textures are associated with the positive emotion of happiness and rough textures with negative emotions such as fear, anger, and disgust (Iosifyan and Korolkova 2019). In another example, in the study by Etzi et al. 2016,

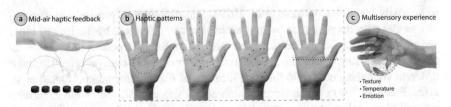

Fig. 2 **a** Mid-air haptic feedback, **b** different haptic patterns on the user's hand, **c** the associations of the haptic patterns with sensory features can produce a multisensory experience

smooth textures were associated with the labels "feminine" and "beautiful" whereas rough textures with the adjectives "masculine" and "ugly".

In summary, by considering these previous findings about how haptic features are associated with other sensory features, developers could design for a particular intended user experience (e.g. a haptic pattern that is **heavy**, **cold**, and **bright**). There are specific situations in which a specific experience may be required. For example, a **pleasant** and **warm** haptic sensation could be suitable for a remote video call (e.g. a virtual handshake), whereas an **unpleasant** and **cold** experience might be required for a virtual horror game (e.g. a spider walking across your hand). Future work in this area consists of a series of studies to explore CCs between specific patters of mid-air haptic feedback on subjects' hand with different features, not only related to touch attributes (e.g. shapes) but towards multisensory features such as temperature, texture, and emotions (see Fig. 2).

The knowledge and findings from more research in this area could give insights into how designers can create more realistic and vivid experiences of touching "real" objects. This in turn could perhaps reduce computational power (e.g. high accuracy needed to render) by exploiting the power of human perception. That is, a better understanding of the capabilities and limits of human perception can lead to more effective interactions (Debarba et al. 2018).

Similarly, the generation of a large dataset of haptic patterns and their associations with sensory features could contribute not only to a better design of haptic experiences in the areas of HCI but also to the body of research on CCs in the area of psychology and cognitive neuroscience. Such advances could lead to haptic designs that are significantly more visceral than those outlined in Chaps. "User Experience and Mid-Air Haptics: Applications, Methods, and Challenges" and "Ultrasound Haptic Feedback for Touchless User Interfaces: Design Patterns".

3.2 Challenge 2: Multisensory Integration

Since experiences in the world can be ambiguous, our perceptual system collects cues from our different senses to resolve potential ambiguities. To resolve these ambiguities, humans follow two general strategies, i.e. *cue combination* and *cue integration* (Ernst and Bülthoff 2004). Whilst *cue combination* accumulates information from different sensory sources to disambiguate uncertainty, *cue integration* integrates information from different sensory sources to find the most reliable estimate by reducing variance as much as possible. In other words, since perception is inherently multisensory (Stein and Meredith 1993), when a single modality is insufficient for the brain to produce a robust estimate, information from multiple modalities can be combined or integrated for better estimation. Examples of these two phenomena are described below.

Cue combination: Imagine you are sitting in a stationary train carriage looking out the window at another nearby train. The other train starts moving and then your brain faces an ambiguous situation: is it *you* or the *other train* that is moving? In this uncertain situation, your brain will raise an answer (right or wrong) by combining multiple sensory cues. Vision alone may not be enough to solve this ambiguity, but, if your brain combines information from your vision (seen parallax motion from outside), vestibular system (your perceived position in space), and proprioceptive system (feeling the motion of the train), this ambiguity can be easily revolved (Ernst and Bülthoff 2004).

Cue integration: In situations when the perceptual event involves more than one sensory estimate, cue integration is employed by our brain. For instance, in a size estimation task, you may use both vision and touch to judge the size of an object. But, if you are simultaneously seeing and touching the object, is the perceived size determined by your vision, by your touch or by something in-between? In this case, information of the different sensory modalities has to be integrated to determine a robust estimate (see Fig. 3). That is, the brain reduces the variance of the size estimate by weighting the influence of each modality (vision and touch) based on their reliability (Ernst and Banks 2002).

A wide range of research has been conducted to investigate how the human senses are integrated, a particular topic of interest is focussed on haptics, for example, visuo-haptic integration (Ernst and Banks 2002) and audio-haptic integration (Petrini et al.

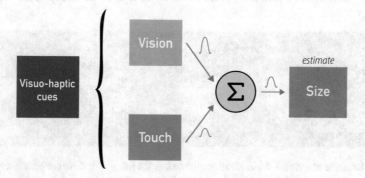

Fig. 3 Humans achieve robust perception by integrating information from different sensory sources to find the most reliable estimate by reducing its variance as much as possible

2012), as well as the integration of haptics and smell (Castiello et al. 2006; Dematte et al. 2006).

However, despite the rapid development of mid-air technologies, efforts to study haptic integration are uniquely focussed on physical touch to date, and it is therefore unknown how mid-air touch is integrated with the other senses. For instance, we do not know if the integration of vision, audio, or smell with mid-air touch is similar to what has been found with actual physical touch, as there are many factors that make physical and mid-air touch different (e.g. physical limits, force, ergonomics, instrumentation). Here, I see an opportunity to expand our knowledge of mid-air interaction by applying the principles of multisensory integration from psychology. Bridging this gap could open up a wide range of new studies exploring the integration of multiple senses with mid-air touch, using the technology recently developed in HCI and further taking advantage of current knowledge in this area. For example, a number of studies have already provided insights that improve our understanding of mid-air haptic stimuli perception in terms of perceived strength (Frier et al. 2019), geometry identification (Hajas et al. 2020b), and tactile congruency (Pittera et al. 2019), providing compelling evidence of the capability of mid-air haptics to convey information (Hajas et al. 2020a; Paneva et al. 2020).

Future research into mid-air haptics should be directed to explore how tactile sensations created by focussed ultrasound are integrated with other senses in order to create **more meaningful experiences** and to **reduce ambiguity** in virtual and digital worlds. For instance, in a virtual world, you might feel a rounded shape rendered on your bare hand in mid-air via an ultrasound haptics device, but by using your sense of touch only it would be very difficult to identify whether that shape is an onion, a peach, or a hedgehog (see Fig. 4). However, by integrating cues from other senses, this uncertainty is reduced, leading to a more **vivid, real,** and **emotional experience**. For example, the 3D shape and texture of a peach's velvety skin can be felt using mid-aid ultrasound, a VR headset can show its bright orange colour giving the perception of a juicy fruit, whilst a sweet smell can be delivered to your nose (see Fig. 4b). This is an example of the new possibilities that can be achieved through multisensory technology but have, to date, been underexplored. With the

Fig. 4 Example of a virtual object identification task in VR integrating different senses: **a** rounded shape, smooth texture and stinky smell, **b** rounded shape, velvety texture and sweet smell; **c** irregular shape, spiky texture, and animal-like smell

accelerated digitisation of human interaction due to social distancing, multisensory digital experiences become increasingly relevant and compelling.

This push towards mid-air touch integration can be done by a combination of VR simulations and computational methods. The development of fundamental principles involving mid-air touch integration can contribute not only to design experiences but also to the literature on sensory integration models and their comparison with the previous proposed models involving physical interaction.

3.3 Challenge 3: Agency and Responsibility

One crucial experience that humans have whilst interacting with the world is the sense of agency (SoA), often referred to as the feeling of being in control (Kühn et al. 2013). Whilst recent multisensory technology and intelligent systems help users by making some computing tasks easier and more immersive, they might affect the SoA experienced by users, thus having implications on the feeling of control and responsibility felt whilst interacting with technology. Particularly for touchless systems, designing mid-air interactions that preserve the user's SoA becomes a challenging task as these interactions lack the typical characteristics of touching an object, and therefore, they might be considered less robust compared with physical interactions. However, the SoA can be improved when the user receives appropriate multisensory cues. In the next sections of this chapter, I explain an overview of what the SoA is, why it is important in our interactions with technology and how it can be increased with a multisensory approach.

3.3.1 The Sense of Agency

The SoA refers to the experience of being the initiator of one's own voluntary actions and through them influencing the external world (Beck et al. 2017). Georgieff and Jeannerod 1998 defined this phenomenon as a "who" system that permits the identification of the agent of an action and thus differentiates the self from external agents. The SoA reflects the experience that links our free decisions (*volition*) to their external outcomes, a result of action-effect causality in which the match between the intended and actual result of an action produces a feeling of controlling the environment (Synofzik et al. 2013), such as happens when we press the light switch and perceive the light coming on (e.g. *I did that*). To experience a SoA, there must be an intention to produce an outcome, and then, three conditions need to occur, (1) the occurrence of a voluntary *body* movement, (2) the execution of an *action* that aims at the *outcome*, and (3) the external *outcome* itself (see Fig. 5a). These conditions are present during our everyday life as we constantly perform goal-directed motor actions and we observe the consequences of those actions (Hommel 2017). This action-effect causality is particularly important in our agentive interactions with technology representative in HCI.

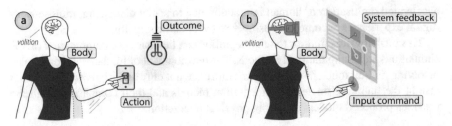

Fig. 5 Elements that compose the SoA in daily life tasks and in our interaction with technology

3.3.2 The Sense of Agency in HCI

When we interact with systems, actions are represented by user input commands, and outcomes are represented by system feedback. Input modalities serve to translate user's intentions into state changes within the system, whilst system feedback informs the user about the system's current state (see Fig. 5b). In this interplay, the SoA is crucial to support a feeling of being in control. For instance, when we manipulate a user interface (e.g. on a computer or smartphone), we expect the system to respond to our input commands as we want to feel that we are in charge of the interaction. If this stimulus–response interplay elicits a SoA, then the user will perceive an instinctive feeling that "I am controlling this".

Due to the ubiquity of our interaction with systems for work or leisure purposes, we usually do not think about our SoA during the interaction, and it may go unnoticed (Moore 2016). However, a clear example that highlights the importance of our SoA in HCI is when this experience is disrupted. When there is a mismatch between user expectations and the actual sensory feedback from the system, the user experiences a sudden interruption in the feeling of control. This can negatively affect acceptability (Berberian 2019) and usability (Winkler et al. 2020), e.g. poor game controllers may cause frustration (Miller and Mandryk 2016).

In summary, if a system does not support a SoA, the user might feel discouraged from using it (Limerick et al. 2015) and lose self-attribution of their actions' outcomes. For this reason, the SoA is gaining increasing attention from the field of HCI. Developing interaction techniques that increase user's SoA will provide the feeling of "I did that" as opposed to "the system did that", thus supporting a feeling of being in control.

3.3.3 Supporting Agency through Multisensory Mid-air Haptics

The SoA has been suggested to "underpin the concept of responsibility in human societies" (Haggard 2017). Whilst mid-air interactions are becoming increasingly popular, a major challenge is how responsibility is shared between humans and touchless systems. That is, whilst causality and accidents are usually attributed to human errors, today crucial actions have been delegated to computers in contexts

Fig. 6 Example mid-air haptics in vehicles **a**, home appliances **b**, and aviation **c**

involving people. A notable example of this agency delegation is characteristic of autonomous systems. Today, such systems are found in vehicles, machines, and aircrafts and could potentially reduce the SoA since increasing levels of automation can decrease the user's feeling of being in control. This raises the question: "who is in control now"? (Berberian et al. 2012).

Given that mid-air technologies have been recently integrated into automotive applications (Hessam et al. 2017), home appliances (Van den Bogaert et al. 2019), and aviation interactions (Girdler and Georgiou 2020) (as depicted in Fig. 6), there are increasing opportunities to develop multisensory interactions for autonomous systems that preserve a user's SoA.

Particularly in driving scenarios, previous studies have employed haptics to make the driver aware of semi-autonomous vehicles' intentions, by means of force feedback (Ros 2016), so that agency is shared between the user and the vehicle (i.e. the system is not fully in control but delegates appropriate level of control to the operator). However, this has not been explored with mid-air interaction yet, despite the proven benefits of combining gestures with mid-air haptic feedback for in-vehicle tasks (Harrington et al. 2018), e.g. as discussed in Chap. "Ultrasound Mid-Air Tactile Feedback for Immersive Virtual Reality Interaction". For example, by minimising the visual demand associated with touchscreens in vehicles, mid-air ultrasonic feedback reduces the number of off-road glance time and "overshoots" (Harrington et al. 2018; Large et al. 2019). This is because "employing haptics naturally reduces the need for vision as users are not required to visually confirm selection or activation", promoting more safe driving practices (Harrington et al. 2018).

More opportunities to improve the user's SoA through mid-air interactions have been demonstrated in the literature. For example, the study by Cornelio et al. (2017) showed that both physical and touchless input commands produce a user's SoA and also showed that mid-air haptic feedback produces a SoA comparable to that felt with typical vibrotactile feedback. Similarly, Evangelou et al. (2021) showed that mid-air haptic feedback can promote implicit SoA as well as protect against latency-induced reductions in the explicit judgements of agency.

Additionally, analogue studies have shown that the SoA can be modulated by sensory and emotional information not only related to the somatosensory channel (Beck et al. 2017; Borhani et al. 2017) but also in response to other sensory cues. For instance, showing increased SoA with positive pictures (Aarts et al. 2012), or pleasant smells (Cornelio et al. 2020), and decreased SoA with negative sounds (Yoshie and Haggard 2013; Borhani et al. 2017). This evidence suggests that sharing control between systems and the operators could be aided by multisensory information. This is because the SoA arises by a combination of internal motoric signals and sensory evidence about our own actions and their effects (Moore et al. 2009).

Those previous findings could be used as a foundation to conduct new studies to explore how multisensory mid-air interaction can improve the user's SoA. An action plan that I see is to link the study of agency modulation from the areas of psychology and neuroscience (e.g. using affective sensory cues) with the study of agency modulation in the area of HCI (e.g. using mid-air haptics to increase the SoA) in order to introduce an approach of multisensory mid-air interactions featuring ultrasound haptic feedback.

Future work in mid-air haptic technologies integrated with autonomous systems should focus on how to include multisensory mid-air interactions (involving, e.g,. the integration of various senses and crossmodal correspondences), in order to make the operators more aware of the system's intentions, actions, and outcomes. In other words, exploiting the benefits of mid-air technologies and multisensory experiences to **share agency between the operator and the system**.

In summary, although recent technology posits the user in environments that are not fully real (e.g. virtual or augmented) and where users' actions are often influenced (e.g. autocompletion predictors) or even automated (e.g. autonomous driving), multisensory signals can help users to feel agency even though they are not the agent of the action or when several commands were not executed (Banakou and Slater 2014; Kokkinara et al. 2016).

Finally, advances in the development and robustness of novel interaction paradigms, which involve multisensory mid-air technologies, can be integrated in the future policy making and legal systems. For example, giving insights to craft guidelines for autonomous driving, preserving moral responsibility, and a safe operation through technology in the future when fully autonomous systems are ubiquitous.

Indeed, legal systems have already started crafting guidelines for autonomous vehicles (Beiker 2012) that preserve moral responsibility (De Freitas et al. 2021), as well as drafting theoretical foundations for the next generation of autonomous systems (Harel et al. 2020). In the future, mid-air interactions can be part of these efforts to promote responsibility during interaction.

4   Discussion, Conclusions, and Future Directions

Whereas humans experience the world through multiple senses, our interaction with technology is often limited to a reduced set of sensory channels. Today, we see increasing efforts to digitalise the senses in order to design more meaningful and emotionally-loaded digital experiences (Velasco and Obrist 2020). Mid-air haptics produced by focussed ultrasound provides a step forward to the digitalisation of touch, enabling interaction paradigms previously only seen in sci-fi movies (Cwiek et al. 2021). For example, it is now possible to touch holograms (Kervegant et al. 2017; Frish et al. 2019) as well as levitate objects (Marzo et al. 2015) and interact with them (Freeman et al. 2018; Martinez Plasencia et al. 2020). However, recent advances in mid-air technology have been focussed on hardware and software development, and therefore, little is known about how these technologies influence human behaviour, and how designers can exploit our knowledge of human perception to improve interaction with such technologies.

In this chapter, I proposed three areas of development to advance mid-air air haptics from a multisensory perspective. I first discussed how crossmodal correspondences can be used to design mid-air haptic patterns that create multisensory experiences, by exploiting the ability of the human brain to associate crossmodal information of different senses. Then, I outlined the lack of research around mid-air touch in the study of multisensory integration and highlighted the need for more research to advance our understanding of mid-air touch with respect to our current understanding about physical touch. Finally, I describe a crucial experience in both our daily life and our interaction with technology—the sense of agency—and discuss how a multisensory approach to mid-air technologies can promote a sense of responsibility, particularly in the context of autonomous systems.

To achieve the multisensory approach suggested in this chapter, it is important to consider methods used to measure user experiences. Favourably, the literature provides different methods to quantify the extent to which people perceive a multisensory experience. For instance, in the case of CCs, visual analogue scales (VAS) are used as a measurement instrument to quantify a sensory attribute by ranging across a continuum of values (Cline et al. 1992). For example, the degree of association between sensory features usually ranges across a continuum from not at all to extremely (Crichton 2001). With this method, researchers have found CCs between different sensory modalities such as smells (e.g. lemon scent) and bodily features (e.g. thin body silhouettes) (Brianza et al. 2021) or between body attributes (e.g. hardness) and haptics metaphors (e.g. vibration patterns on the skin) (Tajadura-Jimenez et al. 2020). The opportunities for designing multisensory mid-air interactions can be extended by means of these associations which can enrich a sensory attribute or provide the perception of amplified sensory features.

In the case of multisensory integration, a large range of studies have provided computational methods to quantify the extent to which a person integrates different senses. One example is maximum-likelihood estimation (MLE), which is often employed to integrate different sources of sensory information when the goal is to produce the most reliable estimate (Kendall and Stuart 1979). More recently, sensing technologies and artificial intelligence (AI) techniques have been employed to digitally replicate how the human body integrates different senses (Zhu et al. 2020). These techniques have been considered a promising approach towards robotic sensing and perception (Tan et al. 2021). The efforts of digitalising the sense of touch in the literature give us growing opportunities to introduce a wide range of new studies to explore the integration of mid-air touch with other senses.

In terms of quantifying the SoA, implicit methods can be found in the literature. For example, the intentional binding paradigm (Haggard et al. 2002) provides an implicit measure of the SoA by indicating a relationship between agency experience and perception of time. In this paradigm, the level of agency can be assessed as perceived differences in time between voluntary actions and their resultant outcomes. Using this method, the previous studies in HCI have shown evidence of the level of control of mid-air interactions (e.g. a mid-air button) in comparison with a physical interaction (e.g. a keyboard button) (Cornelio et al. 2017).

The methods described above can be used in the efforts of introducing multi-sensory mid-air interactions. Whilst prior methods are typically done with physical touch, a wide range of studies is yet to come to understand for mid-air touch what we currently know about physical touch.

In the future of mid-air technology, a multisensory view can change how mid-air interactions are studied, designed, and put into practice. This view includes the integration of multisensory experiences for mid-air haptics, particularly focussing on the sense of touch but also studying its relation, association, and integration with other senses in order to convey more meaningful digital experiences to humans that in turn promote agency and responsibility. The new knowledge acquired to achieve this goal will generate underlying principles resulting in the design of more solid application scenarios in the future, that take into consideration not only engineering advances but also human behaviour and perception, thus augmenting the capabilities of our digital social interaction. That is, we need to foster a new and inclusive ecosystem of multidisciplinary research around mid-air interactions involving psychology, neuroscience and HCI, so that the impact of these technologies is not limited to hardware and software, but also provide an impact on society with respect to accelerated digitisation of human experiences.

I particularly emphasise the importance of preserving a SoA in a world that is increasingly automated. Since the SoA arises through a combination of internal motoric signals and sensory evidence about our own actions and their effects (Moore et al. 2009), a multisensory view can significantly make technology users more aware of their actions and the consequences of these, thus promoting a feeling of responsibility. Emerging research is already examining how to improve the SoA in HCI. For example, by exploring motor actuation without diminishing the SoA (Kasahara et al. 2019), exploring appropriate levels of automation (Berberian et al. 2012), or exploring how the SoA can be improved through olfactory interfaces (Cornelio et al. 2020). Despite such efforts, it has been suggested that "the cognitive coupling between human and machine remains difficult to achieve" (Berberian 2019), so further research is needed.

Nonetheless, research on mid-air interactions can be included in this body of research exploring agency, responsibility, and the human sensory system, so that we design digital experiences in which users can see, hear, smell, touch, and taste just like they do in the real world. Future directions around multisensory integration can break from the conventional studies in mid-air technologies and thus help to achieve this goal.

References

Aarts H, Bijleveld E, Custers R, Dogge M, Deelder M, Schutter D, van Haren NE (2012) Positive priming and intentional binding: eye-blink rate predicts reward information effects on the sense of agency. Soc Neurosci 7(1):105–112. https://doi.org/10.1080/17470919.2011.590602

Banakou D, Slater M (2014) Body ownership causes illusory self-attribution of speaking and influences subsequent real speaking. Proc Natl Acad Sci 111(49):17678–17683. https://doi.org/10.1073/pnas.1414936111

Beck B, Di Costa S, Haggard P (2017) Having control over the external world increases the implicit sense of agency. Cognition 162:54–60. https://doi.org/10.1016/j.cognition.2017.02.002

Beiker SA (2012) Legal aspects of autonomous driving. Santa Clara l Rev 52:1145

Berberian B (2019) Man-machine teaming: a problem of agency. IFAC-PapersOnLine 51(34):118–123. https://doi.org/10.1016/j.ifacol.2019.01.049

Berberian B, Sarrazin J-C, Le Blaye P, Haggard P (2012) Automation technology and sense of control: a window on human agency. PLoS ONE 7(3):e34075. https://doi.org/10.1371/journal.pone.0034075

Borhani K, Beck B, Haggard P (2017) Choosing, doing, and controlling: implicit sense of agency over somatosensory events. Psychol Sci 28(7):882–893. https://doi.org/10.1177/0956797617697693

Brianza G, Cornelio P, Maggioni E, Obrist M (2021) Sniff before you act: exploration of scent-feature associations for designing future interactions. In: IFIP conference on human-computer interaction. Springer.https://doi.org/10.1007/978-3-030-85616-8_17

Carvalho FM, Spence C (2018) The shape of the cup influences aroma, taste, and hedonic judgements of specialty coffee. Food Qual Prefer 68:315–321. https://doi.org/10.1016/j.foodqual.2018.04.003

Castiello U, Zucco GM, Parma V, Ansuini C, Tirindelli R (2006) Cross-modal interactions between olfaction and vision when grasping. Chem Senses 31(7):665–671. https://doi.org/10.1093/chemse/bjl007

Cline ME, Herman J, Shaw ER, Morton RD (1992) Standardization of the visual analogue scale. Nurs Res. https://doi.org/10.1097/00006199-199211000-00013

Cornelio P, De Pirro S, Vi CT, Subramanian S (2017) Agency in mid-air interfaces. In: Proceedings of the 2017 CHI conference on human factors in computing systems. https://doi.org/10.1145/3025453.3025457

Cornelio P, Maggioni E, Brianza G, Subramanian S, Obrist M (2020) SmellControl: the study of sense of agency in smell. In: Proceedings of the 2020 international conference on multimodal interaction. https://doi.org/10.1145/3382507.3418810

Cornelio P, Velasco C, Obrist M (2021) Multisensory integration as per technological advances: a review. Front Neurosci 15:614. https://doi.org/10.3389/fnins.2021.652611

Crichton N (2001) Visual analogue scale (VAS). J Clin Nurs 10(5):706–706

Cwiek A, Fuchs S, Draxler C, Asu EL, Dediu D, Hiovain K, Kawahara S, Koutalidis S, Krifka M, Lippus P (2021) The bouba/kiki effect is robust across cultures and writing systems. Philos Trans Royal Soc B Biol Sci. https://doi.org/10.1098/rstb.2020.0390

De Freitas J, Censi A, Smith BW, Di Lillo L, Anthony SE, Frazzoli E (2021) From driverless dilemmas to more practical commonsense tests for automated vehicles. Proc Natl Acad Sci 118(11). https://doi.org/10.1073/pnas.2010202118

Debarba HG, Khoury J-N, Perrin S, Herbelin B, Boulic R (2018) Perception of redirected pointing precision in immersive virtual reality. https://doi.org/10.1109/VR.2018.8448285

Dematte ML, Sanabria D, Sugarman R, Spence C (2006) Cross-modal interactions between olfaction and touch. Chem Senses 31(4):291–300. https://doi.org/10.1093/chemse/bjj031

Ernst MO, Banks MS (2002) Humans integrate visual and haptic information in a statistically optimal fashion. Nature 415(6870):429–433. https://doi.org/10.1038/415429a

Ernst MO, Bülthoff HH (2004) Merging the senses into a robust percept. Trends Cogn Sci 8(4):162–169. https://doi.org/10.1016/j.tics.2004.02.002

Etzi R, Spence C, Zampini M, Gallace A (2016) When sandpaper is 'Kiki' and satin is 'Bouba': an exploration of the associations between words, emotional states, and the tactile attributes of everyday materials. Multisensory Res 29(1–3):133–155. https://doi.org/10.1163/22134808-000 02497

Evangelou G, Limerick H, Moore J (2021) I feel it in my fingers! Sense of agency with mid-air haptics. In: 2021 IEEE world haptics conference (WHC). IEEE.https://doi.org/10.1109/WHC 49131.2021.9517170

Freeman E (2021) Enhancing ultrasound haptics with parametric audio effects. In: Proceedings of the 2021 international conference on multimodal interaction. https://doi.org/10.1145/3462244. 3479951

Freeman E, Williamson J, Subramanian S, Brewster S (2018) Point-and-shake: selecting from levitating object displays. In: Proceedings of the 2018 CHI conference on human factors in computing systems. https://doi.org/10.1145/3173574.3173592

Frier W, Pittera D, Ablart D, Obrist M, Subramanian S (2019) Sampling strategy for ultrasonic mid-air haptics. In: Proceedings of the 2019 CHI conference on human factors in computing systems. https://doi.org/10.1145/3290605.3300351

Frier W, Seo K, Subramanian S (2016) Hilbert curves: a tool for resolution independent haptic texture. In: Proceedings of the 29th annual symposium on user interface software and technology. https://doi.org/10.1145/2984751.2984774

Frish S, Maksymenko M, Frier W, Corenthy L, Georgiou O (2019) Mid-air haptic bio-holograms in mixed reality. In: 2019 IEEE international symposium on mixed and augmented reality adjunct (ISMAR-Adjunct). IEEE.https://doi.org/10.1109/ISMAR-Adjunct.2019.00-14

Georgieff N, Jeannerod M (1998) Beyond consciousness of external reality: a "who" system for consciousness of action and self-consciousness. Conscious Cogn 7:465–477. https://doi.org/10. 1006/ccog.1998.0367

Girdler A, Georgiou O (2020) Mid-air haptics in aviation—creating the sensation of touch where there is nothing but thin air. arXiv preprint arXiv:2001.01445

Haggard P (2017) Sense of agency in the human brain. Nat Rev Neurosci 18(4):196. https://doi. org/10.1038/nrn.2017.14

Haggard P, Clark S, Kalogeras J (2002) Voluntary action and conscious awareness. Nat Neurosci 5(4):382–385. https://doi.org/10.1038/nn827

Hajas D, Ablart D, Schneider O, Obrist M (2020a) I can feel it moving: science communicators talking about the potential of mid-air haptics. Frontiers Comput Sci. https://doi.org/10.3389/ fcomp.2020.534974

Hajas D, Pittera D, Nasce A, Georgiou O, Obrist M (2020b) Mid-air haptic rendering of 2D geometric shapes with a dynamic tactile pointer. IEEE Trans Haptics. https://doi.org/10.1109/TOH.2020. 2966445

Hanson-Vaux G, Crisinel A-S, Spence C (2013) Smelling shapes: crossmodal correspondences between odors and shapes. Chem Senses 38(2):161–166. https://doi.org/10.1093/chemse/bjs087

Harel D, Marron A, Sifakis J (2020) Autonomics: in search of a foundation for next-generation autonomous systems. Proc Natl Acad Sci 117(30):17491–17498. https://doi.org/10.1073/pnas. 2003162117

Harrington K, Large DR, Burnett G, Georgiou O (2018) Exploring the use of mid-air ultrasonic feedback to enhance automotive user interfaces. In: Proceedings of the 10th international conference on automotive user interfaces and interactive vehicular applications. https://doi.org/10.1145/ 3239060.3239089

Hessam JF, Zancanaro M, Kavakli M, Billinghurst M (2017) Towards optimization of mid-air gestures for in-vehicle interactions. In: Proceedings of the 29th Australian conference on computer-human interaction. https://doi.org/10.1145/3152771.3152785

Ho H-N, Van Doorn GH, Kawabe T, Watanabe J, Spence C (2014) Colour-temperature correspondences: when reactions to thermal stimuli are influenced by colour. PloS One 9(3). https://doi. org/10.1371/journal.pone.0091854

Hommel B (2017) Goal-directed actions. In: The Oxford handbook of causal reasoning, pp 265–288

Iosifyan M, Korolkova O (2019) Emotions associated with different textures during touch. Conscious Cogn 71:79–85. https://doi.org/10.1016/j.concog.2019.03.012

Kasahara S, Nishida J, Lopes P (2019) Preemptive action: accelerating human reaction using electrical muscle stimulation without compromising agency. In: Proceedings of the 2019 CHI conference on human factors in computing systems. https://doi.org/10.1145/3290605.3300873

Kendall M, Stuart A (1979) Estimation: maximum likelihood. In: The advanced theory of statistics, vol 2, pp 38—81

Kervegant C, Raymond F, Graeff D, Castet J (2017) Touch hologram in mid-air. In: ACM SIGGRAPH 2017 emerging technologies, pp 1–2. https://doi.org/10.1145/3084822.3084824

Kokkinara E, Kilteni K, Blom KJ, Slater M (2016) First person perspective of seated participants over a walking virtual body leads to illusory agency over the walking. Sci Rep 6(1):1–11. https://doi.org/10.1038/srep28879

Koutsabasis P, Vogiatzidakis P (2019) Empirical research in mid-air interaction: a systematic review. Int J Human-Comput Interact 35(18):1747–1768. https://doi.org/10.1080/10447318.2019.157 2352

Kühn S, Brass M, Haggard P (2013) Feeling in control: neural correlates of experience of agency. Cortex 49(7):1935–1942. https://doi.org/10.1016/j.cortex.2012.09.002

Large DR, Harrington K, Burnett G, Georgiou O (2019) Feel the noise: mid-air ultrasound haptics as a novel human-vehicle interaction paradigm. Appl Ergon 81:102909. https://doi.org/10.1016/j.apergo.2019.102909

Limerick H, Moore JW, Coyle D (2015) Empirical evidence for a diminished sense of agency in speech interfaces. In: Proceedings of the 33rd annual ACM conference on human factors in computing systems. ACM. https://doi.org/10.1145/2702123.2702379

Long B, Seah SA, Carter T, Subramanian S (2014) Rendering volumetric haptic shapes in mid-air using ultrasound. ACM Trans Graph (TOG) 33(6):1–10. https://doi.org/10.1145/2661229.266 1257

Maggioni E, Cobden R, Dmitrenko D, Obrist M (2018) Smell-O-Message: integration of olfactory notifications into a messaging application to improve users' performance. In: Proceedings of the 20th ACM international conference on multimodal interaction. https://doi.org/10.1145/3242969. 3242975

Martinez Plasencia D, Hirayama R, Montano-Murillo R, Subramanian S (2020) GS-PAT: high-speed multi-point sound-fields for phased arrays of transducers. ACM Trans Graph 39(4). Article 138. https://doi.org/10.1145/3386569.3392492

Marzo A, Seah SA, Drinkwater BW, Sahoo DR, Long B, Subramanian S (2015) Holographic acoustic elements for manipulation of levitated objects. Nat Commun 6:8661. https://doi.org/10.1038/ncomms9661

Matsubayashi A, Makino Y, Shinoda H (2019) Direct finger manipulation of 3D object image with ultrasound haptic feedback. In: Proceedings of the 2019 CHI conference on human factors in computing systems. https://doi.org/10.1145/3290605.3300317

Miller MK, Mandryk RL (2016) Differentiating in-game frustration from at-game frustration using touch pressure. In: Proceedings of the 2016 ACM on interactive surfaces and spaces. ACM. https://doi.org/10.1145/2992154.2992185

Moore JW (2016) What is the sense of agency and why does it matter? Front Psychol 7:1272. https://doi.org/10.3389/fpsyg.2016.01272

Moore JW, Wegner DM, Haggard P (2009) Modulating the sense of agency with external cues. Conscious Cogn 18(4):1056–1064. https://doi.org/10.1016/j.concog.2009.05.004

Narumi T, Nishizaka S, Kajinami T, Tanikawa T, Hirose M (2011) Augmented reality flavors: gustatory display based on edible marker and cross-modal interaction. In: Proceedings of the SIGCHI conference on human factors in computing systems.https://doi.org/10.1145/1978942. 1978957

Obrist M, Subramanian S, Gatti E, Long B, Carter T (2015) Emotions mediated through mid-air haptics. In: Proceedings of the 33rd annual ACM conference on human factors in computing systems. https://doi.org/10.1145/2702123.2702361

Ozkul C, Geerts D, Rutten I (2020) Combining auditory and mid-air haptic feedback for a light switch button. In: Proceedings of the 2020 international conference on multimodal interaction. https://doi.org/10.1145/3382507.3418823

Paneva V, Seinfeld S, Kraiczi M, Müller J (2020) HaptiRead: reading braille as mid-air haptic information. arXiv preprint arXiv:2005.06292. https://doi.org/10.1145/3357236.3395515

Parise CV (2016) Crossmodal correspondences: standing issues and experimental guidelines. Multisensory Res 29(1–3):7–28. https://doi.org/10.1163/22134808-00002502

Petrini K, Remark A, Smith L, Nardini M (2012) When vision is not an option: development of haptic–auditory integration. Seeing Perceiving 25:205–205. https://doi.org/10.1163/187847612X648341

Pittera D, Gatti E, Obrist M (2019) I'm sensing in the rain: spatial incongruity in visual-tactile mid-air stimulation can elicit ownership in VR users. In: Proceedings of the 2019 CHI conference on human factors in computing systems. https://doi.org/10.1145/3290605.3300362

Rakkolainen I, Freeman E, Sand A, Raisamo R, Brewster S (2020) A survey of mid-air ultrasound haptics and its applications. IEEE Trans Haptics. https://doi.org/10.1109/TOH.2020.3018754

Romanus T, Frish S, Maksymenko M, Frier W, Corenthy L, Georgiou O (2019) Mid-air haptic bio-holograms in mixed reality. In: 2019 IEEE international symposium on mixed and augmented reality adjunct (ISMAR-Adjunct). IEEE.https://doi.org/10.1109/ISMAR-Adjunct.2019.00-14

Ros F (2016) Stewart: a haptic interface designed for a self-driving car. Available from http://felixros.com/stewart2.html

Rutten I, Frier W, Van den Bogaert L, Geerts D (2019) Invisible touch: how identifiable are mid-air haptic shapes? In: Extended abstracts of the 2019 CHI conference on human factors in computing systems. https://doi.org/10.1145/3290607.3313004

Salgado Montejo A, Alvarado JA, Velasco C, Salgado CJ, Hasse K, Spence C (2015) The sweetest thing: the influence of angularity, symmetry, and the number of elements on shape-valence and shape-taste matches. Front Psychol 6:1382. https://doi.org/10.3389/fpsyg.2015.01382

Smith BC (2016) Aristotle was wrong and so are we: there are far more than five senses. K. Quinn. aeon, aeon. https://youtu.be/zWdfpwCghIw

Spence C, Gallace A (2011) Multisensory design: reaching out to touch the consumer. Psychol Mark 28(3):267–308. https://doi.org/10.1002/mar.20392

Spence C, Parise CV (2012) The cognitive neuroscience of crossmodal correspondences. i-Perception 3(7):410–412. https://doi.org/10.1068/i0540ic

Sridhar S, Feit AM, Theobalt C, Oulasvirta A (2015) Investigating the dexterity of multi-finger input for mid-air text entry. In: Proceedings of the 33rd annual ACM conference on human factors in computing systems. https://doi.org/10.1145/2702123.2702136

Stein BE, Meredith MA (1993) The merging of the senses. The MIT Press

Synofzik M, Vosgerau G, Voss M (2013) The experience of agency: an interplay between prediction and postdiction. Frontiers Psychol 4. https://doi.org/10.1422/77217

Tajadura-Jimenez A, Väljamäe A, Kuusk K (2020) Altering one's body-perception through E-textiles and haptic metaphors. Frontiers Robot AI 7:7. https://doi.org/10.3389/frobt.2020.00007

Tan H, Zhou Y, Tao Q, Rosen J, van Dijken S (2021) Bioinspired multisensory neural network with cross-modal integration and recognition. Nat Commun 12(1):1–9. https://doi.org/10.1038/s41467-021-21404-z

Van den Bogaert L, Geerts D, Rutten I (2019) Grasping the future: identifying potential applications for mid-air haptics in the home. In: Extended abstracts of the 2019 CHI conference on human factors in computing systems. https://doi.org/10.1145/3290607.3312911

Van Doorn G, Woods A, Levitan CA, Wan X, Velasco C, Bernal-Torres C, Spence C (2017) Does the shape of a cup influence coffee taste expectations? A cross-cultural, online study. Food Qual Prefer 56:201–211. https://doi.org/10.1016/j.foodqual.2016.10.013

Velasco C, Jones R, King S, Spence C (2013) The sound of temperature: what information do pouring sounds convey concerning the temperature of a beverage. J Sens Stud 28(5):335–345. https://doi.org/10.1111/joss.12052

Velasco C, Obrist M (2020) Multisensory experiences: where the senses meet technology. Oxford University Press, Oxford. https://doi.org/10.1093/oso/9780198849629.001.0001

Vogiatzidakis P, Koutsabasis P (2018) Gesture elicitation studies for mid-air interaction: a review. Multimodal Technol Interact 2(4):65. https://doi.org/10.3390/mti2040065

Walker P, Scallon G, Francis B (2017) Cross-sensory correspondences: heaviness is dark and low-pitched. Perception 46(7):772–792. https://doi.org/10.1177/0301006616684369

Winkler P, Stiens P, Rauh N, Franke T, Krems J (2020) How latency, action modality and display modality influence the sense of agency: a virtual reality study. Virtual Reality 24(3):411–422. https://doi.org/10.1007/s10055-019-00403-y

Yoshie M, Haggard P (2013) Negative emotional outcomes attenuate sense of agency over voluntary actions. Curr Biol 23(20):2028–2032. https://doi.org/10.1016/j.cub.2013.08.034

Zhu M, He T, Lee C (2020) Technologies toward next generation human machine interfaces: from machine learning enhanced tactile sensing to neuromorphic sensory systems. Appl Phys Rev 7(3):031305. https://doi.org/10.1063/5.0016485

Augmenting Automotive Gesture Infotainment Interfaces Through Mid-Air Haptic Icon Design

Eddie Brown, David R. Large, Hannah Limerick, William Frier⊙, and Gary Burnett

Abstract A growing body of work is demonstrating the potential benefits of haptic interfaces for the automotive domain, including the use of ultrasound haptic interfaces. In this chapter, we present our work into the development of an in-vehicle mid-air gesture interface for drivers, utilising ultrasound haptic feedback. Our interface uses carefully designed "ultrahapticons" to give feedback and present information to users. We discuss the design and evaluation of our ultrahapticons, giving insight into the design of ultrasound haptic feedback for a gesture interface and contributing a set of effective haptic patterns that can be applied in new application areas.

1 Introduction

Haptic interfaces offer clear potential in the automotive domain given their lack of dependence on the traditional, and already potentially overloaded, visual and auditory channels of the human sensorium, and have been shown to alleviate visual and cognitive load while driving (Gaffary and Lécuyer 2018). As discussed in Chap. "Opportunities for Multisensory Mid-Air Interactions Featuring Ultrasound Haptic Feedback", they also have the potential to encourage a sense of responsibility, which is critical in this context. Indeed, interfaces delivering active haptic feedback have already been successfully employed in various locations within cars, such as the steering wheel, seat and foot pedals, where they can provide driver assistance, alerts, and warnings (see: Riener et al. 2017).

The emergence of mid-air ultrasound haptics as a novel method of human–computer interaction (Iwamoto et al. 2008; Carter et al. 2013; Large et al. 2019) provides further scope in this context, as the need for contact with a physical surface is no longer required. This means, for example, that driver assistance and warnings

D. R. Large · G. Burnett
University of Nottingham, Nottingham, England

E. Brown (✉) · H. Limerick · W. Frier
Ultraleap Ltd, Bristol, UK
e-mail: Eddie.Brown@ultraleap.com

© The Author(s), under exclusive license to Springer Nature Switzerland AG 2022
O. Georgiou et al. (eds.), *Ultrasound Mid-Air Haptics for Touchless Interfaces*,
Human–Computer Interaction Series, https://doi.org/10.1007/978-3-031-04043-6_5

119

may be delivered to any part of the body and at any time (for instance, see: Gil et al. 2018). Moreover, binding mid-air haptics to gesture interfaces can provide agency to contactless interaction, thereby enhancing the utility and usability of gesture interfaces within the automotive domain and providing scope to enrich the affective in-vehicle experience (e.g. as discussed in Chaps. "User Experience and Mid-Air Haptics: Applications, Methods, and Challenges" and "Opportunities for Multisensory Mid-Air Interactions Featuring Ultrasound Haptic Feedback"). This makes mid-air gesture (MAG) interaction a particularly attractive user interface solution in contemporary, manually driven vehicles, where issues of driver distraction and workload still persist, but it also offers huge potential across all levels of vehicle automation (Society of Automotive Engineers 2016). Indeed, novel, MAG interfaces could also be uniquely employed to keep the driver in (or "on") the loop of control (Merat et al. 2019) during lower and intermediate levels of automation or may be harnessed to provide novel and engaging user experiences in higher levels of automation where vehicle occupants are no longer required to drive. Nevertheless, issues such as haptic discrimination, task compatibility, resilience and learning still exist and can hinder the success and adoption of haptic automotive user interfaces and vehicular applications, especially if haptic sensations and gestures are indiscriminate, articulatory vague or lack feature specificity (Brown et al. 2020).

In this chapter, we present an overview of, and key findings from, our pioneering human-centred approach to the design of an in-vehicle, MAG interface. This approach, which is framed and grounded within established human cognitive processes, was used to design and validate exemplar ultrasound, mid-air haptic icons ("ultrahapticons") attuned to the automotive domain. Nevertheless, the method and approach are equally applicable in many other domains and readers may find benefit in adopting this. We outline the approach taken, so this may be employed by other researchers and practitioners in the field and provide full details of all sixteen ultrahapticons, including their metaphorical inspiration and haptic implementation, enabling designers to replicate, develop, and adapt these for their own applications. Further details of the empirical studies upon which the approach is based can be found in Brown et al. (2020, 2022).

2 Formative Studies

Previous, formative investigations into mid-air haptic interfaces in the automotive domain have produced encouraging results (Harrington et al. 2018; Large et al. 2019; Shakeri et al. 2018; Young et al. 2020). For example, Harrington et al. (2018) and Large et al. (2019) created a mid-air haptic interface comprising virtual buttons and a slider-bar arranged as they might be on a traditional, two-dimensional touchscreen interface. The authors reported significant reductions in eyes-off-road time (EORT) as well as a subjective preference for mid-air haptics and gestures, compared to a traditional touchscreen interface and the same MAG interface provided without haptics, also evaluated during the study. Shakeri et al. (2018) revealed benefits to EORT by pairing mid-air haptics with visual, auditory and peripheral lighting effects, and comparing these to visual-only feedback. However, both of these formative studies revealed shortcomings in participants' ability to consistently detect and distinguish different mid-air haptic sensations; moreover, Shakeri et al. (2018) postulated that in some situations, the cognitive effort required to do so may have outweighed any perceived benefits. In addition, Young et al. (2020) concluded that subtle differences may not be perceived when used concurrently with driving.

Needless to say, mid-air haptic technology is continually evolving. Indeed, Shakeri et al. (2018) utilised Amplitude Modulation (AM) (Iwamoto et al. 2008), which is generally perceptively weaker than contemporary rendering approaches like Spatiotemporal Modulation (STM) (Frier et al. 2018) and limits the design of haptic patterns (e.g. as Chap. "Ultrasound Haptic Feedback for Touchless User Interfaces: Design Patterns" reveals). Although Young et al. (2020) employed STM, they were unable to take advantage of the contemporary "Dynamic Tactile Pointer" method of rendering sensations (Hajas et al. 2020). Therefore, although the aforementioned, formative studies show clear potential, ongoing improvements in haptic resolution afford exciting new opportunities for researchers and practitioners to re-imagine and optimise mid-air haptic sensations, for example, by employing the approach outlined in this chapter. Furthermore, we remind readers that although this work is situated in the automotive domain, the design and evaluation approach we use can be used equally well to inform the design of haptic icons to deliver practical benefits across a wide range of other application areas, such as those explored elsewhere in this book.

3 Stimulus Creation: Ideation and Prototyping

The aim of our work was to design and evaluate distinct and salient **Mid-Air Haptic Icons** (**MAHIs** or "**ultrahapticons**") that could be symbiotically paired with hand poses in an exemplar MAG In-Vehicle Infotainment System (IVIS). Grounded in human factors engineering and human cognitive processes, the approach was inspired by related work in semantic information transfer using conventional vibrotactile haptics and gesture elicitation studies (e.g. Brunet et al. 2013; Enriquez et al. 2006; MacLean 2008; Seifi 2019). The ultimate goal was to develop unique haptic icons that were **distinguishable**, **learnable**, **salient** and **recognisable**—key factors in tactile information design known to improve stimulus clarity and reduce overall cognitive effort (MacLean 2008). The entire process (from stimulus elicitation to validation) is shown as a flow chart in Fig. 1.

Method: The first stage involved a participatory design exercise, aiming to capture participants' metaphorical associations with different infotainment features and to elicit a possible mid-air haptic embodiment of these. Seven common in-vehicle info-tainment features/interactions were selected: Fan Speed, Cabin Temperature, Seat Temperature, Navigation, Phone Calls, Audio, and Home Screen. In our study, seven-teen study participants were recruited for one-to-one design sessions. In line with

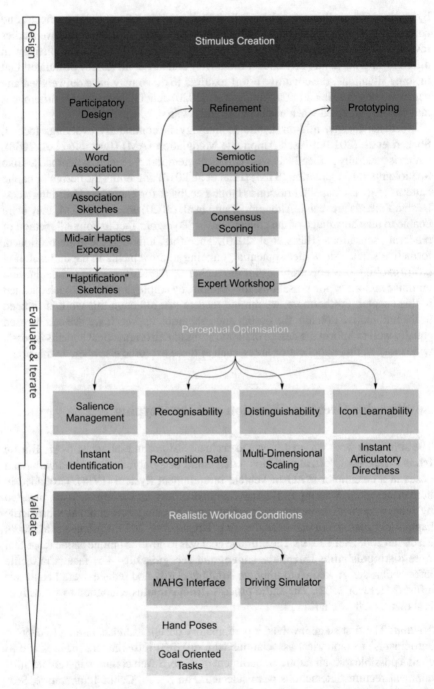

Fig. 1 A flow chart depicting the methodology for developing and testing mid-air haptic icons for an In-Vehicle Infotainment System (IVIS)

the top-down semiotic approach (Danesi 2007), the first step was to understand the participants' expectations and schemas. Thus, they were asked to verbalise the mental model they associated with each infotainment feature, focussing on tactile, visual and auditory elements (i.e. physical sensations, mental images or objects, and sounds). Participants were then asked to sketch their visual, auditory and tactual associations. To eliminate any effects of participants' differing artistic capabilities, they were encouraged to follow a "think-aloud" protocol as they sketched; this enabled the investigator to understand participants' thought processes if the sketch was insufficiently communicative on its own.

Participants were then informed of twelve adjustable, mid-air haptic parameters that could be manipulated to create different sensations, for example, planar shapes, spatial travel direction, diameter, temporal rhythm, etc. Where possible, exemplar sensations conforming with each parameter were demonstrated to participants using the Ultraleap STRATOS explore array. Based on this information, participants were then asked to highlight elements of their designs that they thought most embodied their chosen metaphor, and to suggest how they might use the aforementioned mid-air haptic sensations with a nominal open palm gesture or hand pose to encapsulate these characteristics. Finally, participants were asked to consider how each feature might be adjusted, considering factors such as along which axis the hand pose should move (e.g. up/down, right/left, etc.).

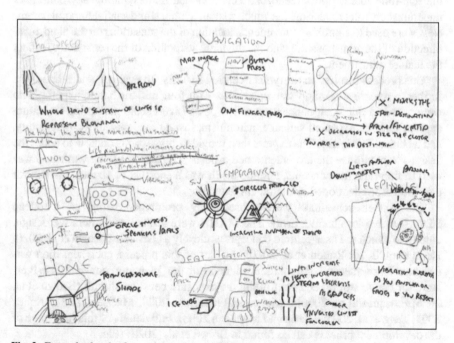

Fig. 2 Example sketch of a participant's metaphorical associations with IVIS features

Results: This elicited 119 possible designs (an example is shown in Fig. 2). Sketched designs were subsequently analysed for their semiotic composition to determine the most intuitive design or designs for each feature (or "referent"). To achieve this, participants' designs were classified into distinct prevailing styles (or "proposals"). Where participants had proposed multiple styles for a single referent, these were analysed for "maximum consensus" (i.e. the percentage of participants eliciting the most popular proposal) and "consensus-distinct ratio" (i.e. the spread of participants displaying the most popular proposal), in line with Enriquez et al. (2006). Singular incidences of proposals were eliminated, resulting in a shortlist of twenty-three ultrahapticons for the seven infotainment features.

Analysis: Proposed ultrahapticons were broken down into exemplar level semiotic components, i.e. the feature "constructs" and "intents" (Seifi 2019). *Constructs* are defined as physical characteristics of a feature that, collectively, comprise the holistic mental model (e.g. the rails of a rocking chair), whereas an *intent* is defined as a symbolic construct that is used to express meaning or behaviour (e.g. blurred lines indicating movement of the rocking chair). This revealed eighty-eight distinct semiotic features, which were analysed further for consensus, resulting in sixty-five commonly occurring components. These components were subsequently decomposed into their value level elements to understand participants' expectation of the real-time interactional feedback. This included understanding any consensus regarding construct rendering, i.e. which spatial, temporal and spatiotemporal parameters were used to signify feature intents, location of the sensations on the hand, axial direction of the adjust gesture, and the dynamic adaptation of the sensation to reflect the feature adjustment.

This process resulted in thirty user-centred MAHIs. To evaluate and refine these further, a remote workshop was conducted with four mid-air haptic experts, who were asked to rate each concept on a five-point Likert scale pertaining to feature appropriateness, expected salience, naturalism, instant recognisability, perspicuity, and technical feasibility. The experts then provided suggestions on how to adapt the designs to maximise the aforementioned aspects. The data from the workshop was used to fine-tune the concepts, and the result was a shortlist of sixteen MAHIs for the seven aforementioned infotainment features.

The sixteen sensations were subsequently prototyped using an Ultraleap STRATOS Explore haptics array. The MAHIs were refined using iterative design, aiming to match the user-centred concepts as closely as possible (Brown et al. 2020; Hajas et al. 2020; Rutten et al. 2020). As part of this process, each sensation was designed for two second presentation, aligned with the "glancing" convention in literature for haptic stimuli and controlling the exposure between stimuli (Brown et al. 2006; Enriquez et al. 2006; Enriquez and MacLean 2008; MacLean and Enriquez 2003; Tang et al. 2005; Ternes and MacLean 2008). Full details of this first stage of the development process can be found in Brown et al. (2020) (Fig. 3).

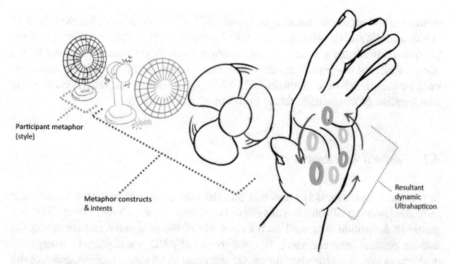

Participant metaphor
(style)

Metaphor constructs
& intents

Resultant
dynamic
Ultrahapticon

Fig. 3 A pictorial representation of the semiotic decomposition process to achieve a mid-air haptic icon from a participant metaphor

4 Perceptual Optimisation

The next stage of developing semiotic mid-air haptics for gestural interfaces was to perceptually optimise the sixteen MAHIs (see: MacLean 2008). This involves employing a different cohort of users to determine how recognisable the derived haptic icons are and to evaluate how distinguishable they are from one another. A further aim of this activity is to quantify each icon's fidelity to the design intent and to determine their "instant articulatory directness"—in other words, the ability of each icon to signify their root metaphor without a further cue (recall from Chap. "Opportunities for Multisensory Mid-Air Interactions Featuring Ultrasound Haptic Feedback" that ambiguity may occur in the absence of more reliable sensory signals). Combined, these data provide an indication of how easily each MAHI could be learned and reveal if and how certain characteristics of the sensations might conflict with each other. Haptic perception studies commonly employ paired comparisons to establish dissimilarity between stimuli. However, this can become too cumbersome for large numbers of stimuli (Bonebright et al. 2005) and an alternative, employed here, is to use perceptual multi-dimensional scaling (see: Rocchesso et al. 2019).

Method: Utilising an Ultraleap STRATOS Explore array, the MAHIs were presented to twenty-five participants, with the aim of providing a compromise between comfort and optimal acoustic pressure, i.e. participants were seated at a desk with their left hand located 20 cm above the ultrasound array; this configuration is also in keeping with the expected in-car location. In addition, threads of acoustically permeable speaker material allowed participants to rest their open hand, thereby minimising fatigue. This also ensured that MAHIs were actuated onto every participant's hand in a controlled and consistent manner. Noise-cancelling Bluetooth headphones connected to video conferencing software were worn by participants throughout the experiment in order to inhibit any spurious noises generated from the ultrasound array while still allowing researcher–participant communication. Before taking part, participants had no prior knowledge of what the MAHIs were. Full details of this second stage of the development process can be found in Brown et al. (2022).

4.1   Instant Identification

In a control scenario, it is important that the user is able to instantly identify the semantic meaning of the control system taxonomy. Instant identification (IID) is a metric to determine how well each icon matched the design intent (conveying the mid-air gestural user interface). In order to quantify IID, we captured participants' opinions of how well-matched the haptic sensation and a visual representation of the haptic icon design were.

Method: In our study, participants began by having each of the sixteen sensations played (in an order dictated by a balanced-Latin square) onto their left hand. Discrete sensations were played three times each, whereas continuous sensations played out for six seconds. Participants were then asked to describe what they had felt. After this, they were shown a visual representation of the haptic icon design and asked to describe how well the diagram matched the sensation they had felt. To quantify IID, and to minimise any confounding effects or demand characteristics, and enable direct comparison, three haptics experts independently assessed participants' descriptions by subjectively evaluating how closely these matched the exemplar definitions. Exemplar definitions had previously been curated around the core semiotic features and locations on the hand and were based on the rationale that object recognition processing is influenced by its "anatomical substrate" (Kaneshiro et al. 2015). For example, the sensation associated with propeller fan was expertly described as, "continuous anti-clockwise rotation of three haptic circles on the centre of the palm". Participants' descriptions were subsequently allocated two points for an exact match, one point for a minor error, or no points in situations when the participant's description was incorrect. A mean value of the median arbitrated scores for each participant was calculated as a percentage of the maximum possible score. Resulting IIDs ranged from 82% for "Thermometer" to 18% for "Propeller fan", with a mean IID (for all haptic icons) of 47%.

The IID metric is useful at understanding the quality of the haptic icon designs, and it can also give an indication of how easily the features of the icons will be able to convey the meaning when presented as a taxonomy. However, limitations exist with quantising the accuracy of the participants' descriptions for the sensations. Moreover, any prior knowledge of mid-air haptics may influence users' ability to accurately articulate the icons. For example, users with no prior knowledge of mid-air haptics may be able to generally articulate the location in which a sensation is actuated but those possessing lexical knowledge or expertise in mid-air haptics may be able to interpret micro-geometry of the sensations (e.g. haptic rings versus haptic points).

4.2 Recognisability and Distinguishability

Recognisability relates to a user's ability to identify a stimulus once it had been learned and is important in the initial adoption and continued use of the haptic icons. In order to quantify recognisability, users can be provided with visualisations of the haptic icons and asked to select which of the visualisations most closely matches the haptic icon they have just experienced.

Method: In our study, participants were exposed to each MAHI three times or for six seconds, as before, and in an order dictated by a balanced-Latin square. After each haptic stimulus had been delivered, the researcher displayed visual representations of all the icons side-by-side on a display monitor (Fig. 4). Adopting a forced-choice approach, participants were required to select which of the visualisations they thought they had just felt, and to give a Likert rating between one and ten to represent how confident they felt in their selection (where one indicated "not at all confident", and ten, "very confident"). Responses were then entered into a 16×16 confusion matrix that presented (as a percentage) the number of times participants correctly matched a MAHI to its visual representation (Table 1).

Results: The most recognisable MAHI was "Ice" which comprised a pulsating haptic bar on the thumb and was correctly recognised by all participants 100% of the time (denoted by [j] in Fig. 4). In contrast, "Sofa cushion", embodied by a circular sensation that expanded and contracted from the centre of the palm, was only recognised 28% (0.28) of the time (denoted by [L] in Fig. 4). Mean recognition rate (RR) was 0.66 (or 66%), and all the icons achieved an RR above the chance level of 6% ($1/16 = 0.06$). These results are similar to those reported in Rocchesso et al. (2019), who found a mean recognition rate of 0.57 (or 57%) for sixteen variants of planar shape-based icons (cross, circle, square).

Distinguishability describes whether the icon's features (i.e. its constructs and intents (Jovicic 2009) are unique enough to be distinguished from others in the set. It is important in enabling a user to be certain that they have selected the correct feature amongst those available. In order to quantify distinguishability, users can be asked to explain which aspect of the sensation informed their previous selection.

Method: In our study, participants' explanations were used in conjunction with their subjective confidence rating to interpret why certain MAHIs may be similar, noting that a low confidence rating may indicate that a participant had previously guessed rather than inaccurately recognised the icon. Incorrect recognition data from the confusion matrix were used to visualise the representational similarity between different haptic icons. In other words, situations in which one haptic icon had been

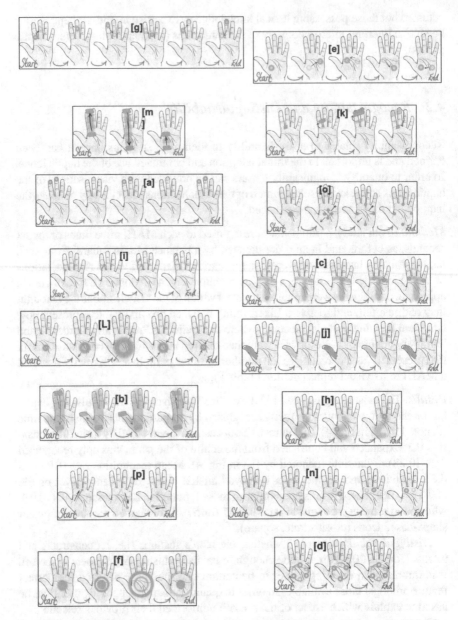

Fig. 4 Sketched depictions of all mid-air haptic icon stimuli used in the perceptual optimisation study. *Note* Further details of all ultrahapticons are provided in Sect. 5

Table 1 Confusion matrix, where rows (CMx) designate the metaphor label condition while columns (CMy) denote predicted responses given; diagonal values indicate where a correct selection was made (CMxy)

Icon label [transpose]	[a]	[b]	[c]	[d]	[e]	[f]	[g]	[h]	[i]	[j]	[k]	[l]	[m]	[n]	[o]	[p]
Bass speaker [a]	0.80	0.00	0.04	0.00	0.00	0.00	0.00	0.00	0.08	0.00	0.04	0.00	0.04	0.00	0.00	0.00
Seat profile view [b]	0.00	0.76	0.00	0.00	0.00	0.00	0.00	0.16	0.00	0.00	0.00	0.00	0.08	0.00	0.00	0.00
T-junction [c]	0.00	0.00	0.68	0.04	0.04	0.04	0.00	0.04	0.00	0.00	0.04	0.00	0.00	0.12	0.00	0.00
Propeller fan [d]	0.00	0.00	0.00	0.56	0.08	0.20	0.00	0.00	0.00	0.00	0.00	0.04	0.00	0.04	0.08	0.00
Bouncing telephone handset [e]	0.00	0.00	0.00	0.08	0.64	0.04	0.04	0.04	0.00	0.00	0.00	0.00	0.00	0.16	0.00	0.00
Waypoint blip [f]	0.00	0.00	0.04	0.04	0.04	0.44	0.00	0.00	0.00	0.00	0.04	0.24	0.00	0.04	0.12	0.00
Flames [g]	0.00	0.04	0.00	0.04	0.00	0.00	0.52	0.00	0.00	0.00	0.32	0.00	0.04	0.00	0.04	0.00
Heating elements [h]	0.00	0.04	0.00	0.00	0.04	0.00	0.00	0.64	0.00	0.00	0.00	0.00	0.12	0.00	0.04	0.12
Coiled telephone wire [i]	0.12	0.00	0.00	0.00	0.00	0.00	0.12	0.00	0.76	0.00	0.00	0.00	0.00	0.00	0.00	0.00
Ice [j]	0.00	0.00	0.00	0.00	0.00	0.00	0.00	0.00	0.00	1.00	0.00	0.00	0.00	0.00	0.00	0.00
Sound waves [k]	0.00	0.00	0.00	0.00	0.00	0.00	0.12	0.00	0.00	0.00	0.84	0.00	0.04	0.00	0.00	0.00
Sofa cushion [l]	0.00	0.00	0.16	0.16	0.04	0.16	0.00	0.08	0.00	0.00	0.00	0.28	0.00	0.04	0.08	0.00
Thermometer [m]	0.00	0.08	0.00	0.00	0.00	0.04	0.04	0.00	0.00	0.00	0.08	0.00	0.76	0.00	0.00	0.00
Telephone rotary dial [n]	0.00	0.04	0.04	0.08	0.04	0.00	0.00	0.04	0.08	0.00	0.00	0.04	0.00	0.64	0.00	0.00
Compass [o]	0.00	0.00	0.04	0.00	0.00	0.08	0.00	0.16	0.04	0.00	0.00	0.12	0.08	0.04	0.40	0.04
House roof [p]	0.00	0.00	0.00	0.08	0.04	0.00	0.00	0.04	0.00	0.00	0.00	0.00	0.04	0.04	0.00	0.76

confused with another suggested that an element of similarity existed between these. This process converts similarity metrics into distances in Euclidian space that can be visualised through multi-dimensional scaling (Fig. 5). In essence, icons that are close together are deemed to be more similar to one another or possess similar elements.

Results: "Compass" (four focal points emerging from a central position on the hand to represent north, south, east and west denoted by [o] in Fig. 4) was most commonly confused with other haptic icons (i.e. least frequently recognised) and is therefore positioned closest to the origin, where no discernible differentiating dimensions exist. In contrast, "Ice" was never confused with another icon (recall, recognition rate was 100%) which is illustrated by its location—furthest from both the origin

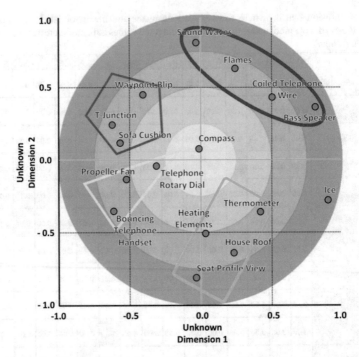

Fig. 5 Haptic icon similarity data visualised through multi-dimensional scaling

and any other data points (denoted by [j] in Fig. 4). It is also evident that there are a number of clusters of data points. These have been enclosed by different coloured planar shapes for clarity, although these shapes bear no resemblance to icon design. The shapes delineate shared commonality amongst MAHIs. In other words, haptic icons that exist within the same cluster have common elements, although it is not possible to infer what the similarity dimensions are from the visualisation alone. However, participants had already verbalised their decision-making process when making classifications, and therefore, it is possible to overlay these qualitative data to help understand which elements were similar between these icons (or, in other words, why certain icons may have been confused). For example, for icons situated within the blue ellipse (the loosest cluster), many participants identified that the sensations were actuated onto the index and middle fingers, suggesting that the location on the fingers was the core confusing attribute. For icons in the green rectangle, several participants mentioned that sensations travelled up and down the palm in some manner; this suggests that the location on the palm and the fact the sensations were rendered dynamically along a pre-defined path may have contributed to confusion. The yellow triangle cluster contains icons that were confused seemingly for their apparent circular path of staccato-like focal points around the palm. The icons within the tightest cluster (red pentagon) all exhibit divergent behaviour (i.e.

focal points splitting in opposite directions, or circles expanding and contracting). Indeed, many participants reported feeling the sensations "growing and shrinking".

4.3 Instant Articulatory Directness

The final factor to consider is *instant articulatory directness* (IAD). IAD provides a measure of how intuitive the connection between the metaphor and the icon is, and thus provides an indication of how easily it may be learned. Blattner et al. (1989) provide a useful taxonomy that describes the stimulus-meaning relationship in iconography as a continuum that ranges from *representational* at one end to *abstract* at the other. A representational relationship is one where the form directly depicts that of the metaphor or accurately reconstructs the sensory experience (e.g. Propeller fan: "The three circles represent each fan blade, and the rotational movement represents the fan blades spinning to generate air flow"). With abstract icons, the representation of semantics is arbitrary meaning that the association is not intrinsic and therefore must be learned or conveyed by other means (e.g. Sofa cushion: "The expanding soft circle represents the compression of a sofa cushion as you sit on it"). Between these extremes, relationships are deemed to be *semi-abstract*; in other words, these icons possess elements or features that imply the whole. For the purpose of classification in the current project, Blattner et al. (1989) continuum was interpreted as a rating scale from one to five, where one indicated "fully abstract" and five, "fully representational" and each MAHI was assigned a rating indicating its relationship with the root metaphor.

Method: In our study, participants were asked to select the text-based metaphor label to which they believed the sensation was semiotically tethered; they had no prior knowledge of the metaphor, and no visualisation was provided. Participants were also asked to articulate why they believed the sensation mapped onto their chosen metaphor. Responses were processed in the same manner as the recognisability data—in a confusion matrix that was normalised to give the frequency of classifications as a proportion of total responses.

Results: The mean percentage of correctly identified metaphors was 35%. Values ranged from 68% for "Seat profile view", to only 8% for "Sofa cushion". In general, results suggest that, although some of the metaphors were well conveyed for some people, others will likely need further explanation or clarification. IAD results were then compared to the abstract/representational ratings. This revealed a strong, significant, positive Spearman's Rank correlation ($rs = 0.786$, $p = 0.001$). As might be expected, the data show a trend towards more representational icons having higher scores for IAD.

A further observation is that representational icons which convey the physical characteristics of a metaphor were more easily discernible than those which convey the non-physical properties (such as the sensory experience) of the metaphor (e.g. motion and rhythm in "Waypoint blip" and "Bass speaker"). This is likely to be because users' expectations are built on visual encoding—in other words, we make judgements on how something is going to feel based on how it looks. This aspect was intentionally removed during this stage of the process (i.e. participants had no visual stimuli on which to build their expectations). Nevertheless, the results appear to suggest that visual encoding may well also apply to mid-air haptics (Breitschaft et al. 2019). In other words, IAD was higher when the metaphor contained familiar physical attributes that the user could readily visualise (as opposed to sensations, for example).

IAD also seemed to be directly affected by the ambiguity of the metaphor label. Labels like "T-Junction" or "Seat Profile View" are very specific and leave little open for interpretation, which may have allowed the participants to build a clearer visualisation and/or expectation. In contrast, labels such as "Sofa Cushion" and "Ice" are arguably more ambiguous. For these reasons, participants' expectations will likely need to be established prior to use by providing bespoke learning, for example, through the provision of visual animations that exhibit the "haptification" of the metaphor.

4.4 Deriving the Exemplar Haptic Icons

Whereas traditional multi-dimensional scaling studies have focussed on stimulus differentiation for the thresholds of base parameters in tactile signals (frequency, amplitude, etc.) (MacLean and Enriquez 2003), our approach aims to uncover distinctions based on spatiotemporal behaviour and metaphorical design. This enables any perceptual anomalies to be identified and the prototypes to be adjusted to better reflect the design intent. The set of exemplar haptic icons thus derived reflect those that achieved the highest consensus in the original participatory design study and subsequently received the highest aggregated scores for instant identification, instant articulatory directness, recognisability and distinguishability for the associated function (future work will explore how these metrics could be weighted.). All sixteen MAHIs and their salience scores are shown in Table 2. From those presented, we selected seven for our exemplar icon set to be taken foreword for implementation in the concept in-vehicle, MAG interface (these are shaded in Table 2), although a case can be made for selecting alternatives.

Indeed, the intended application or hardware implementation may also influence icon selection. For example, "Bass speaker" was commonly reported by participants in our study as a sensation on their wrist, despite the design comprising two repeating focal points at the ends of the middle and index fingers. This is an example of "grating lobes"—a phenomenon which occurs as a result of the rectilinear arrangement of the ultrasonic transducers (Price and Long 2018) and would also likely have occurred in the Shakeri et al. (2018) study given that they used a similar haptics array and sensation for their two-finger hand pose interaction. In this situation, the design of the ultrasound array can help—a "sunflower" arrangement of transducers, such as those now employed in the Ultraleap STRATOS Inspire array, is known to mitigate

Table 2 Cumulative perceptual scores for all icons. Shaded rows indicate exemplar icons for a concept IVIS

MAHI label	IVIS feature	Instant identification	Recognition rate	Instant articulatory directness	Totals
Seat profile view	Seat temperature	0.64	0.76	0.64	2.04
Thermometer	Cabin temperature	0.82	0.76	0.28	1.86
T-junction	Navigation	0.41	0.68	0.68	1.77
Telephone rotary dial	Telephone calls	0.52	0.64	0.6	1.76
Ice	Cabin temperature	0.66	1	0.08	1.74
Bass speaker	Audio	0.73	0.8	0.13	1.66
House roof	Home screen	0.45	0.68	0.52	1.65
Sound w aves	Audio	0.55	0.84	0.2	1.59
Coiled telephone w ire	Telephone calls	0.34	0.76	0.36	1.46
Flames	Cabin temperature	0.57	0.52	0.32	1.41
Bouncing telephone handset	Telephone calls	0.50	0.64	0.24	1.38
Heating elements	Seat temperature	0.32	0.64	0.2	1.16
Propeller fan	Fan speed	0.18	0.56	0.36	1.10
Compass	Navigation	0.20	0.4	0.4	1.00
Waypoint blip	Navigation	0.25	0.44	0.28	0.97
Sofa cushion	Home screen	0.34	0.28	0.08	0.70

this issue. If using a rectilinear transducer array, "Bass speaker" could be replaced by "Sound waves" to avoid the issue of grating lobes; this performed only marginally worse than "Bass speaker" in our study. It is also possible that further refinement or alternatives are required for some icons. For example, although "Propeller fan" achieved very high consensus in the original participatory design study, it did not perform particularly well during the perceptual optimisation study, yet no suitable alternative was identified.

5   Mid-Air Haptic Icon Designs

The following section presents all sixteen of the haptic icons with comprehensive descriptions of their behaviour. Although the haptic icons have been developed for an in-vehicle infotainment system interface, the intention is that other researchers, designers or practitioners may use these or develop them further for their own applications.

5.1 Telephone Calling Features

"Coiled Telephone Wire" (Representational Class)

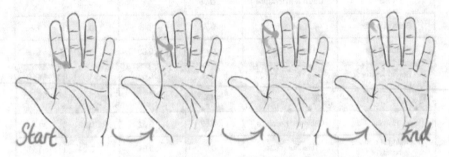

The coiled telephone wire ultrahapticon emulates the metaphor of coiling the wire of a traditional telephone around the finger. The user shall receive a single focal point (green dot) that travels along a path (green lines) rendered at around a 35° angle from right to left in three sequential locations going up the index finger towards the tip.

"Bouncing Telephone Handset" (Semi-Abstract Class)

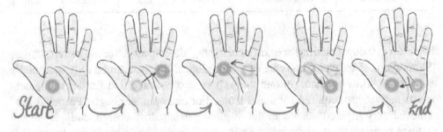

The bouncing telephone handset ultrahapticon emulates the handset of an old telephone, bouncing in its cradle as it rings—the focal rings represent the speaker and microphone sections of the handset. The user shall receive a focal ring "bouncing" between four locations to the temporal rhythm of a retro telephone ringtone. The full sensation consists of a one-second loop of six taps over the four locations (with two taps at the final location, i.e. base of thumb). After the first three taps, there is a small pause before the next three follow.

"Telephone Rotary Dial" (Representational Class)

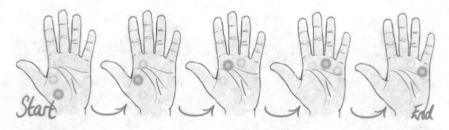

The telephone rotary dial ultrahapticon emulates the finger holes of a rotary dial on an old-fashioned telephone. When accepting an incoming phone call, the user shall receive five sequential, equally spaced haptic circles that are rendered from the bottom left of the palm in a semi-circular path to the base of the little finger knuckle; each haptic circle is sequentially stronger intensity than the last. If the user were rejecting an incoming phone call, they would receive a similar sensation, but it would be mirrored so that the sensation starts at the base of the little finger, follows the medial edge of the palm and ends at the base of the thumb. The sequence of intensity when rejecting an incoming call is also reversed so that each haptic circle is 0.1 less than its previous, i.e. from 1 (full intensity) to 0.6 intensity.

5.2   Audio Features

"Bass Speaker" (Semi-Abstract Class)

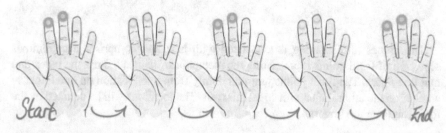

For the base speaker ultrahapticon, the driver shall receive a continuous pulsing sensation at the ends of the fingertips that resembles the user's metaphor of bass sound waves emanating from a speaker.

"Sound Waves" (Semi-Abstract Class)

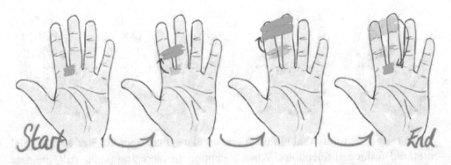

The sound waves ultrahapticon signifies sound waves travelling along the user's fingers. The user shall receive a small two-bar sensation that starts in between the middle and index finger knuckle that increases in size as it travels up the fingers.

5.3   Cabin Temperature Features

"Flames" (Abstract Class)

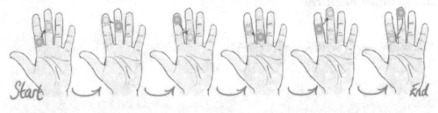

The flames ultrahapticon is associated with heat and comprises a continuous sensation of focal points representing the metaphor of flames licking the index and middle fingers. The focal points jump randomly from one location on one finger to another on the other finger with equal intervals. The locations will be dictated by the three joints on the fingers.

"Ice" (Abstract Class)

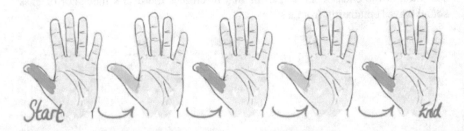

The ice ultrahapticon is associated with cold and signifies the cool aspect of temperature. The user shall receive a solid double bar on the thumb representing a block of ice, that actuates at four pulses per second. It is anticipated that the ice ultrahapticon can be used in conjunction with "flames" to create a representation of a temperature scale.

"Thermometer" (Representational Class)

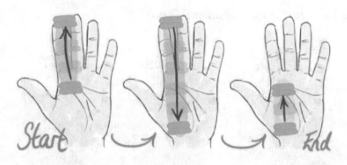

The thermometer ultrahapticon conveys the rising and falling mercury in a thermometer and subsequently represents temperature. The user shall feel a "double bar" haptic sensation initially actuated halfway up the palm. This double bar then accelerates up the index and middle fingers and slows as it reaches the fingertips, where it pauses momentarily. From here, the double bar moves back down the hand, accelerating past the starting point and moving to the bottom of the palm where it pauses momentarily again. Finally, the double bar returns to the starting position.

5.4   Seat Temperature (Heater and Cooler) Feature

"Profile View of a Seat" (Representational Class)

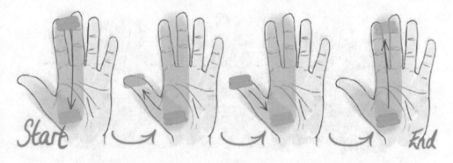

The profile view of a seat was identified as a metaphor for seat temperature and the ultrahapticon conveys the shape of the driver's seat. The user shall feel a "double bar" haptic sensation, initially at the tips of the index and middle fingers. The double bar then accelerates down the index and middle fingers, decelerating as it reaches the base of the thumb/bottom of palm where it pauses momentarily. After reaching the base of the thumb, the double bar then accelerates towards the tip of the thumb where it decelerates and pauses momentarily again. After this, it accelerates down to the base of the thumb, pauses momentarily and then accelerates back up the index and middle fingers and culminates with another subtle deceleration/pause.

"Heating Elements" (Representational Class)

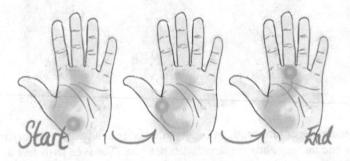

The heating elements ultrahapticon conveys heating elements embedded in a car seat and is associated with the seat temperature feature. The user shall feel a focal ring at the base of the thumb. This sensation travels in an S-shape path (representing a direct translation of the heating element) up the palm to finish at the base of the middle finger knuckle.

5.5   Fan Speed Feature

"Propeller Fan" (Representational Class)

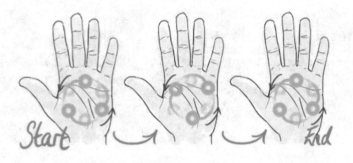

For the propeller fan ultrahapticon, the user shall receive a continuous anti-clockwise rotation of three haptic focal points to represent the users' metaphor of a rotating propeller fan.

5.6   Navigation Features

"T-Junction" (Representational Class)

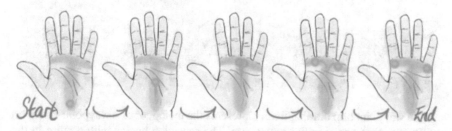

The T-junction ultrahapticon represents the geometry of a junction on a road which was commonly elicited as participants' mental model for navigation. The user receives a dynamic sensation that starts with a single focal point at the middle bottom of the palm. This then travels up the palm. Once the haptic focal point reaches the centre of the knuckles, it splits into two separate focal points—one travels left across the knuckles and the other follows right along the knuckles, thereby dynamically forming the "T".

"Compass" (Semi-Abstract Class)

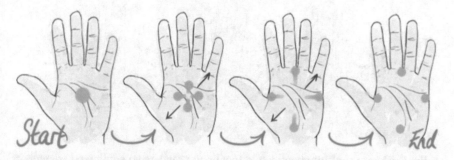

The compass ultrahapticon represents three separate metaphors: "the compass", "crossroads" and "X marks the spot". A single focal point starts in the centre of the palm. This splits into four focal points of equal size. The four focal points move in synchrony towards equidistant locations at the distal, proximal, lateral and medial extremes of the palm. To avoid confusion with expanding circle sensations such as the "Waypoint Blip" and "Sofa Cushion" (as seen in our study), it is suggested that the sensation could work in the opposite direction, i.e. the sensation begins with the four focal points at the extremities of the palm and these come together into a single focal point in the centre of the palm.

"Waypoint Blip" (Semi-Abstract Class)

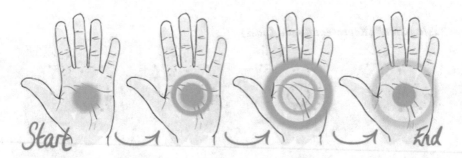

The waypoint blip ultrahapticon represents the metaphor of a waypoint visual on a GPS interface and signifies navigation. The sensation begins with a pulse in the centre of the palm and this spreads outwards, increasing in size, and then fades away.

5.7   Home Screen (Landing Page) Feature

"House Roof" (Representational Class)

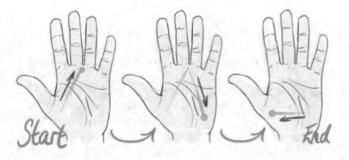

For the house roof ultrahapticon, a focal point renders an equilateral triangle in the palm of the hand. This represents the roof of a house, which was proposed by participants to indicate the "Home" function. The focal point starts at the base of the thumb and completes three separate strokes to delineate the sides of a triangle. At each vertex of the triangle, there is a momentary pause before the rendering continues.

"Sofa Cushion" (Abstract Class)

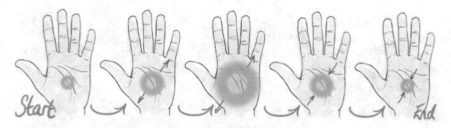

For the sofa cushion ultrahapticon, a ring starts in the centre of the palm. It expands in thickness and diameter and then shrinks back to its original dimensions. This ultrahapticon represents the compression of a cushion as one sits on a sofa.

6 Contextual Validation

As a final note in this chapter, it is important to consider the context in which the haptic icons will be employed. In our work, the haptic icons are intended to complement an in-vehicle, MAG interface. Driving is already a highly demanding task (Mehler and Reimer 2019), and the concern is that this inherent primary task demand will affect the efficacy and usability of our chosen haptic icon designs when used concurrently with driving. Thus, contextual validation is important. Driving simulators provide an ideal setting to conduct driving-related research in a safe and controlled environment (Large and Burnett 2015). We therefore present a brief overview and preliminary results from our driving simulator study that aimed to evaluate the haptic icons in their intended setting.

Method: In practice, we utilised a simplified interface employing three features to ensure that the study was not unduly onerous for participants. The experimental interface utilised a grab-to-initiate gesture, after which one of three hand poses were required for feature selection—each resulting in the activation of their respective MAHI for audio, fan speed and seat temperature functions (Fig. 6). Feature adjustment was made by raising the requisite hand pose up and down, in line with recommendations (see: May et al. 2017; Hessam et al. 2017).

The study compared the MAG interface with a control condition employing nominal confirmation feedback (i.e. where haptic sensations were the same regardless of feature and a pinch gesture was used to adjust feature settings), and captured traditional driving performance data and relevant metrics. These included eye tracking to measure distraction and cognitive tunnelling, subjective measures (e.g. NASA-TLX (Hart and Staveland 1988) to measure perceived workload) and simulator control data to understand the effects of the MAHG interface on vehicle control. In addition, UX questionnaires and semi-structured interviews were utilised, and where relevant,

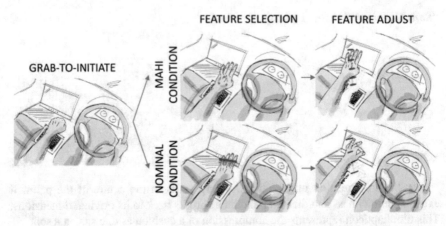

Fig. 6 Storyboard of the mid-air haptic gesture interactions evaluated in the study. Purple sketch elements depict haptic sensations actuated onto the underside of the hand

these were structured in line with the technology acceptance model (Venkatesh and Davis 2000).

Results: Preliminary findings indicate that the mid-air haptic icons were preferred by over 60% of drivers, when compared to a control condition employing nominal confirmation feedback (i.e. where haptic sensations were the same regardless of feature). When used for feature selection, the haptic icons enabled participants to complete the interaction without taking their eyes off the road. Participants also commented that the haptic icons supported the recall of the hand poses used for feature selection. However, the study also revealed the importance of other design elements that need to be considered. For example, the onboarding of the interface was a cumbersome and inefficient process, and this needs to be refined so that a user may learn the interface without the need for detailed, and time-consuming guidance (particularly, during "real-world" use). In addition, the manner in which user intent is distinguished from routine hand movements requires further refinement. Contemporaneous methods have employed temporal feedforward mechanisms (i.e. hand pose dwell time). However, this, in combination with the additional time delay caused by relaying haptic feedback, would create unacceptable latency in the context of driving. We therefore selected a user-triggered feedforward mechanism (i.e. the grab gesture to start interacting) which had previously been dismissed in earlier studies as being annoying and distracting (Riener et al. 2013) and adding to cognitive load (Delamare et al. 2015). Nevertheless, the driver gripping the steering wheel could potentially be mistaken for the grab-to-initiate gesture, thereby resulting in the premature initiation of mid-air haptics. This suggests that the MAHI interaction zone needs to be clearly delineated from other active driving hand-zones. Other usability aspects that will be explored in future work include defining a mechanism to guide the user's hand to the interaction zone with haptics, designing to encourage and manage task interleaving behaviour, and defining the limits of the travel envelope in which a driver can move their hand to adjust a feature as well as how feedback on incremental adjustment is best conveyed in the mid-air haptic medium.

7 Conclusion

In this chapter, we have presented an overview of, and key findings from, our pioneering human-centred approach to the design of an in-vehicle, MAG interface. Sixteen haptic icons (ultrahapticons) were created following an icon elicitation exercise. These were perceptually optimised in a subsequent study to ensure they were distinguishable, learnable, salient and recognisable—key factors in tactile information design. From this, an exemplar set of seven ultrahapticons were selected and a sample of these was subsequently evaluated in a driving simulator study. The chapter provides an overview of the methodological approach—allowing other researchers and developers to adopt this in their own work, as well as a comprehensive taxonomy of all sixteen of our ultrahapticons. Although the work is grounded in automotive interface design, it is envisaged that the approach is equally applicable in other domains and application areas (such as those explored elsewhere in this book), and the anticipation is that other researchers, designers and practitioners may use our ultrahapticons directly or develop their own using our approach.

Acknowledgements The project was funded by the Knowledge Transfer Partnerships (KTP) programme (ref: KTP11513). Knowledge Transfer Partnerships aim to help businesses improve their competitiveness and productivity through the better use of the knowledge, technology and skills that reside within the UK knowledge base and are funded by UK Research and Innovation through Innovate UK, part of the UK Government's industrial strategy.

References

Blattner MM, Sumikawa DA, Greenberg RM (1989) Earcons and icons: their structure and common design principles. Human-Computer Interact 4(1):11–44

Bonebright TL, Miner NE, Goldsmith TE, Caudell TP (2005) Data collection and analysis techniques for evaluating the perceptual qualities of auditory stimuli. ACM Trans Appl Percept (TAP) 2(4):505–516

Breitschaft SJ, Clarke S, Carbon CC (2019) A theoretical framework of haptic processing in automotive user interfaces and its implications on design and engineering. Front Psychol 10:1470

Brown E, Large DR, Limerick H, Burnett G (2020) Ultrahapticons: "Haptifying" drivers' mental models to transform automotive mid-air haptic gesture infotainment interfaces. In: AutomotiveUI '20: 12th international conference on automotive user interfaces and interactive vehicular applications, September 2020, pp 54–57

Brown E, Large DR, Limerick H, Frier W, Burnett G (2022) Validating the salience of haptic icons for automotive mid-air haptic gesture interfaces. Ergonomics Human Factors

Brown LM, Brewster SA, Purchase HC (2006, April) Tactile crescendos and sforzandos: applying musical techniques to tactile icon design. In: CHI'06 extended abstracts on Human factors in computing systems, pp 610–615

Brunet L, Megard C, Paneels S, Changeon G, Lozada J, Daniel MP, Darses F (2013, April) "Invitation to the voyage": the design of tactile metaphors to fulfill occasional travelers' needs in transportation networks. In: 2013 world haptics conference (WHC). IEEE, pp 259–264

Carter T, Seah SA, Long B, Drinkwater B, Subramanian S (2013, October) UltraHaptics: multi-point mid-air haptic feedback for touch surfaces. In: Proceedings of the 26th annual ACM symposium on User interface software and technology, pp 505–514

Danesi M (2007) The quest for meaning: a guide to theory and practice in semiotics

Delamare W, Coutrix C, Nigay L (2015, June) Designing guiding systems for gesture-based interaction. In: Proceedings of the 7th ACM SIGCHI symposium on engineering interactive computing systems, pp 44–53

Enriquez M, MacLean K (2008, March) The role of choice in longitudinal recall of meaningful tactile signals. In: 2008 symposium on haptic interfaces for virtual environment and teleoperator systems. IEEE, pp 49–56

Enriquez M, MacLean K, Chita C (2006, November) Haptic phonemes: basic building blocks of haptic communication. In: Proceedings of the 8th international conference on multimodal interfaces, pp 302–309

Frier W, Ablart D, Chilles J, Long B, Giordano M, Obrist M, Subramanian S (2018, June) Using spatiotemporal modulation to draw tactile patterns in mid-air. In: International conference on human haptic sensing and touch enabled computer applications. Springer, Cham, pp 270–281

Gaffary Y, Lécuyer A (2018) The use of haptic and tactile information in the car to improve driving safety: a review of current technologies. Frontiers ICT 5:5

Gil H, Son H, Kim JR, Oakley I (2018, April) Whiskers: exploring the use of ultrasonic haptic cues on the face. In: Proceedings of the 2018 CHI conference on human factors in computing systems, pp 1–13

Hajas D, Pittera D, Nasce A, Georgiou O, Obrist M (2020) Mid-air haptic rendering of 2D geometric shapes with a dynamic tactile pointer. IEEE Trans Haptics 13(4):806–817

Harrington K, Large DR, Burnett G, Georgiou O (2018, September) Exploring the use of mid-air ultrasonic feedback to enhance automotive user interfaces. In: Proceedings of the 10th international conference on automotive user interfaces and interactive vehicular applications, pp 11–20

Hart SG, Staveland LE (1988) Development of NASA-TLX (Task Load Index): results of empirical and theoretical research. In: Advances in psychology, vol 52. North-Holland, pp 139–183

Hessam JF, Zancanaro M, Kavakli M, Billinghurst M (2017, November) Towards optimization of mid-air gestures for in-vehicle interactions. In: Proceedings of the 29th Australian conference on computer-human interaction, pp 126–134

Hutchins EL, Hollan JD, Norman DA (1985) Direct manipulation interfaces. Human Comput Interact 1(4):311–338

Iwamoto T, Tatezono M, Shinoda H (2008, June) Non-contact method for producing tactile sensation using airborne ultrasound. In: International conference on human haptic sensing and touch enabled computer applications. Springer, Berlin, Heidelberg, pp 504–513

Jovicic J (2009) The quest for meaning: a guide to semiotic theory and practice. Univ Tor Q 78(1):149–149

Kaneshiro B, Perreau Guimaraes M, Kim HS, Norcia AM, Suppes P (2015) A representational similarity analysis of the dynamics of object processing using single-trial EEG classification. PLoS ONE 10(8):e0135697

Large DR, Burnett G (2015) An overview of occlusion versus driving simulation for assessing the visual demands of in-vehicle user-interfaces. In: 4th international conference on driver distraction and inattention, Sydney, New South Wales, Australia

Large DR, Harrington K, Burnett G, Georgiou O (2019) Feel the noise: mid-air ultrasound haptics as a novel human-vehicle interaction paradigm. Appl Ergon 81:102909

MacLean K, Enriquez M (2003, July) Perceptual design of haptic icons. In: Proceedings of EuroHaptics, pp 351–363

MacLean KE (2008) Foundations of transparency in tactile information design. IEEE Trans Haptics 1(2):84–95

May KR, Gable TM, Walker BN (2017, September) Designing an in-vehicle air gesture set using elicitation methods. In: Proceedings of the 9th international conference on automotive user interfaces and interactive vehicular applications, pp 74–83

Mehler B, Reimer B (2019) How demanding is "just driving?" A cognitive workload-psychophysiological reference evaluation

Merat N, Seppelt B, Louw T, Engström J, Lee JD, Johansson E, Green CA, Katazaki S, Monk C, Itoh M, McGehee D (2019) The "out-of-the-loop" concept in automated driving: proposed definition, measures and implications. Cogn Technol Work 21(1):87–98

Price A, Long B (2018, October) Fibonacci spiral arranged ultrasound phased array for mid-air haptics. In: 2018 IEEE international ultrasonics symposium (IUS). IEEE, pp 1–4

Riener A, Ferscha A, Bachmair F, Hagmüller P, Lemme A, Muttenthaler D, Pühringer D, Rogner H, Tappe A, Weger F (2013, October) Standardization of the in-car gesture interaction space. In: Proceedings of the 5th international conference on automotive user interfaces and interactive vehicular applications, pp 14–21

Riener A, Jeon M, Alvarez I, Frison AK (2017) Driver in the loop: best practices in automotive sensing and feedback mechanisms. In: Automotive user interfaces. Springer, Cham, pp 295–323

Rocchesso D, Cannizzaro FS, Capizzi G, Landolina F (2019, September) Accessing and selecting menu items by in-air touch. In: Proceedings of the 13th biannual conference of the Italian SIGCHI chapter: designing the next interaction, pp 1–9

Rutten I, Frier W, Geerts D (2020, September) Discriminating between intensities and velocities of mid-air haptic patterns. In: International conference on human haptic sensing and touch enabled computer applications. Springer, Cham, pp 78–86

Seifi H (2019) Personalizing haptics. Springer International Publishing

Shakeri G, Williamson JH, Brewster S (2018, September) May the force be with you: ultrasound haptic feedback for mid-air gesture interaction in cars. In: Proceedings of the 10th international conference on automotive user interfaces and interactive vehicular applications, pp 1–10

Society of Automotive Engineers (SAE) (2016) J3016A: taxonomy and definitions for terms related to driving automation systems for on-road motor vehicles. Available at https://www.sae.org/sta ndards/content/j3016_201609/. Accessed: 23 July 2021

Tang A, McLachlan P, Lowe K, Saka CR, MacLean K (2005, October) Perceiving ordinal data haptically under workload. In: Proceedings of the 7th international conference on Multimodal interfaces, pp 317–324

Ternes D, MacLean KE (2008, June) Designing large sets of haptic icons with rhythm. In: International conference on human haptic sensing and touch enabled computer applications. Springer, Berlin, Heidelberg, pp 199–208

Venkatesh V, Davis FD (2000) A theoretical extension of the technology acceptance model: four longitudinal field studies. Manage Sci 46(2):186–204

Young G, Milne H, Griffiths D, Padfield E, Blenkinsopp R, Georgiou O (2020) Designing mid-air haptic gesture controlled user interfaces for cars. In: Proceedings of the ACM on human-computer interaction, vol 4(EICS), pp 1–23

Ultrasound Mid-Air Tactile Feedback for Immersive Virtual Reality Interaction

Thomas Howard, Maud Marchal, and Claudio Pacchierotti

Abstract Ultrasound mid-air haptic (UMH) devices are promising for tactile feedback in virtual reality (VR), as they do not require users to be tethered to, hold, or wear any device. This approach is less cumbersome, easy to set up, can simplify tracking, and leaves the hands free for concurrent interactions. This chapter explores work conducted at CNRS-IRISA dealing with the challenges arising from the integration of UMH interfaces in immersive VR through three main axes. These are discussed in the wider context of the state of the art on UMH for augmented and virtual reality, and illustrated through several VR use-cases. A first axis deals with device integration into the VR ecosystem. Interaction in immersive VR is based on the synergy between complex input devices allowing real-time tracking of the user and multimodal feedback devices delivering a coherent visual, auditory and haptic picture of a simulated virtual environment (VE). Using UMH in immersive VR therefore hinges on integrating UMH devices such that their operation does not interfere with other input and feedback devices. It is also critical to ensure that UMH feedback is adequately synchronized and co-located with respect to other stimuli, and delivered within a workspace that is compatible with that of VR interaction. Regarding this final point, we propose PUMAH, a robotic solution for increasing the usable workspace of UMH devices. The second and third axes, respectively, focus on stimulus perception and rendering of VE properties. Virtual object properties can be rendered in a variety of ways, through, e.g., amplitude modulation (AM) or spatiotemporal modulation

T. Howard (✉)
Univ Rennes, INSA Rennes, Inria, CNRS, IRISA, Rennes, France
e-mail: thomas.howard@irisa.fr

M. Marchal
Univ Rennes, INSA Rennes, Inria, CNRS, IRISA, Rennes, France
e-mail: maud.marchal@irisa.fr

IUF, Paris, France

C. Pacchierotti
CNRS, Univ Rennes, Inria, IRISA, Rennes, France
e-mail: claudio.pacchierotti@irisa.fr

© The Author(s), under exclusive license to Springer Nature Switzerland AG 2022   147
O. Georgiou et al. (eds.), *Ultrasound Mid-Air Haptics for Touchless Interfaces*,
Human–Computer Interaction Series, https://doi.org/10.1007/978-3-031-04043-6_6

(STM), with many parameters (modulation frequency, spatial sampling, etc.) coming into play, raising questions about the limits of the design space. To tackle this challenge, we begin by conducting psychophysical experimentation to understand the usable ranges for stimulus parameters and understand the perceptual implications of stimulus design choices. We propose an open-source software framework intended to facilitate UMH stimulus design and perceptual evaluation. These results in turn serve as the basis for the design and evaluation of rendering schemes for VR. Using amplitude variations along a focal point path in STM, we investigate the possibility of rendering geometric details and in a second step, sensations of stiffness in VR.

1 Introduction

The preceding chapters offered a broad view of ultrasound mid-air haptics (UMH), highlighting challenges and perspectives in design and interaction across multiple application domains. In contrast, the present chapter focuses specifically on applications to immersive virtual reality (VR). As such, it serves as somewhat of a bridge between the broader application-independent considerations tackled previously and lower-level UMH rendering and device integration considerations which are dealt with in depth in subsequent chapters. Our work echoes previous considerations relating to UMH's role in supporting multimodal interaction, user experience, and agency in interactions, in the context of using UMH to support VR interaction where inputs to different sensory modalities are fully independent from one another.

The field of VR has developed dramatically over the past decade, thanks in large part to the wide availability of cheap, high-quality head-mounted displays (HMDs), and high-performance graphics processors.

Echoing the early evolution of human–computer interaction (HCI), haptics has been absent or at least slow to be integrated into the VR interaction loop. As was previously noted in relation to touchless user interfaces (Chap. "Augmenting Automotive Gesture Infotainment Interfaces Through Mid-air Haptic Icon Design"), interaction with digital content inherently lacks natural touch, and VR is no exception to this. Yet, in VR interactions dominated by vision and audio, the addition of the sense of touch has been shown to enhance interaction [e.g., Meli et al. (2018)], increase realism [e.g., Meli et al. (2014), de Tinguy et al. (2020)], and improve immersion [e.g., Popescu et al. (2002), Ramsamy et al. (2006)].

Immersive VR relies on the use of a HMD worn by the user, blocking out vision and hearing of the real environment while rendering a full 3D visual scene with immersive audio and, depending on the application, some forms of haptic feedback. In its current form, immersive VR however does not occlude the user's real-world perception of smell, taste, and touch, both though user's proprioception and contact with the real environment.

Interaction is considered as the reciprocal action of the user on the computer system implementing a VR environment through various input devices, and of said computer system on the user through various feedback devices (see Fig. 1). Haptic

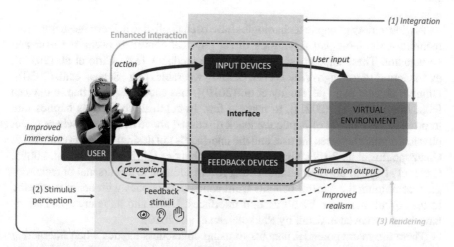

Fig. 1 The HCI interaction loop as applied to immersive VR. Multiple input devices acquire the user's state and actions, which can be mapped to the user's avatar, i.e., their virtual representation in the simulated virtual environment (VE), or to other VE properties. The state of said VE and its actions on the avatar in turn generate outputs which are fed to the multiple feedback devices interfacing with the user. In immersive VR, these feedback devices have the specific characteristic of blocking out real-world sensory inputs for vision and hearing thanks to the HMD, replacing them with sensory inputs related to the VE. Regarding touch, the real-world sensory inputs from the user's proprioception and contact with the their physical environment are not masked, but rather overlaid with virtual sensory inputs from various haptic feedback devices. The broad areas where haptic feedback can provide benefits are circled in green, purple, and red, respectively, for enhanced interaction, improved realism, and improved user immersion. The shaded boxes highlight the three axes discussed in this chapter: device integration (red), stimulus perception (blue), and rendering (yellow)

feedback enhances interaction by enriching the action of the system on the user, providing additional immediate and informative feedback, in particular during contact with and manipulation of virtual objects (green frame in Fig. 1). We define realism as the quality of the representation of a virtual environment (VE) to the user in a way that is accurate and true to the VE's internal structure and rules. Haptic feedback can increase realism by providing sensations corresponding to the virtual physical processes occurring in the virtual environment (purple frame in Fig. 1). Immersion can be understood as the result of a human–computer interface's capability to remove or mask as many real-world sensations as possible, and to substitute them with sensations corresponding to the VE (Mestre et al. 2006). Haptic feedback thus improves immersion by stimulating an otherwise unused sensory modality, which would tend to anchor the user in the perception of the real environment rather than that of the VE (red frame in Fig. 1). In addition, or as a by-product of the former, added haptics in interaction with virtual environments appears to have positive effects on user presence (Kreimeier et al. 2019), engagement and affective response (Rutten et al. 2020), as well as factors relating to embodiment, in particular sense of agency (Cornelio Martinez et al. 2017).

A wide variety of haptic technologies have been applied to achieve these improvements, for the most part relying on direct physical contact between the user and an actuator. These encompass grounded force feedback [e.g., Cirio et al. (2013)], exoskeletons [e.g., Lugo-Villeda et al. (2009)], wearables [e.g., Salazar et al. (2020)], tangible objects [e.g., de Tinguy et al. (2019)], and encounter-type haptic devices [e.g., Mercado et al. (2021)], to name a few. In contrast, contactless haptics aim to provide the benefits of haptic feedback discussed above in contexts where direct physical contact between the user and the interface is not desired (Arafsha et al. 2015; Chatzopoulos et al. 2017). Ultrasound mid-air haptics (UMH) (Hoshi et al. 2009a; Carter et al. 2013) provides an interesting recent addition to this arsenal of technologies, combining the general benefits from contactless haptics with benefits specific to the stimuli delivered by ultrasound interfaces. UMH and its many applications have been reviewed in detail by Rakkolainen et al. (2020).

There are many potential benefits to using contactless haptics when interacting with virtual environments. Removing unwanted physical contact with a controller or actuator may improve interaction by freeing up the hand from constraining devices. This in turn can facilitate better manipulation of virtual objects and ease tracking. Freeing up the hand also allows concurrent manipulation, for example of tangible objects, without impeding real-world touch feedback when it is desired. Physical contact may also be undesirable for the sake of improved immersion. Contactless interfaces achieve the best possible interface transparency by preventing any haptic stimuli arising from the contact of the actuator on the user's skin (Rakkolainen et al. 2020). This improved immersion also translates to an advantage for VE designers as contactless devices do not constrains VR interaction design to match the unavoidable perceived actuator properties (e.g., forcing the user's avatar to wear gloves or a wristband to match haptic devices worn in the real world and thus maintain immersion). A final potential advantage from the absence of contact comes from the perspective of user safety and hygiene. As no physical contact between the user and actuator takes place, there is a reduced risk of user injury from the device or contact with contaminated surfaces. While the latter point may not be as prominent of an issue as it is in digital signage (Corenthy et al. 2018), it may still be relevant, e.g., in medical AR and VR applications. It should be noted that some of these benefits are not specific to immersive virtual environments and are also discussed in Chaps. "Augmenting Automotive Gesture Infotainment Interfaces Through Mid-Air Haptic Icon Design" and "Modulation Methods for Ultrasound Midair Haptics" through the lens of touchless user interfaces for interacting with digital content.

In addition to the general benefits of contactless haptic interfaces over contact haptics, UMH devices provide many specific opportunities for VR applications. Ultrasound devices are capable of delivering a variety of sensations ranging from light pressure and vibrotactile stimuli (Carter et al. 2013) to sensations of airflow (Hasegawa et al. 2017) and thermal stimuli (Kamigaki et al. 2020), all within a continuous 3D workspace and with a very high temporal resolution. These high-dimensional stimuli are potentially capable of encoding a lot of information through rapidly and finely reconfigurable spatial, temporal, and intensity characteristics (Mulot et al. 2021b). The device's workspace and lack of physical constraints on the stimuli mean that stimuli do not necessarily need to be restricted to a single point on the skin or even just the hand, but can potentially target any exposed skin on the user's body (Gil et al. 2018; Suzuki et al. 2018). UMH interfaces are highly interesting in the multi-modal context of augmented and virtual reality interaction as they allow the generation of a wide variety not only of tactile sensations, but also auditory stimuli as well as the levitation of particles. This provides potential for multi-sensory stimulation based on a single device (Ochiai et al. 2017; Shakeri et al. 2019). The manner in which UMH can support multimodal interaction are also discussed in detail in Chaps. "Opportunities for Multisensory Mid-Air Interactions Featuring Ultrasound Haptic Feedback" and "Multimodal Interaction with Mid-Air Haptics". Finally, UMH device have the potential to be embedded within walls, tables (Kervegant et al. 2017), other furniture and objects (Vi et al. 2017), and even the headset (Sand et al. 2015) which can be advantageous in terms of footprint, leaving the VR workspace unobstructed.

The present chapter is intended to provide an overview of the current state of research conducted at CNRS on the subject of integrating ultrasound mid-air haptics to immersive virtual reality. This work is discussed in the context of the broader state of the art for UMH in the hopes of also serving as an introduction to UMH for researchers and designers hoping to apply this technology to immersive interaction with virtual environments.

2 State of the Art and Challenges for Integrating UMH in Immersive VR

Some of the earliest proposed use-cases for UMH feedback concerned augmented reality (AR) interactions which share many common aspects and challenges with immersive VR. As early as 2009, Hoshi et al. (2009a) presented a proof-of-concept integration of multiple focused ultrasound arrays, a hand tracking system, and a holographic visual display to add a tactile dimension to holograms. This was later expanded upon in work by Inoue et al. (2014) and Kimura et al. (2016). Augmented reality screens with tactile feedback also feature prominently in early use-cases for UMH (Monnai et al. 2014; Rümelin et al. 2017; Yoshino and Shinoda 2013). More recently, this concept of touchable holograms has been refined to leverage improved AR HMDs to deliver more complex visual feedback and interface with more diverse external inputs, as seen, e.g., in demonstrators by Kervegant et al. (2017) or the touchable bio-holograms from Romanus et al. (2019). Finally, a recent development has seen a shift from passive displays to interfaces allowing manipulation with UMH feedback (Kimura et al. 2016; Makino et al. 2016; Matsubayashi et al. 2019; Yoshida et al. 2017). Please refer to Chap. "Touchless Tactile Interaction with Unconventional Permeable Displays" UMH for details on augmented-reality user interfaces as well as Chap. "Superimposing Visual Images on Mid-Air Ultrasonic Haptic Stimulation" for a detailed discussion of the challenge of congruence between vision and haptics in such systems.

As consumer VR headsets became more widely available, several proof-of-concept interaction use-cases for UMH were developed specifically in VR. Hwang et al. (2017) presented the Airpiano, a VR piano playing simulation where key presses were rendered through amplitude-modulated (AM) focal points projected on the user's fingertips. UMH has also been applied to enhancing VR gaming experiences by providing abstract cues supporting the interaction (Georgiou et al. 2018) or sensations of supernatural phenomena (Martinez et al. 2018). In the domain of medical VR applications, Karafotias et al. (2017) explored the potential for using UMH feedback to support applications for pain distraction, while Balint and Althoefer (2018) present a proof-of-concept reconfigurable medical palpation simulation based on UMH feedback.

Figure 1 highlights the categories of challenges relating to the integration of UMH feedback to VR experiences. To synthesize insights from our work on this topic, we can group the challenges we tackled into three categories: *device integration* (red in Fig. 1), *stimulus perception* (blue in Fig. 1), and *rendering* (yellow in Fig. 1).

The challenge of device integration (see Sect. 3) relates to incorporating UMH devices into VR interactions in a way that safely enables full use of the UMH feedback device to support the VR interaction without degrading the interfaces between any other input or feedback devices and the user. Our present work does not explicitly tackle the subject of safety; however, details on this can be found in Chaps. "Safety of High-Intensity Ultrasound" and "Ultrasound Exposure in Mid-Air Haptics".

Along with properly integrating UMH devices into VR interaction, it is necessary to understand how users perceive the generated stimuli (see Sect. 4). This is critical to guide tactile rendering design, overcome inherent limitations to UMH devices, and leverage cross-modal interactions which inevitably occur in the multimodal context of immersive VR.

Finally, these insights into the relationship between stimulus design and perceived haptic properties allow tackling of the challenges of rendering for VR interaction (see Sect. 5). These are twofold: on the one hand, we seek to understand what properties of virtual objects and contacts can be effectively rendered using UMH, and on the other, we seek to understand how to best render these properties given the UMH stimulus design space and constraints. This discussion on rendering will build on technical aspects of UMH rendering, a large part of which are subsequently discussed in detail in Chaps. "Introduction to Ultrasonic Mid-Air Haptic Effects", "Modulation Methods for Ultrasound Midair Haptics", "Sound-Field Creation for Haptic Reproduction", and "The Physical Principles of Arrays for Mid-Air Haptic Applications".

While our work has not tackled challenges beyond these three groups, further aspects to consider with respect to integrating UMH feedback to VR interaction have been studied by others, such as the need to understand users' affective responses to UMH stimuli (Eid and Al Osman 2015; Obrist et al. 2015) and the impact of UMH feedback on sense of agency (Cornelio Martinez et al. 2017; Evangelou et al. 2021) (see also Chap. "Opportunities for Multisensory Mid-air Interactions Featuring Ultrasound Haptic Feedback"). The following three sections discuss each of the listed challenge groups, presenting topic-specific state of the art as well as a survey of the work conducted at CNRS on each of these topics.

3   Integrating UMH Devices into the VR Ecosystem

As shown in Fig. 1, interaction in immersive VR relies on a set of input devices tracking the users' position, state, and receiving explicit input actions. These inputs feed into a computer running the simulation of the VE in interactive time (this usually means latency is kept below 75 ms (Waltemate et al. 2016) and frame rates above 60 fps). This simulation in turn generates outputs for the video, audio, and haptic feedback devices.

Proper UMH device integration into the interaction loop requires:

1. Getting the UMH device to not impede user input and ensuring the input devices provide adequate information for the simulation to generate relevant outputs to the UMH device (see Sect. 3.1).
2. Ensuring the UMH device does not break immersion through its physical footprint or the delivery of unwanted stimuli. Ensuring co-location and synchronization between the UMH rendering of a virtual scene with other existing haptic, audio, and visual renderings of the same scene, without degrading the interface between any of the other feedback devices and the user.
3. Ensuring the UMH devices' rendering workspace adequately covers the VR interaction workspace (see Sect. 3.3).

These challenges are addressed through a combination of hard- and software design as well as adequate interaction design.

3.1   Integrating with Input Devices

Since the real environment and user's body are hidden from the user in immersive VR, it usually does not pose many constraints on the obtrusiveness of tracking hardware. However, despite it having been shown that UMH feedback can in some cases be delivered through fabric (Suzuki et al. 2018), UMH generally requires the user's skin to be unobstructed in order for the stimuli to be effectively delivered. This poses certain constraints on the tracking hardware with regard to obtrusiveness, both of the tracking devices themselves and of their fixation on the user's skin.

Furthermore, the high freedom of spatial reconfigurability of UMH stimuli means that the full potential of the technology is best achievable only if the user's pose is tracked with a high level of detail, i.e., the tracking system provides a high number of degrees of freedom (DoF). This is especially challenging when it comes to tracking the hands, which usually are the focus of interaction with UMH devices, and present a high number of DoFs and relatively small anatomical features. This challenge is more general to immersive VR and is usually tackled through sensorized in-hand controllers (e.g., Valve Index Controllers[1]), tracking gloves (e.g., ManusVR[2]), or hand

---

[1] https://www.valvesoftware.com/en/index/controllers.

[2] https://www.manus-vr.com/vr-products.

exoskeletons (e.g., SenseGlove[3]) which provide accurate high-DoF hand tracking over large VR workspaces. These solutions however are mostly incompatible with UMH as they tend to completely occlude the skin in the interaction region.

Another point to consider is that contrary to, e.g., wearable devices, UMH stimuli are generated in the VE world frame of reference. Thus, a relatively high tracking accuracy is required to ensure UMH stimuli are actually delivered to the target area on the user's skin (corresponding to the area of virtual contact). This requirement can be somewhat moderated by taking into account the relatively low spatial precision of UMH stimuli. Focal points are perceptible up to a couple of mm laterally in planes parallel to the array's x–y plane and up to a couple of cm vertically around the nominal focal point position. On the one hand, this property can be an issue for rendering (which we discuss in more detail in Sect. 5.1) but it can also be seen as an advantage with respect to requirements posed for tracking, as there is no reasonable argument for demanding sub-mm accuracy in tracking if the rendering's accuracy cannot follow.

To satisfy requirements toward integration with tracking hardware, most literature solutions in AR and VR interaction rely on optical tracking systems, as these share a similar requirement for unobstructed line-of-sight to the user's skin as UMH devices. These range from custom-built [e.g., Hoshi et al. (2009a), Monnai et al. (2014)] to commercial [e.g., Leap Motion[4] used in Inoue et al. (2014), Matsubayashi et al. (2019), Romanus et al. (2019)] tracking systems, and in the case of AR interaction often leverage inside-out tracking capabilities provided by AR headsets [e.g., the Hololens[5] used in Kervegant et al. (2017) or Magic Leap[6] used in Romanus et al. (2019)].

The majority of work conducted at CNRS presented in this chapter makes use of the HTC Vive Pro system[7] which uses outside-in optical tracking. In it, multiple IR lasers projected from base stations placed around the edges of the VR interaction zone scan the workspace and are picked up by active sensors within the headset, controllers, and trackers, allowing triangulation of the user's body parts and tracked objects. This type of tracker is rather bulky and usually used with straps and is thus not ideal for UMH interaction as they require adequate placement of the straps to keep interaction zones on the skin (e.g., the palm and fingertips) unobstructed. However, there are possibilities for creating adhesive fixtures on the hairy skin, usually not a target for UMH, such as the one we developed in the work by de Tinguy et al. (2020). Most of our use-cases focused on single hand interactions (Howard et al. 2019b, 2021; Marchal et al. 2020), sometimes with additional input through a handheld controller in the hand not interacting with UMH. The use of a tracker allows input over a workspace of the size of the VR interaction zone and however does not provide fine pose information for the hand.

---

[3] https://www.senseglove.com/product/developers-kit/.

[4] https://www.ultraleap.com/product/leap-motion-controller/.

[5] https://www.microsoft.com/en-us/hololens/hardware.

[6] https://www.magicleap.com/en-us/magic-leap-1.

[7] https://www.vive.com/us/product/#pro%20series.

Overall, because of the large interaction zones, 3D workspace, and freedom of user movement, accurate tracking—in particular of the hands—remains an open challenge for haptics in VR interaction in general and even more so in UMH feedback for VR because of the added constraint of keeping the skin free and unobstructed to receive ultrasound tactile feedback.

3.2 Integrating with Feedback Devices

UMH feedback in VR appears to yield the most engaging results in congruent mul-timodal contexts, where the relatively low-fidelity UMH sensations are supported with proper visual and auditory cues to create a compelling experience (Georgiou et al. 2018; Martinez et al. 2018) (see also Chaps. "Opportunities for Multisen-sory Mid-Air Interactions Featuring Ultrasound Haptic Feedback" and "Multimodal Interaction with Mid-Air Haptics").

Integrating UMH into immersive VR likely relies on adequate co-location and syn-chronization of the UMH stimuli with the visual (see Chap. "Superimposing Visual Images on Mid-air Ultrasonic Haptic Stimulation") and auditory stimuli provided through the HMD as well as other haptic stimuli from various other haptic inter-faces. While the extent of this reliance has not been studied for UMH in particular (with the exception of Pittera et al. (2019b), who show that some spatial incongruence may be tolerated), it is reasonable to assume its existence based on prior results on spatially [e.g., Saint-Aubert et al. (2018)] and temporally [e.g., Di Luca and Mahnan (2019)] incongruent stimuli when interacting with virtual environments. Achieving this co-location relies on linking the UMH device frame of reference in which stimuli are positioned with the VE world frame of reference in which other stimuli are posi-tioned, and can be achieved through an initial calibration. While this co-location does not necessarily pose any technical issues with regard to visual or auditory stimuli, co-location with other haptic stimuli can be problematic, either because the actuators delivering those stimuli obstruct the user's skin at the target location, or because of masking effects. We, e.g., regularly observed masking effects when providing simul-taneous UMH and wearable vibrotactile feedback, even when the latter was spatially removed from the site of UMH stimulation. We hypothesize this is mainly due to the differences in stimulus intensities that are achievable between both technologies; however, we have not yet been able to formally evaluate this hypothesis.

Currently, all software dealing with correctly timing outputs for visual, audio, and haptic feedback needs to be developed from scratch, which can prove complex due to the differences in frame rates and requirements between the feedback devices. In order to generate inputs at the frequencies required by UMH devices' transduc-ers (currently usually 40 kHz) and to guarantee the desired temporal modulation of stimulus parameters, the generation of UMH stimuli needs to run on a dedicated thread ensuring output frequency for commands to the device is strictly respected. Considering that in addition, tracking input in immersive VR applications is usually available at frame rates similar to those of the visual feedback, it become apparent that a non-trivial oversampling problem needs to be solved in order to generate UMH feedback that evolves in response to user motion and input. Common solutions to the issue are to generate haptic stimuli independent of user motion, i.e., in a passive manner [e.g., the stimuli used in the perception experiments discussed in Sect. 4.2; Howard et al. (2019a), Mulot et al. (2021b)], to use pre-defined complex stimulus patterns that are triggered by events in the VR interaction [e.g., button-press feedback in Ito et al. (2019) or the sensations corresponding to supernatural phenomena in Martinez et al. (2018)], or to extract frame-rate-independent characteristic values from the tracking input from which UMH feedback can be procedurally generated at whichever frequency is best suited to the UMH device. Such features could, e.g., either be user motion speed or the user's estimated position with respect to pre-defined virtual object features, as is the case in existing works on UMH texture rendering (Beattie et al. 2020; Freeman et al. 2017).

Beyond co-location and synchronization of UMH stimuli with other sensory inputs, it is necessary to ensure UMH devices do not generate unwanted stimuli which may break immersion. By their very nature, UMH devices are somewhat at an advantage over contact haptic devices in this regard as their contactless operation guarantees that with adequate placement, they will not generate unwanted haptic stimuli through contact with the actuator. However, UMH devices can still generate unwanted haptic sensations through two mechanisms. The first is the unintentional generation of airflow around the focal point. This point has been addressed in early literature on UMH device design (Hoshi et al. 2009a; Yoshino and Shinoda 2013). The second is through the generation of side lobes, i.e., other potentially perceptible high-pressure areas occurring in the device workspace due to its function principle. This issue can be addressed to a certain extent through UMH device design (Price and Long 2018), or by using tracking input to activate UMH feedback only when the user is reasonably close to the intended point of stimulation.

Aside from unintended haptic stimuli, UMH devices may produce unintended auditory stimuli. This issue is somewhat secondary in immersive VR as users generally wear headphones occluding outside sounds which may arise from device operation. It can also be addressed to a certain extent through optimizations to rendering algorithms (Hoshi 2016).

It should be pointed out that on the topic of integration with other feedback devices, UMH also brings key opportunities to interaction with virtual environments. For example in the context of AR, the absence of equipment on the user's hand allows seamless integration of the real and virtual visual cues in the interaction area (Kervegant et al. 2017; Romanus et al. 2019). While this does not apply to integration with VR visual feedback, as the user's hand is fully occluded from view, it does apply to concurrent manipulation of tangible objects in a VR setting as the user's hand is kept free from any encumbering device. We plan to investigate this last point in future works.

3.3 Workspace Compatibility

Despite the reasonably large workspace of UMH devices and the ability to freely place and move focal points within it, the workspace of ultrasound arrays rarely matches the large size of VR interaction zones. It is therefore necessary to find solutions to make these workspaces compatible (Fig. 2).

This can be achieved either through software approaches, hardware approaches, or any combination of both. Software approaches to this problem rely on designing the VR interaction to fit within the rendering area of the focused ultrasound array. This can mean shrinking the effective interaction area [e.g., Georgiou et al. (2018), Martinez et al. (2018)], or leveraging redirection techniques. To the best of our knowledge, the latter have not yet been explored for UMH feedback, but there is extensive literature on the subject relating to passive haptic feedback [e.g., Carvalheiro et al. (2016)] which may be applied in this context. Hardware approaches on the other hand aim at enlarging the actual workspace within which UMH feedback can be delivered. This has been achieved through the use of multiple synchronized and larger arrays, an approach discussed in detail in Chap. "Sound-Field Creation for Haptic Reproduction". For example, Inoue et al. (2014) developed a prototype UMH holographic display using four arrays in a cubic arrangement to enable a stronger focus in the center and multi-directional stimuli. A similar arrangement was used in Kimura et al. (2016) and Yoshida et al. (2017), and another with larger arrays was used by Matsubayashi et al. (2019). More recently, passive acoustic reflectors have also been proposed to enlarge the workspace of an array without increasing its complexity (Ariga et al. 2020). Finally, an alternative approach consists in making the UMH arrays mobile, either by mounting them on the user (Sand et al. 2015) or onto robotic manipulators, in an approach akin to encounter-type haptics (Brice et al. 2019).

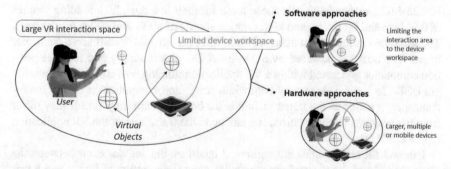

Fig. 2 The workspace compatibility problem: the rendering workspace of UMH devices is usually small compared to the size of VR interaction spaces, limiting the set of virtual objects for which UMH feedback can be provided (left). This issue can be tackled through software (top right), hardware (bottom right), or combined approaches

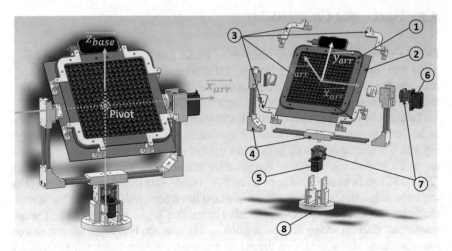

Fig. 3 Assembled (left) and exploded (right) view of the PUMAH. The array (1) is mounted on an aluminum holding plate (2) using 3D-printed ABS clips at the corners (3). The plate rotates around the x_{arr}-axis (tilt) within an aluminum tubing and ABS frame (4), which itself rotates around the device vertical axis z_{base} (pan). The axes are driven by HiTec HS645-MG (5) and HS625-MG (6) servomotors. They are mounted on bearings held within aluminum chassis (7), relieving the motor shafts of any radial loads. The complete system is mounted on a 3D-printed ABS foot (8), which can be screwed to a supporting structure or mounted on a tripod using M6 screws. Adapted from Howard et al. (2019b)

To enlarge the rendering workspace of a UMH device, we have developed an open-source robotic solution for making ultrasound arrays mobile called PUMAH[8] (Howard et al. 2019b).

The device functions as a servo-driven pan and tilt mount for a focused ultrasound array (see Fig. 3). The pan and tilt servomotors are HiTec HS645-MG and HS625-MG,[9] respectively. We chose these for their low cost, high holding torques of 0.94 N m and 0.66 N m, and high rotation speeds of 300/s and 400/s, respectively. The servomotors are driven using a Pololu Mini Maestro-24[10] USB servo controller board. The board is powered by a 5 V, 2.4 A DC power supply and receives position commands generated within a VR application running on a computer connected via USB. To limit unnecessary bandwidth usage and computations on the microcontroller, updates to the target positions for both axes are only sent if they differ from the previous target position, at a rate up to the frame rate of the VR application (approx. 90 Hz).

Pan and tilt error angles are computed based on the angular error between the array normal and the vector from the device pivot (intersection of $Pivot_x$ and $Base_z$ in Fig. 3) to a target defined on an application-specific basis. They are then used as

---

[8] https://gitlab.com/h-reality/pumah.

[9] https://hitecrcd.com/products/servos.

[10] https://www.pololu.com/product/1356.

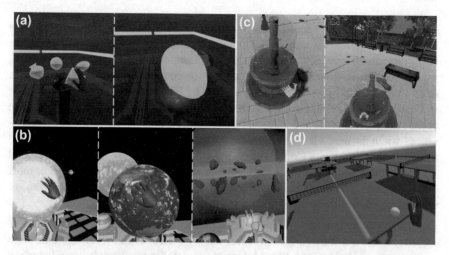

Fig. 4 Interaction use-cases developed to showcase PUMAH's capabilities: **a** touchable holograms; **b** virtual solar system; **c** mid-air haptic fountain; **d** haptic table-tennis. Reproduced from Howard et al. (2021)

commands for the servomotors on each axis. Targets can range from static positions in the VE coordinate frame to dynamic tracking of the user's hand. There are two main steps to integrate the device into a VR environment: an initial calibration and a definition of the target orientation (e.g., through user hand tracking). For calibration, we drive the device to the {0° tilt, 0° pan} position and acquire a known position and orientation of the device base using an HTC Vive tracker. The virtual model of the device (and the virtual scene elements built around it) are then rotated and translated such that they coincide with positions of their real-world counterparts. Once the virtual and real devices are aligned, a target in the workspace needs to be defined and its position computed or acquired through tracking. The vector between the device pivot and target is computed at every frame. The tilt and pan angular errors can be computed by projecting this vector onto the array y–z plane and device base x–z-plane, respectively. To verify the correct execution of the tracking and angle computations, the virtual model of the device is rotated accordingly, thus acting as an ideal representation of our system's target behavior. The computed tilt and pan error angles are then translated into target pulse width modulation (PWM) values for the servomotors based on prior modeling of the relationship between PWM and servo shaft angle.

Our hardware tests and human subject study in an ecological VR setting [reported in Howard et al. (2019b)] show that a 14-fold increase in workspace volume is achievable, with focal point repositioning speeds over 0.85 m/s through device movement alone, and with feedback accuracy below 18 mm in the worst case scenario. We also show that through repositioning of the array to better align it with the user's hand, the PUMAH enables significantly higher stimulus intensities to be delivered throughout the interaction workspace.

We designed a set of interaction use-cases for PUMAH leveraging the device's capabilities in relation to extending the workspace (a and b in Fig. 4) and providing multi-directional feedback (c and d in Fig. 4) (Howard et al. 2021). At the same time, we applied software approaches as previously discussed, designing the interactions to naturally fit within the workspace provided by PUMAH.

Our use-cases are built as four distinct virtual scenes (see Fig. 4). All interactible objects are placed inside the PUMAH's workspace and produce various tactile sensations when the user's hand avatar collides with them. All sensations are generated using Ultrahaptics' Unity Core Asset.[11] To avoid collision between the PUMAH and the user's hand, solid virtual objects are placed in the PUMAH's location in most of the scenes. If the user's hand gets too close to the array, red bounding boxes are shown around the device position to warn the user.

(a) *Touchable holograms*: A holographic projector displays a circular menu of 4 shapes around it (see Fig. 4a). Users use a Vive controller to navigate through the menu of holograms. Fixed intensity vibrotactile feedback is provided when the user's hand collides with the virtual objects. To experience the increase in workspace provided by the PUMAH, the scene also features a button allowing switching between full use of the PUMAH's workspace and use of only the static array's workspace.

(b) *Virtual solar system*: Here, the user can interact with three celestial bodies within a model of the solar system (see Fig. 4b). The sun is similar to the touchable holograms, but also emits solar flares which can be felt as sweeping vibrotactile sensations. For the earth, different sensations are produced when the ocean or land are touched. Finally, the rings of Saturn produce various impact sensations.

(c) *Mid-air haptic fountain*: A fountain is co-located with the PUMAH in the virtual scene, allowing the user's hand to interact with the flowing water from various angles (see Fig. 4b). The tactile sensation is continuously updated to give an impression of water flow around the hand. This demo particularly showcases an application for multi-directional feedback enabled by the PUMAH.

(d) *Haptic table-tennis*: Here, the PUMAH provides haptic feedback for a game of VR ping-pong (see Fig. 4d). Vibrotactile impacts are rendered with an intensity proportional to the ball's impact force on the hand. Because the virtual impacts are so short, we render impacts as a decaying vibration on the hand over a few frames following the actual virtual impact so as to enhance user's perception of the stimuli. This demo was meant to showcase an application or multi-directional UMH feedback and the high device repositioning speed.

4   Perception of UMH Stimuli

Because UMH interfaces are so novel, relatively little is known about the specifics of how UMH stimuli are perceived, nor about the relationship between a stimulus'

---

[11] https://developer.ultrahaptics.com/downloads/unity-plugin/.

parameter and its perceptual qualities. Understanding both these points is a critical challenge for all UMH applications, immersive VR included, for three main reasons. First, it is a key step in determining the usable ranges and discernible levels of stimulus parameters for rendering. Second, it can provide crucial insights into ways for improving the perception of stimuli and overcoming certain limits of UMH technology such as weak perceived intensity and poor spatial definition of the stimuli. Finally, in the context of immersive VR or other multi-modal applications, it is essential to understand how UMH stimuli interact with other haptic, audio, and visual stimuli in order to effectively design interactions.

Early work on perception of UMH stimuli has found that UMH devices are most effective at stimulating the glabrous skin, where they primarily stimulate the Pacinian corpuscles, and as such UMH devices act essentially as vibrotactile devices. There is some evidence that with the proper choice of stimulus parameters, UMH devices are also capable of stimulating non-glabrous skin (Gil et al. 2018) and also activate Meissners corpuscles (Gil et al. 2018; Obrist et al. 2013) as well as slow-adapting tactile receptors (Inoue et al. 2015). Rakkolainen et al. (2020) provide an overview of the state of the art on UMH stimulus perception which goes into more detail on these aspects.

To determine the usable ranges and discernible levels of UMH stimulus parameters, psychophysics studies are conducted with the aim of determining detection and discrimination thresholds. Several studies have focused on this, with some of our own work on the topic (Howard et al. 2019a; Marchal et al. 2020; Mulot et al. 2021b) discussed in more detail in the present section, however given the complexity of UMH stimuli there is still much to be discovered on this subject. We provide an in-depth overview of the state of the art on the subject in the work published by Mulot et al. (2021b).

We have not directly tackled the topic of overcoming limitations of UMH devices with regard to the perceived qualities of the stimuli. However, the framework described in Sect. 4.1 is intended to simplify studies on the topic, such as those conducted by Frier et al. (2018, 2019) on the impact of sampling strategies on perceived stimulus intensity.

Finally, the study of multimodal integration of UMH stimuli has not yet been tackled by our team or most others working on the subject. A notable exception to this is a recent publication by Pittera et al. (2019b) which investigated the effect of presenting spatially incongruous visual and UMH feedback in VR, showing that it can be used to generate the illusion of avatar ownership despite the incongruence.

4.1 DOLPHIN: A Framework for Designing and Studying Perception of UMH Stimuli

A key takeaway from our work on perception of ultrasound tactile feedback was that the high dimensionality of the stimulus design space makes the design and

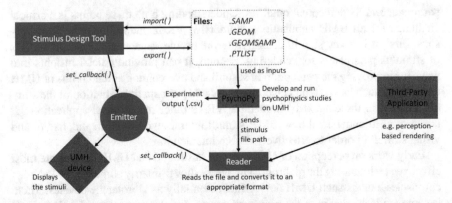

Fig. 5 The DOLPHIN software framework for designing and studying perception of UMH stimuli. Framework components are highlighted in blue, 3rd party components in red. Arrows and their corresponding text show how the different parts are linked. The core of the framework is a stimulus design tool providing full control over spatial, temporal, and intensity aspects of the stimuli in an accessible fashion. Export from the design tool is possible in four formats corresponding to the shape (.GEOM), the sampling strategy (.SAMP), or both (.GEOMSAMP, .PTLIST) with the generic .PTLIST format intended for use in external tools. Stimulus files can be used in experiments or third-party applications thanks to a reader program which sends data to the emitter for rendering. Re-drawn from Mulot et al. (2021b)

study of ultrasound haptic stimuli a very complex task. Indeed, the choice of an UMH stimulus' shape, spatial, temporal, and modulation parameters all interact and impact a user's perception of the stimulus properties as well as perceptual thresholds. To efficiently explore perceptual implications of choices made within this design space, we developed DOLPHIN[12] (Mulot et al. 2021b), an open-source framework facilitating the design of UMH stimuli and designed to interface with 3rd party rendering applications as well as perceptual evaluation tools (see Fig. 5).

At the core of this framework is a stimulus designer tool (see Fig. 5) which helps users configure UMH stimuli, controlling both their geometric shape properties as well as the sampling strategy used to render them. Expanding on the concept introduced by Frier et al. (2019), we define the combination of a spatial discretization of an abstract shape and a set of rules for the temporal display of order and intensity modulation of the resulting points as a sampling strategy (see Fig. 6). Since all UMH stimuli based on focal points can be defined as a temporal sequence of focal point locations in space, DOLPHIN's approach to stimulus design based on discretized geometries remains extremely general and adaptable to almost any UMH rendering scenario.

As touched upon previously, an UMH stimulus has two main aspect. The first concerns the stimulus' spatial properties, i.e., its geometry and position in space (see Fig. 6a). Most of the time the shape can be represented as a parametric function $f : [0, 1]^k \rightarrow \mathbb{R}^3$ whose number of parameters differs depending on the specifics

---

[12] https://gitlab.com/h-reality/dolphin.

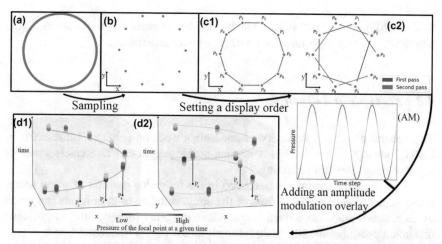

Fig. 6 A sampling strategy represents the process of transforming an abstract geometric shape (**a**) into a UMH stimulus (**d1**, **d2**) through 3 successive steps: spatial discretization (**b**), definition of a temporal display order (**c1** and **c2** show two examples of this for the same spatial discretization), and overlay of a time-dependent amplitude modulation (AM). **d1** and **d2** show the respective application of AM to (**c1**) and (**c2**), with the vertical axis representing time, weak intensities shown in blue and high intensities shown in red. In this example, the dwell time is a third of the AM period. Reproduced from Mulot et al. (2021b)

of the shape. For time-dependent shapes such as a rotating line, a time parameter can be included here. The second aspect of the UMH stimulus is its sampling strategy (see Fig. 6). We define a set of N sampled points $P^s = \{q_i, 0 \leq i < N\}$ s.t. $\forall i, \exists t_{1,i}, \ldots, t_{k,i}, q_i = f(t_{1,i}, \ldots, t_{k,i})$ as a point on the shape. Based on this, the temporal sampling order can be formally defined as a finite series $P^{s,o} = ((P_j, T_j))_j$ where $P_j \in P^s$ for all j and T_j is the dwell time on point P_j. A fully defined configuration is obtained for each timestep $C_k = (P_{j_k}, I_k)$ where $0 \leq j_k < N$ and $I_k = \frac{p(P_j)}{p_{\text{peak}}(P_j)}$ represents the pressure to peak pressure ratio for the device at the position P_j, with $p : \mathbb{R}^3 \to \mathbb{R}^+$. The sampling strategy encompasses all information about how to sample a shape, transforming a potentially continuous shape into a discrete and finite representation. Since the sampling strategy itself is independent of the underlying abstract shape, a same sampling strategy can be applied to different shapes.

DOLPHIN's designer tool provides the user with information about the physical attributes of the designed stimulus and allows haptic previews of the designed stimuli as well as numerous stimulus import and export functions for incremental design and interfacing with 3rd party applications. A more detailed description of the software's inner workings and the interface with 3rd party applications is presented in Mulot et al. (2021b). The framework's objective is thus not only to accelerate the design and psychophysics evaluation process, but also to lower the barriers of entry to the field of UMH, ease communication in the field by standardizing the stimulus design workflow, and ease replication of UMH perceptual experiments.

4.2   Perceptual Thresholds

This section presents a summary of our team's work on perceptual thresholds in UMH, focusing on the need to determine usable ranges and discernible levels of stimulus parameters for rendering.

All perception experiments described in the following used an identical setup, where subjects were seated in front of the array, with one of their hands supported by an armrest, placed at a fixed height above the array (usually 10 cm to achieve maximum possible intensity or 20 cm to allow the largest horizontal extent of perceptible stimuli) with the palm parallel to the array plane. The array used was an Ultraleap STRATOS Explore device, for which changes in intensity ranging between 0 and 100% correspond to acoustic pressure at the focal point between approx. 0–1125 Pa for stimuli centered in a plane 20 cm above the array. Subjects always wore noise-canceling headphones playing pink noise to mask the device operating noise. Instructions were displayed on a computer screen placed directly in front of them, and they provided responses to the experimental questions through a keyboard operated with their non-dominant hand.

Intensity detection thresholds All our experiments aimed at determining detection thresholds used 1-up, 1-down staircase methods, with the threshold estimate taken as the mean of the last 8 of 9 reversals. 15 healthy subjects (8 male, 7 female; ages 22–32 ($M = 25$); 2 left-, 13 right-handed) participated in a first experiment aimed at evaluating the 50%-detection threshold for a single focal point generated 20 cm above the array using AM, both in a passive touch (immobile hand) and an active touch (moving hand) condition (see Fig. 7a). The focal point's amplitude was modulated at a frequency 200 Hz as this is close to peak sensitivity for vibrotaction in humans.

We determined the 50%-detection threshold for a single focal point generated with AM, finding it to be largely independent of hand movement and on average between 48.7 and 49.5% intensity, i.e., approx. 560 Pa peak acoustic pressure (see Fig. 7b).

Our second experiment evaluated the detection threshold for a 15 cm line pattern rendered through spatiotemporal modulation (STM) (Kappus and Long 2018). Given that user motion had no impact on AM focal point detection, we hypothesized this to hold true for STM and only investigated an active condition. Instead, we chose to investigate possible effects of line orientation relative to the hand. Subjects were presented with lines aligned with the device x- or y-axis at a height of 20 cm (see Fig. 8a). We selected a focal point movement speed of 7 m/s, which is close to the best perceived intensity (Frier et al. 2018). The experiment was performed in two parts: the first one investigated the detection threshold regardless of the perceived pattern (50%-detection), while the second one investigated the intensity required for users to reliably feel the displayed pattern as a line (50%-identification threshold).

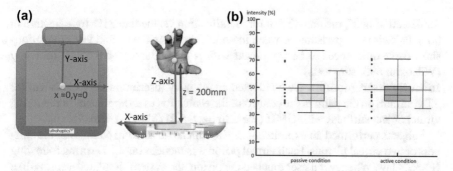

Fig. 7 a Schematic of the stimulus and user hand placement. A fixed AM focal point was generated at $(0, 0, 20\,cm)$ in the array's frame of reference, and the user's hand was either placed with the center of the palm fixed at the focal point position (passive touch condition) or free to explore the plane at $z = 20\,cm$ in the array's frame of reference. **b** Mean subject 50%-detection threshold estimates for both conditions. Blue dots show the actual values, boxes the interquartile range (IQR), the blue horizontal line shows the median while the red lines show the mean plus or minus one standard deviation. Adapted from Howard et al. (2019a)

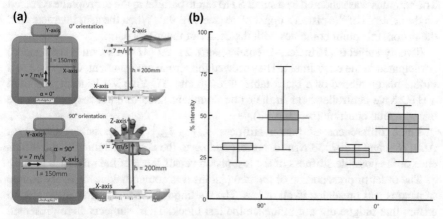

Fig. 8 a Schematic of the stimuli and user hand placement. 15 cm STM lines were displayed in a plane 20 cm above the array in one of two possible orientations relative to the user's hand. **b** Mean subject 50% detection (yellow) and identification (blue) thresholds. The boxplots show the median, IQR, and total spread of values while the horizontal red lines show the mean for all subjects. Adapted from Howard et al. (2019a)

Subjects responded to the binary questions "Did you feel a stimulus?" and "Did you feel a line?" for the detection and identification experiments, respectively. 7 healthy subjects (5 male, 2 female, ages 22–32 (mean: 27.2), all right-handed) participated in the STM detection thresholds experiment, and 12 different healthy subjects (9 male, 3 female, ages 22–47 (mean: 28.3), 11 right handed, 1 left handed) participated in the STM identification thresholds experiment.

For both the 0° and 90° orientations, the measured identification thresholds are well above the detection thresholds (median 46% for identification vs. median 29.6%

for detection in $0°$, median 47.8% for identification vs. median 31% for detection in $90°$). Pairwise comparisons between these thresholds in the $0°$ and $90°$ orientations show these differences to be significant with $p < 0.05$ and $p < 0.01$, respectively (Wilcoxon rank-sum tests).

Intensity discrimination We conducted an intensity discrimination experiment for STM stimuli on the palm in the context of the evaluation of an approach for rendering virtual object stiffness with UMH (see also Sect. 5.2) (Marchal et al. 2020).

Subjects performed an experiment in VR which consisted in comparing the stiffness of two virtual pistons. Each virtual piston was modeled as a 1-D spring following Hooke's law. Whenever a user touched the piston, the system simulated a spring-like feedback, where the pressure generated at the focal point by the array was defined by $p = k(z_0 - z) + p_0$ if the user touched the piston, 0 otherwise. k is the simulated stiffness of the piston (in Pa/m, sound pressure over displacement), z the current stroke of the piston, $z_0 = 30$ cm its free length, $\Delta z = z_0 - z$ its current travel, and $p_0 = 146.87$ dB SPL (441 Pa) the absolute detection threshold we registered at 30 cm (when $\Delta z = 0$). The pistons were fully compressed at $z = 20$ cm ($\Delta z_{max} = 10$ cm). The stimulus was rendered as a small STM circle parallel to the array plane centered on the centroid of the piston's upper plate (see Fig. 9a). When the user interacts with the piston, this point coincides with the center of the user's palm.

Twenty subjects (16 males, 4 females, ages 21–29 ($M = 24$), all right-handed) participated in the experiment. They viewed the virtual environment, composed of a virtual piston placed on a black table, through an HTC Vive VR headset, and used a HTC Vive controller held in their non-dominant hand to enter responses to the experimental question (see Fig. 9b).

Three differences of piston stiffness $|k_{ref} - k_{test}|$ were possible: 0.001176, 0.001764, and 0.002353 N/mm, corresponding to the absolute values of the difference of the possible stiffness of the test piston versus those of the reference piston.

The order of presentation of the two pistons was counterbalanced: Every couple of pistons was presented in all orders. The starting reference was also alternated to ensure that fatigue did not influence the last block. Thus, subjects were presented with 90 trials per reference stiffness (270 in total), divided into 5 blocks of 6 trials in a randomized order for each block.

Figure 10 shows the psychometric functions obtained for each of the three considered references stiffnesses. For the reference stiffness K_{ref1}, we obtained a 75%-Just Noticeable Difference (JND) value of 20% and the Point of Subjective Equality (PSE) at +2.16%. For K_{ref2}, the 75%-JND was of 32% and PSE of +3.65%. Our results for K_{ref3} differed from the others as we were not able to reach proportions of correct answers close to 1 on the right-hand side of the curve. This could have been due to the pressure being delivered at K_{ref3} being close to the device maximum output (at 80% of the maximum). Also in this condition, subjects often reported feeling the displayed shape changing from a circle into something else. We therefore evaluated the psychometric only taking into account the stiffness intensities for which users reported feeling a circular shape (blue points in Fig. 10), yielding a 75%-JND of 18% and PSE of +0.58%.

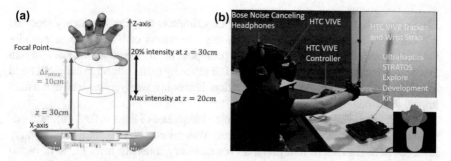

Fig. 9 Intensity discrimination experiment: **a** schematic of the feedback design, the user feels an STM stimulus centered on their palm as they interact with a virtual piston. The intensity goes from its minimum values at a height of 30 cm above the board to its maximum at a height of 20 cm above the board. **b** Experimental setup and view of the VE through the HTC Vive HMD. Users hold their dominant hand outstretched over a table holding the UMH device to press on the virtual piston, while wearing noise-canceling headphones to avoid any bias due to device operating noise. Reproduced from Marchal et al. (2020)

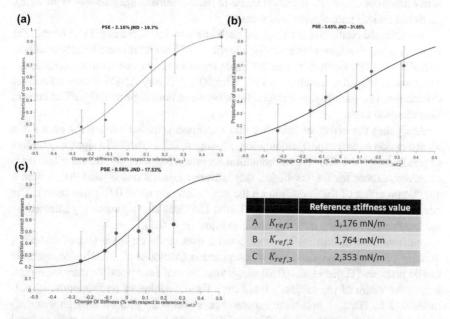

Fig. 10 Psychometric curves for the three reference stiffness values, fitting a cumulative Gaussian to the data. We plot the proportion of correct answers as a function of the percentage increase in stiffness with respect to the reference $k_{\text{ref},i}$. The vertical dashed and solid lines represent the PSE and the 75%-JND, respectively. Error bars represent standard deviation. Adapted from Marchal et al. (2020)

Line orientation discrimination In our experiments, subjects repeatedly reported a certain degree of confusion regarding the orientation of STM lines, especially those rendered at lower intensities. This prompted us to investigate line orientation discrimination performance and the effect of intensity on it. Although subject's hand movement was not found to impact detection thresholds, we hypothesized that it may impact discrimination of orientations.

Subjects were presented with a randomized sequence of lines in four different orientations, $\alpha = f0°; 45°; 90°; 135°$, at three different intensity levels, a low-intensity level (54% of maximum intensity), an intermediary intensity level (77% of maximum intensity), and a high intensity level (100% of maximum intensity). For each stimulus, they were asked to attribute it to one of the four possible orientations. The low intensity level was chosen to be above the 50%-identification threshold of 90% of the sample population (see Sect. 4.2).

Subjects performed two trial blocks with 120 trials each (10 for each pair of intensity and orientation levels), one block in a passive touch condition, one in an active touch condition. 10 healthy subjects (8 male, 2 female, ages 22–44 ($M = 27.2$), all right handed) participated in the study.

We obtained confusion matrices for each intensity level (see Fig. 11). Overall, the majority of orientations were correctly identified. 0° lines were occasionally confused with 45° or 135°, but never with 90° lines (both in active and passive conditions). The most confused orientation is 135° with 90°. A 2-way ANOVA showed neither orientation, nor intensity, nor interactions between both significantly affect correct identification rates.

Analyzing the effect of intensity and condition (passive vs. active) on correct identification rates for the 0° orientation, a 2-way ANOVA showed a significant effect of condition ($p < 0.01$) on discrimination accuracy. No other significant effect were observed, except for the confusion rate between orientations 0° and 90°, where a significant effect of the condition on the confusion rate ($p < 0.05$) was found. The confusion rate between orientations 90° and 135° was also significantly affected by the interaction between intensity and condition ($p < 0.1$).

Curvature discrimination We conducted a user study on the effect of sampling strategy parameters on curvature discrimination (Mulot et al. 2021b) for dynamic tactile pointers (Hajas et al. 2020) displaying arcs of four possible curvature radii across the width of the subject's hand for a fixed duration of two seconds. 19 volunteers (2 f., 16 m., 1 non-binary, mean age $\pm$ std = 23 $\pm$ 3.4), all right-handed) participated in the experiment. The four different ratios of curvature radii to hand width were equal to $\frac{1}{\pi}$ (semi-circle), $\frac{3}{2\pi}$, $\frac{5}{2\pi}$, ∞ (straight line). For the computations, the radius to hand width ratio for the straight line was set to 1.99 which is the smallest ratio ensuring the height difference at the edge of the hand remained smaller than the radius of a focal point (see Fig. 12).

We evaluated five sampling strategies with different numbers of spatial sampling points ($n = $ 10, 50, 200, 400, and 800), resulting in dwell times on each point of $t = \frac{2}{n}$ s. Based on Hajas et al.'s work (2020), the static amplitude modulation frequency was set 200 Hz. Each stimulus was displayed 10 cm above the array and the tactile pointer always moved from the thumb side toward the pinkie.

PASSIVE CONDITION — Minimum intensity (54%)

Actual \ Perceived	0°	45°	90°	135°
0°	99.3%	0.7%	0%	0%
45°	4%	94%	2%	0%
90°	0%	3.4%	95.6%	1%
135°	4%	1%	5.7%	89.3%

PASSIVE CONDITION — Intermediary intensity (77%)

Actual \ Perceived	0°	45°	90°	135°
0°	99.3%	0.7%	0%	0%
45°	6%	93%	1%	0%
90°	0%	3.9%	95.1%	1%
135°	2%	1%	3.1%	93.9%

PASSIVE CONDITION — Maximum intensity (100%)

Actual \ Perceived	0°	45°	90°	135°
0°	99.2%	0.8%	0%	0%
45°	7%	89%	2%	2%
90°	0%	5.3%	92.7%	2%
135°	3%	0%	1%	96%

ACTIVE CONDITION — Minimum intensity (54%)

Actual \ Perceived	0°	45°	90°	135°
0°	97%	2%	0%	1%
45°	2%	96%	2%	0%
90°	2%	2%	96%	0%
135°	2%	1%	1%	96%

ACTIVE CONDITION — Intermediary intensity (77%)

Actual \ Perceived	0°	45°	90°	135°
0°	93%	5%	0%	2%
45°	3%	97%	0%	0%
90°	1%	4%	95%	0%
135°	3%	2%	1%	94%

ACTIVE CONDITION — Maximum intensity (100%)

Actual \ Perceived	0°	45°	90°	135°
0°	95%	3%	0%	2%
45°	2%	95%	0%	3%
90°	1%	2%	92%	5%
135°	1%	1%	5%	93%

Fig. 11 Mean confusion matrices for each condition. Correct identification rates are highlighted in green. The most prevalent confusions are highlighted in orange, the second most prevalent in yellow. Reproduced from Howard et al. (2019a)

The experiment was divided into five blocks corresponding to each of the five studied sampling strategies. Each block followed a two-alternatives forced choice protocol where pairs of stimuli with different curvatures were presented with a 1.5 s break between them, after which users had to indicate which felt closest to a straight line. Stimulus pairs were repeated three times per block, yielding a total of thirty-six trials per block. The pair order within blocks and the order of blocks were randomized.

For each user and each strategy, we plotted the proportion of 'stimulus is flatter than the reference' answers against the relative difference in curvature for each of the four references, as shown in Fig. 13. For a reference stimulus with radius r_1 and test stimulus with radius r_2, the x value corresponding to the pair was $\frac{c_2 - c_1}{c_1}$, where $c_i = \frac{1}{r_i}$ corresponds to the curvature of an arc with radius r_i. We added the hypothetical point at $(0, 0.5)$ corresponding to a fully random answer when both stimuli are identical. We then fitted the set of observations with a cumulative Gaussian centered on 0 and used the curves to calculate the 75%-JND estimate in curvature for this user, strategy, and reference. The obtained JND is thus expressed as the Weber fraction in curvature (see Fig. 13).

Outlier JND values (values greater than $Q_{75\%} + 1.5 IQR$ where $Q_{75\%}$ is the 75% quartile and IQR is the interquartile) were removed, yielding mean subject JND distributions for each strategy (see Fig. 13f). These distributions were assumed to be normal (Shapiro-Wilk test did not reject H_0 with $p > 0.05$ for all five distributions). We therefore performed an ANOVA which revealed no significant difference between strategies in terms of mean resulting JND in curvature ($F = 1.676$, $p = 0.165$). We conclude that when designing dynamic tactile pointers, the number of points used for the sampling strategy does not have a significant impact on users' ability to

(a)

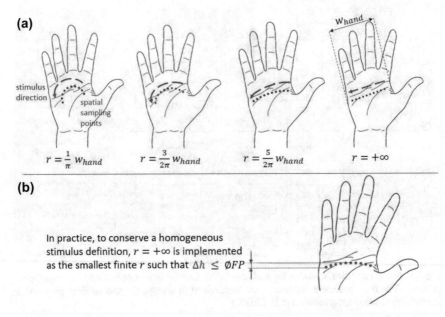

(b)

In practice, to conserve a homogeneous
stimulus definition, $r = +\infty$ is implemented
as the smallest finite r such that $\Delta h \leq \varnothing FP$

Fig. 12 Curvature discrimination experiment stimuli: **a** we used four different curvature radii for curves scanning across the hand from the thumb toward the pinkie (as indicated by the red arrow). The curvatures were defined in relation to subject hand width w_{hand} using a ratio k such that $r = k.w_{hand}$. **b** In theory, the flat line stimulus would require $k = +\infty$; however, in practice we consider a curve to be effectively flat if k is sufficiently large so as to ensure that the difference in height between the center and the end of a curve is inferior to the diameter of a focal point $\varnothing FP$ (yielding $k \geq 1.99$). Each curve was uniformly divided into n spatial sampling points ($n = 10, 50, 200, 400,$ and 800). In the interest of readability, only the sampling points for stimuli with $n = 10$ are graphically represented by the purple dots

discriminate arc curvatures. The mean JNDs obtained were 0.98, 0.98, 1.33, 1.05, and 1.11 for the strategies with $n = 10, 50, 200, 400,$ and 800 points, respectively.

The presence of success rates above 50% in most cases shows that curvature discrimination is indeed possible for UMH dynamic tactile pointers, regardless of the sampling strategy used for rendering. However, curvature discrimination still appeared rather complex to perform on the haptic stimuli alone, echoing prior results on shape identification and discrimination for UMH. The number of spatial sampling points (and thus the dwell time per point) did not appear to significantly impact discrimination performance, meaning that UMH stimulus designers have more freedom when designing such stimuli as the strategy will likely not adversely impact stimulus discrimination.

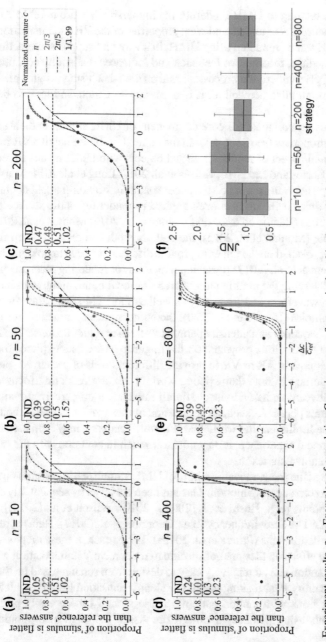

Fig. 13 Experiment results. **a–e** Examples of cumulative Gaussian curves fit to a single subject's results for each strategy, with one curve fit per reference stimulus. The proportions of "stimulus flatter than reference" answers from the user are plot against the Weber fraction in curvature. For a stimulus with radius r_i, the curvature c_i is defined as $\frac{1}{r_i}$ and the Weber fraction with stimulus 1 as a reference is defined as $\frac{c_2 - c_1}{c_1}$. JND estimates for this strategy are reported on the left. **f** Box plot of the mean JNDs obtained for each strategy, using the average of the four JNDs corresponding to the different reference stimuli for each user and strategy. Red lines represent the mean and one standard deviation. Adapted in part from Mulot et al. (2021b)

5   UMH Rendering

Challenges relating to UMH rendering for immersive VR are twofold. On the one hand, it is necessary to understand what properties of the VE and interaction between user and VE can be rendered using UMH, in a way that supports interaction by providing immediate, informative feedback and increases realism by accurately representing the VE's underlying processes. And on the other, using insights gleaned from the study of stimulus perception, it is necessary to understand how to best render said properties.

As discussed previously, a core component of UMH stimuli is their spatial and geometric properties (see Sect. 4.1). In the context of 3D immersive VR interaction, a fundamental aspect of rendering virtual objects with UMH is thus to render their 3D shape (Korres and Eid 2016; Korres et al. 2017; Long et al. 2014; Martinez et al. 2019) and position in space, i.e., to render spatial information about contacts.

Beyond this, UMH has also been applied to rendering tactile surface properties such as textures (Beattie et al. 2020; Freeman et al. 2017; Monnai et al. 2015). In the first example (Monnai et al. 2015), the authors modulate the waveform for an AM focal point projected on the finger to provide different textures to holographic UI elements. Freeman et al. (2017) presented a method for rendering macroscopic texture features by varying the motion path of an STM focal point, along with its intensity, modulation waveform and frequency as well as the STM shape draw frequency. In the last examples (Beattie et al. 2020), the authors present a method for extracting STM draw frequency and intensity parameters from graphics textures. These are then applied to a small circle projected on the fingertip as the user explores the visually rendered textures in AR or VR to provide different levels of perceived roughness.

It is important to note that existing work on texture rendering focuses on congruence between tactile and visual stimuli rather than on perceived realism of the tactile textures per se. As such, an application of these methods to VR should always consider the limitation that while UMH texture feedback may help create a coherent multi-modal experience, it may not have much in common with the represented real-world equivalent texture.

Because of the freely movable nature of UMH stimuli, early research on rendering also focused on rendering motion. This has been achieved by sequentially displaying AM focal points [e.g., Hoshi et al. (2009b, 2010), Wilson et al. (2014)], adequate selection of STM draw frequency [e.g., Georgiou et al. (2017), Hajas et al. (2020)], or even tactile illusions (Pittera et al. 2019a). While each of these methods has been shown to be effective, they are not specific to immersive VR. Interaction with virtual objects in motion can be relatively easy to design from scratch based on the research cited above or by, e.g., making use of Ultraleap's Sensation Editor[13] which provides preset sensations with motion patterns. These stimuli can be easily ported to VR environments using Ultraleap's Unity Core Asset.[14] Stimuli incorporating motion

---

[13] https://developer.ultrahaptics.com/downloads/sensation-editor/.

[14] https://developer.ultrahaptics.com/downloads/unity-plugin/.

have been showcased in VR demos using UMH feedback (Georgiou et al. 2018; Martinez et al. 2018).

Since UMH relies on a fluid coupling between the actuator and the skin (vibrations and pressure are transmitted through the air), physical properties that can be rendered in an ecological manner encompass interactions with fluids (Barreiro et al. 2020; Jang and Park 2020). Barreiro et al. (2020) simulate the pressure field on the surface of the skin as a result of the hand coming into contact with virtual fluids, and then use a custom algorithm to extract an STM stimulus path and intensity modulation from the data in interactive time. While this example is implemented with the virtual scene displayed on a screen, there are no inherent limitations to porting the visual display to a HMD and thus applying them to immersive VR. Jang and Park (2020) propose an alternative particle-based fluids simulation from which they extract modulation parameters for multiple AM focal points projected on the user's hand. They demonstrate the function of this approach in an immersive VR use-case where users interact with various liquid streams, sprays, rainfall, or fountains.

Finally, UMH feedback has also largely been applied to the rendering of abstract information to support interaction. Some of these cues are purely abstract [e.g., Dzidek et al. (2018), Van den Bogaert and Geerts (2020)], others are designed to be evocative of underlying virtual mechanism [e.g., mid-air buttons (Ito et al. 2019)]. Dzidek et al. (2018) design and evaluate a set of abstract UMH stimuli to support a wide range of interactions in an AR demonstrator. Van den Bogaert and Geerts (2020) present a study on the selection of abstract UMH patterns intended for providing users with feedback when interacting with menus in mid-air in AR. Their study demonstrate a notable preference for relatively simple stimulus design when the aim is to support interaction, with a strong focus on the use of stimulus intensity and temporal parameters (continuous vs. discrete) as rendering parameters. In a VR application, Frutos-Pascual et al. (2019) demonstrate the usefulness of abstract UMH feedback cues to the palm to indicate successful grasping of virtual objects, in particular during manipulation of smaller objects.

Building on the understanding of stimulus perception discussed in Sect. 4, we are interested in understanding what properties of interactions with virtual objects can be effectively rendered with mid-air ultrasound haptics. On this topic, we have explored the use of stimulus intensity to encode information about shape and stiffness of virtual objects.

5.1 Rendering Local Shape

As previously discussed, the ability to rapidly move the focal point in the UMH device's 3D workspace makes it an ideal candidate for rendering shape and geometric features. As such, STM patterns displayed in planes parallel to the device can be perceived relatively accurately, as the extent of the perceptible high-pressure region around the focal point is usually considered to be on the order of one wavelength of ultrasound in air, i.e., approx. 8 mm (see Fig. 14-left). However, due to

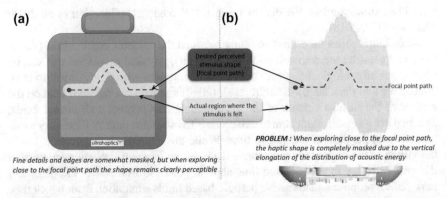

(a)

Desired perceived
stimulus shape
(focal point path)

Actual region where the
stimulus is felt

ultrahaptics▽

*Fine details and edges are somewhat masked, but when exploring
close to the focal point path the shape remains clearly perceptible*

(b)

Focal point path

PROBLEM : *When exploring close to the focal point path,
the haptic shape is completely masked due to the vertical
elongation of the distribution of acoustic energy*

Fig. 14 Examples of shapes rendered in **a** a plane parallel to the device and **b** a plane perpendicular to the device. The red dotted line shows the focal point path while the yellow area schematically represents the area in which a stimulus is perceptible. As the user's hand explores the shapes close to the focal point path, it becomes obvious that lateral deviations of this path within a plane parallel to the device (**a**) can relatively easily be detected whereas vertical deviations within a plan perpendicular to the device (**b**) cannot

the function principle of focused ultrasound arrays, these perceptible high-pressure regions around the focal point tend to extend vertically over heights up to several cm, meaning that rendering small changes in height of a shape above the board is compromised, as close to the focal point path, these are completely masked by the vertical elongation of the focal point (see Fig. 14-right). It should also be noted that even in the most favorable case, i.e., rendering a shape in a plane parallel to the device, shape identification performance has been shown to be quite poor (Rutten et al. 2019), although some methods have been proposed to improve it [e.g., Hajas et al. (2020)].

We therefore proposed rendering such local shape features along the array's z-axis by keeping the focal point path in a plane parallel to the device, but varying the stimulus intensity along that path to generate the illusion of bumps or holes as the user explores the stimulus (Howard et al. 2019a) (see Fig. 15-left).

We investigated the effectiveness of this rendering approach by performing a shape identification experiment in which users had to identify a given pattern among 5 possible shapes: a bump, a hole, and three lines of different intensities (low, medium and high) acting as confounders. Similar to our perception experiments on STM shape detection and identification thresholds (see Sect. 4.2), we once again performed a preliminary investigation into potential effects of line orientation on shape identification performance (see Fig. 15-right).

For this initial investigation, we chose to use the largest possible difference between baseline and peak intensity for the bump and hole patterns to maximize chances of correct identification.

12 healthy subjects (8 male, 4 female; ages 23–30 ($M = 25.3$); 10 right-handed, 2 left-handed) took part in the experiment. They performed two blocks of 90 trials,

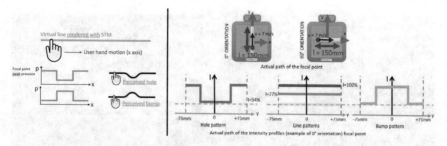

Fig. 15 (Left) Proposed rendering concept for small changes in height of a shape above the board: shapes are rendered as STM patterns within a plane parallel to the device, while the intensity of the focal point is varied as a function of the linear coordinate along the shape. Drops in intensity are expected to be perceived as holes while increases in intensity are expected to be perceived as bumps. (Right) Stimuli used for our user study evaluating this approach: subjects were presented with one of five patterns (hole, 3 lines of different intensities, bump) in one of two possible orientations. Adapted in part from Howard et al. (2019a)

with blocks divided according to pattern orientation, and 30 trials occurring for each possible shape. The order of trials was fully randomized and the block order counterbalanced.

Overall, our results showed that identification rates were well above chance (30% correct) for all shapes in both considered orientations, indicating that subjects were capable of correctly attributing the stimuli to the intended shapes. However, confusion rates between presented shapes ranged from 9.7% (confusion between bumps and holes) to as high as 25.3% (confusion between bumps and lines), indicating that the rendering approach is currently insufficient to reliably generate the desired percepts, at least with UMH feedback alone. Similarly to our prior study on STM line detection thresholds, shape orientation did not appear to have a significant impact on identification or confusion of shapes. A detailed analysis of identification and confusion rates is presented by Howard et al. (2019a).

While these results highlight certain limitations of this rendering approach, they are nonetheless encouraging as performances were well above chance level in the studied haptic-only identification task. In the future, we wish to investigate how congruent visual stimuli may affect perceived realism of the haptic shapes and possibly increase shape identification performance.

5.2 Rendering Stiffness

We applied insights into the discrimination of intensities discussed in Sect. 4.2 to rendering stiffness of virtual elements through the variation of stimulus intensity proportionally to the virtual reaction force. It should be kept in mind that this approach to rendering stiffness differs from actual force feedback as one would obtain from interacting with a real stiff object or, e.g., a grounded force feedback device, simply

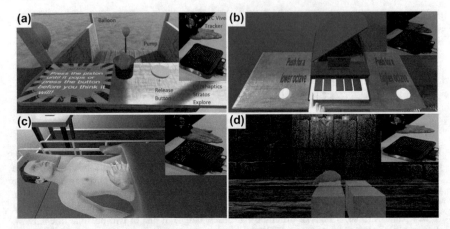

Fig. 16 Four VR scenes exemplifying our approach to rendering stiffness of virtual objects: **a** users inflate balloons at a carnival fair by pressing on a piston whose stiffness increases proportionally to the balloon's inflation; **b** users play a virtual piano. The action of pressing down on the keys is rendered using an STM stimulus, and the key's stiffness (a function of its place in the register) affects the stimulus intensity; **c** virtual medical palpation: users are instructed to find stiffer parts on a virtual patient's abdomen based on the STM stimulus used to render the contact; **d** virtual puzzle game requiring users to press down on identical-looking blocks in ascending order of stiffness to unlock a treasure. Adapted from Marchal et al. (2020)

because there is no solid boundary resisting the user's motion. Similar to the prior discussion on texture roughness rendering, this approach to rendering stiffness aims at creating a perceptually coherent evocation of stiffness rather than rendering it in a manner true to life. However, when asked whether the sensation delivered by the UMH device in the study discussed in Sect. 4.2 resembled stiffness, 80% of subjects responded that it did. The remaining 20% could not clearly describe the physical nature of the stimulus but still recognized an increase in force. When asked to describe the sensations they felt, answers ranged from "feeling a real piston" to feeling a "stream," "circular air flows," and "some kind of resistance." It therefore appeared reasonable that this approach to rendering could elicit a perceptual experience which was coherent with the idea of virtual object stiffness.

The perceptual study conducted on intensity discrimination (see Sect. 4.2) showed that users could not only discriminate between three and five intensity levels within the perceptible range, but also correlated changes in perceived intensity during pressing of a virtual object with the object's stiffness. This rendering approach was therefore implemented in a 4-part VR use-case (see Fig. 16). The first depicted a scene at a carnival fair featuring a pump for inflating virtual balloons (see Fig. 16a). Users inflated the balloon by repeatedly pressing on the pump. A small STM circle of varying intensity was displayed at the contact location between the virtual piston's handle and the user's hand, with the intensity gradually increasing as the pressure inside the balloon increases, providing the user with the feeling of a pump with increasing stiffness.

The second use-case implemented a scenario similar to that presented by Hwang et al. (2017), presenting a small 1-octave virtual piano whose octave could be lowered or raised using a pair of virtual buttons on the side (see Fig. 16b). Real piano keys are generally weighted, with a higher key stiffness for the lower register and lower stiffness for the higher register. We render four octaves, each with a variable degree of stiffness rendered through a small STM circle projected on the user's fingertip when it contacts a key.

The third use-case presents a proof of concept of an application to virtual medical palpation (see Fig. 16c), where users can palpate a virtual character's abdomen, sensing regions of different stiffness in a task where they are instructed to point out the stiffer regions than the surrounding tissue.

Finally, a last use-case presents a virtual treasure-hunt game in a fantasy setting where users must press on four blocks in order of increasing stiffness in order to unlock the treasure (see Fig. 16d). The blocks are visually identical, forcing the user to rely purely on the haptic feedback to solve the puzzle.

While functional, this approach is still somewhat limited by multiple factors. First, the usable intensity ranges for UMH stimuli is generally quite restricted. For example, with the Ultraleap Stratos Explore[15] device used in our work, given the detection thresholds (see Sect. 4.2) and JNDs for stiffness (see Sect. 4.2), it is expected that only up to five levels of stimulus intensity can be distinguished. In the future, it may be possible to increase this resolution by using more powerful devices or possibly using other parameters such as STM draw frequency (Frier et al. 2018) to increase the stimulus's apparent intensity. An additional limitation comes from the fact that for stimuli whose base intensity was above 162.43 dB SPL, users no longer appeared to be able to discriminate intensity in a way that fit observations made at lower intensities as the perceived nature of the sensation changed from appearing as a small circle to something entirely different (Marchal et al. 2020). Further investigation into the acoustic phenomena occurring in this situation may provide solutions for overcoming this issue.

6 Conclusion and Perspectives

This chapter presented a brief overview of research conducted at CNRS-IRISA on the topic of bringing ultrasound mid-air haptic (UMH) feedback to virtual reality interactions, within the context of the broader state of the art of UMH for 3D user interfaces both in augmented and in virtual reality.

We tackled three groups of challenges, relating to device integration, stimulus perception and rendering, with the aim of better understanding the contributions UMH can make to immersive VR experiences, as well as to propose and evaluate novel approaches for designing these interactions.

---

[15] https://www.ultraleap.com/product/stratos-explore/.

This work has yielded a novel robotic system aimed at enlarging a UMH interface's workspace, making it more compatible with the requirements of immersive VR (Howard et al. 2019b). It also led to the development of a software framework facilitating the design and evaluation of UMH stimuli (Mulot et al. 2021b) as well as numerous insights into UMH stimulus perception (Howard et al. 2019a; Marchal et al. 2020; Mulot et al. 2021a, b). Finally, some novel rendering approaches for virtual object properties based on stimulus intensity variation were also proposed (Howard et al. 2019a; Marchal et al. 2020).

There is still much to be learned on the topic of integrating UMH into immersive VR. Fundamentally, the absence of physical contact in UMH interaction and the characteristics of UMH stimuli provide both limitations that need to be worked around and opportunities for designing unique immersive VR interaction techniques.

We plan to extend our work on adapting the workspace of UMH devices to VR interactions, through hard- and software solutions that will enable, e.g., novel bimanual and fine manipulations with UMH feedback. There are also many exciting avenues for exploration on the use of UMH with concurrent haptic feedback, and manipulation combining UMH with tangible objects. Approaches of this type could allow to complement UMH stimulus properties and overcome the technology's limitations; however, they pose major challenges both in terms of device integration and rendering. Finally, there is also a need to investigate solutions to effectively overcome issues associated with the physical footprint of UMH devices, through, e.g., approaches to collision avoidance in VR and visual occlusion in AR. Many of the technical aspects of rendering and integration touched upon in this chapter will become clearer in the upcoming chapters focused on the theory, technological implementation, and safety of UMH.

On the topic of UMH stimulus perception, there is still much to be learned from the psychophysical study of UMH stimuli. Even more importantly, it will be necessary to study cross-modal interactions between UMH and other haptics, as well as between UMH, visual, and auditory feedback, as immersive VR interaction is inherently multimodal. The next chapter (Chap. "Multimodal Interaction with Mid-Air Haptics") will tackle this aspect in more detail.

These insights will lead to the development of many novel approaches and application scenarios for UMH rendering. Furthermore, there is an urgent need for investigating novel interaction techniques and metaphors to leverage the unique properties and compensate for the limitations of UMH technology.

The development of more advanced VR interaction techniques leveraging UMH will open up perspectives for studying the impact of UMH on virtual interaction performance, user immersion, and presence, as well as embodiment toward virtual avatars and factors relating to user engagement and affect.

Acknowledgements This project has received funding from the European Union's Horizon 2020 program under grant agreement No 801413; project "H-Reality."

References

Arafsha F, Zhang L, Dong H, El Saddik A (2015) Contactless haptic feedback: state of the art. In: 2015 IEEE International symposium on haptic, audio and visual environments and games (HAVE). IEEE, pp 1–6

Ariga K, Fujiwara M, Makino Y, Shinoda H (2020) Midair haptic presentation using concave reflector. In: International conference on human haptic sensing and touch enabled computer applications. Springer, Berlin, pp 307–315

Balint P, Althoefer K (2018) Medical virtual reality palpation training using ultrasound based haptics and image processing. In: Proc. Jt. Work. New Technol. Comput. Assist. Surg

Barreiro H, Sinclair S, Otaduy MA (2020) Path routing optimization for STM ultrasound rendering. IEEE Trans Haptics 13(1):45–51

Beattie D, Frier W, Georgiou O, Long B, Ablart D (2020) Incorporating the perception of visual roughness into the design of mid-air haptic textures. In: ACM Symposium on applied perception, pp 1–10

Brice D, McRoberts T, Rafferty K (2019) A proof of concept integrated multi-systems approach for large scale tactile feedback in VR. In: International conference on augmented reality, virtual reality and computer graphics. Springer, Berlin, pp 120–137

Carter T, Seah SA, Long B, Drinkwater B, Subramanian S (2013) Ultrahaptics: multi-point mid-air haptic feedback for touch surfaces. In: Proceedings of the 26th annual ACM symposium on user interface software and technology, pp 505–514

Carvalheiro C, Nóbrega R, da Silva H, Rodrigues R (2016) User redirection and direct haptics in virtual environments. In: Proceedings of the 24th ACM international conference on multimedia, pp 1146–1155

Chatzopoulos D, Bermejo C, Huang Z, Hui P (2017) Mobile augmented reality survey: from where we are to where we go. IEEE Access 5:6917–6950

Cirio G, Marchal M, Otaduy MA, Lécuyer A (2013) Six-DoF haptic interaction with fluids, solids, and their transitions. In: 2013 World haptics conference (WHC). IEEE, pp 157–162

Corenthy L, Giordano M, Hayden R, Griffiths D, Jeffrey C, Limerick H, Georgiou O, Carter T, Müller J, Subramanian S (2018) Touchless tactile displays for digital signage: mid-air haptics meets large screens. In: Extended abstracts of the 2018 CHI conference on human factors in computing systems, pp 1–4

Cornelio Martinez PI, De Pirro S, Vi CT, Subramanian S (2017) Agency in mid-air interfaces. In: Proceedings of the 2017 CHI conference on human factors in computing systems, pp 2426–243

de Tinguy X, Pacchierotti C, Marchal M, Lécuyer A (2019) Toward universal tangible objects: optimizing haptic pinching sensations in 3d interaction. In: 2019 IEEE Conference on virtual reality and 3D user interfaces (VR). IEEE, pp 321–330

de Tinguy X, Howard T, Pacchierotti C, Marchal M, Lécuyer A (2020) Weatavix: wearable actuated tangibles for virtual reality experiences. In: International conference on human haptic sensing and touch enabled computer applications. Springer, Berlin, pp 262–270

Di Luca M, Mahnan A (2019) Perceptual limits of visual-haptic simultaneity in virtual reality interactions. In: 2019 IEEE world haptics conference (WHC). IEEE, pp 67–72

Dzidek B, Frier W, Harwood A, Hayden R (2018) Design and evaluation of mid-air haptic interactions in an augmented reality environment. In: International conference on human haptic sensing and touch enabled computer applications. Springer, Berlin, pp 489–499

Eid MA, Al Osman H (2015) Affective haptics: current research and future directions. IEEE Access 4:26–40

Evangelou G, Limerick H, Moore JW (2021) I feel it in my fingers! Sense of agency with mid-air haptics. IEEE World Haptics

Freeman E, Anderson R, Williamson J, Wilson G, Brewster SA (2017) Textured surfaces for ultra-sound haptic displays. In: Proceedings of the 19th ACM international conference on multimodal interaction, pp 491–492

Frier W, Ablart D, Chilles J, Long B, Giordano M, Obrist M, Subramanian S (2018) Using spatiotemporal modulation to draw tactile patterns in mid-air. In: International conference on human haptic sensing and touch enabled computer applications. Springer, Berlin, pp 270–281

Frier W, Pittera D, Ablart D, Obrist M, Subramanian S (2019) Sampling strategy for ultrasonic mid-air haptics. In: Proceedings of the 2019 CHI conference on human factors in computing systems, pp 1–11

Frutos-Pascual M, Harrison JM, Creed C, Williams I (2019) Evaluation of ultrasound haptics as a supplementary feedback cue for grasping in virtual environments. In: 2019 International conference on multimodal interaction, pp 310–318

Georgiou O, Biscione V, Harwood A, Griffiths D, Giordano M, Long B, Carter T (2017) Haptic in-vehicle gesture controls. In: Proceedings of the 9th international conference on automotive user interfaces and interactive vehicular applications adjunct, pp 233–238

Georgiou O, Jeffrey C, Chen Z, Tong BX, Chan SH, Yang B, Harwood A, Carter T (2018) Touchless haptic feedback for VR rhythm games. In: 2018 IEEE Conference on virtual reality and 3D user interfaces (VR). IEEE, pp 553–554

Gil H, Son H, Kim JR, Oakley I (2018) Whiskers: exploring the use of ultrasonic haptic cues on the face. In: Proceedings of the 2018 CHI conference on human factors in computing systems, pp 1–13

Hajas D, Pittera D, Nasce A, Georgiou O, Obrist M (2020) Mid-air haptic rendering of 2d geometric shapes with a dynamic tactile pointer. IEEE Trans Haptics 13(4):806–817

Hasegawa K, Qiu L, Noda A, Inoue S, Shinoda H (2017) Electronically steerable ultrasound-driven long narrow air stream. Appl Phys Lett 111(6):064104

Hoshi T (2016) Gradual phase shift to suppress noise from airborne ultrasound tactile display. In: Proceedings of the ACM CHI workshop mid-air haptics displays: systems for un-instrumented mid-air interactions. Session 2: Provide vis. haptic feedback

Hoshi T, Abe D, Shinoda H (2009a) Adding tactile reaction to hologram. In: RO-MAN 2009—The 18th IEEE international symposium on robot and human interactive communication. IEEE, pp 7–11

Hoshi T, Iwamoto T, Shinoda H (2009b) Non-contact tactile sensation synthesized by ultrasound transducers. In: World haptics 2009—Third joint EuroHaptics conference and symposium on haptic interfaces for virtual environment and teleoperator systems. IEEE, pp 256–260

Hoshi T, Takahashi M, Iwamoto T, Shinoda H (2010) Noncontact tactile display based on radiation pressure of airborne ultrasound. IEEE Trans Haptics 3(3):155–165

Howard T, Gallagher G, Lécuyer A, Pacchierotti C, Marchal M (2019a) Investigating the recognition of local shapes using mid-air ultrasound haptics. In: 2019 IEEE World haptics conference (WHC). IEEE, pp 503–508

Howard T, Marchal M, Lécuyer A, Pacchierotti C (2019b) PUMAH: pan-tilt ultrasound mid-air haptics for larger interaction workspace in virtual reality. IEEE Trans Haptics 13(1):38–44

Howard T, Gicquel G, Marchal M, Lécuyer A, Pacchierotti C (2021) PUMAH: pan-tilt ultrasound mid-air haptics. In: WHC 2021-IEEE World haptics conference

Hwang I, Son H, Kim JR (2017) AirPiano: enhancing music playing experience in virtual reality with mid-air haptic feedback. In: 2017 IEEE World haptics conference (WHC). IEEE, pp 213–218

Inoue S, Kobayashi-Kirschvink KJ, Monnai Y, Hasegawa K, Makino Y, Shinoda H (2014) Horn: the hapt-optic reconstruction. In: ACM SIGGRAPH 2014 emerging technologies, pp 1–1

Inoue S, Makino Y, Shinoda H (2015) Active touch perception produced by airborne ultrasonic haptic hologram. In: 2015 IEEE World haptics conference (WHC). IEEE, pp 362–367

Ito M, Kokumai Y, Shinoda H (2019) Midair click of dual-layer haptic button. In: 2019 IEEE World haptics conference (WHC). IEEE, pp 349–352

Jang J, Park J (2020) SPH fluid tactile rendering for ultrasonic mid-air haptics. IEEE Trans Haptics 13(1):116–122

Kamigaki T, Suzuki S, Shinoda H (2020) Noncontact thermal and vibrotactile display using focused airborne ultrasound. In: International conference on human haptic sensing and touch enabled computer applications. Springer, Berlin, pp 271–278

Kappus B, Long B (2018) Spatiotemporal modulation for mid-air haptic feedback from an ultrasonic phased array. J Acoust Soc Am 143(3):1836–1836

Karafotias G, Korres G, Teranishi A, Park W, Eid M (2017) Mid-air tactile stimulation for pain distraction. IEEE Trans Haptics 11(2):185–191

Kervegant C, Raymond F, Graeff D, Castet J (2017) Touch hologram in mid-air. In: ACM SIGGRAPH 2017 emerging technologies, pp 1–2 (2017)

Kimura Y, Makino Y, Shinoda H (2016) Computer-created interactive 3d image with midair haptic feedback. In: International AsiaHaptics conference. Springer, Berlin, pp 491–494

Korres G, Eid M (2016) Haptogram: ultrasonic point-cloud tactile stimulation. IEEE Access 4:7758–7769

Korres G, Aujeszky T, Eid M (2017) Characterizing tactile rendering parameters for ultrasound based stimulation. In: 2017 IEEE World haptics conference (WHC). IEEE, pp 293–298

Kreimeier J, Hammer S, Friedmann D, Karg P, Bühner C, Bankel L, Götzelmann T (2019) Evaluation of different types of haptic feedback influencing the task-based presence and performance in virtual reality. In: Proceedings of the 12th ACM international conference on pervasive technologies related to assistive environments, pp 289–298

Long B, Seah SA, Carter T, Subramanian S (2014) Rendering volumetric haptic shapes in mid-air using ultrasound. ACM Trans Graph (TOG) 33(6):1–10

Lugo-Villeda LI, Frisoli A, Pabon S, Padilla MA, Sotgiu E, Bergamasco M (2009) Light-exoskeleton and data-glove integration for enhancing virtual reality applications. In: 2009 International conference on advanced robotics. IEEE, pp 1–6

Makino Y, Furuyama Y, Inoue S, Shinoda H (2016) Haptoclone (haptic-optical clone) for mutual tele-environment by real-time 3d image transfer with midair force feedback. In: CHI, pp 1980–1990

Marchal M, Gallagher G, Lécuyer A, Pacchierotti C (2020) Can stiffness sensations be rendered in virtual reality using mid-air ultrasound haptic technologies? In: International conference on human haptic sensing and touch enabled computer applications. Springer, Berlin, pp 297–306

Martinez J, Griffiths D, Biscione V, Georgiou O, Carter T (2018) Touchless haptic feedback for supernatural VR experiences. In: 2018 IEEE Conference on virtual reality and 3D user interfaces (VR). IEEE, pp 629–630

Martinez J, Harwood A, Limerick H, Clark R, Georgiou O (2019) Mid-air haptic algorithms for rendering 3d shapes. In: 2019 IEEE International symposium on haptic, audio and visual environments and games (HAVE). IEEE, pp 1–6

Matsubayashi A, Makino Y, Shinoda H (2019) Direct finger manipulation of 3d object image with ultrasound haptic feedback. In: Proceedings of the 2019 CHI conference on human factors in computing systems, pp 1–11

Meli L, Scheggi S, Pacchierotti C, Prattichizzo D (2014) Wearable haptics and hand tracking via an RGB-D camera for immersive tactile experiences. In: ACM SIGGRAPH 2014 posters, pp 1–1

Meli L, Pacchierotti C, Salvietti G, Chinello F, Maisto M, De Luca A, Prattichizzo D (2018) Combining wearable finger haptics and augmented reality: user evaluation using an external camera and the microsoft hololens. IEEE Rob Autom Lett 3(4):4297–4304

Mercado V, Howard T, Si-Mohammed H, Argelaguet F, Lécuyer A (2021) Alfred: the haptic butler—on-demand tangibles for object manipulation in virtual reality using an ETHD. IEEE World Haptics

Mestre D, Fuchs P, Berthoz A, Vercher J (2006) Immersion et présence. Le traité de la réalité virtuelle. Ecole des Mines de Paris, Paris, pp 309–38

Monnai Y, Hasegawa K, Fujiwara M, Yoshino K, Inoue S, Shinoda H (2014) HaptoMime: mid-air haptic interaction with a floating virtual screen. In: Proceedings of the 27th annual ACM symposium on user interface software and technology, pp 663–667

Monnai Y, Hasegawa K, Fujiwara M, Yoshino K, Inoue S, Shinoda H (2015) Adding texture to aerial images using ultrasounds. In: Haptic interaction. Springer, Berlin, pp 59–61

Mulot L, Gicquel G, Frier W, Marchal M, Pacchierotti C, Howard T (2021a) Curvature discrimination for dynamic ultrasound mid-air haptic stimuli. In: WHC 2021-IEEE World haptics conference

Mulot L, Gicquel G, Zanini Q, Frier W, Marchal M, Pacchierotti C, Howard T (2021b) DOLPHIN: a framework for the design and perceptual evaluation of ultrasound mid-air haptic stimuli. In: ACM Symposium on applied perception

Obrist M, Seah SA, Subramanian S (2013) Talking about tactile experiences. In: Proceedings of the SIGCHI conference on human factors in computing systems, pp 1659–1668

Obrist M, Subramanian S, Gatti E, Long B, Carter T (2015) Emotions mediated through mid-air haptics. In: Proceedings of the 33rd annual ACM conference on human factors in computing systems, pp 2053–2062

Ochiai Y, Hoshi T, Suzuki I (2017) Holographic whisper: rendering audible sound spots in three-dimensional space by focusing ultrasonic waves. In: Proceedings of the 2017 CHI conference on human factors in computing systems, pp 4314–4325

Pittera D, Ablart D, Obrist M (2019a) Creating an illusion of movement between the hands using mid-air touch. IEEE Trans Haptics 12(4):615–623

Pittera D, Gatti E, Obrist M (2019b) I'm sensing in the rain: spatial incongruity in visual-tactile mid-air stimulation can elicit ownership in VR users. In: Proceedings of the 2019 CHI conference on human factors in computing systems, pp 1–15

Popescu GV, Burdea GC, Trefftz H (2002) Multimodal interaction modeling. In: Handbook of virtual environments. CRC Press, pp 475–494

Price A, Long B (2018) Fibonacci spiral arranged ultrasound phased array for mid-air haptics. In: 2018 IEEE International ultrasonics symposium (IUS). IEEE, pp 1–4

Rakkolainen I, Freeman E, Sand A, Raisamo R, Brewster S (2020) A survey of mid-air ultrasound haptics and its applications. IEEE Trans Haptics 14(1):2–19

Ramsamy P, Haffegee A, Jamieson R, Alexandrov V (2006) Using haptics to improve immersion in virtual environments. In: International conference on computational science. Springer, Berlin, pp 603–609

Romanus T, Frish S, Maksymenko M, Frier W, Corenthy L, Georgiou O (2019) Mid-air haptic bio-holograms in mixed reality. In: 2019 IEEE International symposium on mixed and augmented reality adjunct (ISMAR-adjunct). IEEE, pp 348–352

Rümelin S, Gabler T, Bellenbaum J (2017) Clicks are in the air: how to support the interaction with floating objects through ultrasonic feedback. In: Proceedings of the 9th international conference on automotive user interfaces and interactive vehicular applications, pp 103–108

Rutten I, Frier W, Van den Bogaert L, Geerts D (2019) Invisible touch: how identifiable are mid-air haptic shapes? In: Extended abstracts of the 2019 CHI conference on human factors in computing systems, pp 1–6

Rutten E, Van Den Bogaert L, Geerts D (2020) From initial encounter with mid-air haptic feedback to repeated use: the role of the novelty effect in user experience. IEEE Trans Haptics

Saint-Aubert J, Regnier S, Haliyo S (2018) Cable driven haptic interface for co-localized desktop VR. In: 2018 IEEE Haptics symposium (HAPTICS). IEEE, pp 351–356

Salazar SV, Pacchierotti C, de Tinguy X, Maciel A, Marchal M (2020) Altering the stiffness, friction, and shape perception of tangible objects in virtual reality using wearable haptics. IEEE Trans Haptics 13(1):167–174

Sand A, Rakkolainen I, Isokoski P, Kangas J, Raisamo R, Palovuori K (2015) Head-mounted display with mid-air tactile feedback. In: Proceedings of the 21st ACM symposium on virtual reality software and technology, pp 51–58

Shakeri G, Freeman E, Frier W, Iodice M, Long B, Georgiou O, Andersson C (2019) Three-in-one: levitation, parametric audio, and mid-air haptic feedback. In: Extended abstracts of the 2019 CHI conference on human factors in computing systems, pp 1–4

Suzuki S, Takahashi R, Nakajima M, Hasegawa K, Makino Y, Shinoda H (2018) Midair haptic display to human upper body. In: 2018 57th Annual conference of the society of instrument and control engineers of Japan (SICE). IEEE, pp 848–853

Van den Bogaert L, Geerts D (2020) User-defined mid-air haptic sensations for interacting with an AR menu environment. In: International conference on human haptic sensing and touch enabled computer applications. Springer, Berlin, pp 25–32

Vi CT, Ablart D, Gatti E, Velasco C, Obrist M (2017) Not just seeing, but also feeling art: mid-air haptic experiences integrated in a multisensory art exhibition. Int J Hum-Comput Stud 108:1–14

Waltemate T, Senna I, Hülsmann F, Rohde M, Kopp S, Ernst M, Botsch M (2016) The impact of latency on perceptual judgments and motor performance in closed-loop interaction in virtual reality. In: Proceedings of the 22nd ACM conference on virtual reality software and technology, pp 27–35

Wilson G, Carter T, Subramanian S, Brewster SA (2014) Perception of ultrasonic haptic feedback on the hand: localisation and apparent motion. In: Proceedings of the SIGCHI conference on human factors in computing systems, pp 1133–1142

Yoshida K, Horiuchi Y, Inoue S, Makino Y, Shinoda H (2017) HaptoCloneAR: mutual haptic-optic interactive system with 2d image superimpose. In: ACM SIGGRAPH 2017 emerging technologies, pp 1–2

Yoshino K, Shinoda H (2013) Visio-acoustic screen for contactless touch interface with tactile sensation. In: 2013 World haptics conference (WHC). IEEE, pp 419–423

Multimodal Interaction with Mid-Air Haptics

Jin Ryong Kim

Abstract Multimodal human–computer interfaces utilize sensory information from different modalities to create richer and more immersive user experiences. The use of ultrasound haptics in a multimodal interface is compelling: It requires no physical contact, has high spatial and temporal resolution, and can even be physically co-located with other sensory information (e.g., visual content in mid-air). In this chapter, we explore examples of multimodal interface that use ultrasound haptics, and reflect on the technical and design challenges of creating a high-quality multimodal ultrasound haptic interface.

1 Introduction

Humans perceive the world through multiple modalities, including the basic senses of sight, hearing, smell, taste, and touch (and more nuanced sensory information as discussed in Chap. "Opportunities for Multisensory Mid-air Interactions Featuring Ultrasound Haptic Feedback"). For example, a person in a coffee shop can see nearby people, hear the ambient noise in that setting, smell the coffee in their cup, and feel its warmth while holding it. These modalities work together to provide them with a rich and reliable sense of their surroundings. Humans instinctively interact with the world through multiple sensory modalities, exploring and understanding the environment through rich sensory information.

A multimodal human–computer interface is an interface that provides different types of sensory stimuli at the same time (e.g., visual, auditory, haptic, olfactory, etc.) (Freeman et al. 2017). Multimodal interfaces are necessary to support multisensory experiences, which can offer many benefits to usability and user experience. They can also lead to more "natural" interaction with digital environments, providing multiple types of sensory information, similar to what we perceive when we interact with physical environments. It is, indeed, challenging to create high-quality multimodal interfaces: This requires an in-depth understanding of human perception

J. R. Kim (✉)
Department of Computer Science, The University of Texas at Dallas, Richardson, TX, USA
e-mail: Jin.Kim@UTDallas.edu

© The Author(s), under exclusive license to Springer Nature Switzerland AG 2022   185
O. Georgiou et al. (eds.), *Ultrasound Mid-Air Haptics for Touchless Interfaces*,
Human–Computer Interaction Series, https://doi.org/10.1007/978-3-031-04043-6_7

and device output capabilities, and how these can be combined to create interactions with a convincing multisensory experience. However, the benefits of multimodal interaction are compelling.

Ultrasound haptics can make a significant contribution to a multimodal user experience. Unlike other haptic devices, ultrasound haptics allow bare-hand input actions paired with mid-air tactile sensations, leading to more "natural" haptic interactions. Ultrasound haptics can be harmonized with other output modalities without physical or mechanical constraint and can even be co-located with additional sensory information (e.g., superimposed haptic and visual content, as explored in Chap. "Superimposing Visual Images on Mid-air Ultrasonic Haptic Stimulation"). This haptic technology also has a high degree of spatial and temporal resolution, supporting a wide variety of tactile sensations (e.g., as explored in Chaps. "User Experience and Mid-air Haptics: Applications, Methods and Challenges" and "Ultrasound Haptic Feedback for Touchless User Interfaces: Design Patterns"). These mid-air tactile sensations can be utilized in many ways, e.g., for feedback that confirms gestural actions in mid-air (like pressing a button), or to support tangible interactions with an increased sense of realism and immersion.

Although ultrasound haptics technology offers many benefits, there are limitations. For one, its intensity is often too weak to present strong tactile sensations (e.g., like force feedback). The perceptible strength of the ultrasound haptic cues is relatively weak compared to contact-based haptic devices. Due to its weakness in presenting pressure-based force, tactile presentation is also limited. However, we believe that mid-air haptics can largely benefit from the combination with other modalities, helping to overcome its weaknesses to create stronger and more reliable haptic experiences.

This chapter provides an overview of several systems that use ultrasound haptic feedback as one aspect of a multimodal interface. As will be shown, ultrasound haptic feedback can be used to improve the user experience across many different application domains and will benefit from its combination with other sensory information (e.g., vision, audio). We discuss challenging issues to be considered when designing multimodal interfaces with ultrasound haptic feedback. We then introduce four use cases and explore the benefits of multimodality in each case. We encourage designers and practitioners to consider how ultrasound haptics can be used alongside other modalities to create a better interactive experience for their users. We also encourage researchers to explore further how this technology can be effectively combined with other types of sensory information.

2 Multimodal Interfaces Using Ultrasound Haptics

In this section, we review multimodal interfaces that utilize mid-air haptics as part of a multisensory experience, examples of which are shown in Fig. 1. These other modalities include vision (Sect. 2), audio (Sect. 2.2), and other types of cutaneous

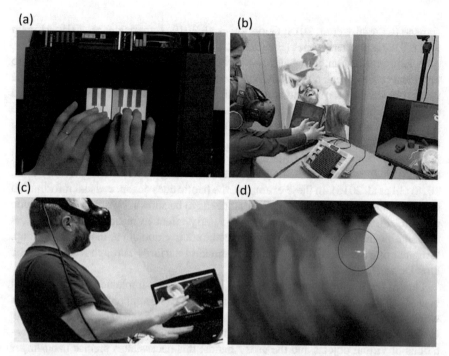

Fig. 1 Multimodal interfaces using ultrasound haptics. **a** Haptomime (Monnai et al. 2014), **b** Mid-air haptics with VR (Martinez et al. 2018), **c** VR rhythm game (Georgiou et al. 2019), and **d** Cross-field Aerial Haptics (Ochiai et al. 2016)

touch (Sect. 2.3). In each section, we consider the benefits of multimodal presentation and discuss the challenges of successful multimodal integration.

2.1 Visual Feedback

Visual and ultrasound haptic feedback is the most common modality combination found in the literature (and, indeed, in this book). Presenting tactile information that matches visual cues is intuitive and can increase a sense of immersion and realism. Haptics and visual information can be superimposed in the same physical space (as discussed in Chap. "Superimposing Visual Images on Mid-Air Ultrasonic Haptic Stimulation"), e.g., using autostereoscopic displays (Kim et al. 2019; Matsubayashi et al. 2019), VR displays (Bhardwaj et al. 2021; Martinez et al. 2018; Puertolas Balint et al. 2018), and AR displays (Dzidek et al. 2018; Romanus et al. 2019) (see Fig. 1a and b for (Martinez et al. 2018; Monnai et al. 2014), respectively). Visual and haptic cues can also be physically separated, and several studies have shown the effectiveness of combining ultrasound haptics with distal 2D displays, including digital signage (Corenthy et al. 2018; Georgiou et al. 2019; Limerick et al. 2019; Monnai et al. 2014) and smartphones (Freeman et al. 2014).

A key goal of combining ultrasound haptic displays with visual displays is to provide a sense of realism for tangible interactions, i.e., by allowing users to feel the virtual objects they can see and interact with. However, tactile information can be used to provide other usability benefits (Van den Bogaert et al. 2019), including guidance (Freeman et al. 2019; Martinez et al. 2018), confirmation (Corenthy et al. 2018; Freeman et al. 2014; Limerick et al. 2019; Martinez et al. 2018; Monnai et al. 2014), information representation (Bhardwaj et al. 2021; Kim et al. 2019; Matsubayashi et al. 2019; Romanus et al. 2019), and status/warning information (Corenthy et al. 2018; Gil et al. 2018). In these examples, the haptic cues enhance visual information or reduce the amount of information that needs to be shown, by offloading to haptic modality instead. The latter can be particularly effective in domains where users face significant sensory demands, e.g., the automotive domain as discussed in Chap. "Augmenting Automotive Gesture Infotainment Interfaces Through Mid-air Haptic Icon Design".

One of the most challenging issues in designing and implementing multimodal visuo-haptic interfaces is providing congruent spatial and temporal feedback: in other words, making sure visual and haptic cues appear in the right place at the right time. In a typical mid-air user interface, most interactions occur between visual representations of virtual objects and the user's hands; this necessitates precise hand/finger tracking without latency to avoid misalignment (in both space and time) between the visual and haptic cues, to guarantee a sense of realism and control. This requirement becomes even more critical when using the autostereoscopic display and VR/AR glasses where there may be visual–physical conflicts. Users heavily rely on visual cues to locate and manipulate virtual objects (i.e., stereoscopic images) with their physical hands. Still, confusion can occur between visual cues and proprioception as users rely on proprioceptive cues about hand depth (van Beers et al. 2002). Therefore, it is important to provide spatiotemporal synchrony between virtual hands and 3D environments, to avoid the jarring feeling of incongruent multimodal feedback. The issue of aligning visual and haptic information is further discussed in Chap. "Superimposing Visual Images on Mid-air Ultrasonic Haptic Stimulation".

2.2 Auditory Feedback

Auditory feedback has also been effectively integrated with ultrasound haptic displays. AirPiano (Hwang et al. 2017) is a piano-playing system that uses auditory and haptic feedback so that when users press piano keys in mid-air (rendered in VR), they *feel* the piano key and *hear* the sound it produces. The spatial and temporal congruency of visual, auditory, and haptic feedback is designed to provide a strong sense of agency, leading to an engaging piano-playing experience. A similar multi-sensory musical experience took the form of a VR drumming game (Georgiou et al. 2018), incorporating mid-air haptics and auditory feedback so that users could *see*, *hear*, and *feel* the drums as they tapped them in mid-air (see Fig. 1c). In that system, two types of hand gesture interactions (i.e., tap and swipe) led to haptic and audio cues for confirmation so that the user knew they had correctly activated the game elements. Ozkul et al. (2020) combined auditory and mid-air haptic feedback for a light switch button, highlighting a possible usage context for mid-air haptics in the home. Auditory feedback was used for short confirmation together with mid-air haptic feedback.

In these examples, the auditory feedback is generally intended to complement haptic feedback given for confirmation about input actions. AirPiano provides piano-key press confirmation, the drumming game provides confirmation of gestural game actions, and the light switch button uses audio and haptic feedback for button press confirmation. This use of multimodal feedback mimics the sensory experiences we have in the physical world, where physical actions often result in auditory and tactile cues (e.g., the sound and feeling of pressing a mechanical button). Auditory feedback can potentially play different roles in a multimodal haptic interface. Free-man (2021) found that auditory cues presented from an ultrasound haptics device have the potential to influence haptic perception, creating the sensory illusion that a haptic surface *felt rough* because it *sounded rough*. There is presently a lack of research investigating audio–haptic interactions. Still, this modality combination is compelling because, as this example shows, audio can do more than redundantly encode confirmation feedback.

The previous section highlighted the importance of spatial and temporal congruence between visual and haptic cues. This congruence is also critical for a practical audio–haptic experience, especially the temporal synchrony between cues. When giving discrete confirmatory feedback, the auditory cues should be carefully designed to match the user's expectation of what should happen and to fit the characteristics of the haptic feedback. For example, consider the feedback for a haptic button press; users may find it jarring if a "heavy" button sound is presented with a brief tactile "click" from a haptics device, or tactile feedback is given when the finger first touches a button, while the auditory feedback is only given after the button has been sufficiently depressed. As a little-explored modality combination, more research is needed to understand better how these modalities can be used together in the most effective way.

2.3   Touch Feedback

While one might think of ultrasound haptics as the only tactile component in a multimodal interface, several systems have been developed using multiple types of cutaneous touch feedback. Cross-field Aerial Haptics (Ochiai et al. 2016) uses femtosecond-laser light fields and ultrasonic haptics to create unique touch sensations drawing on different elements of cutaneous tactile perception (see Fig. 1d). It is interesting to see that the acoustic field affects the tactile perception of the laser haptics, yielding superimposed haptic displays that support cues with varying resolution (i.e., ultrasonic focal points are orders of magnitude larger than the femtosecond lasers). Sonovortex (Hashizume et al. 2017) is another example, combining an ultrasound haptic display with an aerodynamic vortex display. This unified haptic display also provides multiple resolutions of haptic feedback and can provide a larger haptic interaction area (i.e., ultrasound haptics at close range, aerodynamic vortex over a larger range). Finally, a mid-air thermo-tactile system (Singhal et al. 2021) provides thermo-tactile feedback in mid-air by creating an ambient thermal atmosphere with a thermal chamber and mid-air haptic display. As people perceive tactile and thermal stimuli with two different sensory receptors (i.e., mechanoreceptors and thermoreceptors), a larger range of tactile sensations can be achieved than with ultrasound haptics or thermal device on their own.

A key benefit of combining different tactile displays is that a wider range of cutaneous tactile sensations can be presented. To date, there has been little investigation of how such sensations are perceived (Rakkolainen et al. 2020), although this is a compelling topic for future work. One of the challenging issues in designing multiple touch feedback is tactile masking, where a stronger stimulus dominates the tactile perception and diminishes certain aspects of cutaneous tactile perception. For example, considering thermal cues that are so intense, the mid-air haptic feedback may not be perceived. More research is needed to understand cross-modal interference between different aspects of tactile perception, to better inform the creation of multi-haptic interfaces in the future.

2.4 Summary

In this section, we identified three modality combinations often found in the literature: visual and ultrasound haptic feedback, auditory and ultrasound haptic feedback, and cutaneous tactile and ultrasound haptic feedback. Researchers have used multimodality to provide a variety of user experience and usability benefits: for example, to enhance immersion or realism, to create richer sensory experiences, and even to modulate the perception of one modality through the information presented in another.

> A key challenge for all modality combinations is **spatiotemporal congruence**. For a multimodal multisensory interface to be convincing, content must be precisely aligned in both space and time, so that users perceive cues in the **right place at the right time**.

This presents both technical and design challenges. Accurate alignment between output devices is a critical technical issue, yet one must also consider if a design is appropriately aligned (e.g., the example given earlier about audio–haptic button feedback). There are also issues of perceptual dominance and masking to consider;

while this may offer benefits (e.g., enhancing perception across modalities (Freeman 2021)), users may experience a diminished haptic experience if misled or overpowered by other sensory information.

In the remainder of this chapter, we look at four case studies of multimodal systems featuring ultrasound haptics. These demonstrate in more detail how an ultrasound haptics device can be paired with other modalities and reflect on the formative evaluation of these systems.

3 Use Cases

In this section, we introduce four case studies that look at multimodal interfaces featuring mid-air haptic feedback. These example applications illustrate how mid-air haptics is integrated with other forms of sensory feedback to provide a multimodal user experience and to show how it can benefit the users.

3.1 AirPiano: Enhancing Music Playing Experience in VR with Mid-Air Haptics

AirPiano (Hwang et al. 2017) is a virtual reality piano-playing system. It uses a hand tracker to track the fingers in mid-air, an ultrasound mid-air haptics display, and a VR head-mounted display (as shown in Fig. 2). The system delivers vibrotactile sensations from an ultrasound haptics device, simulating the resistive feedback of piano key travel when pressed by the user's fingers.

Visual feedback in the head-mounted display shows a virtual model of the user's hands, as tracked by the hand tracker. When the hand model's finger contacts the surface of a virtual piano key, the visual representation of the key moves down along with the direction of the finger press. When the key is fully pressed, the corresponding piano sound is delivered to the user. Auditory feedback of piano sound was designed to play during the virtual keypress actions. It was only delivered when a key reaches its bottom, above a threshold motion speed (to reduce false-positive keypress actions).

Two haptic rendering schemes were implemented: **Constant Feedback** and **Adaptive Feedback** (see Fig. 3). Constant Feedback provides the maximum intensity of ultrasonic haptic feedback, to deliver clear confirmation of key pressing action. This feedback is provided during the entire period of the key pressing action. Adaptive Feedback was designed to follow the behaviors of mechanical key pressing actions. Like a real piano key press mechanism, the initial intensity was set in proportion to the speed at which the fingertip hits a key: i.e., so that harder "impacts" result in more intense feedback. The intensity decays linearly for a certain period and maintains the intensity level until the key reaches its bottom. Finally, the maximum intensity is provided when the key is fully pressed (mimicking the resistance felt when fully depressing a mechanical).

Constant Feedback is a simple haptic design, representative of most ultrasound haptic buttons found in the literature, as can be seen in Chap. "Ultrasound Haptic Feedback for Touchless User Interfaces: Design Patterns" for the "Floating Screen" design pattern. In contrast, Adaptive Feedback is a more nuanced design, intended to vary the haptic feedback to try to provide a more realistic button press experience.

3.1.1 Benefit of Multimodality

AirPiano is a multimodal interface that supports interplay among three representational modes: visual, auditory, and haptic. Playing a real piano is a great example of a multimodal activity as it involves three main sensory experiences (along with proprioception, etc.) that contribute to the skilled control that a pianist has over their instrument. Users *see* their fingers pressing on piano keys. They *hear* the sound of the piano whenever the key is pressed. And they *feel* the pressing of the piano key through their fingertips. While lacking the resistive force feedback of a physical key press, the ultrasound haptic feedback at least provides valuable tactile cues.

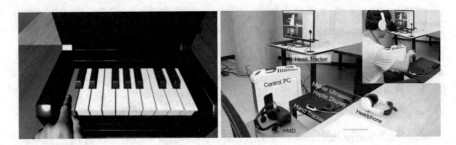

Fig. 2 A VR scene of AirPiano (left) and its setup (right)

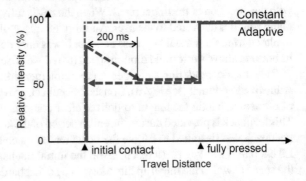

Fig. 3 Haptic feedback rendering of two approaches: Constant Feedback (red) and Adaptive Feedback (blue)

We considered AirPiano both with and without ultrasound haptic feedback. We initially hypothesized that there would be no significant differences between ultrasound feedback and no-feedback conditions. Users are engaged in an immersive environment, and strong visual with auditory cues of piano sound seemed likely to dominate the environment. We also thought that the ultrasound feedback would not be strong enough to impact the user experience. However, in our evaluation, it turned out that the presence of mid-air haptic feedback resulted in significantly higher scores in all subjective measures (for both Constant Feedback and Adaptive Feedback). This was an interesting finding, considering the fact that the perceptible strength of ultrasound haptic feedback is not strong enough to provide solid key-click confirmation. Given that the visual system is dominant, and the perceptual effect of combinatory visual and audio cues is large, the presence of haptic makes significant differences even if its perceptible strength is not strong enough.

We also observed another interesting finding regarding the tactile feedback design. As piano performance is a multimodal musical activity, tactile feedback that confirms the keypress should be designed to follow the realistic settings to harmonize with other modalities to enhance the piano-playing experiences. As we previously mentioned, AirPiano introduced two approaches for tactile rendering. While **Constant Feedback** provides an explicit keypress confirmation to assure that the user is pressing the key, **Adaptive Feedback** simulates more realistic behaviors of piano keys, mimicking the keypress mechanism of a real piano. We observed that the Adaptive Feedback method was the most preferred method among participants during the user study. We further confirmed that the scores in subjective quality measures were higher with Adaptive Feedback than Constant—for reality, enjoyment, comfort, and satisfaction. From the user study results, we may infer that prior piano-playing experience can affect the user experience. Thus, we believe that tactile feedback design is important to be integrated with other modalities.

3.2 Refinity: Haptic-Hologram for Novel Shopping Experience

Refinity (Kim et al. 2019) is an interactive holographic signage for novel retail shopping experience. This work demonstrates a futuristic shopping kiosk that provides free-hand gesture interface for interacting with 3D virtual products. Refinity consists of an autostereoscopic 3D display for holographic content, an ultrasound haptic display for tactile presentation, and a hand motion tracking sensor for sensing input actions and aligning haptic content with the user's hand.

Refinity, as shown in Figs. 4 and 5, combines a 3D display with an autostereoscopic display that provides two stereoscopic views into each eye for parallax and depth

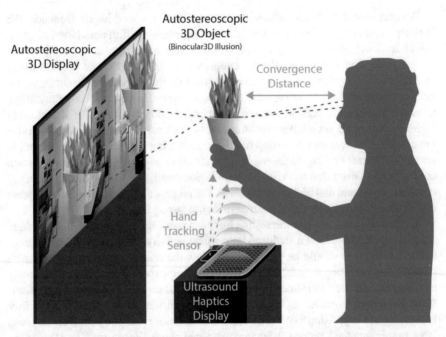

Fig. 4 Overview of the Refinity system. An autostereoscopic 3D display renders 3D visual content in front of the screen. An ultrasound haptics display is used to render a tactile representation of the visual object

perception, resulting in 3D visual content in front of the display. The display has a built-in eye-tracking component to track the user's eyes in real time to adjust the convergence for maximum depth perception. This enables binocular illusions of 3D products to be formed in front of the user's eyes. The mid-air ultrasound haptic display is placed in front of the 3D display, facing upward to generate haptic feedback in the region where 3D content appears. The hand tracking sensor is also placed in front of the user to track their hand movements. The 3D coordinates of the visual and haptic spaces were calibrated and mapped, so that content in both modalities could be aligned—this allowed the user's hands to interact with the virtual objects directly.

Refinity provides several interaction techniques for selection and manipulation (examples of which are shown in Fig. 6). **Pointing gestures** (with an extended index finger) are used to target items on the screen for the purpose of selecting the desired product. Visual feedback of pointer and object highlights are implemented to indicate the current location of the pointer. A **grab gesture** is used as a selection technique to confirm the selection of the product: i.e., once the target object is highlighted, the user can make a grab gesture with their pointing hand, as though they were grasping the object in front of them. **Swipe gestures** are used to switch between products: i.e., the user can make a swipe gesture by rapidly swiping the hand from right to left. **Push gestures** are used to place an item back in its original position, removing it from the interaction area.

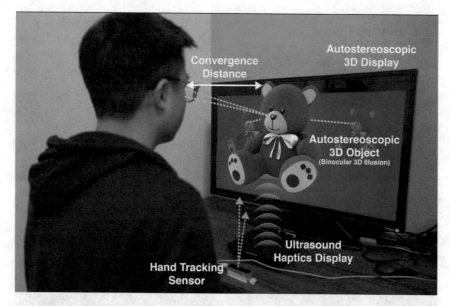

Fig. 5 Refinity system setup. An autostereoscopic 3D object is created in front of the user's eyes for 3D interaction in mid-air

In the Refinity system, ultrasound haptic feedback is used to provide a tangible component for the interaction. Once a product is selected and brought into the fore-ground for closer exploration (via pointing and grabbing), the user can rotate it 360 degrees by reaching out and "holding" it in mid-air. When the users' fingers touch the surface of the virtual object in mid-air, haptic and auditory cues are generated to notify the user that it is being touched. These multimodal cues can be beneficial as they provide guidance information and create a sense of realism.

In addition to confirming input gestures, ultrasound haptic feedback also high-lights salient product features. For example, an ultrasound haptic pattern is generated to simulate different water settings from the showerhead in one of the virtual scenes. Furthermore, as the user interacts with the mid-air 3D faucet, the water flow is sim-ulated to provide the feel of the water. The water flow animation is implemented, reacting to the hand interaction. This is an instance of the Special Effect design pattern discussed in Chap. "Ultrasound Haptic Feedback for Touchless User Inter-faces: Design Patterns". Appropriate sounds and scents were also provided, creating a demonstrator of rich multimodal interaction.

3.2.1   Benefit of Multimodality

The main benefit of multimodal feedback in this context is that it creates a more immersive user experience because users can see and feel holographic 3D content in

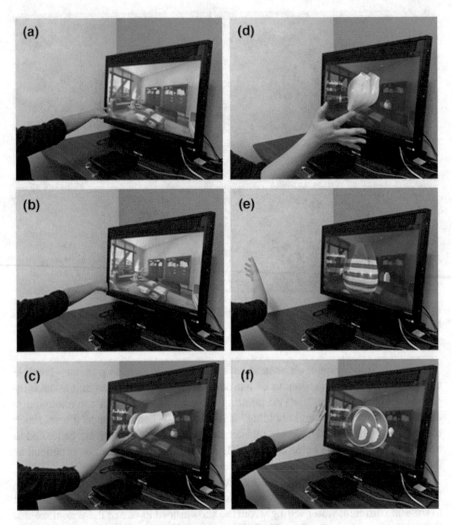

Fig. 6 Examples of mid-air gestural interactions with the 3D product images

front of them. Adding mid-air haptics that provides a "physical presence" of virtual illusion is a natural fit for multimodal interaction.

The Refinity system allows direct manipulation of 3D objects through grasp and rotate gestures. However, there exists an inconsistency of 3D depth perception when the user's hand is involved. Users rely on visual cues to find the target location to touch. However, what they see is a binocular illusion, and this visual perception can conflict with hand involvement. Users cannot know where to focus in this situation. This visual–physical conflict can make it difficult to manipulate the virtual object and may confuse the user's perception of visual and proprioceptive cues. We discerned that additional visual and auditory cues (e.g., highlighting the object or making an appropriate sound when the hand gets closer) along with the sense of touch using mid-air haptic feedback could be a solution to minimize this visual–physical conflict. As direct object manipulation requires handling significant spatial information, we believe that multiple modalities can contribute to resolving the visual–physical conflict and increase the sense of control.

3.3   Mid-Air Thermo-tactile Feedback Using Ultrasound Haptics

The **Thermo-tactile Feedback System** (Singhal et al. 2021) combines an ultrasound haptics device with heat modules, to generate mid-air tactile sensations with an added feeling of warmth. This work demonstrates the use of multiple cutaneous tactile sensations for richer mid-air haptic feedback.

Humans perceive warmth and coldness when their thermoreceptors respond to a stimulus above or below the skin temperature (Darian-Smith and Johnson 1977; Jones and Ho 2008), activating the insula cortex (a region of the brain deep in the cerebral cortex). Haptic devices have been developed to produce such thermal sensations (Freeman et al. 2017). Thermal feedback could be beneficial in VR applications, as users demand more immersive experiences with richer multisensory feedback. Many VR scenarios would benefit from the use of thermal feedback: e.g., users could feel the ambient temperature of a fireplace, feel hot water running from a faucet, or feel the warmth of the coffee cup.

With these benefits in mind, we consider the possibility of creating contactless thermo-tactile sensations. There are a number of studies focusing on non-contact-based thermal feedback, and many of them have used infrared lamps (Hülsmann et al. 2014), heaters (Shaw et al. 2019), fans (Han et al. 2018), and projector lights (Iwai et al. 2018). However, due to their underlying mechanisms, it is almost impossible to localize or control the thermal cues in mid-air. Delivering thermo-tactile feedback using an ultrasound haptic display is a promising direction for providing localized thermal cues in mid-air, directly to the user's bare hand (Singhal et al. 2021). This approach is based on the human ability to identify tactile and thermal cues without masking each other as they are perceived through different receptors (mechanoreceptors and thermoreceptors). By providing localized focused pressure points using ultrasound with ambient global thermal cues to the same area, people can perceive unified thermo-tactile sensation without feeling awkward.

Figure 7 shows the design of the thermo-tactile feedback system, which has an ultrasound haptics display placed inside a temperature chamber. It has two heat modules that contain ceramic heating elements, symmetrically placed at each side of the chamber. Fans are placed behind the ceramic heating elements to push warm air into the chamber. The chamber has an open-top with the shape of two conical frusta

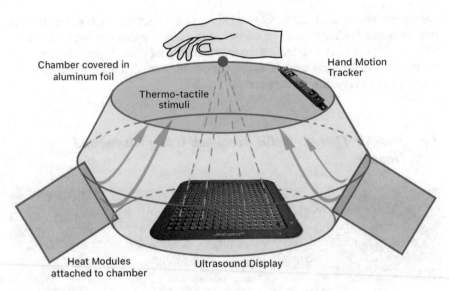

Fig. 7 Overview of the core components in the thermo-tactile feedback system

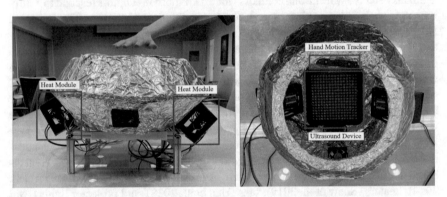

Fig. 8 An image depicting the side and top view of mid-air thermo-tactile system

by sharing a surface in the middle. The chamber is made of cardboard, then wrapped with aluminum foil to retain heat. An ultrasonic haptic display is placed inside the chamber and faced upward. A hand tracking device is installed on the prototype's upper surface to track the user's hand.

The heating elements generate the heat energy to heat and circulate air. Once the heated airflow is inflated, the chamber's temperature can be controlled by adjusting the applied voltage to the heating module. The focused ultrasonic haptic cues with ambient temperature are created on the chamber (i.e., interaction area), generating unified thermo-tactile feedback where users perceive both cues without masking each other. The system can reach up to $54.2\,°C$ in $300\,s$ (Fig. 8).

(a) Campfire Scene   (b) Water Fountain Scene

Fig. 9 We developed two VR scenarios with mid-air thermo-tactile feedback: a campfire scene with warmth from the fire (**a**) and a water fountain scene with the sensation of water (**b**)

3.3.1 Benefit of Multimodality

This system demonstrates the ability to combine different tactile modes: tactile feedback from focused ultrasound and thermal feedback via the heated air. We explored the benefits of this enhanced tactile feedback through a user study. We designed two VR scenes (see Fig. 9) with four haptic feedback conditions to investigate the benefits of thermo-tactile feedback:

- No Feedback: no tactile or thermal feedback;
- Tactile Feedback: activating only focused ultrasound waves;
- Thermal Feedback: activating only thermal system;
- Thermo-tactile Feedback: sactivating both focused ultrasound waves and thermal system.

Sixteen participants were asked to interact with each scene with four randomly presented feedback conditions. After completing each scene, participants were asked to fill out the questionnaire to measure their interaction experiences in immersion, enjoyment, and overall satisfaction.

Figure 10 shows the mean scores of the measures in four feedback conditions for both scenes. It is clearly shown that the thermo-tactile feedback condition was the most effective feedback in all measures in both scenes. We confirmed with a two-way ANOVA that there was a significant difference between tactile feedback and thermo-tactile feedback ($p = 0.001$) and also between thermal feedback and thermo-tactile feedback ($p = 0.006$) for all three measures. The results indicated that virtual experience could be significantly enhanced when coupled with thermal and vibrotactile cues. The users' expectations for sensations are satisfied with the combinatory effect of thermo-tactile feedback, yielding higher immersive VR experiences.

We proposed a method based on the human ability to identify the tactile and thermal patterns without masking each other. We further leveraged ultrasound display's underlying principles that provide acoustic pressure at mid-air with the ambient thermal condition to simultaneously present thermal and vibrotactile cues. The benefit was clear when two modalities were seamlessly coupled to provide a unified perception of thermal and tactile sensations. We believe this is one promising direction

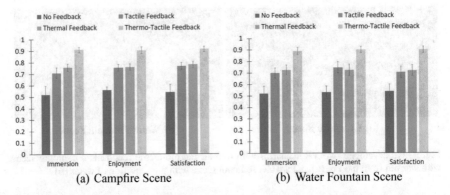

Fig. 10 Mean scores and standard error of all subjective ratings for the campfire scene (**a**) and the water fountain scene (**b**)

to utilize mid-air haptics with other modalities to enhance user experiences in an immersive virtual environment.

3.4 TangibleData: Interactive Data Visualization with Mid-Air Haptics

TangibleData (Bhardwaj et al. 2021) is an interactive 3D data visualization tool that uses free-hand gestures and ultrasound haptic feedback to provide tangible interactions with 3D data visualizations in VR.

Visualizing large data sets in virtual reality (or similar 3D displays) could allow users to explore multi-axis data in an interactive fashion. So-called immersive analytics that allow users to *get into* the data can help provide a better perception of depth, breadth, and height. This enables vast amounts of information to be effectively analyzed from various perspectives. One of the major challenging issues here is occlusion, which occurs when data points are closer to the viewer, leading to the misinterpretation of data. The TangibleData system tackles some of these challenging issues by employing bare-hand interaction with ultrasound haptic feedback, seamlessly coupled with 3D data visualizations. This approach of utilizing hand gestures and direct touch can fundamentally change how people interact with data to improve data comprehension and understanding (Fig. 12).

TangibleData consists of UI components, data processing, and data exploration, running on a VR headset and a mid-air haptics display (see Fig. 11). The UI components support hand gestures and a menu system for the natural manipulation of 3D data representations. Data processing converts the 3D dataset into multisensory

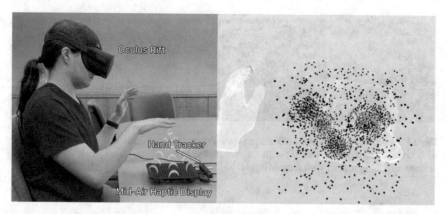

Fig. 11 User study setup and a view of the visual scene

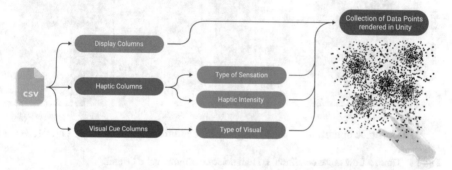

Fig. 12 Process for mapping a 3D dataset to visual and haptic representations. Each data point is mapped to a relevant sensation type

feedback of visual and haptic representations. Data exploration supports two data interaction modes: direct touch mode for intuitive data interaction and indirect touch mode for a better sense of control for exploring the larger dataset. Three applications were presented to show TangibleData's feasibility and performance in different immersive analytics scenarios: 3D scatterplots with several dense clusters, CT-scan lung dataset, and a multi-layered human head anatomy volume rendering dataset (see Fig. 13).

3.4.1 Benefit of Multimodality

We showed that utilizing mid-air haptic feedback can help increase the efficiency of data exploration. Throughout the user study, we investigated the effect of mid-air haptic feedback when combined with data points clustered together to see if adding haptic feedback can help address the occlusion problems. We conducted a within-subjects experiment with two modality conditions (visual only vs. visual+haptic)

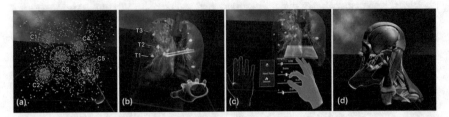

Fig. 13 Example applications: **a** 3D scatterplot with several dense clusters, **b** CT-scan lung dataset with several lung cancer tissues, **c** adjusting values for haptic plane, and **d** human head anatomy volume rendering dataset with muscle layers

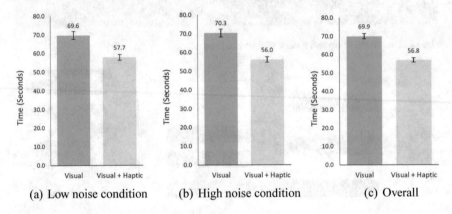

Fig. 14 Time. **a** Low noise condition, **b** High noise condition, and **c** Overall

and two noise conditions (low noise vs. high noise) with 16 participants. The task was to identify a cluster with the highest density among the five clusters as fast and accurately as possible. As you can see in Figs. 14 and 15, visual and haptic feedback conditions performed faster with less error compared to visual-only conditions.

One of the interesting findings was that spatial information could be transferred through bare hands using ultrasonic haptic cues. We noticed that human hands could be natural scanning surfaces placed anywhere in 3D spaces to explore the clustered dataset or volumetric data. By coupling with visual representations of the dataset, we confirmed that multiple sensory feedback improves human understanding of massive 3D data.

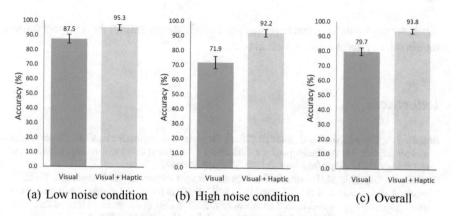

(a) Low noise condition (b) High noise condition (c) Overall

Fig. 15 Accuracy: **a** Low noise condition, **b** High noise condition, and **c** Overall

4 Conclusion

Multimodal human–computer interaction research aims to develop user interfaces and interaction techniques that utilize our full range of sensory capabilities. Multisensory feedback can allow us to explore digital information in richer and more "natural" ways, similar to how we experience the physical world through multiple sensory channels. As this book demonstrates, ultrasound haptic technology has the potential to create a wide range of tactile sensations, which could be integrated into a multimodal user experience.

In this chapter, we reviewed a number of multimodal interfaces that use ultrasound haptics and discussed some of the main challenges to successfully integrating multimodal feedback. We emphasized the benefits and importance of multimodal interaction with mid-air haptics through four use cases. We demonstrated how mid-air haptic could play their role in interplay and leverage natural human capabilities differently. We showed the effect of mid-air haptics in a musical instrument playing scenario and the meaningful impact on user experiences. We explored the feasibility of achieving realism through tangible interaction with 3D binocular illusions in mid-air. We discussed how thermo-tactile feedback could be coupled to deliver thermal and tactile feedback without masking each other. Finally, we also discussed how visual representations of data could be transformed into haptic representations and effectively delivered to the user's hands to help them understand data better and explore it in new ways.

Designing a high-quality multimodal interface is challenging, and this chapter highlights some of the issues designers must deal with. It is crucial that sensory information from different modalities is aligned in both space and time. There are also design challenges associated with combining different sensory cues into a multimodal interface. However, the benefits of multimodality are evident if we design multimodal interfaces that provide multisensory experiences in the right way. We hope that this chapter will inspire others to consider how ultrasound haptics can be integrated with other sensory modalities and hope that our experience can inform the design of future multimodal systems with mid-air haptics.

References

Bhardwaj A, Chae J, Noeske R, Kim JR (2021) Tangibledata: interactive data visualization with mid-air haptics. In: Proceedings of the 27th ACM symposium on virtual reality software and technology, ACM. https://doi.org/10.1145/3489849.3489890

Corenthy L, Giordano M, Hayden R, Griffiths D, Jeffrey C, Limerick H, Georgiou O, Carter T, Müller J, Subramanian S (2018) Touchless tactile displays for digital signage: mid-air haptics meets large screens. In: Extended abstracts of the 2018 CHI conference on human factors in computing systems, ACM, pp 1–4. https://doi.org/10.1145/3170427.3186533

Darian-Smith I, Johnson KO (1977) Thermal sensibility and thermoreceptors. J Invest Dermatol 69(1):146–153

Dzidek B, Frier W, Harwood A, Hayden R (2018) Design and evaluation of mid-air haptic interactions in an augmented reality environment. In: International conference on human haptic sensing and touch enabled computer applications, Springer, pp 489–499. https://doi.org/10.1007/978-3-319-93399-3_42

Freeman E (2021) Enhancing ultrasound haptics with parametric audio effects. In: Proceedings of 23rd ACM international conference on multimodal interaction - ICMI '21, ACM. https://doi.org/10.1145/3462244.3479951

Freeman E, Brewster S, Lantz V (2014) Tactile feedback for above-device gesture interfaces: adding touch to touchless interactions. In: Proceedings of the 16th international conference on multimodal interaction - ICMI '14, ACM, pp 419–426. https://doi.org/10.1145/2663204.2663280

Freeman E, Vo DB, Brewster S (2019) HaptiGlow: helping users position their hands for better mid-air gestures and ultrasound haptic feedback. In: Proceedings of IEEE world haptics conference 2019, the 8th joint eurohaptics conference and the IEEE haptics symposium, IEEE, p TP2A.09. https://doi.org/10.1145/3025453.3025518

Freeman E, Wilson G, Vo DB, Ng A, Politis I, Brewster S (2017) The handbook of multimodal-multisensor interfaces, association for computing machinery and morgan and claypool, chap multimodal feedback in HCI: haptics, non-speech Audio, and Their Applications, pp 277–317. https://doi.org/10.1145/3015783.3015792

Georgiou O, Jeffrey C, Chen Z, Tong BX, Chan SH, Yang B, Harwood A, Carter T (2018) Touchless haptic feedback for vr rhythm games. In: Proceedings of the 2018 IEEE conference on virtual reality and 3D user interfaces (VR), IEEE, pp 553–554. https://doi.org/10.1109/VR.2018.8446619

Georgiou O, Limerick H, Corenthy L, Perry M, Maksymenko M, Frish S, Müller J, Bachynskyi M, Kim JR (2019) Mid-air haptic interfaces for interactive digital signage and kiosks. In: Extended abstracts of the 2019 CHI conference on human factors in computing systems, ACM, pp 1–9. https://doi.org/10.1145/3290607.3299030

Gil H, Son H, Kim JR, Oakley I (2018) Whiskers: exploring the use of ultrasonic haptic cues on the face. In: Proceedings of the 2018 CHI conference on human factors in computing systems, pp 1–13

Han PH, Chen YS, Lee KC, Wang HC, Hsieh CE, Hsiao JC, Chou CH, Hung YP (2018) Haptic around: multiple tactile sensations for immersive environment and interaction in virtual reality. In: Proceedings of the 24th ACM symposium on virtual reality software and technology - VRST '18, pp 1–10

Hashizume S, Koike A, Hoshi T, Ochiai Y (2017) Sonovortex: Rendering multi-resolution aerial haptics by aerodynamic vortex and focused ultrasound. In: Proceedings of ACM SIGGRAPH 2017 posters, ACM, pp 1–2. https://doi.org/10.1145/3102163.3102178

Hülsmann F, Fröhlich J, Mattar N, Wachsmuth I (2014) Wind and warmth in virtual reality: imple-
  mentation and evaluation. In: Proceedings of the 2014 virtual reality international conference, pp
  1–8
Hwang I, Son H, Kim JR (2017) Airpiano: enhancing music playing experience in virtual reality
  with mid-air haptic feedback. In: Proceedings of the 2017 IEEE world haptics conference (- IEEE
  WHC '17, IEEE), pp 213–218
Iwai D, Aoki M, Sato K (2018) Non-contact thermo-visual augmentation by IR-RGB projection.
  IEEE Trans Visualization Comput Graph 25(4):1707–1716
Jones LA, Ho HN (2008) Warm or cool, large or small? the challenge of thermal displays. IEEE
  Trans Hapt 1(1):53–70
Kim JR, Chan S, Huang X, Ng K, Fu LP, Zhao C (2019) Demonstration of refinity: an interactive
  holographic signage for new retail shopping experience. In: Extended abstracts of the 2019 CHI
  conference on human factors in computing systems, pp 1–4
Limerick H, Hayden R, Beattie D, Georgiou O, Müller J (2019) User engagement for mid-air haptic
  interactions with digital signage. In: Proceedings of the 8th ACM international symposium on
  pervasive displays, pp 1–7
Martinez J, Griffiths D, Biscione V, Georgiou O, Carter T (2018) Touchless haptic feedback for
  supernatural vr experiences. In: 2018 IEEE conference on virtual reality and 3D user interfaces
  (VR), IEEE, pp 629–630
Matsubayashi A, Makino Y, Shinoda H (2019) Direct finger manipulation of 3d object image with
  ultrasound haptic feedback. In: Proceedings of the 2019 CHI conference on human factors in
  computing systems, ACM, p paper 87. https://doi.org/10.1145/3290605.3300317
Monnai Y, Hasegawa K, Fujiwara M, Yoshino K, Inoue S, Shinoda H (2014) Haptomime: mid-
  air haptic interaction with a floating virtual screen. In: Proceedings of the 27th annual ACM
  symposium on User interface software and technology, pp 663–667
Ochiai Y, Kumagai K, Hoshi T, Hasegawa S, Hayasaki Y (2016) Cross-field aerial haptics: rendering
  haptic feedback in air with light and acoustic fields. In: Proceedings of the 2016 CHI conference
  on human factors in computing systems, pp 3238–3247
Ozkul C, Geerts D, Rutten I (2020) Combining auditory and mid-air haptic feedback for a light
  switch button. In: Proceedings of the 2020 international conference on multimodal interaction,
  ACM, pp 60–69. https://doi.org/10.1145/3382507.3418823
Puertolas Balint L, Althoefer K et al (2018) Medical virtual reality palpation training using ultrasound based haptics and image processing. In: Proceedings of the conference on computer/robot
  assisted surgery - CRAS '18
Rakkolainen I, Freeman E, Sand A, Raisamo R, Brewster S (2020) A survey of mid-air ultrasound haptics and its applications. IEEE Trans Hapt 14:2–19. https://doi.org/10.1109/TOH.2020.
  3018754
Romanus T, Frish S, Maksymenko M, Frier W, Corenthy L, Georgiou O (2019) Mid-air haptic bio-
  holograms in mixed reality. In: 2019 IEEE International symposium on mixed and augmented
  reality adjunct (ISMAR-Adjunct), IEEE, pp 348–352
Shaw E, Roper T, Nilsson T, Lawson G, Cobb SV, Miller D (2019) The heat is on: Exploring user
  behaviour in a multisensory virtual environment for fire evacuation. In: Proceedings of the 2019
  CHI conference on human factors in computing systems - CHI '19, pp 1–13
Singhal Y, Wang H, Gil H, Kim JR (2021) Mid-air thermo-tactile feedback using ultrasound haptic
  display. In: Proceedings of the 27th ACM symposium on virtual reality software and technology,
  ACM, p Article 28, https://doi.org/10.1145/3489849.3489889
van Beers RJ, Wolpert DM, Haggard P (2002) When feeling is more important than seeing
  in sensorimotor adaptation. Current biology 12(10):834–837. https://doi.org/10.1016/S0960-
  9822(02)00836-9
Van den Bogaert L, Geerts D, Rutten I (2019) Grasping the future: identifying potential applications
  for mid-air haptics in the home. In: Extended Abstracts of the 2019 CHI conference on human
  factors in computing Systems, ACM, p LBW1415. https://doi.org/10.1145/3290607.3312911

Touchless Tactile Interaction with Unconventional Permeable Displays

Antti Sand, Ismo Rakkolainen, Veikko Surakka, Roope Raisamo, and Stephen Brewster

Abstract Unconventional displays, such as 3D displays, projection screens formed of flowing light-scattering particles (fogscreens), and virtual reality (VR) headsets, can create illusions of images floating in mid-air. Paired with hand tracking, gestural interaction with floating user interfaces (UI) is possible on this permeable imagery, thus creating reach-through touchscreens that react and recover instantly from intersecting fingers and objects. The user can explore virtual environments and control floating UIs with hand gestures which could help, for example, in simulated training and in creating an improved feeling of immersion. However, hand-based gestural interaction with such UIs can be difficult without haptic sensations typical in daily activities. Without haptics, the level of immersion and smoothness of interaction suffers if the hands can pass through virtual objects without triggering tactile sensations. Ultrasound haptics is a method to produce a focused airborne acoustic air pressure on a user's skin, thus creating an unobtrusive, mid-air sensation of touch. Fogscreens, VR headsets, or some other unconventional displays together with ultrasound haptics enable tactile interaction with "touchless touchscreens". These tactile, floating UIs open new opportunities, e.g., for immersive interaction, advertisement, and entertainment. It can bring back the missing haptic feedback for these displays.

Keywords Permeable displays · VR · Fog displays · Mid-air haptics

1 Introduction

Displays are everywhere, not just on phones and computers. Ubiquitous displays range from washing machines and other home appliances to public screens in venues such as shopping malls, movie theaters, etc., each requiring specific input modalities.

A. Sand (✉) · I. Rakkolainen · V. Surakka · R. Raisamo
Tampere University, Tampere, Finland
e-mail: antti.sand@tuni.fi

S. Brewster
University of Glasgow, Glasgow, UK

© The Author(s), under exclusive license to Springer Nature Switzerland AG 2022
O. Georgiou et al. (eds.), *Ultrasound Mid-Air Haptics for Touchless Interfaces*,
Human–Computer Interaction Series, https://doi.org/10.1007/978-3-031-04043-6_8

Unconventional displays, such as various kinds of stereoscopic, volumetric, or holographic displays (Benzie et al. 2007), fogscreens, and virtual reality (VR) headsets, can create illusions of images floating in mid-air, but they do not provide any sensation of touch, thus reducing the level of immersion. Ultrasound haptics is a method to produce an unobtrusive, mid-air sensation of touch on a user's skin.

We will focus on two types of unconventional displays, which can employ this mid-air tactile feedback: fogscreens and head-mounted displays (HMD). While appearing dissimilar at first glance, both displays share certain permeability—in fogscreens the display surface is permeable and in VR the presented virtual environments are permeable. This causes them to share also similar usability issues.

When compared with traditional touchscreens or the computer mouse, these displays do not provide the inherent tactile sensation of touching solid surfaces. Tactile sensations are important in interaction, as these sensations can affirm to the user that, e.g., a selection was indeed made. Without them, the user may be left wondering if the gesture was registered or were they simply waving their hands in front of the control.

Extended reality (XR) typically employs vision and audition. If any form of haptics is used, it is often obtrusive. The missing or weak sense of touch in most XR systems is a clear deviation from the real world. It can be disappointing and confusing to reach toward a visually accurate virtual object and then feel rudimentary (or no) tactile signals. Furthermore, the fidelity of current tactile display technologies is very low compared to audio-visual displays or to the capabilities and complexity of human tactile sensing. These tactile shortcomings amount to several orders of magnitude (Biswas and Visell 2019). Haptics can enhance immersion, performance, and interaction of XR and user interfaces (UI).

Traditional, widely used commercial approaches to haptic feedback have been mostly limited to simple surface-based vibrotactile stimuli. Most VR headsets come with hand-held controllers housing vibration motors. This approach provides simple vibrotactile feedback with little precision and is not ideal for sensing surface textures, for example, specialized and cumbersome haptic devices, gloves, and suits disrupt the feeling of presence even more. While wearable haptic devices (Pacchierotti et al. 2017) could be used to solve the issue of missing tactile feedback with permeable screens, they have not yet been a commercial success. Such devices, using many actuators, could offer a richer set of haptic sensations, but with current technology, they are expensive and cumbersome. In any case, wearable haptic devices might not be a good companion for permeable displays in a public setting, as touch-based tactile feedback is not hygienic.

VR headsets with hand trackers allow the user to interact with virtual objects using gestures. Luckily, the missing haptic feedback is no longer confined on a surface but is available also in mid-air without contact. Tactile sensations can be added using acoustic pressure to the skin from several tiny, phased ultrasonic speakers. This ultrasound haptics could be an elegant solution to providing haptic feedback while interacting with permeable displays.

2 Unconventional Display Devices

Display technologies usually take much longer than anticipated to reach maturity (Jepsen 2005). The time from the first prototypes to high-volume sales was around 50 years for the CRT and around 20 years for LCOS. The first HMD was introduced in 1968 (Sutherland 1968), and only now have they started to appear in our homes.

Many display devices have at first been unconventional, but with time have either become more mainstream or forgotten. They can have a good run but become obsolete, like the View-Master by William Gruber, which captivated and immersed its viewers from 1939 to at least the 1990s. Displays can often find a niche market in which to thrive. For example, 3D display devices may be valuable tools for architects or medical professionals, as well as some researchers and data analysts. It is likely that there will never be a universal display for all purposes. Overall, novel display technologies can bring advanced features that in some cases end up competing with traditional lower cost displays if the added value or demand surpasses the added expense. For example, VR headsets are now experiencing a new wave of popularity. Where VPL Research, Sega, and Nintendo failed commercially in the 1980s, it is not exceptional to find HMDs in homes today.

2.1 Permeable Displays

Mid-air and holographic displays have dominated the display imagery in science fiction movies for decades. Ranging from Forbidden Planet to Star Wars to Minority Report and Iron Man, they have captivated the media and the general public's attention. But the idea of an immersive, permeable, or "holographic" display has intrigued people for centuries before any movies. Dioramas (a mobile theater device) immersed the general public into a variety of scenes ever since the early nineteenth century; whereas, wide mural scenic paintings could have filled the viewer's entire field of view.

Permeable imagery floating in mid-air is even more magical and intriguing. Images have been projected to various kinds of water, smoke, haze, or fog screens since at least the fifteenth century. The concept gained popularity and birthed commercial viewings in which attendees would sit in a darkened room occupied by flying demons, hellish scenery, and appropriate audio effects (See Fig. 1). Belgian inventor Étienne-Gaspard Robert coined the term *fantascope* for these "magic" lanterns used to project the images. The macabre atmosphere in the post-revolutionary city of Paris combined with the novelty of moving mid-air projections made Robert the best-known phantasmagoria showman.

Images apparently floating in free space can be generated in numerous ways, e.g., with stereoscopic or multiview displays, or with the old Pepper's ghost illusion (Benzie et al. 2007), but most of them only create illusions of objects in mid-air and they are not truly in air or penetrable. Volumetric displays emit light from the

Fig. 1 Fantasmagorie de Robertson at Cour des Capucines in 1797

actual 3D positions, but the images are usually in a confined display volume, and interaction with them is limited.

Various water and fogscreens are used for example in theme parks and they can create impressive shows (e.g., Disney's Fantasmic show), but they are not walk-through. Most fog and water screens are wet projection surfaces. Alternatively, thin particle clouds have been used, but they need to be planar to create sharp images, except when viewed from afar and directly toward the projector. Smoke is opaque and usually darker, requiring more illumination and resulting in less-than-optimal contrast. Fog machines in concerts can create fine particles from chemicals. However, they accumulate haze after prolonged use in enclosed spaces, which may float around for long periods of time and may have adverse effects on humans.

An unprotected fog flow disperses rapidly due to the turbulence induced by the dynamic pressure differences between the flow and the surrounding air, disrupting the desired smooth and planar surface and thus severely distorting the image. In contrast, the fogscreen (See Fig. 2) uses a thick, nonturbulent (laminar) airflow around a thin, nonturbulent fog flow (both around 1 m/s). The injected particle flow is protected by the surrounding airflow, thus keeping the screen flat and enabling high-quality projected images hovering in thin air.

The fogscreen is thus a great method to create a light-scattering particle screen in terms of high-quality, dry images hovering in mid-air. However, water screens, 3D illusions, volumetric displays, and other types of displays are better than fogscreens for some purposes. There is not a universally best display technology, but all of them have their uses.

Fig. 2 Large fogscreen hanging from the ceiling can show a clear projected image on a thin layer of fog

The fogscreen creates a concise and thin particle projection screen and produces an image quality superior to previous methods. Eventually, the fog flow tends to get slightly turbulent farther away from the device and increasingly starts to break up before reaching the floor. Multiprojector systems can make free space fogscreens appear volumetric (Yagi et al. 2011).

The fogscreen is a permeable projection screen. The tiny micron-scale fog particles are dry to touch, and the screen feels just like air to the hand. The light-scattering fog particles serve as a rear-projected screen with the unconventional feature that the user can unobtrusively interact with the screen and walk or reach right through it.

The mid-air screen opens new use cases as it cannot be broken—it recovers automatically and instantly when penetrated. It also stays clean and hygienic, as there is no permanent surface for dirt, bacteria, and viruses to transfer. It enables also two-sided content, where the two sides do not visually interfere with each other. This can further add value in multi-user scenarios.

The technology enables both large and small screens. A smaller, laptop-sized screen can be used as a computer monitor, with the exception that physical objects can share space with the display medium, thus bringing, for example, augmented reality

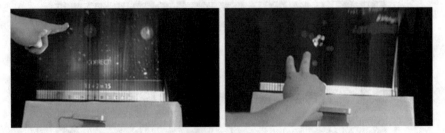

Fig. 3 Left: an interactive math learning application on a 17″ desktop fogscreen with hand tracking. Right: an atomic model visualizer with gestural interaction

(AR) content close to the object of interest without any AR glasses. Furthermore, proximity to the screen will not harm delicate objects when used in that manner.

Gesture tracking can be used for interaction with the display and its content. Figure 3 shows two examples of educational applications using a small fogscreen with a hand tracker.

While a small-size fogscreen could be used as a typical monitor with a keyboard and a mouse, the unique opportunities afforded by it are best employed when used with gestural interaction. This, however, comes with an issue of usability. Touching elements presented on a permeable screen do not provide the tactile sensation of solid touchscreens. With audio-visual feedback alone, the user might be uncertain on whether they performed the intended gesture correctly, or whether the system detected the performed gesture correctly. Wearable actuators, such as haptic gloves, could be used to alleviate the issue, but they may be cumbersome and obtrusive and are often tethered.

2.2 Head-Mounted Displays

The basic principle behind a device that would be called a head-mounted display was presented by Charles Wheatstone (Wheatstone 1838) before the invention of photography. He used custom stereoscopic drawings that were viewable through a device called a stereoscope (See Fig. 4 Left). This simple device was placed in front of the eyes of the user had two mirrors at 45° angles to the user's eyes and stereoscopic picture card pairs on the sides. The drawings, and later photographs, had a slight offset in perspective to mimic the offset of the human eyes.

David Brewster improved on Wheatstone's design in 1849 by adding a pair of lenses (See Fig. 4 Left bottom). This made the device much smaller and more portable. This device was later refined into the well-known View-Master in 1939, but the design remained very similar even in the smartphone-based HMDs, such as the Google Cardboard and Samsung Gear VR, some 200 years after Wheatstone's invention.

Fig. 4 Left: Wheatstone's and Brewster's stereoscopes. Right: Immersion through stereoscopic image pairs in the early twentieth century

Comeau and Bryan (1961) created the first video-based HMD. In 1968, Ivan Sutherland presented an HMD with 3D graphics and head tracking (Sutherland 1968). It is worth noting that the 3D graphics of that time consisted of mostly wireframe rooms and objects.

Today, HMDs take many shapes: AR glasses, VR headsets, head-mounted projector displays, etc. Sometimes a clear distinction between categories can be difficult to make. For example, the Varjo XR-3 HMD streams stereoscopic camera feed into human eye-resolution screens, thus allowing the level of augmentation to be anything from entirely unaugmented reality to a fully virtual environment.

VR headsets allow the users to explore virtual environments. These often come with hand-held controllers, but also hands-free interaction is possible with the use of hand trackers. The user can see their hands in the virtual environment and touch the virtual objects. They can receive audio-visual feedback on their interaction, but ultimately the hand will penetrate the virtual object without providing haptic sensations. This issue is perhaps most emphasized when trying to interact with UI elements using touch. Buttons, knobs, sliders, etc. can be difficult to operate when the hand can slide through them. Wearable controllers could provide coarse vibrotactile feedback, but this would limit hands-free interaction. Some form of touchless tactile interaction could make touching virtual elements easier and more immersive.

3 Touchless Tactile Interaction

Unconventional displays, such as fogscreens, 3D displays, and VR headsets, open new opportunities for gestural interaction. User interfaces on these displays create reach-through touchscreens but tapping on a UI element or a virtual object on such a display would leave the finger intersecting the display surface without any tactile stimulation. This feels unnatural, as visible objects usually feel tactile. It lessens the immersion and makes manipulation of virtual objects cumbersome.

Surface haptics is the traditional method for generating haptic feedback. Smartphones, smartwatches, tablet computers, and gaming controllers house tiny actuators that vibrate the entire device. They are simple, inexpensive, and effective, but the information they can provide is very limited. Further, a high-spatial resolution would also require new methods to propagate the haptic stimuli at a specific location and not to the whole device, such as using constructive wave interference from several actuators (Coe et al. 2021).

Another option is to mediate the sensation in mid-air, without the need for wearable devices. This allows for hands-free interaction and in some cases offer a significantly higher spatial resolution. The ability to "feel" content in mid-air addresses fundamental usability challenges with gestural interfaces (Freeman et al. 2014; Rakkolainen et al. 2020). It helps users to overcome uncertainty about gestures, improves user engagement, immersion, etc.

Mid-air haptics is a group of different technologies that allow for haptic feedback on touchless interaction. Some techniques use directed air jets to create a sensation of touch from a distance, others can produce thermal sensations, but none of them is very accurate or fast. Currently, the most promising approach is using ultrasound haptics.

3.1 Ultrasound Haptics

Focused airborne acoustic air pressure produced by ultrasonic phased arrays can provide mid-air tactile feedback (Iwamoto et al. 2008; Rakkolainen et al. 2020) without mechanically moving parts and with much greater speed and precision. As an ultrasonic actuator matrix can remain at a distance and requires no tethering on the user, this approach is unobtrusive, maintaining the user's freedom to move in the target area.

Compared to wearable vibrotactile actuators, ultrasonic mid-air haptics has some clear benefits. It does not require any wearable actuators or the user to be tethered to the device. It has spatial freedom as the acoustic pressure focal point can be translated quickly inside the interaction volume. It can be used to create volumetric shapes and surfaces and to present surface textures (e.g., Freeman et al. 2017). It can feel like magic to the user.

Ultrasound haptics is particularly good at generating a range of tactile stimuli on the user's palm or fingertips (Sand et al. 2020). For example, a 200 ms burst has been described as "unmistakably a mouse click" (Palovuori et al. 2014).

Common ultrasonic phased arrays offer interaction volumes suitable for desktop use, as the range is limited to tens of centimeters. For large public displays, this is unfeasible. Lately, a solution has been proposed in the form of rotating the array around the pan and tilt axes (Howard et al. 2020). Workspace can also be expanded with a long-distance mid-air haptic display using a curved reflector (Ariga et al. 2021).

Ultrasound haptics is fast and relatively accurate, it offers untethered hands-free interaction, it can present shapes and surfaces to a degree, and it can be a natural transition from traditional input feedback. For these reasons, ultrasound haptics could be a natural match for touchless tactile permeable displays.

4 Touchless Tactile Permeable Displays

Mid-air tactile feedback systems can benefit interaction with displays. They can be used as tactile displays (Sand et al., 2020), and be merged with 3D displays (Hoshi et al. 2009; Inoue et al. 2014; Long et al. 2014; Monnai et al. 2014) or fogscreens (Sand et al. 2015a, b). Stationary ultrasonic arrays require the user to stay close to the array to receive tactile feedback.

The transducer arrays can also be fitted onto an HMD. An HMD with an ultrasound array in a fixed position (Kervegant et al. 2017; Martinez et al. 2018) severely limits the working range. If the array is mounted to the front of an HMD (Sand et al. 2015b), the tactile feedback is always directed outwards to the visual working area of the user, thus its range is mobile and adequate in the range of convenient reach of the arm (See Fig. 5), thus somewhat circumventing the issue of limited interaction volume. For this reason, HMDs match well with mid-air tactile feedback.

This setup allows touchless tactile stimulation when touching virtual objects with one's hands. It has the potential to take VR to a whole new level of immersion. In addition to touching UI controls, such as buttons, the user could also experience ephemeral elements, such as wind and rain, feel a butterfly landing on their hand, etc.

Fig. 5 Ultrasonic mid-air haptics device attached to a head-mounted display always keeps the feedback oriented to the facing direction. The hand tracking sensor on top of the matrix allows the focal point to be directed at the fingertip

Fig. 6 From front left to
back right: leap motion
controller, fogscreen, phased
ultrasonic 16 × 8 array, and
projector (masked with an
R2D2 printout) (Sand et al.,
2015a)

Ultrasound haptics can also go inwards from the HMD to the face (Gil et al. 2018) or lips (Jingu et al. 2021). It can guide the user's attention or evoke emotions. In a teleconference a mother could caress her child with a hand gesture, to be sent to the child's cheek. To accomplish this, short-range low-powered ultrasound haptics could be used toward skin areas adjacent to the HMD.

Permeable screens, such as the fogscreen (See Fig. 6), make the mid-air gestural interaction significantly easier, as the user has a visual reference on roughly where the interaction should take place, for example, how far they need to reach to make a tap gesture. This allows the system to only regard gestures made in a shallow depth volume and frees the user to move and gesture at will without having to worry about unintentional selections.

Challenges of touchless interaction

When touching or tapping with mid-air gestures, there are still some tradeoffs due to technological limitations. It can be difficult to tap on a virtual target in such a uniform way that it can be reliably recognized by the system between various gestures and users.

Many technological challenges can be alleviated with good design, while others require less than optimal interaction methods. One of the most prominent technological challenges related to mid-air gesturing is commonly known as the Midas touch (Kjeldsen and Hartman 2001). Because the gesture tracking technology is constantly tracking the user, there can often be a disparity in what the system detects as a gesture and what the user intends as one. This can lead to constant unintentional selections making the use of the system a very frustrating endeavor. The user might be communicating to another person and, perhaps subconsciously, move their hands, or engage in other physical tasks in the tracking system's interaction space (Walter et al. 2014).

Common remedies for the Midas touch problem include the use of extra actions. In whole-body interaction, the user might be required to take a special body pose, such as a "teapot" (Walter et al. 2013), meaning that the user must place their hands on their hips to indicate to the tracking system that they wish to begin the interaction. When using just pointing and tapping, the user might be required to make a fist or other special gesture to confirm the selection of the pointed object. This can, however, result in the virtual cursor moving away from the intended target as the hand tends to move slightly while the gesture is being made.

The system can analyze also the user's posture and gaze to guess when the user wants their movements to be considered as interacting with the system (Schwarz et al. 2014). However, the Midas touch issue is not limited to just gestural interaction but is prominent in most interaction methods that rely on continuous tracking, for example, in using eye gaze to select targets in gaze-based interfaces (Vrzakova and Bednarik 2013).

The Midas touch phenomenon is worsened by the inherent lack of tactile feedback associated with permeable and virtual displays, as well as mid-air gestural interaction. Traditional physical input devices come with built-in haptic feedback and also inherent limitations—a button can only be pressed so far, and a knob can only be turned one way or the other.

From what we have observed, the Midas touch phenomenon is greatly reduced with fogscreens as the user can have a shallow interaction depth with a clear visible indicator of where it starts. Yet, fog and other common light-reflecting particles reduce the tracking accuracy of many common tracking methods, such as time-of-flight sensors and depth cameras, justifying the need for haptic feedforward. Moreover, users may be wary of gestural interfaces, at least initially, worrying if the system is working or not, and haptic feedback could work to reassure the user that the system is indeed tracking the selections reliably.

To make gesture recognition more reliable, many systems opt for dwelling the pointing finger or hand on top of the target for a certain duration of time. This can help to eliminate unintentional selections but is often much slower and more tiring for the user (van de Camp et al. 2013; Yoo et al. 2015). For example, with a two-meter-wide public fogscreen, a dwell-timer combined with extreme hand extrusion could quickly lead to severe physical strain. In this case, it would perhaps make more sense to interact with the display from a distance as one would with a typical large public display. While the dwell-based selection method has clear drawbacks (time consumption and physical strain), it might still require more technical advances before simple pointing and tapping becomes reliable enough to surpass the need for such clutch actions. One such technical advance could be the addition of ultrasonic actuators to provide the tactile sensation of touching solid surfaces to interact with permeable displays.

Ultrasound haptics suffers also from some limitations, mainly from noticeably weaker feedback compared with standard haptic actuators, as well as from a relatively short interaction distance. The interaction distance with current ultrasound haptics hardware is functional for small-size fogscreens but will not work with larger fogscreens of over one meter of width.

Experimental results

In our preliminary testing, providing ultrasonic tactile feedback to interaction with a fogscreen on a numerical input task (See Fig. 6) did not result in significant differences in the rate of numbers entered or the error rate compared with use without haptic feedback, but the addition of tactile feedback was preferred by the users (Sand et al. 2015a). However, this experiment was conducted using a small 16 × 8 transducer array. A larger ultrasonic array would produce stronger feedback. Further, both the display and the feedback device were novel to the participants and that novelty may also have distracted the participants from the actual task, maximizing their interaction with the tactile feedback instead of optimizing their performance.

In a later study, a similar experiment was repeated using an HMD with the transducer array mounted on the front panel of the HMD (See Fig. 5). While we did not find a significant difference on entered characters per second or error rate compared with use without haptic feedback, subjective values collected using NASA. TLX revealed that ultrasonic haptic feedback lessened the perceived temporal, physical, and mental demand as well as effort with temporal demand having a statistically significant change in t-test ($t12 = 4.38, p < 0.001$) (See Fig. 7). Further, the preference for the tactile feedback was clear with 11 out of 13 participants reporting they preferred having the tactile feedback (Sand et al. 2015b).

Permeable displays have several benefits. In AR use, they allow delicate objects to be placed within the display volume, thus bringing the AR content seamlessly close to the object of interest. As dirt or bacteria cannot catch on, the display is suitable for bakeries, operating rooms, factories, and other places where the user's hands may be dirty. The hygienic aspect makes it suitable also generally during pandemics.

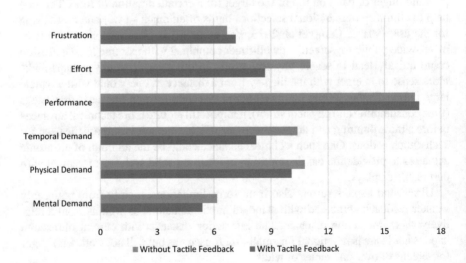

Fig. 7 TLX averages with and without tactile feedback (smaller is better, except in performance, where larger is better)

5 Discussion

Ultrasound haptics offer potential for controllable and expressive touchless tactile feedback. It is a natural match for permeable screens, VR headsets, and other virtual UIs that do not provide inherent tactile sensations. Compared with traditional surface haptics, it allows, for example, rapid translation of the focal point, easy creation of multiple simultaneous focal points, and presentation of shapes and textures.

However, the small range and the strength of stimulation limit its usefulness in many scenarios. Very large permeable screens, such as the one shown in Fig. 2, are not a good match for ultrasound haptics. This is due to the large interaction volume, which would be difficult to serve with ultrasonic actuators. Rotating the array around the pan and tilt axes (Howard et al. 2020), using massively scalable arrays (Suzuki et al. 2021), or using long-distance curved ultrasound reflectors (Ariga et al. 2021) could remedy the issue to a degree, but the dissipation of acoustic radiation over distance would still be problematic. A wearable actuator might still be required for use with large interaction volumes, but the combination of touchless and wearable haptics is not extensively studied.

The strength of stimulation can be affected by the number of transducers, but it is a path of diminishing returns and increasing cost and complexity. Different frequencies can be utilized for stronger stimulations, but current research has focused mainly on 40 kHz (Iwamoto et al. 2008) or 70 kHz (Ito et al. 2016). It is important to note that the size of the focal point is determined by the wavelength of the carrier frequency so that 70 kHz allows a more precise focal point than 40 kHz. More research and technological advancements, such as different transducers, transducer layouts/board designs, and transducer frequencies are needed to improve the strength of the stimulation.

Based on the results of the evaluations described in the previous section, we assume that the best use of mid-air haptic feedback with unconventional permeable displays could be in situations emphasizing user experience: entertainment technology, games, and other user interfaces meant for fun could potentially be even more fun with mid-air haptics. However, in productivity applications, the measurable performance benefits may turn out to be small. At least amplifying an art exhibition with ultrasound haptics left the visitors feeling more immersed and uplifted (Vi et al. 2017). It seems within reason to assume that the same could happen with unconventional displays, but further studies would be needed.

Ultrasound haptics remains an interesting topic for further studies. Little is known about emotional responses to ultrasonic stimulations, and most research has focused exclusively on the palmar side of the hands as the receiving skin location. Ultrasound haptics can create more subtle sensations compared with traditional vibrotactile actuators. This could be useful in therapeutic touch, or wider emotional response invocation, as well as remote touch.

Focusing research on the palmar side of the hands has made sense since it is an area with a high density of mechanoreceptors, which is important given the relatively weak feedback amplitude. The human face, especially the lip area, has also a high density of mechanoreceptors, making it somewhat an obvious research interest, but possibly researchers have thus far avoided focusing the feedback on the face for safety concerns.

Touchless interaction has clear benefits in environments where touch-transferred dirt, viruses, or bacteria might pose harm to others or the system they are interacting with—environments such as operating rooms, factories, bakeries, etc. Further, during pandemics, people might appreciate hygienic "touchless touchscreens" on public interfaces.

Great interest in ultrasound haptics has recently arisen from the automotive industry. As VR gains popularity for simulated training, remote participation, and entertainment, touchless tactile feedback can allow for hands-free interaction and exploration. All of these are fascinating avenues of future research.

6 Conclusions

Unconventional displays, such as fogscreens, various types of 3D displays, and VR headsets, open new opportunities for interaction. Paired with hand tracking they allow for gestural interaction. User interfaces can be presented on permeable screens to create reach-through touchscreens that react and recover instantly from intersecting objects. The user can explore virtual environments and control floating UIs with hand gestures.

Merging touchless interaction with ultrasound haptics enables the user to better interact with and feel virtual objects, as well as experience ephemeral elements. The visual reference provided by fogscreens together with confirming tactile sensation of ultrasound haptics could be one solution for the Midas touch issue of gestural interaction.

Floating UIs using unconventional displays, hand tracking, and ultrasound haptics enable more immersive interaction and enhanced simulated training, and entertainment. However, it has also its limitations, such as limited range, extra weight, relatively weak feedback, etc. The effects of mid-air haptics on interaction have not been extensively studied, but initially it looks like the technology improves user experience and entertainment more than the performance of tasks. The technology is still relatively young, and we expect that many improvements will make it a very intriguing element for many kinds of interaction in the future.

References

Ariga K, Fujiwara M, Makino Y, Shinoda H (2021). Workspace evaluation of long-distance midair haptic display using curved reflector. In: 2021 IEEE world haptics conference (WHC). IEEE, pp 85–90. https://doi.org/10.1109/WHC49131.2021.9517193

Benzie P, Watson J, Surman P, Rakkolainen I, Hopf K, Urey H, Sainov V, von Kopylow C (2007) A survey of 3DTV displays: techniques and technologies. IEEE Trans Circuits Syst Video Technol 17(11):1647–1658. https://doi.org/10.1109/TCSVT.2007.905377

Biswas S, Visell Y (2019) Emerging material technologies for haptics. Adv Mater Technol 4(4):1900042. https://doi.org/10.1002/admt.201900042

Coe P, Evreinov G, Sinivaara H, Hippula A, Raisamo R (2021) Haptic actuation plate for multi-layered in-vehicle control panel. Multimodal Technol Interact 5:25. https://doi.org/10.3390/mti 5050025

Comeau C, Bryan JS (1961) Headsight television system provides remote surveillance. Electronics 86–90

Freeman E, Brewster S, Lantz V (2014) Tactile feedback for above-device gesture interfaces: adding touch to touchless interactions. In: Proceedings of the 16th international conference on multimodal interaction, pp 419–426. https://doi.org/10.1145/2663204.2663280

Freeman E, Anderson R, Williamson J, Wilson G, Brewster SA (2017) Textured surfaces for ultrasound haptic displays. In: ICMI 2017—Proceedings of the 19th ACM international conference on multimodal interaction, vol 2017-Jan. https://doi.org/10.1145/3136755.3143020

Gil H, Son H, Kim JR, Oakley I (2018) Whiskers: exploring the use of ultrasonic haptic cues on the face. In: Proceedings of the 2018 CHI conference on human factors in computing systems, pp 1–13. https://doi.org/10.1145/3173574.3174232

Hoshi T, Abe D, Shinoda H (2009) Adding tactile reaction to hologram. In: RO-MAN 2009—the 18th IEEE international symposium on robot and human interactive communication. IEEE, pp 7–11. https://doi.org/10.1109/ROMAN.2009.5326299

Howard T, Marchal M, Lécuyer A, Pacchierotti C (2020) PUMAH: pan-tilt ultrasound mid-air haptics for larger interaction workspace in virtual reality. IEEE Trans Haptics 13(1):38–44. https://doi.org/10.1109/TOH.2019.2963028

Inoue S, Kobayashi-Kirschvink KJ, Monnai Y, Hasegawa K, Makino Y, Shinoda H (2014) HORN. In: ACM SIGGRAPH 2014 emerging technologies on—SIGGRAPH '14. ACM Press, New York, New York, USA, pp 1–1. https://doi.org/10.1145/2614066.2614092

Ito M, Wakuda D, Inoue S, Makino Y, Shinoda H (2016) High spatial resolution midair tactile display using 70 kHz ultrasound. In: Lecture notes in computer science (including subseries lecture notes in artificial intelligence and lecture notes in bioinformatics, vol 9774. https://doi.org/10.1007/978-3-319-42321-0_6

Iwamoto T, Tatezono M, Shinoda H (2008) Non-contact method for producing tactile sensation using airborne ultrasound. In: Haptics: perception, devices and scenarios. Springer Berlin Heidelberg, Berlin, Heidelberg, pp 504–513. https://doi.org/10.1007/978-3-540-69057-3_64

Jepsen M (2005) Smoke, mirrors, and manufacturable displays. Computer 38(8):63–67. https://doi.org/10.1109/MC.2005.271

Jingu A, Kamigaki T, Fujiwara M, Makino Y, Shinoda H (2021) LipNotif: use of lips as a non-contact tactile notification interface based on ultrasonic tactile presentation. In: The 34th annual ACM symposium on user interface software and technology, pp 13–23. https://doi.org/10.1145/3472749.3474732

Kervegant C, Raymond F, Graeff D, Castet J (2017) Touch hologram in mid-air. In: ACM SIGGRAPH 2017 emerging technologies, pp 1–2. https://doi.org/10.1145/3084822.3084824

Kjeldsen R, Hartman J (2001) Design issues for vision-based computer interaction systems. In: ACM international conference proceeding series (Vol. 15-16-November-2001). New York, New York, USA: association for computing machinery, pp 27. https://doi.org/10.1145/971478.971511

Long B, Seah SA, Carter T, Subramanian S (2014) Rendering volumetric haptic shapes in mid-air using ultrasound. ACM Trans Graphics 33(6):1–10. https://doi.org/10.1145/2661229.2661257

Martinez J, Griffiths D, Biscione V, Georgiou O, Carter T (2018) Touchless haptic feedback for supernatural VR experiences. In: 2018 IEEE conference on virtual reality and 3D user interfaces (VR). IEEE, pp 629–630. https://doi.org/10.1109/VR.2018.8446522

Monnai Y, Hasegawa K, Fujiwara M, Yoshino K, Inoue S, Shinoda, H (2014) HaptoMime. In: Proceedings of the 27th annual ACM symposium on User interface software and technology—UIST '14. ACM Press, New York, New York, USA, pp 663–667. https://doi.org/10.1145/264 2918.2647407

Pacchierotti C, Sinclair S, Solazzi M, Frisoli A, Hayward V, Prattichizzo D (2017) Wearable haptic systems for the fingertip and the hand: taxonomy, review, and perspectives. IEEE Trans Haptics 10(4):580–600. https://doi.org/10.1109/TOH.2017.2689006

Palovuori K, Rakkolainen I, Sand A (2014) Bidirectional touch interaction for immaterial displays. In: Proceedings of the 18th international academic MindTrek conference on media business, management, content & services—AcademicMindTrek '14. ACM Press, New York, New York, USA, pp 74–76. https://doi.org/10.1145/2676467.2676503

Rakkolainen I, Freeman E, Sand A, Raisamo R, Brewster S (2020) A survey of mid-air ultrasound haptics and its applications. IEEE Trans Haptics 14(1):2–19. https://doi.org/10.1109/TOH.2020. 3018754

Sand A, Rakkolainen I, Isokoski P, Raisamo R, Palovuori K (2015a) Light-weight immaterial particle displays with mid-air tactile feedback. In: 2015a IEEE international symposium on haptic, audio and visual environments and games, HAVE 2015—Proceedings. https://doi.org/10.1109/HAVE. 2015.7359448

Sand A, Rakkolainen I, Isokoski P, Kangas J, Raisamo R, Palovuori K (2015b) Head-mounted display with mid-air tactile feedback. In: Proceedings of the 21st ACM symposium on virtual reality software and technology—VRST '15, vol 13–15-Nove, pp 51–58. https://doi.org/10.1145/ 2821592.2821593

Sand A, Rakkolainen I, Surakka V, Raisamo R, Brewster S (2020) Evaluating ultrasonic tactile feedback stimuli. EuroHaptics 253–261. https://doi.org/10.1007/978-3-030-58147-3_28

Schwarz J, Marais C, Leyvand T, Hudson SE, Mankoff J (2014) Combining body pose, gaze, and gesture to determine intention to interact in vision-based interfaces. In: Conference on human factors in computing systems—proceedings. Association for Computing Machinery, New York, New York, USA, pp 3443–3452. https://doi.org/10.1145/2556288.2556989

Sutherland IE (1968) A head-mounted three dimensional display. In: Proceedings of the December 9–11, 1968, fall joint computer conference, part I. Association for Computing Machinery, New York, NY, USA, pp 757–764. https://doi.org/10.1145/1476589.1476686

Suzuki S, Inoue S, Fujiwara M, Makino Y, Shinoda H (2021) AUTD3: scalable airborne ultrasound tactile display. IEEE Trans Haptics. https://doi.org/10.1109/TOH.2021.3069976

van de Camp F, Schick A, Stiefelhagen R (2013) How to click in mid-air. In: Lecture notes in computer science (including subseries lecture notes in artificial intelligence and lecture notes in bioinformatics), vol 8028 LNCS, pp 78–86. https://doi.org/10.1007/978-3-642-39351-8_9

Vi C, Ablart D, Gatti E, Velasco C, Obrist M (2017) Not just seeing, but also feeling art: mid-air haptic experiences integrated in a multisensory art exhibition. J 108. https://doi.org/10.1016/j. ijhcs.2017.06.004

Vrzakova H, Bednarik R (2013) That's not Norma(n/l)! a detailed analysis of Midas touch in gaze-based problem-solving. In: Conference on human factors in computing systems—proceedings, vol 2013-April. Association for Computing Machinery, New York, New York, USA, pp 85–90. https://doi.org/10.1145/2468356.2468373

Walter R, Bailly G, Müller J (2013) StrikeAPose: revealing mid-air gestures on public displays. In: Conference on human factors in computing systems – proceedings, pp 841–850. https://doi.org/ 10.1145/2470654.2470774

Walter R, Bailly G, Valkanova N, Müller J (2014) Cuenesics: using mid-air gestures to select items on interactive public displays. In: MobileHCI 2014—Proceedings of the 16th ACM international conference on human-computer interaction with mobile devices and services. Association for Computing Machinery, Inc., New York, New York, USA, pp 299–308. https://doi.org/10.1145/ 2628363.2628368

Wheatstone C (1838) On some remarkable, and hitherto unobserved, phenomena of binocular vision. Philos Trans R Soc Lond 11:371–394

Yagi A, Imura M, Kuroda Y, Oshiro O (2011) 360-degree fog projection interactive display. In: SIGGRAPH Asia 2011 emerging technologies, pp 1–1. https://doi.org/10.1145/2073370.207 3388

Yoo S, Parker C, Kay J, Tomitsch M (2015) To dwell or not to dwell: an evaluation of mid-air gestures for large information displays. In: OzCHI 2015: being human—conference proceedings. Association for Computing Machinery, Inc., New York, New York, USA, pp 187–191. https:// doi.org/10.1145/2838739.2838819

Modulation Methods for Ultrasound Midair Haptics

Keisuke Hasegawa and Hiroyuki Shinoda

Abstract This chapter describes techniques for midair vibrotactile stimulation based on ultrasound foci with temporally varied intensities or positions. This variation of the focal property is called modulations and can be categorized into three fundamental types of methods according to the modulating fashions and obtained vibrotactile effects: amplitude modulation (AM), lateral modulation (LM), and spatiotemporal modulation (STM). Appropriate modulation is useful in designing vibrotactile textures, enhancing the subjective strength of aroused sensation, and transmitting geometrical information about spatial vibrotactile patterns. The aim of this chapter is to provide a brief and simple overview of the main rendering techniques and to discuss their pros and cons, thus providing sufficient engineering insight to the haptics and human–computer interaction (HCI) readers.

1 Introduction

The acoustic radiation force that can be generated by static midair ultrasound foci is not strong enough to be constantly perceived as a static force. Such still ultrasound foci are perceived only when users move their hands around the focal regions in an exploratory manner. An example of tactile displays using a static ultrasound field is an invisible compliant sphere that can be perceived by bare hands surrounded

K. Hasegawa (✉)
Graduate School of Information Science and Technology, The University of Tokyo, 7-3-1 Hongo, Bunkyo-ku, Tokyo, Japan
e-mail: keisuke_hasegawa@ipc.i.u-tokyo.ac.jp

H. Shinoda
Graduate School of Frontier Sciences, The University of Tokyo, 5-1-5 Kashiwanoha, Kashiwa-shi, Chiba-ken, Japan
e-mail: hiroyuki_shinoda@k.u-tokyo.ac.jp

by multiple phased arrays (Inoue et al. 2015). Although, such an approach is valid in displaying a specific type of tactile pattern at a fixed position, instantaneously perceived vibrotactile stimuli cannot be created using this approach.

Vibrotactile stimuli are especially effective in a variety of application scenarios, where people receive prompt and programmable tactile feedback according to their action. For example, vibrotactile haptic feedback can be presented during hand gesture input in human–computer interaction scenarios. While many realizations of midair haptics target the users palms and fingers, an increasingly prominent feature of the midair haptics is that it can stimulate other parts on the human body such as the users' arms, chest, and face.

Temporal or spatial modulation of the radiation force at the ultrasound focus can offer distinctly perceivable vibrotactile sensation as originally shown since the very beginnings of midair ultrasound haptics technology (Hoshi et al. 2010; Iwamoto et al. 2008). This phenomenon is understood as the envelope detection effect of amplitude-modulated sinusoidal stimulation with high carrier frequencies that are normally imperceptible by skin mechanoreceptors. The analogous effect has been reported with a rigid vibrator used as a vibrotactile actuator (Lamoré et al. 1986).

There are four types of known cutaneous mechanoreceptors, each with different response characteristics to vibrotactile stimulation on the surface of skin (Purves et al. 2001). They are categorized into one of the combinations of two temporal characteristics (fast adaptive (FA) or slow adaptive (SA)) and two spatial characteristics (Type I with small receptive fields or Type II with large receptive fields). Spatial and temporal mechanical stimulations on surface of the skin are converted into nerve signals via these mechanoreceptors. Each type of mechanoreceptor responds to different features of the stimulation with some spatial or temporal components being perceived stronger than others. Moreover, specific spatiotemporal patterns of stimulation can be distinctly perceived as different tactile textures from that aroused by other stimulation patterns. Therefore, research efforts have been focused on designing and applying midair haptic modulation techniques that appropriately stimulate a mix of cutaneous mechanoreceptors to induce a wealth of vibrotactile sensations.

Based on this somatosensory insight, subjectively strong midair haptic vibrotactile stimulations have been designed by considering these characteristics of human tactile perception. Specifically, it has been shown that human vibrotactile sensitivity is the highest against 200–250 Hz vibration, which is mainly captured by the Pacinian corpuscles. Other vibrotactile textures and properties can also be tuned by appropriately designed modulation methods. In the simplest example, a sinusoidal vibrotactile midair haptic stimuli of around 200–250 Hz are felt as spatially more spread than the actual stimulation area because of the large receptive fields of the Pacinian corpuscles. If one wants to realize stimuli that are perceived as more localized, then the use of lower modulation frequency that is captured by Type I mechanoreceptors are recommended.

There have been many modulation methods of midair ultrasound haptics devised for displaying vibrational varieties at high spatial and temporal resolutions (Hasegawa and Shinoda 2013), for example, for haptically rendering spatial geometries (Korres and Eid 2016; Martinez et al. 2019), the stiffness of objects (Marchal et al. 2020;

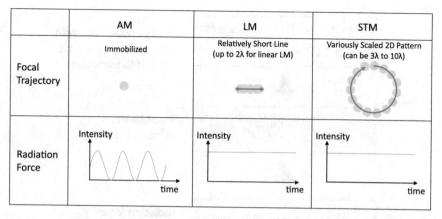

	AM	LM	STM
Focal Trajectory	Immobilized	Relatively Short Line (up to 2λ for linear LM)	Variously Scaled 2D Pattern (can be 3λ to 10λ)
Radiation Force	Intensity / time	Intensity / time	Intensity / time

Fig. 1 Spatiotemporal characteristics of generated ultrasound focus in AM, LM, and STM. Here λ indicates the ultrasound wavelength

Matsubayashi et al. 2021), fluid texture (Jang and Park 2020), and surface roughness in combination with visual cues (Beattie et al. 2020). Each of these modulation methods unlocks new tactile sensations and therefore new applications of the technology. Understanding, developing and discovering new midair haptic modulation methods is therefore an important and active area of research.

In this chapter, we described three well-established midair haptic modulation methods: amplitude modulation (AM), lateral modulation (LM), and spatiotemporal modulation (STM). Figure 1 depicts the spatiotemporal characteristics of these three modulations. A key difference between them is that AM temporally changes the radiation force intensity of a nonmoving ultrasound focus, whereas LM and STM temporally vary the focal position of non-varying radiation force intensity. In the following sections, we introduce the basic principles and effects on vibrotactile perception for each of these modulation methods.

2 Amplitude Modulation (AM)

The AM method was introduced in the early studies on midair ultrasound haptics (Hoshi et al. 2010; Iwamoto et al. 2008), and it is a frequently used vibrotactile stimulation method. This is a method where the radiation force of the midair ultrasound focus is temporally changed. Theoretically, the radiation force is proportional to the square of the root mean square (RMS) value of the acoustic pressure. Hence, the squared envelope of the acoustic waveform at the focal point is equivalent to the vibrotactile waveform (Hasegawa and Shinoda 2018; Hoshi et al. 2010). Based on this principle, AM of the focal acoustic pressure results in mechanical vibration on the skin surface. This vibration waveform can be tuned by adequately designing the modulation envelope of the driving voltage waveform. For example, the aforemen-

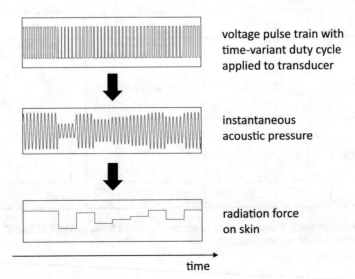

voltage pulse train with
time-variant duty cycle
applied to transducer

instantaneous
acoustic pressure

radiation force
on skin

time

Fig. 2 Relation of a driving pulse train applied to transducers, instantaneous acoustic pressure, and the radiation force in the AM method

tioned squaring effect of the acoustic pressure can engender unwanted vibrotactile harmonics of the acoustic envelope waveform. Therefore, the envelope waveform should be designed so that its square corresponds to the desired vibrotactile waveform.

Designing waveform envelopes for efficient AM midair haptics is often met with a variety of engineering constraints, some of which can be mitigated. For example, some ultrasound phased arrays do not contain analog–digital converters for driving voltage adjustment. Instead, they directly amplify the digital pulses emitted from the controller circuit and input them into ultrasound transducers. The output amplitude of the ultrasound emission from the transducers can be controlled by the duty cycle of the pulse train. Letting d be the duty cycle of the pulses, then the RMS value of the emitted ultrasound amplitude p is given as

$$p = p_0 \sin(\pi d), \tag{1}$$

where p_0 denotes the RMS value of the ultrasound amplitude when $d = 1/2$. Here, it is assumed that the frequency of the pulse train is the same as the resonance frequency of the transducers. Figure 2 shows the relation of the duty cycle of the driving pulse train, instantaneous value of the acoustic pressure, and the radiation force.

Figure 3 shows the vibrotactile characteristics of the AM ultrasound foci that were obtained experimentally (Hasegawa and Shinoda 2018). When the modulation waveform was a sine wave, the detection threshold obtained via user studies was found to be similar to that for the case, where vibrotactile stimuli were produced by mechanical vibrators (Verrillo 1979; Verrilo 1963). Importantly, the obtained

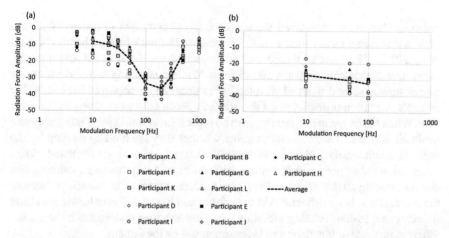

Fig. 3 Detection threshold for AM stimuli with **a** sinusoidal modulation and **b** rectangular modulation. Here 0 dB corresponds to the maximum device output. Adapted from Hasegawa and Shinoda (2018)

threshold curve exhibits its lowest value 200 Hz when the modulation waveform is sinusoidal (Fig. 3a). This suggests that 200 Hz AM focus is perceived as stronger when compared to other frequencies. When using a square waveform, however, the detection threshold is even lower (Fig. 3b), especially for modulation frequencies lower 100 Hz. This is because of the multiple harmonics of the fundamental frequency of the square waves that are not contained in pure sine waves. At the same time, as described in the final part of this section, the second harmonics may spill into audible noises when modulated, which is often unwanted in some application scenarios. These results were obtained in experiments with 320 amplitude quantization levels, which demonstrates that sine waves and square waves were successfully displayed as distinctly different vibrotactile stimuli. The fact that square waves and sine waves of the same frequency are clearly different in terms of textures or detection thresholds has also been confirmed in electrovibration-based (Vardar et al. 2017) and vibrational-actuator-based (MacLean and Enriquez 2003) experiments.

The most prominent feature of midair haptics is that it can offer non-contact tactile stimulation on bare skin. Nevertheless, it is still worth mentioning that AM ultrasound foci can serve as a vibrotactile actuator that has almost flat frequency response across all practical frequencies for tactile use (from 0 up to 1 kHz). In other words, AM foci have no inherent resonance frequencies, whereas most mechanical vibrotactile actuators do. This is a desirable property in that the midair haptics is free from the self-resonance problems of actuators.

In addition to creating subjectively stronger stimuli, another important function of AM is that it can realize a variety of vibrotactile textures by applying modulation waveforms that vary temporally (Hasegawa and Shinoda 2013). For example, a pure sine-wave burst modulation and modulation with a diminishing signal containing multiple frequency components are perceived as completely different. In one of our previous studies, we employed the transient (non-burst) AM ultrasound foci in a system that offers midair images with vibrotactile feedback on bare hands (Monnai et al. 2014). The system offered midair icons that can be selected and dragged, interactive midair number pads, and so forth. While controlling components on the midair screen, several types of vibrotactile textures can be displayed haptically. For example, vibration is displayed on the user's fingertip only when dragging a midair icon. When the fingertip is in contact with no objects in the workspace, no vibrotactile feedback is given. Therefore, users know whether they are holding an icon by the sense of touch, unlike ordinary touch panels that only give visual feedback. When using the number pad, midair buttons with different functions (e.g., deleting one digit or clearing all the input numbers) give different vibrotactile sensations. Each of these sensations has a different AM waveform, and thus a different haptic sensation (clicking, explosion, echoing vibration), helping the user distinguish between the different interactive functions and tasks supported by the system.

One limitation of AM waveforms is that practical implementations often yield a distracting audible noises. This is especially the case when a low refresh rate of the modulation wave is used, which means that the modulation waveform is stair-shaped and thus includes harmonics of the refresh frequency. As the frequency spectrum of these harmonics is broad, some of these frequency components become audible. One effective solution to suppress this audible noise is to prepare band-limited modulation waves by increasing the modulation refresh rate (Hasegawa and Shinoda 2018). Continuously shifting the phases of the driving pulse of the transducers also contributes to the suppression of such noises (Suzuki et al. 2020).

Another limitation of AM-based midair ultrasound haptics is that it is most effective in stimulating the glabrous (hairless) parts of the skin such as the palm and face (Gil et al. 2018), but not the rest of the body surface such as the back of the palms, forearms, arms, and shoulders. Experiments have shown that most hairy parts of the skin, can hardly perceive AM ultrasound foci at comparable acoustic pressure outputs. This could limit some application scenarios such as presenting vibrotactile stimuli to let people pay attention to something, especially since most of our body is usually covered by clothes and the AM-sensitive skin regions that are safely stimulated (i.e., not the face) such as our palms are not always open and visible to the phased array systems.

3   Lateral Modulation (LM)

The LM method (Takahashi et al. 2020, 2018) is a focal modulation technique that can stimulate both glabrous and non-glabrous parts of the skin. While the AM method temporally varies the amplitude of an immobilized ultrasound focus, the LM method temporally changes the focal position while keeping its intensity constant. Thus, the gross acoustic force by LM ultrasound foci on the whole skin surface is time-invariant. However, the acoustic force experienced by a cutaneous mechanoreceptor fixed at a specific location temporally varies according to the focal movement. Therefore, LM ultrasound foci serve as a more powerful vibrotactile stimuli which resembles an

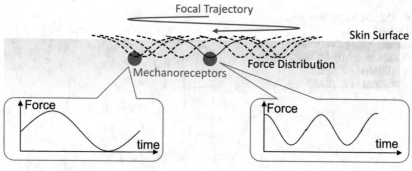

Fig. 4 Schematic depiction of the temporal profiles of received force intensity depending on positions on the skin. Strong second harmonics of the modulation frequency is experienced by mechanoreceptors around the center of the linear focal trajectory, whereas the effect of harmonics is relatively small for mechanoreceptors located near the end of the trajectory

AM stimulation from the standpoint of individual mechanoreceptors as schematically demonstrated in Fig. 4.

There are several parameters describing the movement and physical intensity of the LM ultrasound foci. We call these parameters as the LM modulation parameters and they are the radiation force amplitude, parametric focal trajectory, and modulation frequency (LM frequency). The first study on the LM method (Takahashi et al. 2018) produced movements of an ultrasound focus on a finite-length line as depicted in Figs. 1 and 4. Inspired by the STM method proposed by Frier et al. (2018) which we will introduce in the next section, studies of the LM method later included the case where the ultrasound focus moves along a small circle in a two-dimensional plane that is on the skin surface (Takahashi et al. 2020). In each of these cases, the parametric focal trajectory is described by the focal position with respect to time t with coordinates $(x_L(t), y_L(t))$ for the linear reciprocating focal movement, and $(x_C(t), y_C(t))$ for repetitive circular focal movement. In the experiment performed by Takahashi et al., the focal movement was defined as

$$(x_L(t), y_L(t)) = (l \cos \omega_m t, 0) \tag{2}$$
$$(x_C(t), y_C(t)) = (l \cos \omega_m t, l \sin \omega_m t), \tag{3}$$

with l determining the spatial dimension of the focal trajectory, and ω_m determining the traveling period of the focus is given by $2\pi/\omega_m$. We call l the LM modulation amplitude. For linear focal movement, l is equal to half of the trajectory line segment. For circular focal movement, l is equal to the radius of the trajectory circle. Finally, the LM angular frequency is defined by ω_m.

In the following experiments, the maximum value of l was 7 mm so that the movement of the foci, which is actually a series of discretely positioned foci with a refresh rate of 1 kHz, could be perceived as stationary or as continuous. Meanwhile

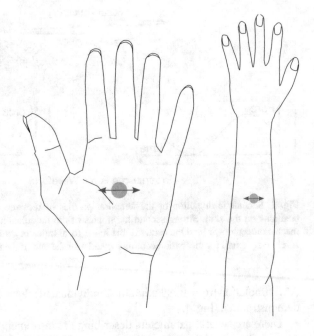

Fig. 5 The LM stimulation positions and focal trajectories on the palm (left) and on the forearm (right) in the experiments. Adapted from Takahashi et al. (2020)

the period of temporal acoustic force on mechanoreceptors is ω_m for both linear and circular focal movements and is in the range of 10–200 Hz. Importantly, the waveform of acoustic force experienced by a mechanoreceptor is no longer a pure sinusoidal wave with frequency ω_m, as it would have been with an AM stimulus. Another important aspect is that this waveform is the same on any position on the circular trajectory except for the phase delays, whereas this is not the case for linear focal movements. In particular, the component with double the frequency of the LM modulation is dominant in the radiation force waveform at the center of the line segment. This strong double-frequency harmonic is what differentiates these two trajectory patterns (Fig. 4).

The experiments to determine detection thresholds of vibrotactile stimuli were performed with AM and LM stimulation on the palm (glabrous, hairless skin) and the forearms (non-glabrous, hairy skin) of the participants while varying the radiation force amplitude (Fig. 5.) The results plotted in Fig. 6 suggest that the detection thresholds of LM stimuli were much lower than AM stimuli of the same modulation frequency. The vertical axis of Fig. 6 is the ratio of the generated radiation force amplitude to the maximum radiation force amplitude that the experimental device could generate. The radiation force amplitude here is defined as the maximum instantaneous output radiation force in one cycle of the modulation period. When comparing LM and AM thresholds for the same radiation force amplitude, one should recall that the acoustic power at the focal point stimulus is about 6 dB higher (i.e., double) in the case of LM since the force amplitude is constant, unlike in the AM case where it oscillates between 0 and 1. Interestingly, the detection threshold

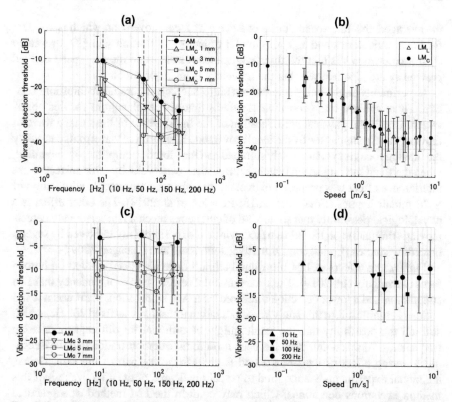

Fig. 6 Detection thresholds for LM stimuli. **a** Detection thresholds for circular LM (LM$_C$) on palms (categorized as glabrous skin) with respect to the LM amplitude and LM modulation frequency. **b** Detection thresholds for circular LM (LM$_C$) and linear LM (LM$_L$) plotted with respect to the moving speed of the focus on palms. **c** Detection thresholds for circular LM on forearms (categorized as hairy skin) with respect to the LM amplitude and LM modulation frequency. **d** Detection thresholds for circular LM plotted with respect to the moving speed of the focus on forearms. Here 0 dB corresponds to the upper limit of the device output. Error bars indicate the standard deviations. Adapted from Takahashi et al. (2020)

is often much lower with LM, compared with AM, even if we account for the 6 dB difference in acoustic output power. The overall tendency is observed that LM stimulation with LM modulation amplitude l no less than 3 mm is felt significantly more strongly than AM stimulation of the same modulation frequency in both the case with the palm and that with the forearm. It is worth mentioning that in the experiments, there were several modulation frequencies with which LM foci generated by four phased array units could certainly be perceived, whereas AM foci generated by the same apparatus could not, even with the maximum output power.

As for the glabrous skin stimulation, the experiments showed that it is not the existence of the aforementioned harmonics that is prominent, especially in linear focal movement, but the moving speed of the focus that essentially governs the LM detection threshold (Fig. 6b). Here, the moving speed of the focus is defined by the averaged absolute speed during one cycle of focal movement, which is $2\omega_m l/\pi$ for linear trajectories and $\omega_m l$ for circular trajectories. The intriguing fact revealed by the experiments is that the threshold values for the same moving speed defined previously are identical whether the trajectory is linear or circular.

Experiments on the hairy skin did not show such clear parameter-threshold relation. There are two main conceivable effects that give explanations for this observation. One is the physical consideration of the interference of the surface wave of moving wavefronts caused by the focal movement. The series of wavefronts caused by the moving focus is synchronously summed and the vibration amplitude is magnified, when the focal moving speed matches the surface wave velocity. This surface-wave interference effect was proposed to explain the enhanced vibrotactile stimulation of STM midair haptics (Frier et al. 2018; Reardon et al. 2019). The other effect is a physiological possibility that some kind of cutaneous mechanism selectively detects moving stimulation on the skin surface, which is experimentally indicated by several preceding studies (Essick and Edin 1995; Johansson and Flanagan 2009).

Finally, the effects of LM ultrasound stimuli have also been studied on human faces (Mizutani et al. 2019). Their experimental results showed a tendency that LM stimulation had a lower detection threshold than AM stimulation, but it was not statistically significant. In this study, the modulation threshold was fixed 200 Hz, which still left the possibility that the results might be different for different modulation frequencies. At this point, there has been no definitive demonstration that the threshold lowering effect of the LM method is valid for every part of the skin. Hence, additional experiments are required to reveal the degree of the effectiveness of this method in various conditions, which may confirm the LM method as a practical passive vibrotactile stimulation technique.

4   Spatiotemporal Modulation (STM)

The STM method was proposed concurrently to and independently of the LM method (Frier et al. 2018). Its principle has much in common with LM, where the focal position is modulated temporally while keeping the focal intensity the same. The main difference between LM and STM is that the focal trajectory dimension is much larger (200 mm in circle perimeter at greatest) than that of LM (14 mm in line segment length at the longest); see Fig. 7. As such, STM enables repositioning the foci along two-dimensional trajectories which shaped into a variety of patterns or shapes ranging from simple circles (Frier et al. 2018) to more complex virtual hand-object intersections (Martinez et al. 2019). As such, the STM method is an alternative and more efficient way of rendering two-dimensional patterns contrasted to the AM-based method of simultaneously generating multiple ultrasound foci and dispersing them along the pattern (Hasegawa et al. 2020; Long et al. 2014; Melde et al. 2016); we refer to this approach as spatial AM method hereafter.

There are several advantages of STM over spatial AM in presenting two-dimensional patterns via vibrotactile sensation. In the AM method, the spatial

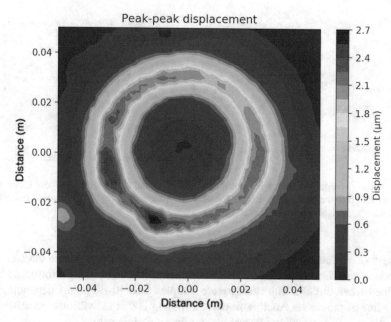

Fig. 7 Example of a STM pattern showing RMS displacement of a circular pattern on a silicone slab measured via a laser Doppler vibrometer. Reproduced from Frier et al. (2018)

acoustic power density is decreased when the generated acoustic power distribution becomes spatially large. This directly weakens vibrotactile sensation for users and the perception of the displayed geometry will likely be less accurate. It is even considered that the displayed radiation force cannot be felt at all when weakened to a degree that is lower than the AM detection threshold. In contrast, the acoustic field generated by STM is a single focus at every moment, which can always concentrate the maximum available device output power on a single point. Therefore, STM can exert the maximum possible radiation force on the skin surface, regardless of the displayed geometry size.

Enhanced vibrotactile sensation by STM was experimentally demonstrated by Frier et al. (2018). They reported that the vibrotactile detection threshold is determined by the focal moving speed, as explained in the previous section (see Sect.3). In their study, it is explained that the subjective stimulation strength reaches its peak value when the focal moving speed was in the range of 5–8 m/s, which matches the surface wave velocity on human skin and causes the wavefront summation effect mentioned in the previous section (Fig. 8).

Frier et al. also indicate that the actual focal movement is not a continuous trajectory but a temporal series of still focal points that changes rapidly at a constant time interval (Frier et al. 2019). They studied the effect of the spatial sampling interval of the focal position on aroused vibrotactile sensation. After performing user studies, it was found that there is an optimal sampling interval that maximizes the perceived

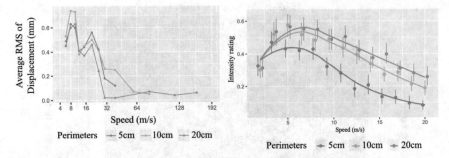

Fig. 8 Left: Average RMS of displacement as a function of the focal movement speed for circular patterns with different perimeters. Right: The subjective intensity ratings of the haptic feedback by perimeter size. Adapted from Frier et al. (2018)

strength of vibrotactile stimuli. In their experimental condition where circular trajectories were displayed twice or ten times per second, the best performance was obtained when circular trajectories were sampled into 10–30 points depending on the radius of the circle. Another important finding is that the vibrotactile sensation disappears with a sampling interval greater than a certain value.

Finally, Ablart et al. studied how different STM circle sensations were perceived as more or less intense, rough, regular, round, and hedonic (Ablart et al. 2019). It was shown that larger circles of perimeter 20 cm reliably displayed different roughness properties depending on their pattern repetition frequency. STM circles with a repetition frequency 25 Hz were perceived as being much rougher than those 75 Hz. This property allowed Beattie et al. to design midair haptic textures sensations that match our visual perception of images roughness (Beattie et al. 2020).

A recent extension of the STM method employs multiple separately moving foci (Barreiro et al. 2020). This multi-focus STM approach is called path routing optimization STM (PRO-STM) and has been used in present the radiation force distribution during the tactile interaction with virtual gaseous objects. The algorithm approximates several routing paths of moving foci so that the scaled time-averaged radiation force distribution is similar to what is originally desired to be presented.

Determination of transducer output signals requires heavy computational resources when simultaneously generating multiple foci while suppressing unwanted artifacts in the ultrasound field. Plasencia et al. developed a phase retrieval algorithm that operates in GPU-based hardware to achieve real-time multiple foci movement with a refresh rate of 17 kHz (Plasencia et al. 2020). This technique offers virtually continuous transition of sequential ultrasound fields, which will contribute to more complicated spatiotemporal ultrasound fields for real-time vibrotactile feedback with a rich variety of textures that can be potentially created.

An STM-based rendering algorithm for displaying three-dimensional shapes has been investigated by Martinez et al. In their work, they examined several conceivable rendering algorithms via user studies and found that presenting the cross section of the virtual object and the user's hand will offer perceivable shape information to users (Martinez et al. 2019). In addition, salient features such as corners of cubes are better rendered with a method that offers additional tactile cues.

5   Hybrid and Variant Modulation Methods

In generating spatiotemporal tactile patterns to the palm, many methods have been invented. One representative method is a variant of the AM methods, where multiple foci with fixed positions are displayed while their intensities are temporally changed. Long et al. created a volumetric shape display system that presents the spatial intersection of the virtual object and the users' hand (Long et al. 2014). Users can move their hands in an exploratory fashion over the virtual object and could correctly recognize three-dimensional shapes among several prepared objects at a correct answer rate of approximately 80%.

There have been several investigations of people's abilities to identify spatial tactile patterns using multi-focus AM stimuli. Among them, the study with participants of the largest age range was conducted by Rutten et al. (2019). The overall accuracy rate of 44% was lower than experiments with similar setups (Korres and Eid 2016; Long et al. 2014), which was ascribed to the smaller numbers of answer choices and younger participants in those experiments.

Hajas et al. presented two-dimensional shapes including circles and polygons by using a single amplitude-modulated focus that slowly moved around a displayed two-dimensional shape trajectory (Hajas et al. 2020). They found that the recognition of a polygon could be more accurate when the focal movement velocity decreased around the vertexes of the shape and made short stops there, compared with the case where the focus traveled along the trajectories at a constant speed. This slowdown strategy around the edge is considered to emphasize the existence of vertexes and edges. Authors called this method dynamic tactile pointer (DTP) and is considered as a hybrid of AM and STM because the focal point (i.e., pointer) intensity is temporally changed while moving dynamically on the shape trajectory.

Matsubayashi et al. devised a rendering technique of spatial radiation pressure distribution that was not composed of multiple discrete foci, but rather of a deformable single focus whose size, shape, and internal spatial power distribution was tunable (Matsubayashi et al. 2021). With this technique, virtual compliance of a floating object is interactively displayed to the fingertips of users according to the change of contact area between the finger and the object.

Another interesting system that offers tactile interaction with falling fluid on the hand was developed by Jang and Park (2020). Based on the real-time simulation of fluid dynamics and fluid–rigid interaction according to the position and posture of the user's hand, the generated ultrasound field is determined so that it gives the proper tactile feedback that corresponds to the calculated force distribution on the hand. In this system, the presented force distribution is realized by simultaneously generating multiple AM foci.

6 Conclusion

We have discussed the main three modulation techniques in midair ultrasound haptics (AM, LM, and STM) which are useful in presenting vibrotactile textures, strengthening sensation intensity, generating perceivable stimuli on hairy skin, and displaying geometrical information. As introduced in this chapter, the technical scope of ultrasound modulation is being constantly expanded introducing new capabilities such as the presentation of tactile texture, roughness information, fluidic interactions, and also the compliance of solid objects. In addition, we have discussed some hybrid or variation methods that are not merely categorized into the above-mentioned three modulation methods, but are understood as a combination of them. They are now an indispensable technical part of midair haptics, though their principles are very simple and easy to implement. Among the three modulation techniques, LM and STM are very new methods that had only been devised a couple of years before this chapter was written. Therefore, these modulation techniques may potentially include novel functions that have not yet been discovered. The authors expect that new modulation technique will continue to be devised and studied via physical and physiological methods. These will surely broaden the application scope of midair ultrasound haptics in a variety of practical contexts.

References

Ablart D, Frier W, Limerick H, Georgiou O, Obrist M (2019) Using ultrasonic mid-air haptic patterns in multi-modal user experiences. In: Proceedings of IEEE international symposium on Haptic, Audio and Visual Environments and Games (HAVE), pp 1–6

Barreiro H, Sinclair S, Otaduy MA (2020) Path routing optimization for STM ultrasound rendering. IEEE Trans Haptics 13(1):45–51

Beattie D, Frier W, Georgiou O, Long B, Ablart D (2020) Incorporating the perception of visual roughness into the design of mid-air haptic textures. In: ACM Symposium on Applied Perception 2020 (SAP '20). Association for Computing Machinery, New York, NY, USA, Article 4:1–10

Essick GK, Edin BB (1995) Receptor encoding of moving tactile stimuli in humans. II. The mean response of individual low-threshold mechanoreceptors to motion across the receptive field. J Neuroscience 15(1):848–864

Frier W et al (2018) Using spatiotemporal modulation to draw tactile patterns in mid-air. In: Ferre M (ed) Haptics: perception, devices and scenarios. Springer, Cham, Switzerland, pp 270–281

Frier W, Pittera D, Ablart D, Obrist M, Subramanian S (2019) Sampling strategy for ultrasonic mid-air haptics. In: Proceedings of the 2019 CHI conference on human factors in computing systems. Association for Computing Machinery, New York, NY, USA, Paper 121, pp 1–11

Gil H, Son H, Kim JR, Oakley I (2018) Whiskers: exploring the use of ultrasonic haptic cues on the face. In: Proceedings of the 2018 CHI conference on human factors in computing systems. Association for Computing Machinery, New York, NY, USA, Paper 658, 1–13

Hajas D, Pittera D, Nasce A, Georgiou O, Obrist M (2020) Mid-air haptic rendering of 2D geometric shapes with a dynamic tactile pointer. IEEE Trans Haptics 13(1):1–12

Hasegawa K, Shinoda H (2013) Aerial display of vibrotactile sensation with high spatial-temporal resolution using large-aperture airborne ultrasound phased array. In: Proceedings of IEEE WHC, pp 31–36

Hasegawa K, Shinoda H (2018) Aerial vibrotactile display based on multiunit ultrasound phased array. IEEE Trans Haptics 11(3):367–377

Hasegawa K, Shinoda H, Nara T (2020) Volumetric acoustic holography and its application to self-positioning by single channel measurement. J Appl Phys 127:244904

Hoshi T, Takahashi M, Iwamoto T, Shinoda H (2010) Noncontact tactile display based on radiation pressure of airborne ultrasound. IEEE Trans Haptics 3(3):155–165

Inoue S, Makino Y, Shinoda H (2015) Active touch perception produced by airborne ultrasonic haptic hologram. In: Proceedings of 2015 IEEE World Haptics Conference (WHC), Northwestern University, Evanston, Il, USA, pp 362–367

Iwamoto T, Tatezono M, Shinoda H (2008) Non-contact method for producing tactile sensation using airborne ultrasound. Proc EuroHaptics 2008:504–513

Jang J, Park J (2020) SPH fluid tactile rendering for ultrasonic mid-air haptics. IEEE Trans Haptics 13(1):116–122

Johansson RS, Flanagan JR (2009) Coding and use of tactile signals from the fingertips in object manipulation tasks. Nature reviews. Neuroscience 10(5):345–359

Korres G, Eid M (2016) Haptogram: ultrasonic point-cloud tactile stimulation. IEEE Access 4:7758–7769

Lamoré PJ, Muijser HH, Keemink CJ (1986) Envelope detection of amplitude-modulated high-frequency sinusoidal signals by skin mechanoreceptors. J Acoustical Soc Am 79:1082–1085

Long B, Seah SA, Carter T, Subramanian S (2014) Rendering volumetric haptic shapes in mid-air using ultrasound. ACM Trans Graph 33(6), Art. no. 181

MacLean K, Enriquez M (2003) Perceptual design of haptic icons. Proc EuroHaptics 2003:351–363

Marchal M, Gallagher G, Lécuyer A, Pacchierotti C (2020) Can stiffness sensations be rendered in virtual reality using mid-air ultrasound haptic technologies? Proc Eurohaptics 2020:297–306

Martinez J, Harwood A, Limerick H, Clark R, Georgiou O (2019) Mid-air haptic algorithms for rendering 3D shapes. In: Proceedings of IEEE international symposium on Haptic, Audio and Visual Environments and Games (HAVE), pp 1–6

Matsubayashi A, Yamaguchi T, Makino Y, Shinoda H (2021) Rendering softness using airborne ultrasound. Proc IEEE World Haptics Conf (WHC) 2021:355–360

Melde K, Mark AG, Qiu T, Fischer P (2016) Holo-grams for acoustics. Nature 537:518–522

Mizutani S, Fujiwara M, Makino Y, Shinoda H (2019) Thresholds of haptic and auditory perception in midair facial stimulation. In: IEEE international symposium on Haptic Audio-Visual Environments and Games (HAVE2019), Sunway, Malaysia, 3–4 Oct 2019

Monnai Y, Hasegawa K, Fujiwara M, Yoshino K, Inoue S, Shinoda H (2014) Haptomime: mid-air haptic interaction with a floating virtual screen. In: Proceedings of 27th Annual ACM Symposium User Interface Software Technology, pp 663–667

Plasencia DM, Hirayama R, Murillo RM, Subramanian S (2020) GS-PAT: high-speed multi-point sound-fields for phased arrays of transducers. ACM Trans Graph 39, 4, Article 138 (July 2020), 12 pages

Purves D, Augustine GJ, Fitzpatrick D et al (eds) (2001) Neuroscience, 2nd edn. Sinauer Associates, Sunderland (MA)

Reardon G, Shao Y, Dandu B, Frier W, Long B, Georgiou O, Visell Y (2019) Cutaneous wave propagation shapes tactile motion: evidence from air-coupled ultrasound. In: Proceedings of IEEE World Haptics Conference (WHC), pp 628–633

Rutten I, Frier W, Bogaert L, Geerts D (2019) Invisible touch: how identifiable are mid-air haptic shapes? In: Extended abstracts of the 2019 CHI conference on human factors in computing systems (CHI EA '19). Association for Computing Machinery, New York, NY, USA, Paper LBW0283, 1–6

Suzuki S, Fujiwara M, Makino Y, Shinoda H (2020) Reducing amplitude fluctuation by gradual phase shift in midair ultrasound haptics. IEEE Trans Haptics 13(1)87–93

Takahashi R, Hasegawa K, Shinoda H (2020) Tactile stimulation by repetitive lateral movement of midair ultrasound focus. IEEE Trans Haptics 13(2):334–342

Takahashi R, Hasegawa K, Shinoda H (2018) Lateral modulation of midair ultrasound focus for intensified vibrotactile stimuli. In: Proceedings of EuroHaptics LNCS 10894, pp 276–288

Vardar Y, Güçlü B, Basdogan C (2017) Effect of waveform on tactile perception by electrovibration displayed on touch screens. IEEE Trans Haptics 10(4):488–499

Verrillo RT (1979) Comparison of vibrotactile threshold and suprathreshold responses in men and women. Percep Psychophys 26:20–24

Verrilo RT (1963) Effect of contactor area on the vibrotactile threshold. J Acoustical Soc Am 35:1962–1966

Multiunit Phased Array System for Flexible Workspace

Seki Inoue, Shun Suzuki, and Hiroyuki Shinoda

Abstract Although smaller and thinner ultrasonic mid-air haptic phased arrays are important to business-to-consumer applications, large-scale phased arrays are exploring the possibility of powerful mid-air haptics. For research applications to ultimately "hack" the entire ultrasonic field of a room or public environment, large array operations are inevitable. In this chapter, after the advantages and disadvantages of employing large-scale arrays are summarized, we present an implementation of a scalable phased array unit that can be installed in a distributed fashion and some of its potential applications.

1 Large-Scale Phased Array

In the evolving and growing field of mid-air ultrasonic haptics, several questions are being debated. For example, "How strong can mid-air haptics be?" and "How far does the haptic force reach?" In this chapter, we will attempt to answer these questions and more as they pertain to large-scale phased ultrasonic haptic arrays.

In reality, the mechanical forces exerted by ultrasonic mid-air haptics are weak. According to measurements taken by Hasegawa and Shinoda (2018), the static mechanical force generated by a 2.5 kPa (160 dB sound pressure-level) peek acoustic focus reached 20 mN (2.0 gf). The mechanical pressure was $1.4\,\mathrm{gf/cm^2}$, which is equivalent to the weight of a one-cent euro coin ($1.1\,\mathrm{gf/cm^2}$). Hasegawa's phased array was fairly large and leveraged 996 transducers. This is why the sophisticated temporal and spatial modulations described in the other chapters are vital and are actively researched to acquire stronger mid-air haptic sensations.

S. Inoue (✉) · S. Suzuki · H. Shinoda
The University of Tokyo, 5-1-5 Kashiwanoha, Kashiwa, Chiba, Japan
e-mail: inoue@hapis.k.u-tokyo.ac.jp

S. Suzuki
e-mail: suzuki@hapis.k.u-tokyo.ac.jp

H. Shinoda
e-mail: shinoda@hapis.k.u-tokyo.ac.jp

© The Author(s), under exclusive license to Springer Nature Switzerland AG 2022
O. Georgiou et al. (eds.), *Ultrasound Mid-Air Haptics for Touchless Interfaces*,
Human–Computer Interaction Series, https://doi.org/10.1007/978-3-031-04043-6_10

However, it is not beyond the realm of possibility to obtain stronger kinetic forces. The mechanical pressure derived by the radiation pressure is proportional to the *square* of acoustic energy power. Hence, from the above measurement, a 25 kPa acoustic focus will create a 2 N (200 gf) mechanical force. The force of 2 N is equivalent to PHANToM Touch USB (3.3 N) and may be strong enough to mimic most physical contacts in daily life. The theoretical upper limit is 16 N when the ultrasonic acoustic pressure reaches atmospheric pressure (100 kPa). As the acoustic power density approaches this limit, it becomes more difficult to create a focused wavefront, owing to nonlinear phenomena, such as acoustic saturation, heat loss, and acoustic streaming.

Two strategies are available for acquiring larger acoustic responses. One requires stronger ultrasonic speakers. Another uses more conventional speakers. In other words, it is necessary to increase either the energy density of the phased array or the area of the phased array. The former option can help maintain a small array while keeping the installation easy, but it must overcome the acoustic saturation problem. The latter option is less susceptible to saturation problems. We discuss this in detail in the next section.

One problem that arises when handling a large aperture array is the directivity of the speaker elements. The HORN system shown in Fig. 1 was implemented in 2015 using 3984 ultrasonic speakers (Inoue et al. 2015). To account for the directivity problem, the speakers were arranged to surround the workspace. It converged a 2.5 kPa focal point at 10% of its maximum drive. Although the maximum sound pressure could not be obtained with microphones at that time, it was unofficially estimated that it could create at least a 20 kPa focus. This vividly presented a strong haptic force with a thermally warm sensation.

Apart from the power, a larger aperture size is necessary to create a distant focus. Sufficiently far from the array, the focal size, w_f, generated by the D aperture array is proportional to

$$w_f \propto \frac{r}{D},$$ (1)

where r is the distance from the array's surface (Hoshi et al. 2010). Hence, at a distance comparable to the aperture or further, the focus becomes blurred and dim.

Indeed, a large array system is problematic when considering consumer home applications, such as portability, cost, and safety. However, large-scale arrays expand the range and efficacy of mid-air haptic applications. For example, a large public space may be adaptable to mid-air haptics such that people in the area can be notified and guided by invisible prompts. Imagine a virtual-reality system in which light field, sound field, and mid-air force field of an entire room are under control. People can actively walk around and experience virtual environments without proxy devices, such as glasses, earphones, and gloves. Apart from mid-air vibratory haptics, it has been possible to present warm and cold sensations (Kamigak et al. 2020; Nakajima et al. 2021) and levitate large (~5 cm) objects (Inoue et al. 2019) by large arrays.

Fig. 1 HORN system, which maximizes the effective solid angles of speakers seen from a focal point, adopted from Inoue et al. (2015)

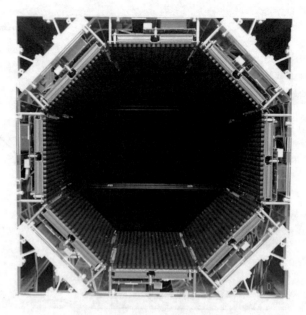

In the rest of this chapter, we discuss the advantages and disadvantages of large aperture arrays; then, we introduce the Airborne Ultrasound Tactile Display version 3 (AUTD v3) system and some future innovations made possible by it.

2 Advantages and Challenges of Large Arrays

2.1 Advantage: Resolution

Small aperture arrays cannot create clear focused air-pressure nodes at a distance, as is well known in lens optics. The size of a focal point at a distance is, as shown in Eq. (1), inversely proportional to the size of the array. Specifically, the focus size, w_f, is defined as the lateral width between the first minima around the focal center (Fig. 2). It is approximated as

$$w_f \approx 2\frac{\lambda r}{D}. \tag{2}$$

Here, D is the aperture of the array, r is the distance of the focus from the array surface, and λ is the wavelength of the ultrasound. Note that this relation falls under the Fresnel approximation and is practically valid if the following factor is smaller than one:

$$Q_{\text{Fresnel}} = \frac{D^4}{16\lambda r^3} < 1. \tag{3}$$

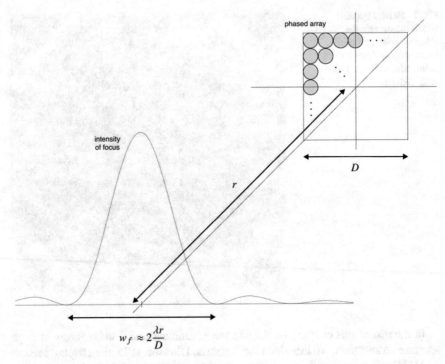

Fig. 2 Schematic of focus-size approximation

Let r_Fresnel be the lower limit of the distance between the focus and the array with which the Fresnel approximation is valid. If we assume $\lambda = 8.5\,\text{mm}$ (40 kHz ultrasound in the air), some typical r_Fresnel are 170 mm when $D = 160\,\text{mm}$, 390 mm when $D = 300\,\text{mm}$, and 2 m when $D = 1\,\text{m}$. Numerical simulations are employed to obtain the focal size at distances nearer than the limit, but it is known that the focal size is approximately $\lambda \sim 2\lambda$. Readers interested in the details are encouraged to refer to p. 128 of Träger (2012). This was demonstrated by measurement by Hasegawa and Shinoda (2018), where in Fig. 3, they show the lateral distribution of acoustic pressure with a variety of array sizes and focal distances. As optical theory states, the farther away the focus and the smaller the array, the larger the focal diameter. Another way to create a smaller focus is to shorten the wavelength (i.e., to use a higher frequency (Ito et al. 2016)). However, this causes stronger attenuation from air absorption (Bass et al. 1995).

2.2 Advantage: Lesser Sensitivity to Acoustic Saturation

Large arrays can focus more strongly than small arrays using stronger elements. This is explained by the acoustic saturation phenomenon. Acoustic saturation is one of

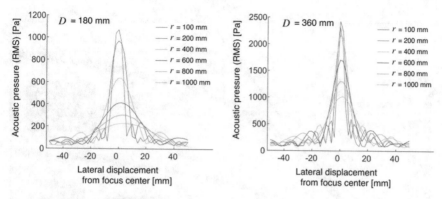

Fig. 3 Measured acoustic pressure field of focus at r distance generated by an array with aperture D, based on Hasegawa and Shinoda (2018)

nonlinear acoustic effects such as acoustic radiation pressure and acoustic streaming. In brief, high-intensity acoustic waves cannot propagate over long distances (Blackstock 1964). The stronger the acoustic wave is the more attenuation it experiences due to the viscosity of the fluid (air). When the intensity of the transmitter is gradually increased, at a certain point, it balances the nonlinear attenuation, and the intensity observed at a receiver stops increasing (i.e., it is saturated).

To minimize attenuation, it is reasonable to avoid forming a high-intensity field early from the focus. In other words, it is important not to localize the intensity as much as possible before reaching the focus. Because the intensity is, by definition, the power transferred per unit area, it is most effective to use the larger cross-section area of the air.

Figure 4 analyzes the effect of acoustic saturation. The upper graph shows the measured peak acoustic pressure of focus, 500 mm above the center of the phased arrays. The two phased arrays consist of four and nine AUTD v3 units, which is further discussed in the following sections. The number of speaker elements is 996 and 2241, respectively. The acoustic pressure of a single speaker was measured at 200 mm above the element. The phases of all elements were fixed to create the focus, and the amplitude of each speaker was gradually increased. The lower graph shows the focus pressure ratio of the nine- to four-unit arrays.

From the upper graph, acoustic saturation is clearly observed. When the sound pressure of each speaker is less than approximately 8 Pa, the focal sound pressure increases linearly. Then, the growth slows down. The blue arrows in the figure indicate the degree of the effect of acoustic saturation.

It should be noted that acoustic saturation is observed regardless of the size of the array. From the lower graph, the ratio between the two arrays is nearly constant along the output power per element, meaning that four- and nine-unit arrays lose the same rate of power when the same element-wise power is induced. This implies that larger arrays are more efficient than compact, powerful arrays regarding energy loss in the air. The loss from the ideal scaling ratio of 9/4 is observed. Because the

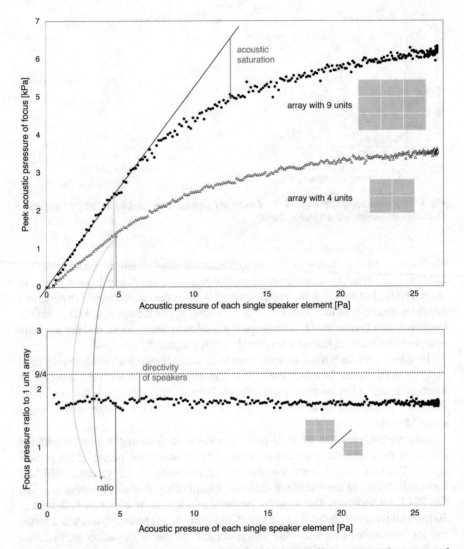

Fig. 4 Relation between acoustic pressure of speaker elements and (upper) acoustic pressure of focus generated by 4, 9 units of AUTD v3, (lower) pressure ratio of 9 units to 4 units

correlation between loss and power is not dominant, we can infer that this is caused by reasons other than acoustic saturation, such as the directivity of speaker elements on the edge of the array.

2.3 Challenge: Directivity

All practical acoustic speakers generally have more or less directivity. Typical ultrasonic transducers with directivity have an on-axis main lobe with a gradually decreasing power profile along the off-axis angles. In addition to the power term, the phase can also vary along the off-axis. The phase directivity can be calibrated on a software stack.

With the increase in the size of the array, speaker elements at the edge of the array cannot fully contribute to the focus. To effectively use every element, the arrays may be arranged three-dimensionally rather than along a single two-dimensional plane. Working examples are seen in Figs. 1, 12, and 14.

2.4 Challenge: Wiring

The power consumed by a single speaker element can reach several hundred mW. To distribute the power lines from a single control panel to the array, several thousand bold wires would be required, causing significant electromagnetic noise and heat. Furthermore, this set up would be inconvenient to handle. This situation was seen in early prototypes of mid-air haptics studies, such as the model shown in Fig. 5.

Moreover, the structured arrangement of arrays discussed in the previous section is nearly impossible to assemble using a direct wiring strategy. Therefore, there is a need for a module-coupling system that can be easily installed by simply connecting small pairs of lines (i.e., power supply and communication lines). Thus, each unit must have an independent network processor to interpret data via a communication line into a waveform signal to drive the ultrasonic transducers.

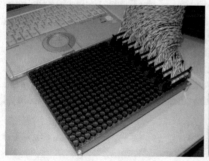 

Fig. 5 Early prototypes of ultrasound phased arrays, adopted from Hoshi et al. (2010) and Carter et al. (2013)

2.5   Challenge: Phase Synchronization

A problem that arises here pertains to the phase synchronization between the units. To control the sound field in a collaborative manner, the phases emitted by each unit must be precisely superimposed onto others at the target point. Specifically, aligning the phase of the ultrasonic wave requires that the clock counter in the processor be aligned with an error smaller than the phase accuracy, which must be less than a microsecond. This is a very high-accuracy level that is an order of magnitude higher than the accuracy of general computer time synchronization methods (e.g., network time protocol).

3   Implementation of AUTD v3

In this section, we introduce our implementation of AUTD v3, the largely scalable phased array. We begin with a summary of the requirements. Although AUTD v3 can drive any ultrasound frequency up to nearly MHz, we assume the frequency to be 40 kHz in the following discussion. Please refer to Ito et al. (2016) for higher-frequency (70 kHz) systems that use AUTD v3.

3.1   Requirement 1: Phase Quantization and Clock Synchronization

Here, we determine the precision to which the phase should be controlled for the generation of tactile stimuli. It would therefore be reasonable to evaluate how the quantization level affects the power and resolution of the focus. Following the convention of digital image/audio encoding, we refer to the amount of phase information per transducer as *phase depth*. For example, a 256 depth has 8 bits of information. In this case, the time width of this quantization unit is 98 ns.

In a study by Suzuki et al. (2021), the effect of phase quantization for a single focus generation was analyzed. Figure 6 shows the variation in sound pressure of the focus for different phase resolutions. Here, the ultrasound phase, ϕ, is digitalized as follows:

$$\phi = 2\pi \frac{1}{x} \left\lfloor \frac{r}{\lambda} x \right\rfloor, \tag{4}$$

where $\lfloor \cdot \rfloor$ is a floor function, x is the number of phase divisions (phase depth), r is the distance between the focus and a speaker element, and λ is the wavelength. As seen in Fig. 6, it can be concluded that 16 depth of phase where the normalized amplitude is 0.993 is sufficient to create a single focal point with less than 1.5% power loss.

The control-time width is 1.6 μs for a depth of 16. Thus, a microsecond of timing error is sufficient for the control. A technique that can achieve this requirement is

Fig. 6 Phase depth and acoustic pressure amplitude at a focal point generated 500 mm above an array with 54×42 transducers, adopted from Suzuki et al. (2021)

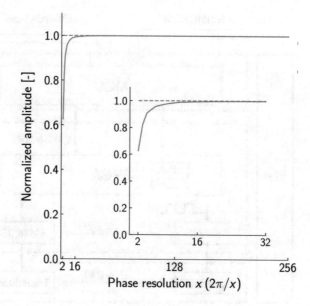

a satellite navigation system, such as the global positioning system. Another is the precision time protocol (PTP; IEEE 1588-2002, IEEE 1588-2008).

3.2 Requirement 2: Refresh Rate and Data Bus Capacity

Humans can sense vibrations along a wide frequency range, but the static pressure is limited to around 500 Hz (Bolanowski et al. 1988). Therefore, according to the sampling theorem, it would be sufficient if the device was to secure a 1 kHz refresh rate to cover the human tactile perception. To determine the required throughput of data transfer, we assume that we have 256 transducers per unit, and we drive them along 256 depths of amplitude. We thus need $8 + 4 = 12$ bits per element, resulting in a nominal transfer rate of

$$12 \text{ bits} \times 1 \text{ kHz} \times 256 = 3 \text{ Mbps}. \tag{5}$$

In this datagram, over 300 units can be connected in 1000 Mbps.

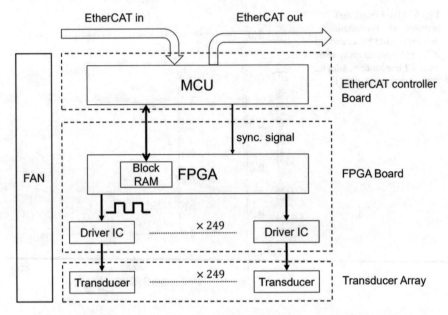

Fig. 7 Hardware system diagram of AUTD v3, adopted from Suzuki et al. (2021)

3.3 Implementation Using EtherCAT

As an example of an implementation that fulfills the requirements mentioned above, we have built an AUTD v3 using the EtherCAT system. EtherCAT is a real-time communication protocol used in factory control systems, robot controls, etc. The physical layer is the same as that of Ethernet, implying that an RJ45 can be used for high quality and low cost. A time synchronization system based on PTP is incorporated as the standard. Additionally, cyclic communications of up to 100 Mbps are possible, meeting the required specifications. For more details and evaluations, please refer to Suzuki et al. (2021).

The configuration of the AUTD v3 is shown in Fig. 7, and its appearance is shown in Fig. 8. It has a microcontroller unit (MCU) with an EtherCAT slave, which controls communications. The field-programmable gate array (FPGA) has sufficient pins to connect to the ultrasonic transducer and generate pulse-width modulation waveforms. The memory bus of the MCU is directly connected to the FPGA, and the MCU can access the FPGA directly as RAM. The sync timing pulse of the EtherCAT slave is directly input to the FPGA.

The performance of time synchronization obtained by this system is shown in Fig. 9. Even with 20 connections, synchronization was achieved with a jitter of less than 100 ns.

Fig. 8 Photograph of **a** an AUTD v3 module and **b** nine connected AUTD v3 modules (Suzuki et al. 2021)

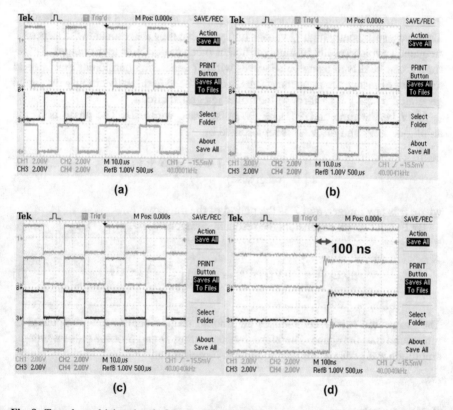

Fig. 9 Transducer driving signal of the 1st, 8th, 14th, and 20th among the 20 connected modules. These figures were captured **a** immediately after start-up, **b** immediately after the start of synchronization, and **c** 1 h after the start of synchronization. **d** Enlarged view during synchronization (Suzuki et al. 2021)

4 AUTD v3 Driver Software

The AUTD v3 mentioned in the previous section is equipped with an FPGA to drive many transducers. This section discusses the signal processing inside the FPGA and some useful functions for tactile presentation. The FPGA code (https://github.com/shinolab/autd3-library-firmware) and the software library code (https://github.com/shinolab/autd3-library-software) of AUTD v3 are both open source. Please refer to the repositories for more details.

4.1 Driving Signal Generation via FPGA

Piezoelectric ultrasonic transducers of 40 kHz are typically used for mid-air haptics. They have sufficiently high Q values, implying that they are resonant with a specific frequency, which results in highly efficient mechano-electric transduction. Therefore, it can be driven using pulse waves without generating harmonics that are odd multiples of resonance frequency. Thus, we only need to digitally amplify the signal generated by the FPGA through the driver integrated circuit.

Let t be the time and $V(t)$ be the pulse-wave width, D. The phase is S, the amplitude is V, and the $V(t)$ is represented by

$$V(t) = \begin{cases} V \ \left(S - \frac{1}{2}D < t + nT \leq S + \frac{1}{2}D\right) \\ 0 \ \ (\text{otherwise}) \end{cases} , \tag{6}$$

where n is any integer, and T is the period of the pulse wave.

By Fourier series expansion, the resonant component, a_f, of $V(t)$ is

$$a_f = \frac{1}{T} \int_0^T dt\, V(t) e^{i\frac{2\pi t}{T}} = \frac{V}{\pi} \sin\left(\frac{D}{T}\pi\right) e^{-2\pi i \frac{S}{T}}. \tag{7}$$

The ultrasound transducer radiates an amount proportional to this component as ultrasound into the space. Therefore, by controlling D and S of the pulse wave, the amplitude and phase of the ultrasound can be controlled.

4.2 Modulation

AUTD v3 has various features that can be used to modulate the ultrasonic beam. In addition to amplitude modulation (AM), it supports spatio-temporal modulation (STM) (Frier et al. 2018), and lateral modulation (LM) (Takahashi et al. 2020) techniques. The latter two present tactile sensations by moving the focal point quickly on skin.

Because AUTD v3 can control each transducer element individually, STM and LM can be realized by temporally switching the sound field patterns. In addition to this software-based control, AUTD v3 is equipped with a function to move a single focus using the hardware timer. This function samples the focal position data at a fixed sampling rate (up to 20 kHz, as in AM) and calculates the phase of each transducer.

4.3 Silent Mode

When AM envelope is applied to an ultrasound wave, it is demodulated into an audible sound via a nonlinear interaction with the air. This phenomenon is called "self-demodulation" and can be applied to parametric speakers and audio spotlights (Westervelt 1963; Yoneyama 1983). Therefore, in mid-air ultrasound tactile presentations, audible sounds can be heard, which could be noisy for users. STM and LM, which maintain a constant sound pressure, also generate noise. This is because the transducer cannot follow the quick phase change, owing to its high Q value. The amplitude of the ultrasound emitted from the transducer fluctuates even when the V and D are maintained constant, and only S is changed, as in Eq. (7). This problem is especially pronounced when many transducers are used, and it significantly impairs the user experience. Therefore, AUTD v3 uses a low-pass filter (LPF) to smooth the fluctuation of D, S, and suppress noise. Please refer to Suzuki et al. (2020) for details.

5 Haptic Navigation

As an application that makes good use of large-scale phased arrays, the non-contact behavior guidance has been summarized in this section. Although the following experiments were conducted in workspaces smaller than a 50 cm cube where hand motion was guided by ultrasound stimulation, the same principle can be applied to larger workspaces.

Tactile and auditory senses have been used to assist or replace vision for disabled users. For example, visually impaired people have long been using canes to perceive the surrounding environment through sound and touch. Tactile paving, which was developed in Japan in the 1960s, assists visually impaired people in walking along, embedding uneven patterns in the road. The patterns notify people of safe routes through the tactile sensation of the soles of their feet. Since the 1990s, navigation systems using wearable tactile devices have also been studied.

Tactile perception has the advantage of being more robust to the environment and intuitive than auditory navigation. Non-contact tactile guidance is even better in that the person being guided does not need to hold or wear a device. It is kept hygienic even in public space for a large number of unspecified users. These features are also effective in evacuation guidance for sighted people. In the following subsection, we introduce more examples of research on non-contact tactile guidance using ultrasound phased arrays. Additionally, there is a study that uses a single array system to guide a user's hand to the sweet spot where better gestural input and better haptic feedback can be provided (Freeman et al. 2019). Next, we focus on wide-range navigations, such as for pedestrians, enabled by a large-scale array.

5.1 Haptic Pursuit

Yoshimoto et al. showed that the human hand can follow a tactile stimulus point without shear stress (Yoshimoto et al. 2019). In their experiment, an ultrasonic focal point moved horizontally along the palm. The participants were instructed to follow the moving focal point.

The results showed that participants could follow a focal point moving at a speed up to 10 cm/s, as shown in Fig. 10. After the focal point begins to move, there is a

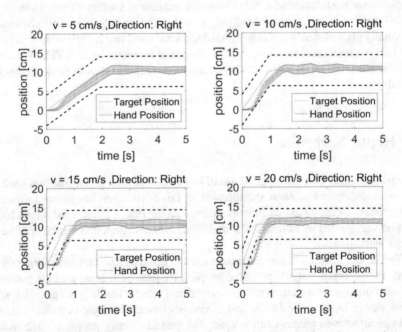

Fig. 10 Motion of the right hand that follows the stimulus point. The stimulus point was at the palm center until time 0. It started moving at time 0 from the palm center with speed v. The dash lines are the upper and lower boundary of the tolerance (4 cm), which is a standard palm size, adopted from Yoshimoto et al. (2019)

lag of approximately 0.5 s before the hand can begin pursuing it. When the speed of the focal point reached 15 or 20 cm/s, the participants could no longer follow its initial movement. Interestingly, however, they were still able to catch up with it later. This is thought to have been caused by the directional cues of the focal point's initial movement.

On the other hand, it was difficult to pursue a focal point moving perpendicular to the palm, even when it was slow. Therefore, this method is limited to guidance in the direction horizontal to the palm.

Tracking is a basic ability of human perception to understand the environment. With vision, we can visually follow a moving object by keeping it at the center of the sight. This smooth pursuit eye movement (SPEM) has already been well-studied. Here, a similar ability in haptic modality was validated.

5.2   Virtual Handrail

Suzuki et al. proposed a method to present a touchable *virtual handrail* (Suzuki et al. 2019), which provides programmable tactile paving in the air. They generated tactile stimulus lines in space using a single focus moving at high-speed back-and-forth via an ultrasonic phased array. Figure 11 illustrates the use of the virtual handrail. It is easy and intuitive to identify the floating line haptically without any learning processes.

Interleaved sampled points with 30 mm intervals on a virtual straight line or semi-circle path were generated, and they continued along the path. When a palm was placed on the virtual line, there was always more than one point felt on the palm because the width interval of 30 mm was chosen to be wider than a palm.

When the moving speed of the focal points was sufficiently high, this moving stimulus created a feeling that the tactile path exists statically. In contrast, a slower moving focal point presents a noticeable direction to users. In the experiment, the whole path at 25 Hz was presented, revealing that humans can move their hands along the path at a speed of approximately 10 cm/s. By following this stimulus path as a virtual handrail, people can proceed to a given destination.

To use ultrasound devices for guidance, devices must be installed along the entire path to the destination. Most studies on non-contact guidance have been limited to experiments in small workspaces. To apply this to people walking around, the system must follow their movements and dynamically produce stimulation patterns depending on the situation and their position. Further studies are expected in this field.

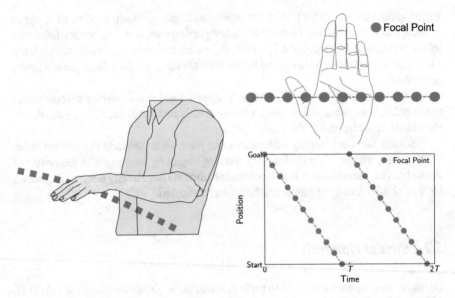

Fig. 11 Virtual handrail. A user can follow the stimulus lines presented in a space to get to the destination, adopted from Suzuki et al. (2019)

5.3 Other Applications

Large-scale arrays have made it possible to conduct many studies apart from the behavioral guidance described in the previous section. Although it is out of the scope of this book, let us introduce some applications other than tactile perception where large-scale arrays can be used.

Furumoto et al. controlled the position and velocity of a helium gas-filled balloon with an ultrasonic array (Furumoto et al. 2019, 2020). The 200 mm object, which could follow users' actions and interact with them, could fly freely in meter-wide workspaces. Figure 12 displays one of their workspaces. This levitating balloon can carry a variety of objects through the air, such as icons or proxy interfaces for three-dimensional design software.

Hasegawa et al. constructed a 384 mm × 302.8 mm array using four units and generated a long and narrow straight airflow in the air using an ultrasound Bessel beam (Hasegawa et al. 2017). The basic principle for this ultrasound-driven airflow is the nonlinear acoustic effect, known as "acoustic streaming," where strong and localized sound propagation directly accelerates the nearby air. The angle of the emitted ultrasonic Bessel beam is electronically controllable, resulting in the traveling direction of the created straight airflow being steerable.

In another work, a 768 mm × 302.8 mm array using eight units was constructed to generate a curved airflow in the air (Hasegawa et al. 2019) (Fig. 13). Although the existence of arc-shaped acoustic patterns has been demonstrated (Zhang et al. 2014), this was the first time that a curved path strong and durable enough to exert an acoustic

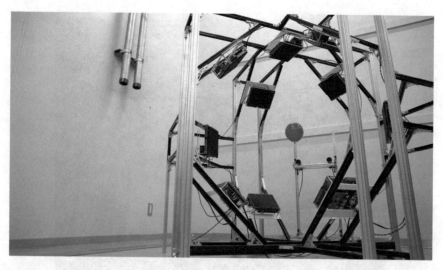

Fig. 12 The balloon interface. The surrounding phased array controls the position of the balloon; thus, it becomes a physical prop that is held in a workspace, even when the user is not holding it. Such a physical prop is an intuitive tool in three-dimensional interfaces, adopted from Furumoto et al. (2020)

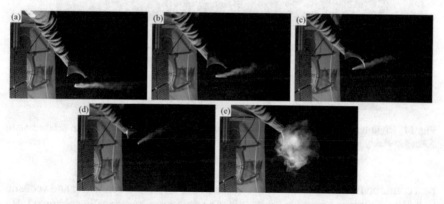

Fig. 13 Top-view figures showing steerable ultrasound airflows guiding water vapor in various directions: **a** perpendicular to the array; **b** 10°; **c** 20°; and **d** 30° tilted from (**a**). When there is no ultrasound emission, the water vapor merely rises (**e**) (Hasegawa et al. 2019)

flow was reported. Such electronically controllable narrow airflows enable us, for example, to present a localized smell to a distant user by propagating a fragrance using the airflow. It can also remove an odor by blowing away the air around the nose. Furthermore, a mid-air cooling sensation created by transporting cold air has been proposed (Nakajima et al. 2018).

Finally, Inoue et al. demonstrated levitation of objects larger than the ultrasound wavelength (Inoue et al. 2019), where the surface of a rigid body was considered to

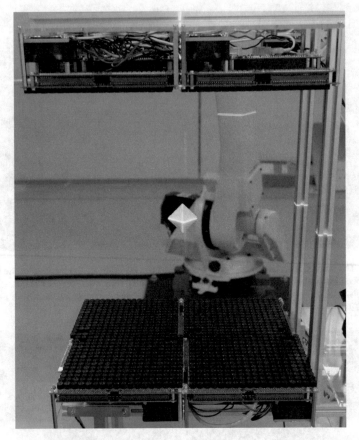

Fig. 14 Rigid-body levitation by top–bottom distributed phased arrays. A 50 mm octahedron of 500 mg is stably levitated (Inoue et al. 2019)

be a continuous surface comprising minute triangles, and the scattering and acoustic radiation pressures occurring on its micro surface were numerically calculated. By controlling the force and torque applied on the object, which were obtained as a combined force of radiation pressures on tiny fragments, stable levitation of a spherical and even a non-spherical object was realized. A sphere with a diameter of 30 mm was lifted by a configuration of four-unit (996 transducers) on the bottom surface. However, for an octahedron of 50 mm, their algorithm did not converge to a stable solution, requiring another phased array above the octahedron. This result could not have been achieved without AUTD v3. The payload was approximately 600 mg, which is the largest mass that has ever been levitated by ultrasonic phased arrays, to the best of the authors' knowledge (Fig. 14).

6 Conclusion

In this chapter, we have reviewed topics related to large-scale ultrasonic haptics-inducing phased arrays. Larger ultrasonic phased arrays are capable of rendering higher tactile resolutions at longer distances, and they are more efficient than smaller arrays in terms of energy lost by acoustic saturation. Modular distributed systems are needed to overcome directivity and wiring problems. It is crucial to precisely synchronize clocks among units because it impacts the focusing and modulating performance. AUTD v3 is a phased array unit that can be daisy-chained by simple Ethernet and a direct-current power line. It employs EtherCAT to solve the synchronization problem. The simple wiring hardware stack and flexible software-development kit have expanded the domain of mid-air haptics capabilities to include navigation cues, mid-air thermal sensations, personal smell displays, and interfaces using levitated objects.

References

Bass HE, Sutherland LC, Zuckerwar AJ, Blackstock DT, Hester D (1995) Atmospheric absorption of sound: further developments. J Acoust Soc Am 97(1):680–683

Blackstock DT (1964) On plane, spherical, and cylindrical sound waves of finite amplitude in lossless fluids. J Acoust Soc Am 36(1):217–219

Bolanowski SJ, Gescheider GA, Verrillo RT, Checkosky CM (1988) Four channels mediate the mechanical aspects of touch. J Acoust Soc Am 84(5):1680–1694

Carter T, Seah SA, Long B, Drinkwater B, Subramanian S (2013) Ultrahaptics: multi-point mid-air haptic feedback for touch surfaces. In: Proceedings of the 26th annual ACM symposium on user interface software and technology, UIST'13. Association for Computing Machinery, New York, NY, USA, pp 505–514. https://doi.org/10.1145/2501988.2502018

Freeman E, Vo DB, Brewster S (2019) HaptiGlow: helping users position their hands for better mid-air gestures and ultrasound haptic feedback. In: 2019 IEEE World haptics conference (WHC), pp 289–294. https://doi.org/10.1109/WHC.2019.8816092

Frier W, Ablart D, Chilles J, Long B, Giordano M, Obrist M, Subramanian S (2018) Using spatiotemporal modulation to draw tactile patterns in mid-air. In: Proceedings of the international conference on human haptic sensing and touch enabled computer applications (EuroHaptics). Euro Haptics Society, pp 270–281

Furumoto T, Hasegawa K, Makino Y, Shinoda H (2019) Three-dimensional manipulation of a spherical object using ultrasound plane waves. IEEE Robot Autom Lett 4(1):81–88. https://doi.org/10.1109/LRA.2018.2880330

Furumoto T, Fujiwara M, Makino Y, Shinoda H (2020) Balloon interface for midair haptic interaction. In: SIGGRAPH Asia 2020 emerging technologies, SA'20. Association for Computing Machinery, New York, NY, USA. https://doi.org/10.1145/3415255.3422882

Hasegawa K, Shinoda H (2018) Aerial vibrotactile display based on multiunit ultrasound phased array. IEEE Trans Haptics 11(3):367–377

Hasegawa K, Qiu L, Noda A, Inoue S, Shinoda H (2017) Electronically steerable ultrasound-driven long narrow air stream. Appl Phys Lett 111(6):064104

Hasegawa K, Yuki H, Shinoda H (2019) Curved acceleration path of ultrasound-driven air flow. J Appl Phys 125(5):054902

Hoshi T, Takahashi M, Iwamoto T, Shinoda H (2010) Noncontact tactile display based on radiation pressure of airborne ultrasound. IEEE Trans Haptics 3(3):155–165. https://doi.org/10.1109/TOH.2010.4

Inoue S, Makino Y, Shinoda H (2015) Active touch perception produced by airborne ultrasonic haptic hologram. In: 2015 IEEE World haptics conference (WHC). IEEE, pp 362–367

Inoue S, Mogami S, Ichiyama T, Noda A, Makino Y, Shinoda H (2019) Acoustical boundary hologram for macroscopic rigid-body levitation. J Acoust Soc Am 145(1):328–337

Ito M, Wakuda D, Inoue S, Makino Y, Shinoda H (2016) High spatial resolution midair tactile display using 70 kHz ultrasound. In: International conference on human haptic sensing and touch enabled computer applications, vol 9774. https://doi.org/10.1007/978-3-319-42321-0_6

Kamigak T, Suzuki S, Shinoda H (2020) Noncontact thermal and vibrotactile display using focused airborne ultrasound. In: Proceedings of the international conference on human haptic sensing and touch enabled computer applications (EuroHaptics). Euro Haptics Society, pp 271–278

Nakajima M, Hasegawa K, Makino Y, Shinoda H (2018) Remotely displaying cooling sensation via ultrasound-driven air flow. In: 2018 IEEE Haptics symposium (HAPTICS), pp 340–343. https://doi.org/10.1109/HAPTICS.2018.8357198

Nakajima M, Hasegawa K, Makino Y, Shinoda H (2021) Spatiotemporal pinpoint cooling sensation produced by ultrasound-driven mist vaporization on skin. IEEE Trans Haptics (early access)

Suzuki S, Fujiwara M, Makino Y, Shinoda H (2019) Midair hand guidance by an ultrasound virtual handrail. In: 2019 IEEE World haptics conference (WHC). IEEE, pp 271–276

Suzuki S, Fujiwara M, Makino Y, Shinoda H (2020) Reducing amplitude fluctuation by gradual phase shift in midair ultrasound haptics. IEEE Trans Haptics 13(1):87–93

Suzuki S, Inoue S, Fujiwara M, Makino Y, Shinoda H (2021) Autd3: scalable airborne ultrasound tactile display. IEEE Trans Haptics 1. https://doi.org/10.1109/TOH.2021.3069976

Takahashi R, Hasegawa K, Shinoda H (2020) Tactile stimulation by repetitive lateral movement of midair ultrasound focus. IEEE Trans Haptics 13(2):334–342

Träger F (2012) Springer handbook of lasers and optics. Springer, Berlin. https://doi.org/10.1007/978-3-642-19409-2

Westervelt PJ (1963) Parametric acoustic array. J Acoust Soc Am 35(4):535–537

Yoneyama M, Fujimoto J, Kawamo Y, Sasabe S (1983) The audio spotlight: an application of nonlinear interaction of sound waves to a new type of loudspeaker design. J Acoust Soc Am 73(5):1532–1536

Yoshimoto A, Hasegawa K, Makino Y, Shinoda H (2019) Midair haptic pursuit. IEEE Trans Haptics 12(4):652–657

Zhang P, Li T, Zhu J, Zhu X, Yang S, Wang Y, Yin X, Zhang X (2014) Generation of acoustic self-bending and bottle beams by phase engineering. Nat Commun 5(1):4316

Sound-Field Creation for Haptic Reproduction

Atsushi Matsubayashi, Seki Inoue, Shun Suzuki, and Hiroyuki Shinoda

Abstract In ultrasound haptics, a tactile sensation is evoked on human skin that touches the high sound pressure area generated due to the interference of ultrasonic waves. Therefore, by controlling the distribution of sound pressure amplitude using a transducer array, it is possible to create tactile sensations at multiple points simultaneously. In this chapter, we first describe the relationship between the complex gains of the transducer array and the generated sound field. Then, we provide various algorithms to control the amplitude pattern based on this relationship.

1 Acoustic Field Reconstruction

Ultrasound haptics is a technology that uses an array of ultrasound transducers to present tactile sensations remotely. The tactile sensation is caused by a nonlinear phenomenon called acoustic radiation. Assuming that the particle velocity of ultrasound is sufficiently small, the acoustic radiation pressure can be approximated as a quantity proportional to the square of the sound pressure p calculated in the range of linear acoustics (Hasegawa et al. 2000). Therefore, controlling p over certain control points leads to the design of a spatial tactile pattern that spreads over them. In this section, we first describe the forward problem of determining the sound pressure field p created by an ultrasound transducer array and then outline the inverse problem of determining the gain of the transducer array that generates the desired sound pressure distribution.

1.1 Forward Problem of the Acoustic Field

The first step is to formulate the sound field produced by the ultrasound-phased array. The ultrasound transducers that make up the array emit ultrasound waves due

---

A. Matsubayashi (✉) · S. Inoue · S. Suzuki · H. Shinoda
University of Tokyo, Tokyo, Japan
e-mail: matsubayashi@hapis.k.u-tokyo.ac.jp

© The Author(s), under exclusive license to Springer Nature Switzerland AG 2022
O. Georgiou et al. (eds.), *Ultrasound Mid-Air Haptics for Touchless Interfaces*,
Human–Computer Interaction Series, https://doi.org/10.1007/978-3-031-04043-6_11

to the piston motion of their internal diaphragms. The sound field produced by an individual transducer is, in fact, affected by various factors, but let us first assume that it is a point source emitting spherical wave with frequency f_0 at the origin. In this case, the sound pressure field created by the transducer is as follows:

$$p(t, x, y, z) = \frac{q^{amp}}{\sqrt{x^2 + y^2 + z^2}} e^{j(-k\sqrt{x^2+y^2+z^2}+2\pi f_0 t + \theta)}, \tag{1}$$

where q^{amp}, θ are the intensity and phase of the point source, c is the speed of sound, and $k = 2\pi f_0 / c$ is the wave number. This equation can be transformed into the product of the transfer function g, complex gain of the transducer q, and time-dependent term.

$$p(t, x, y, z) = g(x, y, z)q(q^{amp}, \theta)e^{j2\pi f_0 t}, \tag{2}$$

where

$$g(x, y, z) = \frac{1}{\sqrt{x^2 + y^2 + z^2}} e^{-jk\sqrt{x^2+y^2+z^2}} \tag{3}$$

$$q(q^{amp}, \theta) = q^{amp} e^{j\theta}. \tag{4}$$

Focusing on the f_0 frequency component of the sound field $\hat{p}(x, y, z)$, the relation between the complex gain and the sound field is expressed as follows:

$$\hat{p}(x, y, z) = g(x, y, z) \cdot q(q^{amp}, \theta). \tag{5}$$

To extend the transfer function to a general position, let $\mathbf{x}$ be the position of the sound source and $\mathbf{x}'$ be the observed position. In this case, the transfer function $g(\mathbf{x}, \mathbf{x}')$ is as follows:

$$g(\mathbf{x}, \mathbf{x}') = \frac{1}{|\mathbf{x} - \mathbf{x}'|} e^{-jk|\mathbf{x}-\mathbf{x}'|}. \tag{6}$$

Let us consider a case where there are multiple transducers. Suppose that there are N transducers, each with a gain of $q_1, q_2, \ldots q_N$, at $\mathbf{x}_1, \mathbf{x}_2, \ldots \mathbf{x}_N$. The sound pressure at point $\mathbf{y}$ can be expressed using vectors:

$$\hat{p}(\mathbf{y}) = \sum_i g(\mathbf{x}_i, \mathbf{y})q_i = \mathbf{g}^{\top}(\mathbf{y})\mathbf{q}. \tag{7}$$

where

$$\mathbf{g}(\mathbf{y}) = \begin{pmatrix} g(\mathbf{x}_1, \mathbf{y}) \\ g(\mathbf{x}_2, \mathbf{y}) \\ \vdots \\ g(\mathbf{x}_N, \mathbf{y}) \end{pmatrix}, \tag{8}$$

$$\mathbf{q} = \begin{pmatrix} q_1 \\ q_2 \\ \vdots \\ q_N \end{pmatrix}. \tag{9}$$

This equation represents the continuous sound pressure created when the gain of the phased array transducer is given.

In practical situations pertaining to mid-air haptic rendering, we often consider controlling the sound pressure at discrete points in the observation space $\mathbf{y}$. When the discretized control points are represented by $\mathbf{y}_1, \mathbf{y}_2, \ldots, \mathbf{y}_M$, the sound pressure at each point can be expressed as follows:

$$\hat{p}(\mathbf{y}_j) = \sum_i g(\mathbf{x}_i, \mathbf{y}_j) q_i = \mathbf{g}^\top(\mathbf{y}_j) \mathbf{q}. \tag{10}$$

Therefore, the sound pressure vector at control points $\mathbf{y}$ follows the matrix equation:

$$\hat{\mathbf{p}} = G\mathbf{q} \tag{11}$$

where

$$G = (\mathbf{g}(\mathbf{y}_1), \mathbf{g}(\mathbf{y}_2), \ldots, \mathbf{g}(\mathbf{y}_M))^\top. \tag{12}$$

This is the basic equation describing the forward problem of the phased array sound field. The vector of the transducer's gain $\mathbf{q}$ and the sound pressure on the control points $\hat{\mathbf{p}}$ are related by the transfer function matrix G.

As mentioned previously, matrix G represents the transfer function for the case where each transducer can be approximated as a point source. However, similar matrix equations can be obtained for other practical situations pertaining to mid-air haptic rendering. For example, if we consider the transducer as a piston disk of radius a attached to a baffle plate, the transfer function at the far field is as follows:

$$g(x, y, z) = \frac{i\omega\rho u a^2 J_1(ka \sin\theta)}{ka \sin\theta \sqrt{x^2 + y^2 + z^2}} e^{-jk\sqrt{x^2+y^2+z^2}}, \tag{13}$$

where J_1 is a Bessel function of the first order, u is the velocity of the disk, and θ represents the angle between (x, y, z) and the normal of the disk. This approximation has been adopted in several mid-air haptic rendering studies using common cylindrical transducers.

Another example is to consider the effects of scattering. Thus far, we have considered the forward problem in a free-sound field. When considering scattering on the surface of an object such as a hand, according to the style of the boundary element method, the sound field can be represented as follows (Inoue et al. 2016):

$$B\hat{\mathbf{p}} = G\mathbf{q}, \tag{14}$$

Matrix B represents the scattering effect. Even in this case, the same matrix equation can be obtained by designating $\bar{G} = B^{-1}G$:

$$\hat{\mathbf{p}} = \bar{G}\mathbf{q}. \tag{15}$$

Mid-air haptic rendering based on this scattered-field equation can increase the pressure at a single point on the fingertip (Inoue et al. 2016) or create an accurate pressure distribution on the hand surface (Matsubayashi et al. 2020).

1.2 Inverse Problem

The problem we face in controlling ultrasound-phased arrays is the reverse of this forward problem. We must first determine the acoustic radiation pressure at the control points that we want to present to the user and then find the transducer complex gain to output the pressure distribution.

Before discussing the sound pressure distribution control, let us first consider a simple case in which we want to maximize the sound pressure at a single point. The creation of this single focus is the most fundamental control and is practically significant. In this case, Eq. (7) can be written as

$$\mathrm{argmax}_{\mathbf{q}}\hat{p}(\mathbf{y}) = \mathrm{argmax}_{\mathbf{q}}\mathbf{g}^{\top}(\mathbf{y})\mathbf{q}. \tag{16}$$

If we increase the energy of $\mathbf{q}$, p may become infinitely large; however, this is not realistic as a physical transducer has nominal power. That is, there is an upper limit on the absolute value for each component of p. As units are meaningless in this discussion, we set the upper limit to 1. That is, $0 \leq q^{\mathrm{amp}} \leq 1$. Understandably, the solution is when each element is driven at its maximum, and the phases are intensified at the focal point. One of the transducer's complex gains that achieves this is as follows:

$$\mathbf{q} = \begin{pmatrix} \frac{g(\mathbf{x}_1,\mathbf{y})^*}{|g(\mathbf{x}_1,\mathbf{y})|} \\ \vdots \\ \frac{g(\mathbf{x}_N,\mathbf{y})^*}{|g(\mathbf{x}_N,\mathbf{y})|} \end{pmatrix}. \tag{17}$$

where $*$ denotes the complex conjugate.

Next, we consider the case of pressure distribution control. If the complex gain on the control points $\mathbf{p}$ is given, it is reasonable to assume that $\mathbf{q}$ can be obtained using the generalized inverse matrix $G^{\dagger}$.

$$\mathbf{q} = G^{\dagger}\mathbf{p} \tag{18}$$

However, two problems specific to ultrasound mid-air haptic rendering arise here. One is the limitation of the transducer amplitude. As in the case with a single focus, it becomes necessary to drive the transducer at an amplitude lower than the transducer's maximum power. The other is the determination of the phase distribution of the sound field. Humans cannot distinguish the phase differences of ultrasonic waves. We can feel tactile sensations as vibrations below 1 kHz, which is considerably lower than the ultrasound frequency, and we can only distinguish the phase difference even smaller than that (Kuroki et al. 2016). Therefore, we are not interested in the phase of the generated sound pressure distribution, and only the sound pressure amplitude is our target of control. In other words, given the desired amplitude of the sound pressure $\mathbf{p}^{amp}$, we need to find $\mathbf{q}$ such that

$$
\begin{aligned}
\forall j \in \{1, \cdots, M\} : \quad &\{\mathbf{p}^{amp}\}_j = |\{G\mathbf{q}\}_j| \\
\forall i \in \{1, \cdots, N\} : \quad &0 \le |\{\mathbf{q}\}_i| \le 1,
\end{aligned}
\tag{19}
$$

where $\{\mathbf{x}\}_i$ means i component of $\mathbf{x}$.

To date, various approaches have been attempted to solve this complex problem. Long et al. were the first to solve this problem and rendering haptic shape using ultrasound (Long et al. 2014). They proposed a method to determine q after solving an eigenvalue problem to find the sound pressure phase such that the focal points at control points strengthen each other. A little later, Inoue et al. (2015) proposed a method to determine the sound pressure phase first, similar to Long et al. by relaxing the phase optimization problem to a semidefinite programming. In a different approach, a fast method for finding q has been proposed by applying the Gerchberg–Saxton algorithm used in optics (Hertzberg et al. 2010; Inoue et al. 2015; Marzo and Drinkwater 2019). This algorithm has been improved to a faster and more accurate version, GS-PAT, by Plasencia et al. (2020). Matsubayashi et al. (2020) solved the least-squares problem using Levenberg–Marquardt method, which is slower than the other methods but achieves a more accurate reproduction of the sound pressure field. All of the above methods consider q as a continuous quantity. However, in practical applications, the amplitude and phase of the transducers are input in discrete quantities. Suzuki et al. (2021) focused on this and proposed a very fast method to determine q by combinatorial optimization. In the next section, we review these methods.

2 Overview of Various Algorithms

This section outlines the algorithms that have been proposed for generating ultrasonic amplitude distributions and their respective applications.

2.1 Eigenmethod

As described in the previous section, we are only interested in the amplitude of sound pressure on the control points. The eigenmethod proposed by Long et al. in 2014 determines a good candidate for phase distribution that can achieve the target amplitude distribution (Long et al. 2014). This method first considers the transducer gain vector $\bar{\mathbf{q}}_j$, which creates a focus of sound pressure p_j^{amp} on the control point j:

$$\bar{\mathbf{q}}_j = p_j^{amp} \begin{pmatrix} \frac{G_{j,1}^*}{\sum_{i=1}^{N} |G_{j,i}|^2} \\ \vdots \\ \frac{G_{j,N}^*}{\sum_{i=1}^{N} |G_{j,i}|^2} \end{pmatrix} \tag{20}$$

This vector is a minimum-norm solution. $G\bar{\mathbf{q}}_j$ represents the pressure distribution at the control points when a focus is generated at the control point j. Therefore, the following matrix R represents the interaction between focal points:

$$R = G\left(\bar{\mathbf{q}}_1, \cdots, \bar{\mathbf{q}}_M\right). \tag{21}$$

For phase of the focal points $\mathbf{t}$ ($|t_i| \leq 1$) such that $R\mathbf{t}$ is large, the focal points have a constructive effect on each other; thus, the energy efficiency from the transducers is high. This implies that it is easier to achieve the target amplitude distribution under the upper limit of the transducer array. Finding such a $\mathbf{t}$ is equivalent to solving the following eigenvalue problem:

$$R\mathbf{x} = \lambda\mathbf{x} \tag{22}$$

The eigenmethod seeks the eigenvector corresponding to the largest eigenvalue of R and uses its phase for the inverse problem. When phase $\mathbf{t}$ is obtained, the eigenmethod solves the matrix equation with weighted Tikhonov regularization to obtain the transducer gain $\mathbf{q}$.

$$\begin{pmatrix} G \\ \begin{matrix} \sigma_1^{\gamma} & \cdots & 0 \\ \vdots & \ddots & \vdots \\ 0 & \cdots & \sigma_N^{\gamma} \end{matrix} \end{pmatrix} \mathbf{q} = \begin{pmatrix} \mathrm{diag}(\mathbf{p}^{amp})\mathbf{t} \\ 0 \\ \vdots \\ 0 \end{pmatrix}, \tag{23}$$

$$\sigma_i = \sqrt{\left| \sum_{j=1}^{M} \frac{G_{j,i}\, p_j^{amp}}{M} \right|} \tag{24}$$

where $\mathrm{diag}(\mathbf{p}_{amp})$ is a diagonal matrix with $\mathbf{p}_{amp}$ as a diagonal element. γ is a regularization parameter. The solution $\mathbf{q}$ is then truncated so that it does not exceed the

Fig. 1 When a tracked hand touches a virtual object, multiple focal points are generated at the intersection (Long et al. 2014)

maximum output of the transducers ($q_i \in [0, 1]$). The computational complexity of solving this linear equation is $O(N^3)$, which is the bottleneck of this method. Therefore, it should be noted that the computation time of this method becomes extensive when the number of transducers is considerable. The entire process is presented in Algorithm 1.

Algorithm 1 Eigen Method

Input: $\mathbf{p}^{\mathrm{amp}}$ and γ

1: $\mathbf{x} \leftarrow$ Largest eigenvector of R
2: **for** $j = 1$ to M **do**
3: $\quad t_j \leftarrow \frac{x_j}{|x_j|}$
4: **end for**
5: **for** $i = 1$ to N **do**
6: $\quad \sigma_i \leftarrow \sqrt{\left| \sum_{j=1}^{M} \frac{G_{j,i} p_j^{\mathrm{amp}}}{M} \right|}$
7: **end for**
8: Solve $\begin{pmatrix} G \\ \sigma_1^{\gamma} \cdots 0 \\ \vdots \ddots \vdots \\ 0 \cdots \sigma_N^{\gamma} \end{pmatrix} \mathbf{q} = \begin{pmatrix} \mathrm{diag}(\mathbf{p}^{amp})\mathbf{t} \\ 0 \\ \vdots \\ 0 \end{pmatrix}$
9: $\mathbf{q} \leftarrow \mathrm{truncate}(\mathbf{q}, [0, 1])$
Output: $\mathbf{q}$

Algorithm 2 Corrected Eigen Method

Input: $\mathbf{p}^{\text{amp}}$ and γ
1: $\mathbf{x} \leftarrow$ Largest eigenvector of R
2: **for** $j = 1$ to M **do**
3: $\quad t_j \leftarrow \frac{x_j}{|x_j|}$
4: **end for**
5: **for** $i = 1$ to N **do**
6: $\quad \sigma_i \leftarrow \sqrt{\left| \sum_{j=1}^{M} \frac{G_{j,i} p_j^{\text{amp}}}{M} \right|}$
7: **end for**
8: Solve $\begin{pmatrix} G \\ \sigma_1^{\gamma} \cdots 0 \\ \vdots \ddots \vdots \\ 0 \cdots \sigma_N^{\gamma} \end{pmatrix} \mathbf{q} = \begin{pmatrix} \text{diag}(\mathbf{p}^{amp})\mathbf{t} \\ 0 \\ \vdots \\ 0 \end{pmatrix}$
9: $\mathbf{p} \leftarrow G\mathbf{q}$
10: $\mathbf{q} \leftarrow \frac{M}{\sum_j \frac{p_i}{p_i^{\text{amp}}}} \mathbf{q}$
11: $\mathbf{q} \leftarrow \text{truncate}(\mathbf{q}, [0, 1])$
Output: $\mathbf{q}$

Using this algorithm, Long et al. configured a system to present the cross-sectional shape of an object. The object shape is rendered by generating many focal points in real time at the intersection of the hand and the object, as shown in Fig. 1. They demonstrated that this system enabled users to recognize the shape of objects only from haptic sensations. This system is the first reported example of generating a sound pressure distribution with a specific shape for mid-air haptic rendering by determining the optimal sound pressure phase. However, it has been shown that the eigenmethod produces a distribution with slightly less pressure than the given sound pressure amplitude $\mathbf{p}^{\text{amp}}$. Plasencia et al. modified the eigenmethod by multiplying the obtained transducer amplitudes by a correction factor (Plasencia et al. 2020) (shown in Algorithm 2). Comparisons between certain algorithms in their paper are described in Sect. 2.4.

2.2 Semidefinite Relaxation

In 2015, Inoue et al. proposed a shape rendering method based on the generation of sound pressure distribution. Similar to the eigenmethod, this method first obtains the distribution of the optimal sound pressure phase. This method considers the following minimization problem.

$$\begin{aligned} \text{minimize} \quad & \|G\mathbf{q} - \text{diag}(\mathbf{p}^{\text{amp}})\mathbf{t}\|_2^2 \\ \text{subject to} \quad & |t_i| = 1, \quad i \in \{1, \cdots, N\} \end{aligned} \tag{25}$$

Then, it assumes that, when the phase distribution $\mathbf{t}$ is obtained, the transducer gain is determined by $\mathbf{q} = G^-\text{diag}(\mathbf{p}^{\text{amp}})\mathbf{t}$, where G^- is the Tikhonov regularization matrix $G^- = (G^*G + \lambda I)G^*$. In this case, the objective function can be transformed as follows:

$$\|G\mathbf{q} - \text{diag}(\mathbf{p}^{\text{amp}})\mathbf{t}\|_2^2 \tag{26}$$
$$= \|(GG^- - I)\text{diag}(\mathbf{p}^{\text{amp}})\mathbf{t}\|_2^2 \tag{27}$$
$$= \mathbf{t}^*\text{diag}(\mathbf{p}^{\text{amp}})(GG^- - I)^*(GG^- - I)\text{diag}(\mathbf{p}^{\text{amp}})\mathbf{t}. \tag{28}$$

Denoting $M = \text{diag}(\mathbf{p}^{\text{amp}})(GG^- - I)^*(GG^- - I)\text{diag}(\mathbf{p}^{\text{amp}})$, the minimization problem can be expressed as follows:

$$\begin{aligned} \text{minimize} \quad & \mathbf{t}^*M\mathbf{t} \\ \text{subject to} \quad & |t_i| = 1, \quad i \in \{1, \cdots, N\} \end{aligned} \tag{29}$$

To make the problem easier to solve, it can be rewritten as an equivalent problem.

$$\begin{aligned} \text{minimize} \quad & \text{Tr}(TM) \\ \text{subject to} \quad & \text{diag}(T) = 1, \; T \succeq 0, \text{rank}(T) = 1, \end{aligned} \tag{30}$$

where $T = \mathbf{t}\mathbf{t}^*$. If the rank constraint is removed, we obtain a semidefinite programming (SDP) problem, and the global optimal solution can be easily obtained. To solve this SDP problem efficiently, Inoue et al. employed the block-coordinate descent method. The approximate solution of the original problem $\mathbf{t}$ was obtained as the phase of the eigenvector corresponding to the largest eigenvalue of the solution of the relaxed problem T. After phase determination, the transducer amplitude was obtained by solving the Tikhonov regularized linear equation. Similar to the eigen-method, the computational complexity of this part is $O(N^3)$, which is the bottleneck of this method. The details are shown in Algorithm 3.

Using this algorithm, Inoue et al. constructed a system called HORN, which presents volumetric tactile objects in air (Inoue et al. 2015). This system uses a large number of ultrasonic transducers to present a sound pressure pattern of sufficient intensity with some shape. As shown in Fig. 2, this allows the user to interact with a virtual object without any delays and time resolution losses caused by hand tracking.

Algorithm 3 Semidefinite Relaxation i^c denotes the index set $i^c = \{1, \cdots, N\}\backslash\{i\}$, and X_{i^c, i^c} denotes the matrix X minus i rows and i columns.

Input: $\mathbf{p}^{\mathrm{amp}}$, $\mathbf{t}_0$ and $\mu > 0$ (small valued parameter)

$T \Leftarrow \mathbf{t}_0 \mathbf{t}_0^*$

for $k = 1$ to K **do**

   Pick $i \in \{1, \cdots, N\}$

   $\mathbf{h} \Leftarrow T_{i^c, i^c} M_{i^c, i}$

   $\gamma \Leftarrow \mathbf{h}^* M_{i^c, i}$

   if $\gamma > 0$ **then**

      $T_{i^c, i} \Leftarrow -\sqrt{\frac{1-\mu}{\gamma}} \mathbf{h}$

      $T_{i, i^c} \Leftarrow -\sqrt{\frac{1-\mu}{\gamma}} \mathbf{h}^*$

   else

      $T_{i^c, i} \Leftarrow \mathbf{0}$

      $T_{i, i^c} \Leftarrow \mathbf{0}$

   end if

end for

$\hat{\mathbf{t}} \leftarrow$ Largest eigenvector of T

for $i = 1$ to M **do**

   $t_i \Leftarrow \hat{t}_i / |\hat{t}_i|$

end for

$\mathbf{q} \Leftarrow G^- \mathrm{diag}(\mathbf{p}^{\mathrm{amp}})\mathbf{t}$

$\mathbf{q} \leftarrow \mathrm{truncate}(\mathbf{q}, [0, 1])$

Output: $\mathbf{q}$

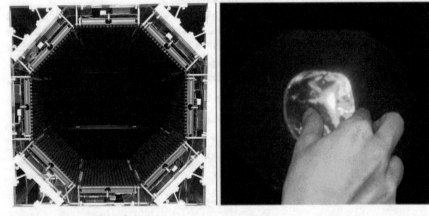

Fig. 2 HORN generates static volumetric haptic image using a large number of transducers surrounding workspace

2.3 Gerchberg–Saxton Algorithm

The methods of first finding the optimum sound pressure phase and then solving the linear equation, as described in the previous sections, are computationally expensive when a large number of transducers are used. In contrast, the methods for iteratively obtaining a solution at high speeds have been studied. One of them is the Gerchberg–Saxton algorithm (GSA) (Gerchberg 1972). The GSA is known as an effective tool to solve phase recovery problems and has attracted attention in a wide range of fields, such as electromicroscopy, computer holography, and astronomy. Phase recovery is the problem of estimating the phase of a physical quantity when only the intensity of the quantity is observed. Our problem can be considered to be a type of phase recovery problem. In terms of acoustic pressure amplitude control using an ultrasound-phased array, which is the subject of this chapter, GSA-based methods have been proposed in the context of hyperthermia (Hertzberg et al. 2010), mid-air haptic rendering (Inoue et al. 2015), and acoustic manipulation (Marzo and Drinkwater 2019). The details of the algorithm differ between these methods, and the method proposed by Marzo and Drinkwater (2019) is presented here.

In this method, each ultrasound transducer is assumed to change only its phase. In one iteration, constraints are placed on each of the two vectors $\mathbf{q}$, $\mathbf{p}$ while alternately propagating between them as follows:

1. Propagate forward: $\mathbf{p} \Leftarrow G\mathbf{q}$

2. Impose constraint: $p_i \Leftarrow p_i^{\mathrm{amp}} \frac{p_i}{|p_i|}$

3. Propagate backward: $\mathbf{q} \Leftarrow G^*\mathbf{p}$

4. Impose constraint: $q_i \Leftarrow \frac{q_i}{|q_i|}$

Algorithm 4 Gerchberg-Saxton Algorithm

Input: $\mathbf{p}^{\mathrm{amp}}$ and $\mathbf{p}^0$ such that $|p_j^{(0)}| = p_j^{\mathrm{amp}}$
1: $\mathbf{p} \Leftarrow \mathbf{p}^0$
2: **for** $k = 0$ to $K - 1$ **do**
3:   $\hat{\mathbf{q}} \Leftarrow G^*\mathbf{p}$
4:   **for** $i = 1$ to N **do**
5:     $q_i \Leftarrow \frac{\hat{q}_i}{|\hat{q}_i|}$
6:   **end for**
7:   $\hat{\mathbf{p}} \Leftarrow G\mathbf{q}$
8:   **for** $j = 1$ to M **do**
9:     $p_j \Leftarrow p_j^{\mathrm{amp}} \frac{\hat{p}_j}{|\hat{p}_j|}$
10:   **end for**
11: **end for**
Output: q

The computational complexity in one iteration is $O(NM)$. In their study, they state that approximately 100 iterations are sufficient. Considering that $N \gg M$ in several applications, this method is fast and was proposed to take advantage of its high speed to perform acoustic manipulation of multiple micro-objects in three dimensions. However, because acoustic manipulation and mid-air haptic rendering have various similarities in terms of the requirements of the target sound field, this algorithm is also useful for mid-air haptic rendering.

2.4 GS-PAT

In 2020, Plasencia et al. proposed an algorithm that is more accurate and faster than the GSA, that is, GS-PAT. The GSA uses G^* as the back-propagation matrix, which is inaccurate in terms of the amplitudes of the transducer. Conversely, GS-PAT uses the normalized matrix F and updates $\mathbf{p}$ in the following manner:

$$
\begin{aligned}
1. \quad \hat{\mathbf{p}} &\Leftarrow GF\mathbf{p} \\
&= G
\begin{pmatrix}
\dfrac{G_{0,0}^*}{\sum_{i=1}^{N} |G_{0,i}|^2} & \cdots & \dfrac{G_{M,0}^*}{\sum_{i=1}^{N} |G_{M,i}|^2} \\
\vdots & \ddots & \vdots \\
\dfrac{G_{0,N}^*}{\sum_{i=1}^{N} |G_{0,i}|^2} & \cdots & \dfrac{G_{M,N}^*}{\sum_{i=1}^{N} |G_{M,i}|^2}
\end{pmatrix}
\mathbf{p}.
\end{aligned}
$$

$$
2. \quad p_i \Leftarrow p_i^{\text{amp}} \frac{\hat{p}_i}{|\hat{p}_i|}, \qquad i \in \{1, \cdots, N\}.
$$

The matrix F is composed of vectors that are minimum-norm solutions when each control point is generated independently, which is identical to the one used in the eigenmethod described in Sect. 2.1. In GS-PAT, the matrix $R = GF$ is calculated in advance to reduce the computational complexity of the matrix-vector product in iterations. When the number of iterations of the algorithm is K, The computational complexity of the GSA is $O(KNM)$, whereas that of GS-PAT is $O(KM^2 + NM^2)$. Considering $M < K < N$ in various practical situations pertaining to multi-point mid-air haptic rendering and multi-object manipulations, GS-PAT has an advantage over the GSA in terms of computation time. Using a middle-end GPU (NVIDIA GTX 1660) with $N = 512$, $M = 32$, $K = 100$, GS-PAT was experimentally shown to be capable of 17000 optimizations per second.

Plasencia et al. also conducted simulations to compare the accuracy of the eigenmethod, the GSA, and GS-PAT for multi-point amplitude control. The results showed that GS-PAT performed well as the other algorithms and was considerably faster. However, when the number of focal points was large ($M \geq 16$), GS-PAT was found to be less accurate than the eigenmethod.

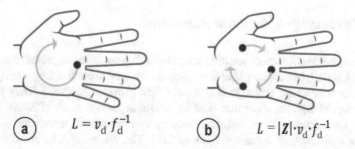

$$L = v_{\mathrm{d}} \cdot f_{\mathrm{d}}^{-1}$$

$$L = |\mathbf{Z}| \cdot v_{\mathrm{d}} \cdot f_{\mathrm{d}}^{-1}$$

Fig. 3 **a** Spatio-temporal modulation, **b** independent control of focal movement speed and refresh rate of haptic stimuli by multi-focus generation (Plasencia et al. 2020)

The fast multi-point pressure rendering achieved by this algorithm has the potential to enable more diverse mid-air haptics sensations. In recent years, it has been reported that, by moving a single focal point at a high speed, it is possible to provide more intense tactile stimulation and recognize the shape of the trajectory (Frier et al. 2018; Takahashi et al. 2018) (see Chap. "Modulation Methods for Ultrasound Midair Haptics," for details). However, how the speed and frequency of the tactile stimuli affect human perception remains to be clarified. Fast multi-focus generation enables independent control of the focus movement speed and the refresh rate of the haptic stimulus in these modulation methods. For example, rotating three focal points on a circle can present haptic sensations at three times the refresh rate of a single point rotated at the same speed (see Fig. 3). This algorithm is expected to reveal a variety of human perceptual characteristics.

Algorithm 5 GS-PAT

Input: $\mathbf{p}^{\mathrm{amp}}$ and $\mathbf{p}^0$ such that $|p_j^{(0)}| = p_j^{\mathrm{amp}}$

1: $\mathbf{p} \Leftarrow \mathbf{p}^0$
2: $R \Leftarrow GF$
3: **for** $k = 0$ to $K - 1$ **do**
4:     $\hat{\mathbf{p}} \Leftarrow R\mathbf{p}$
5:     **for** $i = 1$ to M **do**
6:         $p_i \Leftarrow p_i^{\mathrm{amp}} \frac{\hat{p}_i}{|\hat{p}_i|}$
7:     **end for**
8: **end for**
9: $p_i^{(\Omega)} \Leftarrow (p_i^{\mathrm{amp}})^2 \frac{\hat{p}_i}{|\hat{p}_i|^2}$
10: $\mathbf{q} = F\mathbf{p}^{\Omega}$
11: $\mathbf{q} \leftarrow \mathrm{truncate}(\mathbf{q}, [0, 1])$
Output: $\mathbf{q}$

2.5 Levenberg–Marquardt Algorithm

Basically, there is a tradeoff between accuracy and speed in sound pressure amplitude control. In 2019, Matsubayashi et al. proposed a method to control the sound pressure amplitude accurately, although it is slower than previous methods. They used the Levenberg–Marquardt algorithm (LMA), which is known as an effective solution method for unconstrained nonlinear least-squares problems, to control the sound pressure amplitude in a scattered sound field. The scattering of ultrasonic waves on the surface of the hand is not a problem for macroscopic tactile rendering (e.g., different intensities of tactile rendering for each of the five fingers). However, when more detailed pressure reproduction is required, such as when we want to control the shape of the pressure generated on the fingertips, we need to consider its effect. They described the optimization for controlling the scattering sound field as the following least-squares problem.

$$\text{minimize} \quad \|\text{diag}(\mathbf{p}^{\text{amp}})\mathbf{t} - B^{-1}G\mathbf{q}\|_2^2$$
$$\text{subject to} \quad |t_i| = 1, |q_i| \leq 1, \tag{31}$$

If we fix the transducer amplitude to the maximum value and omit the computationally expensive calculation of B^{-1}, the following problem is obtained:

$$\text{minimize} \quad \|B\text{diag}(\mathbf{p}^{\text{amp}})\mathbf{t} - G\mathbf{q}\|_2^2$$
$$\text{subject to} \quad |t_i| = 1, |q_i| = 1 \tag{32}$$

Furthermore, by setting $\mathbf{q} = [e^{j\theta_1}, \cdots, e^{j\theta_N}]^T$ and $\mathbf{t} = [e^{j\theta_{N+1}}, \cdots, e^{j\theta_{N+M}}]^T$, the problem is simplified to an unconstrained least-squares problem for the phases of sound pressure and transducers. $\boldsymbol{\theta} = [\theta_1, \cdots, \theta_{M+N}]^T$.

Without going into detail, the update step of $\boldsymbol{\theta}$ in the LMA is calculated as follows:

$$\mathbf{h} = -[J(\boldsymbol{\theta})^T J(\boldsymbol{\theta}) + \lambda I]^{-1} J(\boldsymbol{\theta})^T \mathbf{f}(\boldsymbol{\theta}), \tag{33}$$

where

$$\mathbf{f}(\boldsymbol{\theta}) = \begin{pmatrix} \text{Re}[B\text{diag}(\mathbf{p}^{\text{amp}})\mathbf{t} - G\mathbf{q}] \\ \text{Im}[B\text{diag}(\mathbf{p}^{\text{amp}})\mathbf{t} - G\mathbf{q}]. \end{pmatrix}, \tag{34}$$

and $J(\boldsymbol{\theta})$ is a Jacobian matrix of $\mathbf{f}(\boldsymbol{\theta})$. Only if the value of the objective function after the step $\|\mathbf{f}(\boldsymbol{\theta} + \mathbf{h})\|_2^2$ decreases, the phases will be updated $\boldsymbol{\theta} \Leftarrow \boldsymbol{\theta} + \mathbf{h}$. In addition, λ is a damping factor that contributes to the convergence stability of the rhythm and is updated according to the behavior of the objective function after the step. When λ is large, the behavior of the LMA is similar to the steepest descent method, and when λ is small, the LMA converges in a manner similar to the Gauss–Newton method.

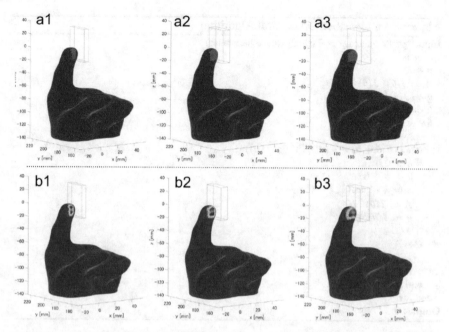

Fig. 4 Pressure amplitude control of the finger surface: (a1-a3) Target amplitude distribution. (b1-b3) Simulation results of the distribution reproduced by LMA (Matsubayashi et al. 2020)

Algorithm 6 describes the details of this process in which the update method for λ follows (Madsen et al. 2004).

Matsubayashi et al. proposed a method to dynamically generate a mesh model of the hand surface and render the sound pressure amplitude on the surface in real time using the LMA described above. They generated pressure amplitude distributions with different widths at the fingertips (see Fig. 4) and verified that these distributions were discriminable via a user study. This is the first reported study of accurately controlling the sound pressure amplitude distribution on the skin surface by considering the scattering on the hand surface.

LMA can be applied not only to the scattered sound field but also to the free field by replacing matrix B with the identity matrix. Sakiyama et al. used LMA in a free-field condition to reproduce the pressure distribution measured by a microphone array to render textures such as fingers, brushes, and towels.

LMA can generate an accurate amplitude distribution, but it is computationally expensive. The bottleneck of this method is that linear Eq. 33 need to be solved for step calculations, whose computational complexity is represented by $O((N + M)^3)$. However, if there is a control point with zero target amplitude, the phase at that point is not considered, and the computational complexity is reduced. The number of zero-amplitude control points can be quite large in situations where we want to prevent the sound pressure from being affected by scattering effects, other than the tactile point position. If the number of control points with nonzero amplitude is M', the

Algorithm 6 Levenberg-Marquardt Algorithm

Input: $\mathbf{p}^{\mathrm{amp}}$, $\boldsymbol{\theta}_0$, and $\gamma > 0$ (small valued parameter)

    $\boldsymbol{\theta} \Leftarrow \boldsymbol{\theta}_0$

    $\nu \Leftarrow 2$

    $A \Leftarrow J(\boldsymbol{\theta})^T J(\boldsymbol{\theta})$

    $\mathbf{g} \Leftarrow J(\boldsymbol{\theta})^T \mathbf{f}(\boldsymbol{\theta})$

    $\lambda \Leftarrow \gamma * \max A_{ii}$

    for $k = 1$ to K **do**

        solve $(A + \lambda I)\mathbf{h} = -\mathbf{g}$

        $\sigma \Leftarrow (F(\boldsymbol{\theta} + \mathbf{h}) - F(\boldsymbol{\theta}))/(\mathbf{h}^T (\mathbf{g} - \lambda \mathbf{h}))$

        if $\sigma > 0$ **then**

            $\boldsymbol{\theta} \Leftarrow \boldsymbol{\theta} + \mathbf{h}$

            $\lambda \Leftarrow \lambda * \max \left(\frac{1}{2}, 1 - (4\sigma - 1)^3\right)$

            $A \Leftarrow J(\boldsymbol{\theta})^T J(\boldsymbol{\theta})$

            $\mathbf{g} \Leftarrow J(\boldsymbol{\theta})^T \mathbf{f}(\boldsymbol{\theta})$

            $\nu \Leftarrow 2$

        else

            $\lambda \Leftarrow \lambda * \nu$

            $\nu \Leftarrow 2 * \nu$

        end if

    end for

Output: $\boldsymbol{\theta}$

---

computational complexity is $O((N + M')^3)$. Using a high-end GPU (NVIDIA GeForce RTX 2080 Ti), it has been shown experimentally that each iteration takes approximately 10 ms when $N + M' = 1500$, $M = 10,000$. In this case, five iterations for one optimization would result in a haptic refresh rate 20 Hz.

2.6 Combinatorial Optimization

In the methods described so far, the amplitude and phase of the transducers were taken as continuous quantities. However, in practical use, they are input as discrete quantities. Furthermore, it has been found that even small amounts of gain information input to each transducer can produce accurate distributions. For example, it was reported that about eight values (3-bit) in phase are sufficient to reproduce some sound field patterns (Morales et al. 2021). Therefore, the inverse problem can be formulated as combinatorial optimization. This is much simpler than the problems we have considered so far, and allows for fast optimization.

In 2021, Suzuki et al. proposed a method to solve the inverse problem by discretizing the gain and applying a greedy algorithm (Suzuki et al. 2021). In this method, the amplitude q^{amp} and phase θ of the transducer are divided into I and J respectively;

Algorithm 7 Combinatorial optimization

Input: p^{amp}
   for $i = 1$ to N **do**
      $q_i \Leftarrow q_*^{amp} e^{-j\theta_*}$ s.t. $q_*^{amp}, \theta_* = \text{argmin } E_i(q_i^{amp}, \theta_i)$
   end for
Output: q

$$q^{amp} \in \left\{ \frac{1}{I}, \frac{2}{I}, \ldots, 1 \right\}, \tag{35}$$

$$\theta \in \left\{ 0, 2\pi \frac{1}{J}, \ldots, 2\pi \frac{J-1}{J} \right\}. \tag{36}$$

In this method, the gain $q_i = q_i^{amp} e^{j\theta_i}$ is determined one by one for all transducers by searching all combinations of these discretized gain sets. Algorithm 7 describes this method. The decision to the gain of the i-th transducer is made by minimizing the difference between the target sound pressure and the sound pressure when the 1 to i-th transducers are driven. Therefore, objective function E_i to decide the gain of the i-th transducer is set as

$$E_i(q_i^{amp}, \theta_i) = \sum_{j=1}^{M} \left| p_j^{amp} - \sum_{k=1}^{i} g(\mathbf{x}_k, \mathbf{y}_j) q_k^{amp} e^{j\theta_k} \right|^2. \tag{37}$$

To minimize the objective function $E_i(q_i^{amp}, \theta_i)$, the brute-force search is used, which means that the objective function is computed for all combinations and the smallest one is selected. The computational complexity of the whole process is $O(IJMN)$, but since this method can generate distributions with sufficient accuracy using small values of I and J, the computation time is short in various practical situations.

Suzuki et al. have implemented the previously described methods (the eigen-method, the semidefinite relaxation, GS-PAT, the LMA, and this method) on a CPU and performed experiments to compare them. The results show that this method has the shorter computation time than the other method when $I = 1, J = 16$. They also performed simulations to generate multiple foci with identical amplitudes. Their results showed that the method could reconstruct the sound pressure given at the control point with at least 80% accuracy which is better than eigenmethod and semidefinite relaxation. LMA gave the most accurate results, but the longest computation time. GS-PAT (Matsubayashi et al. 2020) showed an intermediate performance between this method and the LMA in terms of both accuracy and time.

3 Summary

In this chapter, we introduced the basic equations for controlling the ultrasonic sound field and the various algorithms for solving them. The requirements for sound field control in mid-air haptics rendering are accuracy and speed. The use of GS-PAT or the combinatorial optimization is suitable for fast movement of stimulus points, such as when generating a focus that perfectly follows a fast-moving finger. Note, however, that in such cases, even if the algorithm is fast enough, the effects of hardware and sound transmission delays need to be compensated for. On the other hand, if you want to generate an accurate sound pressure distribution, LMA is superior. Especially in the situation where tactile sensation is generated on a specific part of the hand, taking into account the effect of scattering on the surface of the hand, this algorithm is suitable because the computation time is not much affected by the number of zero pressure points. These and other ultrasonic sound field control algorithms proposed so far, and the applications realized by them have been introduced above, but this is only an overview. Please refer to the respective literature for details.

One of the major advantages of ultrasonic haptic technology is the ability to freely control the pressure applied to the skin surface. This is also important in investigating the sense of touch in the human body. Investigating how the spatial patterns of pressure and the waveforms of the vibrations applied to it affect human perception is the basis for future mid-air haptic rendering technology. It has the potential to define the necessary elements for haptic design and furthermore to create new tactile sensations that do not exist in the real world. For this purpose, further development of algorithms to control the ultrasonic field is expected.

References

Frier W, Ablart D, Chilles J, Long B, Giordano M, Obrist M, Subramanian S (2018) Using spatiotemporal modulation to draw tactile patterns in mid-air. In: International conference on human haptic sensing and touch enabled computer applications. Springer, pp 270–281

Gerchberg RW (1972) A practical algorithm for the determination of phase from image and diffraction plane pictures. Optik 35:237–246

Hasegawa T, Kido T, Iizuka T, Matsuoka C (2000) A general theory of Rayleigh and Langevin radiation pressures. Acoustical Sci Technol 21(3):145–152

Hertzberg Y, Naor O, Volovick A, Shoham S (2010) Towards multifocal ultrasonic neural stimulation: pattern generation algorithms. J Neural Eng 7(5):056002

Inoue S, Makino Y, Shinoda H (2015) Active touch perception produced by airborne ultrasonic haptic hologram. In: 2015 IEEE World Haptics Conference (WHC). IEEE, pp 362–367

Inoue S, Makino Y, Shinoda H (2016) Mid-air ultrasonic pressure control on skin by adaptive focusing. In: International conference on human haptic sensing and touch enabled computer applications. Springer, Heidelberg, pp 68–77

Kuroki S, Watanabe J, Nishida S (2016) Neural timing signal for precise tactile timing judgments. J Neurophysiol 115(3):1620–1629 PMID: 26843600

Long B, Seah SA, Carter T, Subramanian S (2014) Rendering volumetric haptic shapes in mid-air using ultrasound. ACM Trans Graphics (TOG) 33(6):1–10

Madsen K, Nielsen H, Tingleff O (2004) Methods for non-linear least squares problems, 2nd edn, p 60

Marzo A, Drinkwater BW (2019) Holographic acoustic tweezers. Proc Natl Acad Sci 116(1):84–89

Matsubayashi A, Makino Y, Shinoda H (2020) Rendering ultrasound pressure distribution on hand surface in real-time. In: International conference on human haptic sensing and touch enabled computer applications. Springer, Heidelberg, pp 407–415

Morales R, Ezcurdia I, Irisarri J, Andrade MA, Marzo A (2021) Generating airborne ultrasonic amplitude patterns using an open hardware phased array. Appl Sci 11(7):2981

Plasencia DM, Hirayama R, Montano-Murillo R, Subramanian S (2020) Gs-pat: high-speed multi-point sound-fields for phased arrays of transducers. ACM Trans Graphics (TOG) 39(4):138-1

Suzuki S, Fujiwara M, Makino Y, Shinoda H (2021) Radiation pressure field reconstruction for ultrasound midair haptics by greedy algorithm with brute-force search. IEEE Trans Haptics

Takahashi R, Hasegawa K, Shinoda H (2018) Lateral modulation of midair ultrasound focus for intensified vibrotactile stimuli. In: International conference on human haptic sensing and touch enabled computer applications. Springer, Heidelberg, pp 276–288

Superimposing Visual Images on Mid-Air Ultrasonic Haptic Stimulation

Hiroyuki Shinoda and Yasutoshi Makino

Abstract Mid-air haptic stimulation will be accompanied by visual information in many future applications. Vision is a fast and precise means of obtaining spatial information and is how we consume most forms of digital information. The super-imposition of visual and haptic feedback at the same position would provide an intuitive interface that requires minimal learning and could lead to a more engaging and immersive user experience. In this chapter, we introduce typical strategies of visual–tactile superimposition when using an ultrasound haptics device, including: an aerial computer interface with ultrasound haptic feedback, visuo-tactile projection on the skin, holographic transmission of physical entities, and applications with head-mounted displays. We also discuss the problem of positional matching between vision and haptics which is crucial for a high-quality user experience.

1 Introduction

The primary role of human tactile perception is to feel and experience the surrounding environment. However, the tactile modality is not suitable for perceiving and understanding multiple surrounding objects simultaneously. The literature on haptics states that the haptic sense itself has a poor ability to transmit logical and graphical information when it is used alone (Loomis (1981)). In comparison, vision is far superior in obtaining pattern information. In particular, the parallel recognition mechanism of 2D patterns is much faster and more precise than that of haptic perception (Vega-Bermudez et al. (1991)). Therefore, visual information is coupled together with mid-air haptic stimulation in many scenarios (Shinoda (2010)) (as discussed in Chap. "Opportunities for Multisensory Mid-Air Interactions Featuring Ultrasound Haptic Feedback"). In 3D user interfaces depicted in science fiction, people are often surrounded by graphical buttons and icons, which can be touched and controlled. These visual buttons and icons are effective means of displaying the menus of possible operations in the air. An accompanying mid-air haptic stimulus is an indispensable

H. Shinoda (✉) · Y. Makino
The University of Tokyo, 5-1-5 Kashiwanoha, Kashiwa, Japan
e-mail: hiroyuki_shinoda@k.u-tokyo.ac.jp

© The Author(s), under exclusive license to Springer Nature Switzerland AG 2022   281
O. Georgiou et al. (eds.), *Ultrasound Mid-Air Haptics for Touchless Interfaces*,
Human–Computer Interaction Series, https://doi.org/10.1007/978-3-031-04043-6_12

element that facilitates interaction with such an interface (e.g., as discussed in Chaps. "User Experience and Mid-Air Haptics: Applications, Methods, and Challenges" and "Ultrasound Haptic Feedback for Touchless User Interfaces: Design Patterns").

The spatial coincidence between the visual target and haptic stimulus is not an absolute requirement in general visual–haptic interfaces. Design freedom exists, whereby the visual image can be separated from the haptic stimulation. When a computer mouse is used, the mouse pointer appears on the screen while the physical mouse is separate from the screen. However, exact superimposition makes it easier to determine the correspondence between the visual and haptic stimuli, which could lead to intuitive interfaces that require minimal learning process. This principle comes from a fact that has existed since the primitive era, i.e., the primary purpose of visual and haptic perception has been to identify and understand real physical objects, where the visual and haptic entities are always superimposed.

The roles of human senses are shifting with time. Before the development of artificial audio speakers, auditory perception was linked to real entities producing the sound, e.g., a bird singing. Finding the relationship between the sound and its source was crucial for, e.g., catching preys and dealing with attacks from the surrounding environment. However, nowadays, hearing a speech or enjoying music is more important than localizing its sound source. Similarly, the role of vision and haptics is shifting. Therefore, it is not always necessary that visual and haptic stimuli originate from the same entity in future information systems. However, at least as of today, the majority of haptic sensations are still linked to physical objects, including everyday tools and objects handled by fingers as well as interface components like doorknobs and switches. When we use these physical objects, the vision first recognizes their function and required action; next, we reach for the object of interest. Following this, primary idea that the function of an object is combined with and led by a visual image is a promising strategy for the design of near future HCI.

The first example of a contactless mid-air visual–haptic superimposition was demonstrated as "touchable holography" in SIGGRAPH 2009 (Hoshi et al. (2009)), (Hoshi et al. (2010)), (Touchable Holography), a year after the first publication of mid-air haptics (Iwamoto et al. (2008)). In the demo, a 2D floating image was created in mid-air space using a concave mirror as shown in Fig. 1. When an aerial 2D raindrop animation reached the skin surface, the touch sensation was produced by a burst wave of amplitude-modulated radiation pressure from an ultrasound haptics device. This simple conceptual demonstration has evolved into several systems, reviewed in the following sections. Although many studies have already been conducted along this line, we introduced the earliest examples in each form of contactless visual–haptic superimposition.

In this chapter, we review advances in visual-haptic superimposition. We discuss several approaches that can be used to achieve this phenomenon and reflect on the challenges of creating convincing visuo-haptic sensations.

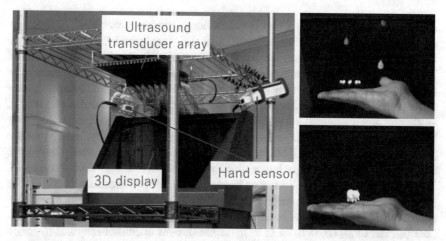

Fig. 1 Touchable holography system (2009) (Hoshi et al. (2009); Hoshi et al. (2010); touchable holography)

2 Realism of Experience Reproduced by Ultrasonic Haptic Displays

The superimposition of visual images onto non-contact haptic stimuli creates virtual objects with physical interactions. Though a general goal of virtual reality technology is to create an experience equivalent to the real world, the goal is often over-specified; sometimes, we have no target real object. It would be beneficial for the users and developers to form a consensus about the realism created by the ultrasound tactile display. At least, three goals of rendering haptic interactions are identified:

- **Class A**: Physically equivalent

    The haptic feedback aims to recreate the exact physical interactions with the target object.
- **Class B**: Perceptually equivalent

    The haptic feedback aims to recreate a similar (ideally equivalent) haptic perception of interacting with the target object.
- **Class C**: Not equivalent, but beneficial to the experience

    The haptic feedback provides a different (distinguishable) perception from the actual contact with the target object, but still improves the interactive experience.

Historically, kinesthetic haptic displays were used to simulate interaction with virtual objects, trying to mimic as closely as possible their physical characteristics, e.g., stiffness, shape, belonging to Class A interactions. This is possible in certain limited cases, but not always. Bulky mechanical devices are needed to generate large forces, which are required to simulate realistic interactions with stiff objects. Even with rigid mechanical systems, it is difficult to reproduce the impact force with a stiff object, such as a table or a wall. In such a case, the feeling of impact is often designed to satisfy Class B interactions (Kuchenbecker et al. (2006)), by superimposing vibrations onto the insufficient and blunt impact response kinesthetic force. Class B interactions are also a typical target of high-definition visual displays. The displayed colors that are synthesized by RGB have different optical spectra from the actual ones, but the perceived colors are identical. Finally, Class C interactions are a reasonable goal in mid-air haptics or wearable haptics (Pacchierotti et al. (2017)), as the maximum applicable force is very limited. In this respect, ultrasound mid-air haptics can produce a realistic feeling of a very lightweight object moving on the palm or a sense of being lightly touched by others. However, in many situations, the objective contact force is larger than the maximum force the device can exert. Users must understand this limitation in advance, which is a necessary condition for practical use. Nevertheless, helpful tactile stimuli can be produced, with significant perceived intensity that has been enhanced by certain methods (Takahashi et al. (2018); Frier et al. (2018)), so as to make the mid-air operation easy and to create realistic and immersive VR experiences. A recent study also showed that non-contact ultrasound stimulation can create a significant pseudo-static pressure (Morisaki et al. (2021)). In the following sections, we review examples of visuo-haptic systems that use mid-air haptic devices to provide a tactile counterpart to interactive visual content.

3 Wearable Versus Stationary Visual Display

Two strategies, namely the wearable and stationary types, are available for displaying visual images in mid-air. Wearable 3D displays, like **head-mounted displays** (HMD) for virtual reality (VR) and augmented reality (AR) content, are promising devices for producing high-quality immersive images around the user. On the other hand, 3D visual displays installed in the environment are being developed to create images for the naked eye—we refer to these as **stationary displays** (SD).

The strength of a SD is that no glasses or user augmentation are required to perceive virtual content. However, enjoying a touchable image anywhere in a room remains a significant technological challenge. As wearable 3D displays become more lightweight and unobtrusive, they will probably be the most natural choice for displaying virtual and augmented objects in everyday interactions.

Mid-air haptics can be combined with both visual rendering approaches. However, mid-air haptics and SDs have one important common trait: they both require no additional device to be worn by the user to facilitate perception. Therefore, the early demonstrations of visual–haptic superimposition were mostly based on SDs, as introduced later in this chapter. Approaches requiring no additional devices on the user's body are particularly beneficial for use in public spaces.

There are other reasons why the use of SDs has been prioritized in this research area. The first is the timing of commercialization. Commercial HMD products emerged in the mid-2010s, whereas a high-quality MMAP[1] was already available in the early 2010s, facilitating 3D visual content that could have haptics superimposed. The second reason is the problems related to sensor feedback. When mid-air haptics is combined with an SD, a common, fixed, coordinate system can be used to align content from each modality. For example, in the visuo-tactile projector introduced below, feedforward control with no sensor feedback can create a virtual existence. However, to integrate mid-air haptics with HMD, the system must precisely measure the positional relationship between the HMD and the ultrasound device in real-time to superimpose the haptic stimulation onto the image. This remains often a challenge in general cases. We also discuss this problem in the following section.

It is interesting to predict and discuss whether SDs or HMDs will be the major partner of mid-air haptics in 10 years. Both outcomes are possible, and this is strongly dependent on the technological advancement and dissemination of SDs and HMDs as well as to the popularity of the applications they are employed in.

4   Display of Mid-air Button: Providing a Response to Active Touch

Touchscreens are popular in many computing devices (e.g., smartphones, tablets, public displays). As many people are already accustomed to interacting with touch-screen interfaces, an easy form of mid-air haptics is to simulate a touch-panel device in the air (i.e., the "floating screen" design pattern from Chap. "Ultrasound Haptic Feedback for Touchless User Interfaces: Design Patterns"). Figure 2 depicts the first demonstration system of the mid-air touch panel HaptoMime (Monnai et al. (2014)). A familiar touch-panel image is produced in the air, which users operate with mid-air gestures that replicate touching icons on a physical touchscreen. The button-alignment information is transmitted to the user visually, and the mid-air haptics provide feedback when interacting with the buttons. Mid-air touch panels are inherently hygienic as users are not exposed to surface contamination. Furthermore, these virtual mid-air screens can disappear when they are not needed. Such non-contact interface satisfies the recent demand, whereby people want to avoid touching devices in public spaces, e.g., to avoid the spread of diseases such as COVID-19. The device will not be compromised even if the user interacts with it with dirty hands. Similarly, doctors can safely interact with such mid-air interface during surgeries.

The above technique is a combination of a gesture interface and a virtual touch panel. The difference from ordinary gesture control is that aerial images restrict the hand position and motion. It is unnecessary to learn gesture rules to transmit their intentions. Moreover, the haptic stimulation feeds back the system response to aid the confirmation of the user's action. This support improves the usability of the

---

[1] MicroMirror Array Plate. A glass-plate-like device including strip mirrors perpendicular to the plate surface. The plate was produced by Asukanet Co., Ltd. as the product name AI plate. A similar device principle was also independently presented by Dr. Satoshi Maekawa, NICT.

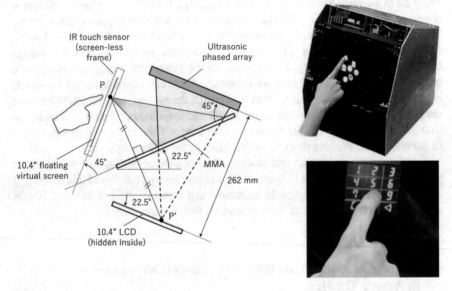

Fig. 2 HaptoMime: mid-air touch panel with haptic feedback (2014)

gesture control while maintaining its important hands-free and contactless feature. A floating touch panel without tactile feedback is also a possible form of the mid-air touch panel. An aerial touch panel can be operated only by visual feedback: a graphical button motion or color change in response to the finger touch motion. In this case, the perceptual load on the user's eyes increases. The haptic sensation notifies the completion of the input action. Without this sensation, the system must implement vision-based approaches to notify the users that their action has been correctly registered. Subsequent studies reported ultrasound also can produce click sensations (Ito et al. (2019)) in addition to simple touch sensations. Such additional tactile information improves usability further, making mid-air panels closer to standard tangible interfaces.

In the HaptoMime system (Monnai et al. (2014)), the fingertip position is sensed by an infrared sensor, which detects the moment the finger touches the floating button. The tactile sensation is then reproduced by irradiating the finger pad with traveling ultrasonic waves. The tactile feeling is programmable by changing the vibration amplitude of the ultrasonic wave with various waveforms. When an icon is dragged, a continuous vibration stimulus is applied during the motion. This tactile feedback tells the user that the icon is indeed being dragged. The aerial images are displayed to the naked eye by transferring a general liquid crystal display (LCD) screen into the air using a micromirror array (ASKA3D plate, renamed from AI plate, manufactured by Asukanet Co., Ltd.). The infrared sensor frame that is used to measure the finger position is located in the same plane of the floating touch panel, on the edge of the rectangular image presentation range. The focusing beam that is emitted from the phased array is reflected by the flat surface of the micromirror array, which enables the ultrasound to focus on a plane that is identical to the aerial image. HaptoMime was an appealing demonstration in 2014 because the tactile perception was stable and believable. Multiple arrays were used to provide a strong tactile sensation, and the finger sensing using an infrared touch sensor was precise and robust. Around the same time, several similar systems were demonstrated for in-vehicle applications following this system (BMW (2017)).

If the objective is to render the interaction with a mechanical keyboard or a smartphone surface, providing feedback through ultrasound mid-air haptics will not provide the same sensation. However, the mid-air tactile feedback can cover the required tactile responses for 2D operation of the floating icons. The usability may be better than that of a normal touch panel without tactile feedback.

The aerial image as shown in Fig. 2 is replaceable with other types of floating images. Any device that creates a floating image in front of a surface can be combined with the ultrasonic stimuli. A fog screen using water mist as a visual screen that scatters a projector light is also an option (Rakkolainen et al. (2015); Norasikin et al. (2019)). Readers should also refer to Chap. "Touchless Tactile Interaction with Unconventional Permeable Displays", which discusses the use of touchless haptic feedback with unconventional permeable displays, including fog screens.

Prior to HaptoMime, Yoshino et al. prototyped a system in which the visual screen was located slightly behind the ultrasound focusing plane (Yoshino and Shinoda 2013), as illustrated in Fig. 3. The system used a translucent visual screen that was almost transparent for ultrasound propagation. A visual projector projected images onto the translucent plane, whereas the ultrasound focus was created immediately before the translucent plane. This is another option for creating a mid-air touch panel, although the visual and tactile stimulation are not perfectly superimposed.

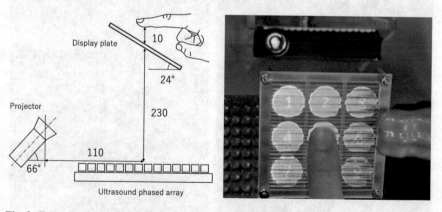

Fig. 3 Example of mid-air touch panel using translucent visual screen (2013)

5 Passive Haptic Stimulation with Projected Image

Another type of superimposition is provided by the visuo-tactile projector or tactile projector presented in (Yoshino et al. (2012); Visuo-Tactile Projector; Hasegawa and Shinoda). As depicted in Fig. 4, passive haptic stimulation is provided with various visual images projected onto the user's skin. In the first demonstration in 2013, an ordinary visual projector projected a virtual object image, e.g., a small virtual creature moving on a table. These were accompanied by ultrasound haptic stimuli. When designing the ultrasound haptic stimuli, we selected waveforms by trial and error. The spatial pressure distribution was a single modulated focus point superimposed onto the visual image. The position and motion of the visual–tactile image were determined in advance (i.e., always moving in synchrony at the same position), and no tracking was necessary. The system was demonstrated in academic conferences, exhibitions, and the open laboratory of the university. Although the haptic signals were not designed to accurately replicate the physical and mechanical characteristics of the projected virtual objects, they provided a sense of reality through haptic stimulation. A frequent question that we received was how we created detailed spatial features of the tactile stimulation pattern. Certain people were surprised when we answered that what we presented was a single focal point with a diameter of 1 cm. They experienced more detailed patterns through their own imaginations; Chap.

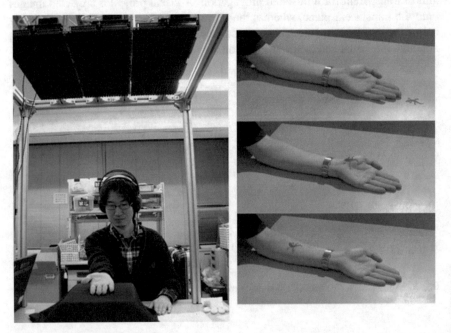

Fig. 4 Visuo-tactile projector (2013) (Yoshino et al. (2012); Visuo-Tactile Projector; Hasegawa and Shinoda 2013)

"Opportunities for Multisensory Mid-Air Interactions Featuring Ultrasound Haptic Feedback" gives insight into why this "illusion" took place.

The variety of presented tactile feelings has now been broadened. Moreover, the displayed small objects can be more realistic and even viewed as 3D objects using projection mapping techniques. In a visuo-tactile projector, it is possible to design experiences that perceptually resemble reality. Several real feelings of light touch or small creatures moving on the skin (with slight wind by acoustic streaming) can be created, whose effect is strengthened by the superimposed visual images.

Such a visuo-tactile projector may be part of entertainment and digital signage. In entertainment applications, ultrasound radiation pressure may be used for purposes other than haptic stimulation. The physical force and air stream that are accompanied by the ultrasound also create physical interactions with the surrounding lightweight or elastic objects. For example, ultrasound can move water or sand surfaces (Visuo–Tactile Projector). Such real-object motions generate a sense of reality as if a creature is present.

An essential parameter in a visuo-tactile projector is the tolerance of the tactile stimulation position. Yoshino et al. clarified the conditions under which visual point images and tactile stimuli are perceived as overlapping (Yoshino et al. (2012)). In the experiment, a point image was projected onto a palm, and amplitude-modulated ultrasounds were applied at 30 and 200 Hz. They evaluated the two-point discrimination threshold on a palm while shifting the focal center from the visual point, whereby the participants noticed the position difference between the visual and tactile stimulations. They concluded that the tolerance on the palm was approximately 1.0–1.3 cm for both a stationary stimulation point and a non-stationary case of 7 cm/s motion along a 16 mm radius circle. The stimulation duration was 3 s. This result was consistent with the localization error of an ultrasound point stimulation on a palm, as evaluated by Wilson et al. (2014).

6   3D Stationary Haptic VR Object with Visual Image

HORN (Inoue et al. (2014), (2015)) is a unique 3D interaction system in which a volumetric haptic entity is created as a stationary or slowly moving 3D sound field. As the acoustic energy density is static, the users do not perceive significant tactile stimuli without hand motion. However, if users actively touch the system, they perceive a virtual object from the acoustic field. A single focal point that is created by omnidirectional converging waves from the surrounding phased arrays produces an invisible elastic sphere in the air. Consider a situation in which an omnidirectional focal point is created around the center of the workspace and a finger approaches the focal center. The finger starts to feel the reaction force around the focal point, and the reaction force is stronger when the finger is closer to the focal center. This means that the finger feels the existence of an elastic object around the focal point. A 3D shape is produced by multiple focal points that form the voxels of the haptic entity. The mechanism of this tactile sensation is considered to be similar to the high sensitivity

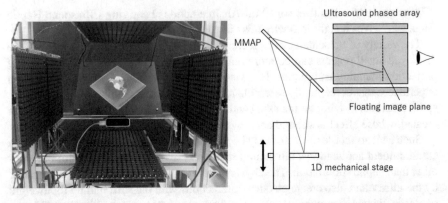

Fig. 5 HORN system (2014)

in lateral modulation (Takahashi et al. (2020)) and spatiotemporal modulation (Frier et al. (2018)). The hand motion produces a relative spatial–temporal change in the radiation pressure on the user's hands, thereby creating significant tactile perception and causing the user to feel the virtual object as a very elastic object.

The optical system of HORN was based on the MMAP introduced in HaptoMime. A floating 2D image was created as a reconstructed image of a normal LCD using MMAP. The depth of the images was controlled by moving the LCD mechanically, as illustrated in Fig. 5. Because the MMAP reconstructs the LCD image at a position that is mirror-symmetrical to the plate, the floating image moves backward when the LCD approaches the MMAP.

7   3D Human–Human Interaction by HaptoClone

Haptic and optical clone (HaptoClone) (Makino et al. (2016)) is an interactive system that produces a realistic 3D visual object with haptic feedback, as illustrated in Figs. 6, 7, and 8. Side-by-side booths are optically connected, whereby 3D images are copied into the booths of each partner. Ultrasonic haptic displays are combined with the transferred 3D images to enable real-time interaction.

The 3D reconstruction of images from adjacent booths is achieved using a pair of MMAPs, as described above. Because the real-time and electrical transmission of 3D images remain challenging, we used high-quality optical transmission by means of MMAP. As depicted schematically in Fig. 7, once an object passes through the micromirror array, its convex and concave surfaces are inverted in the reconstruction. By reflecting the object twice with the two plates, it is possible to optically reconstruct a 3D object at a distance in the adjacent booth. Owing to the symmetry of the MMAP, the positional relationship between the real and virtual images in each booth is perfectly consistent. For example, consider a balloon that is placed in the right booth, and the user touches the reconstructed image of the balloon in the left booth.

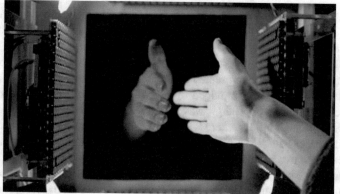

Fig. 6 HaptoClone system (2016). The contrast of the photo was adjusted

Fig. 7 3D image reconstruction with MMAP

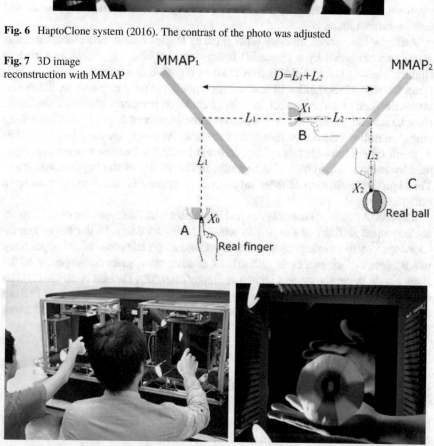

Fig. 8 Photographs of HaptoClone system (2016)

It appears as if the virtual hand in the right booth touches the real balloon in the right booth. It is even possible that the virtual hand actuates the lightweight balloon using the radiation force.

The 3D shapes of the objects in each booth are measured using depth sensors, and the tactile sensation is presented by creating an ultrasonic focus at the domain in which the two objects are judged to have made contact. In the first version of HaptoClone, the acoustic energy was equally distributed to the detected contact points, with no modulation, whereas it was driven in AM and LM (Takahashi et al. (2020)) in recent demos. This system enables real-time tactile interaction with 3D images between two users in different booths. Although the applied force is limited to a normal force perpendicular to the surface, and the force amplitude is not precise, the contact positions and times are accurate, which produces the experience of mutual human–human touch.

An impressive experience that is provided by HaptoClone is human–human interaction, accompanied by realistic 3D images and haptics: e.g., allowing a remote (lightly touching) handshake as illustrated in Fig. 6. It is a scientific tool for clarifying the role of modalities in nonverbal communication. For example, the haptic interaction can be turned on/off, and the affective or emotional effects of the haptic stimulation can be confirmed. Subjectively, the impact of haptics becomes strong when we notice that the partner feels the same. At times, we may feel hesitation to touch others through this system, and the hesitation increases when accompanied by haptics. This effect also depends on the quality of the haptic stimulation. The objective evaluation of these subjective perceptions is one of the current open problems.

The MMAP remains the only method in which mutual and realistic visual images are presented in front of the person with virtually no delay. In the Super Hapto-Clone system, the workspace was expanded, and an optical clone of the upper body was achieved (Serizawa et al. (2020)). As another subsequent development of the HaptoClone system, a system known as HaptoCloneAR (Yoshida et al. (2017)) has also been demonstrated. This system optically constructs additional images in front of the HaptoClone images. An LCD and a half-mirror are used to create a floating information display as AR.

8   Haptic Interaction with Full 3D Computer Graphics

Matsubayashi et al. (2019) prototyped a haptic interaction system using full 3D computer graphics (CG). The aerial CG is produced in real time by a parallax barrier-type display developed by the Hideki Kakeya laboratory at Tsukuba University. The workspace is a cube of approximately 30 cm surrounded by 16 units of ultrasound phased arrays on the up-down-left–right walls, as depicted in Fig. 9.

The displayed pressure distribution on multiple fingers is controlled in this system, reflecting the contact depth between the fingers and virtual object. The virtual object is deformable and possesses specific dynamics. It can simulate object handling using

Fig. 9 Grasping of virtual 3D object with 3D CG. The workspace is surrounded by ultrasound phased arrays (2019)

multiple fingers. The real-time calculation of the sound pressure distribution for this purpose is discussed in Chap. "Sound-Field Creation for Haptic Reproduction" of this book. The spatial and temporal resolutions have been improved across a series of studies. Matsubayashi et al. (2019) confirmed that participants could pick up a virtual object in an area of 20×15 cm and move it to a designated point within 4 s in average without visual information. Local shape (Matsubayashi et al. (2019)) and elasticity (Matsubayashi et al. (2021)) were also tested.

Although full 3D interaction remains a challenge in this context, it is already possible to confirm the human tactile ability to detect the contact condition from the slight difference in the pressure distribution on the skin. The results of this handling simulation system clarify the necessary specifications for creating a realistic virtual object. The fingertip sensation of "holding something" is not created by simply applying a constant force. The human finger is highly sensitive to pressure distribution changes, which enables the detection of a surface, sensing of the surface direction and curvature, and distinguishing of the surface hardness. Surface elasticity is perceived from the spread of the contact area according to the contact depth (Matsubayashi et al. (2021)). These distribution changes occur very sensitively in accordance with the slight differences in the positional relationship between the finger and object. Without reproducing these pressure changes, the entity of a physical object will not be felt. Therefore, precise fingertip measurements are necessary to create a virtual object that is held by the fingers.

Regarding 3D CG technology, a naked-eye 3D image system using ultrasound has been proposed (Hirayama et al. (2019)). The ultrasound moves beads in the air at high speed, which scatters the projected light to create 3D aerial images. This is an interesting application of airborne ultrasound in 3D CG. Note that the display area of shape and stiffness is not limited to the finger pad. The performances of the shape and stiffness sensations in the palm have been evaluated in the studies of Howard et al. (2019) and Marchal et al. (2020).

9 Integration with HMD

Most of the systems discussed so far have combined ultrasound haptics with visual output from stationary displays. An alternative promising combination is mid-air haptics with a wearable HMD (Sand et al. (2015); Pittera et al. (2019); Suzuki et al. (2018); Brice et al. (2019); Howard et al. (2020)). Although this requires the user to adorn a wearable device, a HMD offers great advantages in the sense that visual content is not constrained by the output area of a stationary display (see also Chap. "Touchless Tactile Interaction with Unconventional Permeable Displays"). A HMD can be integrated with a large haptic workspace that is expanded by multi-phased arrays (Suzuki et al. (2018)), a robotic arm (Brice et al. (2019)), or a pan-tilt mechanism to move the phased-array surface (Howard et al. (2020)), creating immersive visuo-haptic interactive systems with a wide interaction area.

A current problem in integration with HMDs is the position transformation between the HMD and the ultrasonic transducers. In many cases, ultrasound phased arrays are implemented in the environment, whereas the HMD moves with the user's head. To match the position of the visual object created by a HMD with the ultrasound focus, the positional relationship between the HMD and phased arrays must be determined precisely in real-time. The measurement remains problematic in practical situations, although it will be solved in the near future.

One solution to this problem is to mount an ultrasonic transducer array onto the HMD Sand et al. (2015). In this case, the ultrasonic transducer array is physically fixed at a known position relative to the visual coordinate system in the HMD. While this allows the haptic output area to move with the user's gaze, there is a limitation that the fingertips or palms need to point toward the face to perceive the haptic feedback because ultrasonic waves are emitted outwards from the face.

Another practical approach is to establish applications that allow a certain visual–tactile deviation. Precise focus on a fingertip in HaptoMime and CG object handling requires exact measurement of the fingertip position. However, in an application in which the tactile stimulation is spread wider in a palm, a rougher measurement is acceptable.

10 Summary and Future Possibilities

In this chapter, we highlighted the advantages of superimposing visual images onto mid-air haptic stimulation. We have introduced typical examples of a mid-air touch panel, visuo-tactile projection, static haptic objects, haptic–optical transmission, 3D CG handling, and the combination with HMD. The variety of tactile feelings we are able to provide with ultrasound haptics is constantly increasing. A significant advancement is non-contact thermal presentation techniques. In addition to heating by infrared (Saga (2019)), effective cooling by mist-vaporization, expedited by ultrasound, is also possible (Nakajima et al. (2021)). Focusing an ultrasound on the skin in

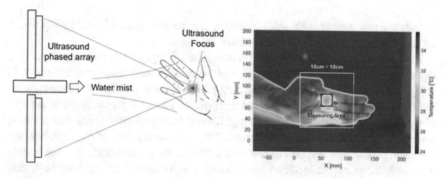

Fig. 10 Display of pin-point cooling sensation by ultrasound focus in water mist (2021)

a water-mist atmosphere produces a rapid cooling sensation in a limited area around the focus, as illustrated in Fig. 10. The combination of such a thermal sensation with a visual display will enable VR experiences with affective or emotional impact. As the range of tactile sensations possible with such devices expands, so too will the range of visual-haptic experiences that can be created.

The technological advancement of visual 3D displays is still necessary to fully benefit from visual–haptic superimposition. Moreover, the precise measurement of the finger/hand motion and positional relativity with respect to the visual rendering is crucial for enhancing practical use. With the further development of these technologies, the possibilities of mid-air haptics will expand significantly. Research on the superimposition of aerial images and ultrasonic tactile presentation is only the beginning. As these technologies progress and improve in realism, visual–haptic images will evolve into what should be known as *materialized graphics* (JST CREST (2018)), behaving as though possessing a physical entity.

The significance of materialized graphics can be understood through the analogy of humanoid robots as a multimodal interface with humans. The human-like behavior and shape of humanoid robots enable communication with humans even if they have no special prior knowledge. Materialized graphics provides a natural interface that humans can handle and manipulate using the skills that are inherent in any human. It may embody a passive object or a living being, including a human. They may be used to mediate human–human or human–robot communication, as well as to evaluate the usability of a prototype before it is created. They can change their appearance and shape, or even instantly disappear when they are unnecessary. The possibility of truly achieving such *materialized graphics* has been increased by a recent finding to reproduce a pseudo-static pressure sensation by ultrasound (Morisaki et al. (2021)).

In certain cases, humans may manipulate physical entities without vision. The sound-image icon (Rim et al. (2020)) is an example of a haptic entity with no visual images, which is a combination of a touchable virtual object and sound (Ochiai et al. (2017)). Controlling smell (Hasegawa et al. (2018)) with airflow (Hasegawa et al. (2017)) created by ultrasonic phased arrays may have an effect on the olfactory senses. This is another modality controllable by ultrasound. Thus, non-contact haptic stimulation that produces physical entities is a research field with infinite possibilities for development, beyond the combination with visual images.

In summary, we have presented an overview of approaches that can be used to superimpose visual and haptic stimuli to create multisensory mid-air experiences. In doing so, we have highlighted the exciting possibilities that arise from this: e.g., the ability to convince users that a simple focal point takes on the physical characteristics of a moving visual object. We also highlighted technical challenges that must be overcome for visual-haptic experiences to be convincing and of high quality. We hope that readers are inspired to consider how mid-air visual interfaces may benefit from ultrasound haptic feedback, and likewise, how mid-air haptic interfaces may benefit from superimposed visual stimuli from cutting-edge displays.

References

https://www.youtube.com/watch?v=1B-7uQ5RD2A "BMW HoloActive TOUCH at CES 2017"

https://www.youtube.com/watch?v=Y-P1zZAcPuw "Touchable Holography" video produced by Takayuki Hoshi in Shinoda laboratory

https://www.youtube.com/watch?v=Bb0hNMxxewg "Visuo-Tactile Projector" video produced by Keisuke Hasegawa in Shinoda laboratory

https://materialized-graphics.hapislab.org/ JST CREST, materialized graphics project since 2018

Brice D, McRoberts T, Rafferty K (2019) A proof of concept integrated multi-systems approach for large scale tactile feedback in VR. In: De Paolis L., Bourdot P. (eds) augmented reality, virtual reality, and computer graphics, lecture notes in computer science, vol 11613

Frier W, Ablart D, Chilles J, Long B, Giordano M, Obrist M, Subramanian S (2018) Using spatiotemporal modulation to draw tactile patterns in mid-air. In: 2018 proceedings of Euro haptics, Part I, pp 270–281

Hasegawa K, Qiu L, Noda A, Inoue S, Shinoda H (2017) Electronically steerable ultrasound-driven long narrow air stream. Appl Phys Lett 111:064104

Hasegawa K, Qiu L, Shinoda H (2018) Midair ultrasound fragrance rendering. IEEE Trans vis Comput Graphics 24(4):1477–1485

Hasegawa K, Shinoda H (2013) Aerial display of vibrotactile sensation with high spatial-temporal resolution using large-aperture airborne ultrasound phased array. In: 2013 Proceedings of the IEEE world haptics conference, pp 31–36

Hirayama R, Martinez Plasencia D, Masuda N, Subramanian S (2019) A volumetric display for visual, tactile and audio presentation using acoustic trapping. Nature 575:320–323

Hoshi T, Takahashi M, Iwamoto T, Shinoda H (2010) Noncontact tactile display based on radiation pressure of airborne ultrasound. IEEE Trans Haptics 3(3):155–165

Hoshi T, Takahashi M, Nakatsuma K, Shinoda H (2009) Touchable holography. In: 2009 proceedings of ACM SIGGRAPH emerging technologies. ACM, New York, NY, USA, Article no. 23

Howard T, Marchal M, Lécuyer A, Pacchierotti C (2020) PUMAH: pan-tilt ultrasound mid-air haptics for larger interaction workspace in virtual reality. IEEE Trans Haptics 13(1):38–44

Howard T, Gallagher G, Lécuyer A, Pacchierotti C, Marchal M (2019) Investigating the recognition of local shapes using mid-air ultrasound haptics. In: 2019 Proceeding IEEE world haptics conference, pp 503–508

Inoue S, Kobayashi-Kirschvink KJ, Monnai Y, Hasegawa K, Makino Y, Shinoda H (2014) HORN: the hapt-optic reconstruction. In: 2014 ACM SIGGRAPH emerging technologies

Inoue S, Makino Y, Shinoda H (2015) Active touch perception produced by airborne ultrasonic haptic hologram. In: 2015 Proceedings of the IEEE world haptics conference (WHC), pp 362–367

Ito M, Kokumai Y, Shinoda H (2019) Midair click of dual-layer haptic button. In: 2019 proceedings of the IEEE world haptics conference, pp 349–352, Tokyo, Japan

Iwamoto T, Tatezono M, Shinoda H (2008) Non-contact method for producing tactile sensation using airborne ultrasound. Proc Euro Haptics 2008:504–513

Kuchenbecker KJ, Fiene J, Niemeyer G (2006) Improving contact realism through event-based haptic feedback. IEEE Trans Visual Comput Graphics 12(2):219–230

Loomis JM (1981) Tactile pattern perception. Perception 10:5–27

Makino Y, Furuyama Y, Inoue S, Shinoda H (2016) HaptoClone (Haptic-Optical Clone) for mutual tele-environment by real-time 3D image transfer with midair force feedback. In: 2016 Proceedings of the chi conference on human factors in computing systems, pp 1980–1990

Marchal M, Gallagher G, Lécuyer A, Pacchierotti C (2020) Can stiffness sensations be rendered in virtual reality using mid-air ultrasound haptic technologies? Proc Euro Haptics 2020:297–306

Matsubayashi A, Makino Y, Shinoda H (2019a) Direct finger manipulation of 3d object image with ultrasound haptic feedback. In: 2019a proceedings of the 2019a CHI conference on human factors in computing systems, Paper no 87, pp 1–11

Matsubayashi A, Oikawa H, Mizutani S, Makino Y, Shinoda H (2019b) Display of haptic shape using ultrasound pressure distribution forming cross-sectional shape.In: 2019b Proceedings of the 2019b IEEE world haptics conference, pp 419–424, Tokyo, Japan

Matsubayashi A, Yamaguchi T, Makino Y, Shinoda H (2021) Rendering softness using airborne ultrasound. In: 2021 proceedings of the IEEE world haptics conference, pp 355–360

Monnai Y, Hasegawa K, Fujiwara M, Yoshino K, Inoue S, Shinoda H (2014) HaptoMime: Mid-air haptic interaction with a floating virtual screen. In: 2014 proceedings of the 27th annual ACM symposium on user interface software and technology (UIST'14). ACM, New York, NY, USA, pp 663–667

Morisaki T, Fujiwara M, Makino Y, Shinoda H (2021) Non-vibratory pressure sensation produced by ultrasound focus moving laterally and repetitively with fine spatial step width. IEEE trans haptics (early access)

Nakajima M, Hasegawa K, Makino Y, Shinoda H (2021) Spatiotemporal pinpoint cooling sensation produced by ultrasound-driven mist vaporization on skin. 2021 IEEE trans haptics (Early access)

Norasikin MA, Martinez-Plasencia D, Memoli G, Subramanian S (2019) SonicSpray: a technique to reconfigure permeable mid-air displays. In: 2019 proceedings of the 2019 ACM international conference on interactive surfaces and spaces (ISS '19), pp 113–122

Ochiai Y, Hoshi T, Suzuki I (2017) Holographic whisper: rendering audible sound spots in three-dimensional space by focusing ultrasonic waves. In: 2017 Proceedings of the 2017 CHI conference on human factors in computing systems, pp 4314–4325

Pacchierotti C, Sinclair S, Solazzi M, Frisoli A, Hayward V, Prattichizzo D (2017) Wearable haptic systems for the fingertip and the hand: taxonomy, review, and perspectives. IEEE Trans Haptics 10(4):580–600

Pittera D, Gatti E, Obrist M (2019) I'm sensing in the rain: spatial incongruity in visual-tactile mid-air stimulation can elicit ownership in VR users. In: 2019 Proceedings of the CHI conference on human factors in computing systems. Association for computing machinery, New York, NY, USA, Paper 132, pp 1–15

Rakkolainen I, Sand A, Palovuori K (2015) Midair user interfaces employing particle screens. IEEE Comput Graph Appl 35(2):96–102

Rim S, Suzuki S, Toide Y, Fujiwara M, Makino Y, Shinoda H (2020) Sound-image icon with aerial haptic feedback. Proc Euro Haptics 2020:497–505

Satoshi S (2019) Thermal-radiation-based haptic display using laser-emission-based radiation control. In: 2019 Proceedings of IEEE world haptics 2019, WP2P.10 (Work-in-Progress Papers)

Sand A, Rakkolainen I, Isokoski P, Kangas J, Raisamo R, Palovuori K (2015) Head-mounted display with mid-air tactile feedback. In: 2015 proceedings of the 21st ACM symposium on virtual reality software and technology (VRST '15), pp 51–58

Serizawa K, Morisaki T, Delfosse C, Fujiwara M, Makino Y, Shinoda H (2020) Super hapto-clone: upper-body mutual telexistence system with haptic feedback. SIGGRAPH '20, emerging technologies, Washington, D.C, USA (moved to a virtual conference)

Shinoda H (2010) Tactile interaction with 3D images. In: 2010 the 17th international display workshops (IDW'10), INP4: 3D interactive systems, pp 1743–1746

Suzuki S, Fujiwara M, Makino Y, Shinoda H (2018) Midair ultrasound haptic display with large workspace. In: 2018 AsiaHaptics 2018, Incheon, Korea

Takahashi R, Hasegawa K, Shinoda H (2020) Tactile stimulation by repetitive lateral movement of midair ultrasound focus. IEEE Trans Haptics 13(2):334–342

Takahashi R, Hasegawa K, Shinoda H (2018) Lateral Modulation of Midair Ultrasound Focus for Intensified Vibrotactile Stimuli. In: 2018 proceedings of Euro haptics, Part II, pp 276–288

Vega-Bermudez F, Johnson KO, Hsiao SS (1991) Human tactile pattern recognition: active versus passive touch, velocity effects, and patterns of confusion. J Neurophysiol 65:531–546

Wilson G, Carter T, Subramanian S, Brewster SA (2014) Perception of ultrasonic haptic feedback on the hand: localisation and apparent motion. In: 2014 Proceedings of the SIGCHI conference on human factors in computing systems (CHI '14), pp 1133–1142

Yoshida K, Horiuchi Y, Inoue S, Makino Y, Shinoda H (2017) HaptoCloneAR: mutual haptic-optic interactive system with 2D image superimpose. In: 2017 Proceedings of SIGGRAPH emerging technologies, Los Angeles, California, USA

Yoshino K, Shinoda H (2013) Visio-acoustic screen for contactless touch interface with tactile sensation. Proc IEEE World Haptics Conf 2013:419–423

Yoshino K, Hasegawa K, Shinoda H (2012) Measuring visio-tactile threshold for visio-tactile projector. Proc SICE Annu Conf 2012:1996–2000

Ultrasound Mid-Air Haptic Feedback at the Fingertip

Kevin Pan, William Frier⊙, and Deepak Sahoo

Abstract Ultrasound haptic feedback is typically used to augment the multi-sensory experience with spatiotemporal patterns projected on the users' hands. Many studies have considered the usability of such techniques on the users' palms as it is more sensitive to ultrasound stimuli. Studies exploring the ultrasound feedback on the users' fingertips have utilized large ultrasound phased arrays to project perceptible haptic stimuli. Spatiotemporal patterns at the fingertips using smaller phased arrays have been largely unexplored due to their weaker sensations. In this chapter, we first present a survey of ultrasound stimuli patterns that have considered the users' fingers for haptic feedback. Then, a set of spatiotemporal stimuli for ultrasound feedback on the finger is presented along with results from a user study and associated examples of mid-air gestures. In the end, the prospect of ultrasound haptic sensations at the fingertip is summarized from a survey.

1 Introduction

Mid-air gestures can be natural and intuitive with haptic feedback, adding realism to virtual interactions (Culbertson et al. 2018; Grandhi et al. 2011). Freehand mid-air interactions with ultrasound haptic feedback are less disruptive than wearable haptic devices and can aid the feeling of immersion and presence (Pacchierotti et al. 2017; Rakkolainen et al. 2021). Current research in mid-air haptics has focused on creating virtual haptic shapes and patterns in mid-air for freehand direct exploration and localization. It has applications of mixed reality and haptic-augmented interfaces in automotive, digital advertising, and sterile medical interfaces (Rakkolainen et al. 2021). Mid-air haptics could enrich the user experience of applications of mid-air interactions, i.e., distant displays, ubiquitous environment, therapeutic assis-

K. Pan · D. Sahoo (✉)
Computer Science, Swansea University, Swansea, UK
e-mail: d.r.sahoo@swansea.ac.uk

W. Frier
Ultraleap Ltd, Bristol, UK
e-mail: william.frier@ultraleap.com

tance, accessibility, cultural heritage, text entry, sharing among devices and others (Koutsabasis and Vogiatzidakis 2019).

Most studies in the literature have explored ultrasound haptic feedback on the users' palm, as it is more sensitive to ultrasound stimuli (Rakkolainen et al. 2021; Sun et al. 2019), but also because it provides a larger canvas for tactile stimulation. Most studies exploring the ultrasound feedback on the users' fingertips have utilized large ultrasound phased arrays to project perceptible haptic stimuli (Matsubayashi et al. 2019). In contrast, spatiotemporal patterns at the fingertips using smaller phased arrays have been largely unexplored due to their limitation of creating stronger forces (Hoshi et al. 2010).

Carter et al (2013) initially proposed ultrasound mid-air haptic feedback at the fingertip with the pinching gesture. They created multiple focal points in mid-air and modulated its amplitude at different frequencies, e.g., 50 Hz and 200 Hz, to present different haptic cues. Since then, many modulation techniques have been developed to improve the ultrasound haptic feedback stimulation force that the users tested by exploring various 3D shapes like points, lines, circle, sphere, and pyramid patterns with their palms (Chilles et al. 2019; Hasegawa and Shinoda 2013; Kappus and Long 2018; Korres and Eid 2016; Long et al. 2014). Other research on ultrasound mid-air haptic feedback has focused on developing stimulation patterns to improve the perception of 3D shapes in mid-air, which users mostly tested with their palms. For example, Wilson et al. (2014) evaluated the localization and apparent motion of focused ultrasound on the user's palm; Frier et al. (2019) explored the effect of spatial sampling strategy on perceived strength of a pattern, e.g., a circle; and Hajas et al. (2020) found that the accuracy and confidence in identifying geometric shapes, e.g., circle, square, and triangle on the palm improved significantly when the moving focal point or haptic pointer slowed down at corners.

Recently, researchers have started exploring ultrasound mid-air haptic feedback with the users' fingers. For example, Howard et al. (2019) reported lower detection and identification thresholds for 15 cm long line patterns extending from the palm to the fingertips than the detection threshold for a single point on the palm. Matsubayashi et al. (2019) demonstrated ultrasound mid-air haptic feedback at the fingertip by stimulating the finger using a large phased array. Their system presented haptic cues when users touched and manipulated 3D virtual objects without wearing any device (Matsubayashi et al. 2019). Previously, researchers have tried ultrasound feedback at the fingertip using smaller phased arrays with limited success. For example, Sand et al. (2015) proposed a head-mounted display with ultrasound feedback for the finger and palm using a smaller phased array, but the stimulation was not strong enough for the fingertip. Palovuori et al. (2014) proposed an immaterial fog-screen display with mid-air ultrasound feedback, but with tileable small phased arrays to create focal point with higher intensity.

In this chapter, we present the prospect of ultrasound haptic feedback at the fingertip using a smaller phased array. To this end, we present the Ghostrokes technique,

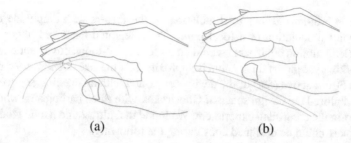

(a)   (b)

Fig. 1 Ghostrokes: Ultrasound mid-air haptic feedback at the fingertip. **a** A user is swiping their hand in mid-air to scroll up/down and left/right. A stroking stimulation using ultrasound mid-air haptics is applied to the fingers in congruence with the finger movement, up/down and left/right. **b** The user could imagine moving their fingers on a trackball to scroll up/down and left/right. The stroking sensation from the ultrasound haptics is meant to elicit the rolling friction between the fingers and the trackball

Fig. 2 The Ultrahaptics evaluation kit with a 16 × 16 ultrasound phased array and a leap motion computer-vision sensor

which evokes a *stroking* sensation on the fingers using a smaller phased array with well-perceived tactile sensation (Fig. 1).

2 Ghostrokes

Ghostrokes is a new touchless technique for haptic feedback on the fingers. It differs from other ultrasound mid-air haptic feedback techniques as it provides a stroking sensation to the fingers only. We implemented it using the Ultrahaptics evaluation kit device (UltraLeap Ltd.) which is based on a phased array with considerably smaller form factor than the system from (Matsubayashi et al. 2019).

We followed a laboratory-based participatory design approach to evaluate as well as explore the design space and applications of Ghostrokes. This device could uniquely enable Ghostrokes with its ultrasound phased array (see Fig. 2) that can

provide ≈ 8.6mm size haptic stimulation on the fingers with amplitude and spatiotemporal modulation of a focal point. The integrated hand and finger tracking
sensor (leap motion controller) would allow for closed-loop/active haptic feedback.
The working volume of this system is approximately the size of an inverted cone that
extends 50 cm above (out) of the device center and with an opening angle of 45°.

We explored the design space of Ghostrokes with three participants who did not
take part in the controlled experiment. We found that ultrasound haptic feedback for
Ghostrokes could be designed considering the following.

2.1   Ultrasound Modulation Technique

A range of ultrasound haptic modulations can be created using amplitude modulation
(AM), spatiotemporal modulation (STM) (Frier et al. 2019), or lateral modulation
(LM) techniques (Takahashi et al. 2018, 2020). All of these techniques apply vibrotactile stimuli to the skin and could thus be used to implement the Ghostrokes sensations. STM relies on the rapid movement of the focal point to create haptic sensation
along a trajectory which could be tailored to create a stroking sensation. LM relies
on small movement of the focal point to create a point haptic sensation which could
be tailored to create a stroking sensation. AM does not require movement of the focal
point to create a point vibrotactile stimulation. However, it could be readily used to
create a stroking sensation, e.g., by moving the AM point along the stroking path in
a similar way to Hajas et al. (2020).

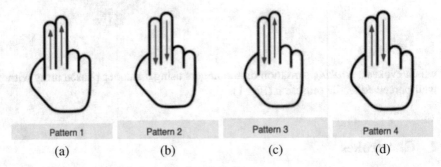

| Pattern 1 | Pattern 2 | Pattern 3 | Pattern 4 |
| (a) | (b) | (c) | (d) |

Fig. 3 The four Ghostrokes patterns on the index and middle fingers: (1) stroking from the base
to the tip of the fingers, (2) stroking from the tip to the base of the fingers, (3) stroking from the
tip to the base of the index finger and stroking from the base to the tip of the middle finger, and
(4) stroking from the base to the tip of the index finger and stroking from the tip to the base of the
middle finger

2.2 Stroking Patterns

A range of stroking patterns could be designed with continuous and discontinuous movements of the focal point. Figure 3 shows four stroking patterns applied to the index and middle fingers [(see Zhang et al. 2020]. To create these patterns, a focal point rapidly jumps between the fingers in a zigzag motion at every step while it moves along the fingers at a slower speed. It creates an illusion of two focal points (or focused ultrasound tactors) moving along the two fingers. More complex patterns could be designed using this technique.

3 Experimental Evaluation

After the preliminary experiments with the three participants mentioned before, the four stroking patterns shown in Fig. 3 were chosen, and a within group lab experiment was performed with the four stimuli presented in random order. The group consisted of 18 participants (8 females and 10 males) aged between 22 and 40 (mean = 27.7 and s.d. = 5.4) and all right handed. The study session including the interview lasted between 40 and 50 min, and each participant was compensated for their time with a gift voucher.

3.1 Procedure

We began the experiment by measuring the lengths of the index and middle fingers of the participant's right hand and then conducted a preliminary sensitivity assessment of their fingers with a two-point discriminator tool (Brand: Touch Test) with 4 mm gap and light pressure applied by the researcher (Lundborg and Rosén 2004). We then continued with a pre-study questionnaire to gather basic demographics before proceeding to carry out the study. An information sheet was given to the participants prior to the experiment. We also explained the information on the sheet to familiarize them with the experimental setup and procedure.

During the study, the participants were asked to sit comfortably on a chair and rest their hand on a support box which housed the Ultrahaptics evaluation kit. They adjusted the height of the chair and the orientation of the box according to their preference. The support box has a 5×11 cm hole on top to expose the fingers to ultrasound stimuli. The participants could align their finger using a guide (see Fig. 4) on top of the Ultrahaptics device where the stimuli would be applied. We used an AM stimuli 200 Hz frequency and full amplitude range (0–1). The hand was placed 15 cm above the Ultrahaptics. The stroking period was set at 3.5 s, which the three previous participants found as a comfortable and natural sensation. We also developed a graphical user interface (see Fig. 5) to assist in the lab study. The room temperature was controlled to maintain the skin temperature and sensitivity constant. Finally, the participants wore studio headphones and an ambient white noise was played to prevent any audible clues from the device.

First, the participants were given one trial of the four patterns in a random order to practice them (using the 'test' button in GUI). During each trial, the stimulation of a pattern was given three times. The participants were then offered to practice any pattern of they wanted which was given to them. There was no limit on how many times they could practice. Then, each participant was given 40 trials (10 × 4 patterns) in random orders. They could see the pictures of the four patterns on a GUI in front of them. After each trial, they reported the pattern they felt. The researcher then recorded it using the GUI which was stored on anonymous files. After 20 trials, the participants reported the area of the finger where they could feel the stimuli. They were then given a 5 min break to rest. Then, the previous steps were repeated. At the end of the study, we asked the participants to fill in a questionnaire to feedback the 'mental demand', 'temporal demand', 'performance', and 'frustration' felt during the study. Lastly, we conducted an interview to gather feedback about their thoughts and suggestions on the Ghostrokes technique.

3.2 Results

We first analyzed the data for errors. The number of errors committed by the participants and the confusion matrix of errors committed for each pattern are shown in Fig. 6. Five participants correctly recognized all the patterns without making any mistake, while participants 4 and 17 made most errors having passed the two-point discrimination touch test with ≈ 75% success rate. The participants made the least

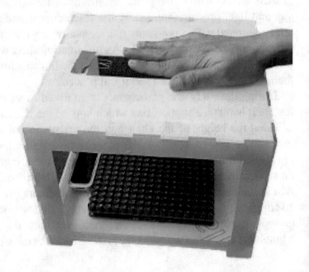

Fig. 4 Experimental setup. It was used during both the practice and test run of the patterns. The large slit allowed the participants to position and rest their hand while exposing their index and middle fingers to the tactile stimulation patterns delivered by the Ultrahaptics device

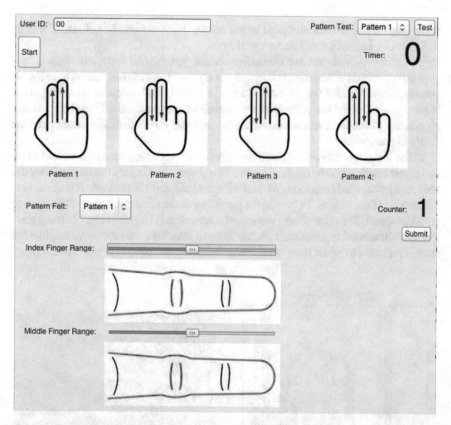

Fig. 5 The graphical user interface for the lab study is shown. It was used to practice and test the patterns. The participants could see it in front of them on screen

error in recognizing pattern 3 and most errors in recognizing pattern 4. Pattern 2 was only confused with pattern 3, but pattern 3 was only confused with pattern 2 only once in 180 trials. Pattern 1 and 4 were sometime confused with one another. This is interesting as all the participants who wanted to practice further had requested to practice patterns 3 and 4 a second time. Their first impression was that these patterns are more difficult than patterns 1 and 2. But none but one of the participants (with shaky hands) requested to try the stimuli for a third time. However, many participants had proceeded to the next stage of testing practicing the initial one trials. We did not record the practice session. In the interview, all participants said that they were confident recognizing patterns 1 and 2 during the first of the three stimuli given during a trial. But they sometimes waited for the second or rarely for the third stimuli to conform when they thought it could be a pattern 3 or 4. The 'I don't know' option was not offered but the participants always guessed a pattern and never said they could not detect a stroking sensation or recognize a pattern. The stimulation areas of the fingers are shown in Fig. 7a. The participants felt the stimuli up to the fingertip which would not have contributed to the errors. The total number of errors was 29 in 720 trials, i.e., an overall accuracy of 96%.

The Shapiro-Wilk test for normality on the 'given' and 'guessed' data gave a $p < 0.01$ for both which means they are not normally distributed. Consequently, we conducted the Kruskal Wallis test and found a $p = 0.0609$. Because $p > 0.05$, there is no significance of the pattern of the stimuli on the error rate. However, this is a significant result for Ghostrokes as all the patterns are statistically similar for the user's to recognize.

In the interview, the participants described the haptic sensation as a stream of air and a soft brush stroking on the fingers and a finger drawing on the finger. They did not feel a hot or cold sensation. We had adjusted the length of the stimuli according to the lengths of the fingers. However, the participants did not perceive any difference of stroking speed. The preliminary workload assessment is shown in Fig. 7b. It suggests that the ultrasound haptic feedback might need attention, and the users might need stronger stimuli to boost their confidence; however, the stimuli is less frustrating.

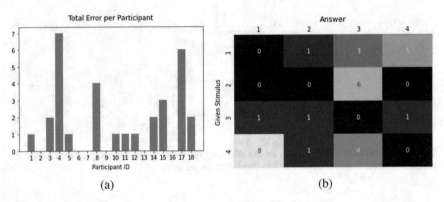

Fig. 6 a The number of mistakes made by the 18 participants is shown. b The confusion matrix of the errors made in recognizing the patterns is shown. A high score implies a large confusion

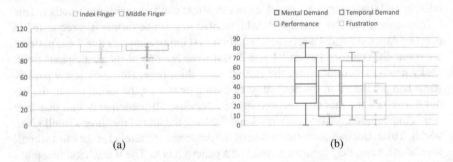

Fig. 7 a The stimulation areas of the fingers are shown. b The confusion matrix of the errors made by the patterns is shown

3.3 Discussion

Rutten et al. (2019) argued that age can be strongly related to a decline in performance in identifying different mid-air haptic shapes. The young age of our participants might have contributed to higher accuracy. They also found that significant differences in accuracy rates for different types of mid-air haptic shapes. It is possible that the haptic patterns chosen in this work could have contributed to higher accuracy.

The lab study was conducted in the passive haptic feedback condition, i.e., the participants kept their hand still throughout the trials. In a deployment scenario, the positions of the fingers might need to be tracked. The stroking stimuli will need to be adapted considering the movement of the fingers to effectively elicit the sensation of the sliding of a tool or stroking a virtual object.

4 Applications

Following the controlled user study in our laboratory, we interviewed the participants for applications of Ghostrokes. The participants were mostly computer science and engineering graduate students working on the university campus under COVID-19 restrictions. We found the following applications of Ghostrokes innovative and relevant. They either represent an active stroking feedback while using a virtual tool or passive stroking feedback by a virtual object.

4.1 Active Stroking Feedback with Virtual Tools

All participants initially mentioned at least one touchless interaction using a virtual tool. Many were public interfaces which might be influenced by the ongoing COVID-19 pandemic. For example, automatic doors in public buildings sometimes open and close unnecessarily when a person is sensed near it, even if they don't want to enter and exit through the said doors. This could lead to inconvenience, waste of energy, and sometimes minor accidents. One suggestion was to rotate an imaginary door handle to open or close the motorized doors. Ghostrokes could mimic the stroking sensation felt while the fingers slide on the door handle while rotating it. A similar suggestion was sliding imaginary doors to open motorized sliding doors, with Ghostrokes mimicking the stroking sensation of the edge of the doors sliding on the fingers. These ideas could be extended to use virtual tools to operate various motorized doors and windows in public buildings, with Ghostrokes simulating the natural stroking sensations on the fingers like using those tools physically.

Participants also suggested applications where the stroking sensations of Ghostrokes could be learned to interact with public interfaces. One suggestion was for active haptic feedback for touchless keypads for ATMs, public phones, cash machines, and elevators. The users can imagine pressing virtual keys/buttons in mid-air and the stroking sensation can guide and notify during the operation. The virtual buttons could be imagined, for example, 15–20 cm above the Ultrahaptics device where the user's eyes meet the physical buttons and the position of the virtual button could be sensed with a depth camera. A stroking stimulation traveling toward the fingertip can notify the proximity of a button, and a stroking stimulation traveling away from the fingertip can notify the pressing of a button. Many participants suggested Ghostrokes as an assistive technology. It could help visually impaired users with touchless information input and output with the above-mentioned public interfaces.

All participants suggested use of Ghostrokes in playing games in virtual or mixed reality (VR/XR) environments. Players could select icons by dragging or pulling them and feel a corresponding stroking sensation. They could drag their hands on surfaces or accessories like the face of a horse or the hilt of a sword to feel them. They could use virtual pointing devices or accessories like an arrow or gun with mid-air gestures and their movement communicated with different stroking patterns on their fingers. They could also feel the pull of the string or trigger with a stroking stimulation. All the participants agreed that when a physical trackpad or mouse is not available, like for touchless interaction with a public display or in a VR environment, a virtual keypad, or trackball mouse could be useful. One participant suggested that Ghostrokes could be useful for extended reality where a small movement of fingers translate to large movement in the virtual world and the stroking feedback can elicit the extent of scaling.

4.2   Passive Stroking Feedback from Virtual Objects

Many participants suggested freehand stroking feedback is suitable for discrete, private, and secure communication in the public or part of a group. One suggestion was to receiving notification, assistance, or instructions as if someone is pulling or a virtual pointer is stroking their fingers to attract their attention to certain task or direction. For example, while exploring a map of a city in the public (for free attractions) or navigating a list of stores or restaurants in a mall (for deals) or wards in a hospital (for an available medical specialist), Ghostrokes can guide the attention to the point of interest on the hovering fingers which others cannot see, hear, or feel.

Other suggested applications of Ghostrokes relied on passive feedback which could be from real or virtual objects. Direction cues of Ghostrokes could assist visually impaired persons with navigation inside buildings. An interesting suggestion was to warn people of potentially dangerous situations like infected surfaces, sharp edges of objects or unseen obstacles. Ghostrokes could be used for nonverbal communication for user's comfort or during stressful situations. For example, stroking feedback could give direction cues on the fingers during a lesson, like learning to drive or playing an instrument. Another notable idea was to receive (passive) stroking feedback for music or musical instrument with vibration traveling through the fingers like while playing drums. Participants also suggested stroking touch by virtual fingers using connected haptic devices for family members (romantic partners) to address isolation, boredom, and loneliness as being stroked is more pleasant than stroking and it decelerates heart rate (Triscoli et al. 2017).

From these suggested applications, we conjecture that the participants considered their mental models of real-life tools and haptics experiences.

5 Conclusion

Ghostrokes is a new ultrasound haptic feedback technique for the fingertips. It can provide easily perceivable haptic cues while implemented on the smaller commercial phased arrays. In this chapter, we have described its design space and the stroking patterns explored and designed with users. We reported the efficacy of recognizing the haptic patterns in a controlled user study and found an overall accuracy of 96%. We also presented a broad range of innovative applications suggested by the study participants following the lab-based user study. We envision Ghostrokes will pave a new way to deploy virtual tools for freehand interactions in real-life use case scenarios like public buildings and personal use case scenario like entertainment and gaming and consider the users' real-life mental models to develop future applications.

Acknowledgements This work was partly supported by Engineering and Physical Sciences Research Council grant EP/M022722/1.

References

Carter T, Seah SA, Long B, Drinkwater B, Subramanian S (2013) UltraHaptics: multi-point mid-air haptic feedback for touch surfaces. In: Proceedings of the 26th annual ACM symposium on user interface software and technology. (St. Andrews, Scotland, United Kingdom) (UIST '13). Association for Computing Machinery, New York, NY, USA, pp 505-514. https://doi.org/10.1145/2501988.2502018

Chilles J, Frier W, Abdouni A, Giordano M, Georgiou O (2019) Laser Doppler vibrometry and FEM simulations of ultrasonic mid-air haptics. In: 2019 IEEE World Haptics Conference (WHC), pp 259–264. https://doi.org/10.1109/WHC.2019.8816097

Culbertson H, Schorr SB, Okamura AM (2018) Haptics: the present and future of artificial touch sensation. In: Annual review of control, robotics, and autonomous systems, vol 1, issue 1, pp 385–409. https://doi.org/10.1146/annurev-control-060117-105043

Frier W, Pittera D, Ablart D, Obrist M, Subramanian S (2019) Sampling strategy for ultrasonic mid-air haptics. Association for Computing Machinery, New York, NY, USA, pp 1–11. https://doi.org/10.1145/3290605.3300351

Grandhi Sukeshini A, Gina J, Irene M (2011) Understanding naturalness and intuitiveness in gesture production: insights for touchless gestural interfaces. Association for Computing Machinery, New York, NY, USA, pp 821–824. https://doi.org/10.1145/1978942.1979061

Pacchierotti C, Sinclair S, Solazzi M, Frisoli A, Hayward V, Prattichizzo D (2017) Wearable haptic systems for the fingertip and the hand: taxonomy, review, and perspectives. IEEE Trans Haptics 10:580–600. https://doi.org/10.1109/TOH.2017.2689006

Hajas D, Pittera D, Nasce A, Georgiou O, Obrist M (2020) Mid-air haptic rendering of 2D geometric shapes with a dynamic tactile pointer. IEEE Trans Haptics 13(4):806–817. https://doi.org/10.1109/TOH.2020.2966445

Keisuke H, Hiroyuki S (2013) A method for distribution control of aerial ultrasound radiation pressure for remote vibrotactile display. SICE Ann Conf 2013:223–228. https://ieeexplore.ieee.org/abstract/document/6736163

Hoshi T, Takahashi M, Iwamoto T, Shinoda H (2010) Noncontact tactile display based on radiation pressure of airborne ultrasound. IEEE Trans Haptics 3(3):155–165. https://doi.org/10.1109/TOH.2010.4

Howard T, Gallagher G, Lécuyer A, Pacchierotti C, Marchal M (2019) Investigating the recognition of local shapes using mid-air ultrasound haptics. In: 2019 IEEE World Haptics Conference (WHC), pp 503–508. https://doi.org/10.1109/WHC.2019.8816127

Kappus B, Long B (2018) Spatiotemporal modulation for mid-air haptic feedback from an ultrasonic phased array. J Acoustical Soc Am 143(3):1836–1836. https://doi.org/10.1121/1.5036027

Georgios K, Mohamad E (2016) Haptogram: ultrasonic point-cloud tactile stimulation. IEEE Access 4:7758–7769. https://doi.org/10.1109/ACCESS.2016.2608835

Koutsabasis P, Vogiatzidakis P (2019) Empirical research in mid-air interaction: a systematic review. Int J Human-Comput Interaction 35(18):1747–1768. https://doi.org/10.1080/10447318.2019.1572352

Long B, Seah SA, Carter T, Subramanian S (2014) Rendering volumetric haptic shapes in mid-air using ultrasound. ACM Trans Graph 33(6), Article 181, 10 pages. https://doi.org/10.1145/2661229.2661257

Lundborg G, Rosén B (2004) The two-point discrimination test–time for a re-appraisal? J Hand Surg 29(5):418–422. https://doi.org/10.1016/J.JHSB.2004.02.008

Matsubayashi A, Yasutoshi M, Hiroyuki S (2019) Direct finger manipulation of 3D object image with ultrasound haptic feedback. Association for Computing Machinery, New York, NY, USA, pp 1–11. https://doi.org/10.1145/3290605.3300317

Palovuori K, Rakkolainen I, Sand A (2014) Bidirectional touch interaction for immaterial displays. In: Proceedings of the 18th international academic MindTrek conference: media business, management, content and services (AcademicMindTrek '14) Association for Computing Machinery, New York, NY, USA, pp 74–76. https://doi.org/10.1145/2676467.2676503

Rakkolainen I, Freeman E, Sand A, Raisamo R, Brewster S (2021) A survey of mid-air ultrasound haptics and its applications. IEEE Trans Haptics 14(1):2–19. https://doi.org/10.1109/TOH.2020.3018754

Rutten I, Frier W, Van den Bogaert L, Geerts D (2019) Invisible touch: how identifiable are mid-air haptic shapes? In: Extended abstracts of the 2019 CHI conference on human factors in computing systems. (Glasgow, Scotland Uk) (CHI EA '19). Association for Computing Machinery, New York, NY, USA, pp 1–6. https://doi.org/10.1145/3290607.3313004

Sand A, Rakkolainen I, Isokoski P, Kangas J, Raisamo R, Palovuori K (2015) Head-mounted display with mid-air tactile feedback. In: Proceedings of the 21st ACM symposium on virtual reality software and technology (VRST '15), Association for Computing Machinery, New York, NY, USA, pp 51–58. https://doi.org/10.1145/2821592.2821593

Sun C, Nai W, Sun X (2019) Tactile sensitivity in ultrasonic haptics: do different parts of hand and different rendering methods have an impact on perceptual threshold? Virtual Reality Intelli Hardware 1(3):265–275. https://doi.org/10.3724/SP.J.2096-5796.2019.0009

Takahashi R, Hasegawa K, Shinoda H (2018) Lateral modulation of midair ultrasound focus for intensified vibrotactile stimuli. In: International conference on human haptic sensing and touch enabled computer applications. Springer, Heidelberg, pp 276–288. https://doi.org/10.1007/978-3-319-93399-3_25

Takahashi R, Hasegawa K, Shinoda H (2020) Tactile stimulation by repetitive lateral movement of midair ultrasound focus. IEEE Trans Haptics 13(2):334–342. https://doi.org/10.1109/TOH.2019.2946136

Triscoli C, Croy I, Olausson H, Sailer U (2017) Touch between romantic partners: being stroked is more pleasant than stroking and decelerates heart rate. Physiol Behav 177:169–175. https://doi.org/10.1016/j.physbeh.2017.05.006

Wilson G, Carter T, Subramanian S, Brewster SA (2014) Perception of ultrasonic haptic feedback on the hand: localisation and apparent motion. In: Proceedings of the SIGCHI conference on human factors in computing systems. (Toronto, Ontario, Canada) (CHI '14). Association for Computing Machinery, New York, NY, USA, pp 1133–1142. https://doi.org/10.1145/2556288.2557033

Zhang C, Sahoo DR, Pearson J, Robinson S, Holton MD, Hopkins P, Jones M (2020) Active Pin-Screen: exploring spatio-temporal tactile feedback for multi-finger interaction. In: 22nd International conference on human-computer interaction with mobile devices and services. (Oldenburg, Germany) (MobileHCI '20). Association for Computing Machinery, New York, NY, USA, Article 18, 11 pages. https://doi.org/10.1145/3379503.3403531

The Physical Principles of Arrays for Mid-Air Haptic Applications

Bruce W. Drinkwater

Abstract Arrays of emitters and receivers are seen in a wide range of applications, from the square kilometre array used in radio astronomy to those used for medical ultrasound imaging. Here, we explore the use of arrays to steer and focus ultrasound for the purposes of mid-air haptics, but many of the basic principles are shared with these other applications. To achieve a mid-air haptic effect, we must use the array to focus ultrasound to a point and thereby create a high-intensity local region. The force then occurs when an object, such as a human hand, is positioned at the focus of the ultrasound beam. Here, the momentum of the sound wave is transferred directly to the object, and the haptic force is proportional to the ultrasonic intensity. High-intensity ultrasound also creates a flow called acoustic streaming, as some of the wave momentum is absorbed by the air causing it to move. These forces and flows interact with the skin where users perceive the presence of a physical object. This chapter will introduce and bring together these ideas to provide an understanding of how mid-air ultrasonic haptics works and how such systems can be designed.

1 Introduction

Mid-air ultrasonic haptics most commonly uses an array of ultrasonic emitters to create a high-intensity region or focal spot targeted on the hand (Carter et al. 2013; Gavrilov and Tsirulnikov 2012; Hoshi et al. 2010). The user senses the acoustic field as it creates forces on the skin and flows near the surface of the skin. This chapter aims to describe the origin of these forces and flows and thereby equip the reader with the knowledge to design high-performance ultrasonic haptics. These phenomena are described using a series of physics-based models, and where possible, these models are further simplified in an attempt to illuminate the physical principles involved.

In Sect. 2 models of a simple circular focussed emitter and an array of emitters are described. The circular emitter model allows some of the key ideas to be introduced

---

B. W. Drinkwater (✉)
Department of Mechanical Engineering, University of Bristol, University Walk,
Bristol BS8 1TR, UK
e-mail: b.drinkwater@bristol.ac.uk

© The Author(s), under exclusive license to Springer Nature Switzerland AG 2022
O. Georgiou et al. (eds.), *Ultrasound Mid-Air Haptics for Touchless Interfaces*,
Human–Computer Interaction Series, https://doi.org/10.1007/978-3-031-04043-6_14

and is appealing as it can be analysed analytically. The next subsection describes a *phased array* in which the phase of the emitted acoustic waves from a number of discrete sources is used to control the location of the focus. This array approach is typical of ultrasonic haptics systems. The acoustic models described here are based on linear acoustic assumptions, e.g. linear superposition of the wave fronts and are of a form widely used in the related field of ultrasonic imaging (Drinkwater and Wilcox 2006). As air is only weakly nonlinear, this model can be expected to maintain good accuracy in most ultrasonic haptic scenarios. However, such models can be expected to perform less well at very high intensities when the ultrasonic waves themselves become distorted and *nonlinear wave propagation* occurs. In this regime a model that includes the nonlinearity of the air would be needed for more accurate results (Treeby and Cox 2010).

In Sect. 3 models of the acoustic radiation and streaming forces are described. These models are widely used in related fields, such as ultrasonic particle manipulation (Bruus 2012). The core model described is termed the *momentum flux integral* and it enables us to analyse either the forces on an object such as the hand or those on the air itself. The model assumes weak nonlinearity, meaning that the forces can be determined from knowledge of the linear components of the acoustic pressure. Hence, the linear acoustics array model and the weak nonlinear formulation of the force model are well-matched. This approach also has the major advantage that it uncouples the wave propagation model from the force model. Hence, if desired, other linear acoustics models could be used to simulate the acoustic field, e.g. finite elements, and the acoustic pressures fed into the momentum flux integral.

Whereas Sect. 3 describes a model of the streaming forces, Sect. 4 explores the fluid flow that results. This is a notoriously difficult field mathematically and so, rather than explore analytical approaches, we adopt a numerical finite element approach. In this way, the flow field can be predicted and if required, animated as a function of time.

In Sect. 5, the acoustic radiation force model is compared to forces measured from a commercial ultrasonic haptics system. The agreement is shown to be generally good. This provides an indication of the level of accuracy possible with these models.

Finally, in Sect. 6, the effect of changing the ultrasonic output in time is explored. This is an important aspect to consider as ultrasonic haptics are very rarely stationary. Indeed there is normally a requirement to change the signals sent to the emitters quite rapidly. If the focal spot is moved fast enough, then the result is the perception of an extended object (Long et al. 2014). However, narrowband emitters lose power if we attempt to change their output too rapidly. A simple model that includes the emitter's impulse response is described and shown to agree well with experiment.

Fig. 1 Circular emitter
geometry and key variables.
Inset shows the relative
acoustic intensity along a
radial slice through the focus

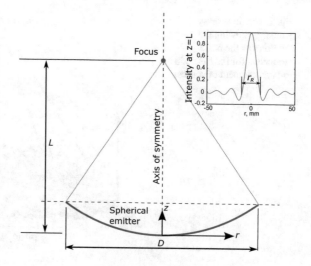

2 Modelling Ultrasonic Fields

2.1 A Simple Analytical Model of a Circular Focussed Emitter

Before describing a model of an ultrasonic haptics array, we consider a model of a spherically focussed circular *piston* emitter as shown in Fig. 1.

For the circular emitter shown in Fig. 1, the focal length, L, is set by the spherical geometry of the emitting surface. This is a classic type of emitter found in many textbooks (Kino 1987) and is useful as the acoustic field has a relatively simple analytical form. As with any acoustic source, we can divide the field in to two regions: the near field and the far field. The length of the near field marks the distance beyond which focussing becomes limited and beam divergence starts to dominate over focussing and can be calculated from $D^2/4\lambda$, where λ is the wavelength and D is the emitter diameter. This reveals that long focal lengths can only be achieved with either large emitters or short wavelengths (i.e. high frequencies). For this simple source, the intensity distribution along a radial line through the focal zone is $2J_1(X)/X$ where $X = \pi r D/\lambda L$ and J_1 is a Bessel function of the first kind. This field shape is shown in the inset in Fig. 1. The width of this focal zone can be obtained from the Rayleigh length, $r_R = 1.22\lambda\mathcal{F}$, where $\mathcal{F} = L/D$ is termed the f-number. It is interesting to note that this estimate for the focal size originates from optical imaging but can equally be applied to acoustics. It tells us something we probably know intuitively already that a sharper focus (or smaller focal region) is obtained either from a larger emitter (large D) or by having a shorter focal length (small L). It can also be seen that the size of the focal region scales linearly with wavelength. These attributes of a circular emitter are also seen in ultrasonic haptics arrays, and we can use this simple model to obtain an estimate of array performance.

Fig. 2 Example array
geometry showing the
definition of the basic
parameters for the case of a
grid arrangement of sources

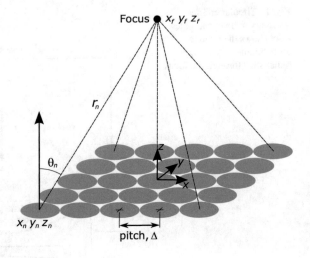

2.2 Modelling a Phased Array

Ultrasonic phased arrays are currently the main method of delivering ultrasonic
haptics in mid-air. By controlling the phase of the emitted waves, the focus can be
moved, tracking the hand, and creating a wide range of haptic effects. In this section,
a simple yet accurate model of an array is described based on modelling ideas used
widely in the field of ultrasonic imaging (Drinkwater and Wilcox 2006; Kino 1987;
Marzo et al. 2018). The model adopted here is from a class of models known as
linear acoustics models as it originates from the linear version of the acoustic wave
equation. In particular, it uses Huygens' principle of the superposition of sources to
describe the interference between the waves emitted from the sources.

Consider the grid array geometry shown in Fig. 2 in which an array is operated
into free space, i.e. an infinite continuum of air containing no reflectors. The acoustic
pressure field of the nth emitter in the array is described by

$$p_n = \frac{p_0}{r} D_f(\theta_n) e^{-ikr_n} e^{-\alpha r_n} \tag{1}$$

$$D_f(\theta_n) = \frac{2J_1(ka\sin\theta_n)}{ka\sin\theta_n} \tag{2}$$

where r_n, θ_n are the polar coordinates of the field with respect to the emitter, with
r_n measured from the emitter centre and θ_n from the emitter surface normal. The
attenuation coefficient is α, $i = \sqrt{-1}$, and the emitter amplitude is labelled p_0 and
is typically determined from experiment using a calibrated microphone (Marzo et al.
2018). Equation 2 shows the directivity function, D_f, which describes the angular
amplitude and phase variation of the emitters. This is the directivity for a flat circular
piston source and depends on the wave number, $k = 2\pi/\lambda$, and the emitter radius, a.

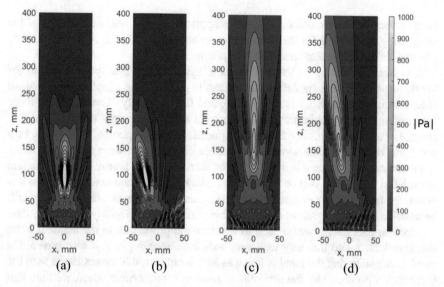

Fig. 3 Pressure distributions from a 10×10 array of 40 kHz emitters, $p_0 = 1.7$ Pa and $\Delta = 10$ mm, **a** focus on a point $(x, y, z) = (0, 0, 100)$ mm, **b** focus on a point $(-25, 0, 100)$ mm, **c** focus on a point $(0, 0, 200)$ mm, and **d** focus on a point $(-25, 0, 200)$ mm

If required, other directivity functions can be used, or measured directivity data can be included. The total acoustic field in 3D Cartesian space due to the array is then

$$p(x, y, z) = \sum_{n=1}^{n=N} p_n A_n e^{i\phi_n} \tag{3}$$

where A_n is an amplitude weighting factor ($A_n = 1$ is used here), ϕ_n is the phase delay applied to each emitter which for the case of a focussed beam at (x_f, y_f, z_f) is

$$\phi_n = k \left(\sqrt{(x_n - x_f)^2 + (y_n - y_f)^2 + (z_n - z_f)^2} - L \right) \tag{4}$$

where the emitters are located at (x_n, y_n, z_n) and the focal length is, $L = \sqrt{x_f^2 + y_f^2 + z_f^2}$, assuming the origin of the co-ordinate system is at the centre of the array. Note that in Eq. 3, N is the total number of emitters, and for the square grid array used as an example here, $N = N_s^2$ where N_s is the number of emitters in each side of the square. If required, the model can be configured for any size or geometry of array.

Figure 3 shows acoustic pressure plots from this model for an example array in which the location of the focus was changed by use of Eq. 4. As can be seen, this works particularly well for the shorter 100 mm focal length. For the longer 200 mm focal length, the focal maximum is not quite at the desired distance, and this is because the focus is now close to the near field length of the array, ≈ 294 mm, meaning that beam divergence is significant. Here, we approximate the near field length of the array using the formula for the circular emitter and setting $D = \Delta \times N_s = 100$ mm, where Δ is the inter-element spacing, or pitch.

It is worth reflecting on the usefulness of applying this free space model to the haptic use case where, by definition, a hand is present. The simplest way forward is to assume that the hand is rigid, large, and flat (or gently curved). Under these assumptions, the acoustic pressure at the hand surface is simply twice that in free space. Let us briefly consider these assumptions. The assumption of rigidity is a very good one, due to the large acoustic impedance difference between air and the hand. If we assume that the hand is made of water, then the energy transmission coefficient at the hand is $\approx 0.1\%$. Not only does this make rigidity a good assumption, but it is beneficial from a safety perspective, as the ultrasonic energy entering the body will be small compared to that in the air. If this assumption of rigidity is relaxed, then a reflection coefficient can be used to describe the proportion in the incident wave that is reflected, and this may well vary with incidence angle. It is also typically a good assumption that the hand is large, as in this context, this means larger than the focal region produced by the available ultrasonic haptic system. Here, we note that the focal regions are of wavelength order and that at the commonly used frequency of 40 kHz, $\lambda = 8.5$ mm. Whilst it is reasonable to assume the hand is large, it may or may not be flat on this scale. Any lack of flatness will result in more complex wave scattering that will depend on the local hand curvature. For example, the presence of surface roughness leads to a more diffuse scattering and hence a reduction in amplitude in the specular direction (Ogilvy 1986). This roughness effect can be approximated as a reflection coefficient. Further complexity comes from edges, but as the hand contains no sharp edges, relatively simple scattering models can be expected to provide accurate predictions. However, to be completely rigorous, the scattering problem due the geometry of a hand must be properly solved, and this is possible using a range of analytical and numerical schemes, e.g. finite elements.

2.3 Implications of the Array Model

With the model described in Eqs. 1–4, it is possible to gain some important insights to the performance of arrays for ultrasonic haptics. We can also understand the performance of the array by approximating it as a similarly sized circular emitter. For example, we note that, just like the circular emitter, if we require a small focal size, then we need some combination of a large array, a short focal length or a small wavelength.

Figure 4a shows how the focal spot size varies with array size. If we normalise both axes, a more generally applicable focussing size performance graph is formed and shown in Fig. 4b. To implement this normalisation, the x-axis becomes $\mathcal{F}$ and the y-axis the focal width divided by the wavelength. Hence, this normalised plot is now applicable to a square grid array of any size and frequency. Also shown in Fig. 4 is the model of the circular focussed transducer described in Sect. 2.1 which can be seen

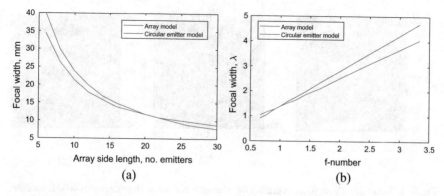

Fig. 4 Focussing performance of a grid array **a** in S.I. units for 40 kHz emitters, $\Delta = 10$ mm, focal length $L = 200$ mm, and **b**, the same data but with the x-axis as f-number, $\mathcal{F} = L/D$, and the y-axis normalised by the wavelength

to give reasonable agreement with the more accurate model of the array described in Sect. 2.2. Some differences remain principally because the array is square rather than circular.

As Eq. 3 is a summation of the contributions of all array elements, it is apparent that adding more emitters can be used to increase the amplitude at the focus. To a first order the pressure amplitude at the focus increases linearly with number of emitters. However, the combined effect of emitter beam divergence, directivity, and attenuation in the air means that the addition of emitters leads to diminishing returns in amplitude as shown in Fig. 5.

Phased arrays generate acoustic fields as the summation of emissions from discretely located emitters. Hence, whilst above we have seen that their behaviour follows that of simple sources, we should also consider effects arising from their discrete nature. Of particular importance is the formation of grating lobes, which

Fig. 5 Array pressure amplitude at the focus for a grid array of 40 kHz emitters, $\Delta = 10$ mm, and $L = 200$ mm. Relative pressure is the true pressure normalised by the pressure at $(0, 0, L)$ of a single emitter located at the origin. The simple linear model neglects beam divergence, directivity, and attenuation

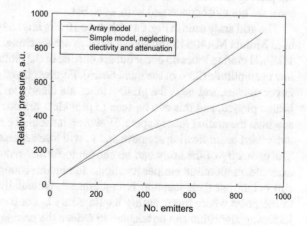

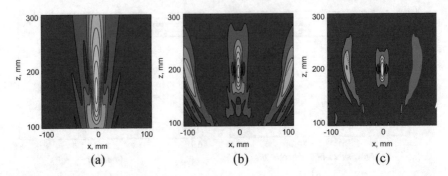

Fig. 6 Effect of transducer pitch on grating lobe formation. A 10×10 grid array of 40 kHz emitters, $L = 200$ mm, with pitch varied **a** $\Delta = 10$ mm, **b** $\Delta = 20$ mm and **c** $\Delta = 30$ mm. The red dashed line shows the grating lobe angles for $m = \pm 1$ in Eq. 5

are beam artefacts caused by aliasing that occur when the source pitch exceeds the Nyquist-Shannon limit. As such, they can be removed if the pitch is always $\leq \lambda/2$, and in many imaging applications, this is the array design rule. The pressure field requirements in ultrasonic haptics are less stringent than in imaging as low-amplitude features may not be sensed/perceived. For this reason, in ultrasonic haptics, it is common to design arrays with larger pitches and accept that some grating lobes will be present. Figure 6 shows, for the case of an example grid array, how the grating lobes start to encroach on the main lobe as the pitch increases. For a regularly spaced array used for beam steering, the angle θ_m at which the grating lobes appear can be found from

$$\theta_m = \sin^{-1}\left(\sin\theta_s - \frac{m\lambda}{\Delta}\right) \tag{5}$$

where θ_s is the steering direction (i.e. $\theta_s = 0$ means that the steering direction is directly in front of the array), and m is an integer (can be positive or negative) termed the grating lobe order. As the first order grating lobes are seen closest to the main lobe, we are most concerned with, $m = \pm 1$.

The grid array used in Fig. 6a with $\Delta = 10$ mm is arranged such that the commonly used Murata MA40S4S transducer casings are touching. In this configuration, $\Delta = 1.2\lambda$ and grating lobes do occur but are outside of the plotted region and are relatively low in amplitude (25% of the main beam). Figures 6b and c show the same array with larger pitches, and now, the grating lobes are clearly visible. The result from Eq. 5 is also plotted, and this can be seen to provide a reasonable prediction of the angle at which the grating lobes appear. However, it should be noted that Eq. 5 is based on unfocused beam steering scenario and so will lose accuracy for shorter focal lengths. The geometry of the array can be chosen to further reduce grating lobes using, for example, randomised emitter locations. In random configurations, the grating lobes still occur, but their location is randomised, potentially reducing their amplitude to the point where the resulting haptic effect is not perceivable. Additionally, the focussing algorithm can be adapted to reduce the grating lobes (Long et al. 2014).

3 Theory of Acoustic Radiation Forces and Streaming

Building on the foundation laid by Rayleigh (1905), we model acoustic radiation forces using the momentum flux integral (Lighthill 1978; Westervelt 1957). This defines the acoustic radiation force vector, $\mathbf{F}_A$, as an integral over a surface, S, that encloses the object on which we aim to find the applied steady force.

$$\mathbf{F}_A = \iint\limits_{S} \left[-\frac{1}{2\rho c^2} \langle p^2 \rangle \mathbf{n} + \frac{1}{2}\rho \langle |\mathbf{v}|^2 \rangle \mathbf{n} - \rho \langle \mathbf{v}(\mathbf{v} \cdot \mathbf{n}) \rangle \right] ds \qquad (6)$$

where $\langle p^2 \rangle$ and $\langle |\mathbf{v}|^2 \rangle$ are the time-averaged acoustic pressure and particle velocity, respectively, $\mathbf{n}$ is a unit vector defining the surface normal, ρ is the fluid (air) density, and c is the speed of sound in the fluid (air). The term in the square brackets is known as the *radiation pressure* (Livett et al. 1981) which is then integrated over the object or region of interest to obtain the radiation force. As this effect is a time average, Eq. 6 is only correct over a timescale of many periods of the wave. If we say that *many* means more than ten periods and the frequency is 40 kHz, then the timescale should be > 0.25 ms.

Equation 6 assumes that thermal and viscous effects can be neglected and that the nonlinearity is *weak*. Whilst these assumptions may seem restrictive, this model has provided accurate predictions in ultrasonic manipulation devices operating at high intensities both in air (Fushimi et al. 2019) and in water (Bruus 2012). In Sect. 5, good agreement with experiment for a commercial ultrasonic haptics system is shown, thereby providing further evidence that these assumptions are typically met. However, such agreement should not be taken as implying that these assumptions are universally valid.

It is useful to note that for a sinusoidal field, the velocity contribution to Eq. 6 can be obtained from the acoustic pressure gradient as

$$\mathbf{v} = -\frac{1}{ic\rho k}\nabla p \qquad (7)$$

where ∇ is the gradient operator. We can now see that the key to calculating the radiation forces is to find the acoustic pressure and its gradient on the surface of the object.

Equation 6 is a general expression that can be applied to any object in an acoustic field, or to a region of the air itself. To use this equation to obtain the acoustic radiation force on an object, the first step is to solve the acoustic scattering problem to find the acoustic pressure and particle velocity on the object. Many scattering problems are intractable analytically, and hence, numerical methods such as finite elements are often required. However, fortunately for us, it is often possible to simplify the scattering that occurs in ultrasonic haptics and compute it with relatively simple numerical schemes (see Sect. 3.1). In some, simple scenarios we can assume that the incident field is a plane wave, and the object is large, rigid, and lies normal to the

Fig. 7 Effect of surface
reflection coefficient on the
terms in Eq. 6. Here, we
assume normal incident
plane waves of amplitude
$p_i = 1$ Pa. A positive force
component is in the direction
of the beam

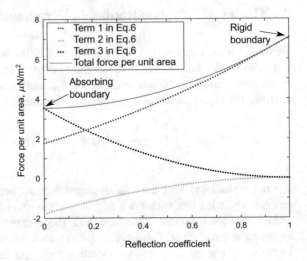

propagation direction. In this case, only the first term in the square brackets in Eq. 6
needs to be evaluated which leads to the often seen acoustic radiation force formula

$$\mathbf{F}_A = -\frac{A}{2\rho c^2} \langle p^2 \rangle \mathbf{n} = -\frac{2W}{c} \mathbf{n} \qquad (8)$$

where A is the surface area of the large planar object, W is time average power of
the incident plane wave. Note here that the $-\mathbf{n}$ term means that the force is in the
direction of the incident beam, hence it is more usual to see $F = 2W/c$ quoted as the
acoustic radiation force on a rigid planar object and the force assumed to be in the
beam direction. It is interesting to note that if the surface is completely absorbing,
then manipulation of Eq. 6 leads to the other much quoted equation for the radiation
force, $F = W/c$. Figure 7 shows how the total force varies with reflection coefficient
of the surface and the relative contributions of the three terms of Eq. 6. From this
graph, it is apparent that for reflection coefficients near unity, as might be expected in
ultrasonic haptics, it is the first term that dominates. It can also be shown that when
the surface is angled the second term becomes significant.

It is possible to apply the momentum flux integral to a region of the air itself. In
this case, the first two terms in the square brackets in Eq. 6 are equal and opposite,
and so, the third term dominates. The magnitude of this third term is dependent on
the energy lost during acoustic propagation through a volume of air. This loss can be
modelled as an exponential attenuation law, such that the acoustic pressure decays at
$e^{-\alpha x}$ where α is termed the attenuation coefficient and as defined here is in units of
Nepers per metre (note that the loss in dB/m $= 8.686\alpha$). In this case, manipulation
of Eq. 6 leads to the force on an elemental volume, dv of the air, termed the acoustic
streaming force, which is then given by Prieur and Sapozhnikov (2017)

$$\mathbf{F}_S = \frac{2\alpha \mathbf{I}}{c} \, dv \tag{9}$$

where $\mathbf{I}$ is the time average intensity of the wave. Equation 9 is generally applicable to any wave field when the intensity is found from $\mathbf{I} = \langle p\mathbf{v} \rangle$. For a plane wave of amplitude, p, the time-averaged intensity becomes $I = \langle p^2 \rangle / \rho c = W/A$, and so, we can write the more commonly seen version as

$$\frac{\mathbf{F}_S}{dv} = \frac{2\alpha W}{Ac} \mathbf{e} \tag{10}$$

where A is some notional area normal to the wave propagation direction, $\mathbf{e}$. The above acoustic radiation force, $\mathbf{F}_A$, and the streaming force, $\mathbf{F}_S$ can both be potentially sensed by a hand, and the total *available* force is the sum of these component forces.

3.1 Acoustic Radiation Force on Large Objects

To simulate the acoustic radiation force on real objects, it is necessary to solve the scattering problem for that geometry. A classical approach to such problems is to use the Kirchhoff approximation. This assumes that the surface is locally flat with no secondary scattering and no shadowing. Inherent in this approximation is the assumption that the object does not change the incident wave field, i.e. we can predict the wave field that insonifies the object using a model that does not include the object. In the ultrasonic haptics case, this means we can use free-field linear acoustics models such as the array model described in Sect. 2.2 to find the acoustic pressure at the surface of a hand.

The Kirchhoff approximation leads to a dramatic simplification of the scattering problem such that objects can be discretised into scattering facets (Fawcett 2001). This approximation is generally good for objects that are relatively large and flat or gently curved but can be extended to include additional features such as sharp edges (Tran Van Nhieu 1996). For our purposes, the Kirchhoff approximation leads to the result that the acoustic pressure on a rigid surface is twice that of the incident wave, i.e. $p_s = 2p_i$. The rigid boundary condition also means that the velocity component normal to the surface should be set to zero (Inoue et al. 2019). Hence, the incident pressure amplitude can be computed by our free-field array model, multiplied by two, and fed into Eq. 6 to find the radiation force. Furthermore, Fig. 7 shows that if a surface reflection coefficient, R, is present and is close to unity, then we can instead use $p_s = (1 + R)p_i$ with good accuracy.

The total force on an object is then the sum of the forces on the facets, $\mathbf{F}_A^n$. As the force given by Eq. 6 is always normal to the facet this then needs resolving in the required direction, $\mathbf{n_d}$ and so the total force in the desired direction can be written as

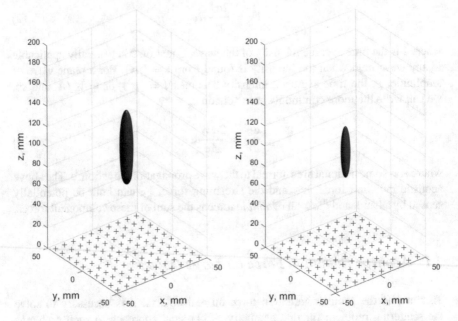

Fig. 8 Example array model showing iso-contours at half maximum. The left hand plot shows the acoustic pressure amplitude and the right hand the radiation pressure on a large flat object at a particular z-location. This is for a 10×10 array with $L = 100$ mm, $\Delta = 10$ mm

$$\mathbf{F}_A^d = \sum_{n=1}^{n=N} \mathbf{F}_A^n \cdot \mathbf{n_d} \tag{11}$$

Now consider an example in which a 10×10 grid array of 40 kHz transducers is used to produce a focus at $L = 100$ mm. This array gives the acoustic pressure field shown in Fig. 8 in the vicinity of the focal region. Also shown in the same figure is the radiation pressure from Eq. 6 on the x–y plane, i.e. normal to the beam and parallel to the array. Hence, this plot represents the radiation pressure that might be felt on a hand at different z locations. It is apparent that the radiation pressure feature is more compact than the acoustic pressure, and this can be explained from the squared dependency seen in Eq. 6.

Figure 9 shows an example of the use of Eq. 11 applied to angled circular reflective targets. For this case, simple geometric arguments can be used to estimate that the force is proportional to $\cos^2(\theta_i)$ where θ_i is the angle between the beam axis and the surface normal. As can be seen the summation of forces on facets approach gives very good agreement with this geometric estimate.

Fig. 9 Effect force in the z-direction for inclined circular reflective targets. Simulations were based on the Ultraleap device used for the experiments (see Sect. 5), i.e. a 10 × 10 grid array of 40 kHz emitters focussed on a $\phi = 35$ mm target at $L = 170$ mm and $p_0 = 2.15$ Pa

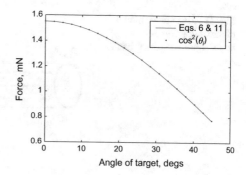

3.2 Plane Wave Interpretation of the Theory

Despite its apparent complexity, it is possible to apply the momentum flux integral (i.e. Eq. 6) in a simple way to ultrasonic haptics and achieve reasonable accuracy. We now make the simplifying assumptions that the incident waves are plane and the hand is rigid, large, flat, and oriented normal to the beam axis. Imagine the ultrasonic beam as a cylindrical region of plane waves as shown in Fig. 10.

Now, a rigid obstacle (such as a hand) placed at a distance X experiences an acoustic radiation force

$$F_A = \frac{2W_X}{c} = \frac{2W_0}{c} e^{-2\alpha X} \tag{12}$$

from which it can be seen that the force decreases with distance due to attenuation in the air. Note here that the factor of 2 in the exponent can be traced back to the fact that the force depends on pressure squared.

The total force applied to the air is the integral of the streaming force from 0 to X given by

$$F_S = \frac{W_0}{c} \left(1 - e^{-2\alpha X}\right) \tag{13}$$

This streaming force is transferred to the hand in the form of an air jet. In Fig. 11, we assume that the jet loses all its momentum in the x-direction and so all the accumulated streaming force is applied to the hand. Hence, the presence of attenuation

Fig. 10 Plane wave geometry that can be used to form a simplified model of the acoustic radiation force on a large, rigid, and planar hand

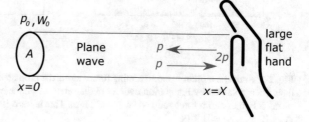

Fig. 11 Plane wave model
of streaming forces on a
large, rigid, and planar hand

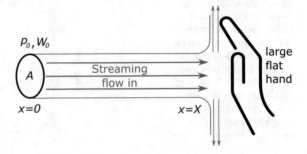

causes an exchange between direct radiation force and streaming forces (Cady and Gittings 1953), and we can write the ratio of radiation to streaming forces as

$$\frac{F_A}{F_S} = \frac{2}{e^{2\alpha X} - 1} \tag{14}$$

For air, the attenuation factor depends strongly on the humidity and using 52% relative humidity at 20 °C, $\alpha = 0.13$ Np/m (Lighthill 1978). This means that the wave energy will have dropped to $1/e$ of its original value after ≈ 3.8 m. The low-attenuation values of air mean that the total streaming force experienced by the air, which can then be passed on the hand through momentum transfer, is small compared to the direct radiation force. For scenario described above, after 1 m of propagation, $F_A/F_S = 6.6$.

We can now produce a back of the envelope estimate of the radiation force on a hand at the focus. We first assume that the focal zone is shaped as for the circular emitter described in Sect. 2.1. Then, we calculate the average intensity within a

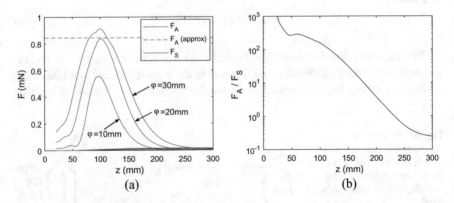

Fig. 12 Acoustic radiation and streaming forces along the propagation axis of the beam. The forces have been obtained by integration over a circular area, of diameter, ϕ, oriented in the $x = y = 0$ plane. **a** Forces and **b** force ratio when $\phi = 20$ mm. This is for a 10×10 array with $L = 100$ mm, $\Delta = 10$ mm, $p_0 = 1.7$ Pa

circle defined by the Rayleigh length, i.e. $I_{ave} = 1/\pi r_R^2 \int^{r_R} 2\pi r I(r) dr$, which leads to $I_{ave} = 0.41 I_{max}$ for the $2J_1(X)/X$ shaped focus. We then use this average intensity as that of a plane wave and via Eq. 8, this leads to the dashed line in Fig. 12a.

Figure 12a shows both this simple plane wave model and the results from the application of the momentum flux integral. In particular, we can see that for the smaller diameter, $\phi = 10$ mm, integration surface, the force is relatively lower than for the larger areas. It is also apparent that the force is not too different when integrated across either $\phi = 20$ mm or $\phi = 30$ mm and both are close to the average intensity plane wave result.

Figure 12b shows that the radiation force dominates over the streaming force around the focus but that the ratio then drops approximately exponentially beyond this. Eventually, a cross-over distance is reached where the accumulated streaming force exceeds the radiation force. Whilst the streaming force is typically small, it should be noted that on some occasions, the streaming may be sensed directly via hairs or as a cooling sensation (Nakajima et al. 2021), making the streaming velocity a more relevant measure than streaming force.

4 Modelling Acoustic Streaming Flow

To simulate how the air responds to the streaming forces, we must construct a fluid mechanics model, and there are a vast number of such models to choose from (Lighthill 1978; Nyborg 1953). For example, Fig. 13 shows streaming predictions using the finite element method (Comsol). The approach taken was to apply the streaming forces from Eq. 9 as a volume force in a steady-state fluid mechanics model. Such models require the boundary conditions to be defined as these have a strong influence on the motion of the fluid. An example model is shown in Fig. 13a which uses axis-symmetry on the left, has an open boundary at the bottom and rigid boundaries on the remaining sides. In this way, the acoustic beam propagation axis is in the z-direction with a focus at $z = 0$ and the upper rigid boundary represents a hand or other solid object as in Fig. 11. Figure 13c shows the flow velocity in the beam direction, which increases through the focus and then drops to zero at the rigid wall. The wall then redirects this flow radially, with a maximum radial velocity near the wall. Because the right hand boundary at $r = 0.2$ m is also rigid, a flow loop is formed. Figure 13d plots the maximum axial and radial streaming velocities, where the maximum axial velocity occurs just after the focus and the maximum radial velocity near the rigid top surface. Time dependent models can also be used to reveal the time taken for the streaming to become fully developed, and this was found to be ≈ 1 s for the models explored here.

The laminar and turbulent flow regimes can be found by considering the Reynolds number, $Re = \rho d U_s / \mu$, where $\mu = 18.5 \times 10^{-6}$ Pa s is the viscosity of air, d is a characteristic dimension, e.g. $d \approx \lambda$ and U_s is the streaming velocity. For the cases shown in Fig. 13b, $Re = 50-200$, meaning that some effects from turbulence can be expected. This is seen in the finite element predictions which suggest that including

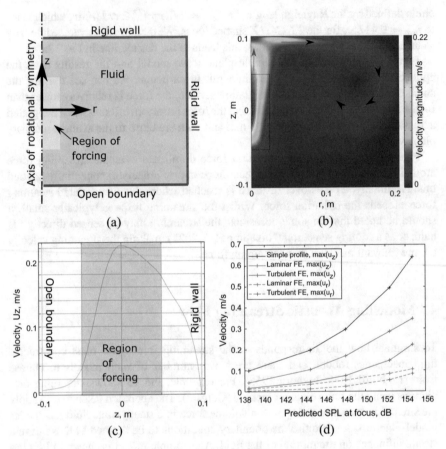

Fig. 13 Acoustic streaming model of a 10×10 array with, $L = 120$ mm, $\Delta = 10$ mm, the focus located at $(z, r) = (0, 0)$ and a wall located 100 mm from the focus. **a** Modelled geometry and boundary conditions, **b** example turbulent finite element prediction of the streaming velocity magnitude for $p_0 = 2.21$ Pa, **c** streaming velocity from the same model in the beam direction along the central beam axis, i.e. $r = 0$ and **d** variation of streaming velocity with array output level

turbulence in the model (i.e. a K-epsilon eddy viscosity model of turbulence) leads to lower streaming velocity. This effect is due to the flow spreading more beyond the focus when turbulence is included.

If we assume that the streaming at the focus results in a simple fluid jet with a known axis-symmetrical flow velocity profile, $U_s = U_0 S(r)$, where $S(r)$ defines the shape of the velocity profile and U_0 is the velocity at the centre of the beam/jet, then it is possible to estimate the axial streaming velocity from basic fluid mechanics analysis of a fluid jet losing its momentum to a solid wall, i.e. $F_{jet} = \int \rho U^2 \, dA$. Substituting in our assumed velocity profile function and rearranging, we can write

$$U_0 = \sqrt{\frac{F_T}{2\pi\rho \int_0^\sigma r S(r)^2 \, \mathrm{d}r}} \tag{15}$$

where F_T is the total streaming force, i.e. the integral of the streaming forces over the focal volume and σ defines the width of the jet. The reality is that both $S(r)$ and σ are unknown and strictly must be found from a proper fluid mechanics model. However, if we assume that flow profile is a raised cosine function, i.e. $S = \frac{1}{2}(1 + \cos(\pi r/\sigma))$ and the width of the jet is the same as the forcing ($\sigma = 10$ mm in this example), then we can generate the line shown in Fig. 13b. The numerical models all predict lower velocities than this simple model as, in reality, the jet diverges after the focus. Whilst this simple estimate is inaccurate, it clearly captures the correct order of magnitude of the streaming and the correct variation of streaming with acoustic pressure level. Equation 15 also suggests that if the amplitude of the focus is time-modulated sufficiently fast such that the air at the focus *feels* the time average force, then the streaming velocity will scale with the square root of the duty cycle.

5 Comparison to Experiment

A theory is only as good as its ability to match experiment. The performance of the theory described in Sect. 3 was explored using an Ultraleap array and driver board as shown in Fig. 14. The array is arranged in the grid geometry and used Murata

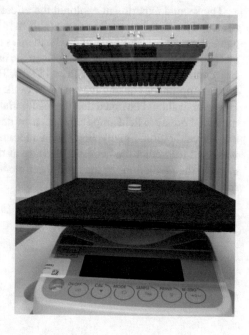

Fig. 14 Experimental apparatus used for comparison with models. The array was positioned 170 mm above a circular target upon which the array was focussed. The target was mounted on a balance to record the forces

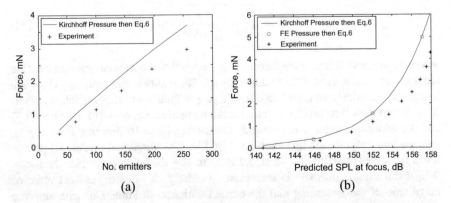

Fig. 15 Comparison between models and experiments for a square grid array of 40 kHz emitters focussed on a circular target of diameter, $\phi = 35$ mm with $L = 170$ mm. **a** Force as a function of the total number of total emitters, $N = N_s^2$ with the amplitude setting 4/10 which corresponded to, $p_0 = 2.15$ Pa and **b** forces of a 10×10 array in which the voltage amplitude used to drive the emitters was varied. The data plotted here are also shown in Tables 1 and 2

MA40S4S, 40 kHz emitters. The simulations used a single emitter pressure calibration curve previously measured by Ultraleap using a suitably calibrated microphone.

In the first experiment, the array size was varied from 6×6 to 16×16 by controlling in software which emitters were excited. This varied the number of emitters, N, and with it the array aperture, D. As can be seen from Fig. 15a the agreement between experiment and the model is generally good with the difference $\approx 20\%$.

The second experiment explored the effect of pressure amplitude on the performance of the simulations. The results shown in Fig. 15b again suggest generally good agreement. At higher pressure levels, there is a discrepancy between the simulation and experiment which reaches 36% when the amplitude was set to 8/10 (in the Ultraleap control software) and the SPL = 157 dB. This error could be a direct result of the higher amplitudes causing the assumed weak nonlinearity to become less accurate. However, it should be noted that the results shown in Fig. 15 are quite sensitive to the modelled pressure field amplitude (i.e. a p^2 dependence), which is dependent on the emitter calibration. Finally, Fig. 15b includes results in which a finite element model was used to predict the acoustic pressure at the object surface, and these are very close to the predictions of the rigid-facet model, validating the use of the Kirchhoff model for this example.

Table 1 Experimental and simulated data shown in Fig. 15a

Array size	Pressure at focus	Force	Force
	Sim	Expt	Sim
	kPa (dB)	mN	mN
6×6	0.43 (143.7)	0.44	0.56
8×8	0.75 (148.4)	0.80	1.03
10×10	1.13 (152.0)	1.16	1.55
12×12	1.55 (154.8)	1.73	2.18
14×14	2.02 (157.1)	2.37	2.93
16×16	2.50 (158.9)	2.96	3.69

Table 2 Experimental and simulated data shown in Fig. 15b and predicted streaming velocities for the same array

Array size	Pressure at focus	Force	Force	Streaming vel.*
	Sim	Expt	Sim	Sim
	kPa (dB)	mN	mN	m/s
10×10	0.31 (140.8)	0.02	0.12	0.033
10×10	0.61 (146.6)	0.33	0.45	0.078
10×10	0.88 (149.8)	0.71	0.94	0.130
10×10	1.13 (152.0)	1.17	1.55	0.196
10×10	1.36 (153.6)	1.49	2.27	0.282
10×10	1.58 (155.0)	2.08	3.07	0.381
10×10	1.79 (156.0)	2.50	3.93	0.460
10×10	1.97 (156.9)	3.05	4.77	0.537
10×10	2.12 (157.5)	3.63	5.53	0.601
10×10	2.23 (157.9)	4.29	6.07	0.650

*Maximum streaming velocity on beam axis in beam direction. Modelled in finite elements using a K-epsilon eddy viscosity model of turbulence (see Sect. 4)

6 Effects of Rapid Phase Changes

For the purposes of ultrasonic haptics, it is necessary to change the signal output by the emitters as a function of time. There are two time varying effects which are particularly common, (1) the drive signal is modulated at a lower frequency, e.g. 200 Hz, to improve the perception of the applied force (Gescheider et al. 2002), and (2) the focal spot is moved to track the hand location or with respect to the hand location to create the perception of shaped objects (Long et al. 2014). The focal spot can be manipulated through Eq. 4 or via more advanced algorithms, but all require the phase to change with time.

Fig. 16 Effect of a sinusoidal modulation of the 40 kHz excitation signals on the applied force. Simulation used Eq. 16. Experiments were taken on an Ultraleap system using and 10×10 grid array focussed on a $\phi = 20$ mm target and $L = 170$ mm

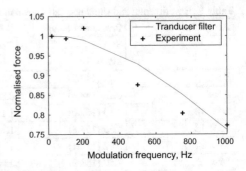

We now consider how these time varying electrical inputs are converted to acoustic outputs. Here, the narrow bandwidth of a typical airborne ultrasound emitter can be thought of as a filter of the input signals. The normalised frequency response function, H, of a typical 40 kHz emitter was found to follow that of a single degree of freedom oscillator (Fushimi et al. 2019) such that

$$H = \left[Q \left(1 - \Omega^2 \right) + i\Omega \right]^{-1} \tag{16}$$

where Ω is the frequency ratio, i.e. $\Omega = \omega/\omega_n$, and Q is the quality factor which is a measure of the damping found from $Q = \omega_n/\Delta\omega$, where $\Delta\omega$ is the bandwidth measured at the half power points. Efficient airborne ultrasound emitters typically have a low damping, which means a narrow bandwidth and a high Q.

As an example of how this filtering affects the response, Fig. 16 shows how the force on a target varies with an applied sinusoidal amplitude modulation. For low-modulation frequencies, the force is maintained whereas higher modulation frequencies cause a force reduction. The key point to note is that the modulation appears in the frequency domain as an input frequency shift and this shift increases with the modulation frequency. The narrow band nature of the emitters means that this frequency shift causes a reduction in the output acoustic pressure and hence applied force.

The link between signal changes and frequency is particularly clear for phase changes, for example, as used to move a focus in space. Whatever the algorithm, to move the focus, the phase (and amplitude) is changed as a function of time. If we consider a plane travelling wave subject to a phase that changes linearly with time as $\delta\phi \times t$ then

$$p = p_0 e^{i[\omega t - kr + \delta\phi.t]} = p_0 e^{i[(\omega + \delta\phi)t - kr]} \tag{17}$$

from which it is immediately apparent that the phase change rate is equivalent to a frequency change. Equation 16 tells us that frequency shift of $\omega_n/2Q$ leads to a halving of power output and therefore force. From Eq. 17, we can convert this frequency shift into a rate of phase change. For example, if $Q = 11.27$ (Fushimi et al. 2019) and one cycle takes $1/40$ ms, then a phase change of $360/2Q = 16°$/cycle results in a halving of the acoustic power output and resulting radiation force. Note that knowledge of the dynamics of the emitters also provides a route to further optimise their performance, by including it in an inversion scheme.

7 Conclusions

We have shown in this chapter that it is possible to model the forces in ultrasonic haptics by combining, (1) a linear acoustics model of the pressure field of an array, (2) a rigid-facet Kirchhoff model of the acoustic scattering at the hand, and (3) the evaluation of the momentum flux integral to obtain the forces. Each of these models is relatively intuitive and hence taken together they provide insight into the governing physics. These models are also surprisingly accurate and have led us to radiation force predictions in good agreement with measured values. These models also enable the prediction of the forces on the air which lead to acoustic streaming. We then considered how this flow can exert a force via momentum transfer to the hand, and this was found to be small when compared to the radiation force. However, it was noted that the streaming flow may be perceived directly via hairs or as cooling and so the streaming velocity may on occasion be a more relevant measure than streaming force. Hence, the streaming forces were applied to a body of fluid in a finite element flow model to enable the prediction of streaming velocity. This model of the streaming flow patterns completes our journey through the physical phenomena that are found in ultrasonic haptics. The models presented here provide both reasonable accuracy and because of their relative simplicity, they have explanatory power. However, models that include further aspects of the governing physics, such as nonlinear wave propagation, are available and would result in increased accuracy, particularly at higher intensities.

Acknowledgements Thanks go to Drs Rob Malkin and William Frier of Ultraleap Ltd., Bristol, UK, for useful discussions, supply of the experimental equipment and help with the experiments themselves.

References

Bruus H (2012) Acoustofluidics 7: the acoustic radiation force on small particles. Lab Chip 12(6):1014. https://doi.org/10.1039/c2lc21068a

Cady WG, Gittings CE (1953) On the measurement of power radiated from an acoustic source. J Acoust Soc Am 25(5):892–896. https://doi.org/10.1121/1.1907213

Carter T, Seah SA, Long B, Drinkwater B, Subramanian S (2013) UltraHaptics. In: Proceedings of the 26th annual ACM symposium on user interface software and technology, pp 505–514. https://doi.org/10.1145/2501988.2502018

Drinkwater BW, Wilcox PD (2006) Ultrasonic arrays for non-destructive evaluation: a review. NDT E Int 39(7):525–541. https://doi.org/10.1016/j.ndteint.2006.03.006

Fawcett JA (2001) Modeling of high-frequency scattering from objects using a hybrid Kirch-hoff/diffraction approach. J Acoust Soc Am 109(4):1312–1319. https://doi.org/10.1121/1.1350400

Fushimi T, Marzo A, Drinkwater BW, Hill TL (2019) Acoustophoretic volumetric displays using a fast-moving levitated particle. Appl Phys Lett 115(6). https://doi.org/10.1063/1.5113467

Gavrilov LR, Tsirulnikov EM (2012) Focused ultrasound as a tool to input sensory information to humans (review). Acoust Phys 58(1):1–21. https://doi.org/10.1134/S1063771012010083

Gescheider GA, Bolanowski SJ, Pope JV, Verrillo RT (2002) A four-channel analysis of the tactile sensitivity of the fingertip: frequency selectivity, spatial summation, and temporal summation. Somatosens Mot Res 19(2):114–124. https://doi.org/10.1080/08990220220131505

Hoshi T, Takahashi M, Iwamoto T, Shinoda H (2010) Noncontact tactile display based on radiation pressure of airborne ultrasound. IEEE Trans Haptics 3(3):155–165. https://doi.org/10.1109/TOH.2010.4

Inoue S, Mogami S, Ichiyama T, Noda A, Makino Y, Shinoda H (2019) Acoustical boundary hologram for macroscopic rigid-body levitation. J Acoust Soc Am 145(1):328–337. https://doi.org/10.1121/1.5087130

Kino GS (1987) Acoustic waves: devices, imaging, and analog signal processing. Prentice Hall Inc., New Jersey

Lighthill SJ (1978) Acoustic streaming. J Sound Vib 61(3):391–418. https://doi.org/10.1016/0022-460X(78)90388-7

Livett AJ, Emery EW, Leeman S (1981) Acoustic radiation pressure. J Sound Vib 76(1):1–11. https://doi.org/10.1016/0022-460X(81)90286-8

Long B, Seah SA, Carter T, Subramanian S (2014) Rendering volumetric haptic shapes in mid-air using ultrasound. ACM Trans Graph 33(6):1–10. https://doi.org/10.1145/2661229.2661257

Marzo A, Corkett T, Drinkwater BW (2018) Ultraino: an open phased-array system for narrowband airborne ultrasound transmission. IEEE Trans Ultrason Ferroelectr Freq Control 65(1):102–111. https://doi.org/10.1109/TUFFC.2017.2769399

Nakajima M, Hasegawa K, Makino Y, Shinoda H (2021) Spatiotemporal pinpoint cooling sensation produced by ultrasound-driven mist vaporization on skin. IEEE Trans Haptics 1–1. https://doi.org/10.1109/TOH.2021.3086516

Nyborg WL (1953) Acoustic streaming due to attenuated plane waves. J Acoust Soc Am 25(1):68–75. https://doi.org/10.1121/1.1907010

Ogilvy JA (1986) An estimate of the accuracy of the Kirchhoff approximation in acoustic wave scattering from rough surfaces. J Phys D Appl Phys 19(11):2085–2113. https://doi.org/10.1088/0022-3727/19/11/008

Prieur F, Sapozhnikov OA (2017) Modeling of the acoustic radiation force in elastography. J Acoust Soc Am 142(2):947–961. https://doi.org/10.1121/1.4998585

Rayleigh L (1905) On the momentum and pressure of gaseous vibrations, and on the connexion with the virial theorem. Philos Mag 10:364–374. https://doi.org/10.1080/14786440509463381

Tran Van Nhieu M (1996) Diffraction by the edge of a three-dimensional object. J Acoust Soc Am 99(1):79–87. https://doi.org/10.1121/1.414492

Treeby BE, Cox BT (2010) k-wave: MATLAB toolbox for the simulation and reconstruction of photoacoustic wave fields. J Biomed Opt 15(2). https://doi.org/10.1117/1.3360308

Westervelt PJ (1957) Acoustic radiation pressure. J Acoust Soc Am 29(1):26–29. https://doi.org/10.1121/1.1908669

Prototyping Airborne Ultrasonic Arrays

Asier Marzo

Abstract Focused ultrasound is the base mechanism for mid-air tactile feedback generation, acoustic levitation, wireless power transfer, directional audio and other emerging applications. The basic required set-up is an ultrasonic emitter with the capability of focusing its acoustic power at a target point. Ideally, a multi-emitter phased array is used since it is capable of steering and shaping the sound field with millimetre accuracy and a time response in the order of milliseconds. There are compelling commercial products and open designs for this kind of ultrasonic arrays. Here, we review the different elements that compose an ultrasonic array: from the emitters and the driving electronics to the signal generators or algorithms. We review some techniques to simulate the output of ultrasonic arrays or to determine the emission phases for target fields. Also, we provide some suggestions for future challenges related to cost, power and heat reduction.

1 Introduction

Transmitting phased arrays are devices made of multiple emitters that can adjust the phase (i.e. time delay) and amplitude of each element in order to focus their power at specific points or directions. This focusing and steering can be done electronically, at fast speeds and with high-accuracy without the need of mechanically moving the array. Phased arrays are nowadays used in 5G communications (Flamini et al. 2019) but have been commonly used in radar (Fenn et al. 2000), sonar (Baggeroer 2005) and medical ultrasound (Seip et al. 2003). When the arrays are composed of airborne ultrasonic emitters, it is possible to focus the acoustic amplitude at different points in space; by applying a modulation on the emitted wave, these points can be perceived as tactile stimuli by the mechanoreceptors of the human hand (Carter et al. 2013; Gavrilov 2008; Hoshi et al. 2009; Rakkolainen et al. 2019).

Airborne ultrasonic phased arrays (AUPs) can also be used for acoustic levitation (Andrade et al. 2020; Ochiai et al. 2014), wireless power transfer (Morales González

A. Marzo (✉)
UpnaLab, Institute of Smart Cities, Public University of Navarre, Navarre, Spain
e-mail: asier.marzo@unavarra.es

et al. 2021) or the generation of directional audio beams (Bourland et al. 2018; Ochiai et al. 2017). The AUPs can be dynamically focused, this enables to move the particles in levitation, transfer power only to specific receivers in wireless power and deliver sound to moving people in directional audio. An AUP can be used in conjunction with virtual reality systems (Georgiou et al. 2018) to generate the missing tactile sensations when touching virtual objects without forcing the user to wear devices on their hands. Other use cases can be found in hands-free car interfaces (Georgiou et al. 2017) or kiosks with gestural input (Kim et al. 2019).

This chapter focuses on describing the main elements that form an AUP. The main ones are the ultrasonic emitters, the amplification drivers and the signal generators. Some of these elements are commercially available. We will also see common spatial arrangement of the emitters used for the AUP. The chapter finishes with a review on the main simulation techniques and algorithms.

2 Components

A phased array has three main components. Firstly, the ultrasonic elements that transduce the electrical signal into ultrasonic waves. Since we focus on emission arrays, also called transmission arrays, we use ultrasonic emitters, but other types of arrays have elements that receive (receivers) or that perform both functions (transducers). Secondly, the driver electronics that amplify the logic signal into a signal capable of driving the emitters with enough amplitude; in general, emitters based on piezoelectric transduction have high impedance and require high voltage and low current. Thirdly, the signal generators are capable of producing multiple synchronized signals of adjustable phase and amplitude.

2.1 Emitters

The main commercially available ultrasonic emitters used in phased arrays have 1 cm in diameter, larger emitters are available but 1 cm is closer to the operating wavelength (8.46 mm) and thus can create more accurate fields and focal points. These emitters are based on leaky-plate radiation and operate at 40 kHz; some common models are MA40S4S (Murata Electronics, Japan), MSO-P1040H07T (Manorshi, China) or FBULS1007P-T (Ningbo, China). Inside these emitters, there is a thin piezo-electric disc that vibrates in radial mode, the disc is attached to a metal plate so that the radial vibration is transformed into traversal vibration, a metal cone is attached on top of this metal plate and allows to radiate from the metal plate into air despite the large mismatch of acoustic impedance. Variations of these transducers can be found with different diameters (e.g. 1.6 cm) or materials for the casing (plastic or aluminium) Fig. 1a. The cone is exposed directly at the top but protected with a metal grid or a plastic pattern that also helps to tune the directivity pattern. These emitters are mainly available at 40 kHz, but it is also possible to find them operating at 25 or 58 kHz.

In the supplementary information of Marzo et al. (2017), a table with radiation amplitude and aperture can be found for different ultrasonic emitters. These parameters can be used in the equations presented in Sect. 4 to obtain an estimation of the field at different points around the emitters. In general, the emitters are driven with a square wave signal (Marzo et al. 2017) leading to simpler driving electronics and generation with digital components. Excitation signals of 24 Vpp are normal in continuous operation, with the metal-case emitters being able to take up to 50 Vpp continuously. The current consumption varies from 4 to 10 mA depending on the efficiency of the driving electronics. Some ultrasonic emitters are made of a piezo-electric elements directly bonded to a metal case. These transducers are water-proof, robust and easy to cool down (e.g. MCUST18A40B12RS, Multicomp). However, their radiation into air is not as effective as the previously described leaky-plate emitters since closed-case emitters are designed to be bonded into a solid material, for example in distance measure applications in small boats (Giordano et al. 2016).

There are wideband ultrasonic emitters made of a piezo-element attached to a plastic membrane. These emitters are generally sold as pest control technology (e.g. FBUT3813, NingBo). They are less efficient than the previous models but can emit with a wide range of frequencies. In the same spectrum, compression drivers (Fig. 2c) (Ramachandran 2010) have often been used as ultrasonic emitters for levitation experiments and perhaps could be used for haptic applications.

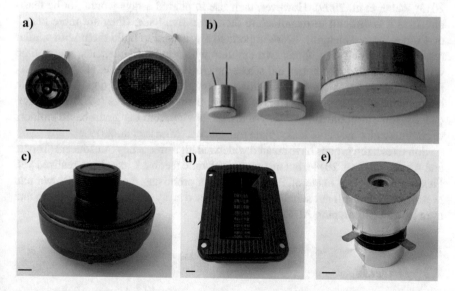

Fig. 1 Different ultrasonic emitters. The black lines at the bottom left of each figure are for reference. They are all 10 mm. **a** Leaky-plate open case operating at 40 kHz of diameter 10 mm and 16 mm. **b** High-frequency transducers with porous matching layer operating at 400, 200 and 100 kHz. **c** Compression drive. **d** Membrane-based tweeter. **e** Langevin horn

Fig. 2 Basic array geometries. **a** a 16 × 16 flat array made with 10 mm diameter emitters. **b** a 16 × 16 flat array using 16 mm emitters. **c** a bowl of radius of 100 mm made with 60 emitters of 16 mm diameter

Commercially available transducers of frequencies larger than 100 kHz are available; they employ a different working principle. The base is a metal case with a piezo attached on the front face from the inside. To provide correct transmission from the case into air, a white porous material is used as the matching layer. These transducers are available operating at 100, 200 and 400 kHz (Fig. 2b). However, they have a diameter of dozens of wavelengths, therefore having little capability to create wave interferences and be used in phased arrays.

Custom-made emitters can be found in the research literature. For example, large bulks of metal clamping piezo-electric elements are called Langevin transducers (Fig. 2d) and are widely used for high-intensity ultrasound applications (Foresti et al. 2013; Weber et al. 2009). However, their use in phased arrays would not be feasible since it is difficult to manufacture them in a small size (they are more than 3 or 4 times the wavelength). More importantly, it is hard to build them with similar resonant frequencies; to obtain two emitters with similar frequencies, the method was to build a dozen of horns and select the closest pair (Weber et al. 2009). Also, these Langevin horns are quite sensitive to continuous emission due to changes in temperature and the required voltage to drive them is dangerous (>200 V). Consequently, some airborne ultrasonic systems are moving from Langevin-based emitters to commercially available leaky-plate transducers (Morris et al. 2019).

Some research groups have created wideband high-frequency transducers (Topete and Alvarez-Arenas 2014), but no arrays for haptic feedback have been realized yet. Flexible transducers made of PVDF are also a promising technology (Brown and Mason 1996) but still not suitable for a full phased array due to their low power, and even less for prototyping AUPs.

2.2 Drivers

The signal coming from the signal generators usually does not have enough amplitude for exciting the emitters with sufficient power. Most of the times, the ultrasonic emitters are the most expensive parts of the arrays. For this reason, they should be driven at their maximum voltage to achieve as much acoustic amplitude as possible with the minimum number of emitters.

If a sinusoidal signal is used, then audio amplifiers (Schappe and Barbosa 2017) or even RF amplifiers (Franklin et al. 2017) can be used to amplify the analog signal. However, most of the AUPs use square waves, which are usually amplified with Mosfet drivers (Marzo et al. 2017). Mosfet drivers are a good option since they are designed to drive the highly capacitive gates of Mosfets; there are several theoretical models to describe an ultrasonic piezo-electric emitter and how their main load is of capacitive nature (IUD 2019).

The drivers can operate in push mode, in which one terminal of the emitter is connected to ground (or voltage) and the other terminal connects to the oscillating signal of the driver (Morales et al. 2021). Another possibility is to drive the emitter in push–pull mode, where both legs connect to two signals that are out of phase (Marzo et al. 2017); thereby, the voltage peak-to-peak that is applied into the emitter is double of the supplied voltage, although two driver channels are needed per emitter in this case.

Most ultrasonic emitters present a high impedance (e.g. 1 kOhm) when compared to traditional speakers; therefore, most drivers are not designed to drive them efficiently. Electrical matching can be done with different circuit networks (Rathod 2019) or with a matching transformer (Svilainis and Motiejūnas 2006) that also increases the voltage delivered to the emitters.

2.3 Signal Generation

Using an off-the-shelf signal generator can be feasible for generating one or two channels. Depending on the requirements for the signal, a scientific instrument (e.g. Keysight Technologies 33210A in the order of EUR 1000) or just a breakout board based on a direct digital synthesis IC (e.g. AD9851 Analog Devices at EUR 15) will suffice. For focusing, a phase resolution of five divisions per period leads to optimum amplitudes at the focal point, since increasing the phase resolution further only improves the amplitude by 5% (Marzo et al. 2017). For more complex amplitude patterns, like the ones shown in Sect. 5.3, a phase resolution of eight divisions per period produces the optimum results, as adding further phase resolution only decreases the mean square error by 3% (Morales et al. 2021). Steering the beam at specific angles will require more phase resolution, especially if the beam needs to target points at long distances from the array. For haptic AUPs, steering with high accuracy is not as important as focusing at different points around the array since the user's hand is not further than 1 m. The low requirements on phase resolution but the necessity of a high number of channels lead to the use of other signal generators in AUPs for haptic.

The traditional 555 IC is used in some projects when only one channel is required; however, it is not possible to synchronize multiple of them. An Arduino UNO can generate at least two channels with phase control (Marzo et al. 2017) and an Arduino MEGA, up to 64 channels with ten divisions per period (Marzo et al. 2017). However, when more channels or phase control are needed, a solution based on an FPGA is commonly employed (Morales et al. 2021; Zehnter and Ament 2019). Hybrid architectures like the BeagleBone (OSUPA 2022) have been successfully used and new microcontrollers like the ESP32 or Raspberry Pi Pico are promising alternative still to be tested since they include protocols for parallel output of data at controlled speeds.

3 Geometries

The location of the ultrasonic emitters determines the main capabilities of the arrays such as the amplitude that can be obtained at the focal points, the dimensions of those points, the undesired secondary lobes that appear and the working volume in which the array can be focused effectively.

A flat geometry is used in most commercial products, since it allows for soldering the emitters directly in a PCB and thus enables easy manufacturing. The rectangular distribution is the simplest because it is panelizable and it does not leave gaps (Fig. 2). A more efficient geometry is the hexagonal packing, which gives more density of emitters but leaves gaps and makes it harder to put components on the other side of the array or to tile various arrays. Arrays with uniform distribution of emitters lead to the generation of undesired focal points (side lobes) that appear outside the main target focal point. To avoid this problem, distributions with quasi-random (Rosnitskiy et al. 2018) or Fibonacci arrangements (Price and Long 2018) have shown to reduce sidelobes; however, their manufacturing in a PCB is more complicated.

Emitters do not need to be constrained to a flat surface if extension wires are used to decouple their driving electronics. Spherical caps (Fig. 2c) generate focal points with more amplitude (Marzo et al. 2017), however the working volume in which they can be focused gets reduced. In other words, flat arrays can focus on a larger volume but with less power. Furthermore, spherical caps have a natural focus which can be used to remove the necessity for complex electronics if only a static focal point is desired. That is, when all the emitters are driven with the same signal, a focal point is generated at the geometric focus.

Height offset on the emitters can be used to produce phase changes at a point without the need of using different electrical signals (Marzo et al. 2017), this technique has been used to generate vortices (Ultrasonic screwdriver 2015), twin-traps or other acoustic fields by placing the emitters at specific positions. This reduces the complexity on the electronics, but the arrays do not have the capability to focus at different points. Passive phase modulators can also be used for focusing and shaping the acoustic field emitted from AUPs (Marzo et al. 2017; Memoli et al. 2017; Norasikin et al. 2018).

Using multiple arrays or extended ones is a technique used to cover a larger working volume (O'Conaill et al. 2020) or being able to focus at different positions around a 3D object (Ohmori et al. 2021). Please refer to Chap. "Multiunit Phased Array System for Flexible Workspace". Other types of spatial distributions such as V-shape or ring shape have been presented in the literature (See supplementary information of Marzo et al. (2015)), but they are not commonly used for haptic arrays.

4 Simulation of the Emitted Field

The piston model is a simplification commonly used to calculate the incident field generated by one or multiple emitters (O'Neil 1949). The model is only applicable for the far-field of the emitters, but this is not an issue since most tactile stimulation takes place centimetres away from the array, the far-field of the employed ultrasonic emitters starts at 3 mm approximately from their top. The near to far-field limit starts at $(2a)^2/4\lambda$, where λ is the wavelength and a is the emitter radius (Lilliehorn et al. 2005). The piston model cannot be used for simulating domains with complex reflecting geometry but this is usually not a problem because tactile systems radiate directly onto the user's hand. Reflections on planar objects can be approximated by mirroring the emitters and adding an attenuation coefficient depending on the material of the reflector. This method is fast and can run in real time for hundreds of emitters (Marzo et al. 2017).

The complex acoustic pressure $p(r)$ at point r due to a piston source emitting at a single frequency can be modelled as:

$$p(\boldsymbol{r}) = AV \frac{D_f(\theta)}{d} e^{i(\varphi + kd)} \tag{1}$$

where A is the transducer output efficiency and V is the excitation signal peak-to-peak amplitude. The term $\frac{1}{d}$ is the divergence, where d is the distance between the centre of the piston and the point r. $k = 2\pi/\lambda$ is the wavenumber and λ is the wavelength. φ is the emitting phase of the source. D_f is the directivity function of the emitter and depends on the angle θ between the emitter normal and the point r. The directivity function of a vibrating piston source can be expressed as:

$$D_f = 2J_1(ka\sin\theta)/ka\sin\theta \tag{2}$$

where J_1 is a first-order Bessel function of the first kind and a is the radius of the piston. This directivity function can be approximated as $D_f = \text{sinc}(ka\sin\theta)$.

The total acoustic field P generated by N transducers is the addition of their emitted complex fields, i.e. $P = \sum_{j=1}^{N} p_j$. The constant A and the piston radius a are needed to characterize a transducer. For instance, the commonly used MA40S4S (Murata Electronics, Japan) can be approximated as: $a = 4.5$ mm and $A = 0.17$ Pa · m/V.

This simple model can be used to simulate the shape and amplitude of the focal points generated by different array geometries. For instance, in Fig. 3, we compare a flat 16×16 array made with 10 mm emitters (MA40S4S) and 16 mm emitters (MSO-P1040H07T). It can be seen that the 16 mm emitters produce a stronger and smaller

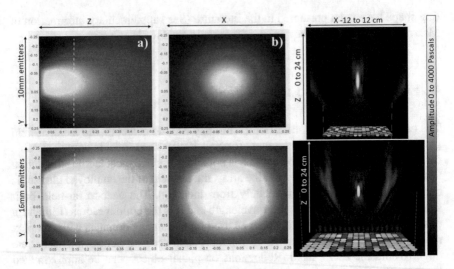

Fig. 3 Amplitude at the focal point when the arrays are focused at each point of the slice. 16 × 16 flat arrays made of Murata MA40S4S 10mm emitters (top row) and 16mm Manorhsi MSO-P1040H07T emitters (bottom row) are compared. On the third column, the shape of a focal point is shown

focal point around a larger working volume but sidelobes are closer to the main focal point. Also, an array made with 16mm emitters is larger and more cumbersome.

5   Focusing Algorithms

Multiple techniques have been developed to determine the required emission phases of each emitter so that the array focuses the acoustic power at different positions. We divide them in three categories: single focal point, multiple focal points and the generation of a 2D amplitude pattern (also called acoustic image) (Fig. 4).

5.1   Simple Focus

To focus the acoustic power at a position in space, the incoming wave from each emitter should arrive at that point with the same phase. This leads to a simple time of flight algorithm $\varphi_n = k \, | f - s_n|$, where φ_n is the emission phase for the n emitter, f is the position of the target focal point, s_n is the position of transducer n, and $|\cdot|$ the distance between those two points. Also please refer to Chaps. "Introduction to Ultrasonic Mid-air Haptic Effects" and "The Physical Principles of Arrays for Mid-air Haptic Applications". Apodization techniques, such as applying a Gaussian

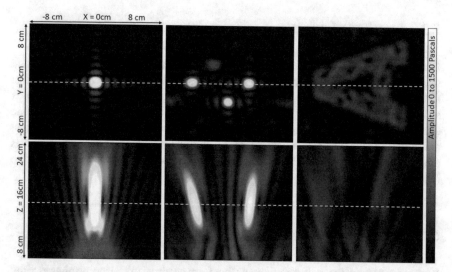

Fig. 4 Amplitude field resulting from focusing a phased array using different algorithms. The array has 16 × 16 1 cm emitters (Murata MA40S4S), the slices are taken 16 cm above the array. **a** Single focal point. **b** Three focal points. **c** Amplitude target of a letter A

profile on the amplitude of the emitters, can be used to reduce the sidelobes (Guo et al. 2013) or give a rounder profile to the focal point.

5.2 Multi-focus

There are three main techniques for creating multiple focal points at target positions. In the first one (Andrade et al. 2018; Watanabe et al. 2018), the emitters are split into different groups using a checkboard pattern or other type of spatial division, each subset of emitters is focused with the simple focus method at a position. This method is fast to compute, leads to smooth transitions, but it does not provide optimum results in terms of amplitude, since the emitters may interfere between subsets.

The creation of multiple focal points can be set as an optimization problem with the emission phases as the variables, and the addition of the amplitude at the target points as the target function. Optimizations solved by mean root squares (Gavrilov 2008; Long et al. 2014) or Broyden–Fletcher–Goldfarb–Shanno (BFGS) (Marzo et al. 2015) have been used with success.

Iterative back propagation (IBP) (Marzo and Drinkwater 2019) can also be used to find emission phases that create maximum amplitude at the target points. Variations of this method such as GS-SPAT (Plasencia et al. 2020) lead to fast calculations that allow the movement of the focal points at high speeds (in excess of 10 kHz). For details, please refer to Chap. "Sound-Field Creation for Haptic Reproduction".

5.3 Amplitude Images

For some applications, it is desired to project an amplitude pattern that resembles that of an image, it could be a simple shape such as a circle or a more complex one like a dove. However, for haptic applications, simple shapes are enough since complex shapes cannot be discerned correctly by humans. Holograms for acoustics (Melde et al. 2016) is an emergent field with the aim of modulating acoustic waves into target amplitude fields, normally a passive phase modulator of high spatial resolution is employed, but algorithms adapted to phased arrays are also present in the literature (Morales et al. 2021).

6 Conclusion

We have presented the main components that form an ultrasonic airborne phased array used for mid-air haptic stimulation. We have analysed the main types of commercially available ultrasonic emitters, driver electronics and signal generators. We showed some of the common geometries for the spatial disposition of the emitters. Algorithms and simulation methods for phased arrays were briefly introduced. There are multiple companies that commercialize phased arrays; also it is still possible to build arrays at home and customize them in shape or power. This fosters novel applications and a growing community of both researchers and enthusiasts that will experiment with phased array for mid-air haptic feedback.

Acknowledgements This research was funded by Jovenes Investigadores Grant (UPNA, Spain) and from the European Union's Horizon 2020 research and innovation programme under grant agreement No 101017746, TOUCHLESS.

References

Andrade MA, Camargo TS, Marzo A (2018) Automatic contactless injection, transportation, merging, and ejection of droplets with a multifocal point acoustic levitator. Rev Sci Inst 89(12):125105

Andrade MA, Marzo A, Adamowski JC (2020) Acoustic levitation in mid-air: recent advances, challenges, and future perspectives. Appl Phys Lett 116(25):250501

Baggeroer A (2005) Sonar arrays and array processing. AIP Conf Proc Am Inst Phys 760:3–24

Bourland AC, Gorman P, McIntosh J, Marzo A (2018) Project telepathy. Interact 25(5):16, 250501

Brown LF, Mason JL (1996) Disposable PVDF ultrasonic transducers for nondestructive testing applications. IEEE Trans Ultras Ferroelectr Freq Control 43(4):560 (1996)

Carter T, Seah SA, Long B, Drinkwater B, Subramanian S (2013) UltraHaptics: multi-point mid-air haptic feedback for touch surfaces. In: Proceedings of the 26th annual ACM symposium on user interface software and technology, pp 505–514

Fenn AJ, Temme DH, Delaney WP, Courtney WE (2000) The development of phased-array radar technology. Lincoln Lab J 12(2):321

Flamini R, Mazzucco C, Lombardi R, Massagrande C, Morgia F, Milani A (2019) Millimeter-wave phased arrays for 5G: An industry view on current issues and challenges. In: 2019 IEEE international symposium on phased array system and technology (PAST). IEEE, pp 1–2

Foresti D, Nabavi M, Klingauf M, Ferrari A, Poulikakos D (2013) Acoustophoretic contactless transport and handling of matter in air. Proc Natl Acad Sci 110(31):12549, 250501

Franklin A, Marzo A, Malkin R, Drinkwater B (2017) Three-dimensional ultrasonic trapping of micro-particles in water with a simple and compact two-element transducer. Appl Phys Lett 111(9):094101

Gavrilov LR (2008) The possibility of generating focal regions of complex configurations in application to the problems of stimulation of human receptor structures by focused ultrasound. Acoust Phys 54(2):269

Georgiou O, Biscione V, Harwood A, Griffiths D, Giordano M, Long B, Carter T (2017) Haptic in-vehicle gesture controls. In: Proceedings of the 9th international conference on automotive user interfaces and interactive vehicular applications adjunct, pp 233–238

Georgiou O, Jeffrey C, Chen Z, Tong BX, Chan SH, Yang B, Harwood A, Carter T (2018) Touchless haptic feedback for VR rhythm games. In: 2018 IEEE conference on virtual reality and 3D user interfaces (VR), IEEE, pp 553–554

Giordano F, Mattei G, Parente C, Peluso F, Santamaria R (2016) Integrating sensors into a marine drone for bathymetric 3D surveys in shallow waters. Sens 16(1):41

Guo J, Chen L, Zhang Y, Yang K, Li J, Gao X (2013) Method of ultrasonic phased array imaging based on segment amplitude apodization. In: 2013 far east forum on nondestructive evaluation/testing: new technology and application. IEEE, pp 181–188

Hoshi T, Iwamoto T, Shinoda H (2009) Non-contact tactile sensation synthesized by ultrasound transducers. In: World haptics 2009-third joint euroHaptics conference and symposium on haptic interfaces for virtual environment and teleoperator systems, IEEE, pp 256–260

Introduction to ultrasonic drivers (2019). https://www.piezodrive.com/ultrasonic-drivers/intro-ultrasonic/

Kim JR, Chan S, Huang X, Ng K, Fu LP, Zhao C (2019) Demonstration of Refinity: An interactive holographic signage for new retail shopping experience. In: Extended abstracts of the 2019 CHI conference on human factors in computing systems, pp 1–4

Lilliehorn T, Simu U, Nilsson M, Almqvist M, Stepinski T, Laurell T, Nilsson J, Johansson S (2005) Trapping of microparticles in the near field of an ultrasonic transducer. Ultrasonics 43(5):293

Long B, Seah SA, Carter T, Subramanian S (2014) Rendering volumetric haptic shapes in mid-air using ultrasound. ACM Trans Graph (TOG) 33(6):1

Marzo A, Drinkwater BW (2019) Holographic acoustic tweezers. Proc Natl Acad Sci 116(1):84

Marzo A, Seah SA, Drinkwater BW, Sahoo DR, Long B, Subramanian S (2015) Holographic acoustic elements for manipulation of levitated objects. Nat Commun 6(1):1

Marzo A, Barnes A, Drinkwater BW (2017) TinyLev: A multi-emitter single-axis acoustic levitator. Rev Sci Inst 88(8):085105

Marzo A, Ghobrial A, Cox L, Caleap M, Croxford A, Drinkwater B (2017) Realization of compact tractor beams using acoustic delay-lines. Appl Phys Lett 110(1):014102

Marzo A, Corkett T, Drinkwater BW (2017) Ultraino: An open phased-array system for narrowband airborne ultrasound transmission. IEEE Trans Ultrason Ferroelectr Freq Control 65(1):102

Melde K, Mark AG, Qiu T, Fischer P (2016) Holograms for acoustics. Nature 537(7621):518

Memoli G, Caleap M, Asakawa M, Sahoo DR, Drinkwater BW, Subramanian S (2017) Metamaterial bricks and quantization of meta-surfaces. Nat Commun 8(1):1

Morales González R, Marzo A, Freeman E, Frier W, Georgiou O (2021) UltraPower: powering tangible & wearable devices with focused ultrasound. In: proceedings of the fifteenth international conference on tangible, embedded, and embodied interaction, pp 1–13

Morales R, Ezcurdia I, Irisarri J, Andrade MA, Marzo A (2021) Generating airborne ultrasonic amplitude patterns using an open hardware phased array. Appl Sci 11(7):2981

Morris RH, Dye ER, Docker P, Newton MI (2019) Beyond the Langevin horn: transducer arrays for the acoustic levitation of liquid drops. Phys Fluids 31(10):101301

Norasikin MA, Martinez Plasencia D, Polychronopoulos S, Memoli G, Tokuda Y, Subramanian S (2018) SoundBender: dynamic acoustic control behind obstacles. In: proceedings of the 31st annual ACM symposium on user interface software and technology, pp 247–259

Ochiai Y, Hoshi T, Rekimoto J (2014) Pixie dust: graphics generated by levitated and animated objects in computational acoustic-potential field. ACM Trans Graph (TOG) 33(4):1

Ochiai Y, Hoshi T, Suzuki I (2017) Holographic whisper: rendering audible sound spots in three-dimensional space by focusing ultrasonic waves. In: proceedings of the 2017 CHI conference on human factors in computing systems, pp 4314–4325

O'Conaill B, Provan J, Schubel J, Hajas D, Obrist M, Corenthy L (2020) Improving immersive experiences for visitors with sensory impairments to the aquarium of the pacific. Extended abstracts of the 2020 CHI conference on human factors in computing systems, pp 1–8

Ohmori T, Abe Y, Fujiwara M, Makino Y, Shinoda H (2021) Remote friction control on 3-dimensional object made of polystyrene foam using airborne ultrasound focus. Association for Computing Machinery, New York, NY, USA. https://doi.org/10.1145/3411763.3451598

O'Neil H (1949) Theory of focusing radiators. J Acoust Soc Am 21(5):516

Open source ultrasonic phased array. https://hackaday.io/project/159467-open-source-ultrasonic-phased-array

Plasencia DM, Hirayama R, Montano-Murillo R, Subramanian S (2020) GS-PAT: high-speed multi-point sound-fields for phased arrays of transducers. ACM Trans Graph (TOG) 39(4):138

Price A, Long B (2018) Fibonacci spiral arranged ultrasound phased array for mid-air haptics. In: 2018 IEEE international ultrasonics symposium (IUS). IEEE, pp 1–4

Rakkolainen I, Sand A, Raisamo R (2019) A survey of mid-air ultrasonic tactile feedback. In: 2019 IEEE international symposium on multimedia (ISM). IEEE, pp 94–944

Ramachandran N(2010) Modeling and control of acoustic levitation for dust control application. Southern Illinois University at Carbondale

Rathod VT (2019) A review of electric impedance matching techniques for piezoelectric sensors, actuators and transducers. Electron 8(2):169

Rosnitskiy PB, Vysokanov BA, Gavrilov LR, Sapozhnikov OA, Khokhlova VA (2018) Method for designing multielement fully populated random phased arrays for ultrasound surgery applications. In: IEEE transactions on ultrasonics, ferroelectrics, and frequency control 65(4):630

Schappe RS, Barbosa C (2017) A simple, inexpensive acoustic levitation apparatus. Phys Teach 55(1):6

Seip R, Chen W, Tavakkoli J, Frizzell L, Sanghvi N (2003) High-intensity focused ultrasound (HIFU) phased arrays: Recent developments in transrectal transducers and driving electronics design. In: proceeding 3rd international symposium therapeutic ultrasound, pp 423–428

Svilainis L, Motiejūnas G (2006) Power amplifier for ultrasonic transducer excitation. Ultra-garsas/Ultrasound 58(1):30

Topete J, Alvarez-Arenas TG (2014) Annular multifrequency piezoelectric array for enhanced wideband ultrasonic response. SENSORS, 2014 IEEE. IEEE, pp 102–105

Ultrasonic screwdriver in air-angular momentum transfer to matter (2015) https://www.youtube.com/watch?v=vqe3YvhivYU

Watanabe A, Hasegawa K, Abe Y (2018) Contactless fluid manipulation in air: droplet coalescence and active mixing by acoustic levitation. Sci Rep 8(1):1

Weber J, Rey C, Neuefeind J, Benmore C (2009) Acoustic levitator for structure measurements on low temperature liquid droplets. Rev Sci Inst 80(8):083904

Zehnter S, Ament C (2019) A modular FPGA-based phased array system for ultrasonic levitation with MATLAB. In: 2019 IEEE international ultrasonics symposium (IUS), IEEE, pp 654–658

Safety of High-Intensity Ultrasound

Andrew Di Battista

Abstract Ultrasound mid-air haptics requires exceptional sound pressure levels (SPL) (>145 dB) to produce perceptible haptic feedback. However, the effects of exposure to such high SPL on humans/animals are not fully understood. Existing exposure guidelines are based on limited outdated studies and additional uncertainties stem from the lack of standards concerning ultrasound acoustic measurements. Yet, in order for ultrasound-based technologies to breakthrough into mainstream consumer products, a safety record needs to be established. This chapter begins with a critical summary of the existing safety data and international guidelines and continues with a report of several recent research endeavours to investigate health-related effects of ultrasound exposure. These include experiments concerning audiological effects, skin and eye exposure to mid-air haptics feedback and investigations into the effectiveness of common types of ear defenders at attenuating ultrasound. While humans may not be able to hear *ultra*sound, many animals, including common household pets, can. This chapter includes a summary of key concerns with respect to animal safety. Although future work will be required, it is hoped that the information in this chapter will help steer HCI developers to produce designs that are both innovative and safe.

1 International Guidelines for (Ultrasound) Noise Exposure

Prior to the advent of ultrasound mid-air haptics (and similar technologies), exposure to such extraordinary SPLs was limited to industrial environments, e.g. factory workers operating ultrasonic welding and cleaning machines. Much of the research informing international safety guidelines originates from occupational health and

A. D. Battista (✉)
Ultraleap Ltd, Bristol, England
e-mail: andrew.di.battista@ultraleap.com

safety studies on these workers. Specifically, they examined the effects on *auditory* function, both in terms of immediate and long-term hearing loss. Thus, we refer to *exposure* in this context as the sound levels reaching the *ears* of an individual. There have been several review articles published on this topic (Acton 1974; Leighton 2016; Lenhardt 2008; Smagowska 2013; Wiernicki and Karoly 1985). The intention in this section is to provide only a brief summary of the key conclusions. Similarly, the amazing signal processing properties of the mammalian ear are also a topic better suited to further reading (Dobie and Hemel 2004; The Open University 2020).

1.1 Effects of Noise Exposure

The main issue is concerned with Temporary Threshold Shift (TTS) and Permanent Threshold Shift (PTS). Exposure to loud noises can cause a temporary loss in hearing sensitivity (i.e. TTS) measured in dB. Those readers who have ever been to a lively music gig will undoubtedly have experienced 'ringing' in their ears for many hours after the performance. In that case, your over-stimulated nerve cells will have suffered from excitotoxicity (pathological levels of neurotransmitters) which interrupt their normal function. The inner hair cells of the cochlea are mechanically driven by sound to produce excitatory nerve signals to the audio cortex of the brain. Therefore, noise exposure can lead to further physical damage to these cells that cannot be reversed; in fact, the brain compensates by *recruiting* neighbouring hair cells to boost the loss in signal. This is not a long-term nor sustainable solution and is the main cause of hyperacusis (hyper-sensitivity to certain sound frequencies). So while it may seem like your hearing has returned to normal when the ringing stops, you have in fact done some degree of 'wear-and-tear' to your auditory function. In short, repeated and/or prolonged TTS can contribute to *permanent* hearing loss, i.e. PTS.

A noise source that is not powerful enough to induce a TTS may still cause distress in the form of annoyance, sleep-deprivation, headache, nausea, etc. (further details are discussed in Physiological Effects.). They are collectively known as *subjective effects* because they affect each individual differently. A prime example would be those living near major international airports and flight paths (Research and Department 2020).

1.2 Non-linear Acoustic Effects

The astute reader may now be asking themselves, if *ultra*sound is inaudible to humans, how can it have any effects on hearing? Firstly, it is important to mention that the often quoted audible frequencies (20–20,000 Hz) are based on an average human response. There are individuals who can hear well into the mid-20s kHz range; for others, particularly as we age, the upper frequency threshold drops dramatically.

However, one would expect a 40 kHz ultrasonic transducer to be well beyond human perception!

The mechanisms by which ultrasound can affect auditory function are not totally understood. Non-linear effects of sound propagation at high SPL can produce *inter-modulation* (IM) distortion (the mixing of frequencies which generates sums and differences of frequencies found in the original signal). This is one source of audible noise that is in fact exploited for use in the parametric audio effect. It is well known that in the case of ultrasound mid-air haptics, a modulated feedback point can produce audible noise. Interaction with the mechanisms of the ear can also produce *subharmonics* (fractional frequencies at powers of two (f/2, f/4, f/8, …) (Huang et al. 2012). It is possible that these audible noises are more likely responsible for the subjective effects of exposure, rather than the ultrasound itself. Separating ultrasound from other confounding factors is a challenge posed to safety researchers (see Subjective Effects).

1.3   Summary of Guidelines

Based on these concerns, the international regulatory community has produced guidelines for maximum permissible levels (MPL) for ultrasound exposure (summarised in Table 1). Figure 1 is an attempt to re-interpret the MPLs by aligning them to known auditory and subjective effects.

The highest permissible levels are granted by the ACGIH (145 dB) with no limit on duration. The motivating factor behind this recommended MPL is that such levels are not associated with *permanent* hearing loss. In fact, in one study (Parrack 1966) exposure to 148–154 dB SPL at 37 kHz for 5 min resulted in less than 20 dB TTS with a rapid and complete recovery. Note, this is comparable to direct exposure to a haptic feedback point. As already mentioned, repeated exposure of this nature is *not* recommended as it could lead to long-term hearing damage. Other regulators are motivated by the need to eliminate the risk of any effect, including subjective effects, hence an MPL of 110 dB. It should be re-emphasised that these exposure levels are those measured *at the ear*. Further, these MPLs are designed for occupational health and safety (8 h work day, exposures to employees) and do not strictly apply to the general public or consumer products.

The main criticism of the guidelines stems from the fact that much of the scientific data incorporated into them is from the mid-twentieth century and consists of tests carried out on factory workers, predominantly middle aged men. Much more data is required if we are to assess the risk to younger people, women and other vulnerable groups known to have considerably greater sensitivity to higher frequency sound.

Table 1 Summary of international guidelines for Maximum Permissible Levels (MPLs) (Lawton 2013)

Organization	MPL
ACGIH (American Conference of Governmental Industrial Hygienists). (2004)	115 dB
	+30 dB if no coupling (i.e. airborne)
	independent of duration
ILO (International Labour Office (United Nations)). (1977)	110 dB
	+6 dB, 1–4hrs
	+12 dB, 15min-1hr
	+18 dB, 5–15min
	+24 dB, 1–5min
IRPA (International Non-Ionizing Radiation Committee). (1984)	110 dB occupational/100 dB public
	+3 dB 2–4hr daily,
	+6 dB 1–2hr daily,
	+9 dB <1 hr
Health Canada (1991)	110 dB
	Independent of duration

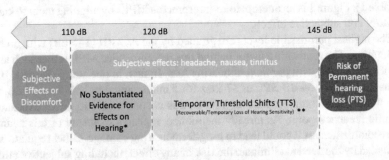

Fig. 1 MPLs aligned with known (or hypothesised) auditory and subjective effects from ultrasound noise exposure. * Guidelines for the safe use of ultrasound: Part II Industrial and Commercial Applications, Health Canada Safety Code 24. ** The 145 dB upper limit is based on the generation of audible *subharmonics* that may cause hearing damage. It has not been established that ultrasound SPLs *below* 145 dB may also contribute to TTS

2 Estimating Typical Exposure from Ultrasound Mid-Air Haptics

Now that we have guidelines, the next relevant question is what is the expected exposure levels from using a ultrasound mid-air haptic device? Because of the complexities of acoustic fields at ultrasonic frequencies, this is not a simple question to answer (M.Bomford and O'Brien 2019). Figure 2 shows SPL exposure measurement results from a simple experimental set-up to simulate a real ultrasound mid-air haptic use case. The array was switched on for continuous output (Fig. 2a). When a hand was placed over the array to interact with the focal point, exposure levels predictably reduced (Fig. 2b). Thus, combining ultrasound mid-air haptic with hand tracking to trigger the device is not only important for user experience, but a safety feature too.

As a side note, another possible safety feature is using advanced signal processing techniques to produce 'null points' (regions of relatively low sound pressure) at locations that are near the user's head/ears. The mechanism is the same for producing haptic focal points; a point in space is assigned a desired SPL (for more information, refer to Chap. "Sound-Field Creation for Haptic Reproduction"). There are many design challenges to overcome, but such a technique would further contribute to lowering the ultrasound exposure risk.

It should be emphasised that this experiment does not cover all scenarios of head positions and array output. As an extreme example, a direct focal point (or grating lobe) to the ear would lead to > 145 dB exposure. However, the experiment does inform us on the 'typical' exposure levels from prescribed use of ultrasound mid-air haptics.

We may broadly estimate that exposure levels are approximately 115–125 dB SPL. Looking back at Fig. 1, it is clear that ultrasound mid-air haptics does not quite conform to recommended MPLs, should we wish to avoid *any* subjective effects. It has also been the focus of more recent research to explore these effects as well as to confirm that no hearing damage is taking place.

The fluctuations in SPL due to the movement of the HATS is easily explained when considering the *spatial response* to ultrasound of the human *pinna* (outer ear) (Fig. 3). The angle of incidence of a focal point to the ear can lead to ≈ 30 dB difference in the level of exposure. From Fig. 3c, we may conclude that (at least for 40 kHz ultrasound) incident angles from *below and in front* (a common interaction location for a mid-air haptic device) and from *above and behind* result in the highest exposures. It is worth noting that no hand interaction/deflection featured in these measurements; it is reasonable to conclude from Fig. 2b that this would have a mitigating effect.

3 Recent Safety Research

3.1 Audiology

There have been a handful of recent studies concerned with high-intensity airborne ultrasound exposure and the audiological effects on humans. In DiBattista (2019), sixteen people (ten exposed, six control) were exposed to a mid-air haptic device in a scenario identical to Fig. 2a for 5 min. Pure tone audiometry (PTA) was conducted prior to and immediately after exposure. There was no significant change in hearing sensitivity found at any frequency tested. As a follow-up to this pilot study, in Carcagno et al. (2019) similar exposure levels consisting of modulated and

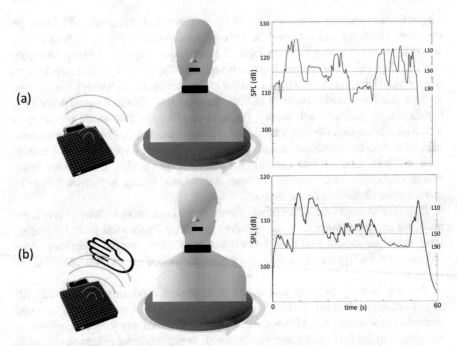

Fig. 2 Exposure levels at the ear using Brüel & Kjær (B&K) (Nærum, Denmark) type 4191 micro-phone fitted in the ear of a B&K type 4100 head and torso simulator (HATS). The free-field response of the 4191 microphone was converted to a pressure-field response using a real-time equalisation filter). The array was placed at 'arm's length' and the HATS model rotated pseudo-randomly on a turntable ($\pm \sim 90^o$) while facing the array. The array was programmed to continuously emit a moving focal point to produce a 'circle sensation' (3 cm radius, 100 rps, (x,y,z): (0,0,20 cm), 40 kHz, 155 dB SPL). **a** Pressure at the ear, no hand interaction with array **b** pressure at the ear, with hand gestures generated by the researcher interacting with the focal point. L10, L50, L90 are Ln statistical measures that indicate levels exceeded for n% of the time. All SPL measurements correspond to 1/3 octave-band f_c: 40 kHz. Ultrasonic frequencies are Z-weighted

unmodulated 40 kHz tones we presented to eighteen (nine exposed , nine control) females (mean age 21 years) for duration totalling 40 min. In addition to audiometry, electro-physiological responses recorded subclinical measures of hearing deficits: speech-in-noise understanding, supra-threshold auditory brain-stem response wave I amplitude and latency, and frequency following response levels to amplitude mod-ulated (AM) tones. There were no significant hearing deficits detected. Moreover, electroencephalographic recordings did not show significant phase-locked activity to the modulated AM tones and subharmonics of the ultrasound tone we not detected either.

This lack of neural/brain response to ultrasonic stimuli is further supported by magnetoencephalography (MEG) and functional magnetic resonance imaging (fMRI) (Kühler et al. 2019). In this case, nothing was detected above 24 kHz; the

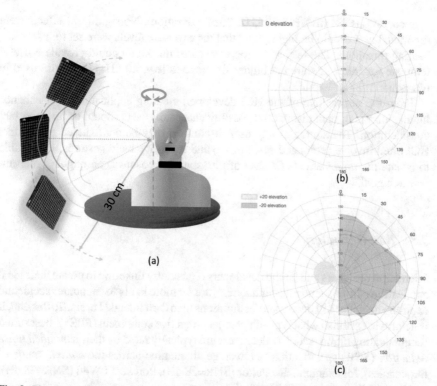

Fig. 3 Pinna-related spatial response using Brüel & Kjær (B&K) (Nærum, Denmark) type 4191 microphone fitted in the ear of a B&K type 4100 head and torso simulator (HATS). The free-field response of the 4191 microphone was converted to a pressure-field response using a real-time equalisation filter). **a** An array was positioned at a distance of 30 cm and a focal point (40 kHz, 155 dB SPL) was directed at the ear. The array was repositioned to elevation angles of ±20°. The HATS was rotated in stages of 15°; the turntable axis was aligned with the entrance of the pinna which was flush with the outer microphone grill. All SPL measurements correspond to 1/3 octave-band f_c: 40 kHz. Ultrasonic frequencies are Z-weighted. **b** SPL at the pinna (0 elevation), 0 − 180° azimuth. **c** SPL at the pinna (±20° elevation), 0 − 180° azimuth

maximum frequency presented to test subjects in this experiment (however, the exposure levels were limited to 115 dB SPL).

3.2 Subjective Effects

There have been few innovations in the field of airborne ultrasound subjective effects research in the last 50 years. A more recent attempt focussed on effects from exposure to 20 kHz ultrasound (Fletcher et al. 2018). In a blinded study, test subjects were asked to perform a computer-based cognitive task while under control and exposure conditions (84 dB SPL, 20 kHz, 20 min duration). No significant effects were reported, but it should be highlighted that the exposure levels were set to just below hearing threshold. The testing protocols used in this study could provide a useful template for future research at higher frequencies (e.g. 40 kHz) like those used in ultrasound mid-air haptic.

From the perspective of the HCI developer, creating applications that enhance interaction rather than distract (or possibly nauseate!) users should be an important consideration. The source of any user discomfort may be confounded by the fact HCI often involve prolonged screen-time and repetitive hand gestures. Being able to isolate the *direct* effects (if any) of ultrasound exposure is an ongoing relevant research goal.

3.3 Ear Defenders

Interaction designers and haptic developers (constantly tinkering to create their ideal application of ultrasound mid-air haptics!) are far more likely to encounter accidental exposure at higher SPL levels and/or durations then their intended users. To this end, it is helpful to establish what type of personal protective equipment (PPE) is best suited for attenuating ultrasound. Ear defenders are typically rated by their *simplified noise reduction* (SNR) specification (an average attenuation across the *audible* range of frequencies), for example, 3M Peltor (SNR=28 dB), Portwest PW40 (SNR=28 dB), and Laser-Lite ear plugs (SNR=35 dB).

Figure 4 shows the ultrasound (40 kHz) attenuation results from this small range of ear defenders. The best performance was achieved from a normal set of music headphones (Bose TP-1A) followed closely by ear plugs. Both the 3M Peltor and PW40 have similar PVC constructions which may be a factor for their considerable drop in SNR performance at 40 kHz. It is possible that the stiffer internal pads may not have adequately conformed to the HATS head. Further testing is certainly warranted, but these results highlight the fact that we cannot assume acoustic properties readily observed in the audible spectrum are applicable to ultrasound.

While all the ear defenders offer some level of protection, it is left to the reader to decide which they would rather wear.

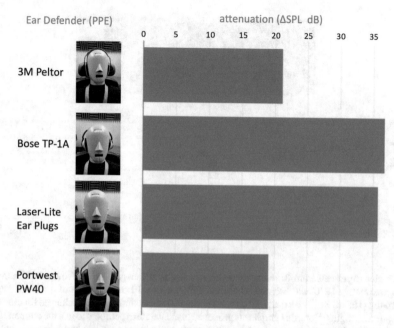

Fig. 4 Attenuation of 40 kHz ultrasound from various ear defenders/headphones. The best performing PPE are the Bose headphones and close second are the Laser-lite ear plugs. Both consists of a softer foam material compared to the harder plastic outer surfaces of the Peltor and PW40

3.4 Heating and Mechanical Effects

Hair and Skin

Heating on skin is mitigated due to the fact that ~99.9% of energy is reflected from the surface due to the acoustic impedance mismatch with air. The situation changes when an impedance matching layer is introduced; in nature, this takes on the form of small hairs/fur.

In an experiment involving a goat hair brush, an ultrasonic focal point (40 kHz, 155 dB SPL) was focussed and temperature increase measured (Pico USB TC 08 Thermocouple Data Logger) over time. Figure 5a shows the results for the 10 mm section (the hair length that resulted in the most dramatic temperature rise). The temperature increase was also sensitive to hair orientation and density. SPLs of more than 130 dB were required to observe any changes at all (Fig. 5b).

This suggests that hairs on arms and faces are unlikely to be involved in any significant heating phenomena. It also suggests that a hairy/fur-covered surface is an effective sound absorbing/dispersing material at the frequencies tested and could play a role in *ultra*-soundproofing applications. The temperature increase raises another concern with regard to animal safety, which will be discussed further in (Effects on Animals).

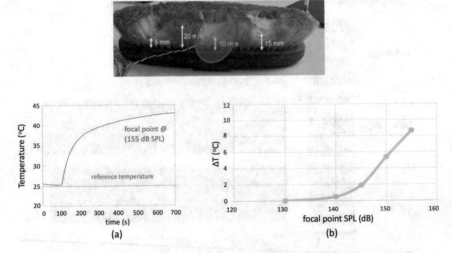

Fig. 5 Heating effects from 40 kHz ultrasound exposure on 10 mm goat hair. **a** Temperature increase of approximately 18^oC was achieved (baseline 25^oC) over a 10 min exposure of a mid-air haptic focal point (155 dB SPL, 40 kHz, z=20 cm). **b** Maximum temperature increase achieved for different focal point strengths. Note, this graph was produced in a separate experiment to (**a**); the temperatures changes at 155 dB do not correspond. The slightest change in hair orientation had a dramatic impact on peek temperature change and the extreme result of (**a**) was not readily repeatable

Eyes

Figure 6 shows the set-up and results from an initial experiment to detect corneal displacement from focussed airborne ultrasound. A haptic focal point (40 kHz, 155 dB SPL) is directed towards a sheep's eye, suspended in the wedge of an absorbent foam material. The eye is inserted with a catheter which is connected to a column of water; this replicates normal intra-ocular pressure (30 cm water $\equiv$ 22 mmHg). A laser Doppler vibrometer (LDV) (Polytec) measures velocity/displacement from pulsed ultrasound. Additionally, a linear AM chirp signal was also generated in order to observe any resonance frequencies of the eye.

A similar set-up to Fig. 6a incorporated thermocouples used for a separate experiment to measure the temperature change from prolonged exposure (see Fig. 6b).

The corneal deflection of the sheep's eye (25 μm) is comparable to that of applantion tonometry, an established technique used for diagnosing glaucoma (a condition that is characterised by abnormally high intra-ocular pressure). Applantion tonometry uses a calibrated puff of air, to flatten a small area of the cornea (as measured via a light sensor system); the force required is correlated to the internal pressure of the eye. A routine screening tool, this gentle 'poke' in the eye is not associated with deleterious effects on vision and may even have therapeutic effects (Schwartz et al. 2014).

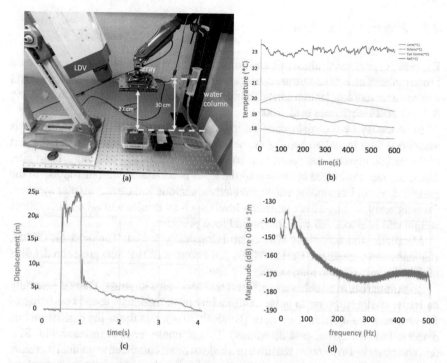

Fig. 6 Corneal displacement from focussed airborne ultrasound **a** Experimental set-up: (not shown) three thermocouples (Pico USB TC 08 Thermocouple Data Logger) were also used to log temperatures in the centre of the eye, the sclera and inside the lens. **b** Sheep eye temperatures during continuous exposure to 40 kHz ultrasound haptics feedback (155 dB SPL). The overall decreasing trend is likely due to cooling effects of acoustic streaming. **c** Input Stimulus 0.5s unmodulated pulse at 40 kHz (155 dB SPL). A delay of 0.5 s was used, so the array is emitting between time indexes (0.5s, 1s). **d** Spectrum of linear AM chirp response (sweep from 20–500 Hz). Two resonant peaks 30 Hz 50 Hz are clearly visible

Temperature changes (Fig. 6b) are negligible (they appear to even decrease, possibly due to acoustic streaming effects). Similar to bare skin, the surface of the eye presents a significant impedance mismatch with air.

Another consideration with respect to accidental eye exposure is the innate blink reflex which would limit exposure duration to a few hundred milliseconds; this is the safety argument behind the regulation of class 2 lasers (BS EN 60825-1).

4   Effects on Animals

Ultrasound is a term with anthropocentric origins. For many creatures in the animal kingdom (including household pets), ultrasound is clearly audible. For example, cats, rats and mice are able to detect ultrasonic frequencies as high as 60–100 kHz (Hefner and Hefner 1985, 2007; Neff and Hind 1955) while dogs are generally limited to approximately 45–50 kHz (Hefner 1983).

4.1 Physiological Effects

Exposure to persistent (ultrasonic and human audible) noise has been shown to have a broad range of effects on normal operation of the mammalian body. There are several extensive review articles that can be found in (Baumans and Castelhano-Carlos 2009; Sales et al. 1988; Turner et al. 2005).

In summary of the main conclusions, prolonged exposure to intense noise is associated with increased activity of the autonomic nervous system (ANS), the part of the nervous system that controls unconscious processes like breathing, heart rate, digestion, etc. Prolonged activation of the ANS is correlated with disruption to the gastrointestinal, immunological, reproductive, nervous and cardiovascular systems. Consequently, it may affect hormone levels such as insulin and adrenaline, affect weight and is associated with increased blood pressure.

Metabolic and behaviour effects are intrinsically linked; Turner et al. (2005), Baumans and Castelhano-Carlos (2009) and Broucek (2014) also present a detailed review on animal behaviour, subject to noise.

To summarise, most behaviour effects are associated with stress. There is generally an initial startle response to noise exhibited by most mammals tested consisting of freezing and fleeing from the source (Broucek 2014); this forms the basic principle discussed in (Ultrasonic pest deterrents). This response tends to increase with SPL and was observed to be more sensitive to a sudden onset compared to gradual increase.

There is little known about noise-induced hearing loss to animals as a result of *ultrasound* exposure. Most exposure studies involving animals have used them as proxies for humans; thus, only human audible frequencies were tested.

As already discussed, intense ultrasonic energy can produce harmful heating effects in extreme cases. There have been reports (Smagowska 2013) that a mouse can be killed from as little as 10 s exposure to a 20 kHz signal at 160 dB. Slightly less intense exposure to 18–20 kHz at 144 dB–155 dB can prove lethal after several minutes exposure and similar results have also been produced in guinea pigs and rabbits.

4.2 Ultrasonic Pest Deterrents

In a bid to exploit animal sensitivity (in conjunction with the human inability) to hear ultrasound, many manufactures have produced pest control devices based on ultrasound; an ultrasound-emitting device is positioned in a location in the garden or home that emits ultrasound, typically at +100 dB, in order to drive away rats, cockroaches, rabbits, and virtually any unwanted pests. There are many parameters to consider frequency and noise types, power output and effective range and the type of creatures being targeted.

There has been much criticism over manufacturers' bold claims with regard to efficacy and specificity in targeting of these devices. This has even led to the US Federal Trade Commission to issue a warning against the industry (Commission 2001).

The primary concern is the lack of evidence to support the manufacturers' claims. Indeed, there have been several studies showing the lack of efficacy of ultrasound as a pest deterrent:

A report from (Algers 1984) concluded the ultrasonic deterrent devices were not suitable for rodent control on farms owing to the lack of efficacy and to the disturbance to stock animals.

In Greaves and Rowe (1969), rodents did notice ultrasound but ultimately were not deterred when searching for food. However, such devices could potentially be used to steer pests to poisoned bait. In laboratory condition where devices emitted very high SPL (>120 dB), the habituation of rodents to the noise could partially be attributed to induced deafness (either temporary or permanent).

A review of six commercial devices was conducted in Shumake (1983): over-all rapid habituation leads to no discernible effect after 3–7 d. As already mentioned, ultrasound waves are highly directional and attenuate quickly, as discussed in (Chap. "Ultrasound Exposure in Mid-Air Haptics"); it is hypothesised that many animals can locate the noise source and avoid it if they want to.

Not all reports suggest the pest repellency of ultrasound noise is unjustified. In a study to test the effects of ultrasound noise on canines, several commercial and modified commercial devices were tested on 14 dogs (Blackshaw et al. 1990). Specifications varied from 60–120 dB SPL (at 1 m) and frequencies spanning both human audible and ultrasonic ranges as high as 55 kHz. Behavioural indicators (ears pricked, aversion) were observed in only the highest powered modified device (17.5–55 kHz sweep 118–120 dB at 1 m) in 13 out of 14 subjects. Other devices were concluded to have little or no effect. It was not established if long-term habituation could occur.

Schemes that targeted specific species by matching them with species-related calls showed improved results. A review of pest deterrent technologies for wildlife control (M.Bomford and O'Brien 1990) reported that distress calls and predator mimicking have been shown to be effective. Examples include repelling starlings with simulated bird of prey noises and using whale songs to deter seals. Generally, louder is more effective and broadband noise has proven better than pure tones.

4.3 Additional Considerations

Does this mean that an ultrasound mid-air haptic device also doubles as a pest deterrent? Because of the tonal qualities of the noise, the intermittent use (likely indoors), it is doubtful that the technology would pose a serious threat to nature.

The type of exposure from haptic feedback devices are not likely to mimic the intentional exposure described in the above sections. Moreover, the movable pinna of many mammalian species may offer additional noise avoidance protection. The main consideration would be to avoid using ultrasound mid-air haptics in an area where a animals/pets are confined and cannot freely escape unwanted exposure. HCI designers will need to consider applications that could involve proximity to animals with particular emphasis on pets.

5   Concluding Remarks

Responsible HCI designers should be aware and considerate of the possible undesirable effects of ultrasound exposure from mid-air haptics devices. By selecting an
appropriate application environment and providing clear and accurate safety advise
to users, the risk of harmful effects can be mitigated.

Most of the discussion presented in this chapter is based on the assumption that
ultrasound mid-air haptic devices operate at ~ 155 dB SPL and produce exposures
(at the ear) in the comparatively modest range of ~ 115–125 dB SPL.

Of course, as developers constantly search for new applications and inevitably
drive up the power, attention should be focussed on the implications for safety (and
not just performance). As a basic example, ensuring that haptics 'engage' only when
a hand is present (using hand tracking technology) reduces exposure considerably.

Future research into ultrasound exposure requires time and carefully planned
steps. It is not ethical to expose an individual to potentially damaging levels of
ultrasound that could induce TTS. Indeed, much of the data from the mid-twentieth
century was derived from *observational* studies of workforces. The strategy for
investigating the safety of mid-air haptics lies with establishing the *existence* and
severity of any subjective or audiological effects at 'typical' exposure levels and
incrementally push towards higher SPL. As technological advancements hopefully
improve to reduce exposure levels, the safety data will meet at a happy medium.

Most international guidelines for ultrasound safety are centred around the avoidance of *any* subjective effects from noise exposure. This may seem somewhat stringent, especially when we consider the harmful effects from other consumer devices
due to prolonged screen-time, muscle fatigue and joint pain from typing, etc. In these
instances, consumers rather than manufacturers are expected to follow warning label
advice and bear some responsibility for proper use of the device. It is possible that
future regulation of airborne ultrasonic devices may evolve in the same fashion.
Many first time users of ultrasound mid-air haptics are blown away by the seemingly
magical effect of touch without actually touching anything. The challenge will be to
inform the public on the how to operate these devices effectively and safely.

References

Acton W (1974) The effect of airborne ultrasound on humans. Ultrasonics :124–128
Algers B (1984) A note on behavioural responses of farm animals to ultrasound. Appl Animal
    Behav Sci :387–391
Baumans V, Castelhano-Carlos M (2009) The impact of light, noise, cage cleaning and in-house
    transport on welfare and stress of laboratory rats. Lab Animals :311–327
Blackshaw J, Cook G, Harding P, Day C, Bates W, Rose J, Bramham D (1990) Aversive responses
    of dogs to ultrasonic, sonic and flashing light units. Appl Animal Behav Sci :1–8
Broucek J (2014) Effect of noise on performance, stress, and behaviour of animals. Slovak J Animal
    Sci :111–123

Carcagno S, DiBattista A, Plack CJ (2019) Effects of high-intensity airborne ultrasound exposure on behavioural and electrophysiological measures of auditory function. Acta Acustica United Acustica. https://doi.org/10.3813/AAA.919395

Commission FT (2001) ftc warns manufacturers and retailers ultrasonic pest control. www.ftc.gov/news-events/press-releases/2001/05/ftc-warns-manufacturers-and-retailers-ultrasonic-pest-control

DiBattista A (2019) The effect of 40khz ultrasonic noise exposure on human hearing. In: 23rd International Congress on Acoustics (ICA). http://pub.dega-akustik.de/ICA2019/data/articles/001374.pdf

Dobie RA, Hemel SV (2004) Hearing loss: determining eligibility for social security benefits. National Academies Press. https://www.ncbi.nlm.nih.gov/books/NBK207834/

Fletcher MD, Jones SL, White PR, Dolder CN, Leighton TG, Lineton B (2018) Effects of very high-frequency sound and ultrasound on humans. part ii: a double- blind randomized provocation study of inaudible 20-khz ultrasound. J Acoustical Soc Am. https://doi.org/10.1121/1.5063818

Greaves J, Rowe F (1969) Responses of comensal rodent populations to an ultrasound generator. J Wildlife Manage :409–417

Hefner H (1983) Hearing in large and small dogs: absolute thresholds and size of the tympanic membrane. Behav Neurosci :310–318

Hefner H, Hefner R (1985) Hearing range of the domestic cat. Hearing Res :85–88

Hefner H, Hefner R (2007) Hearing ranges of laboratory animals. J Am Assoc Lab Animal Sci :11–13

Huang S, Dong W, Olson E (2012) Subharmonic distortion in ear canal pressure and intracochlear pressure and motion. J Assoc Res Otolaryngol :461–471

Kühler R, Weichenberger M, Bauer M, Hensel J, Brühl R, Ihlenfeld A, Ittermann B, Sander T, Kühn S, Koch C (2019) Does airborne ultrasound lead to activation of the auditory cortex? Biomed Eng-Biomed Tech :481–493. https://doi.org/10.1515/bmt-2018-0048

Lawton B (2013) Exposure limits for airborne sound of very high frequency and ultrasonic frequency. https://eprints.soton.ac.uk/351902/

Leighton T (2016) Are some people suffering as a result of increasing mass exposure of the public to ultrasound in air? In: Proceedings Royal Society. https://doi.org/10.1098/rspa.2015.0624

Lenhardt M (2008) Airborne ultrasonic standards for hearing protection. In: 9th International congress on noise as a public health problem (ICBEN). http://icben.ethz.ch/2008/PDFs/Lenhardt.pdf

MBomford, O'Brien P (1990) Sonic deterrents in animal damage control: a review of device tests and effectiveness. Wildlife Soc Bull :411–422

MBomford, O'Brien P (2019) Airborne ultrasound noise at workplaces. In: Proceedings of the 23rd international congress on acoustics, pp 6333–6337

Neff W, Hind J (1955) Auditory thresholds of the cat. J Acoustical Soc Am :480–483

Parrack H (1966) Effect of air-borne ultrasound on humans. Int Audiol :294–308

Sales G, Wilson K, Spencer K, Milligan S (1988) Environmental ultrasound in laboratories and animal houses: a possible cause for concern in the welfare and use of laboratory animals. Lab Animals :369–375

Schwartz D, Samples J, Korosteleva O (2014) Therapeutic ultrasound for glaucoma: clinical use of a low-frequency low-power ultrasound device for lowering intraocular pressure. J Therapeutic Ultrasound

Shumake S (1983) Electronic rodents repellent devices: a review of efficacy test protocols and regulatory actions. In: Great plains wildlife damage control workshop

Smagowska B (2013) Effects of ultrasounic noise on the human body—a bibliographic rerview. Int J Occupational Safety Ergon :195–202

Smagowska B (2013) Effects of ultrasounic noise on the human body—a bibliographic review. Int J Occupational Safety Ergon :195–202. https://doi.org/10.1080/10803548.2013.11076978

The Open University (2020) Openlearn: Hearing. https://www.open.edu/openlearn/science-maths-technology/biology/hearing/content-section-0?intro=1

Turner J, Parrish J, Huges L, Toth L, Caspary D (2005) Hearing in laboratory animals: strain differences and nonauditory effects of noise. Comparitive Med :12–23
UK Civil Aviation Authority (2020) Aircraft Noise and Health Effects - a six monthly update. https://publicapps.caa.co.uk/docs/33/CAP1883_March2020.pdf
Wiernicki C, Karoly W (1985) Ultrasound: biological effects and industrial hygiene concerns. Am Ind Hygeine Assoc J :488–496

Ultrasound Exposure in Mid-Air Haptics

Takayuki Hoshi

Abstract In this chapter, we review the effects of exposure of the human body to ultrasonic waves and discuss the tolerance sound pressure levels reported in the literature. We then consider the theory of nonlinear absorption and discuss its implications for the optimal safety distance that should be maintained from ultrasonic devices during operation. The aims of this chapter are to provide insight into what is currently known about the safety of mid-air ultrasound and to highlight areas where more research is needed.

1 Introduction

Ultrasound haptic devices use high-intensity ultrasound, typically focused to produce one or more "focal points." The sound pressure level (SPL, with a reference value of 20 μPa) at the center of a typical ultrasonic focal point is approximately 140 dB or more. Therefore, if users stand near ultrasound haptic devices and are exposed to ultrasonic waves daily, it is necessary to be familiar with how these waves and their intense SPL affect the human body.

Tolerance to ultrasound exposure has often been debated. Currently, an SPL of 110 dB is internationally recommended as the acceptable tolerance level regardless of the frequency of the ultrasound (Health Canada 1991). However, it has been pointed out that this tolerance level is based on a limited amount of research papers published in the mid-1900s and should be revisited, owing to lack of evidence and recent technological developments (Leighton 2016). Further, owing to the extent of technical knowledge available at that time, tolerance was discussed based on the observations and experimental results obtained for lower-frequency ultrasound devices, producing approximately 20 kHz. In contrast, the ultrasound devices used for mid-air haptics operate at higher frequencies of approximately 40 kHz. Therefore, the manner in which such high-frequency waves affect the human body may differ from those reported for lower-frequency waves.

T. Hoshi (✉)
Pixie Dust Technologies, Inc., Tokyo, Japan
e-mail: star@pixiedusttech.com

This chapter presents a bird's-eye view of the effects of ultrasound on the human body and is complementary to the discussions of Chap. "Safety of High-Intensity Ultrasound". The focus of this chapter, however, is on critically reviewing the references cited in the guidelines provided by Health Canada (1991), a report that later became the basis for several other guideline reports on ultrasound exposure. The surveyed studies in Health Canada (1991) were the publication year, upper/lower bounds of the frequencies reported, and the contents of each reference. Through this review, we demonstrate that the current tolerance guidelines are lacking in evidence, and that most references pertain to low-frequency ultrasounds at approximately 20 kHz.

In this chapter, we also review more recent reports (Wakabayashi et al. 2020; Nagatani et al. 2021; Ito and Nakagawa 2013; Carcagno et al. 2019; Batista 2019; Mizutani et al. 2019; Howard et al. 2019; Takahashi et al. 2020) on higher-frequency ultrasound at approximately 40 kHz and make a comparison table of the perception thresholds of the various effects, relevant to mid-air haptics. Based on this comparison, we recognize what happens when the SPL exceeds each threshold and discuss the interim tolerance.

In the second part of this chapter, we discuss the relationship between the tolerance SPL and distance from an ultrasonic focal point (e.g., the distance between a user and an ultrasound haptics device). It is known that the higher the frequency of the ultrasonic waves, the faster it attenuates in air. Even when geometric spreading, absorption, and scattering effects are ignored, nonlinear absorption occurs for high-intensity ultrasound waves. Based on this, theoretical derivations suggest that a saturation effect occurs, indicating the existence of an upper limit in SPL as a function of distance from the focal point, regardless of the SPL at the center of the focal point. We present some experimental results supporting this observation.

2 Conventional Exposure Tolerance

2.1 Safety Standards

Safety standards are relevant to the ultrasound haptics community because of the importance of avoiding harmful effects of prolonged ultrasound exposure. Several national guidelines and research reports regarding the tolerances of ultrasound exposure are currently available. However, many of these are reprints of past reports and review papers (Leighton 2016). The concept of safety standards, on which these guidelines are based, can be classified into two categories: the range in which ultrasonic perception does not occur is regarded as safe, and the range in which hearing is not excessively fatigued is regarded as safe. Readers should also refer to Chap. "Safety of High-Intensity Ultrasound" for further discussions on safety standards relating to ultrasound haptics.

The Safety Standard of Health Canada (1991) can be cited as a representative example of safety in the range where ultrasonic perception does not occur (i.e., the user feels nothing from the emitted ultrasonic waves). Several safety standards refer back to this one, including that of the US Occupational Safety and Health Administration (OSHA) (2013). It discusses the effects of ultrasonic radiation on the human body, carefully citing early (mid-1900s) research. Lawton (2001) summarized supplementary information about these previous papers. The Safety Standard of Health Canada (1991) identified three effects of ultrasonic waves on the human body: "rising skin temperature," "change in auditory threshold," and "perception of tinnitus, dizziness, and so on." Based on these effects, they recommended a maximum permissible SPL of 110 dB from the perceptual threshold of the ultrasound.

It is often assumed that if ultrasound does not cause excessive hearing fatigue, then it is safe for people to be exposed to. This notion is implemented in the safety standards of the International Radiation Protection Association International Non-ionizing Radiation Committee (INIRC/IPRA), currently known as the International Non-ionizing Radiation Protection Committee (ICNIRP) (International Radiation Protection Association (IRPA) 1984). It sets the SPL of 110 dB as a permissible value for workers who are exposed for 8 hours a day, 5 days a week. The report also assesses that a prolonged and continuous ultrasound energy exposure for the general public can be calculated by subtracting 10 dB from the safety limit set by ICNIRP, that is, the SPL of 100 dB, to account for environmental uncertainties outside of the working environment.

Collectively, these works provide baseline recommendations for safe exposure to ultrasound.

2.2 Frequency of Ultrasound

As far as the Safety Standard of Health Canada (1991) is concerned, most references cited as the basis for conventional tolerance reported the effects at approximately 20 kHz, with very few references discussing higher frequencies, e.g., 40 kHz. However, various standards set tolerances up to frequencies as high as 50–100 kHz. It is suspected that they may have extended the known tolerance set at approximately 20 kHz to higher frequencies, without sufficient evidence that this can be done in a valid way. This has not been pointed out until recently as far as we know and has implications for mid-air haptics devices that typically use frequencies of 40 kHz.

To address this concern effectively, we investigate the Safety Standard of Health Canada (1991) in detail and discuss the effects of airborne ultrasounds on the human body as reported in the following sections of the standard:

Section 2.2: Airborne Ultrasound (lead sentences)
Section 2.2.1: Heating and Cavitation
Section 2.2.2: Auditory Effects—Hearing and Physiological
Section 2.2.3: "Subjective" Effects
Section 4.2.1: Human Exposure Limits.

The other sections of Health Canada (1991) discuss the effects of contact exposure or protective measures for airborne ultrasound exposure and are therefore not relevant to mid-air haptics.

We have compiled a list of research papers referenced in Health Canada (1991) and summarized their studied frequency range in Table 1.

Note that some references in Table 1 include the audible range, whereas some do not report their own observational or experimental results. The values of the latter type of references are written as "not available" (N/A). We could not source certain reference materials by online search, presumably because those papers can only be found in print. The frequency values from such references are marked as "to be confirmed" (TBC).

Certain references report survey data on factory workers who use ultrasonic instruments such as ultrasonic cleaners, and their frequency range is specified as "ultrasonic instruments (over 20 kHz)" but do not specify further. The frequency characteristics of the ultrasonic instruments were measured in Parrack (1966), Acton and Carson (1967), Crabtree and Forshaw (1977). Their noise included frequencies up to 40 kHz ultrasounds, and the SPL of the ultrasound waves did not exceed 120 dB, usually less than 100 dB, in the 1/3-octave or octave bands. It should be noted that in such situations, the contribution of ultrasound waves to the effects on the human body is unclear and easy to misunderstand as noted by Acton and Carson (1967):

> The various subjective effects were observed in persons exposed to high levels of upper audio frequency noise produced as a by-product of industrial processes using ultrasonics. When the high-audio frequency noise from the larger washers was attenuated by 17 to 19 dB, but the fundamental ultrasonic frequency of 20 kHz was attenuated only by 10 dB, these effects were completely abated. A machine operating at 16 kHz, but without any intense low-ultrasonic frequencies in the noise (small washer), also produced these effects. Furthermore, the laboratory experiments show that whereas the SPL of 101 dB at 20 kHz (inaudible) produced no subjective effects, the SPL of 78 dB at 16 kHz produced effects in two subjects to whom it was audible. This seems to indicate, contrary to what has been claimed previously (Skillern 1965), that the high-frequency audible noise was, in fact, responsible for these subjective effects.
>
> (Note: The historical unit kc/s was used in the original text, but we have converted it to kHz for the sake of readability.)

It should therefore be noted that phenomena and perceptions that occur at 20 kHz do not necessarily also occur in higher ultrasonic bands. Despite this, only two studies have investigated pure tones at a frequency of approximately 40 kHz [37 kHz (Parrack 1966) and 40 kHz (Herbertz 1984)]. Furthermore, in the ultrasonic frequency range, the measured SPLs can often deviate by several decibels depending on the protection grids used on the microphone (Barrera-Figueroa 2019). Most references in Table 1 do not provide such details of their measurement, e.g., microphone model number and the measurement setup. Finally, the ultrasonic exposure studies referenced in Health Canada (1991) mostly use the 1/3-octave band to measure ultrasound SPL. In the case of mid-air haptics, however, a pure tone ultrasound frequency is used. These are just some of the limitations and difficulties faced when comparing safety standards, guidelines, previous studies that mix audible and ultrasonic frequencies in industrial settings, and the emerging use case of mid-air haptics.

Table 1 Summary of the references cited in the Safety Standard of Health Canada (1991)

#	Section	Topic	Reference	Year	Lower freq. (Hz)	Higher freq. (Hz)	Target animal
1	2.2	Ultrasonic sickness	Davis	1948	N/A	N/A	Human
2	2.2.1	Heating	Neppiras	1980	N/A	N/A	N/A
3	2.2.1	Heating	Allen et al.	1948	20,000	20,000	Mouse, insect
4	2.2.1	Heating	Von Gierke	1949	100	12,000	Human, rat
5	2.2.1	Heating	Von Gierke et al.	1952	400	6000	Rat
6	2.2.1	Heating	Parrack	1966	17,000	37,000	Human (ca 1950)
7	2.2.1	Heating	Danner et al.	1954	18,000	20,000	Mouse
8	2.2.1	Heating	Acton	1974	N/A	N/A	Human
9	2.2.2	Auditory effect	Dobroserdov	1967	20,600	20,600	Human
10	2.2.2	Auditory effect	Knight	1968	Ultrasonic instruments (over 20 kHz)		Human
11	2.2.2	Auditory effect	Acton and Carson	1967	Ultrasonic instruments (over 20 kHz)		Human
12	2.2.2	Auditory effect	Grigor'eva	1966	20,000	20,000	Human
13	2.2.2	Auditory effect	Grzesik and Pluta	1983	Ultrasonic instruments (over 20 kHz)		Human
14	2.2.2	Auditory effect	Grzesik and Pluta	1986	Ultrasonic instruments (over 20 kHz)		Human
15	2.2.2	Auditory effect	Grzesik and Pluta	1980	TBC	TBC	Human
16	2.2.3	Subjective effect	Skillern	1965	Ultrasonic instruments (over 20 kHz)		Human
17	2.2.3	Subjective effect	Acton	1968	Ultrasonic instruments (over 20 kHz)		Human
18	2.2.3	Subjective effect	Crabtree and Forshaw	1977	Ultrasonic instruments (over 20 kHz)		Human

(continued)

Table 1 (continued)

#	Section	Topic	Reference	Year	Lower freq. (Hz)	Higher freq. (Hz)	Target animal
19	2.2.3	Subjective effect	Herman and Powell	1981	N/A	N/A	Human
20	2.2.3	Subjective effect	Acton	1975	N/A	N/A	Human
21	2.2.3	Subjective effect	Herbertz and Grunter	1981	TBC	TBC	Human
22	2.2.3	Subjective effect	Herbertz	1984	8000	40,000	Human
23	2.2.3	Subjective effect	Von Gierke	1950	N/A	N/A	Human, guinea pig
24	2.2.3	Subjective effect	Dallos and Linnell	1966	1000	10,000	*Chinchilla*, guinea pig
25	4.2.1	Exposure limit	auf der Maur	1985	TBC	TBC	Human
26	4.2.1	Exposure limit	United States Air Force	1976	N/A	N/A	Human
27	4.2.1	Exposure limit	International Radiation Protection Association (IRPA)	1984	N/A	N/A	Human

The upper and lower-frequency bounds are filled when the reference reports its own observational or experimental results. It should be noted that these frequency bounds are the same when the reference pertains to a single pure tone. "Not available" (N/A) means that the values were not mentioned or the papers did not report their own results, and "to be confirmed" (TBC) means that the values were not confirmed because we could not source the papers by online search.

2.3 Historical Background

Many standards mention "rising skin temperature (heating)," "change in auditory threshold (auditory effect)," and "perception of tinnitus, dizziness, and so on (subjective effect)" as the key dimensions that one needs to consider when measuring the effects on the human body of ultrasound exposure. The historical background and discussion of these effects can be found in the references cited in Health Canada (1991).

Figure 1 presents a tally histogram showing the number of references (as listed in Table 1) for every five years of publication, thus offering a chronolectal perspective of the different research trends. These articles can be grouped into three periods: the first period covers 1945–1954, when ultrasonic sickness was first noticed through high-intensity ultrasounds, and the thermal death of small animals was studied. The second period covers 1965–1969, when subjective effects and hearing loss were

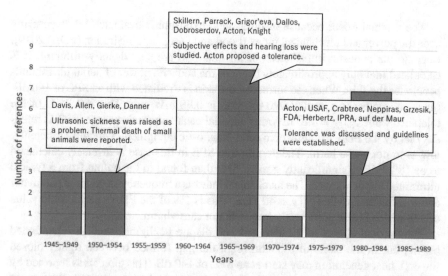

Fig. 1 Histogram depicting the numbers of references cited in the sections that discuss ultrasound exposure tolerance. Historically, there were three categories: (1) ultrasonic sickness and thermal death, (2) subjective effects and hearing loss, and (3) tolerance and guidelines

intensively studied. The third period covers 1975–1989, when tolerance levels were discussed based on research and multiple organizations determined interim exposure limits.

3 Perceptual/Harmful Thresholds

In this section, we review the effects of ultrasound exposure on the human body and list their thresholds. We refer to both the references cited in the Safety Standard of Health Canada (1991) and more recent reports on this topic.

3.1 Tactile Sensation (Heat)

When ultrasonic waves are applied to the skin, some of their energy is absorbed and converted into heat. When the temperature of the skin rises because of the heat, a sense of warmth can occur to some extent. In the field of medical engineering, ultrasonic waves in the megahertz range produce notable thermal effects on skin, whereas ultrasonic waves in the kilohertz range (i.e., for mid-air haptics devices) mostly produce mechanical effects (Sussman and Bates-Jensen 2012). Therefore, the generation of heat at 40 kHz is expected to be negligible.

The thermal effect because of ultrasound exposure is evaluated by considering acoustic power and mechanical index (Food and Drug Administration (FDA) 2019). Because the acoustic impedances of air and skin are significantly different, it is calculated that only approximately 0.1% of the acoustic power of aerial ultrasounds penetrates the skin. When the surface of the skin is irradiated with an SPL of 160 dB, the sound power transmitted into the skin is 0.98 mW/cm^2. This is 1.35‰ of the tolerance value $I_{SPTA} = 720$ mW/cm^2 (spatial peak temporal average (SPTA) intensity) set by the FDA for ultrasonic echo diagnostic equipment, which is sufficiently low as to not cause harm. The permissible SPL in this case is inversely calculated to be 188.7 dB, a significantly greater SPL than found in the output from a typical ultrasound haptics device. The mechanical index is a frequency-dependent parameter and is calculated to be 0.019 at 40 kHz. This is 1% of the FDA's permissible value of 1.9, which is also sufficiently low as to not cause harm.

The thermal effects of 40 kHz and 160 dB are negligibly small, as mentioned before, but in the clefts of the skin (e.g., the gap formed between tightly closed fingers), heat generation may start at an SPL of 140 dB. This effect was reported by Acton (1974). Although some of the details in that study are unknown, the chosen ultrasound frequency seems to be 20 kHz, considering the historical background and context for that work. It seems unlikely that an ultrasound haptics device would lead to excessive heat, as that work suggests may be possible. Ultrasound haptic devices use a different ultrasound frequency, and while the SPL of an ultrasound focal point often exceeds that reported threshold SPL of 140 dB, anecdotal evidence from the ultrasound haptics community suggests that burns or other negative thermal effects have not been experienced or reported.

With respect to the thermal effect, it has been reported that mice have died because of ultrasonic waves (Danner et al. 1954). The entire bodies of hairless mice were exposed to ultrasounds at 22 kHz with an SPL of 162 dB, and they died after 40 min continuous exposure, owing to a 15–20 °C increase in rectal temperature. It was also observed that the rectal temperature of haired mice was higher because the hair acted as an impedance-matching layer. Based on these results, it was estimated that a human could be killed by ultrasounds with an SPL of 180 dB (Parrack 1966). However, it should be noted that it is unlikely that such a strong ultrasonic field can ever cover the entire human body. Moreover, even if a part of the skin generates some heat, the heat spreads throughout the other body parts and the core body temperature does not increase. Therefore, it is unlikely that ultrasound exposure from a mid-air haptics device would cause human death.

The use of high-intensity 40 kHz ultrasound irradiation on mice has been proposed for wound healing (Wakabayashi et al. 2020). The irradiation was local (approximately on a circular area of diameter 9 mm, hairless), and the ultrasounds were modulated by a 10-Hz rectangular wave with an irradiation time of 60 min. The applied acoustic power $2I = 5.1$ W/cm^2 (the coefficient 2 multiplied by the incident acoustic power I implies the summation of the incident and reflected waves), and the incident SPL was calculated as 164.5 dB. The temperature of the surface of the skin changed from 27.8 to 28.6 °C, that is, the temperature change caused by the modulated ultrasounds on the surface of the mouse's skin was less than 1 °C after

60 min of irradiation. This result is in stark contrast to that of Danner et al. (1954), mostly due to the difference in frequency and focused exposure.

3.2 Auditory (Threshold Shift)

Hearing loss/threshold shift is caused by auditory fatigue and is classified into temporal threshold shift (TTS) and permanent threshold shift (PTS). TTS has been reported to be associated with ultrasound exposure. TTS in the audible band was produced when people were exposed to sound/ultrasounds of 17–37 kHz at an SPL of 148–154 dB, and recovery from the shift was rapid and complete (Parrack 1966). However, no detailed data or explanations are available, and it is not known which SPL was the threshold value of the TTS at 37 kHz. Here, we consider the lower SPL of 148 dB, to be on the safe side.

3.3 Auditory (Hearing)

In the following discussion, we use the term "hearing" to describe the subjective auditory perception of ultrasounds. It includes the sensation caused by changes in the atmospheric pressure and could probably be related to the sensation expressed in Leighton (2016) as an "uncomfortable feeling of pressure in the ears." Because it is difficult to distinguish among these perceptions in a perceptual threshold experiment, they are often treated as belonging to the same category for convenience.

There are no hair cells corresponding to the ultrasonic frequencies in the cochlear basement membrane of the inner ear. Therefore, ultrasonic frequencies are not included in the human audible range making it very unlikely that these frequencies are perceived through the normal auditory mechanism. However, even in such a situation, it is known that high-intensity ultrasounds create the sensation that high-frequency audible sound exists. The perceived frequency of this effect was determined through a pitch-matching experiment and found to be 11–13 kHz for participants in their twenties (Nagatani et al. 2021). The experiment was conducted using 40 kHz at 140 dB. Such an effect has also been reported in bone-conducted ultrasounds using a contact-type ultrasonic transducer (Ito and Nakagawa 2013). It is speculated that exposure to high-intensity airborne ultrasounds may have an effect similar to bone conduction, although there is a difference between air conduction and bone conduction.

A recent study reported that ultrasounds could not be heard at 40 kHz and 120 dB (Carcagno et al. 2019), and that no auditory brainstem response was observed, indicating that no psychological or physiological response can occur. The tested SPL of 120 dB was determined by a preliminary study on ultrasound exposure using an ultrasound-based mid-air haptic device under typical usage conditions (Batista 2019).

To the best of our knowledge, there is only a lone report regarding the threshold SPL of hearing of 40 kHz ultrasounds, which was at 142 dB (Herbertz 1984). Further follow-up tests are required, but it is speculated that there may be perceptual thresholds around these SPLs.

It has been reported that airborne ultrasounds can be heard not only through air conduction (that is, by the ears) but also through bone conduction (that is, by the body) (Mizutani et al. 2019). As mentioned in Sect. 3.1, the acoustic impedances of air and skin are significantly different allowing just 0.1% of the acoustic power of airborne ultrasounds to penetrate the skin. If that acoustic energy penetrates deep enough and is powerful enough, then bone-conducted ultrasonic perception of airborne ultrasound is a possibility. The reported perceptual threshold SPLs, the lowest among the experimental results, are 167.0 dB for the cheeks beside the nose and lower jaw without modulation, 167.3 dB for the outer corners of the eyes with amplitude modulation (AM), and 166.3 dB for the cheeks beside the nose with lateral modulation (LM).

3.4   Tactile Sensation (Pressure, Vibration, and Airflow)

Ultrasound-based mid-air haptic devices apply acoustic radiation pressure on the surface of the skin, which is a nonlinear effect of high-intensity ultrasonic waves (Iwamoto et al. 2008; Hoshi et al. 2010). When the amplitude of the ultrasonic wave is constant, a static pressure is generated. After the onset of ultrasonic wave irradiation is felt, the sensation is soon lost owing to adaptation. Vibrotactile stimulation can be achieved by modulating ultrasonic waves. The human tactile sensation is most sensitive to vibrations of about 200 Hz. In the previous study reported that the perceptual thresholds of the RMS sound pressure were 560 Pa for AM and 338 Pa for spatiotemporal modulation (STM) (Howard et al. 2019). These correspond to the SPLs of 148.9 and 144.6 dB, respectively. A different study reported that the perceptual threshold for AM was −28.5 dB, and the lateral modulation (LM) was −36.5 dB, with the maximum output of the ultrasonic phased array being 0 dB (Takahashi et al. 2020). In this study, the same phased array used in Mizutani et al. (2019) was employed, and its maximum SPL at the focal point was 171 dB. Assuming that the abovementioned relative values are for sound pressure, which is inversely proportional to the focal distance, 250 mm in Mizutani et al. (2019) and 200 mm in Takahashi et al. (2020), respectively, the maximum SPL is estimated to be 172.9 dB. Thus, the SPLs of 144.4 and 136.4 dB are the perceptual thresholds for AM and LM, respectively.

Perceptual thresholds on the forehead, outer corners of the eyes, cheeks, and lower jaw have also been reported (Mizutani et al. 2019). When a 200 Hz vibration stimulus was applied through AM, the SPL of approximately 170 dB was the perceptual threshold, which was almost unchanged at any site. For LM, the sensitivity was the highest on the cheek beside the nose, and an SPL of 166.5 dB was the reported perceptual threshold. In addition, acoustic streaming was generated simultaneously with the radiation pressure, which caused a sensation of air flowing on the skin. The sensitivity to this air flow is the highest in the lower jaw, and SPLs of 163.5 dB without modulation, 166.0 dB for AM, and 163.0 dB for LM have been reported as the perceptual thresholds.

4 Harmful Effect Thresholds Lower Boundaries

Table 2 summarizes the thresholds of the effects of 40 kHz ultrasounds on the human body, as derived from discussion in this chapter. Among these effects on the body, the ones to avoid and mitigate are **heat** and **TTS**, whose threshold SPLs for 40 kHz ultrasound are 140 and 148 dB, respectively. We note that there exists great variability between individuals with respect to their hearing and perceptual thresholds, so some individual variability can be expected. However, based on the discussions in this chapter, we conclude that there is no evidence that 40 kHz airborne ultrasound below a SPL of 140 dB poses risk to the human body. However, as a precaution, if a person experiences any discomfort, they should stop exposure regardless of the emitted SPL, to be on the safe side. Note that the threshold pressure refers to the appropriate point of exposure on the body (i.e., a safe SPL of 140 dB near the ear) rather than the peak output from an ultrasound device; the following section considers how SPL attenuates with distance.

These propositions are only provisional and should be reconsidered when new observational and experimental results are obtained. Furthermore, the interim tolerance of 140 dB is valid only for 40 kHz, and further work is required to improve our understanding of ultrasound exposure for other frequencies. The table also lists the thresholds of the effects of 20 kHz ultrasounds for comparison.

Table 2 Summary of effects of 20 and 40 kHz airborne ultrasounds on the human body

Effect		Body part	Threshold SPL (dB)	
			20 kHz	40 kHz
Tactile	Heat	Skin surface	159 (Acton 1974)	188.7 (estimated)
		Skin cleft	140 (Acton 1974)	140 (speculated)
	Vibration/airflow	Palm	N/A	136.4
		Face	N/A	163.0 (lower jaw)
Auditory	TTS	Ear	120 (Dobroserdov 1967)	148
	Hearing	Ear	100.3 (Herbertz 1984)	142.0
		Face	N/A	166.3 (cheek beside nose)

The perception thresholds of tactile sensation and hearing on the face have not been reported for 20 kHz and are expressed as "not available" (N/A)

5   Upper Boundary of Sound Pressure Level of Airborne Ultrasounds at User's Position

So far, we have investigated the SPL of ultrasound and its effects on the human body following published literature and safety standards. In this section, we investigate an attenuation effect that occurs to high-intensity ultrasound, therefore viewing the problem of ultrasonic safety and tolerance from the more relevant viewpoint of mid-air haptics where acoustic energy is focused to a point and decays geometrically with distance from the source. To that end, we present a theoretical upper bound of the SPL, a certain distance from the focal point, and also provide experimental data to support this.

5.1   Nonlinear Absorption

The instantaneous speed of sound is high when the sound pressure is high and low when the sound pressure is low. When the SPL is so high that this effect cannot be ignored, it is observed that the sound pressure waveform, which was initially a sine wave, becomes distorted as it propagates (Fig. 2a). This distortion effect generates harmonic components in the frequency domain, and the amplitude of the fundamental frequency component decreases proportionally to the amount of sound energy transitioning to the new harmonic components.

As the distortion of the waveform progresses, the waveform eventually rises almost vertically and turns into a shock wave (Fig. 2b). When it progresses further,

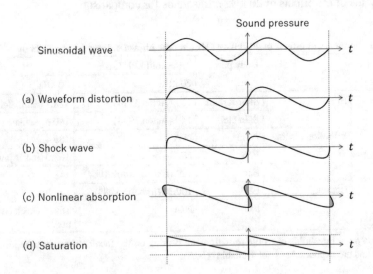

Fig. 2 Nonlinear propagation process of a sound wave (Hoshi and Ooka 2021)

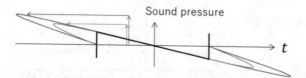

Fig. 3 Explanatory illustration of saturation. The higher the intensity, the greater the nonlinearly of the absorbed ultrasounds. Therefore, the amplitude of the sawtooth wave is maintained

nonlinear absorption occurs, in which the physically nonexistent part protruding from the vertical (gray area displayed in Fig. 2c) dissipates. That is, the acoustic energy of the entire waveform begins to decrease. Finally, a sawtooth wave is generated (Fig. 2d). Its amplitude approaches a constant steady state value even when the sound pressure of the original sine wave approaches infinity (Fig. 3).

5.2 Spherical Wave

In this section, we describe the application of the theory of nonlinear absorption to ultrasonic mid-air haptics. We assume that a single focal point generated by an ultrasonic phased array is similar to the source of sound of a spherical wave (Fig. 4) in the half-space in the direction of propagation. For simplicity, the directivity of the focal point as a sound source and the grating and side lobes are ignored in the following theoretical discussion.

The amplitude of the saturated sound pressure of the fundamental frequency component of a spherical wave $p_1(p_0)$ [Pa] is calculated using the following equation (Rudenko 1977):

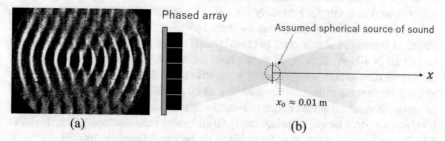

(a)   (b)

Fig. 4 Ultrasonic focal point generated by a phased array. **a** Schlieren photo of the focal point, taken by Katokoken Co., Ltd. The phased array was set on the left side and radiated ultrasounds in the right direction in this photo. Based on this observation, we approximate the focal point by a spherical source of sound, and the ultrasonic wave propagates like a spherical wave in the half-space in the direction of propagation. **b** Illustration of the setup scenario. As a rough value, the equivalent radius of the spherical source of sound is assumed to be 10 mm

Table 3 Values used in the equation

ρ	1.293 kg/m^3
c	340 m/s
β	1.2
ω	2.513×10^5 rad/s (i.e., 40 kHz)

$$p_1(p_0) = \begin{cases} \dfrac{2\rho c^3 J_1\left(\frac{\beta\omega p_0 x_0}{\rho c^3}\ln\frac{x}{x_0}\right)}{\beta\omega x \ln\frac{x}{x_0}}, & 0 \le x \le x_0 \exp\left(\frac{\rho c^3}{\beta\omega p_0 x_0}\right) \\ \dfrac{2\rho c^3 x_0}{\frac{\rho c^3 x}{p_0}+\beta\omega x_0 x \ln\frac{x}{x_0}}, & x_0 \exp\left(\frac{\rho c^3}{\beta\omega p_0 x_0}\right) \ll x \end{cases},$$

where ρ [kg/m^3] is the density of air, c [m/s] is the speed of sound in air, β is the nonlinear coefficient of air, and ω [rad/s] is the angular frequency of the ultrasound. The values of these quantities are specified in Table 3.

x_0 [m] is the radius of the spherical source of sound assumed to be 10 mm for simplicity (Fig. 4). p_0 [Pa] is the initial sound pressure at x_0. J_1 and ln are the Bessel function of the first kind of order one and the natural logarithm. When the initial sound pressure tends to infinity $p_0 \to \infty$, the limit value of $p_1(\infty)$ becomes

$$p_1(\infty) = \frac{2\rho c^3}{\beta\omega x} \frac{1}{\ln\frac{x}{x_0}}.$$

The same equation for the limit value was also derived in Blackstock (1964). It should be noted that Rudenko (1977) and Blackstock (1964) discuss particle velocity instead of sound pressure, but in this case, the particle velocity is converted into sound pressure assuming that the acoustic impedance is ρc.

This attenuation can be interpreted as the product of the geometric spreading effect $1/x$ and the nonlinear absorption effect $1/\ln(x/x_0)$. Figure 5 presents the limit value $p_1(\infty)$ as an upper boundary for a 40 kHz spherical wave and for reference, $p_1(p_0)$ for the initial sound pressures from 140 to 180 dB. The distance from the center of the sound source (i.e., the focal point) where the saturated SPL decreases to 140 dB is 40 cm. That is, no matter how strong the ultrasonic waves emitted by the source are the combined effect of geometric spreading and nonlinear absorption will ensure that the effective exposure SPL at 40 cm will not exceed the provisional permissible value proposed in this chapter. In most mid-air haptic use cases, the user is at least an arm's length (approximately 60 cm) away from the focal point, therefore the ultrasonic exposure at their face will likely be much less than 140 dB.

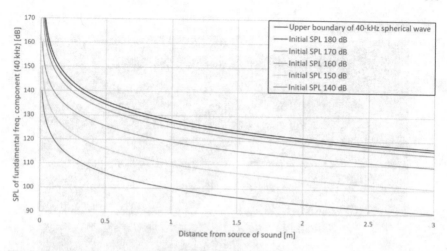

Fig. 5 Upper boundary of 40-kHz spherical wave and the distributions of SPL for the initial value from 140 to 180 dB

5.3 Experiments and Results

In this section, we present the results of the experimental measurement of ultrasound radiated from a focal point (Hoshi and Ooka 2021). The purpose is to verify the theoretically predicted upper boundary of high-intensity ultrasound.

The measurement was conducted using an ultrasonic phased array and an optical microphone in an anechoic chamber of dimensions $5 \times 5 \times 5$ m^3, which was not intended to absorb the ultrasonic frequency range but could block out any external environmental noise. The phased array was composed of 271 ultrasonic transducers (Nippon Ceramic Co., Ltd., T4010B4, 10 mm diameter) in a hexagonal arrangement on its surface. The transducers were driven such that a single focal point was generated at 200 mm away. The phased array was set on a turntable with an offset such that the focal point was generated at the center of rotation of the turntable (Fig. 6). To measure high-intensity ultrasound directly, an optical microphone (XARION Laser Acoustics GmbH, Eta100 Ultra, Freq. 10 Hz to 1 GHz, SPL 80–180 dB) was employed. It was calibrated using another calibrated microphone (ACO Co., Ltd., TYPE4158N, 1/4 in.) without a protection grid.

The fluctuation in the measurements was checked before the experiment. With the maximum output of the phased array, the sound pressure was measured 10 times at $x = 2$ m. The maximum SPL was 117.46 dB, and the minimum SPL was 111.48 dB (Fig. 7). Therefore, the fluctuation was calculated as ± 3 dB. Hereafter, we plot the average value of 10 measurements for each point, which is assumed to be close to the true value.

The distribution of sound pressure was measured in 5 cm increments at the output setting values of 1.0 and 0.1 times the maximum output of 160 dB. The results are presented in Fig. 8. It was confirmed that the measured values did not exceed

Phased array

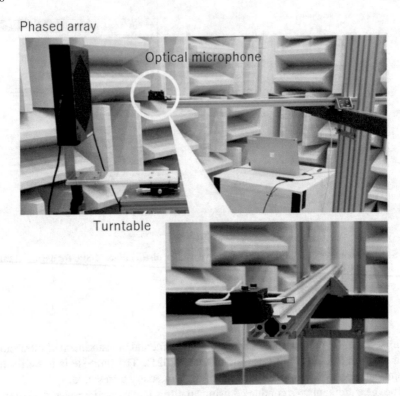

Fig. 6 Experimental setup in the anechoic chamber

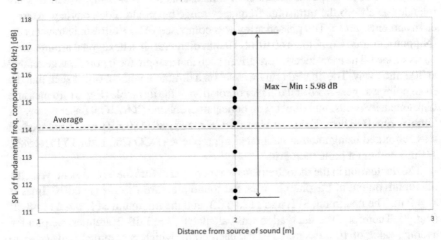

Fig. 7 Plot of 10 measurements carried out at 2 m with the maximum output of the phased array. The difference between the maximum and minimum values is approximately 6 dB

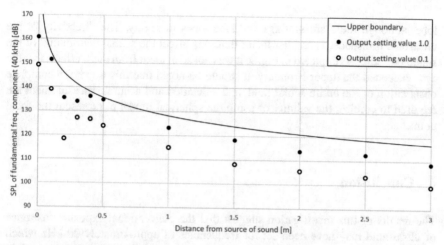

Fig. 8 Plot of the SPLs at the output setting values of 1.0 and 0.1. No data point exceeds the upper boundary specified by the theory

the upper boundary of the spherical wave. The irregular variation of the SPLs at a distance less than 0.5 m is probably due to the near field of the focal point.

The distribution of sound pressure was also measured in 5° increments from the front (0°) to the side (90°) at various distances, with respect to the maximum output. The results are presented in Fig. 9. The colors of the points represent the measurement angles. It was confirmed that the measured values for all the angles did not exceed the upper boundary of the spherical wave. This upper boundary was derived under the assumption that there is a single spherical source of sound, that is, only the main

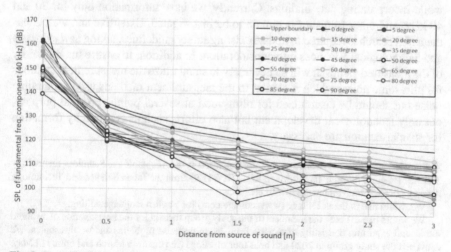

Fig. 9 Plot of the SPLs in the various directions from 0° to 90°. No data point exceeds the upper boundary specified by the theory

lobe, although there are gratings and side lobes in reality. The directivity of the ultrasonic transducer is another factor that may affect the spatial distribution of the sound pressure. As depicted in Fig. 9, it was not so evident from these effects that the SPL exceeded the upper boundary. It should be noted that this was not a complete observation of the entire sound field, and a detailed and accurate measurement are required to confirm the validity of using the spherical model to represent the focal point.

6 Conclusion

The results of this investigation suggest that the conventional exposure tolerance of ultrasound may have been set for frequencies of approximately 20 kHz which were commonly used at the time of enactment, and that different frequencies such as 40 kHz should be considered separately. A review of the related research indicated that hazards including heat in the skin gap (at a threshold SPL of 140 dB) and temporary hearing loss (at a threshold SPL of 148 dB) can be prevented when the SPL of 40 kHz ultrasounds is lower than 140 dB at the point of exposure to the body.

Furthermore, based on the theory of nonlinear absorption, it has become possible to connect the tolerance of ultrasonic exposure with the distance from the sound source. Theoretical predictions indicate that no matter how high the amplitude at the center of the 40 kHz ultrasonic focal point is, and exposures are limited to 140 dB at 40 cm away from the focal point. This theory was supported by experimental measurements presented in the previous section.

The safety and exposure tolerance of ultrasound should continuously be discussed while incorporating new findings. Currently, we have information only for 20 and 40 kHz, and other frequencies remain to be investigated. Extensive and well documented research is required to update existing safety guidelines, taking new evidence and technological advances into consideration. In addition, to ensure the reliability of the measured values, it will be necessary to standardize the measurement methods for ultrasonic noise, which is similar to the measurement methods used for audible noise but should be customized for ultrasound at several points. For that purpose, not only technological development but also efforts such as community formation for standardization are necessary.

Acknowledgements This work was partially supported by the Adaptable and Seamless Technology Transfer Program through Target-driven R&D (A-STEP) from the Japan Science and Technology Agency (JST) Grant Number AS3015012R.

We would like to thank Editage (www.editage.com) for English language editing.

We would like to thank the members of the study group formed for the investigation of airborne ultrasound exposure, consisting of experts from Japan on noise problems and/or ultrasonics. We convened the study group in 2020 and held four meetings (in person in March and online in May, July, and September). This chapter is based on the discussion carried out by this study group. Table 4 presents the member list of the study group, and Fig. 10 displays the group photo of the meeting held on March 4, 2020, in Tokyo, Japan.

Table 4 Member list of the study group convened on airborne ultrasound exposure

Name	Affiliation
Hironobu Takahashi	National Institute of Advanced Industrial Science and Technology
Ryuzo Horiuchi	National Institute of Advanced Industrial Science and Technology
Hiroyuki Shinoda	The University of Tokyo
Kentaro Nakamura	Tokyo Institute of Technology
Koki Sugita	Honda Electronics Co., Ltd.
Masahiro Toyoda	Honda Electronics Co., Ltd.
Mari Ueda	Kanagawa Institute of Technology
Masaaki Hiroe	Kobayasi Institute of Physical Research
Masato Morikawa	RION Co., Ltd.
Tetsuya Ozaki	RION Co., Ltd.
Seiji Nakagawa	Chiba University
Shinichi Sakai	Smart AE
Tomoo Kamakura	Smart AE/The University of Electro-Communications
Shuichi Harashima	Shinko Shoji Co., Ltd.
Suzuno Koga	Shinko Shoji Co., Ltd.
Takanobu Nishiura	Ritsumeikan University
Takayuki Hoshi	Pixie Dust Technologies, Inc.
Tomofumi Fukamiya	Pixie Dust Technologies, Inc.
Yoshiki Nagatani	Pixie Dust Technologies, Inc.

Fig. 10 Group photo of the first meeting of the study group convened on airborne ultrasound exposure

References

Barrera-Figueroa S (2019) Completing the traceability chain for airborne ultrasound. In: Proceedings of international congress on acoustics, pp 6381–6388

Batista AD (2019) The effect of 40 kHz ultrasonic noise exposure on human hearing. In: Proceedings of international congress on acoustics, pp 4805–4810

Blackstock DT (1964) On plane, spherical and cylindrical sound waves of finite amplitude in lossless fluids. J Acoust Soc Am 36:217–219

Carcagno S, Battista AD, Plack CJ (2019) Effects of high-intensity airborne ultrasound exposure on behavioural and electrophysiological measures of auditory function. Acta Acoust United Acust 105:1183–1197

Food and Drug Administration (FDA) (2019) Marketing clearance of diagnostic ultrasound systems and transducers

Health Canada (1991) Guidelines for the safe use of ultrasound. Part II—Industrial and commercial applications, safety code 24

Hoshi T, Ooka Y (2021) Experimental verification of nonlinear attenuation of airborne ultrasound. In: Proceedings of symposium on ultrasonic electronics (USE), vol 42, 3Pb4-2

Hoshi T, Takahashi M, Iwamoto T, Shinoda H (2010) Noncontact tactile display based on radiation pressure of airborne ultrasound. IEEE Trans Haptics 3(3):155–165

Howard T, Gallagher G, Lécuyer A, Pacchierotti C, Marchal M (2019) Investigating the recognition of local shapes using mid-air ultrasound haptics. In: Proceedings of IEEE world haptics conference (WHC), pp 503–508

Ito K, Nakagawa S (2013) Bone-conducted ultrasonic hearing assessed by tympanic membrane vibration in living human beings. Acoust Sci Technol 34(6):413–423

Iwamoto T, Tatezono M, Shinoda H (2008) Non-contact method for producing tactile sensation using airborne ultrasound. In: Haptics: perception, devices and scenarios. 6th International conference, Eurohaptics 2008 proceedings. Lecture notes in computer science, pp 504–513

Lawton BW (2001) Damage to human hearing by airborne sound of very high frequency or ultrasonic frequency. Health and safety executive contract research report, 343/2001

Leighton TG (2016) Are some people suffering as a result of increasing mass exposure of the public to ultrasound in air? Proc Roy Soc A 472:20150624

Mizutani S, Fujiwara M, Makino Y, Shinoda H (2019) Thresholds of haptic and auditory perception in midair facial stimulation. In: IEEE International symposium on haptic audio-visual environments and games (HAVE), pp 1–6

Nagatani Y, Ishikawa H, Hoshi T, Nakagawa S (2021) A preliminary study of pitch matching between 40-kHz air-conducted ultrasonic wave and air-conducted audible sound. In: Proceedings of symposium on ultrasonic electronics (USE), vol 42, 1Pa4-3

Occupational Health and Safety Administration (OSHA) (2013) Technical manual. Section III: Chapter 5 Noise. Appendix C—Ultrasound (updated)

Rudenko OV (1977) Theoretical foundations of nonlinear acoustics. Springer, Berlin

Sussman C, Bates-Jensen B (ed) (2012) Wound care—a collaborative practice manual for health professionals, 4th edn. Wolters Kluwer

Takahashi R, Hasegawa K, Shinoda H (2020) Tactile stimulation by repetitive lateral movement of midair ultrasound focus. IEEE Trans Haptics 13(2):334–342

Wakabayashi N, Sakai A, Takada H, Hoshi T, Sano H, Ichinose S, Suzuki H, Ogawa R (2020) Noncontact phased-array ultrasound facilitates acute wound healing in mice. Plast Reconstr Surg 145:348e–359e

References Cited in Health Canada

Acton WI (1968) A criterion for the prediction of auditory and subjective effects due to airborne noise from ultrasonic sources. Ann Occup Hyg 11:227–234

Acton WI (1974) The effects of industrial airborne ultrasound on humans. Ultrasonics 124–128

Acton WI (1975) Exposure criteria for industrial ultrasound. Ann Occup Hyg 18:267–268

Acton WI, Carson MB (1967) Auditory and subjective effects of airborne noise from industrial ultrasonic sources. Br J Ind Med 24:297–304

Allen CH, Frings H, Rudnick I (1948) Some biological effects of intense high frequency airborne sound. J Acoust Soc Am 20:62–65

auf der Maur AN (1985) Limits of exposure to airborne ultrasound. Ann Am Conf Ind Hyg 12:177–181

Crabtree RB, Forshaw SE (1977) Exposure to ultrasonic cleaner noise in the Canadian forces. DCIEM technical report #77X45. Available from DCIEM, 1133 Sheppard Ave. W., P.O. Box 2000, Downsview, Ontario M3M 3B9

Dallos PJ, Linnell CO (1966) Subharmonic components in cochlear-microphonic potentials. J Acoust Soc Am 40:4–11

Danner PA, Ackerman E, Frings HW (1954) Heating in haired and hairless mice in high-intensity sound fields from 6–22 kHz. J Acoust Soc Am 26:731–739

Davis H (1948) Biological and psychological effects of ultrasonics. J Acoust Soc Am 20:605–607

Dobroserdov VK (1967) The effect of low frequency ultrasonic and high frequency sound waves on workers. Hygiene Sanitation 32:176–181

Grigor'eva VM (1966) Effect of ultrasonic vibrations on personnel working with ultrasonic equipment. Sov Phys Acoust II:426–427

Grzesik J, Pluta E (1980) Noise and airborne ultrasound exposure in the industrial environment. In: Proceedings of the 3rd international congress on noise as a public health problem. Freyburg, W. Germany, 25–29 Sept 1978. ASHA reports 10. The American Speech-Language-Hearing Association, Rockville, Maryland, Apr 1980, pp 657–661

Grzesik J, Pluta E (1983) High frequency hearing risk of operators of industrial ultrasonic devices. Int Arch Occup Environ Health 53:77–78

Grzesik J, Pluta E (1986) Dynamics of high-frequency hearing loss of operators of industrial ultrasonic devices. Int Arch Occup Environ Health 57:137–142

Herbertz J (1984) Loudness of airborne ultrasonic noise. In: Ultrasonics international (1983) conference proceedings, S.226–231

Herbertz J, Grunter K (1981) Untersuchungen zur hoerkurvenmaessigen Bewertung von Ultraschall in Luft. Fortschritte der Akustik-DAGA'81. VDE-Verlag, Berlin, pp 509–512

Herman BA, Powell D (1981) Airborne ultrasound: measurement and possible adverse effects. HHS Publication (FDA) 81-8163, May 1981. Available from CDRH, Rockville, MD, USA, 20857

International Radiation Protection Association (IRPA) (1984) Interim guidelines on limits of human exposure to airborne ultrasound. Health Phys 46:969–974

Knight JJ (1968) Effects of airborne ultrasound on man. Ultrasonics 39–42

Neppiras EA (1980) Acoustic cavitation thresholds and cyclic processes. Ultrasonics 201–209, 230

Parrack HO (1966) Effect of air-borne ultrasound on humans. Int Audiol 5:294–308

Skillern CP (1965) Human response to measured sound pressure levels from ultrasonic devices. Ind Hyg J 26:132–136

United States Air Force (1976) Hazardous noise exposure. USAF Regulation 161-35

Von Gierke HE (1949) Sound absorption at the surface of the body of man and animals. J Acoust Soc Am 21:55

Von Gierke HE (1950) Subharmonics generated in the ears of humans and animals at intense sound levels. In: Federation proceedings, vol 9, p 130(a)

Von Gierke HE, Parrack HO, Eldredge DN (1952) Heating of animals by absorbed sound energy. J Cell Comp Physiol 39:487–505

Mid-Air Haptics: Future Challenges and Opportunities

Orestis Georgiou⊙, William Frier⊙, Euan Freeman⊙,
Claudio Pacchierotti⊙, and Takayuki Hoshi

Abstract Ultrasound mid-air haptic technology has advanced in many ways over the past decade and has found meaningful application in a plethora of use cases. As the technology matures further and progresses from lab to market, in this chapter, we take a step back and discuss three specific directions that we think could result in the greatest impact. Namely, we highlight challenges and opportunities in improving (1) the hardware platforms used, (2) the rendering algorithms employed to create rich haptic sensations, and (3) the resulting user experience and added value the technology can instill to different end-user applications. We hope that this "wish-list" inspires the mid-air haptics and human computer interaction (HCI) community and others to join our efforts toward a deeper technology understanding, integration, and readiness.

1 Introduction

Since the discovery of ultrasonic mid-air haptic technology in Japan in 2010 (Hoshi, et al. 2010) and its commercialization by Ultraleap (UK) (https://www.ultraleap.com/) in 2014, we have seen a rapid and diverse advancement in its development—especially within the last few years. The previous chapters of this book have given a

O. Georgiou (✉) · W. Frier
Ultraleap Ltd, Bristol, UK
e-mail: orestis.georgiou@ultraleap.com

E. Freeman
University of Glasgow, Glasgow, UK

C. Pacchierotti
Centre national de la recherche scientifique (CNRS), Institut de Recherche en Informatique et Systèmes Aléatoires (IRISA), Rennes, France

T. Hoshi
Pixie Dust Technologies, Inc., Tokyo, Japan

© The Author(s), under exclusive license to Springer Nature Switzerland AG 2022
O. Georgiou et al. (eds.), *Ultrasound Mid-Air Haptics for Touchless Interfaces*,
Human–Computer Interaction Series, https://doi.org/10.1007/978-3-031-04043-6_18

flavor of this development, spanning hardware designs, improved software algorithms for haptic rendering, a focus on enhanced user experiences and immersive applications, and finally a deeper understanding of the physical and acoustic processes involved when inducing contactless touch. Moreover, this book is living proof of a growing and highly interdisciplinary community of researchers who actively publish beyond HCI and haptics journals and conferences.

Despite all this progress, in their recent review, Rakkolainen et al. (2020) conclude that ultrasound haptics is still in its infancy and highlight five directions that can help the technology mature: (1) a greater understanding of perception through more user studies, (2) new haptic rendering methods to allow higher quality haptic output, (3) an exploration of new haptic sensations and textures, (4) improved acoustic solvers, and (5) new applications that leverage the many benefits of mid-air haptic feedback. We agree with their assessment but would also like to close this book by adding further tracks toward technology maturity and expanding on them through our own lens. The aim of this final chapter is therefore to look at the road ahead and highlight key challenges and opportunities associated with the further advancement of this emergent touchless technology. We hope this inspires the mid-air haptics community and others to join us on this journey, as we take the next steps forward toward a deeper technology understanding, integration, and readiness. We group our discussions under the themes of hardware (Sect. 2), haptic sensations and rendering (Sect. 3), and user experience and applications (Sect. 4).

2 Hardware

The majority of mid-air haptic devices currently being used, such as those produced by Ultraleap, are implemented using an array of 256 Murata MA40S4S transducers operating at 40 kHz. These are standard components that are commonly used in applications such as automotive parking and alarm sensors. Other ultrasonic transducers do exist and have been used in multiple mid-air haptic prototypes. However, the MA40S4S is indeed one of the highest performing air-coupled transducers currently on the market. It is a 10 mm barrel transducer that reliably achieves a pressure of ~114 dB SPL (10 Pa RMS) at 30 cm when driven with a 0–20 V square wave. Despite its performance, there are multiple issues with this and similar transducer devices that can inhibit the commercial exploitation of the technology.

Firstly, they are relatively expensive. Air-coupled ultrasound transducers currently cost between $1 and 3 each (RRP) when ordered in bulk (depending on the brand), with additional driver costs between $0.10–0.30 per channel for each transducer. This results in a per-channel cost of ~$1.2–3.2. For a standard 256-element array, this is a cost of ~$300–800 for the transducers and drivers alone. A reduction in transducer cost would therefore have a significant effect on the commercial opportunities relating to airborne ultrasound technologies in general, lowering the entry cost and making this technology more accessible to new application areas. It should be also emphasized that the current transducers employed for mid-air haptic applications were originally developed with single-element applications in mind and not the multi-element phased array systems needed here.

The second transducer issue is their size. Most 40 kHz transducers are large both in terms of area and volume, each occupying a 10 mm diameter barrel cylinder and 10 mm in height. A reduction in transducer area and volume would significantly improve their integration options inside or on the surface of products, e.g., an automotive dashboard. As noted in the previous chapters, a mid-air haptic device needs to be above a certain minimum area (aperture) to enable focusing acoustic pressure to a point within a reasonable mid-air interaction range, e.g., 10–50 cm. Modular solutions have been proposed to that effect allowing for some product design flexibility.

Another issue with ultrasound transducer technologies used in mid-air haptic applications is their carrier frequency of 40 kHz. This is above the range of human hearing but is not above the hearing range of some animals, including cats and dogs. Higher carrier frequency devices have been presented in a few prototypes (Ito et al. 2016), however, it is not well understood if higher frequencies have any significant positive or negative effects on the haptic sensation itself. For example, higher frequency transducers would produce a smaller, sharper, focal point. That could be good (e.g., higher resolution rendering) or bad (e.g., weaker haptics) and should be studied in depth before new hardware is proposed.

The last two transducer-related issues are power consumption and heat dissipation. The Murata devices, for example, consume ~250 mW when driven at maximum strength with a 0–20 V 50% duty cycle square wave. This results in a standard 256-element array having a power consumption in excess of 64 W in the maximum output scenario. This is not an insignificant amount of power and may cause issues with some consumer applications, e.g., limiting the potential for portable devices with integrated power units. In consequence, the heat generated by this power is also significant. Specifically, most 40 kHz transducers are quite inefficient as less than 10% of the consumed power is converted to ultrasound. The remainder of the power consumed is wasted as heat, either in the transducer or the driver circuit. Therefore, a key challenge is managing the heat dissipation through cooling units, software control, or new materials.

Advances in transducer technology would certainly mitigate many of the above problems. Until then, however, a good approach is to simply reduce the number of transducers to the minimum needed by the application at hand. The 256 element array employed by Ultraleap development kits produced is overkill for many applications. Meaningful mid-air haptic sensations and interactions can be generated with as little as 64 transducers, therefore, slashing costs, power, and heat simultaneously.

The size of the array also directly affects the renderable workspace, which spans the region directly above the device. For example, the Ultraleap Stratos Explore device (16 × 16 transducers array) features a workspace of 0.055 m^3, shaped like an ellipsoid spanning from 40 to 700 mm above the array, with a maximum lateral radius of 320 mm (Howard et al. 2019). Providing haptic feedback in a bigger workspace is of course possible by using larger or multiple ultrasound arrays, but—depending on the application at hand—other approaches might be equally effective. A notable example is that of Sand et al. (2015), who mounted an ultrasound array onto a head-mounted display so that the renderable workspace moves together with the user. More recently, Howard et al. (2019) presented a 2°-of-freedom robot for rotating a 16×16 ultrasound array around the pan and tilt axes, achieving a 14-fold increase in workspace volume with respect to using the array in its standard static position. Innovative approaches such as these ones can significantly reduce the cost of the haptic system with respect to the renderable workspace.

Other hardware-related opportunities that we foresee include the enhancement of mid-air haptic devices with additional sensors and networking capabilities. Already, the technology is directly coupled with independent hand-tracking sensors, however, there are others that could lead to improved operation of the haptics device, such as microphones, thermometers, IR, and humidity sensors, to name a few. Finally, the endowment of mid-air haptic devices with Wi-Fi or other wireless communication modules could enable over-the-air synchronization and distributed operation of multiple devices, potentially opening up a number of new commercial opportunities and applications.

Finally, most mid-air haptic devices look like engineering prototypes, at best enclosed inside a black box with a perforated grid cover to hide their inner workings while still allowing ultrasound propagation. To date, little attention has been given toward product design and product integration requirements. Mid-air haptic devices are for the most part not intended to be stand-alone products. Rather, they are likely to offer the most value to the user experience when integrated inside an automotive dashboard, under a digital signage monitor, or as a VR table-top accessory, etc. As noted in the previous chapters, the location and orientation of mid-air haptic devices have a direct impact on the quality of the haptic sensation. Therefore, any hardware product design effort must also consider system performance as well as ergonomics, UX, esthetics, and limit any interactions with nearby sensors, e.g., how the acoustic fields could influence the performance of nearby microphones and earpieces, or how any electromagnetic fields on the driver circuit boards can interfere with nearby electrical and electronic equipment. Hayward et al. (2020) have for example proposed enclosing the haptic device in a Faraday cage to enable its use with sensitive neurological monitoring devices.

3   Haptic Sensations and Rendering Algorithms

In analogy to 2D and 3D graphical rendering, mid-air haptic rendering relies on spatial and temporal modulation techniques that change properties of the acoustic focus, so as to create vibrations on the skin that imbue tactile properties and characteristics. Initially, the acoustic focus, which forms the basis for mid-air haptics, was amplitude modulated (AM) to create a localized vibrotactile sensation, while later, the focus was moved around in space to create small lateral modulations (LM) (Takahashi et al. 2018) or to trace out larger tactile shapes using so-called Spatio-temporal modulation (STM) (Frier et al. 2018). Techniques that use acoustic holography (Morales et al.

2021), multiple focal points (Carter et al. 2013), or a blend of AM and STM (Hajas et al. 2020) have also emerged and appear to be more suitable at delivering different haptic sensations in different settings. However, none of these modulation techniques adapt or take into consideration the heterogeneity of the human skin, the density, and types of mechanoreceptors being targeted, nor any effects of wave interference on the skin surface (Frier et al. 2022). Also, no mid-air haptic demonstrators and prototypes that we are aware of have ever been tailored to a particular user group demographic or person, despite the great differences and preferences displayed by end-users. Mid-air haptics, unlike many other haptic technologies, has the customization potential to be able to address many of these limitations. Beyond biophysical heterogeneity across users, there is also output heterogeneity across the interaction zone. For instance, Raza et al. (2019) proposed an algorithm that tuned parameters such as intensity and AM frequency so that the haptic sensation was consistent within the interaction volume. To that end, we call for more research to investigate the perception of ultrasound haptic sensations and explore ways these can be improved through more sophisticated rendering methods.

Psychophysics quantitatively investigates the relationship between physical stimuli and the sensations and perceptions they produce. In the case of mid-air haptics, this presents a great challenge since the possible stimuli cover a very large parameter space. Stimuli can vary in size, shape, intensity, target location, temporal, and spatial waveform just to name a few dimensions. Further, mapping all these stimuli parameters onto the perceptual space they relate to is a grand and taxing challenge, especially since the latter combines both functional and non-functional characteristics. What we mean by that is that different haptic stimuli can lead to low-level sensations such as perceptual and two-point discrimination thresholds, mid-level haptic properties such as roughness and curvature, and high-level haptic experiences such as valence and sense of agency. The latter is especially important ever since the discovery that mid-air haptics can be used to target non-glabrous (hairy) skin with the possibility of inducing affective haptics in social touch applications (Pittera et al. 2021). Here, it is also worth mentioning how Frier et al. (2019) showed how perceptual results can be used to optimize haptic performance by using fewer resources than the capabilities of state-of-the-art hardware. Indeed, sometimes, in haptics "less is more" (Berger et al. 2018), meaning that we can achieve higher performance or improved sensations by providing less rich feedback through simpler devices. While counter-intuitive, such results are well-known in the research community and they are at the core of the great popularity of many cutaneous haptics solutions, such as wearable haptic interfaces (Pacchierotti et al. 2017). Indeed, cutaneous haptics has already been successfully employed in many high-impact scenarios, such as medical robotics, industrial remote manipulation, and micro-robotic assembly. However, for this approach to be successful, it is necessary to know which are the most important stimuli and sensations to deliver, so as to focus the limited actuation capabilities of this technology where it counts most; hence, the importance of studying the perceptual aspects of this technology and the needs of the application at hand. An important forward step to that end is the availability of easy-to-use software tools that can facilitate psychophysical studies, enabling researchers who are not experts in the technology to design and output consistent mid-air haptic stimuli. While there exist some attempts in this direction (Mulot et al. 2021), experimental platforms and frameworks for running perceptual studies on ultrasound mid-air haptics are still rare.

This section has so far reflected on the challenges of using perceptual knowledge to inform the design and presentation of haptic sensations. Closely related to this is the challenge of implementing such designs, so that they can be evaluated and deployed in real usage scenarios. As an emerging technology, there are only a limited number of tools to support the design and implementation of haptic sensations. The Ultraleap Sensation Editor and Controls Suite are a few examples from which designers can select and customize a limited number of templates. Better software support is needed to allow haptic designers to be more expressive and to enable them to explore novel and bespoke haptic designs. Such "no-code" and "easy-to-use" software tools will help the technology become more accessible to a wider audience of designers, practitioners, makers, and academics in other disciplines.

Another aspect that has seen rapid developments in recent years is that of ultrasound field computation and display. Early mid-air haptic prototypes were capable of individually controlling the phase and amplitude of hundreds of transducers, to focus waves at different 3D positions in space. However, these early devices were limited to just one focus point, had low resolution, and limited refresh rates (i.e., the rate at which transducer values could be updated). Since then, we have seen a rapid increase in phase and amplitude resolution, thus improving the granularity of the resulting target field and the number of focus points that can be generated simultaneously. There has also been a rapid increase in computational solving speed, thus improving the refresh rate at which focal point properties can be changed, in turn enabling the rendering of more advanced haptic sensations such as multi-point STM (Plasencia et al. 2020) and PRO-STM (Barreiro et al. 2020). Higher refresh rates allow for smoother transitions between fields, thus influencing the amount of unwanted audible sounds, a byproduct of abruptly changing acoustic fields (Suzuki et al. 2020). All this progress has been a result of the adaptation of optical holography techniques (Morales et al. 2021), efficient eigen problem solving operations (Long et al. 2014), the use of Gerchberg-Saxton (GS) type of iterative phase retrieval algorithms (Plasencia et al. 2020), and their efficient implementation on GPUs or FPGAs. In the near future, we expect to see algorithmic advancements and extensions that are closely coupled to advancements in transducer technology as discussed in the previous section. The opportunity here is for improved acoustic holography and solver techniques that can produce sharper focus states while also reducing grating lobe and acoustic streaming phenomena, and also unlocking new spatial frequencies, and thus potentially enhancing the resulting haptic sensations.

Two major limitations of all these solvers are that they are not time-domain accurate and are not aware of any scattering effects caused by users, i.e., they assume a free field where sound waves are not reflected or scattered off any objects or obstacles. The first problem becomes important only when a focal point moves extremely quickly, and the distance between the focus and the ultrasound sources is large, resulting in acoustic interference and aliasing effects to manifest due to heterogeneous speed of sound delays between sound field frames; a kind of acoustic field inertia. Therefore, solvers should not assume that changes to the acoustic field happen instantaneously and should therefore take into consideration the history of pressure fields preceding new update frames (memory), and if possible optimize for future ones (forecast). The second problem becomes important when complex objects enter the interaction region of the ultrasound display. While reflections of ultrasonic waves off of flat surfaces have been leveraged before to create tactile holograms and illusions (Monnai et al. 2014), partial obstruction (e.g., by a car gear-stick) or indeed the ultrasonic scattering off the user's hands have not been considered in depth, with the exception of the work by Inoue et al. (2016). Often, we assume that the user's hand being targeted by a focal point is flat and homogeneous, and thus, the impinging ultrasound experiences a single specular reflection. However, many mid-air interactions described in this book include gestures like pinching, grasping, and pointing. Here, ultrasound may bounce around the semi-clenched palm inducing all sorts of unexpected tactile sensations. Including such calculations into the acoustic solver requires a closer coupling with the hand-tracking system and a modified Huygens model of acoustic propagation.

Another limitation with existing solvers is that there is no feedback control with regards to the state of the ultrasound transducer board or the environment in which it is operating in. For example, transducers may experience a shift in their resonance frequency of up to a few kHz or a complete phase inversion due to small changes in temperature or humidity levels. Including onboard sensor feedback and solver flexibility can account for such dynamic changes and thus improve the haptic performance of the technology significantly.

Finally, and accentuated by the 2020–2022 global chip shortage crisis that has sent semiconductor component costs rocketing, we can identify the need for modular and scalable hardware platforms, as well as simplified and much more efficient solvers that can be implemented on smaller and cheaper processing units or on the cloud. In summary, there are many gains to be made in exploring more sophisticated acoustic solvers and more efficient hardware implementations, toward the goal of creating higher quality mid-air haptic experiences.

4 User Experience and Applications

A holistic approach to UX is required to advance the applicability and design of mid-air haptics and how they can be tailored to particular applications. While we know that the underlying technology can deliver value by increasing interface usability, improving gesture learning and recall, reducing cognitive load, enhancing a sense of agency, reducing visual distraction, supporting error recovery, etc., we do not know which of these to prioritize and optimize for each target application (automotive, AR/VR gaming, training and simulation, public displays, etc.). Therefore, we call for more studies that develop non-singular prototype systems, starting from the ground up, and that do not just demonstrate a specific capability or function but rather deliver value and improved UX throughout. Frameworks to do so have been presented by Kim et al. (2020) for generic haptic experience design, however, expanding and further specializing those toward mid-air haptics comes with its own challenges due to the large haptic design space associated with gesture input and rendering techniques.

Another obstacle we foresee here is the lack of appropriate publication venues being targeted by mid-air haptic researchers. Namely, most published papers on mid-air haptics have to date been addressing the haptics, acoustics, and HCI communities, which to a first approximation reward novelty and methodology. We, therefore, call for more cross-disciplinary collaborations that produce case-study results that present and discuss how different solutions were thought up, designed, developed, and evaluated. Two examples to that end include the works by O'Conaill (2020) and Young et al. (2020), where the authors give more emphasis on the project delivery process, requirement considerations, and the resulting added UX value, rather than just highlighting a singular contribution or incremental improvement. Such explorations would benefit considerably toward the quest for a "killer application" for mid-air haptic technology.

Another largely unexplored aspect of mid-air haptics is how this technology interacts with other sensory and technological modalities. In terms of the multi-sensory aspect, very few studies have investigated the interplay between mid-air touch and visuals, sounds, and smells. We know, for example, that visuo-haptic feedback can improve the precision of mid-air grasping operations of virtual objects (Frutos-Pascual, et al. 2019), while the right audio-haptic composition can improve the experience of a holographic light-switch button (Ozkul et al. 2020). More such studies are required if we are to imbue unobtrusive touch sensations to the emergent metaverse paradigm but also to more near-term applications such as automotive human–machine interfaces and digital signage displays.

In terms of technological interactions and integrations, very few studies have coupled mid-air haptics to other novel sensors or data streams. For example, most realizations of the technology take hand and finger positional data as their main input and output a pre-calibrated mid-air tactile sensation in return. The pre-calibrated tactile sensation typically represents some properties of the widget or object being interacted with, e.g., its location, size, shape, state, function, or texture. Instead, Romanus et al. (2019) have included to the input stream the user's heart rate as measured by a wearable sensor; the heart rate modulates the presented tactile sensation in real-time. In the age of the Internet of things (IoT), where smart sensors are prolific and produce rich data streams about our lives, homes, and daily objects we interact with, we see an opportunity to enrich the mid-air haptic effect, both in space, time, and form as to represent additional properties such as the weather, the flow of incoming traffic, and the urgency of an incoming email.

Multi-haptic explorations have also been very limited. With the exception of works by Ochai et al. (2016) and Fan et al. (2020) where femtosecond-laser light fields and cable-driven force-feedback, respectively, were combined with ultrasonic acoustic fields to produce novel haptic sensations, very few other examples of multi-haptic interfaces exist. We would therefore like to invite the exploration of mixed haptic interfaces where ultrasound mid-air haptics are utilized together with other contact (wearables, tangibles, grounded, surfaces, etc.) or non-contact (infrared, laser, air jets, electrostatic, etc.) haptic stimuli. These novel prototypes could potentially induce new touch sensations and enable new collaboration synergies between academic groups or commercial exploitation opportunities between industry players.

Considering that touch is a fundamentally complex sense, we believe that in order to advance the technology from CRT, to SD, to HD, to 4K (in analogy to visual displays), we need to first deepen our understanding of the whole mid-air haptic pipeline, from hardware to perception to human experience. That is, how do the acoustic vibrations emitted by a device interact with human perceptual systems and in turn, become meaningful tactile sensations that encode information, or cause an affective or emotive response? Obrist et al. (2015), for example, demonstrated a non-arbitrary mapping between emotions and different haptic descriptions (e.g., patterns and frequencies) pointing toward a massive gap in our ability to model and design sensations in a predictable and controlled manner. To make progress in this grand challenge, we advocate for the need to build links between acoustic models of ultrasound vibrations, finite element models of skin vibrations and mechanoreceptor firings, neurocognitive models of low-level tactile thresholds and high-level experiences, and finally connect these to a user-facing interface or application. Implicit in all this is the need for accurate, reliable, and open datasets that can be used to build and validate such models. Particularly, where there is data, there is also the enticing prospect of leveraging artificial intelligence (AI) methods to create predictive and generative haptic design tools and enhanced applications. In this, we highlight the potential for valuable contributions from different disciplines and the benefits of a more multi-disciplinary approach to research on this topic.

Finally, while the scientific community of mid-air haptics is active, international, interdisciplinary, and growing, the industrial community is rather localized and represented by mainly Ultraleap, who is the majority intellectual property (IP) holder, and their direct partnerships with original equipment manufacturers (OEMs) like Hosiden or Bosch who focus on integrating and assembling application-oriented products for a specific market, e.g., automotive human–machine interfaces (HMIs). To that end, we hope to see more companies, both small startups and large OEMs, reach out to academic expert groups (directly or via the haptics and HCI communities) with the aim to engage with this enabling technology and explore its commercial use in a larger variety of end-user applications, for example, in accessibility, automotive, sterile interfaces in medical and public spaces, AR/VR training, robotics, gaming, the arts and immersive experiences, wellness, and e-commerce or product showcasing. We hope that this book can help facilitate such explorations.

5   Conclusions and Perspectives

Digital haptic interfaces have been around for several decades, using diverse form factors and actuation mechanisms to enrich the tactile experience of user interfaces across many application areas. However, except for some notable exceptions (e.g., vibrations on smartphones and game controllers), haptic technologies have yet to reach the diffusion we believe they deserve. The sense of touch is indeed a fundamental part of human experience, enabling and defining how we interact with the world around us—it is impossible to imagine a true immersive interaction without appealing to our most visceral sense. The timeliness for integrating haptics into digital or remote experiences have gained accelerated momentum due to the COVID-19 pandemic, which has forced individuals, businesses, and governments to shift activities from the real to the digital at a rapid pace. However, most of these digital activities are restricted to the visual and auditory modalities, severely limiting the immersiveness and richness of the targeted interactive experience. Nonetheless, the way we teach, learn, socialize, and play involves all our senses, well beyond what we receive during a typical video conference call. What became apparent through this real-to-digital substitution exercise is that audio-visual media was triumphant, while other senses were absent and truly missed. In this respect, ultrasound mid-air haptic technology can play a revolutionary role. Being able to provide compelling and rich haptic sensations without having to touch or wear anything can take haptic technology to the next level, finally able to reach the popularity of audio and visual feedback modalities.

In this chapter, we reflected on our own experiences and the many viewpoints presented in this book to identify a number of promising challenges and opportunities that we think should be addressed to help mature mid-air haptic technology so that its potential can be realized, e.g., hardware and software improvements, new haptic rendering methods, a deeper understanding of UX, and more application-relevant prototype explorations. However, these directions of inquiry are mostly intrinsic to the technology and the scientific and industrial communities involved. Extrinsic factors such as the ethics and standardization efforts of mid-air touch should also be addressed as they hold great potential in accelerating its trajectory. For example, given that touch is a very intimate and expressive sense which is crucial to our development and wellbeing (Field 2014), mid-air haptics researchers and practitioners should anticipate, reflect on, engage with and act upon possible negative societal or environmental impacts of the development of these technologies (e.g., by following a reflective framework for responsible innovation like AREA). Being proactive about engaging with such issues can help with the successful rollout of new technologies by increasing peoples' willingness to accept and adopt them. As an example of why this is important, consider the issues encountered by early attempts to commercialize augmented reality glasses. Many people perceived this technology as being "not for them" and were concerned about potential privacy violations. Such issues largely stemmed from poor communication and engagement with the communities where these devices were deployed. Stakeholders in haptics are encouraged to engage with ethical and social concerns around technologies like this. For example, Jewitt et al. (2021) have presented a manifesto of 10 statements that are aimed to help haptic designers and developers involved in developing digital touch technologies. This could be further specialized to touchless and mid-air haptic solutions to provide a framework for the responsible development and deployment of mid-air haptic interfaces.

Finally, like with any new technology, standards can ensure that mid-air haptic devices and their induced sensations are consistent in terms of quality and operation and that they adhere to any relevant health and safety considerations. Currently, different prototypes produce different acoustic fields, through a different application programming interface (API), using different electronic components, thus inducing a different haptic sensation. All this uncertainty makes it difficult to compare, reproduce, and reuse, therefore hindering the advancement of the technology, its interoperability, and compatibility with other systems and platforms. To avoid a low-growth and divided future, the mid-air haptics community needs to align on terminology, and recommended practices across all levels of the haptic stack.

Ultrasound haptic technology has advanced considerably over the past decade, accompanied by the emergence of new interaction paradigms, new hardware innovations, and new knowledge about our sense of touch and the role it plays in interactive experiences. These new insights have helped establish new areas of haptics and HCI research and have led to the growth of a diverse and multi-disciplinary research community. This book is a product of that community. Its chapters reflect on the formative years of mid-air haptic technology and the many achievements that have led to the current state-of-the-art. Some offer a retrospective review of key research insights and aim to inform designers, practitioners, and researchers so that they can make the best use of it. Others look to the future to inspire and inform the crucial next steps in advancing the technology. We hope that you share our enthusiasm for mid-air haptics and our excitement for where it goes next, and we hope that this book will be a useful companion as you too may decide to contribute to its bright future.

Acknowledgements This project has received funding from the European Union's Horizon 2020 research and innovation program under grant agreements No 801413 (H-Reality), and 101017746 (Touchless).

References

Barreiro H, Sinclair S, Otaduy MA (2020) Path routing optimization for STM ultrasound rendering. IEEE Trans Haptics 13(1):45–51

Berger CC et al (2018) The uncanny valley of haptics. Sci Robot 3(17)

Carter T et al (2013) UltraHaptics: multi-point mid-air haptic feedback for touch surfaces. In: Proceedings of the 26th annual ACM symposium on user interface software and technology

Inoue S, Makino Y, Shinoda H (2016) Mid-air ultrasonic pressure control on skin by adaptive focusing. In: International conference on human haptic sensing and touch enabled computer applications. Springer, Cham

Takahashi R, Hasegawa K, Shinoda H (2018) Lateral modulation of midair ultrasound focus for intensified vibrotactile stimuli. In International conference on human haptic sensing and touch enabled computer applications. Springer, Cham

Fan L, Song A, Zhang H (2020) Haptic interface device using cable tension based on ultrasonic phased array. IEEE Access 8:162880–162891

Field T (2014) Touch, 2nd edn. The MIT Press, Cambridge, Massachusetts, US

Frier W et al (2018) Using spatiotemporal modulation to draw tactile patterns in mid-air. In: International conference on human haptic sensing and touch enabled computer applications. Springer, Cham

Frier W et al (2019) Sampling strategy for ultrasonic mid-air haptics. In: Proceedings of the 2019 CHI conference on human factors in computing systems

Frier W et al (2022) Simulating airborne ultrasound vibrations in human skin for haptic applications. IEEE Access

Frutos-Pascual M et al (2019) Evaluation of ultrasound haptics as a supplementary feedback cue for grasping in virtual environments. In: 2019 international conference on multimodal interaction

Hajas D et al (2020) Mid-air haptic rendering of 2D geometric shapes with a dynamic tactile pointer. IEEE Trans Haptics 13(4):806–817 (2020)

Hayward N et al (2020) A novel ultrasonic haptic device induces touch sensations with potential applications in neuroscience research. In: 2020 IEEE international ultrasonics symposium (IUS). IEEE

Hoshi T et al (2010) Noncontact tactile display based on radiation pressure of airborne ultrasound. IEEE Trans Haptics 3(3):155–165 (2010)

Howard T et al (2019) PUMAH: pan-tilt ultrasound mid-air haptics for larger interaction workspace in virtual reality. IEEE Trans Haptics 13(1):38–44 (2019)

https://www.ultraleap.com/

Ito M et al (2016) High spatial resolution midair tactile display using 70 kHz ultrasound. In: International conference on human haptic sensing and touch enabled computer applications. Springer, Cham

Jewitt C et al (2021) Manifesto for digital social touch in crisis. Frontiers Comput Sci 97

Kim E, Schneider O (2020) Defining haptic experience: foundations for understanding, communicating, and evaluating HX. In: Proceedings of the 2020 CHI conference on human factors in computing systems

Long B et al (2014) Rendering volumetric haptic shapes in mid-air using ultrasound. ACM Trans Graph (TOG) 33(6):1–10

Monnai Y et al (2014) HaptoMime: mid-air haptic interaction with a floating virtual screen. In: Proceedings of the 27th annual ACM symposium on user interface software and technology

Morales R et al (2021) Generating airborne ultrasonic amplitude patterns using an open hardware phased array. Appl Sci 11(7):2981

Mulot L et al (2021) DOLPHIN: a framework for the design and perceptual evaluation of ultrasound mid-air haptic stimuli. In: ACM symposium on applied perception 2021

Obrist M et al (2015) Emotions mediated through mid-air haptics. In: Proceedings of the 33rd annual ACM conference on human factors in computing systems

Ochiai Y et al (2016) Cross-field aerial haptics: rendering haptic feedback in air with light and acoustic fields. In: Proceedings of the 2016 CHI conference on human factors in computing systems

O'Conaill B et al (2020) Improving immersive experiences for visitors with sensory impairments to the aquarium of the pacific. In: Extended abstracts of the 2020 CHI conference on human factors in computing systems

Ozkul C, Geerts D, Rutten I (2020) Combining auditory and mid-air haptic feedback for a light switch button. In: Proceedings of the 2020 international conference on multimodal interaction

Pacchierotti C et al (2017) Wearable haptic systems for the fingertip and the hand: taxonomy, review, and perspectives. IEEE Trans Haptics 10(4):580–600 (2017)

Pittera D et al (2021) "I can feel it coming in the hairs tonight": characterising mid-air haptics on the hairy parts of the skin. IEEE Trans Haptics

Plasencia DM et al (2020) GS-PAT: high-speed multi-point sound-fields for phased arrays of transducers. ACM Trans Graph (TOG) 39(4):138–1

Rakkolainen I et al (2020) A survey of mid-air ultrasound haptics and its applications. IEEE Trans Haptics 14(1):2–19 (2020)

Raza A et al (2019) Perceptually correct haptic rendering in mid-air using ultrasound phased array. IEEE Trans Ind Electron 67(1):736–745 (2019)

Romanus T et al (2019) Mid-air haptic bio-holograms in mixed reality. In: 2019 IEEE international symposium on mixed and augmented reality adjunct (ISMAR-Adjunct). IEEE

Sand A et al (2015) Head-mounted display with mid-air tactile feedback. In: Proceedings of the 21st ACM symposium on virtual reality software and technology

Suzuki S et al (2020) Reducing amplitude fluctuation by gradual phase shift in midair ultrasound haptics. IEEE Trans Haptics 13(1):87–93

Young G et al (2020) Designing mid-air haptic gesture controlled user interfaces for cars. In: Proceedings of the ACM on human-computer interaction, vol 4(EICS), pp 1–23

Printed in the United States
by Baker & Taylor Publisher Services